Flower Shapes

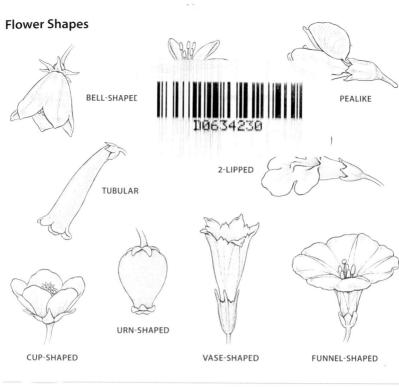

BELL-SHAPED

PEALIKE

TUBULAR

2-LIPPED

CUP-SHAPED

URN-SHAPED

VASE-SHAPED

FUNNEL-SHAPED

Flower Clusters

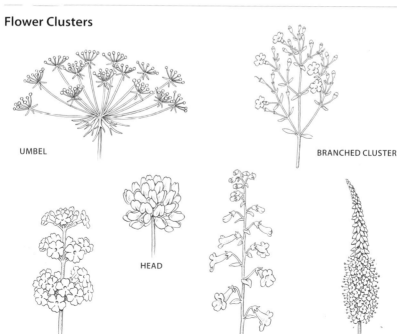

UMBEL

BRANCHED CLUSTER

HEAD

WHORLED CLUSTER

ELONGATED CLUSTER

SPIKELIKE CLUSTER

National Wildlife Federation®

FIELD GUIDE TO
WILDFLOWERS
OF NORTH AMERICA

National Wildlife Federation®

FIELD GUIDE TO
WILDFLOWERS
OF NORTH AMERICA

Written by David M. Brandenburg
Foreword by Craig Tufts, NWF Chief Naturalist

STERLING

New York / London
www.sterlingpublishing.com

This book is dedicated to John Thieret,

the finest field botanist I have ever known.

—*David Brandenburg*

In memory of Craig Tufts, whose childlike sense of wonder

about all living things was an inspiration to so many.

Published by Sterling Publishing Co., Inc.
387 Park Avenue South, New York, NY 10016

© 2010 by Andrew Stewart Publishing, Inc.

Distributed in Canada by Sterling Publishing
c/o Canadian Manda Group, 165 Dufferin Street,
Toronto, Ontario, Canada M6K 3H6

Distributed in the United Kingdom by GMC Distribution Services,
Castle Place, 166 High Street, Lewes, East Sussex, England BN7 1XU

Distributed in Australia by Capricorn Link (Australia) Pty. Ltd.
P.O. Box 704, Windsor, NSW 2756, Australia

Library of Congress Cataloging-in-Publication Data

Brandenburg, David M.
  National Wildlife Federation field guide to wildflowers of North America /
by David M. Brandenburg.
    p. cm.
  Includes bibliographical references and index.
  ISBN: 978-1-4027-4154-8 (pbk.)
  1. Wild flowers—North America—Identification. I. National Wildlife Federation. II. Title.
III.Title: Field guide to wildflowers of North America.

QK110.B73 2010
582.13097—dc22

2009027744

Printed in Singapore
All rights reserved

2 4 6 8 10 9 7 5 3 1

For information about custom editions, special sales, premium and corporate purchases, please
contact Sterling Special Sales Department at 800-805-5489 or specialsales@sterlingpub.com.

National Wildlife Federation® name and logo are trademarks of National Wildlife Federation
and are used, under license, by Andrew Stewart Publishing, Inc.

NATIONAL WILDLIFE FEDERATION® *The mission of the National Wildlife Federation is to inspire Americans to protect wildlife for our children's future.*

Protecting wildlife through education and action since 1936, the National Wildlife Federation® (NWF) is America's largest conservation organization. NWF works with a nationwide network of state affiliate organizations, scientists, grassroots activists, volunteers, educators, and wildlife enthusiasts—uniting individuals from diverse backgrounds to focus on three goals that will have the biggest impact on the future of America's wildlife.

Connect People with Nature

NWF's legacy for connecting people with nature extends back over 50 years, through its award-winning publications *Ranger Rick, Your Big Backyard, Wild Animal Baby,* and *National Wildlife* to its education and outreach programs encouraging generations of children, youth, and adults to appreciate and nurture nature in their own backyards and the world around them. NWF's *Green Hour* program addresses the growing disconnection that children have from nature and encourages parents and caregivers to commit to having children spend one hour a day outside exploring nature. Extending the connection to nature, NWF's *Certified Wildlife Habitat*™ program teaches homeowners, businesses, schools, and other institutions how to create habitat that supports wildlife in their own backyards and provides people with an easy yet effective way to practice their conservation values at home and work. The key focuses of NWF's campus and youth programs are to build the connection to the larger world and to create future generations of conservation leaders.

Protect and Restore Wildlife

Loss of habitat due to oil and gas drilling, urban sprawl, and deforestation is a major threat to the future of America's wildlife. NWF works tirelessly to obtain permanent protection for critical habitat areas—areas that are essential to the recovery of species populations such as wolves, salmon, and the Florida panther. NWF's work also includes protecting lands like the pristine Arctic National Wildlife Refuge, the vanishing wild areas of the western United

States, and the green forests of the Northeast. Water and wetland protection programs focus on restoring the Great Lakes, the Snake River, the Florida Everglades, Louisiana's coastal wetlands, and the Northwest's Puget Sound. In addition to working to restore these habitats today, NWF fights for expanded Clean Water Act protection and campaigns for smarter water and land management for the future. For more than 30 years the Endangered Species Act (ESA) has been the primary tool for conserving endangered and threatened species and their habitats. NWF is committed to upholding the full protection of the ESA, despite attempts to weaken it.

Confront Global Warming

Global warming has become the single greatest threat to wildlife and to the natural resources on which we all depend. Over the lifetime of a child born today, 20–30 percent of wild plants and animals worldwide face an increasingly higher risk of extinction due to global warming. The United States has an historic opportunity to help sustain America's unsurpassed natural legacy. To meet the global warming pollution reductions scientists say are necessary, America must transform its economy to one fueled by clean energy. We must also invest in restoring and protecting natural resources threatened by global warming. NWF is taking action now to address these critical challenges. Working with members, state affiliates, and partners, NWF mobilizes grassroots activists to push for national and state policies that reduce the carbon emissions that cause heat-trapping pollution and that invest in protecting natural resources from global warming. By providing good science and public outreach tools, NWF also educates Americans about personal solutions to global warming they can implement in their everyday lives.

National Wildlife Federation relies on Americans who are passionate about wildlife and wild places to advance our mission: *protecting wildlife for our children's future.* **Visit www.nwf.org or call 800-882-9919 to join us today!**

6

Contents

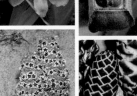

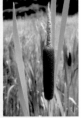
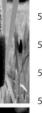

Introduced Species   **563**

Appendices   **601**

Foreword

Where there is even the smallest growing green thing on this planet, you will likely find wildflowers. When rainfall is sufficient and temperature suited for growth, look carefully. You will see them, from huge, showy tropical flowers to the tiniest of bloomers. In extreme cold or heat, in rock or sand, near or in water, wildflowers are everywhere. Recognize them first for their beauty and the curiosity they inspire in us. Then consider them for their austerity and their tenacious ability to thrive in our changing world. Wildflowers are marvels of life no matter where they grow. Go out, meet them and enjoy their company.

Wildflowers shower us with colors and overwhelm us with fragrance. They intrigue us with how they distribute their pollen and seeds, how the combination of flower followed by seed, aided by winds, water, and insect pollinators, assures the plant species of its continuity. The aspects of a wildflower's structure and life cycle all factor precisely into what its role might be in the ecosystem.

I grew up in a neighborhood in coastal New Jersey. The trees, shrubs, wildflowers, grasses, and sedges near the house were the fabric of my playground. My parents and family, friends and naturalist mentors aided and abetted in my curiosity of the natural world. I found that knowing what abounded in my neighborhood, and beyond into the bordering pine barrens, created an insatiable desire to be there, all of the time, to learn, to enjoy, and to ponder what I was seeing near me and, increasingly, just a little farther away. For me, learning to know these new friends—what they did, who visited them, how they grew, and who they fed—became a lifelong process that continues today.

For today's children, whether from urban, suburban, or rural settings, wildflowers and the animals and plants around them can provide joy, peace, excitement, and learning. What is out there to see is boundless. When we begin to learn about the bounty of the natural world, we become enticed to get outside. We learn and gain insight. We keep up our health and physical stamina. As we age, we pass on these attributes of our life to children and others, sharing our wisdom, curiosity, and wonder with those who will be future keepers of wildflowers and the natural world.

David Brandenburg is highly qualified to author this new field guide. A professional botanist with a passion for wildflowers, he has great enthusiasm for both learning and teaching about plants. Dr. Brandenburg has done extensive fieldwork throughout North America and has taught classes, held workshops, and written papers on a wide range of botanical topics. In the *National Wildlife Federation Field Guide to Wildflowers of North America*, he celebrates the diversity of North American wildflowers in grand fashion.

Craig Tufts
CHIEF NATURALIST,
NATIONAL WILDLIFE
FEDERATION

Introduction

Wildflowers might be found almost anywhere—carpeting an alpine meadow, strewn along a woodland stream, floating on a boggy pond, even sprouting in an urban backyard. Their equally far-ranging following includes people of all ages and from all walks of life, people who, like myself, will hike great distances just to catch a glimpse of a particular species. What is it about wildflowers that inspires such passion? The immediate appeal is obvious: the beauty of their many and varied colors, shapes, and fragrances. But perhaps it is also their fleeting nature. Even a common species may appear only briefly. Miss it, and a year or two may pass before another opportunity arises. Cherished too are the sights and smells of a warm desert, a southern bog, or a mountain meadow. Whether you are a beginner delving into the world of wildflowers for the first time or a seasoned naturalist seeking to expand your botanical knowledge, this guide will enhance your capacity to share in the joy and excitement of this pursuit.

Alpine meadows are home to numerous showy wildflowers, including Indian-paintbrushes.

Scope of This Guide

North America north of Mexico is home to more than 20,000 species of plants; nearly half of these qualify as wildflowers, a number far too large to treat in a portable field guide. This guide focuses on genera (singular, genus), groups of closely related species. It describes the principal genera of more than 100 plant families and features photographs and descriptions of more than 2,200 individual species, including the most widespread as well as many that are lesser known. Trees and most shrubs, some of which have spectacular blossoms, are not included because of space limitations; grasses and most sedges are likewise excluded.

The biggest share of the guide is a family-by-family survey of wildflowers native to North America—that is, essentially, plants that were naturally growing here before European colonization. A number of North American native plants have spread well beyond their original boundaries; for example, a species native to the Great Plains may have found its way to New England, or a Rocky Mountain native might now be seen growing along a highway in Michigan. In addition, the natural distributions of some species are changing as a result of regional changes in climate. Such species are considered to be "introduced" in those regions not originally part of their native distribution. Many plants of field and meadow have found their way into North America from other parts of the world. These are marked with the symbol ⬚, or they appear in a separate section, beginning on page 563, which includes a discussion of non-North American wildflowers.

Names and Classification

In scientific classification, plants comprise one of several kingdoms of living organisms. A simple hierarchical breakdown of the plant kingdom (Plantae) separates vascular plants (those having specialized conduits for food and water) from nonvascular plants (mosses and liverworts). Vascular plants are further divided into those that do not produce seeds (ferns, horse-tails, scouring-rushes, and club-mosses) and those that do produce seeds. Seed-producing plants either are gymnosperms, in which seeds are not developed within an ovary (notably the conifers), or they are angiosperms, the true flowering plants, which include the wildflowers. The two major groups of flowering plants are the monocots (with often parallel-veined leaves and flower parts in 3s or multiples of 3) and the dicots (leaf veins generally in a branching pattern, and flower parts in 4s or 5s).

A basic unit of scientific classification is the species, loosely defined as the plants of one kind. Individuals of the same species are structurally similar to one another, and they are capable of interbreeding to produce fertile offspring. A group of related species is called a genus (plural, genera); genera are further grouped into families.

Scientific Names

All plant species are assigned a Latin name, called a binomial because it consists of two parts: a genus name and a specific epithet. In the scientific name for Yellow Trout-lily, *Erythronium americanum*, *Erythronium* is the genus name and *americanum* is the specific epithet. The origins of scientific names are many. Some have classical roots; others may refer to an aspect of the plant (such as broad leaves) or its geographical origin or habitat. All adhere to guidelines set forth in a formal botanical code and are spelled the same the world over; even a guide to wildflowers written in native Japanese will have the scientific names written in their Latin form.

Subspecies and variety (abbreviated "ssp." and "var.") refer to subgroups of a species that exhibit a minor variation in morphology and that sometimes occur in only a portion of the range of that species.

Common Names

There are no official rules for the creation of common names of wildflowers, and these names may vary from region to region and from country to country. Quite a few plants have more than one common name; many are included in this guide.

Changes in Scientific Classification

For generations plants have been classified into families, genera, and species largely on the basis of their morphology—that is, on the similarity of their various parts. Gradually, additional techniques to help assess relationships have been developed as a supplement to the basic morphological data; the most recent of these involves DNA comparisons. Molecular studies have had a substantial impact on earlier classifications, with many plant families and genera redefined and rearranged. Some families have been split into multiple ones, others have been combined with another family, and many new genera have been created. The classification of many plants is currently in a state of flux. It is not uncommon to see the same wildflower species treated in a different genus or even a different family depending on the source one is consulting. Most families in this guide are the traditional ("older") ones.

Pickerel-weed, a colorful eastern wildflower, can form extensive colonies along lakes and ponds.

Habitats

Habitat refers to the natural environment in which a particular species normally grows. Many wildflowers are widespread in North America, and many occur in a variety of habitats; others have specialized requirements in regard to temperature, moisture, soil type, and other conditions and thus are limited to a particular geographical region. Within these regions, species may be associated with a specific habitat type, such as a bog or rocky slope; a few are even confined to a specific substrate like limestone. Some areas of North America, including the southern Appalachians and parts of California, are topographically and climatically diverse, "hot spots" that support a cornucopia of wildflower species. Increased species diversity also occurs where dissimilar habitats are in close proximity, such as where Mount Lemmon towers above the surrounding Sonoran Desert in southern Arizona. A brief mention of some of the habitat terms used in this guide follows.

Across North America, **forests** and **woodlands** are variable, from temperate rain forests in the Pacific Northwest, to coniferous forests that cover extensive sections of Canada and the mountains of the western United States, to broadleaf deciduous forests in the East, to pine-dominated woods in sections of the Southeast. Each forest type supports its own array of wildflowers, and species composition also varies with altitude. In western forests, for example, look for False Lily-of-the-valley at lower elevations and Brewer's Miterwort higher up. Within a given region, woodland habitats are often somewhat unpredictable as to the flora that grows there; there may be no obvious reason why a particular species grows in one undisturbed woods but is absent from another 20 miles away.

Habitats that are more open occur throughout North America, and these may harbor a profusion of plant life. In mountainous regions, **alpine meadows** may be teeming with lupines and Indian-paintbrushes, while **rocky slopes** sustain such species as Rocky Mountain Rockmat, One-flower Kelseya, and Cliff Dwarf-primrose. The grass-dominated **prairies** in the continent's midsection are decorated with coneflowers and prairie-clovers. Colorful cactuses beautify warm and cold **deserts** in arid parts of the West.

Wetland habitats include both standing water and slow- and fast-moving water courses. **Swamps** are wooded; **marshes** are not. Wildflowers associated with **lakes** and **ponds** may grow along wet shores, or they may be aquatic (rooted underwater or free-floating). Golden-club, American White Water-lily, and Common Arrow-head are typical wetland wildflowers. **Bogs** (acidic) and **fens** (alkaline) play host to species uncommon in or absent from other habitats, such as, respectively, some pitcher-plants and sedges.

Coasts bring to mind **sandy beaches** and **dunes**, but search also among **rocky shores**, **coastal bluffs**, and **salt marshes**, all of which have distinctive floras.

California-poppies brighten up a desert in southern California.

Kudzu, a native of eastern Asia, was introduced into the United States in 1876 as an ornamental plant. It has since spread rampantly throughout the Southeast, covering everything in its path.

Conservation

I have a vivid memory of standing in a woodland in Idaho one spring day and staring with profound awe at the incredible display of native wildflowers that carpeted the forest floor. There wasn't a single weed in sight—not one. The exceedingly diverse display of floral shapes and colors was stunning. It was a moment, visual and visceral, that has become increasingly less common.

It's not only the seldom-seen native wildflowers—those with narrow distributions or specialized habitats—that are vulnerable to habitat loss or degradation (I don't recall any rare species in that Idaho woods). Rather, wildflowers are an integral component of natural communities, part of a delicate and myriad mix of plants and animals both common and rare. It is these natural communities that need protection.

The stakes are high. Some of the benefits of plant life are no-brainers. Plants replenish the oxygen in the atmosphere, and they provide many thousands of economic products, including food, fiber, fuel, fragrance, medicine, and building materials. Other benefits may be less obvious. Plants form the framework of most natural communities. They have a major role in water and carbon cycles. They help maintain air quality and control erosion. They provide nourishment, shelter, and nesting sites for wildlife, including birds, mammals, butterflies, and bees.

Habitat Loss

The loss of natural habitat is a high-profile topic and one much talked and written about. Still, it is proceeding at an alarming pace. Housing development, road construction, agriculture, lumbering—and the list goes on—are leaving us with a mere patchwork of unspoiled habitats. In some areas, such as parts of the Midwest and Southeast, some of these remnants are designated as nature preserves. Once fragmented, however, they become less resistant to development, pollution, and pests, and their diversity becomes further compromised.

Invasive Species

Introduced plants, insects, and pathogens can cause serious damage and jeopardize the long-term viability of natural communities. Some invasive plants are detrimental to the point that they interfere with the health and reproduction of native wildflowers, in time displacing them. Non-native plant species are capable of altering a habitat in many ways, including influencing the availability of sunlight, nutrient uptake from the soil, and the susceptibility of an area to fire. A few plants, deemed noxious weeds, can utterly devastate natural communities. Kudzu and Yellow Star-thistle, for instance, may dominate large parts of a landscape, and the aggressive Purple Loosestrife can transform a native wetland into an essentially single-species tract, robbing the habitat of its natural diversity and offering little in the way of food and shelter for wildlife.

Climate Change

The effects of climate change are likely to be complex and variable. Already, some areas of North America have experienced alterations in species composition, with plants and animals less suited to the resultant modifications in temperature and moisture availability being displaced by species that are better adapted. The response of many mountain wildflowers has been to retreat to higher elevations. At some point even this might not be enough, and those species that can't shift their ranges farther northward will be in peril. Some geographic regions in North America have experienced serious water shortages. Droughts not only kill outright, they also leave plants more susceptible to insect infestations.

What You Can Do

The chances are that you purchased this wildflower guide to participate in the sheer pleasure and relaxation that accompany camping, hiking, and nature walks. I strongly encourage you to support local, state, and national organizations that are concerned about and dedicated to conservation issues. It is imperative that we maintain, monitor, and manage extensive areas of existing natural communities. The associations, interactions, and interdependencies found among the plants, animals, microbes, and soils of these communities are intricate and far from completely understood. Ample expanses of native habitats are required to ensure that all of these elements can "stay connected" and remain resistant to outside forces.

Adjunct activities to preserving natural communities include restoring degraded habitats to make them healthy again, and long-term storage of seeds of threatened wildflowers. Endangered species may be cultivated off-site (as in a botanical garden) so that they can later be reintroduced into the wild if needed. Many people have found that gardening with local native species has its rewards: these plants are generally low-maintenance in that they typically require less watering, are resistant to insects, and are usually not invasive. Do your best to ensure that the native plants you purchase for gardening have not been dug from wild populations.

Endangered native wildflowers include Green Pitcher-plant (*Sarracenia oreophila*, below), now found mostly in northeastern Alabama, and Florida Gayfeather (*Liatris ohlingerae*, right), which is endemic to central Florida.

About the Guide

The wildflowers described in this guide are grouped by botanical affinity and arranged hierarchically by family, genus, and species. Family descriptions give the forms of plants in the family as well as general information on leaves, flowers, and fruits. Genus descriptions give the number of North American species in the genus, both native and introduced; include a map displaying the U.S. geographical distribution of the genus; and highlight the combination of botanical features that best define the genus. Species have been chosen to represent the range of variation that occurs among species within that genus in North America. In families for which fruits are especially helpful in the identification process, line drawings of fruits are included after the family text. Families with "unusual" flowers feature labeled drawings of flower structure.

Key to Colors and Shapes

A visual key, arranged first by color and then by shape, has been included to make it easy to find species by their color.

Names

The scientific (Latin) names used in this guide are the ones currently used in several botanical references, particularly BONAP's *Floristic Synthesis of North America* and published volumes of *Flora of North America* (but see "Changes in Scientific Classification," page 11). Common names may vary from region to region and country to country. Quite a few plants have more than one common name, and many of these are included, space permitting.

Distribution Maps

Most species have colored maps (with a correspondingly colored box next to their name) giving their generalized range in the United States (equivalent data is unfortunately not currently available for all of Canada). These maps are only guidelines and do not always indicate every known occurrence; furthermore, plant populations are dynamic, with their ranges expanding and contracting over time. (Note that ranges may appear to extend to the eastern or western U.S. borders even though most species are not actually found directly along a coast.) Maps included with the genus descriptions report the distribution of all native and naturalized species of the particular genus, including those not highlighted in the book, a feature that is helpful when trying to identify the genus of an unknown wildflower species not discussed in the guide. For species included but not mapped, a general geographic range is given.

Species Descriptions

The information supplied for each species is meant to give readers the key features and clues required for identification. Every description begins with the season of bloom and general habitats. (Within a half-page block, species are often grouped that have similar seasons, habitats, or flower colors; in these cases, the information is usually given only for the first listed species.) The rest of the information varies, depending on what is important to know about the particular species. For example, leaf venation is reported only for those species for which it is an important identifying characteristic. Photo captions also include important descriptive information and give the height (average, maximum, or a range) for terrestrial species. Photographs were selected primarily for their value in helping users make identifications of genera and species. Photos of the same species are separated by a hairline space and labeled only once.

Toxic Plants

In this guide, many of the wildflowers commonly associated with human toxicity are labeled as poisonous. Not all poisonous plants, however, are noted as such. Treat every plant as potentially toxic until you are certain that it is not harmful.

What Is a Wildflower?

As treated in this guide, a wildflower is a naturally growing, usually herbaceous (nonwoody) plant having showy or otherwise interesting flowers. Some wildflowers are annual or biennial, completing their life cycle in one or two years, respectively; herbaceous perennials live for three or more years. Wildflowers have reproductive organs—flowers and fruits—and vegetative organs—roots, stems, and leaves.

Flowers and Fruits

The flower contains the reproductive structures, and it is here that fruits and seeds are formed. Flowers may be unisexual, containing only male or only female parts, or they may be bisexual, containing both functional male and female reproductive organs.

The first step in the reproductive process is pollination, the transfer of pollen from the anther of a stamen (the male reproductive organ) to the stigma of a pistil (the female reproductive organ). Pollination is typically accomplished via insects or wind, and the fragrance and colors of a blossom aid in the process by attracting insects. The transplanted pollen grains deliver male sex cells through a slender tube that grows through the style until it reaches the ovary. Fertilization takes place in the ovules of the ovary. The flower's ovary then further develops, its individual ovules maturing into seeds and its outer wall typically becoming the wall of the fruit.

Fruits may be fleshy or dry, and they come in a vast array of sizes, shapes, and textures. Berries are fleshy throughout, except for the seeds. Some fruits (called berrylike in this guide) are similar but vary in technical features; drupes, which differ from berries in that their seeds are tightly bound to a stony pit, are one example.

The term "pod" is used to describe certain dry fruits that usually open at maturity to allow for seed release. Pods include follicles, which split along one side only, and legumes, which ordinarily open along two sides. Capsules are another dry fruit type that opens when ripe. Capsules often split lengthwise along seams.

There are also dry fruits that do not open at maturity; most of these are small and one-seeded. The fruits of some plant families are so small that they appear to be seeds; the cypselae of the aster family (Asteraceae) and the achenes of the buttercup (Ranunculaceae) and rose (Rosaceae) families are often seedlike in appearance. Flowers with multiple pistils (such as buttercups and anemones) may form conspicuous clusters of these tiny one-seeded fruits. Schizocarps, the characteristic fruits of the parsley family (Apiaceae), resemble seeds; each schizocarp separates into two one-seeded sections when ripe.

Roots, Stems, and Leaves

Roots anchor the plant and absorb water and nutrients from the soil or other substrate. Stems support the leaves and flowers and conduct food and water. Stems may be modified into rhizomes (stems, sometimes enlarged, that spread horizontally underground), bulbs (underground stems covered by fleshy leaves), and corms (underground stems covered by papery leaves).

Leaves are the principal photosynthetic organs of the plant, their chemical factories capable of converting carbon dioxide and water—in the presence of light—to organic compounds and oxygen. Some plants lack chlorophyll, the green pigment that makes photosynthesis possible. These include mycotrophic species (such as Indian-pipe), which obtain nourishment through fungi that are interconnected with the roots of other plants, and parasitic plants (such as broomrapes) that attach themselves directly to the stems or roots of compatible host plants. Partially parasitic plants (such as louseworts) are green but obtain some nutrients from other plants.

Flowers

Most flowers comprise layers containing, from outside in, sepals, petals, stamens, and pistil(s). The illustration below shows the structure of a complete flower.

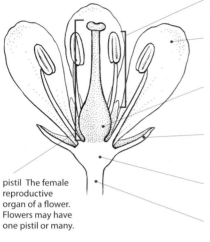

stamen The male reproductive organ of a flower. Flowers usually have several to many stamens.

petal Located above or inside the sepals; often large and colorful. All the petals collectively form the corolla.

ovary Ovule-bearing portion of the pistil. May be superior, positioned above the sepals and petals (as illustrated), or inferior, positioned below them.

sepal Part of the outermost whorl of the flower, often green but sometimes colored and petal-like. A flower's sepals are collectively called the calyx.

pistil The female reproductive organ of a flower. Flowers may have one pistil or many.

receptacle Base of a flower, to which other parts attach; adjoins flower stalk.

flower stalk (pedicel) Connects an individual flower to the supporting stem, branch, or cluster-axis.

One-flower Wintergreen

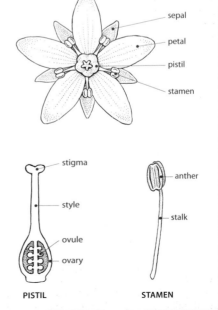

sepal
petal
pistil
stamen

Pistil

The ovary, at the pistil base, contains one or more ovules, which become seeds. The style, often narrow and elongated, connects the ovary to the stigma at the tip, which receives pollen. The stigma can be lobed (as in One-flower Wintergreen), knobby, threadlike, club-shaped, or disk- or button-shaped.

Stamen

A fertile stamen is composed of a thin stalk (filament) tipped with a pollen-bearing anther. Sterile stamens lack pollen and often an anther.

stigma

style

ovule

ovary

PISTIL

anther

stalk

STAMEN

Petals

Petals may be separate and countable (Richardson's Geranium, Twinleaf), or they may be united to each other, either completely from base to tip, as in a morning-glory (Scarlet-creeper), or only partly, with free tips, or corolla lobes (called flower lobes in this guide). The united petals may form a tubular base, or flower tube (Huachuca Mountain Rock-trumpet). Petals or lobes may be back-curved (Turk's-cap Lily), spreading (Venus'-looking-glass), or erect (Alp-lily).

Richardson's Geranium

Huachuca Mountain Rock-trumpet

Venus'-looking-glass

Turk's-cap Lily

Twinleaf

Alp-lily

Scarlet-creeper

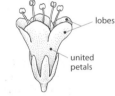

lobes

united petals

FLOWER WITH UNITED PETALS

Sepals

The calyx is comprised of all the sepals (sepal is defined on page 17), and these may be separate (Dissected Toothwort), partly united (One-flower Fringed-gentian), or mostly united and then often cup-shaped or tubular (California Pitcher-sage). The free tips of united sepals are called calyx lobes.

Dissected Toothwort

One-flower Fringed-gentian

California Pitcher-sage

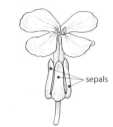

sepals

CALYX OF SEPARATE SEPALS

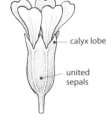

calyx lobe

united sepals

CALYX OF UNITED SEPALS

Tepals

In lilies, irises, and many other flowers, the sepals and petals are very similar to each other and are called tepals. Like sepals and petals, tepals may be united or free.

Scarlet Fritillary

Prairie-celestia

Two-lipped Flowers

In some flowers, the petals are
united at the base, forming a tube
or vase shape that opens (near the
throat) into two lips. The tips of
the lips may be separated into
lobes. (For more flower shapes
see the inside of the front cover.)

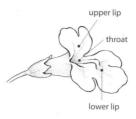

upper lip

throat

lower lip

Yellow Monkey-flower

Flowers with Spurs

Some flowers with united petals
or sepals have an elongated
projection called a spur at
the base. A spur may be long
(Yellow Larkspur) or short.

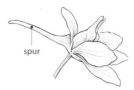

spur

Yellow Larkspur

Flower Arrangement

Flowers may be solitary (a single flower on a stem) or may occur in clusters, which
themselves may form compound clusters. Flowers or flower clusters can be at the tip of
the stem or tucked into the axils of leaves or bracts. There are many types of clusters,
including branched clusters, spikelike clusters, and umbels (umbrella-shaped clusters,
in which all the flower stalks arise from a common point). Clusters may be dense, with
many tightly packed flowers, or open, with the flowers loosely arranged. (For more cluster
shapes see the inside of the front cover.)

SOLITARY FLOWER

FLOWERS IN LEAF AXILS

BRANCHED CLUSTER

Desert Anemone

Sea-milkwort

Long-leaf Bluets

Leaves

A typical simple leaf—that is, a leaf that is not divided into separate leaflets—consists of a leaf blade and a leafstalk.

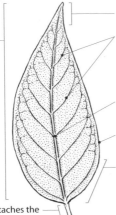

leaf tip The apex of the blade.

blade The expanded portion of the leaf.

veins Veins run through the leaf; side veins extend from the midrib, which is the central vein. Pinnate veins (illustrated here) angle from the midrib and may run to the edge of the blade. Palmate veins emanate from a common point at the leaf base. Some leaves have parallel veins.

midrib The vein that runs along the central axis of the blade, from base to tip.

edge The outer perimeter of the blade, also called the margin; may be toothed or lobed.

leaf base The lowest part of the blade.

leafstalk Attaches the blade to the supporting stem. Stalkless leaves lack a leafstalk (Short-spur Plectritis); some leaves clasp the stem (Green Adder's-mouth Orchid). Some plants (White Avens) have stipules, small leaflike structures near the leafstalk base.

Short-spur Plectritis

Green Adder's-mouth Orchid

White Avens

Compound Leaves

Compound leaves are divided into separate blades, called leaflets, each sometimes with its own stalk. Leaves may have only a few leaflets (Buckbean), or they may be more than once compound—the leaflets again divided—and bear numerous leaflets (Waxy-leaf Meadow-rue).

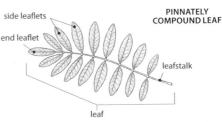
PALMATELY COMPOUND LEAF

leaflets

leafstalk

leaf

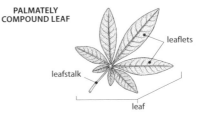
PINNATELY COMPOUND LEAF

side leaflets

end leaflet

leafstalk

leaf

Buck-bean

Waxy-leaf Meadow-rue

Palmately compound leaves have leaflets arising from a single point of attachment on the leafstalk. Pinnately compound leaves have leaflets borne in rows on either side of a central axis. Even-pinnate leaves have paired leaflets; odd-pinnate leaves (illustrated) are terminated by a leaflet.

Segmented Leaves

Some leaves are very deeply cut or lobed, but not quite enough to form true leaflets (separate blades). These divisions, some-times irregular in outline, are called segments in this guide. The overall shape of a segmented leaf can vary widely, from elongated (Small-flower Baby-blue-eyes) to rounded (Balsam-pear); many are hard to distinguish from a true compound leaf (Cut-leaf Cyclanthera). The descriptions fernlike, parsleylike, and carrotlike denote intricately cut leaves.

Small-flower Baby-blue-eyes

Balsam-pear

Cut-leaf Cyclanthera

Leaf Edges

The edges or margins of a leaf (or leaflet) blade may be untoothed (smooth), toothed (with small projections), or lobed (with large indentations). In toothed leaves, the tips of the teeth may be rounded (often called scalloped, as in Ground-ivy), blunt, or pointed; they may be small and uniform or large and coarse, lacking a regular pattern. Some leaves are single-toothed (Woodland-beardtongue); a few are double-toothed, with smaller teeth on the larger teeth (Goat's-beard).

PALMATELY LOBED LEAF

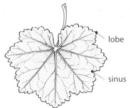
lobe

sinus

Hairy Alumroot

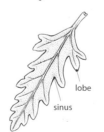

lobe

sinus

PINNATELY LOBED LEAF

Smooth Yellow False Foxglove

Ground-ivy

Woodland-beardtongue

Goat's-beard

Lobed leaf edges have prominent indentations; the projecting parts are the lobes, the indentations are sinuses. Sinuses can be shallow or deep. Lobes themselves may be toothed. The lobes of palmately lobed leaves arise from a common point, like the fingers on a hand. Pinnately lobed leaves have lobes extending from opposite sides of a central midrib.

Bracts

Bracts are modified leaves at the base of a flower or a flower cluster. They range from inconspicuous to showy, and they may resemble leaves (Creeping Eryngo), sepals (Turk's-cap), or even petals (Bunchberry).

Leaf Arrangement

The arrangement of leaves along a stem usually takes one of three forms: opposite, alternate, or whorled. The point at which a leaf attaches to the plant stem is the node. The angle formed between a leaf or leafstalk and the stem is the leaf axil. In some plants, flowers grow in the leaf axils. Basal leaves grow from the plant base.

Stem Leaves

Alternate leaves (Feathery False Solomon's-seal) are borne one at a node along the stem. **Opposite leaves** (Modesty) are borne in pairs at the same node. **Whorled leaves** (Starry Campion) are borne three or more at the same node.

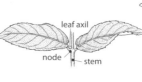

ALTERNATE LEAVES

OPPOSITE LEAVES

WHORLED LEAVES

Basal Leaves

Basal leaves grow at or near the plant base (Wild-comfrey) or they arise from it (Coltsfoot).

BASAL LEAVES GROWING NEAR BASE

BASAL LEAVES ARISING FROM BASE

How to Identify a Wildflower

To quickly identify an unknown wildflower, it helps to be familiar with the characteristics of the various plant families, an ability that comes with time and practice. For beginners, a good place to begin an identification is the Key to Colors and Shapes (page 24). Here, thumbnail photos of many (but not all) flowers in the guide, both native and introduced, are arranged by color and shape. Select the image that most resembles your unknown wildflower and turn to the page or pages indicated. Then check the larger photograph: does it look like your plant? Read the account text and the photo captions; does the information agree with your unknown? Verify the basics:

- Are the leaves simple or compound? Alternate, opposite, or in a basal cluster?
- What is the shape of the leaf? Are its edges smooth, wavy, or toothed?
- Do the flowers have separate petals, or are the petals united into a tubular, funnel, or bell shape?
- How many stamens are present?
- Are the flowers solitary, or are they arranged in clusters? If in clusters, what is the shape of the cluster?
- Does your unknown wildflower grow within the area indicated by the species' range map? If not, examine the genus map to determine whether a related species not included in the guide occurs within the geographical area where you have found your plant.

Perhaps you find a species with blue-violet flowers and long, grasslike leaves. Searching through the thumbnails, you find that it strongly resembles the flowers of blue-eyed-grasses (page 276) in the genus *Sisyrinchium*. Reading through the genus and account texts leaves you with little doubt that your unknown wildflower does, in fact, belong to the genus *Sisyrinchium*.

But what if the flower you are trying to identify does not inhabit the range of the blue-eyed-grass species mapped on page 276 (perhaps you are in Nebraska)? The organization of this guide ensures that you may at least be able to identify your unknown wildflower to its proper genus. Look at the genus map for *Sisyrinchium*, which indicates that other species of blue-eyed-grass occur throughout the United States, and you can assume that the flower you have in hand is a blue-eyed-grass species that is not illustrated.

As another example, let's say that the wildflower you are attempting to identify is in northwestern California, and that it looks like the thumbnail image of American Spikenard. Turn to the genus *Aralia* (page 77) and look at the larger photo. Read the text and captions associated with American Spikenard. If the photo and the text agree with your unknown, but not the distribution map, then examine the genus map to see if a related species is found in California. In this particular instance, this is indeed the case; the species you seek is individually mapped (though not illustrated): California Spikenard.

Metric Conversions

⅛ inch = 3 mm	½ inch = 1.3 cm
3⁄16 inch = 4.5 mm	¾ inch = 2 cm
¼ inch = 6 mm	1 inch = 2.5 cm
⅜ inch = 9.5 mm	1 foot = 30 cm

Flower Sizes

Approximate measurements that correspond to words describing the size of flowers and flower parts (not leaves).

Minute	1⁄16 inch or less
Tiny	⅛–3⁄16 inch
Small	¼–⅜ inch
(No text used)	½–1½ inches
Large	greater than 1½ inches

A Key to Colors and Shapes

This key arranges thumbnail images of many wildflowers in the guide by color and shape; page numbers reference plants with similar looking flowers. The true form of a flower is not always obvious; for example, a flower may appear to have separate petals when in fact the petals are united at their bases. To help beginners, flowers are grouped with the shape they most appear to have. Always refer to the family and genus texts for detailed information.

DISK/RAY TYPES

p. 87

pp. 143–52

pp. 143–52, 570–71

pp. 145–52

CLUSTERS OF SMALL FLOWERS flat-topped or round

pp. 114–30, 570–71

pp. 93–97, 100

p. 211

pp. 56–69, 565–66

pp. 553–54

p. 503

p. 221

p. 53

pp. 56–65, 67–69, 71, 76–77, 565–66

pp. 221–22

p. 363

pp. 249, 454–55, 457

pp. 262, 298–303, 332

pp. 332–33, 421, 430

p. 60

p. 155

pp. 168–80, 574–76

p. 181

pp. 262, 292, 332–33

pp. 321–23, 588

pp. 104–5

p. 108

p. 556

p. 445

CLUSTERS OF SMALL FLOWERS elongated

pp. 205–7

p. 352

pp. 92–100

pp. 211, 249, 433, 474, 454

p. 53

p. 77

pp. 407, 421, 426, 430–32, 434, 449, 591–92

pp. 407, 431, 455, 473, 511, 531

pp. 159–60, 163, 573

p. 213

p. 470

p. 181

pp. 243, 433, 473

p. 350

pp. 455, 511

pp. 213, 296, 496

pp. 278, 283, 587

pp. 215–18, 220, 350–51

p. 452

pp. 496–97

p. 166

pp. 303, 327–28

pp. 496–503

pp. 205–7

continued

 pp. 539–42

 p. 297

 pp. 92–97, 100

 p. 50

 pp. 153, 454

PETALS SEPARATE radial

 pp. 504–8

 pp. 194–95, 578

 pp. 336–37, 339, 341–45, 588–90

 pp. 193–95, 577–78

 pp. 337, 339, 341–45, 589

 pp. 456–60, 463, 466

 pp. 471, 476–77, 479–80, 483, 486–88

 pp. 192–93

 pp. 193–94, 577–78

 p. 498

 p. 451–2

 pp. 456–61

 p. 219

 p. 530

 p. 455

 pp. 364–65, 368–70

 p. 212

 p. 299

 pp. 51–52, 330

 p. 154

 pp. 155–56

 pp. 175, 177, 180

 pp. 260–61

 p. 274

pp. 304–5

pp. 313, 315, 327–28

p. 317

pp. 315–17

p. 318

pp. 311, 328

pp. 331, 463

pp. 357, 466

p. 332

p. 313

pp. 155, 398

pp. 398–401

pp. 398–401, 438

pp. 404, 439–41, 451

p. 600

pp. 362–63

pp. 349–51

pp. 468–70

pp. 453–54, 461

pp. 337, 339, 341–45, 588–98

PETALS SEPARATE bilateral

pp. 557, 600

pp. 226, 230, 233, 237–41

pp. 467–68, 594

p. 376

p. 384

5–86

pp. 386–92, 590

pp. 386–92, 590

pp. 371–74

 *continued*   PETALS UNITED radial

pp. 385–92, 590

 p. 71

 p. 254

 p. 259

 p. 447

 p. 267

 p. 294

 p. 421

 p. 163

 p. 71

 pp. 306–7

 pp. 159–60, 163, 573

 pp. 323, 327

 pp. 325–27

 pp. 410–15, 421–25, 439–40

 pp. 80, 82–83

 pp. 263–64

 p. 73

 p. 448

 p. 549

 pp. 493, 551

 pp. 257–58

 pp. 268–70

 pp. 302, 304, 313

 pp. 307–9

 pp. 414–15, 422

 pp. 447–48

 pp. 547–48, 599

 p. 253

pp. 265, 267, 269–70

pp. 265, 267, 269–70

pp. 215–20

pp. 490–91

pp. 307, 354–55, 548

pp. 348–49

pp. 489, 595–96

pp. 200–204, 579

pp. 490–91, 493

p. 599

PETALS UNITED bilateral

pp. 354–55

pp. 278, 292–93

p. 252

pp. 277–88

pp. 277–88, 586

pp. 516, 532

pp. 518, 541–43, 546, 554, 597–98

pp. 521–22, 527

pp. 530, 596

p. 417

pp. 532–34

p. 534

pp. 46–47

p. 577

DISK/RAY TYPES

pp. 87–92, 569

pp. 111–13

pp. 138–41, 147, 151, 572

pp. 138–42

continued

pp. 138–42

pp. 114–40

pp. 114–33

pp. 114–33

pp. 114–33

CLUSTERS OF SMALL FLOWERS flat-topped or round

pp. 104–7

p. 52

pp. 57, 59, 63–67, 69–70, 565

p. 137

p. 353

pp. 205, 580

p. 583

p. 189

pp. 81–83

pp. 134–37, 426, 435

pp. 168, 171, 173–74, 575

pp. 250, 426

p. 450

pp. 104–7, 571

CLUSTERS OF SMALL FLOWERS elongated

pp. 96, 105–6

p. 179

pp. 135–37

pp. 49–50, 74, 76

PETALS SEPARATE radial

pp. 537–38

p. 297

p. 165

pp. 166, 174, 179

p. 509

pp. 399–403

p. 361

p. 154

pp. 276, 329

p. 312

pp. 399–401

p. 317

pp. 298, 308

p. 326

pp. 198, 272, 329, 331

pp. 444, 593

pp. 344, 551

pp. 562, 600

p. 208

p. 319

p. 561

p. 348

pp. 171, 175, 575

pp. 494–95

p. 335

p. 330

pp. 197–98

pp. 344, 463, 476–85, 595

pp. 463–66, 594

p. 356

p. 154

pp. 464–66, 594

pp. 352, 357

pp. 396, 591

continued

 pp. 361, 364–70

 p. 314

 pp. 315, 317

 pp. 331–32

 pp. 402, 591

 pp. 304, 306

 pp. 182–84

 p. 511

 p. 49

 pp. 469–70

PETALS SEPARATE bilateral

 pp. 557–58

 pp. 250, 252

 pp. 229–36, 583–84

 p. 233

 pp. 378–79

 p. 384

 pp. 248–49, 584

 p. 76

 p. 210

PETALS UNITED radial

 pp. 190–91

 p. 395

 pp. 160–61

 pp. 265, 267

 p. 599

 p. 260

 p. 259

 p. 358

p. 296

pp. 411, 415, 423–24   p. 277   p. 72   pp. 253, 536   pp. 548, 550

PETALS UNITED bilateral

pp. 370, 450, 593   p. 71   pp. 450, 593   pp. 528, 597–98

pp. 295, 519, 597   p. 520   p. 520   p. 536   pp. 541–42

p. 2   pp. 542–45   p. 153   p. 405   pp. 512, 514–15, 598

DISK/RAY TYPES   **CLUSTERS OF SMALL FLOWERS** elongated

pp. 532–33   p. 90   p. 426

PETALS SEPARATE radial

p. 315   p. 331   pp. 402–3   pp. 443–44, 593

continued

 p. 562
 p. 585
 p. 174
 p. 274

PETALS SEPARATE bilateral
PETALS UNITED radial

 pp. 309–10, 585, 588
 p. 157
 p. 389

PETALS UNITED bilateral

 pp. 81–82
 p. 161
 p. 588

 p. 153

DISK/RAY TYPES
CLUSTERS OF SMALL FLOWERS flat-topped or round

 p. 156

 p. 131

 pp. 100–101

CLUSTERS OF SMALL FLOWERS elongated

 pp. 66–67
 pp. 205–6
 pp. 354–55

 p. 349

PETALS SEPARATE radial

 pp. 428–29
 p. 583

 pp. 196, 578
 p. 591

p. 480 · p. 593 · pp. 337–46, 589 · p. 338 · pp. 338–46

pp. 309–11 · p. 314 · p. 274 · pp. 404, 591 · p. 405

PETALS SEPARATE bilateral

p. 318 · pp. 315–16 · p. 468 · p. 234

PETALS UNITED radial

p. 468 · pp. 204, 579 · p. 156 · p. 462

pp. 190–91, 489 · p. 361 · pp. 204, 579 · p. 420 · p. 325

PETALS UNITED bilateral

p. 409 · pp. 190–91 · pp. 46, 281, 290 · p. 187

🌸 continued

pp. 281, 285, 289–90 | pp. 514, 519 | p. 522 | pp. 513, 528 | p. 538

DISK/RAY TYPES

CLUSTERS OF SMALL FLOWERS flat-topped or round

pp. 86–89, 569–70 | pp. 123–24 | p. 510

p. 356 | p. 554 | pp. 408–9, 435, 437, 445 | pp. 215–20

CLUSTERS OF SMALL FLOWERS elongated

92 | p. 294 | pp. 431–33 | pp. 426, 431

pp. 472–74 | pp. 283, 587 | pp. 300, 320 | p. 300 | pp. 451–52

PETALS SEPARATE radial

pp. 311–13 | pp. 311–13 | p. 318 | 76–79, 575

pp. 300, 334, 588

pp. 321, 322, 587

pp. 195–96, 578

p. 51

pp. 260–61, 577, 585

pp. 486–87

pp. 439–41

pp. 336–46, 588–91

pp. 337–43, 589–90

p. 340

pp. 260–61, 271

p. 399

pp. 441–43

p. 365

pp. 488, 504, 509

PETALS SEPARATE bilateral

p. 564

pp. 444–45

pp. 182–84

p. 427

PETALS UNITED radial

pp. 251–52

p. 376

pp. 378–79

pp. 79–82

p. 258

p. 258

p. 420

pp. 48, 72

p. 324

▼ *continued*

pp. 409–12, 414, 423–25, 439–40, 446

pp. 415, 418, 420

p. 71

pp. 79–83

p. 265

p. 163

p. 255

pp. 215–20

p. 218

p. 448

PETALS UNITED bilateral

pp. 201–3, 579

pp. 556, 599–600

p. 447

p. 46

p. 295

pp. 278–86, 586

pp. 277–92

pp. 277–92, 586

pp. 277–92

pp. 405, 406

p. 417

pp. 512–14, 517

p. 515

p. 596

pp. 523–35, 596

p. 528

pp. 539–40

pp. 540, 542, 546

p. 542

p. 546

pp. 290–92, 586

pp. 290–92

pp. 277–92, 586

p. 596

DISK/RAY TYPES

CLUSTERS OF SMALL FLOWERS flat-topped or round

pp. 111–12

pp. 100–103, 566–68

p. 250

pp. 352–53

pp. 189–90, 576

pp. 321–22

pp. 359–61

pp. 94–100

CLUSTERS OF SMALL FLOWERS elongated

p. 99

p. 243

p. 99

pp. 60–61

PETALS SEPARATE radial

pp. 347–48, 362

p. 397

pp. 359–61

pp. 337–42, 589

pp. 273–74

pp. 275–76

p. 316

p. 562

pp. 575–76

continued

pp. 260–61, 585   p. 502   p. 304   p. 167   p. 405

PETALS SEPARATE bilateral

pp. 182–84   p. 277   pp. 359–61, 578   pp. 559–60, 600

p. 334   p. 572   p. 584   p. 346   p. 228

PETALS UNITED radial

pp. 226–33, 240–41, 244, 581–83   pp. 381–83   p. 385   p. 254

p. 264   p. 266   p. 414   pp. 264–68   pp. 47–48

p. 255   p. 255   p. 256   p. 258   pp. 256, 266, 268

pp. 548, 550, 599

pp. 324–25

pp. 409, 412–13, 417, 419, 421

pp. 550, 599

p. 566

PETALS UNITED bilateral

p. 556

pp. 354–55

p. 191

p. 396

pp. 279–83

pp. 516–19

pp. 516–19

pp. 519, 523–24

pp. 531–32

pp. 539–40, 542

p. 542

pp. 544–46

pp. 529–30, 596

p. 545

p. 47

p. 48

p. 78

p. 296

p. 517

DISK/RAY TYPES

CLUSTERS OF SMALL FLOWERS
flat-topped or round

pp. 142–45

pp. 102–3

continued

CLUSTERS OF SMALL FLOWERS elongated

p. 98   pp. 100–101, 566–68   p. 418   p. 242

PETALS SEPARATE radial

p. 573   p. 328   pp. 273–75   p. 275

pp. 275–76   p. 438   p. 593   pp. 458–60   p. 276

PETALS SEPARATE bilateral

pp. 559–60   pp. 198–99   pp. 467–68, 594   p. 233

PETALS UNITED radial

pp. 233, 235–37   pp. 239–45, 581   p. 228   p. 181

pp. 518, 531, 555   pp. 518, 531, 555, 600   p. 257   p. 257   p. 534

pp. 158–59, 162   pp. 162, 573   pp. 263, 265   pp. 162, 573   pp. 264–65

p. 271   p. 325   pp. 253–54   pp. 255–56   p. 264

p. 268   pp. 264, 296   pp. 409, 576   pp. 412–19, 421   pp. 200–201, 579

p. 330   pp. 414, 421   pp. 438, 592   pp. 184–86   pp. 184–86

pp. 184–86, 191, 576   p. 462   pp. 490–91   p. 566   pp. 529–30, 596

PETALS UNITED bilateral

pp. 394–96   pp. 278–89   pp. 278–89, 585   p. 287

✻ continued

pp. 518–19, 524–25, 527, 531–34, 555

pp. 187–88

p. 586

pp. 517, 597

pp. 523, 525, 526

CLUSTERS OF SMALL FLOWERS round   **CLUSTERS OF SMALL FLOWERS** elongated

p. 547

p. 54 **DO NOT HANDLE**

pp. 429, 432, 592

PETALS SEPARATE radial

p. 550

pp. 73–74

p. 180

p. 319

p. 405

p. 301

p. 561

p. 169

p. 75

PETALS UNITED radial

p. 392

p. 80

p. 162

p. 257

CLUSTERS OF SMALL FLOWERS elongated

p. 199

p. 598

p. 452

p. 552

PETALS SEPARATE radial

p. 75

p. 319

p. 318

pp. 77, 78

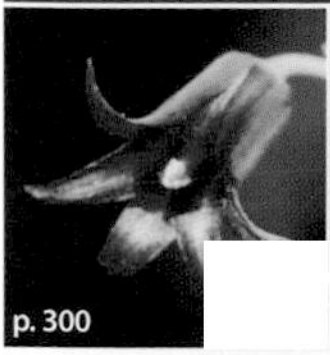

p. 300

p. 301

p. 314

p. 320

p. 314

PETALS SEPARATE bilateral   **PETALS UNITED** radial

pp. 499–503

pp. 372–74

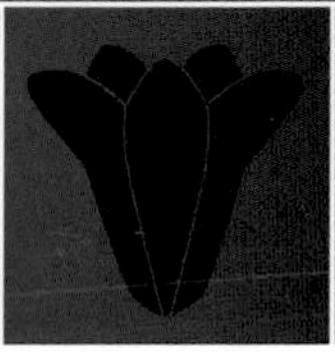

p. 158

PETALS UNITED bilateral   **BICOLORED**

p. 259

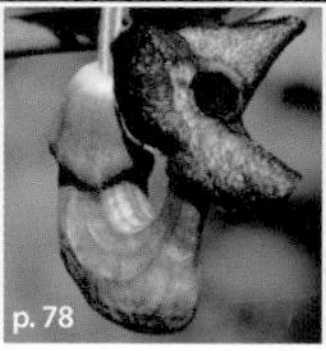

p. 78

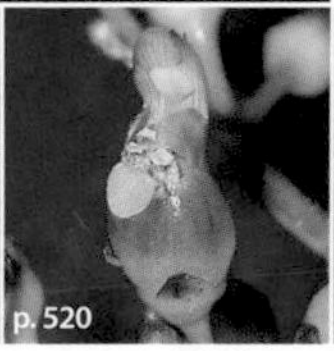

p. 520

p. 376

BICOLORED

p. 329

pp. 468–70

p. 333

p. 392

pp. 390–93, 590

BICOLORED

pp. 241–42, 244–47

p. 600

p. 516

p. 288

p. 180

ACANTHACEAE   ACANTHUS FAMILY

Woody shrubs or annual or perennial herbs. Leaves normally opposite; simple and often untoothed. Flowers usually in clusters; tubular to funnel-shaped (petals united), 4- or 5-lobed, sometimes 2-lipped; sepals 5; stamens 2 or 4; pistil 1. Fruits are capsules.

■ **ARIZONA FOLDWING** (*Dicliptera resupinata*): Spring–fall; rocky slopes, canyons. Leafstalks to ¾ in. long.

■ **BRANCHED FOLDWING** (*D. brachiata*): Summer–fall; moist woods, thickets, stream banks. Similar to Arizona Foldwing, but stalks of larger leaves 1½–2½ in. long; bracts spoon-shaped.

■ **SIX-ANGLE FOLDWING** (*D. sexangularis*): Year-round; roadsides, hammocks. Flowers scarlet; stamens not, or only slightly, protruding.

Genus *Dicliptera* (3 native species). Leaves opposite. Flowers in short-stalked clusters, 2-lipped; flower base enclosed by leaflike bracts; stamens 2.

Arizona Foldwing

Branched Foldwing

HT: to 2 ft.

Six-angle Foldwing

Flowers rose-pink; stamens protruding. Bracts heart-shaped. HT: 1–2 ft.

HT: to 4 ft.

■ **AMERICAN WATER-WILLOW** (*Justicia americana*): Spring–fall; shallow water and shores of rivers, streams, lakes, ditches. Leaves mostly stalkless, slender, willowlike. Flowers have lower lip with spreading side lobes. **SIMILAR LOOSE-FLOWER WATER-WILLOW** (*J. ovata*): Swamps, marshes; southeastern. Flowers in loose clusters, lavender; lower lip similar to that of Hairy Tube-tongue (p. 47).

■ **HUMMINGBIRD-BUSH** (*J. californica*): Mostly spring; desert slopes, flats. Shrub. Leaves egg-shaped (but plants leafless much of the year). Flowers large, scarlet to red-orange (rarely yellow), in clusters at stem ends. Also called Chuparosa.

Genus *Justicia* (17 species, 14 native). Leaves opposite. Flowers in clusters; 2-lipped, with lower lip 3-lobed; stamens 2.

American Water-willow

Flowers light violet to whitish, with purple markings.

Flowers in long-stalked, crowded clusters. HT: 1–3 ft.

Hummingbird-bush

Flowers usually scarlet. HT: 2–6 ft.

■ **HAIRY TUBE-TONGUE** (*Justicia pilosella*): Spring–fall; open woods, hills, grassy places, stream banks. Leaves egg-shaped. Flowers sometimes rose or whitish. Also called False Honeysuckle.

■ **LONG-FLOWER TUBE-TONGUE** (*J. longii*): Rocky slopes. Leaves lance-shaped. Also called Dwarf White-honeysuckle.

Hairy Tube-tongue

Flowers commonly lavender with purple-spotted white throat; tube slender. HT: to 12 in.

Long-flower Tube-tongue

Flowers white; tube long, slender. HT: to 12 in.

■ **CAROLINA RUELLIA** (*Ruellia caroliniensis*): Late spring–fall; woods, fields, roadsides. Mostly has lance-shaped to elliptic leaves along stem; ssp. *ciliosa* (not pictured), eastern TX to NC, has spoon-shaped leaves clustered near base of short stem. Also called Carolina Wild-petunia. **SIMILAR** ■ **FRINGE-LEAF RUELLIA** (*R. humilis*): Leaves stalkless. ■ **LIMESTONE RUELLIA** (*R. strepens*): Stems nearly hairless. Also called Smooth Ruellia.

NOTE Flowers of most ruellias are violet, blue-violet, or pinkish violet. A few species bear white flowers.

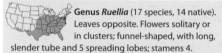

Genus *Ruellia* (17 species, 14 native). Leaves opposite. Flowers solitary or in clusters; funnel-shaped, with long, slender tube and 5 spreading lobes; stamens 4.

Carolina Ruellia

Flowers purplish. Leaves stalked. Stems hairy. HT: to 3 ft.

■ **NARROW-LEAF SNAKEHERB**
(*Dyschoriste linearis*): Spring–summer;
slopes, flats, open woods. Leaves relatively narrow. Flowers have dark purple
marks in throat. Also called Polkadots.

■ **OBLONG-LEAF SNAKEHERB**
(*D. oblongifolia*): Spring–fall; pinelands,
sandhills. Leaves mostly widest above
middle. Flowers ¾–1 in. long.

■ **SWAMP SNAKEHERB** (*D. humistrata*):
Mostly spring–early summer; floodplain
woods. Flowers less than ½ in. long.

NOTE Species are also called twinflower.

Genus *Dyschoriste* (6 native species).
Similar to *Ruellia* (p. 47), but the flower's
narrow, tubular portion is short,
expanding from the throat into a bell shape.

Narrow-leaf Snakeherb

Flowers
lavender to
bluish purple.
HT: 6–15 in.

Oblong-leaf
Snakeherb

Leaves
relatively
broad.
HT: 4–14 in.

Swamp Snakeherb

Flowers
short.
HT: 4–12 in.

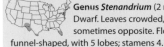

■ **EARLY SHAGGYTUFT** (*Stenandrium
barbatum*): Spring–summer; limestone
flats, rocky hills. Plants mound-forming.
Leaves opposite, densely hairy.

■ **PINELAND PINKLET** (*S. dulce*): Year-
round; moist pinelands, grassy roadsides.
Leaves basal, mostly hairless. Also called
Sweet Shaggytuft.

Genus *Stenandrium* (2 native species).
Dwarf. Leaves crowded, basal or
sometimes opposite. Flowers in clusters;
funnel-shaped, with 5 lobes; stamens 4.

Early Shaggytuft

Flowers
reddish purple with
white streaks. HT: to 3 in.

Pineland Pinklet

Flowers
rose-purple to
pink. HT: to 4 in.

ACORACEAE
SWEETFLAG or CALAMUS FAMILY

Perennial; aromatic. Leaves basal, simple, and elongated, overlapping toward bottom. Flowers tiny, numerous, crowded on fingerlike stalk. Fruits are berries.

■ **AMERICAN SWEETFLAG**
(*Acorus americanus*): Late spring–summer; shallow water, wet ground. The rootstock and crushed foliage are fragrant. Leaves narrowly sword-shaped. Also called Several-vein Sweetflag.
SIMILAR ▣ CALAMUS (*A. calamus*): Mostly central and eastern; an Old World native. Very similar, but sterile, and only the offset midvein of the leaf is conspicuously raised (2–6 raised veins in American Sweetflag). Also called Sweetflag, Single-vein Sweetflag.

Genus *Acorus* (2 species, 1 native). Traditionally, this genus has been included in the family Araceae (p. 73).

American Sweetflag

Flower cluster borne partway up a leaflike stem. HT: to 5 ft.

Flowers greenish to yellowish brown.

AGAVACEAE
AGAVE FAMILY

Perennial. Leaves mostly all clustered at plant base, simple. Flowers in large clusters; 6 tepals (3 petals and 3 petal-like sepals); stamens 6; pistil 1. Fruits are capsules, sometimes fleshy.

■ **AGAVE** (*Agave*; 27 species, 24 native): Mostly spring–summer; slopes, grasslands, shrublands, open woods, roadsides; most common in desert regions. Leaves mostly 6 in.–6 ft. long, often toothed or spiny-edged, with rigid tip. Flowering stalks mostly 3–30 ft. tall. Also called century-plant.

■ **FALSE ALOE** (*Manfreda*; 5 native species): Spring–early fall; rocky or sandy soil. Leaves 4–16 in. long, with flexible tip; not prominently toothed or spiny. Flowering stalks 1–6 ft. tall.

Agave and Relatives (several related genera, numerous species). Leaves generally sharp-pointed. Flower clusters often dense. (Maps show genus distribution.)

Agave

Flowers typically yellowish.

False Aloe

Flowers typically greenish.

■ **YUCCA** (*Yucca*; 28 native species):
Mostly spring–summer; slopes, plains,
grasslands, woods, desert flats. Leaves
occasionally toothed; in many species
edges are frayed into fibrous threads.
Stalks of flower clusters less than 1 in.
in diameter. Plants mostly 3–30 ft. tall.
Some species called Spanish-bayonet,
soapweed.

■ **OUR-LORD'S-CANDLE** (*Hesperoyucca*;
2 native species): Spring; slopes, deserts,
shrublands, open woods. Leaves 6 in.–3 ft.
long. Flowering stalks 3–10 ft. tall, greater
than 1 in. in diameter.

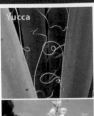
Yucca

Our-Lord's-candle

Flowers large,
white or cream-
colored. Leaf
edges untoothed,
often with fibers.

Flowers similar
to Yucca. Leaf edges
toothed, not fibrous.

■ **SOTOL** (*Dasylirion*; 3 native species):
Mostly late spring–midsummer; open
rocky slopes. Leaves 1–4 ft. long. Flowering
stalks 8–15 ft. tall. Also called desert-spoon.

■ **BEAR-GRASS** (*Nolina*; 14 native
species): Spring–summer; West: open
woods, grasslands, deserts; East:
pinelands. Leaves mostly 1–4 ft. long.
Flowers tiny; flowering stalks to 10 ft. tall.

Sotol

Bear-grass

Flowers
tiny, whitish.
Leaf edges
have sharp,
curved
prickles.

Leaves
untoothed
or toothed,
not prickly.

AIZOACEAE
FIG-MARIGOLD FAMILY

Annual or perennial. Leaves usually opposite and simple; fleshy and usually untoothed. Flowers solitary or in clusters; petals commonly numerous, sometimes none; sepals 3–8; stamens often many; pistil 1. Fruits are usually capsules, occasionally berrylike.

■ **SHORELINE SEA-PURSLANE**
(*Sesuvium portulacastrum*): Early spring–frost (year-round in frost-free regions); sandy beaches, salty coastal areas. Roots at nodes. **SIMILAR** Not rooting at nodes. **SLENDER SEA-PURSLANE** (*S. maritimum*): Similar habitat and range. Only 5 stamens. ■ **WESTERN SEA-PURSLANE** (*S. verrucosum*): Alkaline flats, playa lakes, salty coastal areas. Stamens many.

 Genus *Sesuvium* (4 native species). Plants succulent. Leaves opposite, linear to spoon-shaped. Flowers star-shaped; sepals 5, petal-like (true petals absent), "horn-tipped"; stamens usually numerous. Fruits are capsules.

Shoreline Sea-purslane

Flowers rosy pink; stamens many. Leaves fleshy. Stems sprawling, mat-forming, often reddish.

ALISMATACEAE
WATER-PLANTAIN or ARROWHEAD FAMILY

Annual or more commonly perennial. Leaves simple and usually all basal; generally long-stalked, sometimes floating or underwater. Flowers in clusters; petals 3; sepals 3; stamens 6 to many; pistils numerous. Fruits seedlike, grouped in circles or ball-shaped clusters.

■ **WATER-PLANTAIN** (*Alisma*): Spring–fall; shallow water, muddy shores. Flowers white. Fruits in buttonlike clusters.

RELATED Similar habitats. ■ **FRINGED-WATER-PLANTAIN** (*Damasonium californicum*): Mostly summer. Similar to *Alisma*, but petals toothed; fruit segments pointed. Also called Star-water-plantain. ■ **BURHEAD** (*Echinodorus*): Summer–fall. Fruits in round, burlike clusters.

 Genus *Alisma* (5 species, 3 native). Flowers small, in large, open clusters with whorled branches; stamens 6–9; pistils 15–20. Seedlike fruits in a circle on flattened receptacle.

Water-plantain

Leaves commonly elliptic to egg-shaped. HT: 6 in.–3 ft.

Fringed-water-plantain

HT: to 14 in.

Burhead

HT: 6 in.–3 ft.

■ **COMMON ARROWHEAD**
(*Sagittaria latifolia*): Summer–fall;
muddy shores, marshes, ditches. Also
called Wapato. SIMILAR ■ **GIANT**
ARROWHEAD (*S. montevidensis* ssp.
calycina): Leafstalks spongy, thick; petals
have greenish yellow base; fruiting heads
drooping, clasped by the enlarged sepals.
Also called Hooded Arrowhead.

GRASSLEAF ARROWHEAD (*S. graminea*):
Mostly eastern. Flowers resemble
Common Arrowhead.

NOTE Do not confuse arrowheads with
Arrow-arum (p. 74) or Pickerel-weed
(p. 438). Some arrowheads form ribbon-
or rod-like underwater leaves.

Genus *Sagittaria* (24 species, 23 native).
Flowers in whorls of usually 3, upper ones
all male (many stamens only), lower ones
mostly all female (pistils only). Seedlike fruits flat, winged.

Common
Arrowhead

Grassleaf Arrowhead

Flowers white. Leaves
mostly arrowhead-shaped.
Fruits aggregated in ball-
shaped clusters. HT: 6 in.–3 ft.

Leaves
lance-
shaped.
HT: to 3 ft.

AMARANTHACEAE   AMARANTH FAMILY

Annual or perennial. Leaves alternate or opposite, simple, and untoothed. Flowers tiny, in dense clusters interspersed with many small, papery, often colored bracts. Fruits typically tiny or very small, dry,
thin-walled, 1-seeded.

■ **WOOLLY HONEYSWEET** (*Tidestromia
lanuginosa*): Spring–fall; open places.
Plants mat- or mound-forming. Stems
reddish. Leaves densely whitish-hairy or
gray-hairy.

Genus *Tidestromia* (3 native species).
Leaves mostly opposite. Flowers tiny, in
clusters in leaf axils.

Woolly Honeysweet

Flowers yellowish.
Leaves roundish.
HT: mostly 4–6 in.

■ **PLAINS SNAKE-COTTON** (*Froelichia floridana*): Spring–fall; sandy prairies, roadsides. Also called Florida Snake-cotton.

RELATED *Iresine* (5 native species). Flowers unisexual, in more open clusters than *Froelichia*. ■ **JUDA'S-BUSH** (*I. rhizomatosa*): Mostly fall; river and stream banks, wet woods, sandy soil. Stems mostly unbranched below. Flower clusters on mature female plants fluffy-hairy. **JUBA'S-BUSH** (*I. diffusa*, no photo): Hammocks, floodplains, disturbed places; native chiefly to FL. Stems branched.

Genus *Froelichia* (5 native species). Leaves opposite, mostly on lower half of stem. Flowers tiny, in elongated clusters, densely white-woolly on outer surfaces.

Plains Snake-cotton

Flowers in spikelike, cottony clusters. HT: 1½–5 ft.

Juda's-bush

Flowers in plumelike clusters. HT: 1–3 ft.

■ **TUFTED GLOBE-AMARANTH** (*Gomphrena caespitosa*): Spring–early summer; open places. Plants clumped. Leaves mostly near base, densely gray-hairy. Flowers tiny.

■ **ARRASA-CON-TODO** (*G. serrata*): Year-round; open places. Plants not clumped. Leaves mostly on stem, green. Flower clusters white, often tinged pink or red.

RELATED **SILVERHEAD** (*Blutaparon vermiculare*): Year-round; sandy beaches, saline shores; coastal TX, LA, FL. Similar to globe-amaranths, but leaves narrow, succulent. Also called Bayflower, Samphire. Do not confuse with Alligator-weed (p. 564).

Genus *Gomphrena* (9 species, 7 native). Leaves opposite. Flowers in ball-shaped clusters, often hairy or woolly outside.

Tufted Globe-amaranth

Flower clusters white (flower tips sometimes yellow). HT: 2–6 in.

Arrasa-con-todo

HT: 6–18 in.

Silverhead

HT: to 20 in.

ANACARDIACEAE   CASHEW or SUMAC FAMILY

Trees, shrubs, or woody vines. Leaves normally alternate; simple or more often compound. Flowers in clusters; petals 5; sepals 5; stamens typically 5 or 10; pistil 1, its base surrounded by a ringlike nectar disk. Fruits berrylike.

■ **POISON-IVY** (*Toxicodendron radicans*): Spring–summer; open woods, thickets, roadsides, disturbed places. Normally a woody vine climbing via aerial rootlets on stems. Leaflet edges unlobed or lobed. SIMILAR ■ **PACIFIC POISON-OAK** (*T. diversilobum*): Also called Western Poison-oak. **POISON-OAK** (*T. pubescens*): Southeastern. Shrubby (no aerial stem rootlets). ■ **WESTERN POISON-IVY** (*T. rydbergii*).

Genus *Toxicodendron* (5 native species). Leaves divided into leaflets. Flowers in clusters from leaf axils, unisexual (plants either male or female); stamens 5. NOTE Do not touch; plants have poisonous sap.

Poison-ivy

Fruits cream-colored, tan, or yellowish.

Flowers small, greenish or whitish.

Leaflets 3, middle one long-stalked.

Rootlets present on some stems.

APIACEAE or UMBELLIFERAE   PARSLEY or CARROT FAMILY

Annual, biennial, or perennial; sometimes aromatic. Stems hollow. Leaves alternate or basal, typically compound and divided into segments or leaflets, often large. Flowers tiny, numerous, in flat-topped or rounded umbrella-like clusters (simple umbels), these frequently forming a compound umbel (see illustration below); petals 5, white, yellow, or rarely purple; sepals 5, commonly toothlike or obsolete, rarely conspicuous; stamens 5; pistil 1, styles 2. Fruits seedlike, often winged or ribbed, eventually splitting into 2 segments. NOTE Some species are poisonous if ingested. Contact with the sap of certain species and subsequent exposure to sunlight may result in a painful rash (phytophotodermatitis).

FLOWER

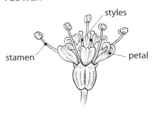

styles

stamen — petal

stamen

styles

petal

COMPOUND UMBEL

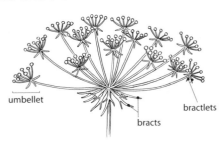

umbellet

bractlets

bracts

Flowers of the parsley family are often arranged in flat-topped or rounded "compound umbels," formed by several long-stalked flower clusters (umbellets) arising from a common point like umbrella ribs. The individual flowers themselves are tiny; the two styles or their enlarged bases (in the center of each flower) are often persistent and visible on the seedlike fruits.

FRUITS OF THE APIACEAE

This is a difficult group for beginners. Many members of the family look alike and are best told apart by technical features, such as those of the seedlike fruits pictured here. (Approximate lengths are given.)

PURPLE-STEM ANGELICA
Flattened and winged; ¼ in. (p. 57).

AMERICAN THOROUGH-WAX
Oblong, with conspicuous ribs; ⅛ in. (p. 57).

SPREADING CHERVIL
Narrowly elliptic, with slender ribs; ¼–⅜ in. (p. 58).

SOUTHERN CHERVIL
Lance-shaped, with thick ribs; ¼–⁵⁄₁₆ in. (p. 58).

WATER-HEMLOCK
Roundish, with corky ribs; ⅛ in. (p. 58).

HONEWORT
Narrow, with slender ribs; ¼ in. (p. 59).

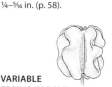

VARIABLE SPRING-PARSLEY
Oblong and often 3- or 4-winged; ⅜ in. (p. 59).

HARBINGER-OF-SPRING
Wider than long, flattened, with slender ribs; ¹⁄₁₆ in. (p. 60).

RATTLESNAKE-MASTER
Covered with papery scales; ¼ in. (p. 60).

AMERICAN BEACH SILVERTOP
With corky-winged ribs; ¼–½ in. (p. 61).

COW-PARSNIP
Flattened and winged; ¼–½ in. (p. 62).

MANY-FLOWER WATER-PENNYWORT
Roundish and flattened; ¹⁄₁₆ in. (p. 62).

PORTER'S WILD LOVAGE
Ovoid, ribbed, narrowly winged; ¼ in. (p. 63).

FERN-LEAF DESERT-PARSLEY
Flattened, narrowly winged; ⅜–¾ in. (p. 63).

WATER-PARSLEY
Barrel-shaped and corky-ribbed, tipped by 2 elongated styles; ⅛ in. (p. 64).

LONG-STYLE SWEET-CICELY
Bristly, with elongated styles; ½–¾ in. (p. 65).

WESTERN SWEET-CICELY
Smooth, with short styles; ½–¾ in. (p. 65).

GAIRDNER'S YAMPAH
Roundish; ¹⁄₁₆–⅛ in. (p. 65).

PRAIRIE-PARSLEY
Elliptic, flattened, corky-winged; ¼–⅜ in. (p. 66).

MOUNTAIN-PARSLEY
Oblong-elliptic, winged; ⅛–¼ in. (p. 66).

THREAD-LEAF MOCK BISHOP'S-WEED
Ovoid, with conspicuous side ribs; ⅛ in. (p. 67).

PRAIRIE-BISHOP'S-WEED
In 2 side-by-side nearly circular segments; ¹⁄₁₆–⅛ in. (p. 67).

BLACK-SNAKEROOT
Roundish, often covered with hooked bristles; ¹⁄₁₆–¼ in. (p. 67).

WATER-PARSNIP
Roundish, with corky-winged ribs; ¹⁄₁₆–⅛ in. (p. 68).

CUT-LEAF-WATER-PARSNIP
Roundish and corky; ¹⁄₁₆ in. (p. 68).

COWBANE
Flattened and winged, with narrow ribs; ³⁄₁₆–¼ in. (p. 68).

RANGER'S-BUTTONS
Wedge-shaped and winged; ¼ in. (p. 69).

YELLOW-PIMPERNEL
Elliptic, with narrow ribs; ³⁄₁₆ in. (p. 69).

HAIRY-JOINT MEADOW-PARSNIP
Oblong-elliptic, winged; ³⁄₁₆ in. (p. 70).

GOLDEN ALEXANDERS
Oblong-ovate, ribbed; ⅛ in. (p. 70).

■ **LYALL'S ANGELICA** (*Angelica arguta*): Summer; moist to wet places in meadows, woods. Leaves large; leafstalk bases enlarged. Also called Sharp-tooth Angelica. **SIMILAR** ■ **KNEELING ANGELICA** (*A. genuflexa*): Some leafstalks sharply bent so that leaflets point downward. ■ **HAIRY ANGELICA** (*A. venenosa*): Open woods, thickets, pinelands, roadsides. Fruits and stalks of flower clusters conspicuously downy.

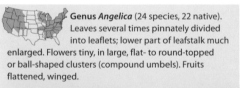

Genus *Angelica* (24 species, 22 native). Leaves several times pinnately divided into leaflets; lower part of leafstalk much enlarged. Flowers tiny, in large, flat- to round-topped or ball-shaped clusters (compound umbels). Fruits flattened, winged.

Lyall's Angelica

Flowers white, in large, flat- to round-topped clusters. Leaves divided into many sharp-toothed leaflets. HT: 2–5 ft.

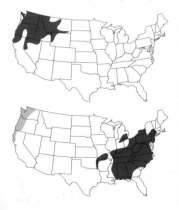

■ **PURPLE-STEM ANGELICA** (*Angelica atropurpurea*): Summer; moist or wet ground. Leaflets sharp-pointed, toothed; leafstalk bases enlarged. Also called Great Angelica. **SIMILAR** ■ **HENDERSON'S ANGELICA** (*A. hendersonii*): Coastal strand and bluffs. Leaflets blunt, woolly-hairy beneath. Also called Coast Angelica. **SEACOAST ANGELICA** (*A. lucida*): Coastal habitats; West Coast and New England. Leaves hairless.

■ **SIERRAN ANGELICA** (*A. lineariloba*): Open rocky slopes, mountain meadows. Unusual in having linear, untoothed leaflets.

Purple-stem Angelica

Sierran Angelica

Flowers white, in large, ball-shaped clusters. Stems dark purple. HT: 3–9 ft.

HT: 2–5 ft.

■ **AMERICAN THOROUGH-WAX** (*Bupleurum americanum*): Summer; slopes, mountain meadows, grasslands. The undivided leaves are unusual for this family. Flowers sometimes purplish.

NOTE *Bupleurum* species are also called thorow-wax. See also ⬚ Round-leaf Thorough-wax (p. 564), which has broadly egg-shaped upper stem leaves that appear to be pierced by the stem.

Genus *Bupleurum* (3 species, 1 native). Leaves simple, untoothed. Flowers tiny, in clusters (compound umbels). Fruits somewhat flattened, ribbed.

American Thorough-wax

Flowers yellow, in rounded clusters. Leaves mostly basal, linear to narrowly lance-shaped. HT: to 20 in.

■ **SPREADING CHERVIL** (*Chaerophyllum procumbens*): Spring; open woods, thickets, roadsides. Stems and underside of leaves hairless to sparsely hairy. Fruits broadest near middle; fruit stalks uniformly threadlike. Also called Wild Chervil.

■ **SOUTHERN CHERVIL** (*C. tainturieri*): Open woods, thickets, fields, prairies. Stems and underside of leaves usually conspicuously hairy. Fruits broadest below middle; fruit stalks thicker toward top. Also called Wild Chervil.

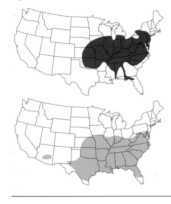

Genus *Chaerophyllum* (2 native species). Leaves dissected into numerous small segments. Flowers tiny, in clusters (compound or occasionally simple umbels). Fruits elongated, somewhat flattened, ribbed.

Spreading Chervil

Flowers white, in small clusters. Leaves parsley- or fern-like. HT: 4–16 in.

Southern Chervil

HT: 4–20 in.

■ **WATER-HEMLOCK** (*Cicuta maculata*): Summer; wet soil. The main side veins on leaflets lead to notches (sinuses) between adjacent teeth, not to tips of teeth (compare *Ligusticum*, *Oenanthe*, and *Sium*, pp. 63, 64, 68). Also called Spotted Cowbane.

■ **BULBLET-BEARING WATER-HEMLOCK** (*C. bulbifera*): Clusters of tiny bulbs (bulblets) present in leaf axils; leaflets less than ¼ in. wide.

NOTE *Cicuta* species are extremely poisonous.

Genus *Cicuta* (4 native species). Sometimes has fleshy, often clustered, carrot-like roots. Leaves pinnately divided 1 or usually 2 or 3 times into sharply toothed, lance-shaped leaflets. Flowers tiny, in rounded or flat-topped clusters (compound umbels). Fruits roundish, with corky ribs.

Water-hemlock

Bulblet-bearing Water-hemlock

Flowers white. Stems often purple-marked. HT: 2–6 ft.

Leaflets narrow; bulblets present. HT: 1–3 ft.

■ **HONEWORT** (*Cryptotaenia canadensis*):
Late spring–summer; woods, stream
banks, floodplains. Leaflets can be
irregularly toothed, double-toothed, or
lobed. Flowers in clusters on unequal
stalks.

Genus *Cryptotaenia* (1 native species).
Leaves divided into 3 leaflets. Flowers tiny,
on stalks of unequal length in loose clusters
(compound umbels). Fruits narrow, with slender ribs.

Honewort

Flowers white.
Leaflets 3, outer
2 often lobed. HT: 1–3 ft.

■ **VARIABLE SPRING-PARSLEY**
(*Cymopterus purpureus*): Spring–early
summer; hills, plains, shrublands. Flowers
yellow or purple. Also called Colorado
Plateau Spring-parsley.

■ **PLAINS SPRING-PARSLEY** (*C. acaulis*):
Flowers commonly white, sometimes
yellow or purple.

■ **WIDE-WING SPRING-PARSLEY**
(*C. purpurascens*): Flowers commonly
purple, sometimes white; this and a few
other *Cymopterus* have united bracts
forming a "cup" around cluster. Also called
Basin White-cup Spring-parsley.

NOTE Spring-parsleys are often wider
than tall. See similar Mountain-parsley
(p. 66) and desert-parsleys (pp. 63–64).

Genus *Cymopterus* (36 native species).
Leaves mostly basal, divided 1 or more
times into small segments. Flowers tiny,
in rounded to flat-topped clusters (compound umbels).
Fruits elliptic to round, winged on sides and usually also
on front and/or back.

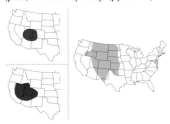

Variable Spring-parsley

Leaves parsley- or
fern-like. HT: 4–10 in.

Plains Spring-parsley

HT: 4–12 in.

Wide-wing Spring-parsley

HT: 2–6 in.

■ **HARBINGER-OF-SPRING** (*Erigenia bulbosa*): Late winter–spring; woods, stream banks. Leaves, 1 or 2 per plant, small at flowering time. Flowers small; anthers (stamen tips) conspicuous, red-brown to blackish red. Also called Pepper-and-salt.

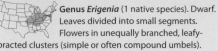

Genus *Erigenia* (1 native species). Dwarf. Leaves divided into small segments. Flowers in unequally branched, leafy-bracted clusters (simple or often compound umbels). Fruits wider than long, flattened, with slender ribs.

Harbinger-of-spring
White petals contrast with dark anthers. Leaves delicate, fernlike. HT: 2–9 in.

■ **RATTLESNAKE-MASTER** (*Eryngium yuccifolium*): Late spring–fall; open woods, prairies, roadsides. Leaves simple. Flowers in ball-shaped clusters. Also called Button-snakeroot. **SIMILAR MARSH ERYNGO** (*E. aquaticum*): Summer; moist or wet places; chiefly southeastern coastal plain. Leaf edges not bristly (but often toothed); flowers bluish. Also called Rattlesnake-master.

■ **LEAVENWORTH'S ERYNGO** (*E. leavenworthii*): Summer–fall; rocky plains, prairies, open woods. Flowers in cone-shaped clusters. This and many other *Eryngium* species are superficially thistlelike; compare with true thistles (*Cirsium*, p. 100).

Genus *Eryngium* (32 species, 29 native). Leaves simple to pinnately or palmately divided, often spiny-edged. Flowers tiny, in dense clusters above whorl of spiny-edged, leaflike bracts. Fruits roundish, covered with tiny scales or bumps.

Rattlesnake-master

Flowers white or greenish white. Leaves bayonet-shaped, stiff, bristly-edged. HT: 1–5 ft.

Leavenworth's Eryngo

Flowers purplish; spiny bracts at base and tip of cluster. Leaves divided, spiny-edged. HT: 1–4 ft.

■ **SAVANNA ERYNGO** (*Eryngium integrifolium*): Late summer–fall; savannas, boggy places, wet pinewoods. Leaves simple, variable, often egg- or lance-shaped; those on upper stem mostly stalkless. Flower clusters several. Plants erect. Also called Blue-flower Eryngo, Bog Eryngo.

■ **CREEPING ERYNGO** (*E. prostratum*): Late spring–fall; wet soil of ditches, meadows, pond margins. Leaves simple, variable, often elliptic and irregularly toothed. Flower clusters solitary from leaf axils, longer than broad. Also called Spreading Eryngo. **SIMILAR BALDWIN'S ERYNGO** (*E. baldwinii*): Chiefly FL. Flower clusters rounded (about as broad as long); bracts typically not conspicuous.

Savanna Eryngo

Flowers bluish, in rounded clusters above conspicuous, toothed, narrow bracts. HT: 8–32 in.

Creeping Eryngo

Stems creeping.

Flowers bluish, in cylindrical clusters above conspicuous, narrow bracts.

■ **AMERICAN BEACH SILVERTOP** (*Glehnia littoralis* ssp. *leiocarpa*): Spring–summer; sea beaches, dunes. Leaves white-woolly beneath. Plants mostly prostrate, often partly buried in sand.

Genus *Glehnia* (1 native species). Plants stemless or short-stemmed. Leaves 1 or 2 times divided into 3 leaflets that are toothed or lobed. Flowers tiny, in rounded clusters (compound umbels). Fruits have corky-winged ribs.

American Beach Silvertop

Flowers whitish, in rounded clusters. Leaves leathery, crinkled. HT: to 4 in.

■ **COW-PARSNIP** (*Heracleum maximum*):
Late spring–summer; moist or wet
ground. Leaflets large, lobed, coarsely
toothed, and commonly conspicuously
hairy beneath. Petals of outer flowers
larger, deeply notched. See also ⬛ Giant
Hogweed (p. 566).

NOTE Some *Heracleum* species cause
phytophotodermatitis (see p. 54).

Genus *Heracleum* (3 species, 1 native).
Leaves large, divided into 3 leaflets; lower
part of leafstalk much enlarged. Flowers
very small or small, in flat-topped clusters (compound
umbels). Fruits flattened, winged.

Cow-parsnip

Flowers white,
in flat-topped
clusters. Leaflets 3,
maplelike. Stems
hairy. HT: 3–10 ft.

■ **MANY-FLOWER WATER-PENNYWORT**
(*Hydrocotyle umbellata*): Spring–fall;
shallow water, wet ground. Leaf edges
scalloped; leafstalk attached near middle
of underside of blade. Flowers numerous,
in long-stalked clusters. Also called
Umbrella Water-pennywort.

■ **AMERICAN WATER-PENNYWORT**
(*H. americana*): Summer–fall; swamps,
stream banks, marshy ground. Leaf edges
shallowly lobed; leafstalk attached near
base of notch on underside of blade.
Flowers few, in nearly stalkless clusters.

RELATED COINLEAF (*Centella erecta*):
Summer; wet places; southeastern.
Leaves shovel-shaped; leafstalk attached
to heart-shaped or squared-off base of
blade (not on underside). Also called Stiff
Spadeleaf.

Genus *Hydrocotyle* (7 species, 6 native).
Stems creeping; often mat-forming. Leaves
simple, kidney-shaped to nearly circular.
Flowers tiny, in clusters (some umbels). Fruits roundish,
flattened. Sometimes included in Araliaceae (p. 76).

Many-flower
Water-pennywort

Flowers whitish.
Leaves round. HT: 3–8 in.

American
Water-
pennywort

Flowers whitish. Leaves
kidney-shaped. HT: 2–5 in.

Coinleaf

HT: 3–10 in.

■ **PORTER'S WILD LOVAGE** (*Ligusticum porteri*): Summer; mountain meadows, stream banks, slopes. Also called Osha.
SIMILAR ■ **GRAY'S WILD LOVAGE** (*L. grayi*): Plants 6–24 in. tall; leaves mostly basal; stem leaves reduced.

■ **AMERICAN WILD LOVAGE** (*L. canadense*): Spring–summer; woods, stream banks.

NOTE Do not confuse *Ligusticum* species with hemlock-parsleys (*Conioselinum*, not covered), in which leaflet side veins are not conspicuous; ⊞ Poison-hemlock (p. 565); or Water-hemlock (p. 58).

 Genus *Ligusticum* (11 native species). Aromatic, often celery-scented. Leaves 1 or more times divided into leaflets; main side veins on leaflets lead to tips of marginal teeth. Flowers tiny, in clusters (compound umbels). Fruits often winged.

Porter's Wild Lovage

American Wild Lovage

Flowers white to pinkish, in clusters. Leaves lacy, carrotlike. HT: 2–4 ft.

Flowers white, in clusters. Leaflets broad, toothed; bases nearly straight. HT: 2–5 ft.

■ **FERN-LEAF DESERT-PARSLEY** (*Lomatium dissectum*): Spring–summer; rocky slopes, shrublands, grasslands. Leaves fern- or parsley-like. Also called Giant Lomatium.

■ **BARE-STEM DESERT-PARSLEY** (*L. nudicaule*): Spring–early summer; open rocky or grassy slopes, flats. Leaves bluish green. Also called Pestle Lomatium.

NOTE Some desert-parsleys are also called biscuit-root. Species are difficult to tell apart. Do not confuse with spring-parsleys (p. 59), which have fruits often winged on 3 or 4 sides.

 Genus *Lomatium* (79 native species). Leaves mostly basal, sometimes also on stems; 1 or more times divided into segments, or sometimes distinct leaflets; often dissected and fern- or parsley-like. Flowers tiny, in clusters (compound umbels). Fruits flattened, with 2 side wings.

Fern-leaf Desert-parsley

Bare-stem Desert-parsley

Flowers yellow, or sometimes purplish, in rounded clusters. HT: 1–5 ft.

Flowers yellow, in ball-shaped clusters on stalks of unequal length. Leaflets elliptic. HT: 1–3 ft.

■ **NINE-LEAF DESERT-PARSLEY**
(*Lomatium triternatum*): Late spring–early
summer; slopes, meadows. Leaves
divided into linear segments. Also called
Ternate Lomatium.

■ **CANBY'S DESERT-PARSLEY**
(*L. canbyi*): Spring; slopes, plains. Leaves
dissected into many small segments.
Petals white, contrasting with dark purple
anthers. Also called Chucklusa.

Flowers yellow. Leaves divided into long, narrow segments. HT: 8–32 in.

Canby's Desert-parsley

Leaves fern- or parsley-like. HT: 4–8 in.

■ **WATER-PARSLEY** (*Oenanthe
sarmentosa*): Late spring–fall; marshes,
ponds, slow streams. Stems soft, weak,
often bent over; new stem tips curled.
Also called Pacific Water Dropwort. Do
not confuse with Water-hemlock (p. 58),
which has leaflets with main side veins
ending in notches between teeth (ending
at tips of teeth in Water-parsley); fruits
rounder and with shorter styles.

Genus *Oenanthe* (1 native species).
Leaves 1 or more times pinnately divided
into toothed or cut leaflets. Flowers tiny,
in clusters (compound umbels). Fruits barrel-shaped,
corky-ribbed, tipped by 2 elongated styles.

Water-parsley

Flowers white, in clusters. Leaflets have side veins ending in teeth. HT: 2–5 ft.

■ **LONG-STYLE SWEET-CICELY**
(*Osmorhiza longistylis*): Spring–summer;
woods, stream banks. Plants anise-scented.
Styles on bristly fruits ⅛–³⁄₁₆ in. long. Also
called Anise-root. **SIMILAR** Common
species not or only faintly anise-scented;
flowers whitish; fruits bristly, with short
styles (¹⁄₁₆ in. or less). **BLAND SWEET-
CICELY** (*O. claytonii*): Eastern. Also called
Clayton's Sweet-cicely. **MOUNTAIN
SWEET-CICELY** (*O. berteroi*): Western.

■ **WESTERN SWEET-CICELY**
(*O. occidentalis*): Anise-scented. Fruits
smooth, with short styles (¹⁄₁₆ in. or less).

 Genus *Osmorhiza* (8 native species).
Sometimes anise-scented. Leaves 1
or more times divided into toothed
leaflets. Flowers tiny, in usually loosely flowered clusters
(compound umbels); white, yellow, purple, or pink.
Fruits narrow, linear to club-shaped, usually bristly.

Long-style
Sweet-cicely

Flowers white, in
clusters. Leaflets
toothed, sometimes
lobed at base.
HT: 1–3 ft.

Western Sweet-cicely

Flowers
pale or
greenish
yellow, in
clusters.
HT: 1–4 ft.

■ **GAIRDNER'S YAMPAH** (*Perideridia
gairdneri*): Summer; open woods,
meadows, slopes. Delicate plant with
caraway-like fragrance. Several similar
species, a few with broader leaf segments.

NOTE The poisonous Bulblet-bearing
Water-hemlock (p. 58), a plant of usually
wet places, is similar to *Perideridia* but
normally has bulblets in some leaf axils.

 Genus *Perideridia* (13 native species).
Leaves 1 or more times divided into very
narrow, grasslike segments. Flowers tiny,
in flat-topped to rounded clusters (compound umbels);
white to pinkish. Fruits roundish.

Gairdner's Yampah

Flowers white to
pinkish, in clusters.
Leaves divided into
narrow segments;
wither early. HT: 1–4 ft.

■ **PRAIRIE-PARSLEY** (*Polytaenia nuttallii*): Spring–early summer; prairies, plains, open woods. Leaf segments irregularly toothed and lobed.

Genus *Polytaenia* (2 native species). Leaves 2 or 3 times divided into relatively narrow segments. Flowers tiny, in flat-topped to somewhat rounded clusters (compound umbels). Fruits elliptic, flattened, corky-winged.

Prairie-parsley

Flowers yellow to greenish yellow. HT: 1–3 ft.

■ **MOUNTAIN-PARSLEY** (*Pseudocymopterus montanus*): Spring–fall; rocky hillsides, meadows, open woods. Leaf segments generally narrow but highly variable in shape and size. Short, stiff hairs at top of main flower stalk (base of flower cluster).

NOTE Stalks of spring-parsleys (p. 59) and desert-parsleys (pp. 63–64) are either hairless or hairy throughout.

Genus *Pseudocymopterus* (2 native species). Leaves 1 or more times pinnately divided into segments. Flowers tiny, in flat-topped clusters (compound umbels); yellow, orangish, reddish, or purplish. Fruits winged.

Mountain-parsley

Leaves often parsley- or carrot-like. HT: 6 in.–3 ft.

■ **THREAD-LEAF MOCK BISHOP'S-WEED** (*Ptilimnium capillaceum*): Spring–fall; marshes, wet woods, pond margins, ditches. Leaves finely divided; terminal segment ¼–¾ in. long. Also called Atlantic Mock Bishop's-weed.

■ **NUTTALL'S MOCK BISHOP'S-WEED** (*P. nuttallii*): Spring–summer; prairies, roadsides, moist or wet soil. Terminal leaf segment ⅜–2 in. long. Also called Ozark Mock Bishop's-weed.

RELATED ■ **PRAIRIE-BISHOP'S-WEED** (*Bifora americana*, no photo): Spring; prairies, rocky hills, roadsides. Similar to mock bishop's-weeds, but flowers showier and with larger petals; fruits in 2 side-by-side, nearly circular segments.

Genus *Ptilimnium* (5 native species). Leaves generally dissected into narrow linear segments. Flowers tiny, in flat-topped clusters (compound umbels). Fruits egg-shaped to round, somewhat corky-winged.

Thread-leaf Mock Bishop's-weed

Nuttall's Mock Bishop's-weed

Flowers white. Leaf segments threadlike. HT: 6–30 in.

Bracts beneath clusters 3-segmented.

Bracts beneath clusters undivided. HT: 1–2 ft.

■ **CANADIAN BLACK-SNAKEROOT** (*Sanicula canadensis*): Spring–summer; woods, thickets. Side leaflets deeply cleft. Flowers greenish white to whitish.

■ **FOOTSTEPS-OF-SPRING** (*S. arctopoides*): Spring; coastal bluffs and dunes. Flowers yellow. Also called Yellow-mats.

■ **PACIFIC BLACK-SNAKEROOT** (*S. crassicaulis*): Spring; woods, slopes. Flowers usually yellow, rarely purplish. Also called Gamble-weed.

PURPLE BLACK-SNAKEROOT (*S. bipinnatifida*): Spring; open or shaded slopes. Range similar to Pacific Black-snakeroot. Flowers purple or yellow.

NOTE Black-snakeroots are also called sanicle.

Genus *Sanicula* (18 native species). Leaves palmately or pinnately divided into leaflets or segments. Flowers tiny, in ball-shaped or headlike clusters; yellow, whitish, or purple. Fruits covered with hooked bristles or tiny bumps.

Canadian Black-snakeroot

Footsteps-of-spring

Leaflets 3. HT: 6 in.–3 ft.

Leaves maplelike, yellowish. HT: prostrate, 2–12 in.

Pacific Black-snakeroot

Purple Black-snakeroot

Leaves maplelike. HT: 1–3 ft.

Leaves toothed and lobed. HT: 6–30 in.

■ **WATER-PARSNIP** (*Sium suave*): Summer; wet places. Upper part of stems conspicuously grooved lengthwise. Leaflets finely toothed, with side veins forming a branching network; main side veins do not clearly end in notches (sinuses) or marginal teeth. Compare the similar Water-hemlock (p. 58), which usually has some leaves 2 or 3 times pinnately divided and side veins of leaflets ending in notches between teeth.

Genus *Sium* (1 native species). Leaves mostly once pinnately divided into lance-shaped leaflets (underwater leaves can be fernlike). Flowers tiny, in flat-topped to rounded clusters (compound umbels). Fruits roundish, with corky ribs.

Water-parsnip

Flowers white, in clusters. HT: 2–5 ft.

WATER-PARSNIP RELATIVES

These species, found in wet places, are similar to Water-parsnip, with white flowers in compound umbels and once-pinnate leaves.

■ **CUT-LEAF-WATER-PARSNIP** (*Berula erecta*): Summer–fall; wet places. Upper stem leaves have irregularly sharply toothed and cleft leaflets (regularly small-toothed in Water-parsnip). Fruits roundish, corky, obscurely ribbed.

■ **COWBANE** (*Oxypolis rigidior*): Summer; wet places. Leaflets untoothed to several-toothed. Fruits ³⁄₁₆–¼ in. long, strongly flattened and winged. **SIMILAR FENDLER'S COWBANE** (*O. fendleri*): Stream banks; southern Rockies. **WATER COWBANE** (*O. filiformis*): Southeastern. Very slender, tubular leafstalks, to 2 ft. long, serve as leaves.

Cut-leaf-water-parsnip

Upper leaflets jagged-toothed. HT: to 3 ft.

Cowbane

Some leaflets have several large teeth. HT: to 5 ft.

Leaflets may be untoothed.

■ **RANGER'S-BUTTONS** (*Sphenosciadium capitellatum*): Summer; wet places. Also called Swamp White-heads.

Genus *Sphenosciadium* (1 native species). Leaves pinnately divided into irregularly toothed leaflets. Flowers tiny, in tightly packed, ball-shaped clusters, these arranged in compound umbels. Fruits wedge-shaped, winged.

Ranger's-buttons

Flowers white, in ball-shaped clusters on hairy stalks. Lower part of leafstalk much enlarged. HT: 2–6 ft.

■ **YELLOW-PIMPERNEL** (*Taenidia integerrima*): Spring–early summer; woods, rocky hillsides. Plants have celery-like aroma. Flowers yellow. SIMILAR ■ **MOUNTAIN-PIMPERNEL** (*T. montana*): Found primarily on shale barrens. Plants have aniselike aroma; fruits have narrow wings. Also called Shale-barren-pimpernel.

Genus *Taenidia* (2 native species). Leaves 1 or more often 2 or 3 times divided into untoothed leaflets. Flowers tiny, in open clusters (compound umbels). Fruits elliptic, with narrow ribs.

Yellow-pimpernel

Leaves divided into egg-shaped or elliptic, untoothed leaflets. HT: 16–32 in.

■ **HAIRY-JOINT MEADOW-PARSNIP** (*Thaspium barbinode*): Spring–early summer; woods, thickets, prairies, stream banks. Flowers pale yellow or cream, on 10–15 equal-length stalks. **SIMILAR** ■ **CUTLEAF MEADOW-PARSNIP** (*T. pinnatifidum*): Late spring–early summer; woods. Leaves fernlike; flowers whitish.

■ **SMOOTH MEADOW-PARSNIP** (*T. trifoliatum*): Spring–early summer; woods, thickets, prairies. Flowers yellow or purple, on 6–10 unequal-length stalks.

Genus *Thaspium* (3 native species). Basal leaves simple or compound; stem leaves divided 1 or more times into toothed leaflets. Flowers tiny, in flat-topped clusters (compound umbels), with all flowers and fruits stalked; compare *Zizia*, below. Fruits winged.

Hairy-joint Meadow-parsnip

All leaves pinnately divided; nodes on upper part of stem hairy. HT: 1–3 ft.

Smooth Meadow-parsnip

Basal leaves heart-shaped; stem leaves have 3 leaflets. HT: 1–2 ft.

■ **GOLDEN ALEXANDERS** (*Zizia aurea*): Spring–midsummer; moist sites. **SIMILAR** ■ **MEADOW ALEXANDERS** (*Z. trifoliata*): Moist woods. Leaflets edged with 5–7 teeth per inch (12–25 in Golden Alexanders).

■ **HEART-LEAF ALEXANDERS** (*Z. aptera*): Moist woods and meadows. Only stem leaves are divided.

Genus *Zizia* (3 native species). Similar to *Thaspium* (above), but with a stalkless flower or fruit in center of each smaller cluster; fruits ribbed, not winged.

Golden Alexanders

Flowers yellow, in clusters. All leaves divided. HT: 1–3 ft.

Heart-leaf Alexanders

Basal leaves heart-shaped; stem leaves divided into 3 leaflets. HT: 1–3 ft.

APOCYNACEAE   DOGBANE FAMILY

Perennial; plants commonly have milky juice. Leaves opposite (rarely alternate), simple, and untoothed. Flowers solitary or in clusters; tubular at base (petals united), with 5 often spreading lobes; sepals 5; stamens 5; pistils 2, united only at tip. Fruits are long, narrow pods, usually 2 from each flower.

■ **EASTERN BLUESTAR** (*Amsonia tabernaemontana*): Spring; woods, stream banks, roadsides. Plants generally hairless or nearly so; flowers hairy inside and outside. Also called Blue-dogbane.

■ **WOOLLY BLUESTAR** (*A. tomentosa*): Desert plains, washes, canyons, roadsides. Plants hairless to densely grayish-hairy; flowers hairy inside, tube hairless outside.

Genus *Amsonia* (16 native species). Plants have milky juice. Leaves alternate (may appear opposite or whorled). Flowers in clusters; narrowly tubular, with 5 often spreading lobes forming a star shape; blue, purple, or whitish.

Eastern Bluestar

Flowers sky blue. HT: 1–3 ft.

Woolly Bluestar

Flowers whitish, or tinged bluish or purplish. HT: 6–24 in.

■ **SPREADING DOGBANE** (*Apocynum androsaemifolium*): Late spring–summer; open woods, slopes, fields, roadsides. Leaves somewhat drooping.

■ **HEMP DOGBANE** (*A. cannabinum*): Moist ground, open places. Leaves horizontal to upright.

OTHER GENUS CLIMBING-DOGBANE (*Thyrsanthella difformis*): River and stream banks, thickets; chiefly southeastern. Twining vine. Leaves opposite. Flower clusters in leaf axils.

Genus *Apocynum* (2 native species). Plants have milky juice. Stems often reddish. Leaves opposite. Flowers 5-lobed, loosely clustered at stem ends.

Spreading Dogbane

Flowers pinkish, bell-shaped; lobes spreading or back-curved. HT: 6 in.–3 ft.

Climbing-dogbane

Flowers pale yellow; lobes back-curved. Vine.

Hemp Dogbane

Flowers white or greenish white, cylindrical to urn-shaped. HT: 1–4 ft.

■ **SACRAMENTO WAXY-DOGBANE**
(*Cycladenia humilis*): Late spring–summer;
rocky slopes, open woods, shrublands.
Plants usually hairless but sometimes
densely short-hairy.

Genus *Cycladenia* (1 native species).
Plants have milky juice. Leaves opposite.
Flowers 5-lobed, mostly 2–6 on stalks
from leaf axils.

Sacramento Waxy-dogbane

Flowers
rose-purple,
funnel-shaped.
Leaves broad,
somewhat fleshy.
HT: 3–10 in.

■ **COCKROACH-PLANT** (*Haplophyton
crooksii*): Summer–fall; slopes, canyons.
Flowers trumpet-shaped. Do not confuse
with Showy Menodora, which has
flower tube much longer than lobes, or
Rough Menodora, which has flowers
with 2 protruding stamens (both species
pictured on p. 358).

Genus *Haplophyton* (1 native species).
Somewhat shrubby. Leaves alternate
or sometimes opposite. Flowers have
5 broad lobes longer than the narrow tube; solitary or few
at stem ends.

Cockroach-plant

Flowers yellow; lobes
overlap, pinwheel-like.
Leaves lance-shaped.
HT: 1–2 ft.

■ **LONG-TUBE ROCK-TRUMPET**
(*Mandevilla macrosiphon*): Mostly
summer; rocky slopes, mesas. Almost
shrubby. Leaves elliptic to nearly round.
Flower tube narrow, 2–4 in. long. Also
called Flor de San Juan.

■ **HUACHUCA MOUNTAIN ROCK-
TRUMPET** (*M. brachysiphon*): Similar to
Long-tube Rock-trumpet; flower tube
1–2½ in. long.

 Genus *Mandevilla* (5 species, 4 native).
Sometimes shrubby. Plants have milky
juice. Leaves usually opposite. Flowers
5-lobed, solitary or few at stem ends.

Long-tube Rock-trumpet

Flowers white,
trumpet-shaped;
lobes overlap,
pinwheel-like.
HT: 6–12 in.

Huachuca Mountain Rock-trumpet

HT: 6–24 in.

ARACEAE
ARUM FAMILY

Perennial. Leaves basal or sometimes alternate; simple or compound. Flowers tiny, densely crowded
onto fleshy, club-shaped stalk (spadix); spadix generally at least partly enclosed by often showy bract
(spathe). Fruits are generally berries or berrylike. **NOTE** Plants have irritating juice.

■ **WATER-ARUM** (*Calla palustris*): Late
spring–summer; shallow water, marshy
shores, sedge mats. Flowers tiny, greenish
white to cream-colored. Berries red. Also
called Wild Calla.

 Genus *Calla* (1 native species). Leaves
several, long-stalked. Spathe at end of
long stalk, clasping (not enclosing) short,
thick spadix. Berries pear-shaped, in clusters.

Water-arum

Spathe white (may be greenish
outside), with elongated
tip. Leaves broadly
heart-shaped.
HT: 4–12 in.

■ **GOLDEN-CLUB** (*Orontium aquaticum*): Late winter–spring; shallow water, swamps, bogs, marshes, streams, pools. Leaves sometimes floating. Flowers tiny, golden yellow; flower stalk greenish or reddish below, white above. Fruits bluish green to brownish.

Genus *Orontium* (1 native species). Leaves long-stalked, appearing before flowers. Spathe apparently absent; spadix at tip of long stalk. Fruits partially embedded in spadix.

Golden-club

Flower stalk ends in bright yellow spadix. Leaves elliptic, bluish green. HT: to 2 ft.

■ **ARROW-ARUM** (*Peltandra virginica*): Spring–summer; shallow water, muddy shores. Spathe green, often partially open. Fruits greenish to purple-green. Also called Tuckahoe. Nonflowering plants are distinguished from arrowheads (p. 52) and Pickerel-weed (p. 438) by marginal leaf vein.

■ **WHITE ARROW-ARUM** (*P. sagittifolia*): Boggy and swampy places. Spathe white, open at top. Fruits red. Also called Spoonflower.

Genus *Peltandra* (2 native species). Leaves long-stalked, arrowhead-shaped, appearing before flowers. Spathe tubular; spadix cylindrical, covered with tiny greenish, yellowish, or whitish flowers. Berries in clusters.

Arrow-arum

Leaf blade has strong vein running along entire margin. HT: 6 in.–3 ft.

White Arrow-arum

HT: to 2 ft.

■ **JACK-IN-THE-PULPIT** (*Arisaema triphyllum*): Spring–early summer; woods, thickets, wet areas. Single or 2 leaves, divided into 3 (or rarely 5) leaflets. Berries orange-red. Also called Indian-turnip.

■ **GREEN-DRAGON** (*A. dracontium*): Woods, thickets, stream banks. Spadix tip whiplike, extending well beyond top of spathe. Also called Dragon-root.

Genus *Arisaema* (2 native species). Leaves long-stalked, palmately divided into leaflets. Spathe partially open near top; lower portion tubular. Flowers tiny, yellowish to greenish. Berries in clusters.

Jack-in-the-pulpit

Spathe ("pulpit") folded hood-like over spadix ("Jack"), green or purple with light stripes. HT: to 3 ft.

Green-dragon

Single leaf, divided into 7-13 leaflets arranged in a semicircle. HT: to 3 ft.

■ **SKUNK-CABBAGE** (*Symplocarpus foetidus*): Late winter–spring; wet areas. Among the earliest of bloomers; spathes sometimes found poking through snow or ice. Leaves broadly heart-shaped; at maturity up to 24 in. long and 16 in. wide. Plants are ill-scented, with somewhat skunklike odor.

Genus *Symplocarpus* (1 native species). Leaves several, appearing after flowers. Spathe partially open. Flowers tiny, yellowish to dark purple-red. Fruits maroon, embedded in spadix.

Skunk-cabbage

Spathe hoodlike, usually maroon, mottled with green or yellow. HT: spathe to 6 in.

■ **YELLOW SKUNK-CABBAGE** (*Lysichiton americanus*): Late winter–spring; wet areas. Plants rank-smelling, bloom very early. Leaves can grow to 5 ft. long and 2 ft. wide; blades often oval. Also called Western Skunk-cabbage.

Genus *Lysichiton* (1 native species). Leaves several, appearing at or soon after flowering. Spathe open, only partially enclosing spadix. Flowers tiny, yellowish green. Fruits berrylike, green or reddish, embedded in spadix.

Yellow Skunk-cabbage

Spathe boat-shaped, yellow (may be green-tinged). HT: flowering stalk 1–2 ft.

ARALIACEAE   GINSENG FAMILY
Woody plants or perennial herbs. Leaves alternate (rarely whorled or basal), mostly divided into leaflets. Flowers tiny, commonly in umbrella-like clusters (umbels); petals 5, whitish or greenish. Fruits are berries or berrylike.

■ **AMERICAN GINSENG** (*Panax quinquefolius*): Summer; woods. Leaflets usually 5, larger ones 1½–2½ in. wide. Flowers greenish white to yellowish green. Fruits red.

■ **DWARF GINSENG** (*P. trifolius*): Spring. Larger leaflets ½–1 in. wide. Fruits yellowish.

Genus *Panax* (2 native species). Leaves in single whorl of usually 3, each palmately divided into 3 or 5 leaflets. Flowers tiny, in solitary, ball-shaped cluster (umbel), on stalk growing from junction of leaves. Fruits berrylike.

American Ginseng

HT: 6–20 in.

Dwarf Ginseng

Flowers white or pink-tinged. Leaflets 3 or 5. HT: 3–8 in.

■ **AMERICAN SPIKENARD** (*Aralia racemosa*): Summer; woods, shaded slopes, stream banks. Plants bushy. Leaves alternate on stem; large, with numerous leaflets. Flower clusters numerous. SIMILAR ■ **CALIFORNIA SPIKENARD** (*A. californica*): Moist, shady places. Also called Elk-clover. **BRISTLY SARSAPARILLA** (*A. hispida*): Woods, clearings; northeastern. Lower stems bristly (smooth on American Spikenard); flower clusters few, long-stalked.

■ **WILD SARSAPARILLA** (*A. nudicaulis*): Spring–summer; woods, shaded sites. Large, solitary leaf arising from plant base long-stalked and branching at top into 3 parts, each subdivided into usually 3 or 5 leaflets. Flower clusters 2–4.

Genus *Aralia* (8 species, 6 native). Leaves alternate or arise from plant base; very large, most often divided into many leaflets. Flowers tiny, white to greenish white, borne in 2 to many rounded clusters (umbels). Fruits berrylike, dark purple to black.

American Spikenard

Flowering stalks overtop leaves. HT: 3–6 ft.

Wild Sarsaparilla

Flowering stalks shorter than leaves. HT: 1–2 ft.

ARISTOLOCHIACEAE · BIRTHWORT FAMILY

Woody vines or aromatic perennial herbs. Leaves alternate, simple, and untoothed; usually heart-shaped at base, palmately veined. Sepals petal-like (true petals absent), usually 3, united at base into bell-shaped or irregularly S-shaped tube; stamens 6 or 12; pistil 1. Fruits are capsules.

■ **ARROWHEAD HEARTLEAF** (*Hexastylis arifolia*): Late winter–spring; woods. Leaves arrowhead-shaped, often mottled, hairless. Flowers purplish to greenish brown outside, dark purple inside. Also called Little-brown-jug.

■ **VIRGINIA HEARTLEAF** (*H. virginica*): Spring. Leaves round-heart-shaped.

NOTE Wild-gingers (p. 78) can be told from heartleafs by their hairy leaves.

Genus *Hexastylis* (10 native species). Leaves arise from plant base; aromatic when crushed. Flowers solitary near ground level, flask- or pitcher-shaped, 3-lobed; stamens 12.

Arrowhead Heartleaf

HT: 3–6 in.

Virginia Heartleaf

HT: to 4 in.

■ **WILD-GINGER** (*Asarum canadense*): Spring–summer; woods. Petal-like lobes ¼–1½ in. long.

■ **LONG-TAIL WILD-GINGER** (*A. caudatum*): Moist woods. Petal-like lobes 1½–3 in. long, tapering.

■ **HARTWEG'S WILD-GINGER** (*A. hartwegii*): Wooded slopes. Upper leaf surface usually has conspicuous silver or white veins. Inside of flower whitish with maroon stripes, white hairs. SIMILAR **MARBLED WILD-GINGER** (*A. marmoratum*): Woods, rocky slopes; southwestern OR, northern CA. Inside of flower dark red with purple hairs.

Genus *Asarum* (6 native species). Rootstock aromatic. Leaves in pairs at plant base, heart- or kidney-shaped. Flowers solitary near ground level, in fork between 2 leafstalks; cup-shaped, with 3 spreading, petal-like lobes; stamens 12.

Wild-ginger
Flowers maroon, hairy. Leaves hairy, especially on stalk.
HT: 6–12 in.

Long-tail Wild-ginger
HT: 2–8 in.

Hartweg's Wild-ginger
HT: to 12 in.

■ **DUTCHMAN'S-PIPE** (*Aristolochia macrophylla*): Late spring–summer; mountain woods. Stems woody, climbing. Flowers greenish yellow to maroon. SIMILAR ■ **CALIFORNIA DUTCHMAN'S-PIPE** (*A. californica*): Stream banks, woods, shrublands. ■ **WOOLLY DUTCHMAN'S-PIPE** (*A. tomentosa*): River and stream banks, woods. Leaves densely soft-hairy beneath. Also called Woolly Pipevine.

VIRGINIA-SNAKEROOT (*A. serpentaria*): Woods; eastern. Flowers difficult to see.

Genus *Aristolochia* (12 species, 10 native). Flowers solitary or few, tubular, typically curved, with usually 3 lobes and circular opening at tip; stamens 6.

Dutchman's-pipe
Flowers S-curved. Leaves heart-shaped. Climbing vine.

Virginia-snakeroot
Flowers near base of plant. HT: to 2 ft.

ASCLEPIADACEAE   MILKWEED FAMILY

Perennial herbs and vines; most have milky juice. Leaves mostly opposite or whorled; simple and untoothed. Flowers in clusters (often umbels), with central corona (see illustration); petals 5, united at base; sepals 5; stamens 5; pistils 2, united only at tip. Fruits are pods. Asclepiadaceae is now sometimes included in the dogbane family (Apocynaceae, p. 71).

FLOWERS OF THE GENUS *ASCLEPIAS*

Milkweed flowers have 5 petals, usually turned downward and obscuring the 5 smaller sepals. Above the petals is a "corona," a circle of 5 scooplike structures, or "hoods," each often with a curved, beaklike projection, or "horn." The horns point toward the flower center, a column formed by the united stamens and the upper portions of the pistils. Milkweed pods split to reveal numerous seeds, each usually bearing a tuft of hairs.

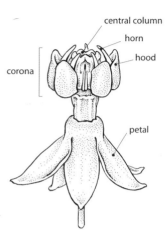

central column
horn
hood
corona
petal

seeds

FLOWER STRUCTURE   **POD**

■ **COMMON MILKWEED** (*Asclepias syriaca*): Summer; meadows, fields, roadsides. Leaves opposite. Flowers purplish pink.

■ **SHOWY MILKWEED** (*A. speciosa*): Prairies, roadsides, floodplains. Leaves opposite.

Genus *Asclepias* (73 species, 72 native). Leaves mostly opposite or whorled. Flower structure illustrated above.

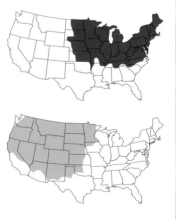

Common Milkweed

Showy Milkweed

Flower hoods short. HT: 2–5 ft.

Flower hoods long. HT: 2–3 ft.

■ **WHORLED MILKWEED** (*Asclepias verticillata*): Summer; prairies, roadsides, open woods. Leaves whorled, numerous, very narrow.

■ **GREEN MILKWEED** (*A. viridiflora*): Leaves opposite.

Whorled Milkweed

Flowers greenish white; horns present, long. HT: 1–3 ft.

Green Milkweed

Flowers pale green; horns absent. HT: 1–2½ ft.

■ **PURPLE MILKWEED** (*Asclepias purpurascens*): Late spring–summer; open woods, thickets. Leaves opposite. Flowers purple-red.

■ **HEART-LEAF MILKWEED** (*A. cordifolia*): Rocky slopes, woods, thickets. Leaves opposite. Flowers red-purple. Also called Purple Milkweed.

Purple Milkweed

Leaves stalked; bases rounded. HT: 2–3 ft.

Heart-leaf Milkweed

Leaves stalkless, heart-shaped. HT: 1–2 ft.

■ **BUTTERFLY-WEED** (*Asclepias tuberosa*): Summer; prairies, fields, roadsides. Leaves mostly alternate, crowded. Plants lack milky juice. Also called Orange Milkweed.

Butterfly-weed

Flowers usually deep orange.

Flowers sometimes bright yellow.

HT: 1–3 ft.

■ **SWAMP MILKWEED** (*Asclepias incarnata*): Summer; wet places. Leaves opposite, mostly narrowly lance-shaped, with pointed tip. Flower horns longer than hoods (see inset).

Swamp Milkweed

Flowers pink to deep rose, often with pale center.
HT: 2–5 ft.

■ NARROW-LEAF MILKWEED

(*Asclepias fascicularis*): Summer; dry ground. Flowers greenish white, often purple-tinged.

■ FOUR-LEAF MILKWEED (*A. quadrifolia*):

Woods. Leaves egg- to broadly lance-shaped. Flowers pinkish to whitish.

■ BROAD-LEAF MILKWEED (*A. latifolia*):

Plains, prairies, mesas. Flowers pale green to yellowish or whitish, sometimes purple-tinged.

■ CLASPING MILKWEED (*A. amplexicaulis*):

Open woods, prairies, fields. Flowers greenish, often flushed purple; hoods pink.

Narrow-leaf Milkweed
Leaves in whorls of 3–5, narrowly lance-shaped. HT: 2–3½ ft.

Four-leaf Milkweed
Midstem leaves in whorls of 4. HT: 1–2½ ft.

Broad-leaf Milkweed
Leaves opposite; blades very broad. HT: 1–2½ ft.

Clasping Milkweed
Leaves opposite, wavy-edged, the rounded bases often clasping stem. HT: 1½–3 ft.

■ FEW-FLOWER MILKWEED

(*Asclepias lanceolata*): Late spring–summer; wet places. Leaves ⅜ in. wide. Flowers occasionally all red.

■ WHEEL MILKWEED (*A. uncialis*):

Plains, hills, shrublands. Leaves narrowly lance-shaped.

■ WHITE MILKWEED (*A. variegata*):

Woods, thickets. Leaves broad. Also called Red-ring Milkweed.

■ SPIDER MILKWEED (*A. viridis*):

Open woods, prairies, pastures. Leaves lance- to egg-shaped. Unusual in having erect petals. Also called Green Antelope-horn.

NOTE These species have opposite leaves.

Few-flower Milkweed
Petals red; hoods usually orange. HT: 2–4 ft.

Wheel Milkweed
Petals purplish or pinkish, form a "star"; hoods short, whitish. HT: 1–4 in.

White Milkweed
Flowers white with central red-purple band. HT: 1–3 ft.

Spider Milkweed
Petals pale green, spreading upward; hoods purplish. HT: 1–2 ft.

MILKWEED VINES

Three common, mostly summer-flowering species are featured. Also called climbing milkweeds.

■ **HONEYVINE** (*Cynanchum laeve*): Summer; woods, fields, disturbed places. Also called Sandvine, Smooth Swallow-wort.

■ **FRINGED TWINEVINE** (*Funastrum cynanchoides* ssp. *cynanchoides*): Streamsides, washes, dry plains.

■ **COMMON ANGLEPOD** (*Gonolobus suberosus*): Woods, thickets.

Milkweed Vines (several related genera, numerous species). Vines, many with milky juice. Leaves opposite, often heart-shaped. Flower clusters in leaf axils; petals mostly spreading or erect; corona variable, its segments petal-like, bladderlike, united into a disk, or rarely absent.

Honeyvine

Fringed Twinevine

Common Anglepod

ASTERACEAE or COMPOSITAE   ASTER or COMPOSITE FAMILY

Also called the daisy or sunflower family. Annual, biennial, or perennial herbs, or sometimes shrubs. Leaves alternate, opposite, basal, or whorled; simple or compound. Flowers small, grouped together on a common receptacle; the entire cluster is called a flower head and resembles a single flower. (A daisy, for example, is a flower cluster.) The flower heads may be solitary or more often occur in clusters.

The individual flowers are of two main types. Disk flowers are typically tubular (petals united) and 5-lobed, with 5 stamens joined by their anthers in a ring around the style of a single pistil. The second type of flower is called a ray flower (or a "ray")—the individual petals comprising it are not recognizable but united and reduced to a single, petal-like blade. Ray flowers generally occur around the margin of the flower head, surrounding the disk flowers located in the center of the head. They are either female (pistillate, with a style present), sterile (with a pistil but infertile), or neutral (lacking a pistil). Some flower heads lack rays and are composed only of disk flowers. Others are comprised of a modified type of ray flower, called "raylike" in this book ("ligulate" in many guides), that is similar to a typical ray flower but has both stamens and a pistil. The style of fertile flowers ends in two branches (Y-shaped).

The flower head is surrounded (at least at its base) by bracts called phyllaries, which are frequently greenish and sepal-like in appearance. The phyllaries of an individual flower head may be similar to one another, or some of them might differ in size, shape, or texture. Additional small bracts (bractlets) are occasionally present beneath the phyllaries. The receptacle that bears the individual small flowers is variously shaped, and in a few species has on its surface papery or bristly bracts called chaff.

At the base of each individual flower is an ovary, which in fertile flowers will develop into a seedlike fruit. At the top of the ovary is a pappus (absent in some species) consisting of various bristles, scales, or little plumes. At maturity the pappus often remains attached to the top of the fruit; it can be a useful identification feature. (See page 84 for labeled illustrations of flower types and structures.)

FLOWERS OF THE ASTERACEAE

Individual flowers are grouped in a head (a type of flower cluster). A head may contain both ray and disk flowers, only disk flowers, or only raylike flowers.

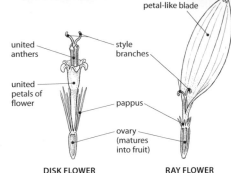

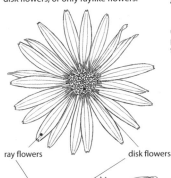

DISK FLOWER

RAY FLOWER

petal-like blade

style branches

united anthers

united petals of flower

pappus

ovary (matures into fruit)

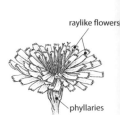

ray flowers

disk flowers

raylike flowers

location of chaffy bracts (chaff), when present

receptacle

phyllaries (flower-head bracts)

phyllaries

FLOWER HEAD WITH BOTH RAY AND DISK FLOWERS

FLOWER HEAD WITH ONLY DISK FLOWERS

FLOWER HEAD WITH ONLY RAYLIKE FLOWERS

FRUITS OF THE ASTERACEAE

Fruit body and pappus are commonly ¹⁄₁₆–³⁄₈ in. long each.

DESERT-CHICORY
(p. 87)

PARACHUTE-PLANT
(p. 87)

WESTERN HAWK'S-BEARD
(p. 89)

NODDING MICROSERIS
(p. 90)

PRAIRIE FALSE DANDELION
(p. 90)

LINDLEY'S SILVER-PUFFS
(p. 90)

PALE AGOSERIS
(p. 90)

SLENDER HAWKWEED
(p. 91)

CAROLINA FALSE DANDELION
(p. 91)

POTATO DWARF-DANDELION
(p. 92)

COMMON BONESET
(p. 97)

DUSTY-MAIDEN
(p. 104)

WHOLE-LEAF ROSINWEED
(p. 114)

ENGELMANN'S DAISY
(p. 115)

GOLDEN CROWNBEARD
(p. 116)

BRITTLE-BUSH
(p. 116)

COMMON SUNFLOWER
(p. 117)

FALSE SUNFLOWER
(p. 118)

PARISH'S GOLDENEYE
(p. 119)

SHOWY GOLDENEYE
(p. 119)

NODDING HELIANTHELLA
(p. 119)

ARROW-LEAF BALSAMROOT
(p. 120)

MULE'S-EARS
(p. 120)

LANCE-LEAF COREOPSIS
(p. 122)

TICKSEED-SUNFLOWER
(p. 124)

DEVIL'S BEGGARTICKS
(p. 125)

COMMON WOOLLY-SUNFLOWER
(p. 128)

COLORADO RUBBERWEED
(p. 132)

ORANGE-SNEEZEWEED
(p. 133)

BROOM SNAKEWEED
(p. 134)

SLENDER SCRATCH DAISY
(p. 138)

MARYLAND GOLDEN-ASTER
(p. 138)

CAMPHORWEED
(p. 139)

NEW ENGLAND ASTER
(p. 142)

TALL FLAT-TOPPED WHITE ASTER
(p. 145)

TOOTHED WHITE-TOP ASTER
(p. 146)

FALSE ASTER
(p. 147)

LAZY DAISY
(p. 148)

EASTERN WESTERN DAISY
(p. 148)

BABY WHITE-ASTER
(p. 149)

COMMON DANDELION
(p. 569)

YELLOW SALSIFY
(p. 569)

■ **TALL RATTLESNAKE-ROOT**
(*Prenanthes altissima*): Late summer–fall; woods. Nodding heads of 4–6 flowers.

■ **WHITE RATTLESNAKE-ROOT** (*P. alba*): Woods. Nodding heads of 7–9 flowers; phyllaries often purple-tinged. **SIMILAR WESTERN RATTLESNAKE-ROOT** (*P. alata*): Northwestern. Flowers 7–16 per head; phyllaries dark green.

■ **ROUGH RATTLESNAKE-ROOT** (*P. aspera*): Prairies, rocky woods. Leaves often hairy. Erect heads of 8–19 yellow to white flowers. **SIMILAR PURPLE RATTLESNAKE-ROOT** (*P. racemosa*): Moist places; chiefly upper Midwest. Leaves hairless; flower heads often pinkish.

Genus *Prenanthes* (14 native species). Plants have milky juice. Leaves basal and alternate. Only raylike flowers; flower-head bracts (phyllaries) in 1 row, with bractlets beneath. Seedlike fruits unbeaked; fruit pappus of bristles. Species are also called white-lettuce. (See p. 83.)

Tall Rattlesnake-root

Flower heads whitish or greenish yellow. HT: 1½–7 ft.

White Rattlesnake-root

Flower heads white, pink, or lavender. HT: 1–5 ft.

Rough Rattlesnake-root

HT: 1–5 ft.

■ **RUSH SKELETON-PLANT** (*Lygodesmia juncea*): Summer; plains, prairies, road-sides. Lower leaves grasslike, upper ones scalelike. Phyllaries ½ in. long. Round swellings on some stems are insect galls. **SIMILAR** ■ **RUSH-PINK** (*L. grandiflora*): Plains. Flowers 5–12; phyllaries ⅝–1 in.

■ **ROSE-RUSH** (*L. aphylla*): Spring–fall; sandy soil, pinelands. Grasslike basal leaves in clusters (at least before bloom time). Flower heads often large. **SIMILAR** ■ **TEXAS SKELETON-PLANT** (*L. texana*): Open woods, shrublands, grasslands. Basal leaves sometimes jagged-edged.

NOTE Species are also called skeleton-weed. See also Ⅰ Chicory (p. 570), which has dandelion-like lower and basal leaves.

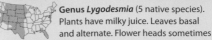

Genus *Lygodesmia* (5 native species). Plants have milky juice. Leaves basal and alternate. Flower heads sometimes solitary; only raylike flowers; flower-head bracts (phyllaries) in 1 row, with bractlets beneath. Seedlike fruits unbeaked; fruit pappus of hairlike bristles. (See p. 83.)

Rush Skeleton-plant

Stems rushlike, twiggy. HT: 6–18 in.

Raylike flowers usually 5, light pink to lavender.

Rose-rush

Heads of 8–10 raylike flowers. HT: 1–2½ ft.

■ **NARROW-LEAF WIRE-LETTUCE** (*Stephanomeria tenuifolia*): Summer; slopes and plains, especially rocky places. Leaves narrow. Flowers pink, lavender, or whitish. Pappus bristles white. Also called Lesser Wire-lettuce. **SIMILAR BROWN-PLUME WIRE-LETTUCE** (*S. pauciflora*): Widespread in Southwest. Pappus bristles brownish yellow. Also called Desert-straw.

■ **PARRY'S WIRE-LETTUCE** (*S. parryi*): Spring; desert slopes. Leaves thick, with sharp-tipped lobes.

RELATED ■ **FALSE WIRE-LETTUCE** (*Pleiacanthus spinosus*): Summer; desert slopes, rocky places. Heads of 3–5 flowers. Pappus bristles minutely barbed (not feathery). Also called Thorny Skeleton-plant.

Genus *Stephanomeria* (14 native species). Flowers similar to *Lygodesmia* (above). Fruit pappus of bristles that are partially or wholly featherlike. (See p. 83.)

Narrow-leaf Wire-lettuce

Parry's Wire-lettuce

Heads of usually 10–13 flowers. HT: 4–16 in.

False Wire-lettuce

Heads of 4 or 5 raylike flowers. Stems twiggy. HT: 6–24 in.

Branches spine-tipped. HT: 4–20 in.

DESERT RELATIVES OF DANDELION

■ **DESERT-CHICORY** (*Rafinesquia neomexicana*): Stems weak, often supported by surrounding vegetation. Leaves basal and alternate, toothed to deeply lobed. Small bractlets at base of phyllaries (flower-head bracts). Seedlike fruits long-beaked; pappus of bristles, feathery on lower part.

■ **WHITE TACKSTEM** (*Calycoseris wrightii*): Plants erect. Upper stems, stalks, and phyllaries have tack-shaped glands. Flowers white, often rose-tinged beneath. Pappus bristles not feathery.

■ **YELLOW TACKSTEM** (*C. parryi*): Similar to White Tackstem, but flowers yellow, sometimes faintly red-tinged.

Desert Relatives of Dandelion (several genera, numerous species). Spring-flowering desert plants with only raylike flowers, as in ▣ Common Dandelion (p. 569). Plants have milky juice. Flower heads sometimes solitary.

Desert-chicory

Flower heads white, often rose-tinged beneath. HT: 6–24 in.

White Tackstem

Flower heads white. HT: 2–12 in.

Yellow Tackstem

HT: 2–12 in.

DESERT RELATIVES OF DANDELION

■ **PARACHUTE-PLANT** (*Atrichoseris platyphylla*): Leaves broadly spoon-shaped, mostly in a basal cluster nearly flat on the ground. Tips of raylike flowers sometimes tinged rose-purple. Seedlike fruits unbeaked; pappus absent. Also called Gravel-ghost.

■ **SNAKE'S-HEAD** (*Malacothrix coulteri*): Stem leaves usually clasping. Phyllaries (flower-head bracts) broad, papery-edged, often with purplish midstripe.

■ **DESERT-DANDELION** (*M. glabrata*): Leaves mostly basal, divided into threadlike segments. Young flower heads have red spot in center.

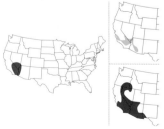

Parachute-plant

Flower heads white, in open clusters.

Leaves gray-green, often mottled. HT: 6 in.–6 ft.

Snake's-head

Flower heads pale yellow or whitish. HT: 6–24 in.

Desert-dandelion

Flower heads yellow. HT: 6–18 in.

DESERT RELATIVES OF DANDELION

■ **SCALEBUD** (*Anisocoma acaulis*): Heads of about 40 raylike flowers. Phyllaries (flower-head bracts) papery, with red-edged tip, dark midvein. Seedlike fruits finely ribbed and hairy; pappus of feathery bristles.

■ **KEYSIA** (*Glyptopleura setulosa*): Leaves conspicuously white-toothed. Heads of 7–14 flowers, aging pinkish or purplish. Bractlets at base of phyllaries have tooth-edged tip. Seedlike fruits have minute bumps, short beak, pappus of hairlike bristles. Also called Holly-dandelion, Crust-leaf.

Scalebud

Leaves in a basal cluster, pinnately divided, segments toothed. HT: 2–9 in.

Flower heads yellow or cream-colored; underside sometimes red-marked.

Keysia

Flower heads white or light yellow. HT: 1–3 in.

■ **WILD LETTUCE** (*Lactuca canadensis*): Summer–fall; open places. Leaves highly variable: toothed or untoothed, unlobed or cut into slender lobes; basal leaves often deeply lobed (see inset). Small, dandelion-like heads of mostly 15–20 usually yellow (sometimes bluish) raylike flowers in large clusters; phyllaries mostly equal in size. Pappus bristles white. Also called Tall or Canadian Lettuce.

■ **TALL BLUE LETTUCE** (*L. biennis*): Moist places. Very similar to Wild Lettuce, but flowers mostly 15–30, typically blue or occasionally cream-colored (sometimes yellowish); pappus bristles dark.

Genus *Lactuca* (10 species, 6 native). Plants have milky juice. Leaves basal and alternate. Flower heads have only raylike flowers; flower-head bracts (phyllaries) in 2 rows, with small bractlets beneath. Seedlike fruits beaked; fruit pappus of hairlike bristles. (See p. 83.)

Wild Lettuce

Leaves highly variable, even on a single stem. HT: 1–8 ft.

Tall Blue Lettuce

Flower heads usually blue. HT: 1–8 ft.

■ **WOODLAND LETTUCE** (*Lactuca floridana*): Mostly summer; thickets, woods, moist or wet places. Leaves basal and on stems, variable, mostly toothed to deeply lobed. Heads to about ½ in. across, of mostly 10–15 bluish or whitish, raylike flowers. Also called Florida Lettuce.

RELATED ■ **BLUE LETTUCE** (*Mulgedium pulchellum*; often treated as *L. tatarica* ssp. *pulchella* or as *L. oblongifolia*): Meadows, clearings, moist places. Leaves narrowly lance-shaped, lobed to unlobed. Heads to about 1 in. across, of mostly 18–50 raylike flowers.

Woodland Lettuce

Flower heads usually blue.

Blue Lettuce

Flower heads blue, showy.

Flower heads in large clusters. HT: 1–6 ft.

Flower heads in open clusters. HT: 6 in.–3 ft.

■ **WESTERN HAWK'S-BEARD** (*Crepis occidentalis*): Late spring–summer; open woods, slopes, meadows. Plants hairy. Leaves gray-hairy, basal and on stems, mostly deeply lobed. Flower heads in clusters of 2–20.

TAPER-TIP HAWK'S-BEARD (*C. acuminata*): Open woods, slopes, meadows; western. Leaves hairy, with long, narrow tip. Flower heads in clusters of 30–100.

■ **MEADOW HAWK'S-BEARD** (*C. runcinata*, no photo): Meadows. Leaves mostly basal, hairless or inconspicuously hairy, untoothed to toothed or shallowly lobed; teeth may be backward-pointing.

NOTE The similar ① Common Dandelion has only basal leaves; flower heads solitary. See also ① Smooth Hawk's-beard (both species shown on p. 569).

Genus *Crepis* (24 species, 12 native). Plants have milky juice. Leaves basal and also often alternate. Only raylike flowers; flower-head bracts (phyllaries) in 1 or 2 rows, with small bractlets beneath. Seedlike fruits many-ribbed, beaked or not; fruit pappus of hairlike bristles. (See p. 83.)

Western Hawk's-beard

Heads large, yellow, many-flowered. HT: 6–18 in.

Taper-tip Hawk's-beard

Heads fewer-flowered. HT: 6–24 in.

■ **NODDING MICROSERIS** (*Microseris nutans*): Spring–early summer; meadows, open woods. Flower heads nodding in bud, erect in flower. Fruit pappus of 15–30 feathery-awned, narrow scales.

OTHER GENERA Flower heads also solitary and yellow, but erect in bud. ■ **PRAIRIE FALSE DANDELION** (*Nothocalais cuspidata*): Spring–early summer; prairies, plains. Leaves basal, often wavy-edged. Fruit pappus of hairlike bristles. See also Pale Agoseris (below). ■ **LINDLEY'S SILVER-PUFFS** (*Uropappus lindleyi*): Spring; open places. Leaves mostly unlobed. Fruit pappus of 5 awn-tipped scales. Also called Starpoint. See also ① Yellow Salsify (p. 569).

Genus *Microseris* (11 native species). Plants have milky juice. Leaves mostly basal. Flower heads normally solitary; only raylike flowers. Seedlike fruits 10–15-ribbed; fruit pappus usually of awned scales. (See p. 83.)

Nodding Microseris

Prairie False Dandelion
HT: 6–12 in.

Lindley's Silver-puffs

Flower heads solitary, yellow. Leaves long and narrow. HT: 6–18 in.

Tips of phyllaries (flower-head bracts) visible. HT: 6–18 in.

■ **PALE AGOSERIS** (*Agoseris glauca*): Late spring–summer; slopes, meadows. Flowers commonly age or dry pinkish. Fruiting heads round, fluffy; fruits have thickish, ribbed beak. Also called Short-beak Agoseris. The similar Prairie False Dandelion (above) has unbeaked fruits; see also ① Common Dandelion (p. 569).

■ **ORANGE AGOSERIS** (*A. aurantiaca*): Summer; slopes, meadows, open woods. Flowers sometimes age or dry purplish or pinkish. Fruits have slender, elongated beak. See also ① Orange Hawkweed (p. 569), which has flower heads in clusters.

NOTE *Agoseris* species are also called mountain-dandelion or goat-chicory.

Genus *Agoseris* (9 native species). Plants have milky juice. Leaves basal. Flower heads solitary; only raylike flowers. Seedlike fruits narrow, ribbed, usually with conspicuous beak; fruit pappus of hairlike bristles. (See p. 83.)

Pale Agoseris

Flower heads yellow, on leafless stalks. Leaves lance-shaped. HT: 6–24 in.

Orange Agoseris

Flower heads orange. HT: 6–24 in.

■ **SLENDER HAWKWEED** (*Hieracium triste*): Summer; meadows, slopes, woods. Typical of many hawkweeds. Leaves chiefly in a basal cluster.

RATTLESNAKE HAWKWEED (*H. venosum*): Late spring–midsummer; open woods; eastern. Basal leaves have reddish purple veins. Flower heads yellow.

■ **SHAGGY HAWKWEED** (*H. horridum*): Summer; open places. Plants very hairy. Both stem and basal leaves. Flower heads yellow. **SIMILAR** ■ **HAIRY HAWKWEED** (*H. gronovii*): Also called Queen-devil.

WHITE-FLOWER HAWKWEED (*H. albiflorum*): Summer; open places; western.

NOTE See also introduced hawkweeds (p. 569).

Genus *Hieracium* (36 species, 29 native). Plants have milky juice. Leaves basal or alternate. Flower heads sometimes solitary; only raylike flowers; flower-head bracts (phyllaries) may have tiny bractlets at base. Seedlike fruits unbeaked; fruit pappus of hairlike bristles. (See p. 83.)

Slender Hawkweed

Flower heads yellow. HT: 4–12 in.

Rattlesnake Hawkweed

HT: 1–2½ ft.

Shaggy Hawkweed

HT: 3–12 in.

White-flower Hawkweed

Flower heads white. HT: 6–24 in.

■ **CAROLINA FALSE DANDELION** (*Pyrrhopappus carolinianus*): Mostly spring; open places. Stem leaves lance-shaped, often toothed or occasionally lobed; basal leaves unlobed to deeply lobed. Heads of mostly 50–150 flowers. **SIMILAR** ■ **TUBER FALSE DANDELION** (*P. grandiflorus*): Plants generally 6–12 in. tall; leaves usually all basal, commonly deeply toothed to lobed, with many lobes pointing outward or upward; heads mostly solitary, of typically 40–60 flowers.

NOTE See also 🅘 Common Dandelion (p. 569), which has leaves all basal (stem leaves present in Carolina False Dandelion), with lobes generally pointing backward; flower heads always solitary.

Genus *Pyrrhopappus* (4 native species). Plants have milky juice. Leaves basal and also often alternate. Only raylike flowers; flower-head bracts (phyllaries) have bractlets at base. Seedlike fruits 5-ribbed, beaked; outer pappus of short hairs, inner pappus of hairlike bristles. (See p. 83.)

Carolina False Dandelion

Flower heads light yellow, sometimes large, solitary or few; dark anthers usually visible in center. HT: 6–30 in.

■ **TWO-FLOWER CYNTHIA** (*Krigia biflora*): Late spring–summer; meadows, thickets, woods. Leaves mostly basal, untoothed, toothed, or lobed; usually 1 or 2 lance-shaped, clasping midstem leaves.

■ **OPPOSITE-LEAF DWARF-DANDELION** (*K. caespitosa*): Spring–summer; open places. Leaves basal and on stems.

■ **POTATO DWARF-DANDELION** (*K. dandelion*): Spring; moist open areas. Plants resemble a dandelion. Leaves all basal, untoothed to lobed. Heads of 25–35 flowers; phyllaries (flower-head bracts) hang down in fruit.

NOTE Ⅰ Common Dandelion (p. 569) has leaves with backward-pointing lobes; heads of 40–100 flowers; fruits beaked.

Genus *Krigia* (7 native species). Plants have milky juice. Leaves mostly basal, or also on stems. Flower heads sometimes solitary; only raylike flowers. Seedlike fruits unbeaked; fruit's outer pappus of tiny scales, inner pappus of longer, hairlike bristles, or pappus absent. (See p. 83.)

Two-flower Cynthia

Flower heads yellow-orange, solitary or few on stalks (often 2) above midstem leaves. HT: 6–30 in.

Opposite-leaf Dwarf-dandelion

Leaves on upper stem appear opposite. HT: 6–18 in.

Potato Dwarf-dandelion

Flower heads solitary. HT: 6–18 in.

■ **AMERICAN TRAILPLANT** (*Adenocaulon bicolor*): Summer–fall; woods. Stems white-woolly near base, sticky-hairy above. Leaves on lower third of plant, typically broadly triangular and wavy-edged to coarsely lobed; leafstalks long, often winged. Fruits form only in outer flowers. Also called Pathfinder.

Genus *Adenocaulon* (1 native species). Leaves basal and alternate. Only disk flowers. Seedlike fruits sticky-hairy, club-shaped. (See p. 83.)

American Trailplant

Flower heads very small. HT: 1–3 ft.

Leaves densely white-hairy beneath.

Flowers whitish.

■ **PEARLY EVERLASTING** (*Anaphalis margaritacea*): Summer–fall; open woods, fields, roadsides. Plants have white, cobwebby or woolly hairs. Leaves narrow, usually white-woolly beneath. Typically unisexual; individual plants either male or female.

NOTE Do not confuse with pussytoes (p. 94), which have leaves mostly basal. Differs from rabbit-tobaccos (see Blunt-leaf Rabbit-tobacco, below) in having slender underground stems (vs. a taproot); leaf edges often downturned or curled under (vs. usually flat); flower heads unisexual (vs. bisexual).

Genus *Anaphalis* (1 native species). Leaves alternate. Only disk flowers, these unisexual; flower-head bracts (phyllaries) bright white, in 8–12 overlapping rows. (See p. 83.)

Pearly Everlasting

Heads small, with yellowish disk flowers surrounded by white, papery bracts. HT: 1–3 ft.

■ **BLUNT-LEAF RABBIT-TOBACCO** (*Pseudognaphalium obtusifolium*): Late summer–fall; open places. Stems frequently white-hairy. Leaves narrow, greenish above, white-woolly beneath. Also called Fragrant Cudweed, Sweet Everlasting, Cat's-foot. Several similar species, with leaves often hairy above and beneath, sometimes also basal. See similar Pearly Everlasting (above).

RELATED *Gnaphalium*: Shorter plants with flower heads in dense clusters.

■ **LOWLAND CUDWEED** (*G. palustre*): Spring–fall; moist open places. Plants commonly woolly. Leaves ⅛–5⁄16 in. wide. Flowers white. Also called Western Marsh Cudweed. **MARSH CUDWEED** (*G. uliginosum*, no photo): Summer–fall; chiefly northeastern and northwestern, possibly entirely or in part introduced from Europe. Similar; leaves to ⅛ in. wide.

Genus *Pseudognaphalium* (21 species, 19 native). Sometimes aromatic. Leaves mostly alternate, sometimes also basal. Only disk flowers; flower-head bracts (phyllaries) unequal, often papery, in 3–7 overlapping rows. Fruit pappus of hairlike bristles. (See p. 83.)

Blunt-leaf Rabbit-tobacco. Phyllaries papery, white. Flower heads small, in clusters. HT: 1–3 ft.

Lowland Cudweed. Flower heads small, in crowded, woolly clusters. HT: 1–6 in.

PLANTAIN-LEAF PUSSYTOES

(*Antennaria plantaginifolia*): Spring; open places; eastern. Plants often mat-forming. Stem leaves narrow; basal leaves 3–5-veined, spoon-shaped or roundish, densely white-hairy beneath. Plants bear male (left) or female (right) flower heads. Also called Woman's-tobacco. Several similar species with 1-veined basal leaves.

■ **SINGLE-HEAD PUSSYTOES** (*A. solitaria*): Spring; woods.

■ **ROSY PUSSYTOES** (*A. rosea*): Summer; open places. Phyllaries brown, white, pink, or yellow.

NOTE See also Pearly Everlasting and Blunt-leaf Rabbit-tobacco (both on p. 93), which have prominent stem leaves.

Genus *Antennaria* (34 native species). Leaves mostly basal. Flower heads sometimes solitary; only disk flowers, these unisexual; flower-head bracts (phyllaries) unequal, often papery, in 3–6 overlapping rows. (See p. 83.)

Plantain-leaf Pussytoes

Phyllaries papery, white. HT: 3–10 in.

Flower heads small, in clusters.

Single-head Pussytoes

Flower heads solitary, whitish. HT: 2–10 in.

Rosy Pussytoes

Flower heads often pinkish. HT: 2–12 in.

■ **SWEETSCENT** (*Pluchea odorata*): Mostly summer–fall; wet, often alkaline places. Plants aromatic. Clusters often flat-topped; phyllaries (flower-head bracts) short-hairy. Also called Saltmarsh-fleabane. SIMILAR Mostly southeastern, in wet places. **CAMPHORWEED** (*P. camphorata*): Clusters rounded; phyllaries minutely gland-dotted. Also called Plowman's-wort. **ROSY CAMPHORWEED** (*P. baccharis*): Leaves stalkless.

■ **STINKING CAMPHORWEED** (*P. foetida*): Mostly summer–fall; wet places. Plants ill-scented. Also called Stinkweed.

■ **ARROW-WEED** (*P. sericea*): Spring–summer; stream banks. Shrub; not aromatic. Branches wandlike. Leaves willowlike, silvery silky-hairy.

Genus *Pluchea* (9 species, 6 native). Plants occasionally woody, often aromatic. Leaves alternate. Only disk flowers. Seedlike fruits cylindrical, 4–8-ribbed; fruit pappus of hairlike bristles. (See p. 83.)

Sweetscent

Flower heads small, pink to rose-purple. Leaves egg-shaped. HT: mostly 1–4 ft.

Stinking Camphorweed

Flower heads often cream-colored. HT: 1–3 ft.

Arrow-weed

Flower heads pinkish to purplish. HT: 3–10 ft.

■ **PALE INDIAN-PLANTAIN**
(*Arnoglossum atriplicifolium*): Spring–early summer; open woods, thickets, roadsides. Stems smooth or with faint ridges. Leaves palmately veined, whitish beneath. Flowers 5 per head, sometimes tinged greenish or purplish. SIMILAR ■ **GREAT INDIAN-PLANTAIN** (*A. reniforme*): Spring–fall; open woods. Stems have prominent ridges and grooves; leaves green above and beneath.

Genus *Arnoglossum* (8 native species). Leaves basal and alternate, palmately veined. Only disk flowers; flower-head bracts (phyllaries) 5. (See p. 83.)

Pale Indian-plantain

Flowers whitish.

Flower heads in more or less flat-topped clusters. HT: 3–9 ft.

Leaves triangular-egg-shaped, coarsely toothed and lobed.

■ **PRAIRIE INDIAN-PLANTAIN**
(*Arnoglossum plantagineum*): Spring–summer; open places. Leaves thick and unlobed, with parallel veins. Heads of 5 flowers; phyllaries (flower-head bracts) winged. Also called Tuberous Indian-plantain. SIMILAR ■ **EGG-LEAF INDIAN-PLANTAIN** (*A. ovatum*): Summer–fall; wet places. Leaves thin and variable, usually egg-shaped; phyllaries not winged.

RELATED ■ **FALSE INDIAN-PLANTAIN**
(*Hasteola suaveolens*): Late summer–fall; woods, thickets, stream banks. Differs from *Arnoglossum* in having many (18–55) flowers per head; 12–14 phyllaries; and a ring of short, narrow bractlets beneath each head. Also called Sweet- or Hastate-Indian-plantain.

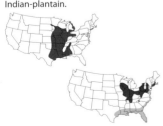

Prairie Indian-plantain

Flowers white or greenish, in more or less flat-topped clusters. Leaves elliptic. HT: 2–3 ft.

False Indian-plantain

Flowers cream-white. Leaves mostly arrowhead-shaped. HT: 3–5 ft.

■ **SILVERBACK LUINA** (*Luina hypoleuca*):
Summer; rocky slopes, cliffs. Leaves
stalkless, egg- to lance-shaped, dark
green above, silvery white and densely
hairy beneath; main leaf veins more
or less parallel. Also called Little-leaf
Silverback.

Genus *Luina* (2 native species). Leaves
alternate, palmately veined. Only disk
flowers; flower-head bracts (phyllaries)
in 1 or 2 rows. Seedlike fruits many-lined; fruit pappus of
many bristles. (See p. 83.)

Silverback Luina

Flower heads
yellowish cream,
in clusters;
style branches
and anthers
conspicuously
protrude. HT: 6–18 in.

■ **SILVERCROWN** (*Cacaliopsis
nardosmia*): Spring–early summer;
meadows, open woods. Leaves mostly
basal and long-stalked, broadly kidney-
shaped to nearly round in outline; to
14 in. wide; silvery-white-hairy beneath.
Also called Cut-leaf-luina.

Genus *Cacaliopsis* (1 native species).
Leaves basal and alternate. Only disk
flowers; flower-head bracts (phyllaries) in
1 or 2 rows, with papery edges. (See p. 83.)

Silvercrown

Flower heads yellow to orange, in
clusters; style branches and anthers
conspicuously protrude. Leaves
deeply palmately lobed, the lobes
coarsely toothed. HT: mostly 1–3 ft.

■ **COMMON BONESET** (*Eupatorium perfoliatum*): Summer–fall; mostly moist or wet places. Leaves opposite (rarely whorled), stalkless, the pairs united and wrapping around stem at their bases.
SIMILAR ■ **UPLAND BONESET**
(*E. sessilifolium*): Drier sites. Leaves stalkless, their bases not joined around stem.
LATE-FLOWERING THOROUGHWORT
(*E. serotinum*): Open places; eastern. Leaves have distinct stalks, ⅜–1½ in. long.

■ **COMMON DOG-FENNEL**
(*E. capillifolium*): Open places. Leaves opposite or some alternate, stalkless, divided into threadlike segments.

 Genus *Eupatorium* (24 species, 23 native). Leaves usually opposite. Only disk flowers; style branches often protruding; flower-head bracts (phyllaries) generally unequal, in mostly 2 or 3 overlapping rows. Seedlike fruits 5-angled; fruit pappus of hairlike bristles. (See p. 83.)

Common Boneset

Flower heads very small, whitish, in flat-topped clusters. HT: 2–5 ft.

Midstem leaves appear pierced by stem.

Common Dog-fennel

Flower heads tiny, whitish, in feathery sprays. HT: 2–6 ft.

■ **WHITE SNAKEROOT** (*Ageratina altissima*): Summer–fall; woods, thickets. Leaves opposite, triangular-egg-shaped, sharply toothed, tapering at tip.
SIMILAR ■ **FRAGRANT SNAKEROOT**
(*A. herbacea*): Slopes, meadows, open woods. Leaves lighter, green to yellow-green (or occasionally grayish green). Also called Western Thoroughwort.

■ **WESTERN SNAKEROOT**
(*A. occidentalis*): Rocky slopes, open woods, stream banks. Leaves alternate above, opposite below. Flowers pinkish, purplish, or sometimes whitish or bluish.

 Genus *Ageratina* (14 species, 13 native). Similar to *Eupatorium* (above), but with phyllaries usually in 2 rows, about equal in length, and not strongly overlapping. (See p. 83.)

White Snakeroot

Western Snakeroot

Flower heads very small, whitish. HT: mostly 1½–3 ft.

Flower heads small, frequently pinkish to purplish. HT: 6–30 in.

■ **MISTFLOWER** (*Conoclinium coelestinum*): Summer–fall; meadows, thickets, woods, stream banks, roadsides. Flowers sometimes whitish or pinkish; style branches conspicuously protruding. Also called Hardy-ageratum, Blue Mistflower. **SIMILAR** ■ **PALM-LEAF MISTFLOWER** (*C. dissectum*): Spring–fall; plains, mesas, stream banks. Leaves deeply lobed or dissected.

RELATED ■ **PINK THOROUGHWORT** (*Fleischmannia incarnata*): Fall; woods, thickets, swamps. Differs from *Conoclinium* in having flowers fewer per head (15–25 vs. 35–70), with a flat receptacle and unequal phyllaries (flower-head bracts). Also called Pink Boneset.

Genus *Conoclinium* (3 native species). Similar to *Ageratina* (p. 97), but receptacle conelike (vs. dome-shaped). (See p. 83.)

Mistflower

Pink Thoroughwort

Flower heads very small, usually blue or blue-lavender. Leaves opposite, stalked, triangular-egg-shaped, toothed. HT: 1–3 ft.

Flower head typically pink to lilac. HT: 1–4 ft.

■ **SPOTTED JOE-PYE-WEED** (*Eutrochium maculatum*): Late summer–early fall; moist or wet places. Leaves sharply toothed, in whorls usually of 4 or 5. Flower heads in more or less flat-topped clusters; mostly 9–20 flowers per head.

OTHERS With flower heads in large, rounded clusters; mostly 4–7 flowers per head (no photos). ■ **SWEET JOE-PYE-WEED** (*E. purpureum*): Stems usually solid, purple only near point of leaf attachment. Leaves in whorls of 3 or 4. Also called Sweet-scented or Purple Joe-pye-weed. ■ **HOLLOW JOE-PYE-WEED** (*E. fistulosum*): Stems usually hollow; generally purple overall, with a pale whitish coating. Leaves in whorls of 4–7.

Genus *Eutrochium* (5 native species). Similar to *Eupatorium* (p. 97), and often included in that genus, but leaves usually whorled (only rarely opposite); flowers usually pinkish or purplish (only rarely whitish). (See p. 83.)

Spotted joe-pye-weed

Flower heads pinkish purple, in large clusters.

Stems usually solid, purple-spotted or sometimes nearly all purple. HT: 2–6 ft.

Leaves whorled.

■ **HAIRY CHAFFHEAD** (*Carphephorus paniculatus*): Fall–early winter; moist or wet places. Stems densely hairy. Leaves elliptic to spoon-shaped, the largest ones basal and on lower stem, reduced upward. Flower heads small. Also called Deer-tongue.

■ **VANILLA-LEAF** (*C. odoratissimus*): Fall; woods, fields, roadsides, boggy places. Plants usually have a pronounced vanilla-like odor. Stems hairless. Also called Deer-tongue, Carolina-vanilla.

 Genus *Carphephorus* (7 native species). Leaves basal and alternate. Only disk flowers; style branches often protruding. Seedlike fruits narrow and 10-ribbed; fruit pappus of 1 or occasionally 2 rows of hairlike bristles. (See p. 83.)

Hairy Chaffhead · Vanilla-leaf

Flower heads pinkish purple, in broadly cylindrical clusters. HT: 1–4 ft.

Flower heads in more or less flat-topped clusters. HT: 1–4 ft.

■ **DOTTED GAYFEATHER** (*Liatris punctata*): Summer–fall; prairies, open places. Leaves narrow. Heads of 3–8 flowers. Fruit pappus bristles feathery. Several similar species, some with minutely barbed pappus bristles.

■ **ELEGANT GAYFEATHER** (*L. elegans* var. *elegans*): Flower heads cream-colored; phyllaries (flower-head bracts) conspicuously spreading, their tips petal-like, lavender or pink. Pappus bristles feathery.

■ **SCALY GAYFEATHER** (*L. squarrosa*): Heads of 20–50 pinkish purple flowers; phyllary tips long-pointed, spreading.

Genus *Liatris* (37 native species). Leaves basal and alternate. Only disk flowers; style branches often protruding. Seedlike fruits 8–11-ribbed; fruit pappus of minutely barbed to featherlike bristles. (See p. 83.) Species are also called blazing-star or button-snakeroot.

Dotted Gayfeather · Elegant Gayfeather

HT: 1–4 ft.

Scaly Gayfeather

Flower heads pinkish purple, nearly stalkless, in spike-like clusters. HT: 6 in.–3 ft.

HT: 1–2 ft.

■ **CLIMBING HEMPWEED** (*Mikania scandens*): Mostly summer–late fall; moist or wet places. Stems round or weakly angled, often climbing on bushes and other vegetation. Leaves untoothed, wavy-edged, or few-toothed; opposite, long-stalked, triangular or heart-shaped. Heads about ¼ in. long, with 4 flowers. Also called Climbing Hempvine, Climbing-boneset. **SIMILAR** ■ **HEARTLEAF CLIMBING HEMPWEED** (*M. cordifolia*): Seeps, stream banks, wet places. Stems distinctly 6-angled; flower heads mostly ³⁄₁₆–³⁄₈ in. long, white. Also called Florida Keys Hempvine.

Genus *Mikania* (3 native species). Vines. Leaves opposite. Only disk flowers; flower-head bracts (phyllaries) 4 (or sometimes 5), overlapping. Fruit pappus of hairlike bristles. (See p. 83.)

Climbing Hempweed

Flower heads very small, in clusters. Twining or sprawling vine.

Flower heads often pinkish or purplish.

Flower heads sometimes whitish.

■ **FIELD THISTLE** (*Cirsium discolor*): Summer–fall; fields, open woods. Ring of leaflike, spiny-edged bracts beneath phyllaries of each flower head.

■ **YELLOW THISTLE** (*C. horridulum*): Spring–summer; open places. Flowers pink, purple, red, yellow, or white; conspicuous spiny-edged bracts beneath each head. Also called Horrid Thistle.

■ **WESTERN THISTLE** (*C. occidentale*): Spring–summer; many habitats. Flowers white, pink, purple, or red.

NOTE Most thistles have pink or purple flowers. See also introduced thistles (p. 567). Do not confuse thistles with burdocks (p. 566), knapweeds (p. 568), or teasels (p. 580).

Genus *Cirsium* (62 species, 59 native). Plants spiny. Leaves basal and alternate. Flower heads sometimes solitary; only disk flowers; flower-head bracts (phyllaries) usually spine-tipped, in 5–20 overlapping rows. Seedlike fruits often egg-shaped. (See p. 83.)

Field Thistle

Yellow Thistle

HT: 6 in.–6 ft.

Western Thistle

Flower heads spiny, pink or purple. Leaves deeply lobed, spiny, white-hairy beneath. HT: mostly 3–6 ft.

Phyllaries have cob-webby hairs. HT: 1–6 ft.

■ **ELK THISTLE** (*Cirsium scariosum*):
Mostly summer; slopes, meadows, open
woods. Several varieties, some with tall
stems, some nearly stemless and with
leaves in a basal cluster. Also called
Meadow Thistle. The name Elk Thistle is
also used for *C. foliosum*, a less common
species of the northern Rockies, with
which this species has been confused.

■ **WHITE THISTLE** (*C. hookerianum*):
Slopes, clearings, meadows. Flowers
generally cream-colored or white,
occasionally pinkish.

Elk Thistle

White Thistle

Flower heads spiny, white, pink, or purple. Stems very leafy. HT: 1–6 ft.

Plants sometimes nearly stemless.

Flower heads spiny, white. HT: 1–5 ft.

■ **AMERICAN BASKET-FLOWER**
(*Plectocephalus americanus*): Spring–
summer; prairies, open places. Leaves
stalkless, lance-shaped, untoothed or
few-toothed; basal leaves typically absent
at bloom time. Inner flowers in head
fertile, cream-colored to pinkish; outer
flowers sterile, pinkish purple, enlarged
and mimicking rays.

NOTE Separated from ⬛ *Centaurea*
(knapweeds, Cornflower, and related
plants, p. 568) on the basis of technical
characters. Do not confuse with thistles
(pp. 100–101), which have leaves spiny;
phyllaries usually spine-tipped.

Genus *Plectocephalus* (2 native species).
Leaves basal and alternate. Flower heads
sometimes solitary; only disk flowers,
some enlarged and resembling ray flowers; flower-head
bracts (phyllaries) in 8–10 overlapping rows, their tips
fringed with spinelike teeth. Seedlike fruits barrel-shaped;
fruit pappus of stiff bristles. (See p. 83.)

American Basket-flower

Flower heads very large; flowers have slender lobes; tips of phyllaries fringed. HT: 1½–5 ft.

■ **STOKE'S-ASTER** (*Stokesia laevis*): Summer; moist or wet woods, bogs, roadsides. Basal leaves elongated, upper stem leaves stalkless. Outer phyllaries (flower-head bracts) leaflike, bristly-edged.

Genus *Stokesia* (1 native species). Leaves basal and alternate. Flower heads sometimes solitary; only disk flowers, some enlarged and mimicking ray flowers. Fruit pappus of a few scales. (See p. 83.)

Stoke's-aster

Outer flowers flared and lobed, resembling rays.

Flower heads large, mostly blue or blue-purple. HT: 1–2 ft.

■ **CAROLINA ELEPHANT'S-FOOT** (*Elephantopus carolinianus*): Summer–fall; woods, thickets, meadows. Flower heads small, grouped in clusters of 10 or more that resemble a single, larger head. Individual heads have 1–5 (often 4) flowers, each with 5 slender lobes extending to one side and mimicking ray flowers. Also called Leafy Elephant's-foot.

NOTE Flowering plants of *E. carolinianus* have large, well-developed stem leaves. The remaining *Elephantopus* species, all southeastern, have chiefly basal leaves at bloom time (the stem leaves reduced or bractlike) and differ from one another in technical characters.

Genus *Elephantopus* (4 native species). Leaves basal and alternate. Flower heads in clusters above leaflike bracts; only disk flowers; flower-head bracts (phyllaries) 8, overlapping, in 2 rows. Fruit pappus of 5 awned scales. (See p. 83.)

Carolina Elephant's-foot

Flower heads often white, above usually 3 triangular, leaflike bracts. Stem leaves alternate. HT: 1–3 ft.

Flower heads sometimes pink to purple.

■ **TALL IRONWEED** (*Vernonia gigantea*): Summer–fall; open places. Heads of mostly 18–24 flowers; tips of phyllaries pointed to rounded. Also called Giant Ironweed. **SIMILAR WESTERN IRONWEED** (*V. baldwinii*): Great Plains, Midwest. Leaves conspicuously hairy beneath; phyllaries commonly resin-dotted, the middle ones often curved outward at tip. Also called Baldwin's Ironweed.

■ **NEW YORK IRONWEED** (*V. noveboracensis*): Open places. Leaves ⅝–1¾ in. wide. Heads of mostly 30–45 flowers.

■ **NARROW-LEAF IRONWEED** (*V. angustifolia*, no photo): Pinelands, open woods, fields. Leaves narrow, ¼ in. or less wide. Heads of mostly 12–20 flowers.

Genus *Vernonia* (17 native species). Leaves alternate, occasionally basal. Only disk flowers; flower-head bracts (phyllaries) in 4–7 overlapping rows. Fruit's inner pappus of long, hairlike bristles, outer pappus of short bristles or slender scales. (See p. 83.)

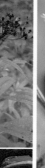

Tall Ironweed

New York Ironweed

Flower heads purplish, in clusters. Leaves lance-shaped. HT: 1–6 ft.

Tips of phyllaries often pointed.

Tips of phyllaries very narrow to threadlike. HT: to 6 ft.

■ **ROSY PALAFOX** (*Palafoxia rosea*): Spring–fall; sandy soil. Leaves narrowly lance-shaped. Heads of all disk flowers; flower tube shorter than its lobes; phyllaries (flower-head bracts) more or less equal. **SIMILAR ■ COASTAL-PLAIN PALAFOX** (*P. integrifolia*): Mostly late summer–fall. Outer phyllaries shorter than inner ones.

■ **DESERT PALAFOX** (*P. arida*): Late winter–spring. Heads of all disk flowers; flower tube longer than its lobes. Also called Spanish-needles.

■ **RAYED PALAFOX** (*P. sphacelata*): Summer–fall. Heads of disk flowers and 3–5 petal-like rays. Also called Othake.

Genus *Palafoxia* (10 native species). Leaves alternate (or the lower ones sometimes opposite). Usually only disk flowers, occasionally also ray flowers. Seedlike fruits hairy; fruit pappus of 4–10 scales. (See p. 83.)

Rosy Palafox

Desert Palafox

Flower heads pink to rose-violet. HT: 6–18 in.

Flower heads pale pink to whitish. HT: mostly 6–30 in.

Rayed Palafox

Ray flowers deeply 3-lobed. HT: 6 in.–3 ft.

■ **GRASS-LEAF BARBARA'S-BUTTONS** (*Marshallia graminifolia*): Late summer–fall; wet woods, boggy places. Basal leaves 1½–10 in. long, ⅛–½ in. wide.

■ **WHITE BARBARA'S-BUTTONS** (*M. caespitosa*): Spring; prairies, rock outcrops. Basal leaves 2–6 in. long, ⅛–⅜ in. wide.

■ **SPOON-LEAF BARBARA'S-BUTTONS** (*M. obovata*, no photo): Spring; woods, fields. Basal leaves commonly spoon-shaped, 2–4 in. long, ¼–½ in. wide. Flower heads white.

■ **BROAD-LEAF BARBARA'S-BUTTONS** (*M. trinervia*): Spring; woods, stream banks. Leaves chiefly on stems, egg-shaped, 1½–4 in. long, ½–1¼ in. wide.

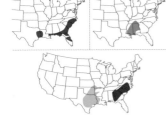

Genus *Marshallia* (7 native species). Leaves basal or alternate. Flower heads sometimes solitary; only disk flowers, each with elongated tube and slender lobes; receptacle bract-covered (chaffy). Fruit pappus of 5 scales. (See p. 83.)

Grass-leaf Barbara's-buttons

Flower heads lavender to purple. Stem leaves linear; basal leaves elongated. HT: 1–3 ft.

White Barbara's-buttons

Flower heads white. HT: 6–18 in.

Broad-leaf Barbara's-buttons

Flower heads pink. HT: 1½–2 ft.

■ **DUSTY-MAIDEN** (*Chaenactis douglasii*): Spring–summer; open, often rocky places. Plants white- or gray-hairy. Leaves pinnately lobed, fernlike. Also called Douglas'-pincushion.

■ **ESTEVE'S-PINCUSHION** (*C. stevioides*): Spring; desert slopes, flats, shrublands. Lower stems often white-hairy. Leaves have 4–8 pairs of lobes. Flowers white to pinkish. Also called Desert-pincushion.

■ **FREMONT'S-PINCUSHION** (*C. fremontii*): Spring; southwestern deserts. Lower stems nearly hairless. Leaves usually have 1 or 2 pairs of lobes. Flowers white to pinkish. Also called Desert-pincushion.

■ **YELLOW-PINCUSHION** (*C. glabriuscula*): Spring; shrublands. Flowers yellow.

Genus *Chaenactis* (17 native species). Leaves basal or alternate. Flower heads sometimes solitary; only disk flowers, the outer ones sometimes enlarged. Seedlike fruits club-shaped; fruit pappus of 4–20 scales. (See p. 83.)

Dusty-maiden

Flower heads white. HT: 4–20 in.

Esteve's-pincushion

Outer flowers enlarged, somewhat asymmetrical. HT: 4–15 in.

Fremont's-pincushion

Outer flowers enlarged, strongly asymmetrical. HT: 4–15 in.

Yellow-pincushion

Outer flowers enlarged. HT: 4–24 in.

■ **FINE-LEAF WOOLLYWHITE**
(*Hymenopappus filifolius*): Spring–fall;
open places. Flower heads mostly 15 or
fewer per stem (sometimes up to 60). Also
called Columbia-cutleaf.

■ **YELLOW WOOLLYWHITE**
(*H. flavescens*): Spring–summer; sandy or
gravelly soil. Flower heads 15–100 per stem.

■ **OLD-PLAINSMAN** (*H. scabiosaeus*):
Spring–early summer; prairies, open
woods. Flower heads mostly 40–100 per
stem. Related species may have flowers
tinged with pink or red.

NOTE Disk flowers of *Hymenopappus*
are goblet- or funnel-shaped, with
back-curved lobes. Phyllaries often have
colored edges or tip.

Genus *Hymenopappus* (10 native
species). Leaves basal or alternate.
Flower heads sometimes solitary; usually
only disk flowers; flower-head bracts (phyllaries) equal.
Seedlike fruits commonly 4-angled, often with pappus of
12–22 scales. (See p. 83.)

Fine-leaf Woollywhite
Stamens and style protruding.

Flower heads relatively few, usually yellowish. Leaves fernlike. HT: 6 in.–3 ft.

Yellow Woollywhite
Flower heads usually many, yellowish. HT: 1–3 ft.

Old-plainsman
Flower heads whitish; phyllaries petal-like. HT: 1–4 ft.

■ **VELVET TURTLEBACK** (*Psathyrotes
ramosissima*): Spring–fall (mostly
spring); desert washes, flats, hills. Leaves
stalked, roundish, toothed. Heads of
16–32 flowers, occasionally purple-
tinged. Seedlike fruits have pappus of
120–140 bristles. Also called Desert-
velvet. **SIMILAR** ■ **MEALY TURTLEBACK**
(*P. annua*): Open, often alkaline places.
Leaves thinly hairy; heads of 10–20
flowers; pappus of 35–50 bristles.

Genus *Psathyrotes* (3 native species).
Leaves basal and alternate, hairy or
covered with minute scales, aromatic.
Flower heads solitary; only disk flowers; flower-head
bracts (phyllaries) in 2 unlike rows. (See p. 83.)

Velvet Turtleback

Flower heads small, yellow, lack rays.
Leaves prominently veiny, whitish or
grayish velvety-hairy. HT: mostly 2–6 in.

■ **EMORY'S ROCK DAISY** (*Perityle emoryi*): Spring–fall; desert slopes and washes. Plants sticky-hairy. Leaves mostly alternate. Disk flowers 4-lobed; rays 3-toothed at tip. (Many *Perityle* species have rayless flower heads; most of these are local and uncommon.)

RELATED ■ MOUNTAIN TAIL-LEAF (*Pericome caudata*): Slopes, rocky places. Leaves mostly opposite. Disk flowers 4-lobed; phyllaries wholly or partially united. Also called Taper-leaf.

 Genus *Perityle* (35 native species). Herbs or shrubs, sometimes aromatic. Leaves opposite or alternate. Flower heads sometimes solitary; usually only disk flowers, sometimes also rays; flower-head bracts (phyllaries) equal, typically in 2 rows. Seedlike fruits often flattened. (See p. 83.)

Emory's Rock Daisy

Flower heads have yellow center, white petal-like rays. Leaves lobed and deeply toothed. HT: 6–24 in.

Mountain Tail-leaf

Flower heads yellow or orange-yellow, lack rays. Leaves triangular or arrowhead-shaped, with long-tapering tip. HT: 2–5 ft.

■ **PINEAPPLE-WEED** (*Matricaria discoidea*): Late spring–fall; open, often disturbed places; native to Northwest, introduced over most of current range. Leaves finely divided into narrow segments; crushed leaves have pronounced pineapple-like scent. Flower heads mostly 4–50 per plant, each of typically 125–500 disk flowers (rays absent). Also called Disc Mayweed, Rayless Chamomile. **SIMILAR VALLEY MAYWEED** (*M. occidentalis*): Spring–summer; alkaline flats, vernal pools, salt marsh borders; southern OR to southern CA. Plants lack strong scent and generally have fewer flower heads per plant (1–15); otherwise differ in technical characters.

NOTE See also ⊞ German Chamomile (p. 570), which has ray flowers.

Genus *Matricaria* (3 species, 2 native). Often aromatic. Leaves basal and alternate, pinnately divided. Flower heads sometimes solitary; usually only disk flowers. Seedlike fruits 5-ribbed; pappus tiny, crownlike. (See p. 83.)

Pineapple-weed

Heads greenish yellow, small, round or acorn-shaped, of many disk flowers. Leaves fernlike. HT: 2–16 in.

■ **DUNE TANSY** (*Tanacetum bipinnatum*): Late spring–summer; beaches, sand dunes. Plants aromatic. Leaves pinnately divided into narrow segments. Flower heads ⅜–¾ in. wide, 1–12 per plant; disk flowers numerous; rays 8–21, very small to inconspicuous or absent. Plants of the West Coast are often called Camphor Tansy or Seaside Tansy; those found from the far north to the Great Lakes region and New England are called Lake Huron Tansy.

NOTE Do not confuse with Ⅱ Common Tansy (p. 571), which has flower heads that are numerous (20–200 per plant) and smaller (³⁄₁₆–⅜ in. wide).

Genus *Tanacetum* (4 species, 1 native). Usually aromatic. Leaves basal or alternate. Flower heads rarely solitary; usually both ray and disk flowers (sometimes rays absent). Seedlike fruits often have gland dots; pappus tiny, crownlike. (See p. 83.)

Dune Tansy

Ray flowers often inconspicuous or absent.

Flower heads buttonlike, yellow. Leaves fernlike. HT: 4–30 in.

Rays sometimes very small but conspicuous.

■ **SWEET COLTSFOOT** (*Petasites frigidus*): Spring; moist or often wet places. Leaves mostly basal, large, variable in shape; plants typically begin blooming before leaves have fully expanded. Individual plants often have either predominantly male or predominantly female flower heads; rays sometimes absent on male heads. Three varieties are recognized: var. *frigidus*, var. *palmatus*, and var. *sagittatus*.

Genus *Petasites* (1 native species). Leaves basal and alternate. Both ray and disk flowers, or sometimes rays absent; flower-head bracts (phyllaries) in 2 rows. Fruit pappus of hairlike bristles. (See p. 83.)

Sweet Coltsfoot

Flower heads in dense clusters, whitish or sometimes pinkish. HT: mostly 6–24 in.

Leaves sometimes triangular to broadly arrowhead-shaped.

Leaves sometimes deeply palmately lobed, the lobes coarsely toothed.

■ **WILD-QUININE** (*Parthenium integrifolium*): Mostly summer; open places. Leaves broad, toothed, to 12 in. long. Flower heads very small, each with 5 tiny rays. Also called Eastern Parthenium, American-feverfew.

■ **LYRE-LEAF PARTHENIUM** (*P. confertum*): Spring–fall; plains, mesas. Leaves 1–3 in. long. Rays minute or absent. Also called Gray's-feverfew, Crowded Rayweed. **SIMILAR MARIOLA** (*P. incanum*): Desert scrub; southwestern. Shrub, 1–3 ft. tall. Leaves lobed, to 1 in. long, gray-hairy.

■ **RAGWEED PARTHENIUM** (*P. hysterophorus*): Spring–fall; disturbed places. Rays minute. Considered by some to be an introduction from tropical America.

Genus *Parthenium* (7 native species). Often aromatic. Leaves alternate. Usually both ray and disk flowers; receptacle bract-covered (chaffy). Seedlike fruits flattened, black, each shed with a phyllary and chaff. (See p. 83.)

Wild-quinine

Lyre-leaf Parthenium

Leaves hairy, lobed; end lobe often largest. HT: mostly 6–18 in.

Ragweed Parthenium

Flower heads whitish, in flat-topped clusters. HT: 1–4 ft.

Leaves fernlike. HT: mostly 1–3 ft.

■ **ECLIPTA** (*Eclipta prostrata*): Mostly summer–fall; muddy banks, wet places. Leaves often shallowly toothed. Flower heads on stalks from leaf axils. Also called Yerba-de-tajo, False Daisy.

Genus *Eclipta* (1 native species). Leaves opposite. Flower heads sometimes solitary; both ray and disk flowers; receptacle bristle-covered (chaffy). Seedlike fruits minutely warty. (See p. 83.)

Eclipta

Flower heads very small; rays many, minute, white. Leaves opposite, narrowly lance-shaped. HT: 6–24 in.

■ **YARROW** (*Achillea millefolium*): Spring–fall; meadows, roadsides, disturbed places. Plants often hairy. Leaves fernlike. Small heads of 10–20 whitish disk flowers and 5–8 (often 5) tiny, white (or pinkish), petal-like rays; stamens yellow. Both native and introduced populations are found. Also called Milfoil.

Genus *Achillea* (4 species, 2 native). Aromatic. Leaves alternate, or sometimes basal. Flower-head clusters somewhat flat-topped; both ray and disk flowers; receptacle bract-covered (chaffy); flower-head bracts (phyllaries) have pale to blackish, papery edges. (See p. 83.)

■ **SIBERIAN YARROW** (*A. alpina*): Mostly summer; open places; chiefly Alaska, Canada. Ray flowers 6–12 (often 6–8).

Yarrow

Flower heads in somewhat flat-topped clusters. HT: mostly 3–25 in.

Siberian Yarrow
Leaves single- or double-toothed. HT: 20–30 in.

■ **BEAR'S-FOOT** (*Smallanthus uvedalius*): Summer–fall; woods, thickets, meadows. Upper stems hairy. Leaves large, angularly lobed; leafstalks winged. Ray flowers ½–1 in. long, toothed at tip. Also called Yellow-flower or Large-flower Leafcup.

RELATED *Polymnia* (3 native species).
■ **PALE-FLOWER LEAFCUP** (*P. canadensis*): Late spring–summer; woods. Upper stems sticky-hairy. Some leaf pairs have leaflike appendages at base of stalk that wrap around stem. Ray flowers to about ⅜ in. long, each 3-lobed at tip, sometimes absent. Also called Small-flower or White-flower Leafcup.

Genus *Smallanthus* (1 native species). Leaves opposite. Flower heads sometimes solitary; both ray and disk flowers; receptacle bract-covered (chaffy). Seedlike fruits somewhat flattened; pappus absent. (See p. 83.)

Bear's-foot

Flower heads large; petal-like rays bright yellow. Larger leaves palmately lobed. HT: 3–9 ft.

Pale-flower Leafcup

Flower heads small; rays white to pale yellow.

Larger leaves pinnately lobed. HT: 2–5 ft.

■ **ABERT'S SANVITALIA** (*Sanvitalia abertii*): Summer–fall; slopes, mesas, canyons, valleys. Disk flowers yellowish; rays 8–11, each about ⅛ in. long, 2-lobed at tip, yellow aging to cream-colored. Also called Abert's Creeping-zinnia, Abert's-dome.

Genus *Sanvitalia* (3 species, 2 native). Leaves opposite. Flower heads solitary; both ray and disk flowers; receptacle bract-covered (chaffy). Fruit pappus of 3 or 4 awns. (See p. 83.)

Abert's Sanvitalia

Flower heads very small; center dome-shaped, yellowish green; petal-like rays tiny, yellow. Leaves opposite, narrowly lance-shaped. HT: 3–15 in.

■ **GOLDENSTAR** (*Chrysogonum virginianum*): Mostly spring; woods. A variable species: plants with or without runners; leaf bases heart-shaped, squared-off, or wedge-shaped; flowering stems leafy or leafless. Flower heads solitary or paired; disk flowers many; rays usually 5, petal-like, 3-toothed at tip; phyllaries (flower-head bracts) in 2 unlike, overlapping rows. Also called Green-and-gold, Gold-star.

Genus *Chrysogonum* (1 native species). Leaves basal and opposite. Both ray and disk flowers; receptacle bract-covered (chaffy). Seedlike fruits (from rays only) flattened, each shed with an inner phyllary and chaff. (See p. 83.)

Goldenstar

Flower heads yellow. Stem leaves opposite, stalked, typically triangular-egg-shaped. Plants generally hairy. HT: mostly 2–16 in.

■ **TEXAS-STAR** (*Lindheimera texana*): Spring; prairies, roadsides. Plants generally hairy. Leaves untoothed or coarsely toothed. Disk flowers commonly 12–25; rays usually 5, petal-like, 2-toothed at tip; phyllaries (flower-head bracts) in 2 unlike, overlapping rows. Also called Texas Yellowstar, Star Daisy, Lindheimer Daisy.

Genus *Lindheimera* (1 native species). Leaves alternate, upper ones sometimes opposite. Flower heads solitary or in clusters; both ray and disk flowers; receptacle bract-covered (chaffy). Seedlike fruits (from rays only) flattened, winged. (See p. 83.)

Texas-star

Flower heads yellow. HT: 4–20 in.

■ **PURPLE CONEFLOWER** (*Echinacea purpurea*): Late spring–summer; woods, thickets, prairies. Basal leaves toothed, hairy, 2–5 in. wide, egg- to lance-shaped with rounded base; stem leaves lance-shaped. Disk flowers green to purple. Also called Eastern Purple Coneflower. **SIMILAR** ■ **SMOOTH PURPLE CONE-FLOWER** (*E. laevigata*): Basal leaves smooth or slightly hairy, to 2½ in. wide, toothed, elliptic to lance-shaped; petal-like rays usually strongly drooping. Also called Appalachian Purple Coneflower.

■ **OZARK CONEFLOWER** (*E. paradoxa* var. *paradoxa*): Basal leaves narrow, ¼–¾ in. wide, untoothed. Also called Yellow or Yellow Purple Coneflower.

Genus *Echinacea* (9 native species). Leaves basal and alternate. Flower heads solitary; both ray and disk flowers; receptacle dome- to cone-shaped, covered with prominent, usually stiff and sharp-pointed bracts (chaff). Seedlike fruits 3- or 4-angled; fruit pappus a toothed crown. (See p. 83.)

Purple Coneflower

Petal-like rays horizontal to drooping, pink to purple.

Flower heads large, solitary, with dome-shaped center. HT: 1½–4 ft.

Ozark Coneflower

Rays strongly drooping, yellow. HT: to 3 ft.

■ **NARROW-LEAF PURPLE CONEFLOWER** (*Echinacea angustifolia*): Late spring–summer; prairies, plains. Basal leaves rough-hairy, to 1½ in. wide, elliptic to lance-shaped, tapering to base. Disk flowers usually purplish; rays ⅝–1½ in. long. Fresh pollen yellow.

■ **PALE PURPLE CONEFLOWER** (*E. pallida*): Prairies, open woods. Rays long and narrow (1½–3½ in. long, ⅛–³⁄₁₆ in. wide), drooping, pink to reddish purple. Fresh pollen usually white.

■ **WAVY-LEAF PURPLE CONEFLOWER** (*E. simulata*): Open rocky woods, prairies. Rays ³⁄₁₆–¼ in. wide, usually rose to pink, but one of a few species with rays occasionally white. Fresh pollen yellow.

Narrow-leaf Purple Coneflower
Flower heads large, solitary; petal-like rays pink to purple, spreading to drooping. HT: 6–24 in.

Pale Purple Coneflower
HT: mostly 1½–3 ft.

Wavy-leaf Purple Coneflower
Rays sometimes white. HT: mostly 1½–3 ft.

■ **CALIFORNIA CONEFLOWER** (*Rudbeckia californica*): Summer–fall; mountain meadows, stream banks. Rays yellow; disk flowers greenish yellow.

■ **CLASPING CONEFLOWER** (*R. amplexicaulis*): Late spring–summer; open moist places. Leaves blue-green. Rays yellow, often splotched brownish red.

■ **CUTLEAF CONEFLOWER** (*R. laciniata*): Summer–fall; moist places. Stems hairless. Leaves deeply cut into coarsely toothed or lobed segments. Pinnate Prairie Coneflower (p. 113) has stems hairy; flower heads grayish or purplish in center.

■ **WESTERN CONEFLOWER** (*R. occidentalis*): Summer–fall; moist places. Leaves egg-shaped. Flower heads dark, lack rays.

Genus *Rudbeckia* (23 native species). Leaves basal and alternate. Flower heads sometimes solitary; both ray and disk flowers; receptacle ball-shaped to columnar, bract-covered (chaffy). Seedlike fruits 4-angled. (See p. 83.)

California Coneflower
Flower heads large; center conical. HT: 2–6 ft.

Clasping Coneflower
Leaves clasp stem. HT: to 3 ft.

Cutleaf Coneflower
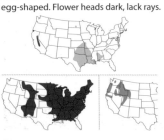
Flower heads large; center ball-shaped, yellow-green to yellowish. HT: 2–9 ft.

Western Coneflower

HT: to 6 ft.

■ **BLACK-EYED-SUSAN** (*Rudbeckia hirta*): Spring–fall; open places. Plants conspicuously, coarsely stiff-hairy. Flower heads have dark brown-purple, dome-shaped center; rays sometimes with red-brown splotch; chaffy bracts minutely bristle-tipped. **SIMILAR EASTERN CONEFLOWER** (*R. fulgida*): Moist or wet places; eastern. Plants sparsely or moderately hairy; chaffy bracts blunt or pointed. Also called Orange Coneflower.

■ **BROWN-EYED-SUSAN** (*R. triloba*): Summer–fall; woods, thickets, roadsides. Plants hairy or not. Leaves unlobed, or lower leaves 3–7-lobed (usually 3). Flower heads large, similar to Black-eyed-Susan; chaffy bracts sharp-pointed. Also called Three-lobe Coneflower.

Black-eyed-Susan

Petal-like rays yellow to orange-yellow. Leaves bristly-hairy, egg- or lance-shaped to elliptic. HT: 1–3 ft.

Brown-eyed-Susan

Lower leaves commonly deeply 3-lobed. HT: mostly 2–4 ft.

■ **PRAIRIE CONEFLOWER** (*Ratibida columnifera*): Spring–fall; prairies. Leaves pinnately divided into 3–14 narrow segments. Disk flowers yellowish green to brownish purple; rays 4–12, spreading or often drooping, to 1⅜ in. long. Also called Mexican-hat.

■ **PINNATE PRAIRIE CONEFLOWER** (*R. pinnata*): Prairies, open woods. Leaves divided into 3–9 segments. Flower heads large, with ball-shaped center; rays 6–15, spreading or often drooping, to 2½ in. long. Also called Gray-head Prairie Coneflower. Do not confuse with Cutleaf Coneflower (p. 112).

■ **SHORT-RAY PRAIRIE CONEFLOWER** (*R. tagetes*): Plains, prairies, rocky hillsides. Rays 5–10, ⅛–⅜ in. long.

Genus *Ratibida* (4 native species). Leaves basal and alternate. Flower heads sometimes solitary; both ray and disk flowers; receptacle ball-shaped to columnar, bract-covered (chaffy); flower-head bracts (phyllaries) unequal, in 2 rows. Seedlike fruits flattened; edges hairy. (See p. 83.)

Prairie Coneflower

Flower heads large; center fingerlike; petal-like rays yellow, dark reddish brown, or 2-colored. HT: 1–3 ft.

Pinnate Prairie Coneflower

Rays yellow. HT: 2–4 ft.

Short-ray Prairie Coneflower

Rays yellow to purple-brown. HT: 6–18 in.

■ **WHOLE-LEAF ROSINWEED** (*Silphium integrifolium*): Summer–fall; prairies, roadsides. Leaves lance- to egg-shaped. Also called Prairie or Entire-leaf Rosinweed.

■ **CUP-PLANT** (*S. perfoliatum*): Wet prairies, open woods, thickets. Upper leaf bases fused, forming a cup around the square stem.

■ **STARRY/WHORLED ROSINWEED** (*S. asteriscus*): Prairies, meadows, open woods. Plants with hairy, alternate or opposite leaves are called Starry Rosinweed; those with hairless to slightly hairy, whorled or opposite leaves are called Whorled Rosinweed.

Genus *Silphium* (12 native species). Plants resinous. Leaves variously arranged. Both ray and disk flowers; receptacle bract-covered (chaffy); flower-head bracts (phyllaries) in 2–4 overlapping rows, the outer ones broad. Seedlike fruits (from rays only) flattened and winged; fruit pappus of 2 awns or absent. (See p. 83.)

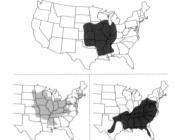

Whole-leaf Rosinweed

Leaves opposite, stalkless.

Flower heads large, yellow; phyllaries broad. HT: 1½–5 ft.

Cup-plant

HT: to 8 ft.

Whorled Rosinweed

HT: to 5 ft.

■ **PRAIRIE-DOCK** (*Silphium terebinthinaceum*): Summer–early fall; prairies, fens. Basal leaves large, toothed, long-stalked, held vertically; blades commonly about 20 in. long, broadly egg-shaped. Also called Prairie Rosinweed.

■ **COMPASS-PLANT** (*S. laciniatum*): Summer–early fall; prairies. Basal leaves very large. Flower heads yellow.

■ **WHITE ROSINWEED** (*S. albiflorum*): Late spring–summer; prairies. Leaves similar to Compass-plant. Petal-like rays white. Also called White Compass-plant.

■ **KIDNEY-LEAF ROSINWEED** (*S. compositum*): Summer–early fall; open places. Basal leaves lobed or unlobed.

Prairie-dock

Compass-plant

Basal leaves lobed. HT: 3–10 ft.

Flower heads large, yellow. HT: 2–10 ft.

White Rosinweed

Flower heads white. HT: to 2½ ft.

Kidney-leaf Rosinweed

Rays few. HT: 2–8 ft.

■ **LYRE-LEAF GREEN-EYES** (*Berlandiera lyrata*): Mostly spring–fall; plains, fields, roadsides. Leaves mostly basal, some with conspicuously large end lobe. Ray flowers often 8, toothed at tip, red-streaked beneath. Phyllaries broad, forming a shallow cup around flower head. Flowers chocolate-scented. Also called Chocolate Daisy, Chocolate-flower.

■ **FLORIDA GREEN-EYES** (*B. subacaulis*): Pinelands, sandy soil. Leaves mostly basal, wavy-edged, lobed. Ray flowers green-streaked beneath.

TEXAS GREEN-EYES (*B. texana*): Rocky or sandy soil; south-central. Leaves all on stems, triangular to lance-shaped.

NOTE Species commonly hybridize, forming intermediates.

Genus *Berlandiera* (5 native species). Leaves basal or alternate. Flower heads sometimes solitary; both ray and disk flowers; receptacle bract-covered (chaffy); flower-head bracts (phyllaries) broad. Seedlike fruits (from rays only) flattened. (See p. 83.)

Lyre-leaf Green-eyes
Flower heads in clusters; disk flowers red or maroon; petal-like rays yellow or orange-yellow. HT: 6–30 in.

Florida Green-eyes
Flower heads solitary; disk flowers yellow. HT: to 1½ ft.

Texas Green-eyes
HT: 1–3 ft.

■ **ENGELMANN'S DAISY** (*Engelmannia peristenia*): Mostly spring–summer; grassy plains, prairies, hills, roadsides. Plants generally hairy. Disk flowers many, yellowish; rays typically 8, untoothed or minutely 2- or 3-toothed at tip, curling under during part of the day. Also called Cutleaf Daisy.

Genus *Engelmannia* (1 native species). Leaves basal and alternate. Both ray and disk flowers; receptacle bract-covered (chaffy); flower-head bracts (phyllaries) in usually 3 overlapping rows. Seedlike fruits flattened, each shed with 1 phyllary and chaff; fruit pappus of 2–4 scales. (See p. 83.)

Engelmann's Daisy

Flower heads yellow. Most leaves deeply pinnately lobed. HT: 6–24 in.

Petal-like rays mostly 8.

Tips of rays sometimes curled under.

■ **COMMON WINGSTEM** (*Verbesina alternifolia*): Late summer–fall; thickets, woods, stream banks. Leaves mostly alternate. Disk flowers in a ball-shaped cluster; rays 2–10 (often 6–8). **SIMILAR YELLOW CROWNBEARD** (*V. occidentalis*): Southeastern. Leaves mostly opposite.

■ **WHITE CROWNBEARD** (*V. virginica*): Late summer–fall; thickets, stream banks, woods. Leaves mostly alternate. Rays 1–7. Also called White Wingstem, Frostweed.

■ **GOLDEN CROWNBEARD** (*V. encelioides*): Spring–fall; open places. Stems not winged. Leaves alternate above, opposite below; triangular, grayish green. Flower heads large; rays mostly 10–15, 3-lobed at tip. Also called Cowpen Daisy.

Genus *Verbesina* (16 native species). Leaves alternate or opposite. Flower heads sometimes solitary; both ray and disk flowers (or sometimes rays absent); receptacle bract- or bristle-covered (chaffy). Seedlike fruits strongly flattened, often winged, with pappus typically of 2 awns. (See p. 83.)

Common Wingstem

Stems winged.

Flower heads large; petal-like rays spreading or drooping, yellow. HT: 3–8 ft.

White Crownbeard

Rays very small, white. Stems winged. HT: 3–7 ft.

Golden Crownbeard

HT: 1–3 ft.

■ **BRITTLEBUSH** (*Encelia farinosa*): Spring, late summer; desert slopes, flats, and washes, coastal scrub. Shrubby. Stems brittle, oozing resin when broken. Leaves silvery gray-hairy, egg- to lance-shaped. Disk flowers many, yellow or brownish purple; rays 11–21, often 3-toothed at tip. Also called Incienso, Golden-hills.

■ **BUTTON BRITTLEBUSH** (*E. frutescens*): Desert washes, flats, and slopes. Shrubby. Leaves green, elliptic to narrowly egg-shaped. Disk flowers many; ray flowers absent.

Genus *Encelia* (8 native species). Herbs or shrubs, often aromatic. Leaves alternate. Flower heads sometimes solitary; both ray and disk flowers (or sometimes rays absent); receptacle bract-covered (chaffy). Seedlike fruits strongly flattened; edges hairy. (See p. 83.)

Brittlebush

Flower heads in clusters; petal-like rays yellow. HT: 1–5 ft.

Button Brittlebush

Flower heads solitary, dome-shaped, yellowish. HT: 2–5 ft.

■ **SEA OXEYE** (*Borrichia frutescens*):
Mostly late spring–fall; salt marshes,
brackish waters, coastal shores. Shrubby.
Leaves opposite, gray-hairy, typically
widest above middle, toothed or
untoothed. Both receptacle bracts (chaff)
and flower-head bracts (phyllaries)
spine-tipped. Disk flowers many,
greenish yellow to brownish yellow;
rays 15–30, often shallowly 3-toothed
at tip. Also called Sea Daisy, Sea Oxeye
Daisy, Bushy Seaside-tansy. **SIMILAR**
■ **BAY-MARIGOLD** (*B. arborescens*):
Shores, beaches, dunes, salt marsh
edges. Leaves generally green, often
hairless; bracts not spine-tipped. Also
called Sea Oxeye.

Genus *Borrichia* (2 native species). Herbs
or shrubs, sometimes aromatic. Leaves
opposite. Flower heads sometimes
solitary; both ray and disk flowers; receptacle bract-
covered (chaffy), the bracts clasping the bases of the disk
flowers. Seedlike fruits 3- or 4-angled; pappus a toothed,
short cup or crown. (See p. 83.)

Sea Oxeye

Flower heads
solitary; petal-like
rays bright yellow.
Leaves somewhat
leathery, gray-green.
HT: mostly 1–3 ft.

COMMON SUNFLOWER (*Helianthus
annuus*): Summer–fall; open places;
widespread. Stems hairy. Leaves mostly
alternate, stalked, toothed; leafstalks to
8 in. long; blades egg-shaped, to 16 in.
long and wide.

■ **TEXAS-BLUEWEED** (*H. ciliaris*): Open
places. Bushy. Leaves to 3 in. long, ¾ in.
wide; mostly opposite, stalkless, bluish
green.

■ **NARROW-LEAF SUNFLOWER**
(*H. angustifolius*): Moist to wet places.
Stems hairy. Leaves to 7 in. long, ⅜ in.
wide; alternate, stalkless, slender. Also
called Swamp Sunflower. **SIMILAR**
■ **WILLOW-LEAF SUNFLOWER**
(*H. salicifolius*): Prairies. Stems hairless.

Genus *Helianthus* (52 native species).
Leaves basal, alternate, or opposite.
Flower heads sometimes solitary; usually
both ray and disk flowers; receptacle bract-covered
(chaffy). Seedlike fruits (from disk flowers only) flattened,
thick, often purplish black; fruit pappus of typically
2 awns that shed easily. (See p. 83.)

Common Sunflower

Flower heads large,
with yellow rays and
red-purple (or sometimes
yellowish) center.
HT: 3–10 ft.

Texas-blueweed

HT: 1–2½ ft.

Narrow-leaf
Sunflower

HT: 2–6 ft.

MAXIMILIAN SUNFLOWER (*Helianthus maximiliani*): Summer–fall; open places; widespread, chiefly Great Plains, Midwest. Leaves mostly alternate; rough-hairy, 1-veined, and usually untoothed; often partially folded lengthwise and curved.

FEW-LEAF SUNFLOWER (*H. occidentalis*): Mostly east-central, Midwest. Flowering stalks almost leafless. Also called Naked-stem or Western Sunflower.

■ **WOODLAND SUNFLOWER** (*H. divaricatus*): Leaves 3-veined, hairy above.

■ **ASHY SUNFLOWER** (*H. mollis*): Leaves 3-veined, densely grayish-hairy. Also called Downy Sunflower.

JERUSALEM-ARTICHOKE (*H. tuberosus*, no photo): Chiefly central, eastern. Flower heads yellow. Plants have conspicuous underground tubers.

Maximilian Sunflower
Flower heads have yellow rays, yellow center. Stems hairy. HT: 2–10 ft.

Few-leaf Sunflower
Leaves mostly basal. Stems hairy. HT: 1½–4 ft.

Woodland Sunflower
Leaves opposite. Stems mostly hairless. HT: 1–5 ft.

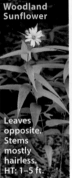
Ashy Sunflower
Leaves opposite. Stems hairy. HT: 1½–4 ft.

■ **FALSE SUNFLOWER** (*Heliopsis helianthoides*): Late spring–early fall; open woods, prairies, thickets, meadows. Leaves all opposite, lance- to egg-shaped, toothed, hairless to moderately rough-hairy; leafstalks ¼–1⅜ in. long. Phyllaries (flower-head bracts) blunt-tipped (see inset). Seedlike fruits 3- or 4-angled, with pappus absent or of minute, toothlike scales. Also called Oxeye, Smooth Oxeye.

NOTE Do not confuse with sunflowers (*Helianthus*), which, in addition to the differences noted in the genus description, often have at least the uppermost leaves alternate; phyllaries (flower-head bracts) with a pointed tip.

Genus *Heliopsis* (3 native species). Very similar to *Helianthus* (p. 117), but ray flowers are female and fertile and when in bloom have a forked style and ovaries that form seedlike fruits. (The rays of *Helianthus* lack a visible style and do not develop seedlike fruits.) (See p. 83.)

False Sunflower
Flower heads large, with yellow center, yellow petal-like rays. Leaves opposite. HT: 1½–5 ft.

■ **SHOWY GOLDENEYE** (*Heliomeris multiflora*): Summer–fall; slopes, open woods, meadows. Leaves mostly opposite (uppermost alternate), generally untoothed. Seedlike fruits hairless; fruit pappus absent.

■ **SKELETON-LEAF GOLDENEYE** (*Viguiera stenoloba*): Summer–fall; slopes, plains, desert scrub. Shrub. Leaves mostly deeply lobed. Seedlike fruits hairless; fruit pappus absent. Also called Resinbush.

■ **PARISH'S GOLDENEYE** (*Bahiopsis parishii*): Spring–fall; rocky slopes, mesas, desert scrub. Shrub. Leaves conspicuously veined. Seedlike fruits hairy; fruit pappus of scales of 2 different sizes.

Goldeneyes (several related genera, 10 native species). Similar to *Helianthus* (p. 117); differ in technical characters such as features of the seedlike fruits. (See p. 83.)

Showy Goldeneye
Flower heads yellow. Leaves narrowly lance-shaped. HT: 1–4 ft.

Skeleton-leaf Goldeneye
Leaves divided into linear segments. HT: 1½–4 ft.

Parish's Goldeneye
Leaves triangular-egg-shaped, usually toothed. HT: 1½–4 ft.

■ **NODDING HELIANTHELLA** (*Helianthella quinquenervis*): Mostly summer; slopes, meadows, open woods. Largest leaves on lower stem, untoothed.

■ **CALIFORNIA HELIANTHELLA** (*H. californica*): Largest leaves below midstem. **SIMILAR** ■ **ROCKY MOUNTAIN HELIANTHELLA** (*H. uniflora*): Largest leaves at midstem.

NOTE Helianthellas, also called little-sunflower or dwarf-sunflower, resemble sunflowers (pp. 117–118), but have seedlike fruits strongly flattened and with persistent awns; leaves untoothed and often larger and more prevalent on lower stems and at plant base.

Genus *Helianthella* (6 native species). Leaves basal and opposite (or uppermost alternate). Flower heads often solitary; both ray and disk flowers; receptacle bract-covered (chaffy). Seedlike fruits flattened; pappus typically of 2 awns and several smaller scales. (See p. 83.)

Nodding Helianthella
Flower heads large, yellow, solitary, often nodding or facing outward. HT: 2–5 ft.

California Helianthella
Flower heads generally erect. HT: 6–24 in.

■ **ARROW-LEAF BALSAMROOT**
(*Balsamorhiza sagittata*): Late spring–
midsummer; slopes, open places.
Leaves distinctly hairy, olive-green to
grayish (young leaves white beneath),
untoothed. Flower heads large, woolly
at base, yellow. **SIMILAR** ■ **DELTOID
BALSAMROOT** (*B. deltoidea*): Leaves
green, sparsely hairy, occasionally short-
toothed; base of flower heads hairy but
mostly not woolly.

■ **SERRATE BALSAMROOT** (*B. serrata*):
Leaves toothed, and a few may be lobed.
Also called Toothed Balsamroot.

HOOKER'S BALSAMROOT (*B. hookeri*):
Western. Leaves deeply pinnately divided
into segments.

Genus *Balsamorhiza* (12 native species).
Leaves basal. Flower heads usually
solitary; both ray and disk flowers;
receptacle bract-covered (chaffy). Fruit pappus absent.
(See p. 83.)

Arrow-leaf Balsamroot — Leaves all basal, long-stalked, arrow-head-shaped. HT: 6–30 in.

Serrate Balsamroot — Leaves lance-shaped, toothed. HT: 4–12 in.

Hooker's Balsamroot — Leaves divided into small segments. HT: 4–12 in.

■ **MULE'S-EARS** (*Wyethia amplexicaulis*):
Late spring–early summer; open places.
Leaves mostly tapered to base, hairless;
basal leaves shiny, lance-elliptic- to lance-
shaped; stem leaves smaller. Also called
Northern Mule's-ears. **SIMILAR**
■ **ARIZONA MULE'S-EARS** (*W. arizonica*):
Leaves short-hairy.

■ **WOOLLY MULE'S-EARS** (*W. mollis*):
Leaves strongly white-hairy when young.
Also called Mountain Mule's-ears.

■ **WHITE MULE'S-EARS**
(*W. helianthoides*): Leaves hairy when
young. Disk flowers yellow; rays whitish.

NOTE Arrow-leaf Balsamroot (above) has
basal leaves less vertically oriented, with a
heart-shaped base.

Genus *Wyethia* (8 native species). Similar
to *Balsamorhiza* (above), but has a few
alternate stem leaves as well as basal
leaves; flower heads sometimes more than 1 per stem;
pappus absent or of short scales. (See p. 83.)

Mule's-ears — Flower heads large, in clusters of 2–8; petal-like rays yellow. HT: 1–2½ ft.

Woolly Mule's-ears — HT: mostly 1–2 ft.

White Mule's-ears — Flower heads large, solitary. HT: 1–2½ ft.

■ **ROUGH-MULE'S-EARS** (*Scabrethia scabra*): Late spring–summer; desert plains, washes, hills. Stems often whitish. Leaves mostly alternate (occasionally opposite) and stalkless, relatively narrow, covered with short, stiff hairs rough to the touch. Also called Sandpaper-mule's-ears, Badland-mule's-ears.

Genus *Scabrethia* (1 native species). Similar to *Wyethia* (p. 120), but leaves are mostly all on stems. (See p. 83.)

Rough-mule's-ears

Flower heads solitary, often large; petal-like rays yellow. HT: 1–2 ft.

■ **HEART-LEAF ARNICA** (*Arnica cordifolia*): Late spring–midsummer; mountain woods and meadows. Leaves stalked, mostly 2–4 pairs.

SPEAR-LEAF ARNICA (*A. longifolia*): Summer–fall; moist places in western mountains. Leaves stalkless, lance-shaped, 5–7 pairs. Also called Seep-spring Arnica. Several similar species.

NODDING ARNICA (*A. parryi*): Late spring–summer; woods, meadows; western mountains. Leaves mostly lance-shaped, 3 or 4 pairs. Unopened flower heads often nodding; rays absent. Also called Parry's Arnica. **SIMILAR**
■ **RAYLESS ARNICA** (*A. discoidea*): Shrublands, open woods. Leaves egg- to lance-shaped, 3–7 pairs; unopened flower heads erect. Also called Coast Arnica.

Genus *Arnica* (26 native species). Plants often hairy. Leaves opposite and basal. Flower heads sometimes solitary; both ray and disk flowers (or sometimes rays absent); flower-head bracts (phyllaries) in 2 rows (or rarely 1). Fruit pappus of minutely barbed to feathery bristles. (See p. 83.)

Heart-leaf Arnica

Flower heads yellow. Stem leaves opposite, heart-shaped. HT: 6–24 in.

Spear-leaf Arnica

HT: 1–3 ft.

Nodding Arnica

Rays absent. HT: 6–24 in.

■ **STIFF GREENTHREAD** (*Thelesperma filifolium*): Spring–fall; slopes, plains, prairies. Leaves divided into threadlike segments. Petal-like rays 8, yellow, sometimes tinged reddish brown at base, their tips 3-toothed; bractlets just below flower heads ³⁄₁₆–⁵⁄₁₆ in. long.

SIMILAR ■ SCAPOSE GREENTHREAD (*T. subnudum*): Slopes, open woods. Leaves mostly on lower ¼ of plant; flower heads all yellow; rays occasionally absent; bractlets smaller. This and following species also called Hopi-tea or Navajo-tea Greenthread.

■ **SLENDER GREENTHREAD** (*T. megapotamicum*): Plains, prairies, mesas, open woods. Bractlets tiny.

Genus *Thelesperma* (9 native species). Leaves mostly basal or opposite. Flower heads sometimes solitary; both ray and disk flowers (or rays absent); receptacle bract-covered (chaffy); flower-head bracts (phyllaries) equal, partially or nearly wholly united, with bractlets beneath. Seedlike fruits somewhat flattened; pappus absent or of 2 short awns or scales. (See p. 83.)

Stiff Greenthread

Slender Greenthread

Flower heads yellowish or yellowish brown, lack rays. HT: 1–3 ft.

Flower heads often have reddish brown center. HT: 6–18 in.

■ **LANCE-LEAF COREOPSIS** (*Coreopsis lanceolata*): Spring–summer; open, often sandy places. Leaves basal and on lower ⅓ of stem. Flower heads large, yellow; petal-like rays 8, their tips conspicuously toothed; lance-shaped bractlets at base of phyllaries. Also called Sand Coreopsis.

■ **BIG-FLOWER COREOPSIS** (*C. grandiflora*): Flowers similar to Lance-leaf Coreopsis. Leaves scattered along stem. Also called Large-flower Coreopsis.

NOTE *Coreopsis* species are also called tickseed.

Genus *Coreopsis* (28 native species). Leaves basal, opposite, or alternate. Flower heads sometimes solitary; both ray and disk flowers; receptacle bract-covered (chaffy); flower-head bracts (phyllaries) mostly 8 in 2 rows, with bractlets beneath. Seedlike fruits flattened, sometimes winged. (See p. 83.)

Lance-leaf Coreopsis

Big-flower Coreopsis

Leaves mostly divided into slender segments. HT: 1–3 ft.

Leaves lance-shaped. HT: 6–24 in.

■ **TALL COREOPSIS** (*Coreopsis tripteris*): Summer; often moist places. Leaves have distinct stalk. Petal-like rays 8, their tips sometimes shallowly toothed; narrow bractlets at base of phyllaries (flower-head bracts).

■ **GREATER COREOPSIS** (*C. major*): Late spring–summer; open woods, clearings. Flower heads similar to Tall Coreopsis, but with mostly yellowish disk flowers. Leaves opposite, stalkless, divided into 3 leaflets. Also called Whorl-leaf Coreopsis.

Tall Coreopsis
Leaves opposite, often divided into 3 leaflets.

Flower heads often large, with reddish brown center, yellow rays. HT: 3–8 ft.

Greater Coreopsis

Leaves appear to be in whorls of 6. HT: 1–3 ft.

■ **THREAD-LEAF COREOPSIS** (*Coreopsis verticillata*): Summer; open woods. Petal-like rays 8; tiny bractlets at base of phyllaries (flower-head bracts). Also called Whorled Coreopsis.

PLAINS COREOPSIS (*C. tinctoria*): Spring–fall; open places; widespread. Leaf segments linear to threadlike. Also called Golden Coreopsis, Calliopsis.

■ **SWAMP COREOPSIS** (*C. nudata*): Spring; moist or usually wet places in pinelands. Leaves lack blades (leafstalks only). Disk flowers yellowish. Also called Georgia or Pink Coreopsis. **SIMILAR** ■ **ROSE COREOPSIS** (*C. rosea*): Late summer; wet places. Leaves narrow. Also called Pink Coreopsis.

Thread-leaf Coreopsis

Flower heads often large, yellow. Leaves divided into threadlike segments. HT: 6–24 in.

Plains Coreopsis

Petal-like rays yellow with reddish brown base, toothed tip. HT: 1–3 ft.

Swamp Coreopsis

Rays pinkish or purplish, toothed. HT: 1–3 ft.

■ **SOUTHWESTERN COSMOS** (*Cosmos parviflorus*): Summer–fall; slopes, meadows, woods, canyons. Leaves opposite, divided into threadlike segments. Ray flowers typically 8, often toothed at tip; 8 bractlets at base of phyllaries are prominent, as long as the rays.

① **GARDEN COSMOS** (*C. bipinnatus*, no photo): Native to Mexico and possibly southwestern U.S., escaped elsewhere. Flower heads 2–3 in. across (vs. ⅝–1 in. across in Southwestern Cosmos).

 Genus *Cosmos* (4 species, 2 native). Leaves opposite. Flower heads sometimes solitary; both ray and disk flowers; receptacle bract-covered (chaffy); flower-head bracts (phyllaries) in 2 rows, with bractlets beneath. Fruit pappus (from disk flowers only) of 2–4 awns with downward-pointing barbs. (See p. 83.)

Southwestern Cosmos

Rays sometimes white.

Flower heads long-stalked; petal-like rays often pink to rose-purple. HT: 1–3 ft.

Conspicuous bractlets beneath flower head.

TICKSEED-SUNFLOWER (*Bidens aristosa*): Summer–fall; moist or wet places; eastern. Leaves pinnately divided into segments or leaflets. Ray flowers 5–10, each ½–1 in. long. Also called Midwestern Tickseed-sunflower, Bearded Beggarticks. **SIMILAR TICKSEED-SUNFLOWER** (*B. polylepis*): Range similar but extends to NM, CO. Bractlets beneath phyllaries very narrow, 12–21 (8–12 in *B. aristosa*). Also called Ozark Tickseed-sunflower.

■ **NODDING BUR-MARIGOLD** (*B. cernua*): Wet places. Leaves undivided. Petal-like rays 6–8, orange-yellow, small (⅛–½ in. long).

SMOOTH BUR-MARIGOLD (*B. laevis*): Wet places; mostly eastern and southwestern. Rays 7 or 8, longer, ⅝–1 in.

 Genus *Bidens* (25 native species). Leaves usually opposite. Flower heads sometimes solitary; both ray and disk flowers (sometimes rays absent); receptacle bract-covered (chaffy); flower-head bracts (phyllaries) have bractlets beneath. Fruit pappus of 2–4 commonly downwardly barbed, often spinelike awns. (See p. 83.)

Tickseed-sunflower

Nodding Bur-marigold

Leaf segments coarsely toothed.

HT: mostly 6 in.–3 ft.

Flower heads often large; petal-like rays golden yellow. HT: 1–4 ft.

Smooth Bur-marigold

HT: to 3 ft.

■ **WATER-MARIGOLD** (*Bidens beckii*): Summer; lakes, ponds, streams. Underwater leaves in threadlike segments.

WHITE BEGGARTICKS (*B. pilosa*): Year-round; moist places; southern. Leaves in 3–7 segments or leaflets, or simple.

■ **DEVIL'S BEGGARTICKS** (*B. frondosa*): Summer–fall; moist places. Leaves divided into lance-shaped leaflets.

■ **SPANISH-NEEDLES** (*B. bipinnata*): Summer–fall; disturbed places. Leaves opposite, divided into small segments.

Water-marigold

Flower heads yellow; rays 8 per head. Above-water leaves opposite, toothed.

White Beggarticks

Rays 3–8, white, disk flowers yellow. HT: 1–4 ft.

Devil's Beggarticks

Rays commonly absent, or yellow and tiny. Leaflike bractlets surround flower head. HT: 6 in.–3 ft.

Spanish-needles

Rays commonly absent, or yellow and tiny. Leaves fernlike. HT: 1–4 ft.

■ **COMMON DOGWEED** (*Thymophylla pentachaeta*): Spring–fall; desert slopes, mesas, plains. Leaves opposite. Rays 12–21, to ¼ in. long. Also called Parralena.

■ **PRICKLE-LEAF DOGWEED** (*T. acerosa*): Open places. Leaves opposite. Rays 7 or 8.

RELATED With phyllaries not united.

■ **FETID-MARIGOLD** (*Dyssodia papposa*): Summer–fall; open places. Leaves pinnately divided into slender, often toothed segments. Rays 5–8. Also called Prairie-dogweed. **DAMIANITA** (*Chrysactinia mexicana*, no photo): Spring–fall; rocky ground; southern NM to south-central TX. Shrubby. Leaves mostly alternate, linear, undivided. Petal-like rays 8–12, ¼–½ in. long. Fruit pappus of hairlike bristles.

Genus *Thymophylla* (8 native species). Plants sometimes shrubby; gland-dotted, aromatic. Leaves opposite or alternate. Flower heads solitary; usually both ray and disk flowers; flower-head bracts (phyllaries) in 2 rows, often partly united, sometimes with tiny bractlets beneath. Fruit pappus of scales. (See p. 83.)

Common Dogweed

Petal-like rays yellow. Leaves pinnately divided into threadlike, sharp-tipped lobes. HT: 4–10 in.

Prickle-leaf Dogweed

Leaves needlelike, unlobed. HT: 4–8 in.

Fetid-marigold

Rays tiny, yellow to orange. HT: 6–18 in.

■ **JAUMEA** (*Jaumea carnosa*): Late spring–fall; salt marshes, tidal flats. Stems sprawling. Leaves stalkless, linear to very narrowly spoon-shaped. Ray flowers 3–10, tiny or very small; phyllaries (flower-head bracts) often purple-tinged. Also called Fleshy or Marsh Jaumea.

Genus *Jaumea* (1 native species). Leaves opposite, succulent. Flower heads solitary; usually both ray and disk flowers. Seedlike fruits 10-ribbed. (See p. 83.)

Jaumea

Flower heads solitary, yellow. Leaves opposite, hairless, fleshy, narrow. HT: mostly 3–10 in.

■ **COMMON SPIKEWEED** (*Centromadia pungens*): Spring–fall; alkaline plains, grassy places, disturbed areas. Stems bear numerous short, leafy side branches. Lowermost leaves opposite, pinnately divided into segments. Stem leaves alternate, rigid, spiny. Ray flowers mostly 15–40, each 2-toothed at tip. Also called Pungent False Tarplant.

Genus *Centromadia* (3 native species). Sometimes aromatic. Leaves alternate above, opposite below. Both ray and disk flowers; receptacle bract-covered (chaffy); flower-head bracts (phyllaries) commonly spine-tipped. Seedlike fruits (from rays only) have tiny beak. (See p. 83.)

Common Spikeweed

Flower heads small, yellow, spiny-bracted. Stem leaves spine-tipped. HT: 6 in.–4 ft.

■ **COMMON MADIA** (*Madia elegans*): Spring–fall; grasslands, open places. A variable species. Plants generally hairy, sometimes sticky. Leaves stalkless, lance-shaped to linear. Ray flowers 5–27. Also called Showy Tarweed.

NOTE *Madia* species are sometimes aromatic; not all are as showy as this one.

Genus *Madia* (10 native species). Leaves opposite below, alternate above. Usually both ray and disk flowers; flower-head bracts (phyllaries) mostly in 1 row. Seedlike fruits wider toward top, often flattened. (See p. 83.)

Common Madia

Flower heads in clusters; petal-like rays yellow, 3-lobed. HT: 6 in.–4 ft.

Rays sometimes maroon-blotched at base.

Phyllaries often hairy.

■ **TIDY-TIPS** (*Layia platyglossa*): Spring–early summer; open places. Leaves narrowly lance-shaped. Disk flowers yellow with often purple anthers. Several similar species. Also called Coastal Tidy-tips.

■ **WHITE TIDY-TIPS** (*L. glandulosa*): Spring–early summer; plains, meadows, open woods. Plants glandular. Disk flowers yellow, often with yellow anthers; rays occasionally yellow, the heads then resemble yellow forms of *L. platyglossa*.

RELATED ■ **ROUGH EYELASH-WEED** (*Blepharipappus scaber*): Spring–summer; woods, clearings. Outwardly similar to *Layia*, differing in technical characters. Leaves linear. Rays purple-veined on underside; disk flowers white with purple anthers.

Genus *Layia* (14 native species). Sometimes aromatic. Leaves mostly alternate, the lowermost ones sometimes opposite. Flower heads sometimes solitary; usually both ray and disk flowers; receptacle bract-covered (chaffy); flower-head bracts (phyllaries) in 1 or 2 rows, each enveloping a ray ovary. Seedlike fruits flattened. (See p. 83.)

Tidy-tips

Petal-like rays often yellow with white, 3-lobed tip.

Rays may be entirely yellow. HT: 6–24 in.

White Tidy-tips
Rays white. HT: 6–24 in.

Rough Eyelash-weed
Rays white. HT: 6–12 in.

■ **COMMON GOLDFIELDS** (*Lasthenia gracilis*): Mostly spring; open places. Plants commonly hairy. Leaves opposite, narrow, mostly untoothed. Disk flowers many, yellowish; rays 6–13, ¼–⅜ in. long, entirely golden or bright yellow or sometimes orange-yellow on lower portion, sometimes darker toward base. Fruit pappus of awned scales.

■ **SMOOTH GOLDFIELDS** (*L. glaberrima*): Spring–early summer; vernal pools, wet grassy areas. Plants hairless. Rays ⅟₁₆ in. or less long.

Genus *Lasthenia* (17 native species). Leaves opposite. Flower heads sometimes solitary; usually both ray and disk flowers; flower-head bracts (phyllaries) in 1 or 2 rows. Fruit pappus of 1–12 scales, or absent. (See p. 83.)

Common Goldfields

Petal-like rays often have toothed tip. HT: 4–16 in.

Smooth Goldfields

Rays inconspicuous. HT: to 14 in.

■ **COMMON WOOLLY-SUNFLOWER** (*Eriophyllum lanatum*): Spring–summer; open places. Leaves and stems gray-woolly. Leaves lance-shaped to fernlike. Flower heads often on long, leafless stalks; rays 5–13, each ¼–¾ in. long, minutely toothed at tip; phyllaries woolly.

■ **PRINGLE'S WOOLLY DAISY** (*E. pringlei*): Shrublands, desert scrub. Plants densely woolly. Leaves wedge-shaped, often 3-lobed at tip.

■ **GOLDEN-YARROW** (*E. confertiflorum*): Sandy or rocky places. Shrub. Stems and leaves woolly when young. Leaf segments narrow. Flower heads small, in crowded clusters; rays 4–6, each ⅛–³⁄₁₆ in. long; phyllaries 4–6. Also called Yellow-yarrow.

Genus *Eriophyllum* (13 native species). Herbs or shrubs. Leaves mostly alternate. Flower heads sometimes solitary; both ray and disk flowers, or rays absent; flower-head bracts (phyllaries) in 1 row. Fruit pappus of 6–12 sometimes awn-tipped scales. (See p. 83.)

Common Woolly-sunflower

Flower heads have yellow center, yellow rays. HT: 6 in.–3 ft.

Pringle's Woolly Daisy

Flower heads very small, lack rays. HT: ½–3 in.

Golden-yarrow

HT: 6–30 in.

■ **WALLACE'S WOOLLY DAISY**
(*Eriophyllum wallacei*): Spring–early
summer; open places in deserts. Ray
flowers 5–10 (often 8), ⅛–¼ in. long, the
tips 2- or 3-toothed. Also called Woolly
Easter-bonnets.

■ **WHITE WOOLLY DAISY** (*E. lanosum*):
Spring. Similar to Wallace's Woolly Daisy,
but rays white. Also called White Easter-
bonnets.

Wallace's Woolly Daisy

Flower heads small,
yellow. Leaves spoon-
shaped, woolly. HT: ½–6 in.

White Woolly Daisy

Flower heads
small; yellow
center, white rays. Plants
sparsely woolly. HT: ½–6 in.

■ **BLACKFOOT DAISY** (*Melampodium
leucanthum*): Spring–fall; rocky slopes,
hills, plains. Sometimes shrubby. Disk
flowers many, yellow; rays 8–13, each
¼–½ in. long, to ⁵⁄₁₆ in. wide, commonly
with purplish veins on lower surface.
Also called Plains Blackfoot, Rock Daisy.
SIMILAR ■ **HOARY BLACKFOOT**
(*M. cinereum*): Plains. Rays often shorter
(⅛–⁵⁄₁₆ in.); outer row of phyllaries united
along ⅓ or less their length (vs. ½ or
more).

NOTE Do not confuse Blackfoot Daisy
with White Zinnia (p. 130), which
has rays 4–7, broad. The other native
Melampodium species, some with yellow
or orangish rays, are uncommon.

 Genus *Melampodium* (7 species, 5
native). Leaves opposite. Flower heads
solitary; both ray and disk flowers;
receptacle bract-covered (chaffy); flower-head bracts
(phyllaries) in 2 unlike, overlapping rows. Each seedlike
fruit surrounded by and shed with an inner phyllary, the
whole often wrinkled or roughened. (See p. 83.)

Blackfoot Daisy

Flower heads
solitary; yellow
center; white rays
2- or 3-toothed at tip.
Leaves opposite, relatively narrow,
untoothed to few-lobed. HT: 6–18 in.

■ **LITTLE GOLDEN ZINNIA** (*Zinnia grandiflora*): Spring–fall; slopes, mesas, plains. Somewhat shrubby. Disk flowers 18–24, orangish, reddish, or greenish; rays 3–6, yellow to yellow-orange, remaining attached and becoming papery after blooming. Also called Plains, Rocky Mountain, or Prairie Zinnia. Do not confuse with paper-flowers (below).

■ **WHITE ZINNIA** (*Z. acerosa*): Somewhat shrubby. Disk flowers 8–13, yellowish or tinged with purple; rays 4–7, white or sometimes faintly yellow, commonly with greenish veins on lower surface, obscurely toothed at tip. Also called Desert or Wild Zinnia. Do not confuse with Blackfoot Daisy (p. 129).

NOTE Some introduced zinnias have red, maroon, or purple rays.

Genus *Zinnia* (5 species, 4 native). Sometimes shrubby. Leaves opposite. Flower heads usually solitary; usually both ray and disk flowers; receptacle bract-covered (chaffy). Seedlike fruits flattened or 3-angled; fruit pappus of 1–3 awns or scales (or sometimes absent). (See p. 83.)

Little Golden Zinnia

Petal-like rays broad, yellowish.

Leaves opposite, very narrow. HT: 3–10 in.

White Zinnia

Rays broad, white. HT: 3–8 in.

■ **WHITE-STEM PAPER-FLOWER** (*Psilostrophe cooperi*): Year-round; desert slopes, plains, washes. Shrubby. Stems densely white-woolly or -felted. Disk flowers yellow or orange; rays 3–6, each ½–¾ in. long, persistent and becoming papery after blooming.

■ **PLAINS PAPER-FLOWER** (*P. villosa*): Spring–fall; plains. Stems gray-green, with cobwebby hairs. Flower heads on stalks to ³⁄₁₆ in. long; rays about ³⁄₁₆ in. long. **SIMILAR** ■ **WOOLLY PAPER-FLOWER** (*P. tagetina*): Desert scrub, grasslands. Flower heads on stalks ½–¾ in.; rays ¼–½ in.

NOTE Paper-flowers are also called paper daisy. The similar Little Golden Zinnia (above) has leaves opposite; ray tips not conspicuously 3-toothed or -lobed.

Genus *Psilostrophe* (6 native species). Sometimes shrubby. Leaves basal or alternate. Flower heads sometimes solitary; both ray and disk flowers; flower-head bracts (phyllaries) in 1 or 2 rows. Seedlike fruits cylindrical to club-shaped, ribbed; fruit pappus of 4–8 scales. (See p. 83.)

White-stem Paper-flower

Petal-like rays 3-toothed at tip.

Flower heads solitary, yellow. Leaves alternate. HT: 8–20 in.

Plains Paper-flower

Rays deeply 3-lobed at tip. HT: 6–16 in.

■ **ALPINE-GOLD** (*Hulsea algida*):
Summer; high rocky slopes. Plants
generally hairy. Leaves commonly spoon-
shaped, partly folded lengthwise; edges
wavy, toothed, or shallowly lobed. Ray
flowers 28–59.

■ **PUMICE ALPINE-GOLD** (*H. vestita*
ssp. *vestita*): Late spring–summer; rocky
slopes, alpine woods. Leaves broadly
spoon-shaped, densely white-woolly.
Flower heads 1–3; rays 12–21, sometimes
red-tinged.

■ **RED-RAY HULSEA** (*H. heterochroma*):
Late spring–summer; open places,
especially after fire. Plants generally
hairy. Leaves toothed. Flower heads 3–5;
rays commonly 28–75. Also called Great
Hulsea, Red-ray Alpine-gold.

 Genus *Hulsea* (7 native species). Sometimes aromatic. Leaves basal, alternate,
or whorled. Flower heads sometimes
solitary; both ray and disk flowers. Seedlike fruits hairy;
fruit pappus of 4 scales. (See p. 83.)

Alpine-gold

Flower heads
solitary; petal-
like rays yellow.
Leaves mostly
basal. HT:
6–18 in.

Pumice Alpine-gold

Rays yellow.
Leaves basal. HT: 6–12 in.

Red-ray
Hulsea

Rays reddish.
Leaves mostly on
stems. HT: 1½–5 ft.

■ **INDIAN-BLANKET** (*Gaillardia
pulchella*): Spring–fall; open places.
Leaves alternate. Ray flowers 3-lobed.
Also called Firewheel, Blanket-flower.

■ **FRAGRANT GAILLARDIA** (*G. suavis*):
Spring. Leaves basal. Ray flowers purplish
or red. Also called Rayless Gaillardia,
Pincushion-daisy, Perfume-balls.

■ **COMMON BLANKET-FLOWER**
(*G. aristata*): Late spring–summer. Leaves
alternate. Also called Great Blanket-flower.

■ **LANCE-LEAF BLANKET-FLOWER**
(*G. aestivalis*): Summer–fall. Leaves
unlobed. SIMILAR **RED-DOME BLANKET-
FLOWER** (*G. pinnatifida*): Spring–fall;
southwestern. Leaves pinnately lobed.

 Genus *Gaillardia* (11 native species).
Leaves basal or alternate. Flower heads
solitary; usually both ray and disk
flowers; receptacle sometimes bristly; flower-head
bracts (phyllaries) in 2 or 3 rows. Fruit pappus of 6–10
sometimes awned scales. (See p. 83.)

Indian-blanket

Petal-like
rays typically reddish
with yellow tip. HT: 6–24 in.

Fragrant Gaillardia

Rays
small
or absent.
HT: 6–30 in.

Common
Blanket-
flower

Rays
yellow
or with
purplish base,
commonly
crowded.
HT: 6–30 in.

Lance-leaf Blanket-flower

Rays
often
yellow,
commonly
well spaced.
HT: 6–24 in.

COMMON SNEEZEWEED (*Helenium autumnale*): Mostly late summer–fall; moist or wet places; widespread. Leaves lance-shaped. Disk flowers 5-lobed; rays fertile. Also called Autumn or Fall Sneezeweed. **SIMILAR** With leaves untoothed.
■ **BIGELOW'S SNEEZEWEED** (*H. bigelovii*): Summer; wet places. Rays ½–1 in. long. **ROSILLA** (*H. puberulum*): Chiefly CA. Rays absent or very small. See also Orange-sneezeweed (p. 133).

■ **PURPLE-HEAD SNEEZEWEED** (*H. flexuosum*): Late spring–summer; wet places. Stems winged. Disk flowers brownish or purple, 4-lobed; rays sterile.

■ **BITTER SNEEZEWEED** (*H. amarum* var. *amarum*): Spring–fall; open places. Stems not winged. Leaves threadlike.

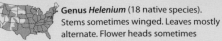

Genus *Helenium* (18 native species). Stems sometimes winged. Leaves mostly alternate. Flower heads sometimes solitary; usually both ray and disk flowers; flower-head bracts (phyllaries) often in 2 rows. Fruit pappus of 5–12 sometimes awn-tipped scales. (See p. 83.)

Common Sneezeweed

Flower heads yellow; center ball-shaped; rays wedge-shaped, 3-lobed. HT: 1½–5 ft.

Stems winged.

Purple-head Sneezeweed

HT: 1–3 ft.

Bitter Sneezeweed

HT: 6–24 in.

■ **COLORADO RUBBERWEED** (*Hymenoxys richardsonii*): Mostly summer; open places. Stems woolly at base, unbranched below flower clusters. Var. *richardsonii* (northern) has 8–14 rays, each ½–⅝ in. long; var. *floribunda* (southern) has 7–9 rays, each ⁵⁄₁₆–⅜ in. long. Also called Pingue. **SIMILAR** ■ **BITTER RUBBERWEED** (*H. odorata*): Mostly spring; flats; hills. Stems not woolly at base, commonly branched throughout; rays 8–13, each about ⅜ in. long. Also called Poison or Western Bitterweed.

■ **OLD-MAN-OF-THE-MOUNTAIN** (*H. grandiflora*): Summer; alpine slopes. Plants hairy. Rays mostly 15–34, each ⅝–1¼ in. long. Also called Alpine-sunflower, Graylocks Rubberweed.

Genus *Hymenoxys* (17 native species). Leaves basal or alternate. Flower heads sometimes solitary; usually both ray and disk flowers; flower-head bracts (phyllaries) unequal, in 2 rows, outer ones typically united at their bases. Fruit pappus often of 2–11 sharp-pointed scales. (See p. 83.)

Colorado Rubberweed

Petal-like rays yellow, 3-lobed at tip. Leaves often cut into very slender segments. HT: 3–14 in.

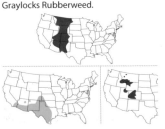

Old-man-of-the-mountain

Flower heads large; rays 3-toothed at tip. HT: 3–12 in.

■ **ORANGE-SNEEZEWEED** (*Hymenoxys hoopesii*): Mostly summer; slopes, meadows, open woods, stream banks. Leaves untoothed, the largest to 12 in. long. Flower heads large; rays 14–26, each ¾–1½ in. long, sometimes drooping. Also called Owl's-claws. Do not confuse with western species of *Helenium* (p. 132), which have winged stems.

RELATED *Tetraneuris* (9 native species): Leaves mostly basal; dried rays turn white and remain attached to flower head; phyllaries typically not united.

■ **ANGELITA DAISY** (*T. acaulis*): Spring–summer; slopes, hills, plains. Rays mostly 8–15, each ⅜–¾ in. long. Also called Stemless Four-nerve Daisy. Some related species have 13–26 rays.

Orange-sneezeweed
Petal-like rays yellow-orange, 3-toothed. Basal and lower stem leaves strap-shaped. HT: 1–3 ft.

Angelita Daisy
Rays yellow, 3-toothed. Leaves all basal, narrow. HT: mostly 2–12 in.

■ **DESERT-MARIGOLD** (*Baileya multiradiata*): Spring–fall; slopes, mesas, plains, roadsides. Plants woolly-hairy, whitish or grayish green. Leaves mostly on lower half of plant, deeply lobed and toothed. Disk flowers numerous, yellow. Also called Showy Desert-marigold. **SIMILAR WOOLLY DESERT-MARIGOLD** (*B. pleniradiata*): Plains, mesas; more or less similar geographic range. Leafless portion of flowering stalks generally only 1–5 in. long (4–12 in. in Desert-marigold); otherwise differs in technical characters.

Genus *Baileya* (3 native species). Stems woolly. Leaves basal and alternate. Flower heads solitary or few; both ray and disk flowers; flower-head bracts (phyllaries) in 2 overlapping rows. (See p. 83.)

Desert-marigold
Flower heads solitary, bright yellow; petal-like rays many, 3-toothed at tip. HT: mostly 6–24 in.

■ **RUBBER RABBIT-BRUSH** (*Ericameria nauseosa*): Late summer–fall; open places. Young twigs typically white-hairy. Leaves threadlike to narrowly spoon-shaped. Disk flowers commonly 5 per head; rays absent; phyllaries unequal, often in vertical rows. (The very similar Green or Yellow Rabbit-brush, *Chrysothamnus viscidiflorus*, has usually greenish twigs.)

■ **WHITE-STEM GOLDENBUSH** (*E. discoidea*): Late summer–fall; slopes. Twigs white-hairy. Disk flowers 10–26; rays absent; phyllaries nearly equal.

■ **NARROW-LEAF GOLDENBUSH** (*E. linearifolia*): Spring–early summer; open places. Twigs hairless. Leaves ⅛ in. or less wide. Flower heads solitary; rays 3–18.

Genus *Ericameria* (34 native species). Shrubs, sometimes aromatic. Leaves alternate. Flower heads sometimes solitary; usually only disk flowers; flower-head bracts (phyllaries) in 1–7 overlapping rows. Fruit pappus of 20–60 hairlike bristles. (See p. 83.)

Rubber Rabbit-brush

Flower heads yellow, in clusters. HT: mostly 6 in.–5 ft.

White-stem Goldenbush
HT: 6–18 in.

Narrow-leaf Goldenbush
HT: 1–5 ft.

■ **BROOM SNAKEWEED** (*Gutierrezia sarothrae*): Summer–fall; plains, prairies, rocky slopes. Shrubby. Stems minutely hairy. Leaves linear. Flower heads very small, cylindrical at base (longer than broad); disk flowers 3–9; rays tiny. Also called Turpentine-weed, Matchweed, Kindling-weed.

RELATED ■ **PRAIRIE BROOMWEED** (*Amphiachyris dracunculoides*): Prairies, plains. Not shrubby. Stems hairless. Flower heads bell-shaped at base (about as broad as long); disk flowers 10–21.

Genus *Gutierrezia* (10 native species). Sometimes shrubby, sometimes aromatic. Leaves basal and alternate, gland-dotted. Flower heads small, sometimes solitary; both ray and disk flowers. Seedlike fruits often hairy; fruit pappus of 5–10 minute scales. (See p. 83.)

Broom Snakeweed
Petal-like rays 3–8. HT: 6 in.–3 ft.

Prairie Broomweed
Rays 7–12. HT: 6 in.–3 ft.

■ **TALL GOLDENROD** (*Solidago altissima*): Late summer–fall; open places. Leaves stalkless, lance-shaped, finely toothed to untoothed; lower leaves often absent at bloom time. Flower heads very small; rays about ⅛ in. long. Also called Late Goldenrod. SIMILAR **CANADIAN GOLDENROD** (*S. canadensis*): Widespread. Leaves sharply toothed. ■ **MISSOURI GOLDENROD** (*S. missouriensis*): Lower leaves typically the longest on stem, present at bloom time.

■ **ROUGH GOLDENROD** (*S. rugosa*): Moist ground. Leaves sharply toothed, basal and lowermost ones usually absent.

NOTE Conspicuous ball-shaped swellings on the stems of some species are caused by insects.

Genus *Solidago* (77 native species). Leaves basal or alternate. Usually both ray and disk flowers; flower-head bracts (phyllaries) mostly unequal, in 3–5 overlapping rows. Fruit pappus of hairlike bristles. (See p. 83.)

Tall Goldenrod

Rough Goldenrod

Leaves 3-veined.

Flower heads yellow, on arching branches in terminal, plumelike sprays. HT: 2–6 ft.

Leaves many-veined. HT: 2–6 ft.

■ **STIFF GOLDENROD** (*Solidago rigida*): Late summer–fall; prairies, meadows, open places. Stems hairy. Leaves egg-shaped to elliptic, densely hairy; upper stem leaves stalkless, stiff, small; basal and lower stem leaves stalked, firm. Flower heads very small.

■ **ROCKY MOUNTAIN GOLDENROD** (*S. multiradiata*): Meadows, slopes, tundra. Upper stems hairy. Basal and lower stem leaves often spoon-shaped. Also called Northern or Alpine Goldenrod.

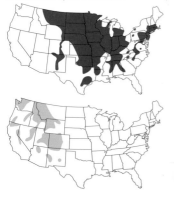

Stiff Goldenrod

Flower heads yellow, in flat-topped clusters. HT: 1–5 ft.

Rocky Mountain Goldenrod

Flower heads yellow, in round-topped clusters. HT: 6–18 in.

■ **BLUE-STEM GOLDENROD** (*Solidago caesia*): Late summer–fall; woods, thickets. Stems often waxy bluish or purplish, straight or sometimes arching. Leaves narrowly lance-shaped or elliptic-lance-shaped, hairless. Flower heads very small. Also called Wreath Goldenrod.

■ **ZIGZAG GOLDENROD** (*S. flexicaulis*): Woods, thickets. Flower-head arrangement similar to Blue-stem Goldenrod. Stems bent at each point of leaf attachment. Leaves elliptic-egg-shaped, hairy beneath; leafstalks winged. Also called Broad-leaf Goldenrod.

Blue-stem Goldenrod

Flower heads yellow, in small clusters in leaf axils. Leaves stalkless, narrow, often toothed. HT: 1–3 ft.

Zigzag Goldenrod

Leaves stalked, broad, sharply toothed. Stems zigzag somewhat. HT: 1–3 ft.

■ **HAIRY GOLDENROD** (*Solidago hispida*): Late summer–fall; sandy or rocky places. Leaves spoon-shaped to elliptic, usually hairy; upper stem leaves small, stalkless; basal and lower stem leaves have winged leafstalk. Flower heads very small.

■ **WHITE GOLDENROD** (*S. bicolor*): Open woods, rocky places. Similar to Hairy Goldenrod except for flower color. Also called Silver-rod.

Hairy Goldenrod

Flower heads entirely yellow, in elongated clusters. HT: 6 in.–3 ft.

White Goldenrod

Disk flowers pale yellow; rays white or cream-colored. HT: 6 in.–3 ft.

■ **SEASIDE GOLDENROD** (*Solidago sempervirens*): Late summer–fall; salt marsh edges, sand dunes, saline areas. Larger leaves 4–16 in. long, untoothed; basal and lower stem leaves have winged stalk that clasps stem. Disk flowers yellow. One of a few goldenrods with ample, petal-like rays (⁵⁄₁₆–¼ in. long).

■ **UPLAND WHITE GOLDENROD** (*S. ptarmicoides*): Prairies, rock outcrops, open places. Leaves narrow, mostly untoothed. Unusual for a goldenrod in having rays that are both white and prominent (¼–⁵⁄₁₆ in. long); disk flowers cream-colored. Also called Sneezewort Goldenrod. Once classified as *Aster ptarmicoides* and still often called Upland White-aster or Stiff-aster.

Seaside Goldenrod

Upland White Goldenrod

Flower heads in dense clusters; petal-like rays showy, yellow. Leaves fleshy. HT: 1½–6 ft.

Flower heads in flat-topped clusters; rays showy, white. Leaves somewhat stiff. HT: 6–30 in.

■ **COMMON GRASS-LEAF GOLDENROD** (*Euthamia graminifolia*): Midsummer–fall; open places. Plants nearly hairless to densely hairy. Leaves narrow, untoothed, with 3 or 5 distinct parallel veins; upper surface obscurely dotted with minute glands. SIMILAR ■ **GREAT PLAINS GRASS-LEAF GOLDENROD** (*E. gymnospermoides*): Open, often sandy places. Plants mostly not hairy. Leaves very narrow, conspicuously gland-dotted and often sticky.

■ **WESTERN GRASS-LEAF GOLDENROD** (*E. occidentalis*): Moist or wet places. Stems have waxy, whitish coating. Flower clusters not flat-topped. Also called Western Goldenrod.

NOTE Species are also called goldentop.

Genus *Euthamia* (5 native species). Similar to *Solidago* (p. 135), but flower heads in small, tight clusters that together form a large, often flat-topped or rounded cluster; leaves narrow, prominently or inconspicuously gland-dotted, with parallel main veins. (See p. 83.)

Common Grass-leaf Goldenrod

Western Grass-leaf Goldenrod

Flower heads tiny, yellow, in often flat-topped clusters; rays minute. Leaves grasslike. HT: 1–5 ft.

Flower heads in rounded or elongated, leafy-bracted clusters. HT: 1½–6 ft.

■ **SLENDER SCRATCH DAISY** (*Croptilon divaricatum*): Summer–fall; open, often sandy places. Plants typically hairy or sticky-hairy. Leaves lance-shaped to linear, often toothed above middle, hairy-fringed along edge at leaf base. Disk flowers mostly 14–22; rays ¼ in. long.

■ **HOOKER'S SCRATCH DAISY** (*C. hookerianum*): Disk flowers mostly 30–70; rays mostly ¼–½ in. long.

Genus *Croptilon* (3 native species). Leaves basal and alternate, narrow. Flower heads sometimes solitary; both ray and disk flowers. Seedlike fruits top-shaped; fruit pappus of hairlike bristles. (See p. 83.)

Slender Scratch Daisy

Petal-like rays 5–11, yellow. HT: 6 in.–3 ft.

Hooker's Scratch Daisy

Rays mostly 13–21. HT: 6 in.–3 ft.

■ **MARYLAND GOLDEN-ASTER** (*Chrysopsis mariana*): Late summer–fall; open woods, fields, sandy places. Plants conspicuously soft-hairy when young. Leaves stalkless, with prominent midvein and inconspicuous, pinnate side veins; lower leaves spoon-shaped. Phyllaries (flower-head bracts) sticky-hairy.

RELATED *Pityopsis* (7 native species). Leaves have several parallel veins.

■ **GRASS-LEAF GOLDEN-ASTER** (*P. graminifolia*): Mostly summer–fall; sandy places. Plants generally silky-hairy. Also called Narrow-leaf Silk-grass.

Genus *Chrysopsis* (11 native species). Sometimes shrubby. Leaves basal and alternate. Both ray and disk flowers. Seed-like fruits flattened; fruit's inner pappus of minute, hairlike bristles, outer one of minute scales. (See p. 83.)

Maryland Golden-aster

Grass-leaf Golden-aster

Petal-like rays yellow. Upper leaves lance-shaped, smaller than lower leaves. HT: 6 in.–3 ft.

Leaves grasslike, the upper usually much reduced. HT: 1–2½ ft.

■ **HAIRY GOLDEN-ASTER** (*Heterotheca villosa*): Spring–fall; open places. Plants generally coarsely hairy. Ray flowers mostly ¼–⁷⁄₁₆ in. long. **SIMILAR** ■ **PRAIRIE GOLDEN-ASTER** (*H. camporum*): Stem leaves generally few-toothed; rays mostly ⁷⁄₁₆–⅝ in. long. Also called Lemon-yellow Golden-aster.

■ **CAMPHORWEED** (*H. subaxillaris*): Crushed leaves have strong odor. Stems branched below flower cluster. Rays mostly ⅛–¼ in. long, with fruits lacking the pappus found on fruits of the disk flowers. **SIMILAR TELEGRAPH-WEED** (*H. grandiflora*): CA and adjacent Southwest. Plants grayish green; stems often unbranched ("telegraph pole"–like).

Genus *Heterotheca* (17 native species). Sometimes aromatic. Similar to *Chrysopsis* (p. 138), differing in technical characters; often has rough-hairy leaf surfaces (vs. hairless, soft-hairy, or woolly in *Chrysopsis*). (See p. 83.)

Hairy Golden-aster

Petal-like rays yellow. Leaves rough-hairy, typically untoothed. HT: 6–18 in.

Camphorweed

HT: 1–6 ft.

■ **CURLY-CUP GUMWEED** (*Grindelia squarrosa*): Summer–fall; open places. Leaves mostly blunt-toothed. Flower rays sometimes absent; phyllaries gummy.

OTHERS With leaves having bristle-tipped teeth; phyllaries only slightly to moderately gummy. ■ **LANCE-LEAF GUMWEED** (*G. lanceolata*): Leaves elongated, 3–12 times as long as wide, rarely untoothed. Also called Narrow-leaf or Spiny-tooth Gumweed. ■ **WAX GOLDENWEED** (*G. ciliata*): Leaves 2–4 times as long as wide. Also called Saw-leaf Daisy. **HAIRY GUMWEED** (*G. hirsutula*, no photo): Widespread (except Southeast). Includes more than 2 dozen previously recognized species and varieties.

Genus *Grindelia* (18 native species). Leaves basal or alternate. Usually both ray and disk flowers; flower-head bracts (phyllaries) many, generally resinous. Fruit pappus of 2–8 bristly awns. (See p. 83.)

Curly-cup Gumweed

Flower heads yellow. HT: mostly 1–3 ft.

Phyllary tips typically hooked or curved.

Lance-leaf Gumweed

Phyllary tips typically straight. HT: mostly 1–3 ft.

Wax Goldenweed

Leaves bristly-toothed; bases clasp stem. HT: 1–4 ft.

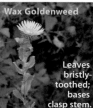

■ **THREAD-LEAF RAGWORT** (*Senecio flaccidus* var. *monoensis*): Summer; open places. Plants not hairy. Leaves linear or divided into threadlike segments. Petal-like rays 8–21, yellow. Also called Mono Ragwort, Comb Butterweed.

■ **CUT-LEAF GROUNDSEL** (*S. eremophilus*): Spring–fall; open places. Leaves deeply and coarsely toothed to pinnately lobed. Rays often 8; phyllaries may be black-tipped. Also called Desert Ragwort.

■ **ARROW-LEAF RAGWORT** (*S. triangularis*): Summer; stream banks, open woods. Leaves triangular or arrowhead-shaped. Rays often 8.

NOTE *Senecio* species are also called ragwort, groundsel, and butterweed.

Genus *Senecio* (55 species, 48 native). Herbs or shrubs. Leaves basal or alternate. Flower heads occasionally solitary; usually both ray and disk flowers; flower-head bracts (phyllaries) in 1 or 2 rows, often with small bractlets beneath. Fruit pappus of hairlike bristles. (See p. 83.)

Thread-leaf Ragwort

Cut-leaf Groundsel
HT: 1–3 ft.

Slender bractlets at base of phyllaries.
HT: 1–5 ft.

Arrow-leaf Ragwort
HT: 1½–4 ft.

■ **WESTERN GROUNDSEL** (*Senecio integerrimus*): Spring–midsummer; open places. Basal leaves prominent. Rays 5–13, each ¼–⅝ in. long. Also called Lamb-tongue Ragwort, Single-stem Butterweed. Rays white to cream-colored in WHITE WESTERN GROUNDSEL (var. *ochroleucus*), northwestern.

■ **SHOWY ALPINE RAGWORT** (*S. amplectens*): Summer; high slopes, alpine ridges. Leaves somewhat strap-shaped, coarsely toothed, often clasping stem. Flower heads nodding or turned to one side; rays 8–13, each ⅝–1 in. long.

■ **NODDING GROUNDSEL** (*S. bigelovii*): Summer; mountain meadows, open woods. Also called Nodding Ragwort.

Western Groundsel

Flower heads in clusters; petal-like rays usually yellow.
HT: 6–18 in.

White Western Groundsel

Rays whitish.

Showy Alpine Ragwort

Flower heads solitary or few; rays yellow.
HT: 6–24 in.

Nodding Groundsel

Flower heads nodding, lack rays.
HT: 1–3 ft.

■ **ROUND-LEAF RAGWORT** (*Packera obovata*): Spring–early summer; woods, grassy places. Plants generally not hairy. Basal leaves spoon-shaped, with narrowly winged stalk. Flower heads yellow; rays ¼–⅜ in. long. Several similar species.

OTHERS With similar flower heads.
■ **GOLDEN RAGWORT** (*P. aurea*): Spring–early summer. Basal leaves heart-shaped at base. ■ **WOOLLY GROUNDSEL** (*P. cana*): Late spring–summer. Basal leaves densely gray- or white-woolly, mostly untoothed; stem leaves reduced. ■ **NEW MEXICO GROUNDSEL** (*P. neomexicana* var. *neomexicana*): Spring–summer. Basal leaves grayish-hairy and often toothed; stem leaves conspicuous.

Genus *Packera* (54 native species). Very similar to *Senecio* (p. 140) and shares general common names. (See p. 83.)

Round-leaf Ragwort

Golden Ragwort

Basal leaves in clusters, spoon-shaped. HT: 6–24 in.

HT: 1–1½ ft.

Woolly Groundsel

New Mexico Groundsel

HT: 6–18 in.

HT: 6–24 in.

■ **BASIN BUTTERWEED** (*Packera multilobata*): Spring–midsummer; slopes, plains, open woods. Upper stem leaves stalkless; basal and lower stem leaves stalked, with sharply toothed lobes. Rays ¼–⅜ in. long. Also called Lobe-leaf Groundsel, Axhead Butterweed.

■ **BUTTERWEED** (*P. glabella*): Open, often moist places. Plants generally hairless. Leaf segments round-toothed; end segment commonly larger. Also called Yellowtop, Cress-leaf Groundsel.
SIMILAR ■ **BOLANDER'S BUTTERWEED** (*P. bolanderi*): Woods, stream banks, wet cliffs. Basal leaves long-stalked, often heart-shaped to roundish, shallowly lobed. Also called Seacoast Butterweed.

Basin Butterweed

Butterweed

Petal-like rays yellow. HT: 6–24 in.

Leaves pinnately divided. HT: 6–30 in.

■ **SPRING-GOLD** (*Crocidium multicaule*): Spring; open places. Stem leaves small, few; basal leaves several, somewhat fleshy. Leaf axils often have woolly tufts of hair. Flower heads have dome-shaped center. Also called Gold-stars.

Genus *Crocidium* (1 native species). Leaves somewhat fleshy, basal and alternate. Flower heads solitary; both ray and disk flowers; flower-head bracts (phyllaries) in 1 row. Seedlike fruits hairy; fruit pappus of hairlike bristles. (See p. 83.)

Spring-gold

Flower heads solitary; petal-like rays yellow. HT: mostly 2–8 in.

ASTERS

■ **NEW ENGLAND ASTER** (*Symphyotrichum novae-angliae*): Late summer–fall; open places. Stems hairy, especially upper. Leaf bases clasp stem, have small, earlobelike appendage on either side. Phyllaries sticky-hairy. This and several other leafy-stemmed species are often called Michaelmas Daisy.

■ **LEAFY-BRACTED ASTER** (*S. foliaceum*): Slopes, open woods, mountain meadows. Leaves to 1 in. wide, mostly untoothed. Outer phyllaries of some varieties notably enlarged. Also called Leafy Aster.

WESTERN ASTER (*S. ascendens*): Woods, plains, slopes, meadows; western. Leaves relatively narrow; stem leaves mostly 3/16–3/8 in. wide. Phyllaries in pronounced vertical rows. Also called Long-leaf Aster.

Asters (several genera traditionally included in *Aster*; 131 species, 130 native). Leaves basal or alternate. Flower heads sometimes solitary; usually both ray and disk flowers; flower-head bracts (phyllaries) in mostly 4–6 overlapping rows. Fruit pappus of hairlike bristles. (See p. 83.)

New England Aster

Leafy-bracted Aster

Rays in shades of violet. HT: 6–24 in.

Petal-like rays usually deep rose-purple. Leaves hairy, stalk-less, mostly untoothed. HT: 1–4 ft.

Western Aster

Rays violet. Leaves elongated. HT: 6–24 in.

ASTERS

■ **PANICLED ASTER** (*Symphyotrichum lanceolatum*): Summer–fall; open, often moist places. The hairlike bristles of the fruit pappus are slightly longer than the shallowly lobed disk flowers; ray flowers sometimes pale pink or pale violet. Also called Lance-leaf Aster.

■ **CALICO ASTER** (*S. lateriflorum*): Woods, thickets. Disk flowers deeply lobed, fairly quickly turning from pale yellow to rose. Also called Side-flower Aster.

Panicled Aster

Flower heads numerous, in a leafy cluster; petal-like rays typically white. Leaves stalkless, relatively narrow. HT: 1–5 ft.

Calico Aster

Flower heads often in cluster along one side of branch. HT: 6 in.–3 ft.

ASTERS

■ **WHITE WOOD ASTER** (*Eurybia divaricata*): Late summer–fall; woods, clearings. Stems somewhat zigzag. Lower leaves long-stalked, egg-shaped, with heart-shaped base. Ray flowers 5–12.

■ **LOW SHOWY ASTER** (*E. spectabilis*): Sandy soil, pinelands. Upper stems sticky-hairy. Basal leaves large, lance- to spoon-shaped. Flower heads in flat-topped clusters; rays 15–35.

White Wood Aster

Flower heads in more or less flat-topped clusters. Leaves sharply toothed. HT: 1–3 ft.

Petal-like rays relatively few, white.

Low Showy Aster

Rays purple. Leaves mostly basal, untoothed. HT: 6 in.–3 ft.

ASTERS

■ **ALPINE ASTER** (*Oreostemma alpigenum*): Summer; rocky slopes, alpine meadows, boggy places. Leaves 1–10 in. long, chiefly in a basal cluster; stem leaves bractlike. Ray flowers 10–40, white, pink, or purple. Long known as Alpine Aster, sometimes now called Mountain-crown to distinguish it from *Aster alpinus*.

■ **ALPINE ASTER** (*Aster alpinus* ssp. *vierhapperi*): Early summer; alpine meadows, tundra; rare in U.S. Rockies, more prevalent in northwestern Canada and Alaska. Stems densely gray- or white-hairy. Larger leaves basal and on lower half of stem; blades mostly ⅜–3 in. long. The only North American native species still included in the genus *Aster*.

Alpine Aster (*Oreostemma alpigenum*)

Flower heads solitary; petal-like rays often violet or lavender. Basal leaves elongated, narrow, untoothed. HT: 2–16 in.

Alpine Aster (*Aster alpinus* ssp. *vierhapperi*)

Flower heads solitary; rays white, pink, or violet. Basal leaves spoon-shaped, untoothed. HT: 2–12 in.

ASTERS

Ionactis (5 native species). Seedlike fruits hairy; fruit's outer pappus of short scales or bristles, inner pappus of long bristles. Sometimes called ankle-aster.

■ **STIFF ASTER** (*I. linariifolia*): Late summer–fall; sandy or rocky places. Leaves stalkless, ½–1½ in. long, mostly ¹⁄₁₆–⅛ in. wide. Also called Flax-leaf Aster.

■ **LAVA ASTER** (*I. alpina*): Late spring–early summer; slopes, hills, plains. Leaves white-edged, ¼–½ in. long. Also called Crag Aster. **SIMILAR** ■ **ROCKY MOUNTAIN ASTER** (*I. stenomeres*): Summer; slopes, clearings. Plants 5–12 in. tall. Leaves green-edged, ½–1 in. long.

Stiff Aster

Flower heads solitary or in clusters; petal-like rays blue to violet. Leaves numerous, stiff, very narrow, HT: 6–24 in.

Lava Aster

Flower heads solitary. Leaves crowded, short, firm. HT: 2–6 in.

ASTERS

Oclemena (3 native species). Seedlike fruits covered with minute gland dots; fruit pappus bristles in 2 or 3 rows, the outer much shorter than the inner. Sometimes called nodding-aster.

■ **WHORLED ASTER** (*O. acuminata*): Late summer–fall; woods. Stems slightly zigzag. Leaves thin, crowded on upper stems. Also called Whorled Wood Aster.

■ **PINEBARREN ASTER** (*O. reticulata*): Mostly spring; wet pinelands, burned areas. Stems straight. Leaves untoothed to coarsely toothed. Rays sometimes pinkish. Also called White-top Aster.

■ **BOG ASTER** (*O. nemoralis*): Summer– early fall; bogs. Rays occasionally white.

Whorled Aster

Petal-like rays white. Leaves sharply toothed, crowded, sometimes appearing whorled. HT: 6 in.–3 ft.

Pinebarren Aster

Rays usually white. Leaves not crowded, veiny. HT: 1–3 ft.

Bog Aster

Rays usually pink. Leaves narrow, numerous. HT: 6–24 in.

ASTERS

Doellingeria (3 native species), *Eucephalus* (10 native species). Seedlike fruits have outer pappus of minute bristles, inner pappus of larger bristles. *Eucephalus* species, sometimes called wayside aster, have scalelike lowermost stem leaves.

■ **TALL FLAT-TOPPED WHITE ASTER** (*D. umbellata*): Midsummer–fall; moist or wet places. Leaves stalkless, elliptic; lowermost stem leaves fall off before bloom time. Also called Parasol White-top.

■ **ENGELMANN'S ASTER** (*E. engelmannii*): Summer; open woods, mountain meadows. Phyllaries (flower-head bracts) often tinged reddish or purplish.

■ **BREWER'S ASTER** (*E. breweri*): Summer; open woods, mountain meadows. Rays absent. Also called Brewer's Golden Aster.

Tall Flat-topped White Aster

Flower heads numerous, in flat-topped clusters; petal-like rays small, white. HT: 1–5 ft.

Engelmann's Aster

Flower heads large; rays white to pink. HT: 1½–4 ft.

Brewer's Aster

Flower heads yellow, lack rays. HT: 1–3 ft.

ASTERS

Sericocarpus (4 native species). Seedlike fruits hairy; pappus of many bristles.

■ **TOOTHED WHITE-TOP ASTER** (*S. asteroides*): Midsummer–early fall; woods, fields. Basal leaves persistent (unlike all other *Sericocarpus*); stem leaves egg-shaped, to 4 in. long. Rays ⅛–¼ in. long.

■ **DIXIE WHITE-TOP ASTER** (*S. tortifolius*): Open woods, pinelands, fields. Leaves hairy, to 1½ in. long. **SIMILAR** ■ **OREGON WHITE-TOP ASTER** (*S. oregonensis*): Woods, meadows. Leaves to 4 in. long, lance-shaped, not twisted.

■ **NARROW-LEAF WHITE-TOP ASTER** (*S. linifolius*): Open woods, fields. Leaves hairless, to 3 in. long. Rays ³⁄₁₆–⁷⁄₁₆ in. long.

Toothed White-top Aster

Flower heads in flat-topped clusters; center cream-colored; petal-like rays 3–7, very small, white. Stem leaves stalkless, often toothed. HT: 6–24 in.

Dixie White-top Aster

Leaves wider toward tip, untoothed, twisted at base. HT: 1–3 ft.

Narrow-leaf White-top Aster

Rays longer. Leaves narrow, untoothed. HT: 6–24 in.

TANSY-LEAF-ASTER AND RELATIVES

■ **TANSY-LEAF-ASTER** (*Machaeranthera tanacetifolia*): Spring–fall; grasslands, desert scrub, open woods, roadsides. Leaves fernlike, sticky-hairy. Ray flowers mostly 12–40; phyllary tips curve out or downward. Also called Tahoka Daisy.

■ **MOJAVE-ASTER** (*Xylorhiza tortifolia*): Spring; desert slopes and flats. Shrubby. Leaves lance-shaped to elliptic, spiny-edged. Rays 18–60; phyllaries sticky-hairy, with threadlike, erect to spreading tips.

■ **HOARY-ASTER** (*Dieteria canescens*): Summer–fall; open places. Variable. Leaves undivided, narrow. Rays 8–25; phyllary tips usually spreading or curved.

Tansy-leaf-aster and Relatives (several genera, about 20 native species). Similar to asters (p. 142), but phyllaries (flower-head bracts) sometimes have outwardly curving tip; leaves sometimes have bristle- or spine-tipped teeth.

Petal-like rays blue-violet. Leaf segments bristle-tipped. HT: mostly 6–24 in.

Rays lavender. HT: 6–30 in.

Rays purple. HT: 6 in.–3 ft.

TANSY-LEAF-ASTER RELATIVES

■ **SPINY GOLDENWEED** (*Xanthisma spinulosum*): Spring–fall; open places. Sometimes shrubby. Plants variable: conspicuously hairy to nearly hairless; basal leaves present or absent. Ray flowers 14–60; phyllaries (flower-head bracts) bristle-tipped (see inset). Also called Cut-leaf Iron-plant, Yellow Spiny Daisy, Lacy Tansy-aster.

■ **GUMWEED-ASTER** (*X. grindelioides*): Spring–summer; open places. Shrubby. Heads of disk flowers only. Also called Goldenweed.

Spiny Goldenweed

Petal-like rays yellow. Leaves pinnately lobed, the lobes bristle-toothed. HT: 6–30 in.

Gumweed-aster

Leaves bristle-toothed. HT: 2–14 in.

Flower heads yellow.

■ **FALSE ASTER** (*Boltonia asteroides*): Midsummer–fall; moist or wet places. Leaves stalkless, mostly untoothed. Flower heads in clusters; rays ¼–½ in. long, usually white, sometimes light purple or pink. Do not confuse False Aster with asters (p. 142), which have a usually flat receptacle (center of head) and a fruit pappus of hairlike bristles; or with ⊞ Ox-eye Daisy (p. 570), which has lobed or deeply toothed leaves.

■ **DOLL'S DAISY** (*B. diffusa*): Prairies, woodland borders, disturbed places. Petal-like rays ¼ in. or less long.

Genus *Boltonia* (5 native species). Stems often in clusters. Leaves basal or alternate. Both ray and disk flowers. Seedlike fruits strongly flattened; fruit pappus of often 2 tiny, spinelike awns and minute bristles or scales. (See p. 83.)

False Aster

Flower heads have yellow, dome-shaped center. HT: 1–5 ft.

Doll's Daisy

Flower heads smaller, in open, much-branched clusters. HT: 1½–5 ft.

■ **LAZY DAISY** (*Aphanostephus skirrhobasis*): Spring–early summer; open places. Plants gray-hairy. Leaves unlobed to deeply pinnately lobed. Ray flowers mostly 25–45; may be tinged red, rose, or purple beneath; phyllaries papery-edged. Also called Arkansas Lazy Daisy. **SIMILAR RIDDELL'S LAZY DAISY** (*A. riddellii*): TX, NM. Rays mostly 40–75.

OTHER GENUS *Astranthium* (3 native species): Similar, but phyllaries not papery-edged; fruits flattened (no photos). ■ **EASTERN WESTERN DAISY** (*A. integrifolium*): Spring; open places. Rays 8–26, white, may be blue- or purple-tinged. Also called Entire-leaf Western Daisy, a name shared with ■ **COMANCHE WESTERN DAISY** (*A. ciliatum*).

Genus *Aphanostephus* (4 native species). Leaves basal or alternate. Flower heads solitary; both ray and disk flowers; flower-head bracts (phyllaries) in 3 or 4 overlapping rows. Seedlike fruits 4-angled, ribbed. (See p. 83.)

Lazy Daisy

Flower heads solitary; petal-like rays white. HT: 4–20 in.

Center of head dome-shaped, yellow.

■ **STEMLESS TOWNSEND DAISY** (*Townsendia exscapa*): Mostly spring; plains, hills, open woods. Leaves slender (often narrowly spoon-shaped), grayish-hairy, untoothed. Flower heads large, essentially stalkless, often tucked among basal leaves. Also called Easter Daisy.

■ **SHOWY TOWNSEND DAISY** (*T. florifer*): Mostly spring–early summer; gravelly flats, hills. Flower heads on sparsely leafy stems; phyllaries mostly ¼–⅜ in. long, their tips short-pointed.

■ **PARRY'S TOWNSEND DAISY** (*T. parryi*): Late spring–summer; meadows, slopes. Flower heads on leafy stems; phyllaries mostly ⅜–⅝ in. long, their tips often long-tapering.

Genus *Townsendia* (26 native species). Leaves basal or alternate. Flower heads solitary; both ray and disk flowers; flower-head bracts (phyllaries) unequal, in 3–7 overlapping rows. Seedlike fruits often flattened and hairy; fruit pappus of bristlelike scales. (See p. 83.)

Stemless Townsend Daisy

Petal-like rays white or very pale pink. Leaves mostly in a basal cluster. HT: 1–2 in.

Showy Townsend Daisy

Rays white to pale pink. HT: 1–6 in.

Parry's Townsend Daisy

Rays purple or bluish. HT: mostly 2–8 in.

■ **BABY WHITE-ASTER** (*Chaetopappa ericoides*): Spring–summer; open places. Leaves very narrow, overlapping, untoothed, about ½ in. long. Flower heads small, with protruding center; mostly 12–24 rays, each to about ¼ in. long and aging pinkish; phyllaries in vertical overlapping rows. Also called Rose-heath, Sand-aster.

■ **COMMON LEAST DAISY** (*C. asteroides*): Basal leaves clustered; stem leaves not overlapping. Ray flowers mostly 5–13.

Genus *Chaetopappa* (8 native species). Leaves basal or alternate. Flower heads solitary; both ray and disk flowers; flower-head bracts (phyllaries) in 2–6 overlapping rows, with white, papery edges. Fruit pappus of bristles or a crown of scales or both. (See p. 83.)

Baby White-aster — Disk flowers yellow; petal-like rays white, sometimes curled under at tip. HT: 2–6 in.

Common Least Daisy — Flower heads on wiry stems. HT: 2–12 in.

■ **DESERT-STAR** (*Monoptilon bellioides*): Spring; sandy or gravelly deserts. Plants bristly-hairy. Stems often reddish purple. Disk flowers yellow; ray flowers sometimes tinged rose-pink or purplish. Fruit outer pappus of scales, inner pappus of 8–15 bristles. Also called Mojave or Bristly Desert-star. **SIMILAR** ■ **DAISY DESERT-STAR** (*M. bellidiforme*): Stems typically yellow-green; fruit pappus a minute crown of scales plus a single feather-tipped bristle. Also called Small Desert-star.

Genus *Monoptilon* (2 native species). Plants have long, white hairs. Leaves basal and alternate. Flower heads solitary; both ray and disk flowers; flower-head bracts (phyllaries) in 1 row. Fruit pappus of scales and bristle(s). (See p. 83.)

Desert-star — Petal-like rays white. Upper leaves often form a loose ring below flower heads. Leaves small, narrow, untoothed. HT: 1–3 in.

PHILADELPHIA FLEABANE (*Erigeron philadelphicus*): Spring–summer; open places; widespread. Leaf bases clasp stem. Ray flowers typically 150–250, very narrow, each 3/16–3/8 in. long. Also called Common or Marsh Fleabane. **SIMILAR** With fewer (50–125) rays. ■ **DAISY FLEABANE** (*E. strigosus*): Leaves mostly untoothed. **EASTERN DAISY FLEABANE** (*E. annuus*): Eastern. Lower leaves often toothed.

■ **CUT-LEAF FLEABANE** (*E. compositus*): Late spring–summer; slopes, rocky places. Leaves basal, fan-shaped, divided into slender segments. Ray flowers 20–60; 1/4–1/2 in. long; white, pinkish, or bluish; sometimes reduced or absent. Also called Cut-leaf Daisy, Dwarf Mountain Fleabane.

Genus *Erigeron* (173 species, 172 native). Similar to asters (p. 142) in basic features, but flower heads generally have more numerous and narrower rays, and most species bloom spring–summer rather than late summer–fall. (See p. 83.)

Philadelphia Fleabane

Flower heads in clusters; petal-like rays often white, sometimes pinkish. HT: 1–3 ft.

Cut-leaf Fleabane

Flower heads solitary. HT: 2–8 in.

■ **SHOWY FLEABANE** (*Erigeron speciosus*): Midsummer–fall; slopes, meadows, open woods. Ray flowers 5/16–5/8 in. long, blue to lavender, or rarely white.

OTHERS Also with variably colored ray flowers. ■ **SEASIDE DAISY** (*E. glaucus*): Spring–summer; coastal bluffs, beaches. Leaves somewhat fleshy; rays 5/16–1/2 in. long. Also called Beach Fleabane.
■ **ROBIN'S-PLANTAIN** (*E. pulchellus*): Mostly spring; woods, fields. Rays 1/4–3/8 in. long. Also called Hairy Fleabane.
■ **SUBALPINE FLEABANE** (*E. glacialis* ssp. *glacialis*): Summer; slopes, meadows, stream banks. Rays 5/16–3/4 in. long.

Showy Fleabane
Petal-like rays 75–150. HT: 6 in.–3 ft.

Seaside Daisy
Rays 80–165. HT: 2–12 in.

Robin's-plantain
Rays 50–80. HT: 6–24 in.

Subalpine Fleabane
Rays 30–80. HT: 6–24 in.

■ **LINE-LEAF FLEABANE** (*Erigeron linearis*): Late spring–midsummer; gravelly slopes, grassy plains. Also called Desert Yellow Fleabane, Linear-leaf Daisy.

■ **BLOOMER'S FLEABANE** (*E. bloomeri*): Open places. Leaves mostly basal. Phyllaries (flower-head bracts) ¼–⅜ in. long. Also called Scabland Fleabane.

■ **RAYLESS SHAGGY FLEABANE** (*E. aphanactis*): Desert flats, hills, plains. Stems have spreading hairs. Leaves basal and often also on stems. Phyllaries ³⁄₁₆–¼ in. long. Also called Basin Rayless Daisy.

NOTE Some *Erigeron* species (such as Cut-leaf Fleabane, p. 150) have flower heads with or without rays.

Line-leaf Fleabane

Bloomer's Fleabane

Flower heads a little taller than wide, lack rays. HT: 2–6 in.

Rayless Shaggy Fleabane

Flower heads solitary; petal-like rays usually bright yellow. Leaves mostly basal, very slender. HT: 3–12 in.

Flower heads wider than tall, lack rays. HT: 3–12 in.

■ **SHORT-RAY FLEABANE** (*Erigeron lonchophyllus*): Summer; moist or wet places. Stems hairy. Stem leaves linear; basal leaves very narrowly spoon-shaped. Flower heads solitary or often in clusters of 3–12; rays tiny, more or less erect rather than spreading, sometimes pale pink.

RELATED *Conyza* (4 species, 2 native). Differs from *Erigeron* in technical characters. **HORSEWEED** (*C. canadensis*): Mostly summer–fall; open, often disturbed places; widespread. Stems have short, bristly hairs. Leaves mostly on stems, narrow, hairy-edged. Flower heads very small, in large clusters; rays sometimes pinkish. Also called Canadian Horseweed, Canadian-fleabane.

Short-ray Fleabane

Horseweed

Ray flowers 70–130, tiny, usually white. HT: 2–20 in.

Rays 25–40, tiny, usually white. HT: 6 in.–6 ft.

■ **WOOLLY SUNBONNETS** (*Chaptalia tomentosa*): Mostly spring; pinelands, wet woods, bogs. Disk flowers whitish; rays frequently 3-toothed at tip. Also called Pineland Daisy. **SIMILAR** ■ **SILVERPUFF** (*C. texana*): Open wooded slopes. Leaves stalked, often lobed; petal-like rays white above and beneath.

NOTE The flower heads of Woolly Sunbonnets are nodding, closed, and pinkish purple in the morning but erect, open, and whitish by afternoon. Many of the flowers of *Chaptalia* are 2-lipped.

Genus *Chaptalia* (3 native species). Leaves basal. Flower heads solitary; both ray and disk flowers. Seedlike fruits narrow, tapered into a neck or beak; fruit pappus of straw-colored or pinkish, hairlike bristles. (See p. 83.)

Woolly Sunbonnets

Petal-like rays white above, commonly pinkish purple beneath. Leaves in a basal cluster, stalkless, densely white-hairy beneath. HT: 6–12 in.

■ **CALIFORNIA TRIXIS** (*Trixis californica*): Spring–fall; rocky slopes, canyons, washes. Unusual in having 2-lipped disk flowers: inner lip 2-lobed and frequently curled back, outer lip normally 3-toothed and spreading, resembling a ray. Bractlets at base of phyllaries lance- to egg-shaped. Also called American Threefold. **SIMILAR** ■ **MEXICAN TRIXIS** (*T. inula*): Sandy areas, brushy places, roadsides. Differs in technical characters. Also called Tropical Threefold.

Genus *Trixis* (2 native species). Shrubby. Leaves alternate. Flower heads some-times solitary; only disk flowers, these 2-lipped; flower-head bracts (phyllaries) narrow, erect, in usually 1 row, with bractlets beneath. Seedlike fruits cylindrical; fruit pappus of hairlike bristles. (See p. 83.)

California Trixis

Flower heads yellow, above conspicuous leaflike bractlets; stamens and styles protrude. Leaves lance-shaped. HT: 1–3 ft.

BALSAMINACEAE   TOUCH-ME-NOT FAMILY

Annual. Stems translucent, watery. Leaves simple and usually alternate. Flowers dangle on stalks from leaf axils; petals 5 (but appear as 3): upper hood-shaped, lower 4 in 2 united pairs and flaring; sepals 3, middle one cornucopia-shaped, ending in a "tail" (spur); stamens 5; pistil 1. Fruits are capsules.

■ **ORANGE JEWELWEED** (*Impatiens capensis*): Summer; damp woods, thickets, stream banks. Spur to ⅜ in. long, usually strongly curved and pointing forward. Also called Spotted Touch-me-not.

■ **YELLOW JEWELWEED** (*I. pallida*): Spur to ¼ in. long, commonly bent downward at a right angle. Also called Pale Touch-me-not. **SIMILAR** ■ **WESTERN JEWELWEED** (*I. noli-tangere*): Flowers spotted with reddish brown; spur to ⅜ in., curved. Also called Western Touch-me-not.

NOTE Jewelweed fruits explode when touched, scattering their seeds.

Genus *Impatiens* (10 species, 5 native). Flowers of native species are yellow to orange, often with reddish brown spots.

Orange Jewelweed

Flowers yellow-orange. HT: 2–5 ft.

Yellow Jewelweed

Flowers pale yellow. HT: 3–5 ft.

BERBERIDACEAE   BARBERRY FAMILY

Shrubs or perennial herbs. Leaves usually alternate or basal, simple or compound. Flowers solitary or in clusters; flower parts mostly in 3s: petals 6–9 (or rarely 0); sepals 6, often petal-like; stamens as many as (or sometimes twice as many as) petals; pistil 1. Fruits are usually berries or pods.

■ **VANILLA-LEAF** (*Achlys triphylla*): Spring–summer; woods, stream banks. Leaflets 3, middle one mostly 3-lobed. Flowers tiny, petal-less; conspicuous features are the many stamens. Pods small, red-purple, half-moon-shaped. Also called Deer-foot. **SIMILAR CALIFORNIA VANILLA-LEAF** (*A. californica*): Similar range. Middle leaflet 6–9-lobed.

NOTE Leaves have vanilla-like fragrance when dried.

Genus *Achlys* (2 native species). Single, long-stalked, circular leaf arising from plant base, divided into 3 wedge- or fan-shaped leaflets with wavy-lobed edges. Flowers in spikelike clusters. Fruits are pods.

Vanilla-leaf

Flowers white, at end of leafless, wandlike stalk. Leaflets fan-shaped. HT: 10–20 in.

■ NORTHERN INSIDE-OUT-FLOWER

(*Vancouveria hexandra*): Spring–summer; woods. Leaflets heart-shaped at base, blunt-toothed above middle.

GOLDEN INSIDE-OUT-FLOWER

(*V. chrysantha*): Siskiyou Mountains (northern CA, southwestern OR). Also called Siskiyou Inside-out-flower.

Genus *Vancouveria* (3 native species). Leaves several, on long stalks arising from plant base, divided into many leaflets. Flowers clustered at ends of wiry, leafless stalks; petals 6, strongly curved backward; stamens 6, forming conelike center. Fruits are pods.

Northern Inside-out-flower

Flowers white; petals swept back. HT: 8–20 in.

Golden Inside-out-flower

Flowers yellow. HT: 8–16 in.

■ BLUE-COHOSH (*Caulophyllum*

thalictroides): Spring; woods. Blooms while leaves are still small. Leaflets rounded at base, often with 2–5 lobes or large teeth above middle. The berrylike fruits are actually fleshy, naked seeds.

Genus *Caulophyllum* (2 native species). Main leaf divided into numerous leaflets (looks like 3 whorled, divided leaves); second, smaller leaf below flowers. Flowers in clusters; sepals 6, pointed, petal-like (true petals inconspicuous); stamens 6. Fruits berrylike.

Blue-cohosh

Flowers yellow-green or purplish. Seeds blue, berrylike, on long stalks. HT: 1–3 ft.

■ **UMBRELLA-LEAF** (*Diphylleia cymosa*): Late spring; wet places in mountains. Nonflowering plants have 1 leaf, flowering plants have 2. Berries blue, on reddish stalks.

Genus *Diphylleia* (1 native species). Leaves long-stalked, 2 per stem, roundly kidney-shaped; each blade more or less cut to form 2 coarsely toothed, 5–7-lobed segments. Flowers in clusters; petals 6; stamens 6. Fruits are berries.

Umbrella-leaf

Flowers white, in clusters held above leaves. Leaves umbrella-like. HT: 1½–3 ft.

■ **TWINLEAF** (*Jeffersonia diphylla*): Spring; woods. Leaf segments nearly symmetrical, triangular, with wavy-lobed edges. Plants bloom while 6–8 in. tall, when leaves are still small. Do not confuse Twinleaf with the more common Bloodroot (p. 398).

Genus *Jeffersonia* (1 native species). Single, long-stalked leaf arises from plant base. Single flower at end of leafless stalk; petals 8; stamens 8. Fruits are greenish to brownish pods with a "hinged" lid.

Twinleaf

Single, white flower; petals drop early. Single leaf, deeply divided, resembles a pair of butterfly wings. HT: to 1½ ft.

■ **MAY-APPLE** (*Podophyllum peltatum*): Spring; woods, clearings. Nonflowering plants have 1 leaf, flowering plants have 2. Leaf segments usually toothed or lobed. Fruits egg-shaped, usually yellowish.

NOTE *Podophyllum* species are poisonous (except the ripe fruit).

Genus *Podophyllum* (1 native species). Leaves long-stalked, 2 per stem, nearly circular, deeply cut into 5–7 segments. Single flower on stalk arising from V formed by leafstalks; petals 6–9; stamens 12–18. Fruits are fleshy berries.

May-apple

Single flower, typically waxy-white, nodding. Leaves umbrella-like. HT: 1–2 ft.

Fruit.

BIGNONIACEAE **BIGNONIA or TRUMPET-CREEPER FAMILY**

Woody plants, often vines. Leaves mostly opposite; compound or sometimes simple. Flowers showy, tubular (petals united), 5-lobed, often 2-lipped; sepals 5, united; stamens 4; pistil 1. Fruits are capsules.

■ **TRUMPET-CREEPER** (*Campsis radicans*): Summer–fall; woods, fields, fencerows, roadsides. Leaves divided into toothed leaflets. Also called Trumpet-vine.

RELATED ■ **CROSSVINE** (*Bignonia capreolata*): Leaves divided into a pair of untoothed leaflets with a tendril at leaflet junction. Flowers red to orange-red.

Genus *Campsis* (1 native species). Climbing or sprawling woody vine. Leaves opposite, pinnately divided into 5–13 sharply toothed leaflets. Flowers in clusters, somewhat leathery. Fruits elongated.

Trumpet-creeper

Flowers red-orange. Vine climbs via aerial roots.

Crossvine

Flowers usually yellowish inside.

BIXACEAE
LIPSTICK-TREE FAMILY

Trees, shrubs, or sometimes perennial herbs; some have visible orange-red sap. Leaves simple or compound, alternate and palmately veined, lobed, or divided. Flowers mostly in clusters; petals 5; sepals 5; stamens many; pistil 1. Fruits are capsules.

■ **WRIGHT'S YELLOWSHOW** (*Amoreuxia wrightii*): Late spring–summer; plains, thickets, roadsides. Uppermost petals have 2 dark splotches at base, middle petals have 1 splotch, lowermost petal not splotched. SIMILAR ■ **MEXICAN YELLOWSHOW** (*A. palmatifida*): Mostly summer; slopes and plains. Leaves typically 7- or 9-lobed. Also called Arizona Yellowshow.

Genus *Amoreuxia* (3 native species). May be somewhat shrubby. Leaves palmately lobed, often dotted on lower surface. Flowers have stamens in 2 sets of unequal length.

Wright's Yellowshow

Flowers large, yellow to orange. Leaves 5- or 7-lobed, coarsely toothed. HT: 6–20 in.

BORAGINACEAE
BORAGE FAMILY

Annual, biennial, or perennial. Stems frequently hairy. Leaves alternate, sometimes also basal (lower ones occasionally opposite); generally simple and untoothed. Flowers often in coiled clusters that uncoil as they mature; funnel- or trumpet-shaped (petals united) and 5-lobed; sepals 5; stamens 5; pistil 1, ovary usually deeply 4-lobed (except in a few genera, such as *Tiquilia* and *Heliotropium*, p. 163). Fruits (nutlets) usually seedlike.

FRUITS (NUTLETS) OF THE BORAGINACEAE

WILD-COMFREY
Covered on all sides with short, hook-tipped bristles; ¼–⁵⁄₁₆ in. (p. 158).

MOUNTAIN FORGET-ME-NOT
Smooth; ¹⁄₁₆ in. (p. 158).

MANY-FLOWER STICKSEED
With hook-tipped bristles; ⅛–³⁄₁₆ in. (p. 159).

COMMON CRYPTANTHA
Frequently with tiny bumps; attachment scar groovelike (sunken); ¹⁄₁₆–⅛ in. (p. 160).

COMMON POPCORN-FLOWER
Attachment scar ridgelike (raised); ¹⁄₁₆–⅛ in. (p. 160).

COMMON FIDDLENECK
With tiny bumps; ⅛–³⁄₁₆ in. (p. 161).

158 • BORAGINACEAE

■ PACIFIC HOUND'S-TONGUE
(*Cynoglossum grande*): Spring–early summer; woods, shrubby slopes. Stems not hairy. Leaves mostly on lower half of stem. Flowers ⅜–⅝ in. across, in clusters held above leaves.

WESTERN HOUND'S-TONGUE
(*C. occidentale*): Range somewhat similar to Pacific Hound's-tongue. Stems hairy. Leaves lack distinct stalk. Flowers smaller, ³⁄₁₆–⁵⁄₁₆ in. across, sometimes tinged brown-rose or reddish purple. See also Ⓘ Common Hound's-tongue (p. 572).

■ **WILD-COMFREY** (*C. virginianum*): Woods, woodland borders. Flowers light blue. Also called Blue Hound's-tongue.

Genus *Cynoglossum* (6 species, 3 native). Plants leafy. Flowers in clusters, funnel- or trumpet-shaped and 5-lobed, the opening (throat) essentially closed by a ring of toothlike appendages. Nutlets covered on all sides with short, hook-tipped bristles. Compare *Hackelia*, p. 159.

Pacific Hound's-tongue

Flowers blue or violet, with white eye. Leaves have distinct stalk. HT: 1–3 ft.

Western Hound's-tongue

HT: 6–24 in.

Wild-comfrey

Leaves clasping. HT: 12–32 in.

■ MOUNTAIN FORGET-ME-NOT
(*Myosotis asiatica*): Summer; mountain meadows, slopes. Flowers ³⁄₁₆–⅜ in. across. See also Alpine Bluebells (p. 162).

SIMILAR ■ **SMALL-FLOWER FORGET-ME-NOT** (*M. laxa*): Wet places. Flowers ¹⁄₁₆–³⁄₁₆ in. across. Ⓘ **EUROPEAN TRUE FORGET-ME-NOT** (*M. scorpioides*): Flowers ³⁄₁₆–⅜ in. across. See also Ⓘ Yellow-and-blue Forget-me-not (p. 573).

RELATED ■ **ALPINE-FORGET-ME-NOT** (*Eritrichium nanum*): Alpine areas. Dwarf.

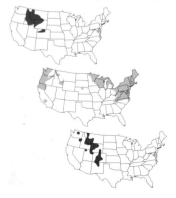

Genus *Myosotis* (11 species, 4 native). Flowers small, in clusters; funnel- to trumpet-shaped and 5-lobed, the opening (throat) mostly closed by a ring of tiny, toothlike projections. Nutlets seedlike, smooth (bristly in *Hackelia*, p. 159). Sometimes called scorpion-grass.

Mountain Forget-me-not

Flowers small, bright blue with yellow (or red) eye. Leaves short-hairy. HT: 2–15 in.

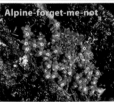

Alpine-forget-me-not

Flowers blue. Leaves tiny, silvery, long-hairy. Plants mat-forming. HT: 2–4 in.

■ **SPRING FORGET-ME-NOT**
(*Myosotis verna*): Spring–early summer;
woods, fields. Fruiting stalks erect at
base. SIMILAR **LARGE-SEED FORGET-
ME-NOT** (*M. macrosperma*): Eastern.
Fruiting stalks spreading at base.

NOTE See also ① Corn-gromwell (p. 573).

Spring Forget-me-not

Flowers
tiny, white.
HT: 2–15 in.

■ **MANY-FLOWER STICKSEED** (*Hackelia
floribunda*): Summer; woods, meadows,
thickets, disturbed places. Nutlets on
down-curved stalks; nutlets of this and
most *Hackelia* species have bristles
generally only on edges. Also called
Large-flower Stickseed.

■ **VIRGINIA STICKSEED** (*H. virginiana*):
Flowers tiny, white or pale blue. Bristles
also on the back of the nutlets.

NOTE Plants in the related genus *Lappula*
(not included), also called stickseed, are
similar but have leaflike bract below each
flower; fruit stalks not down-curved.

Genus *Hackelia* (29 native species).
Flowers small, in clusters; tubular below,
with 5 lobes, the opening (throat) mostly
closed by a ring of tiny, toothlike appendages. Nutlets
seedlike, with hook-tipped bristles.

Many-flower Stickseed

Flowers small, blue
with white-ringed
yellow eye.
HT: 1–4 ft.

Virginia Stickseed

Nutlets
bristly.
HT: 1–4 ft.

■ **COMMON CRYPTANTHA** (*Cryptantha intermedia*): Spring–summer; open slopes, dry ground. Leaves lack side veins. Many similar *Cryptantha* species, most with white flowers. Compare with *Plagiobothrys* species (below). Also called Clearwater Cat's-eye.

■ **PLATEAU YELLOW CRYPTANTHA** (*C. flava*): Open places. A yellow-flowered species. Also called Plateau Yellow Cat's-eye.

 Genus *Cryptantha* (115 native species). Plants bristly. Leaves narrow. Flowers small, in clusters; tubular below, with 5 lobes, the opening (throat) more or less closed by tiny, toothlike appendages. Nutlets seedlike, frequently with tiny bumps; attachment scar groovelike (sunken).

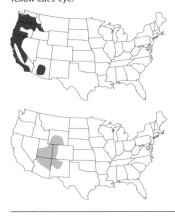

Common Cryptantha

Flowers small, white with yellow eye. HT: 4–20 in.

Plateau Yellow Cryptantha

HT: 6–16 in.

■ **COMMON POPCORN-FLOWER** (*Plagiobothrys nothofulvus*): Spring; grasslands, open woods, roadsides. Leaves purple-staining when crushed. Nutlets seedlike, gnarly. Also called Rusty Popcorn-flower.

NOTE The various types of nutlet surfaces are used to tell popcorn-flower species apart.

Genus *Plagiobothrys* (43 native species). Similar to *Cryptantha* (above), but the nutlet attachment scar is ridgelike, or raised (groovelike, or sunken, in *Cryptantha*).

Common Popcorn-flower

Flowers small, white with yellow eye. Leaves mostly in basal clusters. HT: 8–20 in.

■ **COMMON FIDDLENECK** (*Amsinckia menziesii* var. *intermedia*): Spring–summer; open places. Leaves lack side veins.

■ **MENZIES' FIDDLENECK** (*A. menziesii* var. *menziesii*): Similar to Common Fiddleneck, but flowers smaller and entirely pale yellow with no blotches.

NOTE There are several similar fiddleneck species that are difficult to tell apart.

Genus *Amsinckia* (10 native species). Plants bristly. Leaves narrow. Flowers small, in coiled, 1-sided clusters, uncoiling as they mature; trumpet-shaped and 5-lobed. Nutlets seedlike, with tiny bumps.

Common Fiddleneck

Flowers small, orange-yellow with 5 red-orange blotches. HT: 1–3 ft.

Menzies' Fiddleneck

HT: 6–30 in.

■ **HOARY PUCCOON** (*Lithospermum canescens*): Spring–summer; prairies, roadsides, open woods. Leaves soft-hairy. Also called Hoary Gromwell.

■ **NARROW-LEAF PUCCOON** (*L. incisum*): Similar to Hoary Puccoon, but lobes of flowers have jagged edges. Also called Fringed Gromwell.

■ **WESTERN PUCCOON** (*L. ruderale*): Plains, hillsides, open woods. Leaves many, narrow, short-hairy. Also called Western Stoneseed.

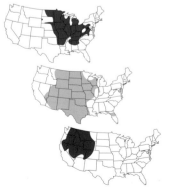

Genus *Lithospermum* (17 species, 16 native). Flowers in clusters, often occurring among leaflike bracts; funnel- or trumpet-shaped and 5-lobed. Nutlets seedlike.

Hoary Puccoon

Flowers orange-yellow. HT: 6–16 in.

Narrow-leaf Puccoon

Flower lobes toothed. HT: 4–12 in.

Western Puccoon

Flowers greenish yellow to yellow. HT: 8–24 in.

■ **SOFT-HAIR MARBLESEED**
(*Onosmodium bejariense*): Spring–
summer; prairies, open woods, roadsides.
Also called Western False Gromwell.

■ **VIRGINIA MARBLESEED**
(*O. virginianum*): Spring–summer;
woods. Tips of flowers long-tapering.
Also called Eastern False Gromwell.

RELATED ■ **GIANT-TRUMPETS**
(*Macromeria viridiflora*): Summer; rocky
slopes, valleys. Flowers long, with
spreading lobes; style and stamens
slightly protruding.

 Genus *Onosmodium* (4 native species).
Plants hairy. Flowers in coiled clusters,
uncoiling as they mature; tubular, with
5 erect lobes; style long-protruding. Nutlets seedlike,
whitish, smooth or pitted.

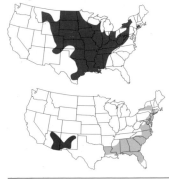

Soft-hair Marbleseed

Flowers in coiled clusters,
white with greenish tips.
HT: 1–4 ft.

Virginia Marbleseed

Tips
of flowers yellow
to orange. HT: 1–2 ft.

Giant-trumpets

Tips
of flowers
spreading.
HT: to 3 ft.

■ **VIRGINIA BLUEBELLS** (*Mertensia virginica*): Spring; woods, floodplains, stream banks. Flowers ¾–1 in. long. Also called Virginia-cowslip.

■ **STREAMSIDE BLUEBELLS** (*M. ciliata*): Summer; moist or wet places. Sepal edges fringed. Also called Fringed-lungwort. **SIMILAR LONG-FLOWER BLUEBELLS** (*M. longiflora*): Plains and hills; northwestern. Tube 2–3 times as long as expanded portion of flower. Also called Trumpet Bluebells.

ALPINE BLUEBELLS (*M. alpina*): Midsummer; higher elevations in middle Rocky Mountains. Flower tube short; flowers wider than long. Do not confuse with Mountain Forget-me-not (p. 158), which has hairy stems.

Genus *Mertensia* (21 native species).
Flowers in clusters; mostly funnel-shaped
and 5-lobed, often expanding abruptly
outward from narrower tube; bluish (or rarely whitish),
but often pink in bud. Nutlets generally wrinkled.

Virginia Bluebells

Flowers blue,
nodding.
HT: 1–2 ft.

Streamside Bluebells

HT: 1–4 ft.

Alpine Bluebells

HT: 4–12 in.

■ **WOODY CRINKLEMAT** (*Tiquilia canescens*): Spring–summer; open rocky areas. Stems have alternate branching pattern, become woody in age. Flowers mostly solitary. Also called Shrubby-coldenia.

■ **ROSETTE CRINKLEMAT** (*T. nuttallii*): Sandy places. Stems have opposite branching pattern, not woody. Flowers in clusters. Also called Nuttall's-coldenia.

Genus *Tiquilia* (9 native species). Sometimes shrubby; plants hairy, commonly mat- or clump-forming. Leaves small. Flowers small, solitary or clustered in leaf axils; broadly funnel-shaped and 5-lobed. Nutlets smooth or textured.

Woody Crinklemat

Flowers small; rose, pink, or white. Leaves lack side veins.

Rosette Crinklemat

Flowers tiny, pink to white. Leaves have side veins.

■ **SALT HELIOTROPE** (*Heliotropium curassavicum*): Spring–fall (year-round in frost-free areas); beaches, salty or alkaline places. Plants hairless. Leaves fleshy. Also called Seaside Heliotrope. See also **Ⅰ** Indian Heliotrope (p. 573).

OTHERS With leaves hairy; flowers white with yellow eye. ■ **SWEET-SCENTED HELIOTROPE** (*H. convolvulaceum*): Sandy soil. Stems erect or sprawling. Leaves egg-shaped to elliptic. Flowers in leaf axils, morning-glory-like. Also called Bindweed Heliotrope. ■ **PASTURE HELIOTROPE** (*H. tenellum*): Open woods, prairies, rocky ground. Stems erect. Leaves very slender. Flowers solitary, deeply 5-lobed. Also called Slender Heliotrope.

Genus *Heliotropium* (18 species, 15 native). Flowers commonly in coiled, 1-sided clusters that uncoil as they mature; sometimes solitary; funnel- to trumpet-shaped and 5-lobed. Nutlets smooth, textured, or hairy.

Salt Heliotrope

Flowers in coiled clusters; small, white with yellow to purplish eye. Usually trailing, sometimes erect. HT: 4–16 in.

Sweet-scented Heliotrope

HT: 5–15 in.

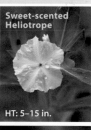

Pasture Heliotrope

HT: 4–16 in.

BRASSICACEAE or CRUCIFERAE   MUSTARD FAMILY

Annual, biennial, or perennial; rarely shrubby; plants exude watery, pungent sap. Leaves alternate or basal (basal sometimes withering early), or rarely opposite or whorled; simple or compound. Flowers typically in elongated clusters (racemes); petals 4, arranged diagonally ("crosswise"), their bases often narrowed ("clawed"); sepals 4; stamens typically 6 (usually 2 short, 4 long); pistil 1. Fruits are pods, commonly either long and thin (silique) or short and broad (silicle). A difficult family, with many look-alike genera and species; mature pods are often needed for identification. In addition, there are numerous widespread exotics.

FRUITS OF THE BRASSICACEAE

Measurements refer to length, except where indicated; they do not include stalks, which are quite long in some species.

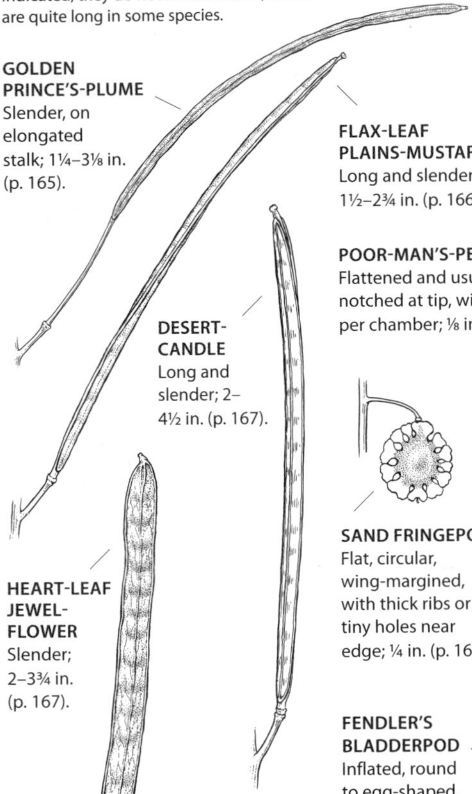

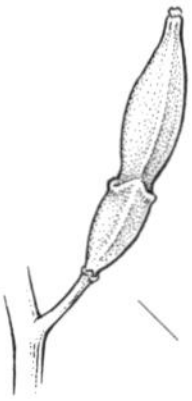

AMERICAN SEA-ROCKET
With 2 unlike segments: upper one larger, bulb-shaped, 1-seeded, detaching from plant at maturity; lower one cylindrical, seedless or 1-seeded, not detaching; ⅜–1¼ in. (p. 168).

GOLDEN PRINCE'S-PLUME
Slender, on elongated stalk; 1¼–3⅛ in. (p. 165).

FLAX-LEAF PLAINS-MUSTARD
Long and slender; 1½–2¾ in. (p. 166).

POOR-MAN'S-PEPPER
Flattened and usually notched at tip, with 1 seed per chamber; ⅛ in. (p. 168).

DESERT-CANDLE
Long and slender; 2–4½ in. (p. 167).

MOUNTAIN-CANDYTUFT
Flat, triangular to narrowly heart-shaped, winged or not; 3⁄16–⅜ in. (p. 169).

SAND FRINGEPOD
Flat, circular, wing-margined, with thick ribs or tiny holes near edge; ¼ in. (p. 169).

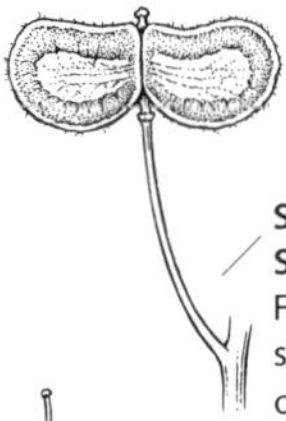

SOUTHWESTERN SPECTACLE-POD
Flat, shaped like spectacles, notched only below; ⅜–⅝ in. wide (p. 170).

HEART-LEAF JEWEL-FLOWER
Slender; 2–3¾ in. (p. 167).

FENDLER'S BLADDERPOD
Inflated, round to egg-shaped, tipped by persistent style; 3⁄16–5⁄16 in. (p. 171).

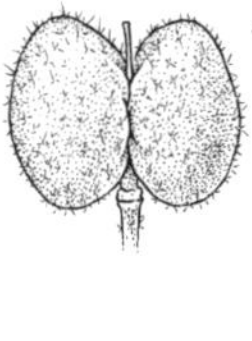

SHARP-LEAF TWINPOD
Inflated and 2-lobed; ¼–⅜ in. (p. 171).

BICOLORED FAN-MUSTARD
Slender; ½–1¼ in. (p. 170).

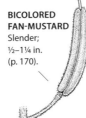

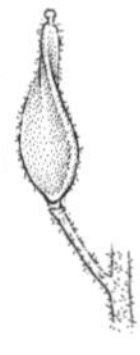

GOLDEN DRABA
Short; ⅜–½ in. (p. 171).

SCALEPOD
Nearly circular; ¼–⅜ in. (p. 171).

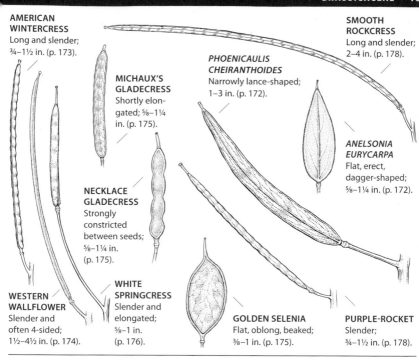

AMERICAN WINTERCRESS
Long and slender; ¾–1½ in. (p. 173).

MICHAUX'S GLADECRESS
Shortly elongated; ⅝–1¼ in. (p. 175).

PHOENICAULIS CHEIRANTHOIDES
Narrowly lance-shaped; 1–3 in. (p. 172).

SMOOTH ROCKCRESS
Long and slender; 2–4 in. (p. 178).

ANELSONIA EURYCARPA
Flat, erect, dagger-shaped; ⅝–1¼ in. (p. 172).

NECKLACE GLADECRESS
Strongly constricted between seeds; ⅝–1¼ in. (p. 175).

WESTERN WALLFLOWER
Slender and often 4-sided; 1½–4½ in. (p. 174).

WHITE SPRINGCRESS
Slender and elongated; ⅝–1 in. (p. 176).

GOLDEN SELENIA
Flat, oblong, beaked; ⅜–1 in. (p. 175).

PURPLE-ROCKET
Slender; ¾–1½ in. (p. 178).

■ **GOLDEN PRINCE'S-PLUME** (*Stanleya pinnata*): Spring–summer; slopes, plains, canyons, deserts. Lower leaves deeply pinnately lobed. Pods slender, stalked. Plants have woody base.

NOTE Some other species of prince's-plume have white flowers or unlobed leaves.

Genus *Stanleya* (7 native species). Leaves alternate, sometimes also basal. Flowers numerous, in long, showy clusters; stamens all of equal length, longer than petals. Pods slender, each on elongated stalk.

Golden Prince's-plume

Flowers yellow; stamens conspicuous. HT: 1½–5 ft.

■ **CUT-LEAF THELYPODY** (*Thelypodium laciniatum*): Spring–summer; rocky slopes, cliffs, outcrops. Lower leaves jagged-toothed to pinnately lobed. Flowers usually whitish, sometimes lavender; stamens conspicuous. **SIMILAR** ■ **WRIGHT'S THELYPODY** (*T. wrightii*): Stem leaves mostly untoothed.

■ **ENTIRE-LEAF THELYPODY** (*T. integrifolium*): Summer–fall; open places. Basal leaves long-stalked, spoon-shaped. Also called Tall Thelypody. **SIMILAR** ■ **CRISPED THELYPODY** (*T. crispum*): Summer; sandy places. Basal leaves often lobed; stem leaves arrowhead-shaped, clasping stem.

Genus *Thelypodium* (16 native species). Leaves basal (commonly withering early) and alternate. Flowers in mostly dense clusters, white to purplish (never yellow). Pods long, narrow, noticeably constricted between seeds, each often held on a shortly elongated stalk.

Cut-leaf Thelypody

Stem leaves stalked, typically irregularly toothed. HT: 1–4 ft.

Entire-leaf Thelypody

Stem leaves stalkless, untoothed. HT: 1½–5½ ft.

■ **FLAX-LEAF PLAINS-MUSTARD** (*Sisymbrium linifolium*): Spring–summer; slopes, plains, prairies. Leaves long, narrow, stalkless. Pods linear. Also called Salmon River Plains-mustard, Slender-leaf Plains-mustard.

OTHER GENUS ■ **SLIM-LEAF PLAINS-MUSTARD** (*Hesperidanthus linearifolius*): Summer–fall; rocky hillsides, open woods, shrublands. Leaves bluish. Inner 2 sepals have swollen base, outer 2 have "bump" near tip. Also called Pink-windmills.

Genus *Sisymbrium* (9 species, 1 native). Leaves alternate, lower ones often deeply lobed or divided. Flowers yellowish to whitish. Pods long, slender.

Flax-leaf Plains-mustard

Flowers yellow; petals not stalked. HT: 6–30 in.

Slim-leaf Plains-mustard

Flowers purplish; petals have stalklike base ("claw"). HT: 1–4 ft.

■ **DESERT-CANDLE** (*Caulanthus inflatus*): Spring; sandy plains, rocky slopes. Stem leaves stalkless, clasping. SIMILAR ■ **THICK-STEM WILD-CABBAGE** (*C. crassicaulis*): Stem leaves not clasping; basal leaves dandelion-like.

■ **HAIRY WILD-CABBAGE** (*C. pilosus*): Spring–summer; plains, open slopes. Stem leaves few, not clasping; basal leaves dandelion-like, often hairy. Also called Chocolate-drops.

Genus *Caulanthus* (17 native species). Leaves alternate and often basal. Petals whitish, purplish, or yellowish, often crinkled; sepals form a mostly urn- to vase-shaped calyx. Pods long, slender.

Desert-candle

Calyx dark purple in bud, becoming whitish below, not hairy. Stems yellowish green, inflated. HT: 1–2 ft.

Hairy Wild-cabbage

Calyx purple-brown, hairy. Stems not inflated. HT: 1–3 ft.

■ **HEART-LEAF JEWEL-FLOWER** (*Streptanthus cordatus*): Spring–summer; slopes, open woods, plains. Stem leaves clasping; bases heart-shaped. Uppermost leaves usually found only below flower clusters. SIMILAR ■ **MOUNTAIN JEWEL-FLOWER** (*S. tortuosus*): Uppermost leaves occur within lower portion of flower clusters, bractlike; sepal tips hairless. Also called Shieldleaf.

Genus *Streptanthus* (35 native species). Leaves alternate and basal; upper leaves usually clasping. Petals purplish to yellowish, often white-edged; sepals form an urn- or flask-shaped calyx, closed at start of flowering, often colored. Pods slender.

Heart-leaf Jewel-flower

Sepals purplish or purple-tinged, with tuft of hairs near tip. HT: 1–3 ft.

■ **AMERICAN SEA-ROCKET** (*Cakile edentula*): Spring–summer; sandy beaches. Leaves wavy-margined to sometimes deeply toothed. Pods distinctive, 2-segmented (see inset). SIMILAR ▣ **EUROPEAN SEA-ROCKET** (*C. maritima*): Chiefly Pacific Coast. Leaves pinnately lobed; pods have 2 hornlike projections on opposite sides near base. Also called Horned Sea-rocket.

Genus *Cakile* (5 species, 4 native). Plants succulent. Leaves alternate, wavy-margined to pinnately lobed. Pods of 2 unlike segments: upper one larger, bulb-shaped, 1-seeded, detaching from plant at maturity; lower one cylindrical, seedless or 1-seeded, not detaching.

American Sea-rocket

Flowers small, purplish to white. Plants fleshy. HT: 6–24 in.

■ **POOR-MAN'S-PEPPER** (*Lepidium virginicum*): Spring–fall; open places. Leaves toothed; basal leaves to 6 in. long. Also called Wild Peppergrass. See also ▣ Field Peppergrass, which has stem leaves with arrowhead-shaped base; ▣ Broad-leaf Pepperweed, with basal leaves to 12 in. (both on p. 575); ▣ Shepherd's-purse; and ▣ Field Pennycress (both on p. 574).

■ **YELLOW PEPPERGRASS** (*L. flavum*): Spring–summer; deserts. Larger leaves pinnately lobed. See also ▣ Shield Peppergrass (p. 575), which has upper leaves heart-shaped and clasping, basal leaves fernlike.

NOTE Species are also called pepperweed and pepperwort.

Genus *Lepidium* (42 species, 30 native). Leaves alternate and often also basal. Flowers white or occasionally yellow. Pods short, flattened, usually notched at tip; 1 seed per chamber (2–8 in *Noccaea*, p. 169).

Poor-man's-pepper

Flowers tiny, white. Pods tiny. HT: 6–24 in.

Yellow Peppergrass

Flowers tiny, yellow. Plants mat-forming.

■ **MOUNTAIN-CANDYTUFT** (*Noccaea fendleri*): Spring–summer; slopes, canyons, meadows. Pods flat, notched, tipped with persistent style. Also called Mountain-pennycress. See also Ⓘ Field Pennycress (p. 574).

OTHER GENUS ■ **FERN-LEAF FALSE CANDYTUFT** (*Smelowskia americana*): Flowers resemble those of Mountain-candytuft. Plants have many-branched hairs. Leaves pinnately lobed. Pods narrow. Also called Alpine Smelowskia.

 Genus *Noccaea* (3 native species). Leaves mostly basal; upper leaves have arrowhead-shaped base clasping stem. Flowers white, pinkish, or purplish. Pods flat, triangular to narrowly heart-shaped, winged or not.

Mountain-candytuft

Flowers white to pinkish purple. Leaves not hairy. HT: 2–16 in.

Fern-leaf False Candytuft

Leaves pinnate, gray-hairy. HT: 2–8 in.

■ **SAND FRINGEPOD** (*Thysanocarpus curvipes*): Spring; slopes, flats, meadows. Upper leaves clasping; bases arrowhead-shaped. Pods thin, wide. Also called Lacepod. **SIMILAR** ■ **MOUNTAIN FRINGEPOD** (*T. laciniatus*): Stem leaves have tapered, nonclasping base.

■ **RIBBED FRINGEPOD** (*T. radians*): Pods ⅜ in. wide. Also called Spoke-pod.

 Genus *Thysanocarpus* (4 native species). Leaves alternate and also often basal. Flowers small; petals white to purplish. Pods flat, circular, and wing-margined, with thick ribs or tiny holes near edge; 1-seeded; do not open.

Sand Fringepod

Pods round with scalloped edge, dangling from gently curving stalk. HT: 6 in.–3 ft.

Ribbed Fringepod

Pods have slender, spokelike ribs; stalks have sharp bend near tip. HT: 6–20 in.

■ **SOUTHWESTERN SPECTACLE-POD**
(*Dimorphocarpa wislizeni*): Spring–fall;
sandy soil. Leaves toothed to pinnately
lobed. Pods ½ in. wide, on stalk about
½ in. long. Also called Tourist-plant.

RELATED ■ **CALIFORNIA SPECTACLE-
POD** (*Dithyrea californica*): Flowers white
to pale lavender. Pods ⅜–½ in. wide, on
stalk ⅛ in. or shorter, notched above
and below.

Genus *Dimorphocarpa* (3 native species).
Plants have branched hairs. Leaves basal
and alternate. Flowers white or purple-
tinged. Pods flat, shaped like spectacles, notched below.

Southwestern
Spectacle-pod

California Spectacle-pod

Flowers
small, white.
Pods turned
upward at
end of stalk.
HT: 1–2 ft.

Pods not
upturned.
HT: 6–30 in.

■ **BICOLORED FAN-MUSTARD**
(*Nerisyrenia camporum*): Early spring–late
fall; hills, plains. Also called Mesa Greggia,
Velvety Nerisyrenia.

■ **WHITE SANDS FAN-MUSTARD**
(*N. linearifolia*): Spring–fall; flats, bluffs,
hills. Also called Narrow-leaf Greggia.

Genus *Nerisyrenia* (2 native species).
Leaves generally alternate. Flowers white
to lavender, showy. Pods slender.

Bicolored Fan-mustard

Leaves
spatula-
to lance-
shaped,
toothed.
HT: 6–24 in.

White Sands Fan-mustard

Leaves numerous,
narrow, untoothed.
HT: 6–18 in.

■ **FENDLER'S BLADDERPOD** (*Physaria fendleri*): Spring; rocky slopes, plains. Leaves mostly narrow. Pods smooth, on straight or curved stalk. Many similar species.

■ **WESTERN BLADDERPOD** (*P. occidentalis*): Slopes. Leaves spoon-shaped. Pods hairy, somewhat flattened, on S-shaped stalk.

NOTE Some species, commonly called twinpod, have inflated, deeply notched (2-lobed) pods. Photo shows Sharp-leaf Twinpod (*P. acutifolia*).

Genus *Physaria* (about 100 native species). Leaves alternate and basal, with branched, star-shaped hairs sometimes resembling silvery scales. Flowers generally yellow, may be whitish or purplish. Pods often inflated, round or egg-shaped, sometimes 2-lobed, tipped by persistent style.

Fendler's Bladderpod
Flowers yellow.
HT: 2–12 in.

Western Bladderpod
HT: 2–6 in.

Twinpod

■ **GOLDEN DRABA** (*Draba aurea*): Summer; rocky slopes and mountain meadows. Stem leaves often egg-shaped; basal leaves spoon-shaped. **SIMILAR** ■ **LEMMON'S DRABA** (*D. lemmonii*): Leaves all basal.

■ **LANCE-POD DRABA** (*D. lonchocarpa*): Summer; rocky slopes. Leaves all basal.

OTHER GENUS SCALEPOD (*Idahoa scapigera*, no photo): Spring; rocky and gravelly places; chiefly northwestern. Leaves basal. Flowers solitary, white. Pods nearly circular. Also called Flatpod.

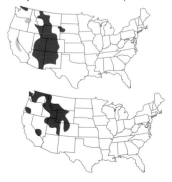

Genus *Draba* (104 species, 103 native). Plants commonly have branched hairs. Leaves mostly in tufts at plant base; stem leaves absent or alternate. Flowers tiny, in elongated clusters, yellow or white. Pods short, hairless to densely hairy, sometimes twisted.

Golden Draba
Flowers yellow.
HT: 3–16 in.

Lance-pod Draba
Flowers white.
HT: 1–5 in.

■ **WEDGE-LEAF DRABA** (*Draba cuneifolia*): Spring; mostly open places. Leaves stiff-hairy, with wedge-shaped base and frequently a few large teeth. Pods ¼–⅜ in. long, minutely hairy.

■ **SHORT-POD DRABA** (*D. brachycarpa*): Leaves fine-hairy. Pods ¹⁄₁₆–³⁄₁₆ in. long, not hairy.

NOTE See also ① Early Whitlow-grass (p. 574), which has flowers with deeply notched petals.

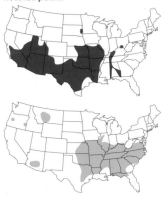

Wedge-leaf Draba

Short-pod Draba

Flowers white. Leaves usually on lower third of stem. HT: 3–10 in.

Upper stem leaves narrower than basal leaves. HT: 2–8 in.

■ **DAGGERPOD** (*Phoenicaulis cheiranthoides*): Spring–early summer; slopes, stony flats, plains. Pods horizontal on stem. Also called Wallflower Phoenicaulis, False Daggerpod (to distinguish it from *Anelsonia*, below).

RELATED ■ **DAGGERPOD** (*Anelsonia eurycarpa*): Summer; slopes, ridges. Dwarf alpine plant with flat, erect, dagger-shaped pods.

Genus *Phoenicaulis* (1 native species). Leaves mostly basal, lance- to spoon-shaped. Flowers showy. Pods narrowly lance-shaped.

Daggerpod (*Phoenicaulis cheiranthoides*)

Flowers pink to red-purple. Leaves softly gray-hairy. HT: 2–8 in.

Daggerpod (*Anelsonia eurycarpa*)

HT: to 2 in.

■ **WESTERN TANSY-MUSTARD**
(*Descurainia pinnata*): Spring; open woods, shrublands, plains, slopes. Variable, with several subspecies. Leaves and stems generally hairy. Pods ³⁄₁₆–½ in. long, on spreading stalk. SIMILAR ■ **SIERRAN TANSY-MUSTARD** (*D. californica*): Summer. Pods ³⁄₁₆ in. or shorter. ■ **MOUNTAIN TANSY-MUSTARD** (*D. incana*): Summer. Pods ³⁄₁₆–³⁄₈ in., on erect stalk often held close to plant. Also called Richardson's Tansy-mustard.

NOTE See also Ⅱ Flixweed (p. 575), which has pods ½–1 in. long.

Genus *Descurainia* (8 species, 7 native). Plants commonly have branched hairs. Leaves alternate and basal, normally divided into many small segments. Flowers yellow or whitish. Pods short to elongated.

Western Tansy-mustard

Flowers small, bright yellow to cream-colored. Leaves lacy or fernlike. Pods on slender stalk. HT: 6–30 in.

■ **AMERICAN WINTERCRESS** (*Barbarea orthoceras*): Spring–summer; moist meadows, woods, stream banks. Basal leaves typically have 2–4 pairs of side lobes; often some upper stem leaves are deeply pinnately lobed. Pods slender. Also called American Yellow-rocket. See also Ⅱ Common Wintercress (p. 575), introduced from Europe, with basal leaves having 1–4 pairs of side lobes, upper stem leaves not deeply pinnately lobed.

OTHERS Also introduced from Europe. Ⅱ **EARLY WINTERCRESS** (*B. verna*, no photo): Disturbed places; mostly eastern and western. Basal leaves have 4–10 pairs of side lobes.

Genus *Barbarea* (4 species, 1 native). Leaves alternate and basal; pinnate, with 1 large, round end lobe, 2 to several pairs of smaller side lobes. Flowers yellow. Pods long, slender.

American Wintercress

Flowers small, yellow. Leaves have 1 large end lobe, smaller, narrower side lobes. HT: 6–30 in.

■ **WESTERN WALLFLOWER** (*Erysimum capitatum*): Spring–summer; rocky slopes, open woods, prairies, deserts. Petals ½–1 in. long. Pods mostly upright.
SIMILAR ■ **PRAIRIE WALLFLOWER** (*E. asperum*): Pods spreading, their sides ribbed and with the surface alternating densely hairy and lightly hairy (giving "striped" appearance).

OTHERS Smaller-flowered, widespread Eurasian species, also called treacle mustard (no photos). ⊡ **WORMSEED WALLFLOWER** (*E. cheiranthoides*): Leaves untoothed or shallowly toothed. Petals ⅛–³⁄₁₆ in. long. ⊡ **SPREADING WALLFLOWER** (*E. repandum*): Leaves distinctly wavy-toothed. Petals ¼–⁵⁄₁₆ in.

Genus *Erysimum* (19 species, 15 native). Leaves alternate and also often basal. Flowers in crowded clusters that elongate in age. Pods slender, often 4-sided.

Western Wallflower

Flowers usually yellow, sometimes orange. Leaves narrow. HT: 6 in.–3 ft.

■ **COMMON YELLOWCRESS** (*Rorippa palustris*): Summer; muddy shores, marshy ground, shallow water. Stems unbranched toward base. Lower leaves (see inset) pinnately lobed. Petals about as long as sepals. Pods on slender stalk. Also called Bog Yellowcress, Marsh Yellowcress.

■ **CURVE-POD YELLOWCRESS** (*R. curvisiliqua*): One of several species with stems branching from the base.

⊡ **CREEPING YELLOWCRESS** (*R. sylvestris*, no photo): Widespread species from Europe. All leaves deeply pinnately lobed. Petals distinctly longer than sepals.

Genus *Rorippa* (20 species, 15 native). Leaves alternate and sometimes also basal, toothed to pinnately lobed. Flowers tiny or small, usually yellow. Pods commonly plump.

Common Yellowcress

Flowers yellow. Pods sausage-shaped, on slender stalk. HT: 1–3 ft.

Curve-pod Yellowcress

Pods curved. HT: 10–20 in.

■ **GOLDEN SELENIA** (*Selenia aurea*):
Spring; rocky prairies and glades, fields,
pastures, road banks. Both stem leaves
and basal leaves present; leaves deeply
pinnately cut into narrow segments.
Petals and mature sepals yellow.

■ **TEXAS SELENIA** (*S. dissecta*): Late
winter–spring; hills, shrublands, flats,
roadsides. Leaves in basal cluster, fernlike,
twice pinnately divided into small lobes.
Pods fleshy at maturity.

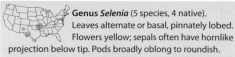

Genus *Selenia* (5 species, 4 native).
Leaves alternate or basal, pinnately lobed.
Flowers yellow; sepals often have hornlike
projection below tip. Pods broadly oblong to roundish.

Flowers
bright yellow.
HT: 2–8 in.

Golden
Selenia

Texas Selenia

HT: to 5 in.

■ **MICHAUX'S GLADECRESS**
(*Leavenworthia uniflora*): Late winter–
midspring; limestone cedar glades, wet
fields, ditches, roadsides. Petals ¼ in. long.
The only gladecress without notched
petals. Also called Small Gladecress.

■ **NECKLACE GLADECRESS** (*L. torulosa*):
Petals ¼–⅜ in. long, notched at tip.
Pods strongly constricted between seeds.
Also called Beaded Gladecress. **SIMILAR**
But without pronounced necklacelike
pods. **LONG-STYLE GLADECRESS**
(*L. stylosa*): Central TN. Flowers larger, with
petals ⅜–⅝ in. long; pods fleshy. Also
called Cedar Gladecress. **TENNESSEE
GLADECRESS** (*L. exigua*): KY to AL.
Flowers rarely entirely yellow; pods
distinctly flattened. Also called Pasture
Gladecress.

Genus *Leavenworthia* (8 native species).
Leaves in basal clusters, deeply pinnately
lobed (but earliest leaves often unlobed).
Flowers white, lavender, or yellow, on long stalks. Pods
sometimes elongated.

Michaux's Gladecress

Necklace Gladecress

Flowers white
with yellow eye.
HT: 2–4 in.

Flowers
white or pale
lavender, with
yellow eye; petals
notched. HT: 2–6 in.

■ **WHITE SPRINGCRESS** (*Cardamine bulbosa*): Spring; moist or wet places. Flowers white (rarely pink-tinged). Also called Bulbous Bittercress.

■ **PINK SPRINGCRESS** (*C. douglassii*): Spring. Similar to White Springcress, but flowers mostly pink to purple. Also called Limestone Bittercress.

■ **LARGE MOUNTAIN BITTERCRESS** (*C. cordifolia*): Summer. Leaves round to kidney-shaped. Flowers white. Heartleaf Bittercress and Lyall's Bittercress are varieties.

Genus *Cardamine* (34 species, 31 native). Leaves alternate, opposite, whorled, or basal. Flowers white, pink, or purple. Pods slender, elongated, opening by each of the 2 sides coiling upward from the base, sometimes explosively.

White Springcress

Pink Springcress

Petals pinkish; sepals purple. HT: 4–12 in.

Stem leaves stalkless, lance-shaped; basal leaves long-stalked, round. HT: 8–20 in.

Large Mountain Bittercress

Stem leaves round. HT: 8–24 in.

■ **PENNSYLVANIA BITTERCRESS** (*Cardamine pensylvanica*): Spring–summer; moist or wet places. **SIMILAR** With most leaves in a conspicuous basal cluster, few on stems. ■ **LITTLE WESTERN BITTERCRESS** (*C. oligosperma*). ⊡ **HAIRY BITTERCRESS** (*C. hirsuta*): Mostly eastern; Eurasian introduction.

Pennsylvania Bittercress

Flowers tiny, white. Leaves pinnate, with end segment large, side leaflets narrow. Basal leaves few. HT: 6–24 in.

■ **CUT-LEAF TOOTHWORT** (*Cardamine concatenata*): Spring; woods.

■ **TWO-LEAF TOOTHWORT** (*C. diphylla*): Spring; woods. Stem leaves 2, nearly opposite, each with 3 broad, toothed leaflets. Also called Broad-leaf Toothwort, Crinkleroot.

■ **CALIFORNIA TOOTHWORT** (*C. californica*): Late winter–spring; woods, slopes, fields. Stem leaves alternate, with 3 (or 5) leaflets; basal leaves round or divided into 3 leaflets. Also called Milkmaids.

NOTE See also Slender and Dissected Toothworts (below).

Cut-leaf Toothwort

Flowers white to purplish. Typically a whorl of 3 stem leaves, each deeply divided into toothed segments. HT: 8–16 in.

Two-leaf Toothwort

HT: 8–16 in.

California Toothwort

HT: 8–24 in.

■ **SLENDER TOOTHWORT** (*Cardamine angustata*): Spring; woods, wooded rocky hillsides, floodplains, stream banks. Stem leaves 2, each with 3 narrow, toothed leaflets; basal leaves have broad leaflets (in foreground of photo). Do not confuse with Two-leaf Toothwort (above), which has stem and basal leaflets similar in shape.

■ **DISSECTED TOOTHWORT** (*C. dissecta*): Woods. Stem leaves 2; stem and basal leaves dissected into narrow segments. Do not confuse with Cut-leaf Toothwort (above), which has upper stems hairy (hairless in Dissected Toothwort), leaves whorled. Also called Fork-leaf Toothwort.

Slender Toothwort

Flowers pale pink-lavender to whitish. HT: 8–16 in.

Dissected Toothwort

Flowers white to pale pink. HT: 8–16 in.

■ **PURPLE-ROCKET** (*Iodanthus pinnatifidus*): Spring; moist or wet woods, thickets. Stems and leaves usually hairless. Upper leaves sometimes clasping stem, lower stem leaves sometimes have pinnately lobed base. Flowers commonly pinkish or purple, ¼–⅜ in. across. Pods ¾–1½ in. long. Do not confuse with ① Dame's-rocket (p. 576), which has stems and leaves fine-hairy; flowers ¾–1 in. across; fruits ½–4 in. long.

Genus *Iodanthus* (1 native species). Leaves alternate, typically conspicuously toothed or partly pinnately lobed. Flowers purplish to almost white. Pods slender.

Purple-rocket

Flowers sometimes nearly white. Leaves sharply and unequally toothed. HT: 1–3 ft.

ROCKCRESSES

■ **SMOOTH ROCKCRESS** (*Boechera laevigata*): Spring–summer; woods, rocky hillsides. Leaves hairless. Flowers small, white. Pods often curved, spreading.

■ **SICKLEPOD** (*B. canadensis*): Upper leaves often hairless, lower leaves hairy. Pods curved, downturned. Also called Sicklepod Rockcress.

Rockcresses (several genera traditionally included in *Arabis*; more than 100 native species). Basal leaves generally stalked; stem leaves stalkless and often clasping, commonly with arrowhead-shaped base. Flowers white, pink, or purple. Pods long, slender.

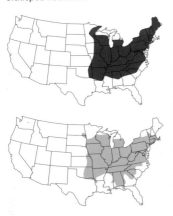

Smooth Rockcress

Leaf bases clasp stem. HT: 1–3 ft.

Sicklepod

Leaf bases do not clasp stem. HT: 1–3 ft.

ROCKCRESSES

■ **HOLBOELL'S ROCKCRESS** (*Boechera retrofracta*): Spring–summer; rocky slopes, gravelly places, open woods. Stem leaves many, conspicuous, hairy; bases clasp stem. Flowers rarely white. Pods down-curved, straight or slightly curved.

■ **DRUMMOND'S ROCKCRESS** (*B. stricta*): Leaves sometimes hairy; stem leaf bases clasp stem. Flowers pale lavender, pink, or white. Pods erect. Also called Canadian Rockcress.

■ **SMALL-LEAF ROCKCRESS** (*B. microphylla*): Most leaves basal; stem leaf bases clasp stem. Pods spreading or nearly erect.

Holboell's Rockcress

Flowers usually purple-pink. HT: 6 in.–3 ft.

Small-leaf Rockcress

Stem leaves few. HT: 1–3 ft.

Drummond's Rockcress

Stem leaves mostly hairless. HT: 1–3 ft.

ROCKCRESSES

■ **HAIRY ROCKCRESS** (*Arabis pycnocarpa*): Summer; open woods, ledges, meadows, stream banks. Stems and lower leaves hairy. Stem leaves clasping or not. Mature pods flattened in cross section. Westernmost populations may have stems hairy only near base; petals pinkish.

■ **TOWER-MUSTARD** (*Turritis glabra*): Spring–summer; open woods, fields, thickets, rocky outcrops. Lower stems and lower leaves hairy. Stem leaves strongly clasping. Pods straight, erect, roundish or 4-angled in cross section. Some authors believe this species was introduced into North America. Also called Tower Rockcress.

Hairy Rockcress

Flowers usually white. Pods short, straight, erect. HT: 1–2½ ft.

Tower-mustard

Flowers pale yellow to cream-colored. HT: 1–5 ft.

ROCKCRESSES

■ **LYRE-LEAF ROCKCRESS** (*Arabidopsis lyrata*): Spring–summer; open woods, fields, sandy soil. Plants commonly hairy on lower half. Stem leaf bases do not clasp stem. Petals ¼–⁵⁄₁₆ in. long. **SIMILAR** ⊞ **MOUSE-EAR CRESS** (*A. thaliana*): Spring; disturbed places; widespread Eurasian species. Basal leaves untoothed or toothed; petals small (³⁄₁₆ in. long).

Lyre-leaf Rockcress

Basal leaves often pinnately lobed, with end lobe largest.

Flowers white. Stem leaves narrow. HT: 4–16 in.

Pods slender.

BROMELIACEAE
BROMELIAD or PINEAPPLE FAMILY

Perennial. Most are epiphytes ("air plants"), growing on trees but obtaining moisture and minerals from rainwater. Leaves linear, usually in vase-shaped clusters at plant base. Flowers often found among colorful bracts, usually arranged in spikelike clusters; petals 3; sepals 3; stamens 6; pistil 1. Fruits are berries or capsules.

■ **CARDINAL AIRPLANT** (*Tillandsia fasciculata*): Spring–summer. Leaves in a basal cluster, tapering,10–20 in. long, 1 in. wide. Also called Quill-leaf Airplant.

▪ **SPANISH-MOSS** (*T. usneoides*): Stems wiry, curled, dangling. Leaves to about 1½ in. long, ¹⁄₁₆ in. wide. Flowers greenish.

■ **BALL-MOSS** (*T. recurvata*): Plants form dense clusters to about 6 in. across. Flowers small, purple.

NOTE Cardinal Airplant is a typical bromeliad, Spanish-moss is unusual; not true mosses.

Genus *Tillandsia* (13 native species). Plants grow on tree trunks and branches. Fruits are capsules.

Cardinal Airplant

Flowers purple, among colorful, often red and yellow-green bracts.

Spanish-moss

Stems and leaves silvery gray.

Ball-moss

Plants in ball-shaped clusters.

BURMANNIACEAE — BURMANNIA or BLUETHREAD FAMILY

Annual or perennial. Stems threadlike. Leaves alternate, commonly scalelike or sometimes absent. Flowers solitary or in clusters; tubular and 3- or 6-lobed at tip; petals and sepals alike (and called tepals), 3 each; stamens 3 or 6; pistil 1. Fruits are capsules.

■ **SOUTHERN BLUETHREAD** (*Burmannia capitata*): Late summer–fall; pond margins, wet woods, bogs, ditches. Stems green, wiry. Leaves scalelike. Flowers 3-ribbed, essentially stalkless, sometimes pale blue-tinged.

■ **NORTHERN BLUETHREAD** (*B. biflora*): Flowers 3-winged, some on short stalks.

RELATED ■ **NODDING NIXIE** (*Apteria aphylla*): Moist woods, hammocks, bog edges. Stems purplish. Leaves tiny, scalelike. Flowers long-stalked; tube rounded.

Genus *Burmannia* (3 native species). With characters of the family. Flower tube ribbed or winged; stamens 3.

Southern Bluethread

Flowers small, whitish, clustered at stem ends. HT: 2–8 in.

Northern Bluethread

Flowers violet. HT: 2–6 in.

Nodding Nixie

Flowers bluish purple to whitish. HT: 2–9 in.

BUXACEAE — BOXWOOD FAMILY

Woody plants or, infrequently, perennial herbs. Leaves opposite or less often alternate; simple. Flowers in clusters, unisexual (male and female flowers normally on same individual plant); petals absent; sepals mostly 4–7; stamens typically 4; pistil 1. Fruits are generally capsules.

■ **ALLEGHENY PACHYSANDRA** (*Pachysandra procumbens*): Spring; woods. Leaves coarsely toothed along upper half. Flower clusters arise from near stem base; consist primarily of male flowers, with few female flowers located near bottom. Also called Allegheny-spurge, Allegheny Mountain-spurge.

Genus *Pachysandra* (2 species, 1 native). With characters of the family. Plants somewhat shrubby. Leaves alternate.

Allegheny Pachysandra

Flowers whitish or pink-tinged, in elongated clusters. Leaves crowded, often mottled. HT: 5–16 in.

CACTACEAE

CACTUS FAMILY

Perennial; succulent. Stems swollen, fleshy, bearing spines from specialized areas (areoles). Leaves typically absent. Flowers solitary; sepals, petals, and stamens many; pistil 1. Fruits mostly fleshy. Cactuses grow chiefly in warm regions and in North America are most abundant in arid parts of the Southwest.

CACTUSES

■ **CHOLLA** (*Cylindropuntia*; 21 native species): Mostly spring–early summer, occasionally fall; open places.

▇ **PRICKLY-PEAR** (*Opuntia*; 41 species, 39 native).

NOTE These are jointed, branched cactuses with yellowish, pink, or red flowers arising from joints of the previous season. In addition to spines, the areoles bear tiny barbed bristles (glochids) that readily detach and penetrate the skin.

Cactuses (several related genera, numerous species). Plants fleshy-stemmed, typically leafless. Flowers showy, with a gradual transition from sepals to petals. (Maps show genus distributions.)

Cholla

Prickly-pear

Branch segments cylindrical. HT: mostly 1–9 ft.

Branch segments flattened. HT: mostly 6 in.–6 ft.

CACTUSES

■ **BARREL CACTUS** (*Ferocactus*; 6 native species): Spring–summer, occasionally fall; open places. Plants ball- to cylinder-shaped, unbranched; sides prominently vertically ribbed. Flowers mostly yellow to reddish, arise from new growth near stem tip; outer sepals not spiny.

▇ **COTTON-TOP CACTUS** (*Echinocactus*; 3 native species): Outer sepals spine-tipped. Also sometimes called barrel cactus.

Barrel Cactus

Areoles and fruits not woolly. HT: mostly 6 in.–5 ft.

Cotton-top Cactus

Areoles and fruits have woolly hairs. HT: mostly 6–24 in.

CACTUSES

■ **HEDGEHOG CACTUS** (*Echinocereus*; 26 native species): Mostly spring–early summer; open places. Plants soft-bodied, usually clump-forming; often pickle-shaped, with ribs made of closely placed "bumps" (tubercles). Flowers mostly pink, magenta, or red, occasionally yellow; stigma lobes green; arise from old growth on sides of plant. Fruits spiny.

Hedgehog Cactus

HT: mostly 6–24 in.

CACTUSES

■ **NIPPLE CACTUS** (*Mammillaria*; 12 native species): Spring–summer; open places. Plants small, ball- to cylinder-shaped; surface covered by spirally arranged "bumps" (tubercles). Flowers variously colored, arise from axils of tubercles (not from the spine-bearing areoles, as in other cactuses). Species with some spines hooked at the tip are sometimes called **FISHHOOK CACTUS**.

Nipple Cactus

Flowers often in rings. HT: 1–4 in., rarely to 12 in.

Fishhook Cactus

Flowers on old growth, not plant tip.

CACTUSES

■ **BALL CACTUS** (*Pediocactus*; 8 native species): Spring–early summer; open places. Plants small, ball-shaped; surface covered by spirally arranged "bumps" (tubercles). Flowers commonly pink, white, or yellow; arise from new growth near plant tip.

Ball Cactus

Yellow-flowered form.
HT: mostly to 8 in.

Magenta-flowered form.

CAMPANULACEAE   BELLFLOWER FAMILY

Annual, biennial, or perennial; some have milky sap. Leaves simple and mostly alternate. Flowers solitary or in clusters, 5-lobed (petals united), sometimes 2-lipped; sepals 5; stamens 5, in a ring around pistil, often united in 2-lipped flowers. Fruits are usually capsules.

■ **HAREBELL** (*Campanula rotundifolia*): Summer; woods, meadows, cliffs, dunes. Flowers lobed up to ⅓ way to base. Also called Bluebells-of-Scotland. **SIMILAR PARRY'S BELLFLOWER** (*C. parryi*): Slopes, stream banks, meadows; Rocky Mountains. Flowers lobed halfway to base.

■ **SOUTHERN HAREBELL** (*C. divaricata*), woods, slopes, and ■ **SCOULER'S HAREBELL** (*C. scouleri*), woods, also called Pale Bellflower, have flower lobes curved backward, style protruding.

NOTE See also ⬆ Creeping Bellflower (p. 576).

Genus *Campanula* (27 species, 21 native). Flowers bell- to funnel-shaped and 5-lobed.

Harebell

Flowers blue.
Stem leaves narrow.
Basal leaves (sometimes absent)
long-stalked, round. HT: 6–24 in.

Southern Harebell

HT: 6–30 in.

Scouler's Harebell

HT: 8–16 in.

■ **ARCTIC BELLFLOWER** (*Campanula uniflora*): Summer; high mountain slopes, tundra. Flowers narrowly bell-shaped. Also called Arctic Harebell.

■ **ROUGH BELLFLOWER** (*C. scabrella*): High slopes. Leaves have stiff hairs. Also called Rough Harebell. **SIMILAR OLYMPIC BELLFLOWER** (*C. piperi*): Olympic Mountains (northwestern WA): Leaves hairless, sharply toothed; flowers larger.

■ **MARSH BELLFLOWER** (*C. aparinoides*): Wet places. Leaves very narrow. Also called Bedstraw Bellflower.

■ **FLORIDA BELLFLOWER** (*C. floridana*): Wet places. Flowers have narrow lobes. Also called Florida Bluebell.

Arctic Bellflower

Flowers small, blue to purplish. HT: 2–16 in.

Rough Bellflower

Flowers small, pale to dark blue. HT: 1½–5 in.

Marsh Bellflower

Flowers small, pale blue to whitish. HT: 8–24 in.

Florida Bellflower

Flowers purplish, star-shaped. HT: 8–16 in.

OTHER BELLFLOWERS

■ **TALL BELLFLOWER** (*Campanulastrum americanum*): Summer–fall; open areas in woods, moist thickets. Leaves stalked. Flowers mostly stalkless; style curves downward, then up at tip. Also called American Bellflower.

■ **CALIFORNIA HAREBELL** (*Asyneuma prenanthoides*): Open woods. Leaves nearly stalkless. Flowers stalked. Also called California Bluebell. The similar Scouler's Harebell (p. 184) has leaves stalked; flowers with wider lobes.

Tall Bellflower

Flowers light blue to violet, with white eye; star-shaped; style protruding. HT: 1½–6 ft.

California Harebell

Flowers bright blue; lobes narrow; style protruding. HT: 6 in.–3 ft.

■ WESTERN PEARL-FLOWER
(*Heterocodon rariflorum*): Spring–summer;
moist meadows, seeps, vernal pools.
Flowers ¼ in. long or smaller. Also called
Rareflower Heterocodon.

Genus *Heterocodon* (1 native species).
Stems 4-angled. Flowers solitary in
axils of upper leaves, cylindrical-bell-
shaped, stalkless.

Western Pearl-flower

Flowers very small, bluish.
Leaves and bracts roundish,
sharply toothed. HT: 2–12 in.

■ VENUS'-LOOKING-GLASS (*Triodanis
perfoliata*): Spring–summer; various, often
disturbed sites.

**■ NARROW-LEAF VENUS'-LOOKING-
GLASS** (*T. leptocarpa*): Prairies, plains, hills.
Leaflike bracts beneath flowers narrowly
lance-shaped or linear. Also called Slim-
pod Venus'-looking-glass.

RELATED **■ COMMON BLUECUP**
(*Githopsis specularioides*): Open places.
Flowers small, often shorter than sepals;
not in axils of large bracts.

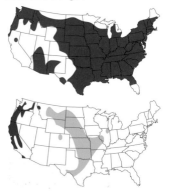

Genus *Triodanis* (7 native species). Stems
angled. Leaves mostly stalkless. Flowers
in axils of leaflike bracts, star-shaped.

Venus'-
looking-
glass

Flowers blue-
violet to violet.
Leaves and
bracts round to
heart-shaped,
clasping stem.
HT: 6 in.–3 ft.

Narrow-leaf
Venus'-
looking-
glass

HT: 6–
30 in.

Common Bluecup

HT: 2–12 in.

- **GREAT BLUE LOBELIA** (*Lobelia siphilitica*): Summer–fall; moist or wet places. Stems smooth to sparsely hairy. Conspicuous earlobelike projections at base of sepals, to ³⁄₁₆ in. long. **SIMILAR**
- **DOWNY LOBELIA** (*L. puberula*): Stems usually fine-hairy throughout; projections at base of sepals inconspicuous.

- **CARDINAL-FLOWER** (*L. cardinalis*): Also called Scarlet Lobelia.

NOTE Some *Lobelia* species are poisonous.

Genus *Lobelia* (25 native species). Flowers 2-lipped; stamens fused into a column, often protruding from split in top of flower tube; *L. siphilitica* and *L. cardinalis* also have windowlike slits along each side of flower tube near base.

Great Blue Lobelia

Cardinal-flower

Flowers large, blue, pale-striped; 2 white bumps on lower lip. HT: 1–4 ft.

Flowers large, scarlet. HT: 1½–5 ft.

- **SPIKE LOBELIA** (*Lobelia spicata*): Spring–summer; various sites. Also called Pale-spike Lobelia.

INDIAN-TOBACCO (*L. inflata*): Summer–fall; various sites; eastern. Weedy. Mature capsules inflated.

- **KALM'S LOBELIA** (*L. kalmii*): Summer–fall; shores, marshes, swamps. Also called Brook Lobelia.

- **WATER LOBELIA** (*L. dortmanna*): Summer–fall; shallow water. Tubular, outcurved leaves clustered at plant base.

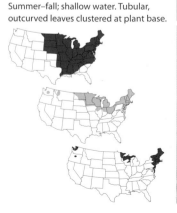

Spike Lobelia

Indian-tobacco

Flowers light blue to whitish. HT: 1–3 ft.

Capsules swollen. HT: 8–32 in.

Kalm's Lobelia

Water Lobelia

Flowers pale blue with white center. HT: 6–24 in.

No stem leaves. HT: 6–30 in.

■ **ELEGANT DOWNINGIA** (*Downingia elegans*): Spring–summer; vernal pools, wet areas. Stamen tube protruding, bent.

■ **BACIGALUPI'S DOWNINGIA** (*D. bacigalupii*), also called Bach's Downingia, and ■ **CUPPED DOWNINGIA** (*D. insignis*), also called Harlequin Downingia, are similar to Elegant Downingia.

■ **TOOTHED DOWNINGIA** (*D. cuspidata*): No protruding stamen tube.

RELATED PORTER-PLANT (*Porterella carnosula*, no photo): Western. Flowers stalked, ovary short.

NOTE Species are also called calico-flower.

Genus *Downingia* (13 native species). Leaves stalkless, untoothed. Flowers 2-lipped, bluish or purplish, stalkless (but ovary elongated, stalklike); stamens fused into a column.

Elegant Downingia
Petals have white patch. HT: 4–16 in.

Bacigalupi's Downingia
Orange-yellow spots on patch. HT: 2–12 in.

Cupped Downingia
Yellowish green spots and purple band on patch. HT: 4–10 in.

Toothed Downingia
Yellow spot on patch. HT: 2–6 in.

■ **GLANDULAR THREADPLANT** (*Nemacladus glanduliferus*): Spring; sandy places, washes, gravelly slopes. Flowers ⅛ in. or less across. Also called Redtip Threadstem.

NOTE Some threadplants have flowers with 5 more or less equal lobes.

Genus *Nemacladus* (13 native species). Stems threadlike. Leaves clustered at plant base. Flowers mostly 2-lipped, on wiry stalks.

Glandular Threadplant
Flowers tiny, whitish; upper 3 lobes have reddish tip. Stems zigzag. HT: 2–10 in.

CANNACEAE
CANNA FAMILY

Perennial. Leaves alternate, simple, and untoothed. Flowers in clusters; petals and sepals each 3; showy parts of flowers are the much-enlarged, petal-like stamens (all but 1 sterile), one bent down forming a lip; pistil 1. Fruits are warty capsules.

■ **GOLDEN CANNA** (*Canna flaccida*): Spring–summer; wetlands. Leaves to 2 ft. long. Flowers up to 4 per cluster; petals narrowly lance-shaped, sepal-like, bent downward. Also called Bandana-of-the-Everglades. **SIMILAR** ■ **LOUISIANA CANNA** (*C. glauca*): Flowers 10 or more per cluster; petals erect.

Genus *Canna* (4 species, 2 native). With characters of the family. Leaves have conspicuous veins.

Golden Canna
Flowers large, yellow.
Leaves long. HT: to 4 ft.

CAPPARACEAE
CAPER FAMILY

Annual (most North American species) or perennial herbs or woody shrubs. Leaves alternate; simple to more often palmately compound. Flowers usually in clusters; petals 4; sepals 4; stamens 6 to many, usually conspicuous; pistil 1, commonly on a stalk and held among stamens. Fruits generally podlike.

■ **YELLOW BEE-PLANT** (*Cleome lutea*): Spring–summer; open places. Pods ⅝–1½ in. long. Also called Yellow Spider-flower.

■ **ROCKY MOUNTAIN BEE-PLANT** (*C. serrulata*): Spring–summer.

RELATED With yellow flowers (no photos). **STINKWEEDS** (*Cleomella*): Western. Pods small, as wide as or wider than long. **SPECTACLE-FRUIT** (*Wislizenia refracta*): Southwestern. Fruits are pairs of rounded nutlets tipped by a tail-like style. Also called Jackass-clover. **BLADDERPOD** (*Isomeris arborea*): Desert hillsides and washes, coastal bluffs; chiefly southern CA. Shrub, 2–7 ft. tall. Pods inflated.

Genus *Cleome* (11 species, 6 native). Leaves palmately divided into 3, 5, or 7 leaflets; unpleasant odor when crushed. Flowers clustered at stem ends; stamens 6, protruding. Pods elongated, on spreading or down-curved stalk.

Yellow Bee-plant
Flowers yellow. Leaflets mostly 5. HT: 1–4 ft.

Rocky Mountain Bee-plant
Flowers pink; stamens conspicuous. Leaflets 3. HT: 1–4 ft.

■ RED-WHISKER CLAMMYWEED

(*Polanisia dodecandra*): Spring–fall; open places. Leaflets 3, broad. Petals in unequal pairs, with narrowed base, notched tip.

■ SLENDER-LEAF CLAMMYWEED

(*P. tenuifolia*): Sandy soil. Leaflets very slender. Petals not notched. Also called Pineland Catchfly.

NOTE Leaves have unpleasant odor when crushed.

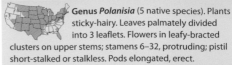

Genus *Polanisia* (5 native species). Plants sticky-hairy. Leaves palmately divided into 3 leaflets. Flowers in leafy-bracted clusters on upper stems; stamens 6–32, protruding; pistil short-stalked or stalkless. Pods elongated, erect.

Red-whisker Clammyweed

Flowers white or pink-tinged; stamens conspicuous, pink to purple. HT: 6 in.–3 ft.

Slender-leaf Clammyweed

HT: 8–32 in.

CAPRIFOLIACEAE   HONEYSUCKLE FAMILY

Mostly shrubs, some vines or perennial herbs. Leaves opposite and generally simple. Flowers solitary or in clusters; petals united, equally or unequally 5-lobed or with lobes forming 2 lips; sepals 5, small; stamens 4 or 5; pistil 1. Fruits are usually berries or berrylike.

■ PERFOLIATE HORSE-GENTIAN

(*Triosteum perfoliatum*): Spring–summer; woods, thickets. Bases of at least middle stem leaves joined, appearing pierced by stem. Fruits yellow-orange. Also called Feverwort, Tinker's-weed. **SIMILAR**

■ ORANGE-FRUIT HORSE-GENTIAN

(*T. aurantiacum*): Leaves not or only weakly joined; fruits orange-red.

■ NARROW-LEAF HORSE-GENTIAN

(*T. angustifolium*): Fruits orange-red. Also called Yellow-flower Horse-gentian.

Genus *Triosteum* (3 native species). Stems hairy. Leaves opposite. Flowers in leaf axils, tubular to bell-shaped and unequally 5-lobed; stamens 5. Fruits berrylike.

Perfoliate Horse-gentian

Flowers mostly dull red to reddish purple. HT: to 4 ft.

Narrow-leaf Horse-gentian

Flowers pale yellow. HT: to 3 ft.

■ **TWINFLOWER** (*Linnaea borealis*): Summer; woods, thickets, clearings, bogs. Main stems trail or creep on or near the ground, sending up erect flowering branches. Flowers in pairs, dangling from Y-shaped stalks. Fruits tiny.

Genus *Linnaea* (1 native species). Somewhat woody; evergreen. Leaves opposite. Flowers bell- to funnel-shaped, 5-lobed; stamens 4; style elongated. Fruits are sticky-hairy nutlets.

Twinflower

Flowers pink to whitish, nodding. Leaves roundish. HT: flowering branches 3–6 in.

■ **LIMBER HONEYSUCKLE** (*Lonicera dioica*): Spring–summer; woods, thickets. Leaves hairless above, white-waxy beneath. Flowers 2-lipped, ⅝–1 in. long. Also called Wild Honeysuckle.

■ **YELLOW HONEYSUCKLE** (*L. flava*): Leaves hairless above, green beneath. Flowers 2-lipped, 1–1⅜ in. long.

■ **HAIRY HONEYSUCKLE** (*L. hirsuta*): Leaves hairy above and beneath. Flowers 2-lipped, ½–¾ in. long.

TRUMPET HONEYSUCKLE
(*L. sempervirens*): Eastern. Flowers long-tubular, not 2-lipped, 1–2 in. long.

NOTE See also Ⅱ Japanese Honeysuckle (p. 577).

Genus *Lonicera* (30 species, 18 native). Mostly shrubs; pictured species are woody, twining or trailing vines. Leaves opposite, uppermost joined around stem in shieldlike fashion below flowers. Flowers bell-, funnel-, or trumpet-shaped, often 2-lipped; stamens 5. Fruits are berries.

Limber Honeysuckle

Flowers pale yellow, tinged purple to red.

Yellow Honeysuckle

Flowers golden yellow to orange.

Hairy Honeysuckle

Flowers yellow to orange.

Trumpet Honeysuckle

Flowers red outside, often yellowish inside.

CARYOPHYLLACEAE   PINK FAMILY

Annual, biennial, or perennial. Stems commonly swollen at points of leaf attachment (nodes). Leaves usually opposite, pairs may be joined at base; simple. Flowers solitary or in clusters; petals 5 (or rarely none), tips often toothed or lobed; sepals 5; stamens 1–10 (often 5 or 10); pistil 1. Fruits are capsules.

■ **SAND-SPURRY** (*Spergularia*): Spring–fall; open places, including salt marshes (often in alkaline soil). Stems can be covered with tiny glands or smooth (lacking glands). Plants erect to prostrate, generally 2–10 in. tall. Leaves commonly fleshy, narrow, generally 2 in. or less in length. Flowers small, often pink but sometimes white; styles 3.

Genus *Spergularia* (11 species, 4 native). Leaves often in tufts; bases often have triangular papery membranes (stipules).

Sand-spurry

SANDWORTS

■ **SLENDER MOUNTAIN SANDWORT** (*Eremogone capillaris* var. *americana*): Late spring–summer; rocky slopes, mountain meadows, open woods. Sepal tips blunt. Also called Thread-leaf Sandwort, Fescue Sandwort. **SIMILAR** ■ **FENDLER'S SANDWORT** (*E. fendleri*): Plains, open woods, slopes. Sepal tips pointed.

■ **MOUNTAIN SANDWORT** (*Minuartia groenlandica*): Ledges, mountain slopes. Also called Greenland Stitchwort. **SIMILAR BEAUTIFUL SANDWORT** (*M. rubella*): Slopes, open woods, gravelly soil; chiefly western. Leaves 3-veined. Also called Boreal Stitchwort.

Sandworts: genera *Eremogone* (14 native species), ***Minuartia*** (33 native species). Leaves opposite, needlelike or narrow, pointed. Flowers white; petals 5, sometimes with notched tip; stamens 10; styles usually 3. Capsules 6-toothed (*Eremogone*) or 3-toothed (*Minuartia*).

Slender Mountain Sandwort

Leaves long. HT: 2–8 in.

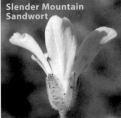
Mountain Sandwort
Leaves short, 1-veined. Plants mat-forming. HT: 1–4 in.

SANDWORTS

■ **SPREADING SANDWORT** (*Arenaria lanuginosa* var. *saxosa*): Spring–summer; mountain forests, stream banks. Leaves 1-veined, mostly ¼–¾ in. long.
SIMILAR ⊞ **THYME-LEAF SANDWORT** (*A. serpyllifolia*): Widespread Eurasian introduction. Leaves 3–5-veined, ¼ in. long or shorter.

■ **GROVE SANDWORT** (*Moehringia lateriflora*): Spring–early summer; woods, meadows, gravelly shores. Also called Blunt-leaf Sandwort.

Sandworts: genera *Arenaria* (9 species, 8 native), ***Moehringia*** (3 species, 2 native). Similar to *Eremogone* and *Minuartia* sandworts (p. 192); leaves broader; capsules 6-toothed, *Moehringia* with white, spongy appendages on seeds.

Spreading Sandwort
Grove Sandwort
Flower stalks mostly at stem ends. HT: 2–24 in.
Flower stalks sometimes on side branches. HT: 2–12 in.

■ **STAR CHICKWEED** (*Stellaria pubera*): Spring; woods, bottomlands. Leaves opposite, to nearly 1½ in. wide. Petals longer than sepals. Also called Great Chickweed. See also ⊞ Common Chickweed (p. 577), which has petals often shorter than sepals.

■ **LONG-STALK STARWORT** (*S. longipes*): Late spring–summer; stream banks, meadows, tundra. Leaves narrower than Star Chickweed, mostly ¼ in. or less wide. Also called Long-stalk Chickweed.

RELATED ■ **STICKY STARWORT** (*Pseudostellaria jamesiana*): Summer; grasslands, meadows, open woods. Petals have V-shaped notch; plants sometimes sticky.

Genus *Stellaria* (29 species, 22 native). Stems sometimes have vertical lines of hairs. Flowers white; petals split ⅔–⅘ their length; styles usually 3. Capsules usually 6-toothed.

Star Chickweed
Long-stalk Starwort
Petals 5, but deeply cut and appearing as 10. HT: 4–16 in.
HT: 2–13 in.

Sticky Starwort
HT: 6–18 in.

■ **FIELD MOUSE-EAR CHICKWEED** (*Cerastium arvense* ssp. *strictum*): Spring–summer; open places. Plants clump- or mat-forming, sometimes hairy. Petals to nearly ½ in. long. Also called Starry Grasswort. **SIMILAR** ■ **NODDING MOUSE-EAR CHICKWEED** (*C. nutans*): Plants soft-hairy; petals to ¼ in. long (as long as sepals). ⊞ **COMMON MOUSE-EAR CHICKWEED** (*C. fontanum* ssp. *vulgare*): Widespread Eurasian introduction. Uppermost bracts in flower clusters have thin, nongreen tips (tips green and herbaceous in *C. nutans*).

Genus *Cerastium* (27 species, 17 native). Differs from *Stellaria* (p. 193) in having flower petals split for ½ or less their length; styles usually 5; capsules usually 10-toothed.

Field Mouse-ear Chickweed

Petals longer than sepals. HT: 2–12 in.

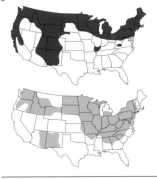

■ **SEA-SANDWORT** (*Honckenya peploides*): Late spring–summer; sea beaches, dunes, sandy flats. Flowers whitish, often unisexual, the males with petals ⅛–¼ in. long, the females with petals to ¹⁄₁₆ in. long.

Genus *Honckenya* (1 native species). Stems trailing, fleshy. Leaves opposite, numerous. Flower petals have narrowed base; stamens 10. Capsules round.

Sea-sandwort

Plants mat-forming. HT: 2–12 in.

■ **STARRY CAMPION** (*Silene stellata*):
Summer; woods, prairies. Flowers
white. **SIMILAR** ■ **BELL CATCHFLY**
(*S. campanulata*): Spring–summer; open
woods, thickets. Leaves opposite; flowers
cream-colored or sometimes greenish or
pinkish.

■ **SNOWY CAMPION** (*S. nivea*): Late
spring–summer; woods. Leaves opposite.

■ **DOUGLAS' CAMPION** (*S. douglasii* var.
douglasii): Summer; grassy or wooded
slopes. Leaves opposite. Also called
Douglas' Catchfly.

NOTE See also introduced campion
species (p. 578).

Genus *Silene* (70 species, 52 native).
Leaves opposite (rarely whorled). Sepals
joined to form cup- or tube-shaped calyx;
petals 5, often with toothed or lobed tip; petal
bases narrowed, with tiny appendages that may form petal-like
ring; stamens 10; styles usually 3, less often 5.

Starry Campion

Snowy Campion

Petals
notched.
HT: 8–25 in.

Douglas'
Campion

Petals fringed.
Leaves whorled.
HT: 12–32 in.

Petals
2-lobed.
HT: 4–16 in.

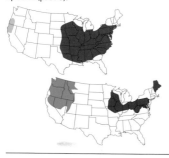

■ **SCOULER'S CATCHFLY** (*Silene scouleri*):
Summer; woods, bluffs, slopes, meadows.
Leaf pairs 3–12 on stem. Flowers generally
½ in. or less across; petals deeply 4-lobed
(or sometimes 2-lobed), the inner lobes
larger. Also called Simple Catchfly.
SIMILAR ■ **PARRY'S CATCHFLY** (*S. parryi*):
Leaf pairs commonly 2–4 on stem.

■ **HOOKER'S CATCHFLY** (*S. hookeri*):
Spring–early summer; rocky slopes, open
woods. Flowers ¾ in. or wider; petals
usually 4-lobed. Ssp. *bolanderi* has flowers
¾–1 in. across; petals linear, whitish.

NOTE See also introduced *Silene* species
(p. 578).

Scouler's Catchfly

Flowers whitish to pinkish
or purple-tinged.
Leaves largest
at plant base,
become
smaller
above.
HT: 6–30 in.

Hooker's
Catchfly

Flowers pink or white.
Leaves smallest at plant base,
become larger above. HT: 2–8 in.

■ **MOSS CAMPION** (*Silene acaulis*): Early summer; rocky ledges, tundra. Leaves ³⁄₁₆–½ in. long, very narrow, crowded near plant base. Petals sometimes notched. Also called Cushion-pink. See also Spreading Phlox and pink-flowered forms of Hood's Phlox (p. 410), both with flower petals united and stamen tips not conspicuous; dwarf-primroses (p. 446); Purple Mountain Saxifrage (p. 509).

■ **WILD-PINK** (*S. caroliniana*): Spring; open woods. Leaves 2–4½ in. long, ½–1¼ in. wide; at plant base and 2 or 3 pairs on stems. Petals sometimes notched. Also called Carolina-pink. See also Moss Phlox (p. 410), which has needlelike leaves to ¾ in. long; petals united.

Moss Campion

Flowers usually pink. Plants mound-forming. HT: 1–3 in.

Wild-pink

Flowers usually pink. HT: 3–8 in.

■ **FIRE-PINK** (*Silene virginica*): Spring; woods, slopes. Petals deeply notched or 2-lobed, often with 2 tiny side teeth.

■ **ROYAL CATCHFLY** (*S. regia*): Summer–fall; rocky places. Petals not lobed, usually rounded or minutely toothed.

■ **INDIAN-PINK** (*S. laciniata*): Spring–summer; open woods, shrublands, cliffs. Upper leaves to ⁵⁄₁₆ in. wide. Flower clusters well developed, with 3 to many flowers; petals 4–6-lobed. Also called Mexican Campion. **SIMILAR CALIFORNIA INDIAN-PINK** (*S. laciniata* ssp. *californica*): CA. Upper leaves to 1¼ in. wide; flower clusters poorly developed, with generally 1–3 flowers.

Fire-pink

Flowers red. HT: 8–32 in.

Royal Catchfly

HT: 2–4 ft.

Indian-pink

Flowers red. HT: 8 in.–4 ft.

CHENOPODIACEAE
GOOSEFOOT FAMILY

Annual or perennial; occasionally shrubs. Leaves simple, usually alternate. Flowers solitary or mostly in clusters; small to minute; petals absent; sepals 1–5; stamens 1–5; pistil 1. Fruits mostly seedlike.

■ **STRAWBERRY-BLITE** (*Chenopodium capitatum*): Summer–fall (fruit); open woods, meadows, disturbed places. Leaves triangular or broadly arrowhead-shaped; coarsely toothed to shallowly lobed. Also called Indian-paint.

NOTE The colorful, strawberry-like fruiting clusters are unusual for the genus; most *Chenopodium* species (often called goosefoot) bear insignificant greenish flowers and fruits.

Genus *Chenopodium* (34 species, 22 native). Flowers typically greenish; sepals usually 5.

Strawberry-blite

Flowers in ball-shaped clusters along upper stems. Fruiting clusters bright red. HT: 6–30 in.

CISTACEAE
ROCK-ROSE FAMILY

Shrubs or perennial herbs. Leaves alternate, opposite, or whorled; simple and untoothed. Flowers solitary or in clusters; petals 5; sepals 5, but appear as 3 because outer 2 are much smaller or narrower; stamens often many; pistil 1. Fruits are capsules.

■ **COMMON FROSTWEED** (*Helianthemum canadense*): Spring–summer; fields, open woods, roadsides. Late-season flowers smaller, lack petals, remain closed. SIMILAR ■ **PINE-BARREN FROSTWEED** (*H. corymbosum*): Sandy areas. Flowers in dense clusters. See also Pitted Stripeseed (p. 551).

■ **COMMON RUSH-ROSE** (*H. scoparium*): Slopes, ridges, sandy flats. Twiggy; leafless in summer. Also called Broom-rose.

NOTE Species are also called rock-rose, sun-rose.

Genus *Helianthemum* (13 native species). Plants sometimes shrubby. Leaves alternate, nearly stalkless. Flowers yellow; stamens mostly 10–50.

Common Frostweed

Common Rush-rose

Flowers solitary. HT: 6–16 in.

Flowers in clusters. HT: 6–18 in.

■ **FALSE HEATHER** (*Hudsonia tomentosa*): Spring–summer; beaches, dunes, open sandy places. Leaves to ⅛ in. long, densely white-hairy, scalelike, closely overlapping and tightly pressed against stem. Plants somewhat resemble a groundcover juniper (*Juniperus*). Also called Sand-heather, Beach-heath.

■ **GOLDEN-HEATHER** (*H. ericoides*): Pine barrens, rocks, dunes. Leaves ⅛–¼ in. long, green, needlelike. Flowers on stalks to ½ in. long.

Genus *Hudsonia* (3 native species). Shrubby. Leaves alternate, evergreen. Flowers yellow; stamens 8–20, conspicuous.

False Heather

Golden-heather

Flowers small, numerous, nearly stalkless. Plants form dense mounds. HT: 4–8 in.

HT: to 7 in.

COMMELINACEAE   SPIDERWORT FAMILY

Annual or perennial; somewhat succulent. Leaves alternate, simple, and untoothed; basal portion forms tubular sheath around stem. Flowers in clusters, often borne in conspicuous bracts, short-lived; petals 3; sepals 3; stamens 6; pistil 1. Fruits are capsules.

■ **ERECT DAYFLOWER** (*Commelina erecta*): Spring–fall; woods, roadsides, hills, dunes. Also called Slender Dayflower. SIMILAR ① **ASIATIC DAYFLOWER** (*C. communis*): Eastern. Lower stems sprawling, often rooting at nodes.

■ **VIRGINIA DAYFLOWER** (*C. virginica*): Summer–fall; moist places. SIMILAR ① **SPREADING DAYFLOWER** (*C. diffusa*): Tropical; southeastern. Leaf sheaths not red-brown-fringed. ■ **WESTERN DAYFLOWER** (*C. dianthifolia*): Woods.

Genus *Commelina* (9 species, 4 native). Flower clusters emerge from folded, boat-shaped bracts; lowest petal slightly to much smaller; stamens 6 (3 fertile and 3 sterile).

Erect Dayflower

2 petals blue, 1 white. Tops of tubular leaf sheaths have flaring edges. HT: 6–30 in.

Virginia Dayflower

All petals blue. Tops of tubular leaf sheaths red-brown-fringed. HT: 1–3 ft.

■ **OHIO SPIDERWORT** (*Tradescantia ohiensis*): Late winter–fall; roadsides, thickets, fields. Leaves to 1¾ in. wide. Also called Bluejacket. **SIMILAR** ■ **WESTERN SPIDERWORT** (*T. occidentalis* var. *occidentalis*): Spring–summer; prairies, plains, woods, fields. Sepals have sticky hairs. Also called Prairie Spiderwort.

■ **ZIGZAG SPIDERWORT** (*T. subaspera*): Spring–fall; woods, ravines, stream banks, bluffs. Stems zigzag.

RELATED ■ **GRASS-LEAF ROSELING** (*Cuthbertia graminea*): Spring–summer; sandhills, pinewoods. Flowers lack leaf-like bracts. Leaves grasslike, to ¼ in. wide. **PIEDMONT ROSELING** (*C. rosea*, no photo): Same range. Leaves ¼–½ in. wide.

Genus *Tradescantia* (30 species, 26 native). Flowers in clusters emerging from leaflike bracts; petals equal in size, blue, purple, pink, or white; stamens 6, all fertile, their stalks (filaments) often have colored hairs.

Ohio Spiderwort

Grass-leaf Roseling

Flowers blue to rose; sepals hairless. HT: 8 in.–3 ft.

Flowers pink to rose. HT: 8–16 in.

CONVOLVULACEAE   MORNING-GLORY FAMILY

Annual or perennial, often trailing or twining; some have milky sap. Leaves alternate and simple. Flowers solitary or in clusters; typically funnel- or trumpet-shaped (petals united), commonly pleated; petals 5; sepals 5; stamens 5; pistil 1. Fruits are capsules.

■ **DICHONDRA** (*Dichondra carolinensis*): Mostly spring; lawns, roadsides, moist or wet ground. Leaves long-stalked, round. Flowers tiny, greenish white. Also called Carolina Pony's-foot.

Genus *Dichondra* (8 native species). Creeping or trailing. Leaves commonly round, stalked. Flowers often solitary in leaf axils, shallowly funnel-shaped, deeply 5-lobed; styles 2.

Dichondra

Plants spreading, often forming dense mats. HT: to 4 in.

■ **SOUTHERN DAWNFLOWER** (*Stylisma humistrata*): Summer–fall; dry woods, thickets, roadsides. Leaves elliptic, ⅜–1 in. wide. Flowers about ¾ in. long.

■ **COASTAL PLAIN DAWNFLOWER** (*S. patens*): Spring–fall; sandy places. Flowers usually solitary. Bracts beneath flowers inconspicuous.

■ **PICKERING'S DAWNFLOWER** (*S. pickeringii*): Mostly summer; sandy soil. Leaves narrow. Flowers 1–5 per stalk. Bracts beneath flowers leaflike.

Genus *Stylisma* (6 native species). Vinelike. Flowers on long stalks from leaf axils; bell- to funnel-shaped; white, pink, or purple; styles 2, each with knobby stigma.

Southern Dawnflower

Flowers white, often 2 or 3 per long, slender stalk. Plants sprawling or trailing.

Coastal Plain Dawnflower

Leaves narrow.

Pickering's Dawnflower

Leaves often held vertically upright.

■ **WILD DWARF-MORNING-GLORY** (*Evolvulus arizonicus*): Spring–fall; open areas. Leaves flat, usually lightly hairy on both sides. Also called Arizona Blue-eyes.

■ **SILVER DWARF-MORNING-GLORY** (*E. sericeus*): Plains, pinelands. Leaves folded, usually silvery-hairy beneath.

■ **SHAGGY DWARF-MORNING-GLORY** (*E. nuttallianus*, no photo): Open areas. Leaves densely silky on both sides. Flowers lavender, short-stalked.

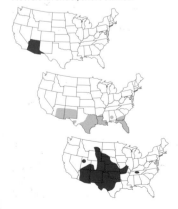

Genus *Evolvulus* (7 native species). Prostrate to erect, not twining. Flowers solitary or few from leaf axils, wheel- to funnel-shaped; styles 2, each divided (4 slender stigmas).

Wild Dwarf-morning-glory

Flowers sky blue with white eye, on slender stalk. HT: 4–16 in.

Silver Dwarf-morning-glory

Flowers white to pale blue, short-stalked. HT: to 8 in.

■ **HAIRY CLUSTER-VINE** (*Jacquemontia tamnifolia*): Summer–winter; roadsides, fields. Begins blooming while still small and erect, eventually twining. Flowers in dense, compact, long-stalked, leafy-bracted clusters; sepals conspicuously hairy. Also called Tie-vine.

■ **SKY-BLUE CLUSTER-VINE** (*J. pentanthos*): Year-round; hammock and swamp margins. No leafy bracts.

Genus *Jacquemontia* (7 species, 6 native). Vines. Flowers mostly in clusters from leaf axils; bell- to funnel-shaped; white, blue, or pinkish; style 1, stigmas 2, flattened.

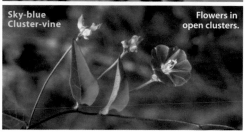

Hairy Cluster-vine — Flowers blue, 5-angled. Leaves commonly heart-shaped. Twining vine.

Sky-blue Cluster-vine — Flowers in open clusters.

■ **HEDGE FALSE BINDWEED** (*Calystegia sepium*): Spring–summer; various habitats. Leaves arrowhead-shaped. Also called Hedge Bindweed. See Field Bindweed (p. 579).

■ **SEASHORE FALSE BINDWEED** (*C. soldanella*): Sea beaches. Leaves kidney-shaped. Also called Beach-morning-glory.

■ **PAIUTE FALSE BINDWEED** (*C. longipes*): Dry places. Shrubby. Flowers cream-colored. Also called Paiute-morning-glory.

■ **SIERRAN FALSE BINDWEED** (*C. malacophylla*): Dry slopes. Leaves triangular, white-woolly. Also called Sierran-morning-glory.

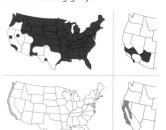

Genus *Calystegia* (16 native species). Mostly trailing or twining, sometimes erect. Flowers usually solitary in leaf axils, funnel-shaped, with 2 leaflike bracts at base (these often covering sepals); style 1, stigmas 2, slender.

Hedge False Bindweed — Flowers white to pinkish.

Paiute False Bindweed — Leaves narrow, with 2 basal lobes.

Seashore False Bindweed — Flowers white-striped pink with yellow eye.

Sierran False Bindweed — Flowers white to yellowish.

■ **TEXAS BINDWEED** (*Convolvulus equitans*): Spring–fall; various habitats. Leaves silky-woolly, variable: narrowly oblong to egg- or arrowhead-shaped; untoothed, toothed, or lobed. Flowers ⅝–1¼ in. long; sepals ¼–½ in. long. See also the more widespread ⊡ Field Bindweed (p. 579), which has leaves not densely hairy; sepals less than ¼ in. long. See also ⊡ Alamo-vine (p. 579), which has leaves palmately lobed; flowers larger.

Genus *Convolvulus* (4 species, 2 native). Similar to *Calystegia* (p. 201), but with bracts found well below base of flowers.

Texas Bindweed

Flowers white to pink, often with red eye. Trailing or twining.

■ **WILD-POTATO-VINE** (*Ipomoea pandurata*): Summer–fall; fields, roadsides, thickets, open woods. Leaves heart-shaped. Flowers 2–3 in. long. Also called Big-root Morning-glory, Man-of-the-earth.

■ **SMALL WHITE MORNING-GLORY** (*I. lacunosa*): Summer; moist fields, roadsides, disturbed areas. Leaves 3-lobed or heart-shaped. Flowers ⅝–1 in. long, may be pink-tinged. Also called Whitestar.

NOTE See also ⊡ Alamo-vine (p. 579).

Genus *Ipomoea* (47 species, 34 native). Mostly twining. Flowers solitary or in clusters from leaf axils; bell-, funnel-, or trumpet-shaped; style 1, stigma 1, ball-shaped or with 2 or 3 somewhat ball-shaped lobes (knobby).

Wild-potato-vine

Flowers large, white with purple-red eye. Twining vine.

Small White Morning-glory

Flowers usually white, shorter than leaves. Twining.

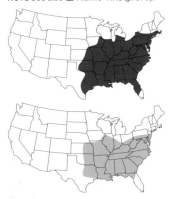

■ **SHARP-POD MORNING-GLORY**
(*Ipomoea cordatotriloba*): Spring–fall;
fields, thickets, pastures. Leaves heart-
shaped to 3- or 5-lobed. Flowers 1–2 in.
long. Also called Tie-vine.

■ **SALTMARSH MORNING-GLORY**
(*I. sagittata*): Marshes, ditches, moist
roadsides. Leaves narrowly arrowhead-
shaped. Flowers 2½–3½ in. long. Also
called Glade Morning-glory.

■ **BUSH MORNING-GLORY**
(*I. leptophylla*): Prairies, plains. Leaves
narrow. Flowers 2–4 in. long.

NOTE See also ⊞ Common Morning-glory
and ⊞ Ivy-leaf Morning-glory (p. 579).

Sharp-pod Morning-glory

Flowers purple-rose
with dark eye.
Twining vine.

Saltmarsh Morning-glory

Flowers
rose-purple
to lavender.
Trailing
or twining.

Bush Morning-glory

Flowers
purple-red to
pink. Plants erect,
bushy. HT: 1–3 ft.

■ **GOAT-FOOT MORNING-GLORY**
(*Ipomoea pes-caprae*): Year-round; sea
beaches, dunes. Leaves nearly round,
folded, notched at tip. Also called
Railroad-vine.

■ **BEACH MORNING-GLORY** (*I. imperati*):
Spring–fall; sea beaches, dunes. Leaves
irregularly 3–7-lobed, often notched at
tip. Also called Fiddle-leaf Morning-glory.

Goat-foot Morning-glory

Flowers rosy pink,
dark purplish inside.
Trailing or creeping.

Beach Morning-glory

Flowers white
with yellow eye.
Trailing or creeping.

■ **REDSTAR** (*Ipomoea coccinea*): Summer–fall; fields, thickets, roadsides. Leaves mostly heart-shaped, untoothed to angularly toothed. Flowers sometimes yellow or orange; sepals ¼–⁵⁄₁₆ in. long. Fruits downturned. Also called Red Morning-glory. **SIMILAR** ⊡ **SCARLET-CREEPER** (*I. hederifolia*): Southeastern; tropical American introduction. Sepals ³⁄₁₆ in. long; fruits erect.

■ **TRANS-PECOS MORNING-GLORY** (*I. cristulata*): Hills, canyons. Leaves range from unlobed and untoothed to deeply 3–7-lobed. Sepals similar to Redstar.

NOTE See also ⊡ Cypress-vine (p. 579), which has leaves with many narrow segments.

Redstar

Flowers commonly red with yellow or orange eye, trumpet-shaped. Stamens and style protruding. Twining vine.

Trans-pecos Morning-glory

Some leaves deeply lobed.

CORNACEAE   DOGWOOD FAMILY

Trees or shrubs, rarely perennial herbs. Leaves simple and usually opposite. Flowers in clusters, individually small; petals 4; sepals inconspicuous; stamens 4; pistil 1. Fruits berrylike.

■ **BUNCHBERRY** (*Cornus canadensis*): Spring–summer; woods, swamps, bogs. Leaves seemingly whorled, 6 on flowering stems, 4 on nonflowering stems. Flowers tiny, in dense cluster surrounded by 4 conspicuous, petal-like bracts, the whole resembling a single flower; each flower has deep purple nectar-producing disk. Fruits bright red. Also called Dwarf Cornel. **SIMILAR** ■ **WESTERN CORDILLERAN BUNCHBERRY** (*C. unalaschkensis*): Tiny petals purple toward tip.

Genus *Cornus* (19 species, 16 native). With characters of the family. Only a few species have showy bracts.

Bunchberry

Large white bracts surround cluster of cream-colored flowers. Plants often form patches. HT: 3–9 in.

CRASSULACEAE   STONECROP FAMILY

Mostly perennial; commonly succulent. Leaves basal or alternate, or sometimes opposite or whorled; usually simple. Flowers in clusters; petals 4 or 5; sepals 4 or 5; stamens 8 or 10; pistils 4 or 5. Fruits are groups of 4 or 5 small pods, frequently colored (not green).

■ **CANYON LIVE-FOREVER** (*Dudleya cymosa*): Spring; rocky cliffs, outcrops. Basal leaves generally widest at or above middle. SIMILAR ■ **LANCE-LEAF LIVE-FOREVER** (*D. lanceolata*): Basal leaves lance-shaped, widest below middle.

■ **CHALK LIVE-FOREVER** (*D. pulverulenta*): Spring–summer; rocky cliffs. Plants coated with white, waxy powder. Basal leaves oblong to spoon-shaped. Flowers sometimes apricot-yellow.

Genus *Dudleya* (26 native species). Succulent. Basal leaves densely clustered, generally much longer and wider than the alternate stem leaves. Flower parts in 5s.

Canyon Live-forever

Chalk Live-forever

Flowers yellow to red. HT: 4–18 in.

Flowers mostly deep red. HT: to 30 in.

■ **LANCE-LEAF STONECROP** (*Sedum lanceolatum*): Summer; rocky places. Basal leaves lance-shaped. Also called Narrow-leaf Stonecrop.

■ **BROAD-LEAF STONECROP** (*S. spathulifolium*): Summer; rocky places. Basal leaves spoon-shaped, in flat, tightly overlapping layers. Also called Pacific Stonecrop.

■ **WOODLAND STONECROP** (*S. ternatum*): Spring; rocky woods, cliffs. Lower leaves round, in whorls of 3. Also called Wild Stonecrop.

NOTE See also ⊞ Mossy Stonecrop (p. 580), which has tiny leaves.

Genus *Sedum* (41 species, 30 native). Succulent. Leaves typically basal and on stems, generally thick. Flower parts in 4s or 5s.

Lance-leaf Stonecrop

Flowers yellow. HT: 2–10 in.

Broad-leaf Stonecrop

Flowers yellow. HT: 2–12 in.

Woodland Stonecrop

Flowers white. HT: 3–8 in.

■ **WIDOW'S-CROSS** (*Sedum pulchellum*): Spring–early summer; cliffs, rock outcrops, rocky soil. Leaves narrow, cylindrical; leaves on flowering stems have 2 tiny lobes at base that clasp stem. Also called Pink Stonecrop, Lime Stonecrop.

RELATED ■ **ELF ORPINE** (*Diamorpha smallii*): Spring; rock outcrops. Petals 4, white; other flower parts commonly pinkish. Differs from *Sedum* in having petal tips hooded (vs. flat); pistils partially united (vs. separate).

Widow's-cross

Flowers pink to pinkish white, in branched sprays. HT: mostly 4–12 in.

Elf Orpine

Plants red, growing carpetlike on rocks. HT: 1½–4 in.

■ **KING'S-CROWN** (*Rhodiola integrifolia*): Summer; moist ground in mountains. Leaf midrib not easily visible. Petals usually 4. **SIMILAR** ■ **ROSEROOT** (*R. rosea*): Cliffs. Flowers yellow.

■ **QUEEN'S-CROWN** (*R. rhodantha*): Wet places in mountains. Leaf midrib prominent on lower surface. Petals usually 5. Also called Rose-crown.

Genus *Rhodiola* (3 native species). Fleshy. Leaves alternate, broad, flat. Flower parts in 5s; or flower parts mostly in 4s and flowers then normally unisexual, generally with male and female flowers on separate plants.

King's-crown

Flowers dark red to maroon-purple. HT: 2–12 in.

Queen's-crown

Flowers rose-pink, partly closed. HT: 6–12 in.

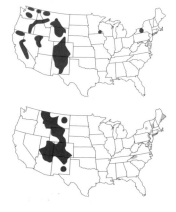

■ **ALLEGHENY STONECROP**
(*Hylotelephium telephioides*): Summer–fall; cliffs, crevices, rocky woods. Plants often purple-tinged. Also called American Orpine, Wild-live-forever.

NOTE See also □ Orpine (p. 580), which has deep pink to purple-red petals.

Genus *Hylotelephium* (4 species, 1 native). Plants fleshy. Leaves all on stems, alternate or occasionally opposite, broad and flat. Flower parts in 5s.

Allegheny Stonecrop

Petals white to light pink; pistils white to pink. Leaves broad. HT: 8–24 in.

CUCURBITACEAE   **CUCUMBER, GOURD, or PUMPKIN FAMILY**

Annual or perennial. Stems commonly angled, often rough to the touch, climbing by coiled tendrils or trailing. Leaves alternate, often palmately lobed or divided. Flowers solitary or in clusters; petals 5, usually united below; sepals 5; stamens 5 (or 3, if 2 pairs fused); pistil 1. Flowers unisexual, males and females usually on same plant. Fruits are berries or berrylike, often with tough rind (gourd or melon).

FRUITS OF THE CUCURBITACEAE

BUFFALO GOURD
2–4 in. wide (p. 208).

COYOTE MELON
3–3½ in. wide (p. 208).

MELON-LOCO
To 4 in. long (p. 208).

CUTLEAF GLOBE-BERRY
To ¾ in. long (p. 208).

WILD-CUCUMBER
1–2 in. long (p. 209).

ONE-SEEDED BUR-CUCUMBER
About ½ in. long (p. 209).

CREEPING-CUCUMBER
To ¾ in. long (p. 209).

COASTAL MANROOT
¾–1⅜ in. wide (p. 210).

CALIFORNIA MANROOT
1½–2 in. wide (p. 210).

■ BUFFALO GOURD (*Cucurbita foetidissima*): Spring–summer; prairies, plains, roadsides. Plants have rank odor. Fruits 2–4 in. across. Also called Calabazilla.

■ COYOTE MELON (*C. palmata*): Mesas, plains, sandy places. Leaves lobed halfway to base. Fruits 3–3½ in. across. Also called Coyote Gourd. **SIMILAR ■ FINGER-LEAF GOURD** (*C. digitata*): Leaves divided to base into 5 narrow segments.

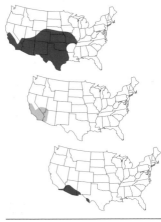

Genus *Cucurbita* (7 species, 5 native). Trailing vines. Flowers solitary in leaf axils, deeply cup- to bell-shaped, with 5 spreading lobes. Fruits (ours) are round, hard-shelled gourds, whitish-striped, mottled green, ripening yellowish.

Buffalo Gourd

Flowers large, yellow. Leaves triangular in outline.

Coyote Melon

Flowers large, yellow. Leaves 5-lobed.

■ MELON-LOCO (*Apodanthera undulata*): Spring–fall; plains, mesas. Fruits to 4 in. long, dark green, 10-ribbed.

OTHER GENUS Also southwestern.
■ CUTLEAF GLOBE-BERRY (*Ibervillea tenuisecta*): Climbing or trailing vine. Leaves deeply 3- or 5-lobed or divided into narrow segments. Flowers small, greenish yellow, males and females on separate plants. Fruits round, to ¾ in. long. Also called Deer-apples. **SIMILAR ■ LINDHEIMER'S GLOBE-BERRY** (*I. lindheimeri*): Woods, thickets, prairies. Leaves 3- or 5-lobed; fruits to nearly 2 in. long. Also called Balsam Gourd.

Genus *Apodanthera* (1 native species). Trailing vine; unpleasant odor. Leaf edges wavy, jagged-toothed. Flowers have slender tube, 5 spreading lobes; male flowers in clusters, females solitary. Fruits are hard-shelled gourds.

Melon-loco

Flowers large, yellow, star-shaped. Leaves round-kidney-shaped, with broadly notched base.

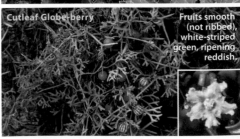

Cutleaf Globe-berry

Fruits smooth (not ribbed), white-striped green, ripening reddish.

■ **CUT-LEAF CYCLANTHERA** (*Cyclanthera dissecta*): Summer–fall; rocky soil, canyons. Leaves divided into 3–7 segments. Flowers white, cup-shaped, small, about ¼ in. across. Fruits about 1 in. long. Also called Cocklebur Melon.

OTHER GENUS *Brandegea* (1 native species). ■ **DESERT STARVINE** (*B. bigelovii*): Mostly spring; washes, canyons. Trailing, scrambling, or climbing vine. Leaves variable, unlobed to deeply palmately lobed (not divided into leaflets). Flowers ⅛ in. or less across. Fruits about ¼ in. long.

Genus *Cyclanthera* (1 native species). Climbing vine. Leaves palmately divided into segments. Male flowers in clusters, females solitary. Fruits prickly.

Cut-leaf Cyclanthera
Leaf segments often toothed or lobed. Fruits prickly.

Desert Starvine
Flowers white, star-shaped. Upper leaf surface covered with whitish dots.

■ **WILD-CUCUMBER** (*Echinocystis lobata*): Summer–fall; moist woods, thickets, riverbanks, roadsides. Stems hairless. Fruits 1–2 in. long, solitary, greenish but aging straw-colored. Also called Wild Balsam-apple.

OTHER GENERA With similar leaves. ■ **ONE-SEEDED BUR-CUCUMBER** (*Sicyos angulatus*): Summer–fall. Stems sticky-hairy. Fruits about ½ in. long, in clusters, green or greenish yellow. Also called Star-cucumber. ■ **CREEPING-CUCUMBER** (*Melothria pendula*): Spring–fall. Flowers small. Fruits to ¾ in. long, solitary, white-speckled green ripening to blackish.

Genus *Echinocystis* (1 native species). Climbing vine. Leaves somewhat maplelike, 5-angled or lobed. Flowers star-shaped, males in clusters, females solitary. Fruits inflated.

Wild-cucumber
Flowers whitish, 6-lobed. Fruits covered with weak prickles.

One-seeded Bur-cucumber
Flowers whitish, 5-lobed. Fruits hairy, bristly.

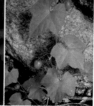
Creeping-cucumber
Flowers yellow, 5-lobed. Fruits smooth (not bristly or prickly).

■ **COASTAL MANROOT** (*Marah oreganus*): Spring; slopes, fields, meadows. Leaves 4–8 in. long. Fruits football-shaped, prickly to nearly smooth, ¾–1⅜ in. across. Also called Oregon Wild-cucumber.

■ **CALIFORNIA MANROOT** (*M. fabaceus*): Late winter–spring; slopes, roadsides, dunes. Leaves 2–4 in. long. Flowers yellow-green to white. Fruits 1½–2 in. across.

NOTE Manroots are also called bigroot.

Genus *Marah* (6 native species). Trailing or climbing vines. Leaves 5–7-lobed. Flowers 5–8-lobed, saucer- to bell-shaped; males in clusters, females solitary. Fruits prickly.

Coastal Manroot

Flowers white.

California Manroot

Fruits round, prickly.

CUSCUTACEAE   DODDER FAMILY

Mostly annual. Plants lack green pigment (chlorophyll), parasitic, rootless at maturity. Stems threadlike, twining, often yellowish or orange. Leaves apparently absent (represented by small scales). Flowers small, in clusters; urn- to bell-shaped and 4- or 5-lobed (petals united); sepals 4 or 5; stamens 4 or 5; pistil 1. Fruits are capsules.

■ **DODDER** (*Cuscuta*): Summer–fall; grows on various species of plants, including some agricultural crops. Parasitic. Stems slender, with tiny rootlike structures that penetrate host plant to obtain water and nutrients. When a Dodder seed germinates, the seedling must find a host before the seed's food reserves run out.

Genus *Cuscuta* (42 species, 37 native). With characters of the family. Species are difficult to tell apart.

Dodder

Flowers small, whitish. Stems wiry, yellowish or orange.

CYPERACEAE   SEDGE FAMILY

Annual or mostly perennial. Stems usually solid (unlike grasses, family Poaceae, not covered), sometimes 3-sided. Leaves grasslike, often in 3 vertical rows. Flowers tiny, in clusters among small, scalelike bracts; sepals and petals none or represented by bristles, hairs, or scales. Fruits (achenes) small, seedlike.

■ **NARROW-LEAF WHITE-TOP SEDGE** (*Rhynchospora colorata*): Spring–fall; damp and wet places. Lowermost bracts ¹⁄₁₆–³⁄₁₆ in. wide at base. **SIMILAR**

■ **BROADLEAF WHITE-TOP SEDGE** (*R. latifolia*): Lowermost bracts ¼–⁷⁄₁₆ in. wide at base.

NOTE There are 4 species of *Rhynchospora* with bright white bracts; the 2 not presented here have local distributions.

Genus *Rhynchospora* (68 native species). With characters of the family. Most species lack showy bracts.

Narrow-leaf White-top Sedge
Leaves grasslike.
HT: 8–24 in.

Petal-like bracts white with green tip.

■ **FRASER'S SEDGE** (*Cymophyllus fraserianus*): Spring–early summer; mountain woods. Leaves to 2 in. wide. Flowers in clusters at ends of long stalks.

Genus *Cymophyllus* (1 native species). With characters of the family. Evergreen. Leaves strap-shaped.

Fraser's Sedge
Flowers white. Clumps of broad, often arching leaves. HT: 8–16 in.

DIAPENSIACEAE

DIAPENSIA FAMILY

Perennial herbs or dwarf shrubs; evergreen. Leaves basal, alternate, or sometimes opposite; simple. Flowers solitary or in clusters, 5-lobed (petals united at least at base); sepals 5; stamens 5, additional sterile (antherless) stamens sometimes present; pistil 1. Fruits are capsules.

■ **DIAPENSIA** (*Diapensia lapponica*): Mostly late spring–early summer; gravelly or rocky alpine summits, tundra. Plants sometimes red-tinged. Leaves crowded and overlapping, ¼–½ in. long; shiny green, often turning bronze in fall; single groove on upper leaf surface. Flowers on short stalks held above leaves. Also called Pincushion-plant.

 Genus *Diapensia* (1 native species). Dwarf shrub; appears herbaceous. Leaves mostly opposite. Flowers bell-shaped, with 5 rounded lobes; 3 bracts just beneath each flower; stamens 5, conspicuous.

Flowers white, solitary. Leaves narrow. Plants form cushionlike mounds or mats. HT: 2–4 in.

■ **PYXIE-MOSS** (*Pyxidanthera barbulata*): Spring; pine barrens, moist or wet sand. Flowers nearly stalkless, often numerous. Leaves crowded, ³⁄₁₆–³⁄₈ in. long, narrow and pointed. **SIMILAR SANDHILL PYXIE-MOSS** (*P. brevifolia*): Dry sandhills; NC, SC. Leaves ¹⁄₁₆–³⁄₁₆ in. long.

NOTE These are not true mosses.

Genus *Pyxidanthera* (2 native species). Dwarf shrubs; appear herbaceous. Leaves mostly alternate or in clusters. Flowers wheel- to broadly bell-shaped, with 5 well-spaced, blunt lobes; stamens conspicuous.

Flowers usually white. Plants form dense, moss-like mats. HT: about 1 in.

■ **GALAX** (*Galax urceolata*): Late spring–early summer; woods, mostly in mountains. Leaves heart-shaped to nearly round, finely toothed, shiny green commonly becoming coppery bronze in winter. Also called Beetleweed.

Genus *Galax* (1 native species). Leaves on long stalks arising from plant base. Flowers small, crowded in a narrow, spikelike cluster; petals nearly separate; 5 fertile and 5 sterile stamens, alternate and joined at bases.

Galax

Flowers white, clustered at end of leafless, wand-like stalk. Leaves long-stalked. HT: 8–24 in.

■ **SHORTIA** (*Shortia galacifolia*): Spring; moist slopes, stream banks, rock outcrops. Plants sometimes form patches. Leaves round, toothed, shiny green, sometimes purple-tinged. Also called Oconee-bells.

Genus *Shortia* (1 native species). Leaves on long stalks arising from plant base. Flowers bell-shaped, with 5 lobes; 3–5 bracts below each flower; 5 fertile and 5 tiny, scalelike sterile stamens around ovary.

Shortia

Flowers solitary, nodding, white to pinkish white, toothed. Leaves long-stalked. HT: 4–8 in.

DIOSCOREACEAE — YAM FAMILY

Perennial, mostly vines. Leaves alternate, sometimes opposite or whorled; palmately veined and usually simple. Flowers in clusters; usually unisexual; tepals 6 (3 petals and 3 sepals, all alike); stamens 6; pistil 1. Fruits are triangular capsules. Species in this family are not related to sweet potato, which is often called "yam."

■ **WILD YAM** (*Dioscorea villosa*): Spring–summer; woods, thickets, marsh and swamp edges, roadsides. Leaves mostly alternate (some may be whorled); prominent "parallel" veins arch from base to tip of blade. Also called Yam-root, Colic-root. Plants with lower leaves in whorls of 4–7 sometimes treated as a distinct species, *D. quaternata*. **SIMILAR** ■ **FLORIDA YAM** (*D. floridana*): Differs in technical characters.

NOTE Some introduced species produce conspicuous aerial tubers in the leaf axils.

Genus *Dioscorea* (6 species, 2 native). With characters of the family. Plants are either male or female.

Wild Yam

Male flowers minute.

Fruits winged.

Leaves heart-shaped. Twining vine.

DROSERACEAE — SUNDEW FAMILY

Mostly perennial. Leaves arise from plant base, simple, modified to capture insects. Flowers in clusters; petals 5; sepals 5; stamens 5–20; pistil 1. Fruits are capsules.

■ **VENUS' FLYTRAP** (*Dionaea muscipula*): Spring; wet sandy roadsides, pine savannas, bog margins. Leaves modified to catch insects, with tiny, sensitive trigger hairs on upper surface that, when touched, spring the trap. Leaf blades normally reddish above; about 1 in. wide, up to 2¾ in. long.

Genus *Dionaea* (1 native species). Leaves erect or lying down; stalks often broadly winged; blades have 2 kidney-shaped lobes with eyelashlike bristles along edges.

Venus' Flytrap

Flowers white, on leafless stalks; petals have conspicuous veins. HT: flowering stalk 4–14 in.

■ **ROUND-LEAF SUNDEW** (*Drosera rotundifolia*): Summer; bogs, fens, swamps, damp sandy areas. Flowers on leafless stalks.

■ **THREAD-LEAF SUNDEW** (*D. filiformis*): Damp sandy areas, gravelly pond margins. Leaves coiled when young. Also called Dew-thread.

 Genus *Drosera* (10 species, 9 native). Leaves bear reddish to purple, sticky, insect-trapping hairs. Flowers in often 1-sided clusters; petals sometimes toothed at tip.

Round-leaf Sundew

Leaves round, on narrow stalks.

Flowers white to pink. HT: 2–12 in.

Thread-leaf Sundew

Flowers rose-pink to purple. Leaves wandlike. HT: 4–12 in.

ERICACEAE   HEATH FAMILY

Mostly shrubs, usually in acidic soils. Leaves alternate (or occasionally opposite or whorled) and simple; may be leathery and evergreen. Flowers in clusters, or rarely single; petals 4 or 5, usually united; sepals 4 or 5; stamens typically 8 or 10 (occasionally 5); pistil 1. Fruits are capsules, berries, or berrylike.

■ **BOG-ROSEMARY** (*Andromeda polifolia*): Spring–summer; bogs, fens. Flowers in often nodding clusters. Most commonly seen is var. *glaucophylla*, which has leaves minutely hairy beneath (white-waxy in var. *polifolia*).

Genus *Andromeda* (1 native species). Shrub; evergreen. Leaves untoothed, leathery, whitish beneath. Flowers urn-shaped, 5-lobed; stamens 10. Fruits are round capsules.

Bog-rosemary

Flowers small, pink or sometimes white. Leaves narrow; edges curled under. HT: 4–24 in.

■ **COMMON BEARBERRY** (*Arctostaphylos uva-ursi*): Spring–early summer; sandy or rocky soil. Dwarf evergreen. Stems trailing, often mat-forming. Also called Kinnikinnick.

RELATED ■ **ALPINE BEARBERRY** (*Arctous alpina*): Late spring–early summer; woods, heaths, arctic and alpine tundra; mostly in far north (Alaska and Canada). Dwarf, not evergreen. Leaves conspicuously veiny, toothed. Also called Black Bearberry. SIMILAR ■ **RED ALPINE BEARBERRY** (*A. rubra*): Fruits red.

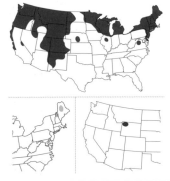

Genus *Arctostaphylos* (62 native species). Mostly shrubs and small trees; evergreen or deciduous. Leaves alternate. Flowers urn- or vase-shaped, 5-lobed; stamens 10. Fruits berrylike.

Common Bearberry

Flowers small, pink to white, in nodding clusters. Leaves shiny, untoothed. Fruits red. HT: 2–6 in.

Alpine Bearberry

Flowers mostly whitish. Fruits purplish black. HT: to 6 in.

■ **WHITE MOUNTAIN-HEATHER** (*Cassiope mertensiana*): Summer; mountain slopes and meadows. Plants often mat-forming. Leaves tiny, boat-shaped, crowded and overlapping. Also called Western Moss-heather.

Genus *Cassiope* (3 native species). Dwarf shrubs; evergreen. Leaves opposite, in 4 vertical rows, closely pressed against and concealing stem. Flowers bowl- or widely bell-shaped and 5-lobed; stamens 10. Fruits are capsules.

White Mountain-heather

Flowers small, nodding, white; sepals often red. HT: 4–12 in.

■ **TRAILING-ARBUTUS** (*Epigaea repens*):
Spring; sandy or rocky soil. Also called
Mayflower.

 Genus *Epigaea* (1 native species). Dwarf
shrub; evergreen; hairy. Leaves alternate.
Flowers tubular, with 5 spreading lobes;
2 bracts beneath each flower; stamens 5. Fruits berrylike.

Trailing-arbutus

Flowers pink to white.
Leaves leathery, untoothed.
Stems creeping. HT: 2–3 in.

■ **WINTERGREEN** (*Gaultheria
procumbens*): Summer; woods. Flowers
nodding, white. Wintergreen odor. Also
called Eastern Teaberry, Checkerberry.

■ **SLENDER WINTERGREEN**
(*G. ovatifolia*): Woods, heaths, mountain
bogs. Similar to Wintergreen; flowers
tiny, bell-shaped, white or pale pink. Also
called Western Teaberry.

■ **CREEPING SNOWBERRY** (*G. hispidula*):
Boggy places. Flowers and fruits white.
SIMILAR **ALPINE WINTERBERRY**
(*G. humifusa*): Wet forests in western
mountains. Flowers white to light pink;
fruits red.

Genus *Gaultheria* (6 native species).
Shrubs; evergreen. Leaves alternate,
leathery. Flowers urn- to bell-shaped and
5-lobed (but 4-lobed in *G. hispidula*); stamens usually 8 or
10. Fruits are capsules surrounded by fleshy coat.

Wintergreen

Fruits red.

Slender Wintergreen

HT: 2–6 in.

Flowers small, urn- to
barrel-shaped. Leaves few,
near top of stem.
HT: 2–6 in.

Creeping Snowberry

Stems
creeping.

■ **SALAL** (*Gaultheria shallon*): Spring–midsummer; woods, thickets, bluffs. Stems creeping, spreading, or erect. Leaves finely sharp-toothed. Flowers in clusters, small, hairy. Also called Lemon-leaf.

Salal

Flowers urn-shaped, drooping. Leaves egg-shaped. HT: mostly 1–6 ft.

Flowers white or pinkish.

Fruits blackish, dark bluish, or dark purplish.

■ **BOG-LAUREL** (*Kalmia polifolia*): Spring–early summer; bogs, swampy places. Leaves essentially stalkless, whitish beneath. Also called Pale-laurel, Swamp-laurel. **SIMILAR ALPINE-LAUREL** (*K. microphylla*): Western mountains. Leaves half as long (to ¾ in.).

■ **SHEEP-LAUREL** (*K. angustifolia*): Woods, swamps, bog margins. Leaves in 3s; lower leaves drooping, stalked, green beneath. Also called Lambkill. **SIMILAR** ■ **SOUTHERN SHEEP-LAUREL** (*K. carolina*): Leaves usually hairy beneath.

MOUNTAIN-LAUREL (*K. latifolia*, no photo): Woods; eastern. Large shrub or small tree. Leaves mostly alternate. Flowers white or pink-tinged.

Genus *Kalmia* (7 native species). Shrubs; evergreen. Leaves opposite, whorled, or alternate; leathery and untoothed. Flowers bowl- or saucer-shaped and 5-lobed; stamens 10, anthers fit into pouches inside corolla. Fruits are capsules.

Bog-laurel

Flowers rose-pink, mostly at stem ends. Leaves in pairs; edges curled under. HT: 6–24 in.

Sheep-laurel

Flowers well below stem tips, among leaves. HT: 6 in.–3 ft.

■ **COMMON LABRADOR-TEA** (*Ledum groenlandicum*): Summer; bogs, swamps, bluffs, shores. Leaves to about 2½ in. long, rusty-hairy beneath. Also called Rusty Labrador-tea. SIMILAR **MARSH LABRADOR-TEA** (*L. palustre* ssp. *decumbens*): Bogs and tundra; Alaska and far north. Plants 4–20 in. tall; leaves narrow, to 1 in. long. ■ **TRAPPER'S-TEA** (*L. glandulosum*): Mountain meadows. Leaf edges not strongly curled, pale and gland-dotted beneath. Also called Glandular Labrador-tea.

OTHER GENUS ■ **SAND-MYRTLE** (*Leiophyllum buxifolium*): Spring–summer; pine barrens, sandhills, rock outcrops. Leaves ¼–½ in. long, not aromatic. Flowers sometimes pink-tinged.

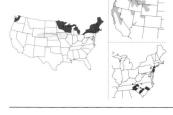

Genus *Ledum* (3 native species). Shrubs; evergreen; aromatic. Leaves alternate, leathery, untoothed. Petals 5, not united; stamens mostly 5–10. Fruits are capsules.

Common Labrador-tea

Flowers white, star-shaped; stamens conspicuous. Leaf edges curled under. HT: 1–3 ft.

Sand-myrtle
Leaves hairless, shiny. HT: 6 in.–3 ft.

■ **ALPINE-AZALEA** (*Loiseleuria procumbens*): Mostly summer; alpine ridges, tundra. Plants often mat-forming. Leaves about ¼ in. long. Flowers small, about ¼ in. across, rarely white. Not a true azalea.

OTHER GENUS Found in similar habitats. ■ **LAPLAND ROSEBAY** (*Rhododendron lapponicum*): Shrub; covered with minute scales. Leaves rust-colored beneath. Flowers ⅜–¾ in. across, magenta to purple or rarely white.

Genus *Loiseleuria* (1 native species). Dwarf shrub; evergreen. Leaves mostly opposite, leathery, untoothed. Flowers in clusters, 5-lobed; stamens 5. Fruits are capsules.

Alpine-azalea
Flowers usually rose-pink, bell-shaped. Leaf edges curled under. HT: to 6 in.

Lapland Rosebay

Style and stamens conspicuous. HT: 4–20 in.

■ **PINK MOUNTAIN-HEATHER**
(*Phyllodoce empetriformis*): Summer;
mountain slopes and meadows. Leaves
needlelike. Flowers pink to dark rose.

■ **RED MOUNTAIN-HEATHER** (*P. breweri*):
Flowers pink; stamens protruding.

■ **MOUNTAIN-HEATH** (*P. caerulea*):
Flowers rose-lavender; sepals sticky-hairy.
Also called Purple Mountain-heather.

■ **YELLOW MOUNTAIN-HEATHER**
(*P. glanduliflora*): Flowers dull yellow to
greenish white, sticky-hairy.

Genus *Phyllodoce* (5 native species).
Dwarf shrubs; evergreen. Leaves alternate,
crowded, resemble fir needles. Flowers
small, 5-lobed; stamens 10. Fruits are capsules.

Pink Mountain-heather

Red Mountain-heather

Flowers bell-shaped. HT: 4–16 in.

Flowers cup-shaped. HT: 6–12 in.

Mountain-heath

Yellow Mountain-heather

Flowers urn-shaped. HT: 2–6 in.

Flowers urn-shaped. HT: 6–18 in.

■ **COMMON CRANBERRY** (*Vaccinium
macrocarpon*): Summer; bogs, swamps,
wet shores. Stems slender, creeping.
Flower stalks arise from below stem tips,
bear 2 small, green, leaflike bracts above
middle. Also called Large Cranberry.

■ **SMALL CRANBERRY** (*V. oxycoccos*):
Flower stalks arise from stem tips, bear 2
tiny, reddish bracts near middle or below.

■ **MOUNTAIN-CRANBERRY** (*V. vitis-idaea*
ssp. *minus*): Bogs, rocky places; mostly
northern. Leaves black-dotted beneath.
Flowers bell-shaped.

Genus *Vaccinium* (25 native species).
Shrubs; evergreen or deciduous. Leaves
alternate. The 3 species pictured here are
dwarf evergreens with 4-lobed flowers, red berries.

Common Cranberry

Small Cranberry

Leaf edges often curled under; tips pointed. HT: to 4 in.

Mountain-cranberry

HT: to 4 in.

Flowers small, pink to white; lobes commonly swept back. Leaf tips blunt. Fruits red. HT: to 6 in.

ERIOCAULACEAE
PIPEWORT FAMILY
Mostly perennial. Leaves arise from plant base, grasslike. Flowers unisexual, males and females together in dense clusters at ends of long stalks. Fruits are capsules.

■ **TEN-ANGLE PIPEWORT** (*Eriocaulon decangulare*): Spring–fall; wet shores, ditches, savannas, shallow water. Flowers, individually hardly visible, are grouped in roundish "buttons" at ends of leafless stalks. Flowering stalks 8–12-ribbed. SIMILAR ■ **SEVEN-ANGLE PIPEWORT** (*E. aquaticum*): Wet shores, bogs, shallow water. Stalks 5–7-ribbed, 2–8 in. tall. Also called Northern Pipewort.

Genus *Eriocaulon* (11 species, 10 native). Leaves grasslike, in basal clusters. Flowers tiny, 2-petaled, occur among scalelike bracts in densely packed clusters. Also called hatpins.

Ten-angle Pipewort

Flower clusters whitish, ball-shaped but flattened above. Leaves grasslike. HT: 1–3 ft.

EUPHORBIACEAE
SPURGE FAMILY
Annual or perennial herbs, or shrubs, trees, or vines; many have irritating milky sap. Leaves usually alternate (sometimes opposite or whorled) and simple. Flowers unisexual; petals 5 or none; sepals 5 or none; stamens 1 to many; pistil 1. Fruits are segmented capsules.

■ **TREAD-SOFTLY** (*Cnidoscolus urens* var. *stimulosus*): Spring–fall (year-round in FL); dry sandy places. Male flowers have about 10 stamens; females below males, fewer, calyx sheds early. Also called Spurge-nettle, Bull-nettle.

OTHERS ■ **TEXAS BULL-NETTLE** (*C. texanus*, no photo): Open woods, fields, sandy soil. Flowers hairy.
■ **MALA-MUJER** (*C. angustidens*): Rocky slopes. Leaves white-spotted.

NOTE Plants have stinging hairs.

Genus *Cnidoscolus* (3 native species). Plants have milky sap. Leaves alternate, palmately lobed; lobes toothed or spiny. Flowers in clusters, trumpet-shaped, formed of united sepals (calyx); true petals absent.

Tread-softly
Flowers white, with usually 5 petal-like lobes.
Leaves somewhat maplelike. Stinging hairs abundant. HT: 6 in.–3 ft.

Mala-mujer
Leaves long-toothed. HT: 6 in.–4 ft.

■ **FLOWERING SPURGE** (*Euphorbia corollata*): Spring–fall; fields, roadsides, prairies, open woods. Leaves narrow. Each "flower" is a group of tiny flowers mimicking a single 5-petaled flower with a central, stalked, 3-lobed ovary.

■ **SNOW-ON-THE-MOUNTAIN** (*E. marginata*): Prairies, pastures, roadsides. "Flowers" similar to Flowering Spurge. Bractlike leaves, called floral leaves, have wide, white borders.

■ **FIRE-ON-THE-MOUNTAIN** (*E. cyathophora*): Woods, ravines, roadsides. "Flowers" greenish, lack petal-like lobes. Stem leaves usually alternate. SIMILAR **TOOTHED SPURGE** (*E. dentata*): Open places; eastern and central U.S. to AZ. Base of floral leaves green or whitish; stem leaves opposite.

Genus *Euphorbia* (62 species, 52 native). Plants have milky sap. Leaves mostly alternate. Each "flower" is a small cup with 1 female and several tiny male flowers within, small appendages (sometimes petal-like) along rim.

Flowering Spurge
"Flowers" small, white. HT: 1–3 ft.

Snow-on-the-mountain
"Flowers" white; floral leaves white-edged. HT: 1–3 ft.

Fire-on-the-mountain
Base of floral leaves red. HT: 1–3 ft.

■ **MOJAVE SPURGE** (*Euphorbia schizoloba*): Late winter–summer; slopes. Leaves ¼–¾ in. long. Female flower (center of cluster) stalked, hanging down.

SIMILAR With half-moon-shaped ("2-horned") appendages. **SHORT-HORN SPURGE** (*E. brachycera*, no photo): Rocky Mountain region, western Great Plains. Also called Horned Spurge. ■ **CHINESE-CAPS** (*E. crenulata*): Dry places. ■ **WOOD SPURGE** (*E. commutata*, no photo): Woods. Also called Tinted Woodland Spurge. See also 🔳 Cypress Spurge and 🔳 Leafy Spurge (both on p. 581).

■ **CANDELILLA** (*E. antisyphilitica*): Spring–fall; rocky deserts, slopes. Leaves tiny, falling early. Also called Wax-plant.

Mojave Spurge
"Flowers" small; petal-like appendages yellow, jagged-toothed. HT: 6–16 in.

Chinese-caps
HT: 6–24 in.

Candelilla
Flower clusters near stem tops. Stems rushlike, grayish green, leafless, in clumps. HT: 8–24 in.

"Flowers" small, whitish with dark center, starlike.

■ **WHITE-MARGIN SANDMAT**
(*Chamaesyce albomarginata*): Late winter–fall; dry slopes, flats, roadsides. Each "flower" is a cluster mimicking a single flower. Also called Rattlesnake-weed, White-margin Spurge.

NOTE Most *Chamaesyce* species are not showy; a few are quite weedy.

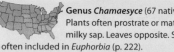

Genus *Chamaesyce* (67 native species). Plants often prostrate or matted, have milky sap. Leaves opposite. Similar to and often included in *Euphorbia* (p. 222).

White-margin Sandmat

"Flowers" small, white with usually maroon eye. Leaves roundish. Plants mat-forming.

■ **QUEEN'S-DELIGHT** (*Stillingia sylvatica*): Spring–fall; open woods, sandhills, prairies, roadsides. Leaves crowded, ⅜–1 in. wide, often finely toothed.

■ **TEXAS QUEEN'S-DELIGHT** (*S. texana*): Spring–summer; hills, fields. Similar to Queen's-delight, but leaves ⅛–³⁄₁₆ in. wide. **SIMILAR** ■ **QUEEN'S-ROOT** (*S. linearifolia*): Spring; deserts. Leaves about ¹⁄₁₆ in. wide, often curved, untoothed. Also called Linear-leaf Stillingia.

■ **ANNUAL STILLINGIA** (*S. spinulosa*): Spring; dry sandy places. Leaves 3-veined, lance- to diamond-shaped, to ⅝ in. wide. Also called Broad-leaf Stillingia.

NOTE Species are also called toothleaf.

Genus *Stillingia* (7 native species). Plants typically have milky sap. Leaves alternate. Flowers tiny, in spikelike clusters; male flowers (stamens 2) along upper part of spike, females below. Fruits 3-lobed.

Queen's-delight

Flowers in yellowish, spikelike clusters. HT: 1–3 ft.

Texas Queen's-delight

Annual Stillingia

Leaf edges have conspicuous pointed teeth. HT: 3–12 in.

Leaves narrow. HT: 8–20 in.

■ **CALIFORNIA CROTON** (*Croton californicus*): Spring–fall; sandy places. Upper leaf surface nearly covered with branched hairs. Male and female flowers on separate plants. **SIMILAR** ■ **TEXAS CROTON** (*C. texensis*): Prairies, plains, roadsides. Upper leaf surface only dotted with branched hairs, brighter green.

ALSO SIMILAR With female and petaled male flowers on the same plant (no photos). **WOOLLY CROTON** (*C. capitatus*): Often sandy soil; east-central U.S. Plants densely fuzzy-woolly. Also called Hogwort. ■ **TOOTH-LEAF CROTON** (*C. glandulosus*): Various habitats. Leaves toothed, with 1 or 2 minute cuplike glands on leafstalk near base of blade. Also called Vente-conmigo.

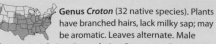

Genus *Croton* (32 native species). Plants have branched hairs, lack milky sap; may be aromatic. Leaves alternate. Male flowers: petals 0 or 5, sepals 4 or 5, stamens 5 to many; female: petals 0 (rarely 5), sepals 5–9. Fruits are capsules.

California Croton
Leaves grayish olive.
HT: 6–30 in.

Male flowers.

Fruits.

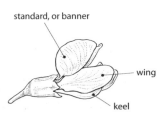

FABACEAE or LEGUMINOSAE   LEGUME, PEA, or BEAN FAMILY

Annual or perennial herbs, woody or herbaceous vines, or shrubs or trees. Leaves alternate or occasionally basal, usually compound. Flowers most often in clusters; petals 5; sepals 5 (sometimes united into a tube below); stamens 5 to many (often 10); pistil 1. Fruits are pods (legumes).

FLOWERS OF THE FABACEAE

Many plants in Fabaceae have "pealike" flowers, with 5 unequal petals: an uppermost petal, often the largest, called the "standard" (or "banner"); 2 side petals, the "wings" (often with narrowed base); and 2 lowermost petals, usually united into a single, boat-shaped "keel." The 10 stamens commonly have 9 united and 1 free.

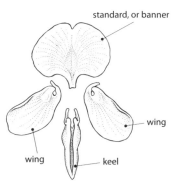

standard, or banner

wing

wing   keel

standard, or banner

wing

keel

stamens (9+1)

FRUITS (PODS) OF THE FABACEAE
Approximate lengths are given.

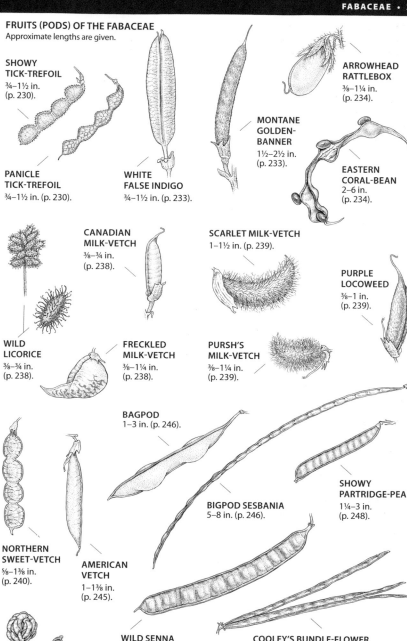

SHOWY TICK-TREFOIL
¾–1½ in. (p. 230).

PANICLE TICK-TREFOIL
¾–1½ in. (p. 230).

WHITE FALSE INDIGO
¾–1½ in. (p. 233).

MONTANE GOLDEN-BANNER
1½–2½ in. (p. 233).

ARROWHEAD RATTLEBOX
⅜–1¼ in. (p. 234).

EASTERN CORAL-BEAN
2–6 in. (p. 234).

CANADIAN MILK-VETCH
⅜–¾ in. (p. 238).

SCARLET MILK-VETCH
1–1½ in. (p. 239).

PURPLE LOCOWEED
⅜–1 in. (p. 239).

WILD LICORICE
⅜–¾ in. (p. 238).

FRECKLED MILK-VETCH
⅜–1¼ in. (p. 238).

PURSH'S MILK-VETCH
⅜–1¼ in. (p. 239).

BAGPOD
1–3 in. (p. 246).

BIGPOD SESBANIA
5–8 in. (p. 246).

SHOWY PARTRIDGE-PEA
1¼–3 in. (p. 248).

NORTHERN SWEET-VETCH
⅝–1⅜ in. (p. 240).

AMERICAN VETCH
1–1⅜ in. (p. 245).

WILD SENNA
2½–4 in. (p. 248).

COOLEY'S BUNDLE-FLOWER
1¼–2¾ in. (p. 249).

ILLINOIS BUNDLE-FLOWER
½–1 in. (p. 249).

CATCLAW SENSITIVE-BRIAR
1½–4 in. (p. 250).

■ **HOG-PEANUT** (*Amphicarpaea bracteata*): Summer–fall; woods, thickets. Keel petals nearly straight; lobes of calyx (united sepals) half or less the length of tubular base. Long, slender, creeping runners at plant base bear bud-shaped flowers that produce 1-seeded, plump, fleshy pods that mature underground.

NOTE Do not confuse with wild-beans (p. 227), which have a tiny pair of bracts beneath each flower (absent in Hog-peanut) and keel petals strongly curved upward into a beak. In milk-peas (below), the calyx lobes are as long as the tubular base.

Genus *Amphicarpaea* (1 native species). Twining vine. Leaves divided into 3 leaflets. Flowers pealike (p. 224). Pods flattened, 2–4-seeded.

Hog-peanut

Flowers purple to white. Leaflets 3. Stems wiry, climbing or sprawling.

■ **EASTERN MILK-PEA** (*Galactia regularis*): Spring–summer; woods, fields, roadsides, sandhills. Flowers ½–¾ in. long. Also called Trailing Milk-pea.
SIMILAR ■ **DOWNY MILK-PEA** (*G. volubilis*): Stems twining, tangle-forming, with spreading hairs; flowers ⁵⁄₁₆–½ in. long. Also called Twining Milk-pea.

■ **ELLIOTT'S MILK-PEA** (*G. elliottii*): Pinelands, thickets. Stems twining.

NOTE Do not confuse milk-peas with Hog-peanut (above) or wild-beans (p. 227).

Genus *Galactia* (17 native species). Vines. Leaves usually divided into 3 leaflets (rarely 1, 5, 7, or 9). Flowers pealike (p. 224). Pods flattened.

Eastern Milk-pea

Elliott's Milk-pea

Flowers lavender to pink-purple. Leaflets 3. Stems trailing, smooth or minutely hairy.

Flowers white. Leaflets 5–9 (often 7).

■ **TRAILING WILD-BEAN** (*Strophostyles helvola*): Spring–fall; open woods, fields, roadsides. Flowers age greenish. Also called Annual Wild-bean.

■ **PINK WILD-BEAN** (*S. umbellata*): Flowers about ⅜ in. long. Also called Perennial Wild-bean. **SIMILAR** ■ **SMALL-FLOWER WILD-BEAN** (*S. leiosperma*): Flowers about ¼ in. long; pods hairy.

NOTE Wild-beans differ from milk-peas (p. 226) in having beaked flowers, all clustered at very tip of stalk. See also Hog-peanut (p. 226).

Genus *Strophostyles* (3 native species). Scrambling or vining. Leaves divided into 3 leaflets. Flowers pealike (p. 224), with keel petals strongly curved upward into a beak. Pods twist after opening.

Trailing Wild-bean

Pink Wild-bean

Leaflets narrow, unlobed.

Flowers pink or purplish. Leaflets 3, often lobed. Trailing or twining.

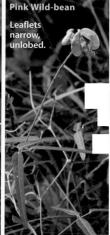

■ **LONG-LEAF COLOGANIA** (*Cologania angustifolia*): Summer–fall; grasslands, canyons, mountain woods. Leaflets variable in shape, but generally narrower than those of other *Cologania* species; sometimes folded in half lengthwise. Flowers solitary or few from leaf axils. Also called Narrow-leaf Tick-clover.

Genus *Cologania* (4 native species). Twining or trailing, sometimes erect. Leaves divided into usually 3 leaflets (sometimes 5). Flowers pealike (p. 224). Pods mostly flattened.

Long-leaf Cologania

Flowers reddish purple. Leaflets usually 3, mostly long and narrow.

■ **BUTTERFLY-PEA** (*Clitoria mariana*):
Spring–summer; open woods, fields,
roadsides. Leaflets 3. Flowers 1½–2½ in.
long, solitary or few from leaf axils. Also
called Atlantic Pigeon-wings.

RELATED ■ **BUTTERFLY-PEA**
(*Centrosema virginianum*): Spring–fall;
open woods, clearings. Similar to *Clitoria
mariana*, but has green, sepal-like bracts
partly hiding calyx; flowers ¾–1¼ in. long.
Also called Spurred Butterfly-pea.

Genus *Clitoria* (3 species, 2 native).
Scrambling or vining. Leaves divided into
3 leaflets. Flowers pealike (p. 224) but
upside down (circular standard petal on bottom); bluish,
pinkish, or purplish. Pods flattened.

Butterfly-pea
(*Clitoria mariana*)

Lobes of calyx
(united sepals)
shorter than
tubular base.
Usually trailing
or sprawling.

Butterfly-pea
(*Centrosema
virginianum*)

Calyx lobes
longer than tube.
Trailing or twining.

■ **BAY-BEAN** (*Canavalia rosea*): Year-
round; coastal beaches and dunes.
Plants sometimes twining. Pods thick
but flattened, 4–6 in. long. Also called
Seaside-bean, Seaside Jackbean.

Genus *Canavalia* (3 species, 1 native).
Leaves divided into 3 leaflets. Flowers
pealike (p. 224). Pods flattened.

Bay-bean

Flowers lavender
to rose-pink.
Leaflets 3, broadly
elliptic to nearly
round. Mostly
trailing vine.

■ **TEXAS SNOUT-BEAN** (*Rhynchosia senna* var. *texana*): Spring–summer; plains, mesas, slopes. Leaflets 3. **SIMILAR** ■ **HAIRY SNOUT-BEAN** (*R. tomentosa*): Dry woods. Stems erect, hairy.

■ **DOLLARLEAF** (*R. reniformis*): Sandy soil. Stems erect. Leaves mostly kidney- to heart-shaped (uppermost leaves occasionally divided into 3 leaflets).

NOTE Do not confuse *Rhynchosia* species with Pencil-flower (below).

OTHER GENUS With similar flowers. **FLORIDA-ALICIA** (*Chapmannia floridana*): Spring–fall; sandy pinewoods, scrub; FL. Leaves odd-pinnate, divided into 3–9 (often 5 or 7) leaflets.

Genus *Rhynchosia* (15 native species). Erect, trailing, or twining. Leaves divided into 3 leaflets (sometimes reduced to 1), often sprinkled with tiny, yellowish resin dots. Flowers pealike (p. 224). Pods small, 1- or 2-seeded.

Texas Snout-bean

Flowers small, yellow, sometimes red-tinged. Mostly trailing or twining.

Dollarleaf HT: 2–8 in.

Florida-alicia Flowers at end of sticky-hairy stalk. HT: 16–32 in.

■ **PENCIL-FLOWER** (*Stylosanthes biflora*): Spring–summer; open woods, woodland borders, roadsides. Lower segment of pods reduced to a hairy white stalk, upper segment somewhat leathery and fertile (seeded).

NOTE Do not confuse *Stylosanthes* with snout-beans (above), which have stipules free from leafstalk and stem, and leaflets that are generally broader.

RELATED ■ **VIPERINA** (*Zornia bracteata*): Spring–fall; sandy soil. Stems trailing. Leaves divided into usually 4 narrow leaflets. Flowers yellowish to orange, pealike (similar to Pencil-flower), in stalked clusters from leaf axils; base of flower enclosed by 2 elliptic, leaflike bracts. Pods bristly. Also called Bracted Zornia.

Genus *Stylosanthes* (5 species, 4 native). Leaves divided into 3 leaflets; stipules (appendages at base of leafstalk) partly united to leafstalk, forming tube around stem. Flowers solitary or few, pealike (p. 224). Pods tiny, 2-segmented.

Pencil-flower Flowers small, orange-yellow. Leaflets 3. HT: 4–16 in.

Viperina Flowers yellowish to orange. HT: 3–6 in.

■ **WILD COW-PEA** (*Vigna luteola*): Year-round; sea beaches, hammocks, thickets. Pods hairy, downturned. Also called Hairy-pod Cow-pea.

NOTE Many *Vigna* species have purple to blue-purple flowers.

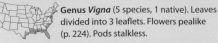

Genus *Vigna* (5 species, 1 native). Leaves divided into 3 leaflets. Flowers pealike (p. 224). Pods stalkless.

Wild Cow-pea

Flowers yellow. Leaflets 3. Trailing or climbing vine.

■ **SHOWY TICK-TREFOIL** (*Desmodium canadense*): Summer; prairies, thickets, stream banks, clearings. Leaflets 3. Flowers rose-purple, aging dark blue. Pod segments (3–5) rounded below. Also called Canadian Tick-trefoil.

■ **PANICLE TICK-TREFOIL** (*D. paniculatum*): Woods, fields. Leaflets often narrow. Pod segments triangular below. Also called Narrow-leaf Tick-trefoil.

■ **FEW-FLOWER TICK-TREFOIL** (*D. pauciflorum*): Woods. Flowers white. Pods deeply notched.

NOTE Many species, difficult to tell apart.

Genus *Desmodium* (45 species, 42 native). Leaves divided into 3 leaflets. Flowers pealike (p. 224); pink or purple, or occasionally white. Pods segmented, visibly constricted between segments (easily separated at maturity), covered with tiny, hooked hairs.

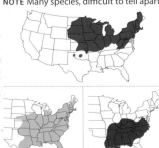

Showy Tick-trefoil

Panicle Tick-trefoil

HT: 1–3 ft.

Few-flower Tick-trefoil

HT: 2–3 ft.

HT: 6–30 in.

■ **ROUND-HEAD BUSH-CLOVER**
(*Lespedeza capitata*): Spring–fall; open
woods, prairies, roadsides. Flowers white
with purple inside, in dense clusters.

■ **HAIRY BUSH-CLOVER** (*L. hirta*):
Summer–fall; woods, clearings. Flowers
similar to Round-head Bush-clover.

Genus *Lespedeza* (15 species, 11 native).
Leaves divided into 3 leaflets. Flowers
pealike (p. 224). Pods small, 1-seeded.

Round-head Bush-clover

Flower
clusters
short-
stalked.
Leaflets
narrow.
HT: 2–5 ft.

Hairy Bush-clover

Flower
clusters
long-
stalked.
Leaflets
broad.
HT: 2–5 ft.

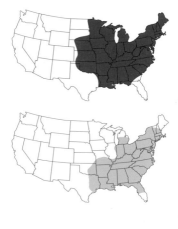

■ **SLENDER BUSH-CLOVER** (*Lespedeza
virginica*): Summer–fall; open woods,
clearings, roadsides. Flowers purplish.

VIOLET BUSH-CLOVER (*L. violacea*):
Eastern. Flowers purplish; clusters are on
stalks longer than the leaves.

CREEPING BUSH-CLOVER (*L. repens*):
Eastern. Stems prostrate; hairs pressed
against stems. **SIMILAR TRAILING
BUSH-CLOVER** (*L. procumbens*): Also
eastern. Stem hairs spreading.

NOTE ⚠ Korean-clover and ⚠ Japanese-
clover (both on p. 582) have more
prominent stipules (appendages at base
of leafstalk).

Slender Bush-clover

Flower
clusters
short-
stalked.
Leaflets
narrow.
HT: 1–3 ft.

Violet Bush-clover

Flower clusters
long-stalked.
Leaflets broad.
HT: 6–30 in.

Creeping Bush-clover

Stems trailing.

■ **UINTA CLOVER** (*Trifolium dasyphyllum*): Summer; slopes, mountain meadows, alpine tundra. Leaves all basal; leaflets 3, mostly untoothed (unusual for genus). Also called Alpine Clover, Whiproot Clover. **SIMILAR** ■ **PARRY'S CLOVER** (*T. parryi*): Stems short; leaflets often toothed; whorl of small, sepal-like bracts beneath flower cluster; flowers reddish purple.

■ **DWARF CLOVER** (*T. nanum*): Leaves all basal; leaflets toothed. Flowers, only 2 or 3 per cluster, held just above leaves. Also called Tundra Clover.

Genus *Trifolium* (89 species, 66 native). Leaves usually palmately divided into 3 equal-size, usually toothed leaflets. Flowers small, in dense, often ball-shaped clusters; pealike (p. 224). Pods tiny.

Uinta Clover
Flowers purplish and whitish. HT: 1–5 in.

Dwarf Clover
Flowers lilac-purple with some white. HT: about 1 in.

■ **LONG-STALK CLOVER** (*Trifolium longipes*): Summer; prairies, meadows, slopes. Flower clusters held well above leaves. Also called Summer Clover.

■ **LARGE-HEAD CLOVER** (*T. macrocephalum*): Spring–early summer; rocky flats, slopes, meadows. Flowers pinkish, in large clusters. Also called Big-head Clover.

■ **COW CLOVER** (*T. wormskioldii*): Spring–summer; coastal beaches to mountain meadows. Leaflets 3. Flowers purple-pink, often white-tipped. **SIMILAR** ■ **WHITE-TIP CLOVER** (*T. variegatum*): Flowers lilac to dark purple, white-tipped.

Long-stalk Clover
Flowers whitish or with some purple. Leaflets 3. Leaves basal and on erect stems. HT: 4–8 in.

Large-head Clover
Leaflets 5–9, often folded. HT: mostly 4–10 in.

Cow Clover
Circular, jagged-lobed bract below clusters. HT: 2–24 in.

■ **WHITE FALSE INDIGO** (*Baptisia alba*): Spring–summer; open woods, prairies, roadsides. Leaflets 3. Pods hairless, black at maturity (see inset).

■ **BLUE FALSE INDIGO** (*B. australis*): Open woods, grasslands, glades, bluffs.

■ **YELLOW FALSE INDIGO** (*B. tinctoria*): Open woods, clearings.

NOTE Species are also called wild-indigo.

Genus *Baptisia* (15 native species). Leaves divided into 3 leaflets. Flowers in elongated clusters mostly at stem ends, pealike (p. 224), with all 10 stamens separate. Pods inflated, papery or woody.

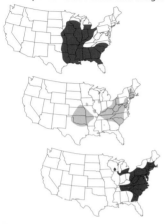

White False Indigo

Blue False Indigo

Flowers lavender to violet-blue. HT: 1–5 ft.

Yellow False Indigo

Flowers white to cream-colored. HT: 1–5 ft.

Flowers yellow. HT: 1½–3½ ft.

■ **MONTANE GOLDEN-BANNER** (*Thermopsis montana*): Spring–summer; open woods, slopes, meadows, stream banks. Pods straight (see inset). Also called Mountain Golden-pea. **SIMILAR** ■ **PRAIRIE GOLDEN-BANNER** (*T. rhombifolia*): Plains and hills. Pods C-shaped to nearly circular. **ALLEGHENY MOUNTAIN GOLDEN-BANNER** (*T. mollis*): Woods, slopes, ridges; southern Appalachian region. One of 3 similar species. Differs from Yellow False Indigo (above) in its persistent stipules (appendages at base of leafstalk, falling early in Yellow).

NOTE Species are also called golden-bean, false lupine.

Genus *Thermopsis* (10 native species). Similar to *Baptisia* (above), but with flat pods. Flowers always yellow.

Montane Golden-banner

Flowers golden yellow. Leaflets 3. HT: 1–2 ft.

■ **ARROWHEAD RATTLEBOX** (*Crotalaria sagittalis*): Summer–early fall; open places. Plants hairy. Uppermost leaves bear downward-pointing, arrowhead-shaped stipules (appendages at base of leafstalk). Leaves ½–2½ in. long. Pods plump, blackish in age.

■ **LOW RATTLEBOX** (*C. pumila*): Various sites. Leaves divided into 3 leaflets.

NOTE ⒈ Showy Rattlebox (p. 584) has leaves undivided, 2–6 in. long.

Genus *Crotalaria* (15 species, 5 native). Leaves simple or divided into 3 leaflets. Flowers pealike (p. 224), with 10 alternately long and short stamens. Pods inflated.

Arrowhead Rattlebox
Flowers yellow. Leaves undivided. HT: 4–16 in.

Low Rattlebox
Flowers often red-streaked. HT: 4–12 in.

■ **EASTERN CORAL-BEAN** (*Erythrina herbacea*): Mostly spring–summer; open sandy woods, pinelands, coastal strand. Plants shrubby, prickly; become soft-wooded shrubs or small trees in southernmost part of range. Leaflets 3, often broadly 3-lobed. Flowers borne on separate, leafless stems. Pods open to reveal hard, red, poisonous seeds (see inset). Also called Cherokee-bean, Cardinal-spear. **SIMILAR** ■ **WESTERN CORAL-BEAN** (*E. flabelliformis*): Rocky slopes. Flowers and leaves on same stem; leaflets round-triangular, not lobed.

NOTE *Erythrina* species are poisonous.

Genus *Erythrina* (3 species, 2 native). Mostly woody; often prickly. Leaves divided into 3 leaflets. Flowers tubular, with uppermost petal (the standard) much the largest. Pods commonly constricted between seeds.

Eastern Coral-bean
Flowers bright red; stamens protruding. HT: 2–5 ft.

■ **SILVERY LUPINE** (*Lupinus argenteus*):
Spring–fall; slopes, plains, meadows,
open woods. **SIMILAR** ■ **SUNDIAL
LUPINE** (*L. perennis*): Open woods,
clearings, roadsides. The most common
eastern species. Also called Wild Lupine.

■ **HARLEQUIN LUPINE** (*L. stiversii*):
Foothill woodlands. Flowers 3-colored.

■ **SULPHUR LUPINE** (*L. sulphureus*):
Open wooded and grassy slopes.

NOTE Most lupine species have blue to
violet flowers and are difficult to tell apart
(Harlequin Lupine and forms of Sulphur
Lupine are unusual). Lupines in Texas are
often called Texas Bluebonnet.

Genus *Lupinus* (151 species, 149 native).
Sometimes shrubby. Leaves mostly
palmately divided into 5–15 (rarely fewer)
leaflets. Flowers in elongated clusters, pealike (p. 224).
Pods flat. Do not confuse with *Pediomelum* (p. 237).

Silvery Lupine

Flowers blue
to lavender.
Leaflets 6–10,
hairy at least
beneath. Stems
silvery-hairy.
HT: 6–24 in.

Harlequin Lupine

Flowers yellow,
rose-pink,
and white.
HT: 4–20 in.

Sulphur Lupine

Flowers
yellow.
HT: 1–3 ft.

■ **COULTER'S LUPINE** (*Lupinus
sparsiflorus*): Spring; sandy places.
Leaflets 5–11. Uppermost flower petal
has white patch with red-dotted yellow
center. Also called Mojave Lupine.

■ **MINIATURE LUPINE** (*L. bicolor*): Spring;
open woods, grassy places, disturbed
areas. Leaflets 5–7, narrow. Uppermost
flower petal often nearly white with
blue-purple spots.

■ **BREWER'S LUPINE** (*L. breweri*): Late
spring–summer; mountain woods and
meadows. Leaflets 5–10.

NOTE In many blue- or violet-blue-
flowering lupines, the uppermost petal
often has a white or yellow patch that
commonly ages to red-purple.

Coulter's Lupine

Leaflets
narrow.
HT: 6–18 in.

Miniature Lupine

HT: 6–16 in.

Brewer's Lupine

Plants silvery-hairy.
HT: 2–12 in.

■ **LARGE-LEAF LUPINE** (*Lupinus polyphyllus*): Late spring–summer; moist or wet places; naturalized in western Great Lakes region and New England. Stems stout. Leaves both basal and on stem, large, divided into 5–17 (commonly 9–15) leaflets. Uppermost flower petal sometimes has white, yellowish, or red-violet blotch.

■ **STINGING LUPINE** (*L. hirsutissimus*): Mostly spring; shrublands, disturbed areas (especially following fire). Leaves divided into 5–8 rounded leaflets. Uppermost flower petal may be yellow-blotched. Also called Nettle Lupine. **DO NOT TOUCH** plants have stinging hairs.

Large-leaf Lupine

Flowers blue to purplish. HT: 2½–5 ft.

Stinging Lupine

Flowers red-violet. Plants have stinging hairs. HT: 1½–3 ft.

■ **BUSH LUPINE** (*Lupinus arboreus*): Spring–summer; coastal flats and bluffs, dunes. Shrubby. Plants nearly hairless to hairy. Flowers most often yellow; purplish or whitish in some populations. Also called Yellow-bush Lupine, Tree Lupine. SIMILAR ■ **SILVER BUSH LUPINE** (*L. albifrons*): Sandy or rocky places. Plants conspicuously silvery-hairy; flowers purplish (never yellow), back of uppermost petal hairy (not hairy in Bush Lupine). Also called White-leaf Bush Lupine. Do not confuse with Silvery Lupine (p. 235), which is not shrubby.

Bush Lupine

Flowers usually yellow. Leaflets 5–12. HT: 2–5 ft.

■ **PRAIRIE-TURNIP** (*Pediomelum esculentum*): Spring–summer; prairies, plains, hills. Leaflets mostly 5. Also called Indian-breadroot, Pomme de Prairie.

■ **SILVER-LEAF SCURF-PEA** (*P. argophyllum*): Prairies, plains, hills. Leaves (at least upper) divided into 3 silvery white leaflets.

NOTE Lupines have commonly more than 5 leaflets, small and large anthers (all alike in *Pediomelum*), and 2–12-seeded pods.

RELATED ■ **SAMPSON'S-SNAKEROOT** (*Orbexilum pedunculatum*): Open woods, pinelands, roadsides. Leaflets 3, narrow, middle one with longer stalk.

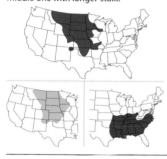

 Genus *Pediomelum* (21 native species). Leaves palmately divided into 3, 5, or 7 leaflets. Flowers pealike (p. 224). Pods small, 1-seeded, stalkless, all but tip enclosed in enlarged fruiting calyx (united sepals).

Prairie-turnip
Leaflets hairy beneath. Stems have spreading hairs. HT: 3–20 in.

Silver-leaf Scurf-pea

HT: 1½–3 ft.

Flowers blue or purple (aging tan).

Sampson's-snakeroot

HT: 1–3 ft.

■ **SLIM-FLOWER SCURF-PEA** (*Psoralidium tenuiflorum*): Spring–summer; prairies, plains, hills, open woods. Leaflets gland-dotted. Flowers rarely white. Pods ellipsoid. **SIMILAR** ■ **LEMON SCURF-PEA** (*P. lanceolatum*): Pods nearly round.

RELATED Also gland-dotted, but differ from *Psoralidium* in having broader leaflets with middle one stalked. ■ **CALIFORNIA-TEA** (*Rupertia physodes*): Spring; open places. Also called Rupert's Scurf-pea. ■ **LEATHER-ROOT** (*Hoita macrostachya*): Late spring–summer; moist places.

Genus *Psoralidium* (3 native species). Similar to *Pediomelum* (above), but stalked pods are exposed at maturity.

Slim-flower Scurf-pea
Flowers blue to violet. Leaflets mostly 3, narrow. HT: 1–3 ft.

California-tea
Flowers white or yellow. HT: 1–2½ ft.

Leather-root

Flowers blue or purple, on often hairy stalk. HT: to 5 ft.

■ **WILD LICORICE** (*Glycyrrhiza lepidota*): Spring–summer; prairies, thickets, stream banks, roadsides. Plants somewhat sticky-hairy. Leaflets have tiny dots on lower surface. Pods burlike, densely covered with hooked bristles. Also called American Licorice.

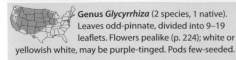

Genus *Glycyrrhiza* (2 species, 1 native). Leaves odd-pinnate, divided into 9–19 leaflets. Flowers pealike (p. 224); white or yellowish white, may be purple-tinged. Pods few-seeded.

Wild Licorice

Flowers in elongated clusters. Leaflets 9–19. HT: 1–3 ft.

■ **CANADIAN MILK-VETCH** (*Astragalus canadensis*): Spring–summer; thickets, open woods, prairies, shores. Pods hairless or occasionally short-hairy.

■ **FRECKLED MILK-VETCH** (*A. lentiginosus*): Plains, hillsides, shrublands. Leaflets numerous. Flowers purple to yellowish white; flower's keel tip spotted. Pods inflated, sometimes purple-spotted. Also called Mottled Locoweed.

NOTE *Astragalus* is a large genus, and species are difficult to tell apart. Species are sometimes called locoweed, a name shared with the similar *Oxytropis* (p. 239).

Genus *Astragalus* (about 350 species, most native). Leaves commonly basal and alternate, usually odd-pinnate, divided into several to numerous leaflets. Flowers pealike (p. 224). Pods flat to plump, often inflated.

Canadian Milk-vetch

Flowers yellowish white. Leaflets 11–35. HT: 1–4 ft.

Freckled Milk-vetch

HT: 6 in.–3 ft.

■ **SCARLET MILK-VETCH** (*Astragalus coccineus*): Spring; gravelly ridges, canyons. Plants silvery-hairy. Pods curved, white-woolly.

■ **PURSH'S MILK-VETCH** (*A. purshii*): Spring–summer; plains, hillsides. Plants silvery-hairy. Pods white-woolly. Also called Woolly-pod Locoweed.

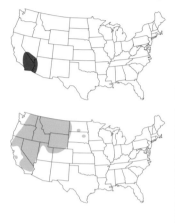

Scarlet Milk-vetch. Flowers red. Leaflets 7–15. HT: to 8 in.

Pursh's Milk-vetch. Flowers purplish to yellowish white. Leaflets 7–19. HT: 2–6 in.

■ **PURPLE LOCOWEED** (*Oxytropis lambertii*): Spring–summer; prairies, plains, slopes. Also called Lambert's Crazyweed.

■ **WHITE LOCOWEED** (*O. sericea*): Flowers white to pale yellow, with purple-tipped keel. Also called Silky Crazyweed.

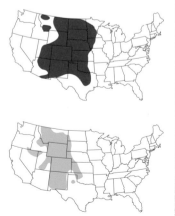

Genus *Oxytropis* (about 30 species, most native). Similar to *Astragalus* (p. 238), but all leaves arise from plant base (no stem leaves), and flower's keel has definite, short beak (keel tip blunt or round in *Astragalus*).

Purple Locoweed. Flowers pink-purple to violet. Leaflets 7–17, silvery-hairy. HT: 4–16 in.

White Locoweed

HT: mostly 6–12 in.

■ **NORTHERN SWEET-VETCH**
(*Hedysarum boreale*): Spring–summer;
grasslands, open woods. Pods have round
segments. Also called Boreal Sweet-
vetch. **SIMILAR** But with prominent side
veins on leaflets. ■ **ALPINE SWEET-
VETCH** (*H. alpinum*): Woods, meadows,
stream banks. Pod segments ¼ in.
long. ■ **WESTERN SWEET-VETCH**
(*H. occidentale*): Slopes, meadows,
canyons. Pod segments ⅜–½ in. long.

■ **YELLOW SWEET-VETCH**
(*H. sulphurescens*): Open woods, slopes,
meadows. Also called White Sweet-vetch.

NOTE Milk-vetches and locoweeds (pp.
238–239) have side petals (wings) longer
than keel; pods not segmented.

Genus *Hedysarum* (4 native species).
Leaves odd-pinnate, divided into mostly
7–19 leaflets. Flowers pealike (p. 224),
with keel (lowest petals) longer than wings (side petals).
Pods flat, segmented, visibly constricted between seeds.

Northern Sweet-vetch

Flowers
pink to
purple-red.
Leaflets 7–
15; side veins
inconspicuous.
HT: 6–24 in.

Yellow Sweet-vetch

Flowers
yellow to
whitish.
HT: 6–24 in.

■ **SILKY SOPHORA** (*Sophora nuttalliana*):
Spring–summer; grassy plains, rocky
hillsides. Leaflets mostly 11–23, elliptic,
often folded along midrib, gray-green,
fine-hairy. Pods 1–4-seeded.

■ **SILVERY SOPHORA** (*S. stenophylla*):
Spring–early summer; sandy soil, dunes.
Leaflets 9–15, very narrow, silvery silky-
hairy.

NOTE Some *Sophora* species are
poisonous. Do not confuse with milk-
vetches or locoweeds (pp. 238–239),
which have 9 joined stamens (1 free);
pods not constricted between seeds.

Genus *Sophora* (3 native species). Leaves
odd-pinnate, divided into 5–23 leaflets.
Flowers pealike (p. 224); stamens 10, all
separate. Pods generally strongly constricted between
seeds (in some species pearl-necklace-like), often beaked.

Silky Sophora
Flowers white
to yellowish
white. HT:
6–18 in.

Silvery Sophora

Flowers
blue-violet.
HT: 6–16 in.

■ **GOAT'S-RUE** (*Tephrosia virginiana*): Spring–summer; open woods, roadsides, sandy places. Also called Hoary-pea.

■ **LINDHEIMER'S HOARY-PEA** (*T. lindheimeri*): Leaflets 9–13, elliptic to round, white-edged. Flowers purple-rose.

SPIKED HOARY-PEA (*T. spicata*): Southeastern. Stems often rusty-hairy. Leaflets mostly 9–13. Flowers whitish, aging pink or maroon.

■ **SCURF HOARY-PEA** (*T. chrysophylla*, no photo): Plants prostrate, mat-forming. Leaflets 5–9. Flowers similar in color to Spiked Hoary-pea.

Genus *Tephrosia* (14 native species). Leaves odd-pinnate, divided into mostly 5–29 leaflets, commonly with conspicuous parallel side veins that extend to leaflet edges. Flowers pealike (p. 224). Pods flat, stalkless.

Goat's-rue
Flowers 2-colored: yellowish white and pinkish purple. Leaflets usually 13–25. Plants commonly gray-hairy. HT: 1–2 ft.

Lindheimer's Hoary-pea
HT: to 3 ft.

Spiked Hoary-pea
HT: 1–2 ft.

■ **AMERICAN WISTERIA** (*Wisteria frutescens*): Spring–early summer; woods, thickets, stream banks. Flowers blue-purple, lilac, or whitish, in hanging clusters. Pods hairless. **SIMILAR** ① **CHINESE WISTERIA** (*W. sinensis*): Eastern. Pods velvety-hairy.

Genus *Wisteria* (3 species, 1 native). Woody vines. Leaves odd-pinnate, divided into 7–19 leaflets. Flowers pealike (p. 224). Pods elongated, usually constricted between seeds.

American Wisteria

Flowers often blue-purple. Leaflets 7–15. Climbing vine.

■ **GROUNDNUT** (*Apios americana*): Summer–fall; thickets, stream banks, woods, meadows. Leaflets 5 or 7. Root tubers sometimes occur in necklacelike strands. Also called Potato-bean, Indian-potato.

Genus *Apios* (2 native species). Twining vines. Plants have milky sap. Leaves odd-pinnate, divided into 5 or 7 leaflets. Flowers pealike (p. 224). Pods linear.

Groundnut

Flowers purple-red to brownish maroon. Stems sprawling or climbing.

■ **LEADPLANT** (*Amorpha canescens*): Late spring–summer; prairies, roadsides, open woods. Plants shrubby, grayish-hairy. Leaves nearly stalkless; leaflets 15–50, each ⅜–¾ in. long. Flowers in dense, spikelike clusters near upper stems.

FALSE INDIGO-BUSH (*A. fruticosa*): Spring–summer; woods, stream banks, marsh edges, roadsides; widespread. Shrub. Leaves on stalks to 1 in. long; leaflets 9–23, each ¾–2 in. long.

Genus *Amorpha* (13 native species). Shrubs or shrubby; sometimes gland-dotted. Leaves odd-pinnate, divided into 9 to many leaflets. Flowers small, with 1 petal (the standard) and 10 protruding stamens. Pods 1- or 2-seeded.

Leadplant

Flowers purplish; anthers (stamen tips) yellow-orange. HT: 1–3 ft.

False Indigo-bush

HT: 3–10 ft.

■ **PURPLE PRAIRIE-CLOVER** (*Dalea purpurea*): Late spring–summer; prairies, plains, hillsides. Leaflets 3–7 (often 5). Flowers in dense, cylindrical clusters.

■ **WHITE PRAIRIE-CLOVER** (*D. candida*): Prairies, open woods, hillsides. Leaflets 5–9 (often 7).

Genus *Dalea* (59 native species). Plants usually sprinkled with minute dots (glands). Leaves odd-pinnate, divided into 5 to many leaflets (occasionally 3). Flowers pealike (p. 224) or not, with 5–10 stamens. Pods tiny, 1-seeded.

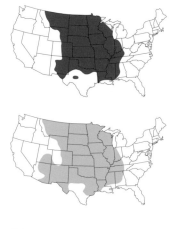

Purple Prairie-clover

Flowers small, rose to dark purple. HT: 1–3 ft.

White Prairie-clover

Flowers small, white. HT: 1–3 ft.

■ **GOLDEN PRAIRIE-CLOVER** (*Dalea aurea*): Late spring–summer; prairies, open woods, hillsides. Leaflets 3–7 (often 5). Also called Silktop Dalea.

■ **SUMMER-FAREWELL** (*D. pinnata*): Summer–fall; sandy places. Leaflets 3–11, threadlike. Also called Eastern Prairie-clover.

Golden Prairie-clover

Flowers small, yellow. Plants silky-hairy. HT: 1–3 ft.

Summer-farewell

Flowers small, white, in headlike clusters. HT: 1–3 ft.

■ **COASTAL INDIGO** (*Indigofera miniata*): Spring–fall; woods, open areas, disturbed places. Sprawling or trailing. Leaflets 5–9. Flowers about ½ in. long, wings (side petals) held horizontally. Pods to 1 in. long, several-seeded, opening when ripe. Also called Scarlet-pea.

■ **CAROLINA INDIGO** (*I. caroliniana*): Mostly summer; sandy woods. Shrubby. Leaflets 9–13. Flowers to ⁵⁄₁₆ in. long. Pods to ⁵⁄₁₆ in. long, 1–3-seeded, remaining closed. Also called Wild Indigo.

Genus *Indigofera* (12 species, 5 native). Sometimes shrubby. Leaves odd-pinnate, divided into 5–19 leaflets. Flowers pealike (p. 224), commonly reddish. Pods few- to many-seeded.

Coastal Indigo

Carolina Indigo

Flowers salmon-pink to reddish. HT: to 8 in.

Flowers pinkish to yellow-brown. HT: to 5 ft.

■ **BEACH-PEA** (*Lathyrus japonicus*): Spring–summer; sea beaches and shores of Great Lakes. Leaflets 6–12, somewhat fleshy. Also called Sea-vetchling.

■ **SILKY BEACH-PEA** (*L. littoralis*): Sea beaches. Leaflets 4–8, silky, densely gray-hairy. Also called Silky Beach Vetchling.

NOTE Do not confuse beach-peas with vetches (*Vicia*, p. 245).

Genus *Lathyrus* (40 species, 29 native). Mostly trailing, climbing, or sprawling. Stems often angled or winged. Leaves even-pinnate, divided into 2–16 leaflets tipped with tendril or bristle; stipules (leaflike appendages at leafstalk base) often prominent. Flowers pealike (p. 224). Pods flattened.

Beach-pea

Flowers blue-purple to rose or 2-colored: purple and white. Trailing or sprawling.

Silky Beach-pea

Flowers 2-colored: pink-purple and white. Prostrate or upward-growing.

■ **MARSH-PEA** (*Lathyrus palustris*): Spring–summer; moist or wet places. Leaflets 4–8 (often 6), opposite. Also called Marsh Vetchling.

■ **CREAM-PEA** (*L. ochroleucus*): Thickets, meadows, open woods. Leaflets 4–8 (often 6), opposite. Also called Cream Vetchling. **SIMILAR** ■ **NEVADA-PEA** (*L. lanszwertii*): Meadows, slopes, open woods. Leaflets broad to narrow, a little offset to opposite; flowers purple to white. Also called Nevada Vetchling.

■ **SNUB-PEA** (*L. sulphureus*): Shrublands, open forests, slopes. Leaflets 6–10, often alternate. Also called Snub Vetchling.

NOTE See also ⊡ Everlasting-pea (p. 582), with stems broadly winged; leaflets 2.

Marsh-pea
Flowers red-purple.

Cream-pea
Flowers whitish.

Snub-pea
Flowers bronze-yellow or purple-tinged.

■ **AMERICAN VETCH** (*Vicia americana*): Spring–summer; meadows, thickets, woods. Stipules (appendages at base of leafstalk) often toothed. Flowers about ¾ in. long. Pods visibly stalked.

■ **WOOD VETCH** (*V. caroliniana*): Woods, thickets, meadows. Stipules untoothed. Flowers about ½ in. long. Pods nearly stalkless. Also called Carolina Vetch.

■ **DEER-PEA** (*V. ludoviciana*, no photo): Open woods, fields, roadsides, plains, slopes. Stipules untoothed. Flowers about ¼ in. long, blue-purple or lavender. Also called Louisiana Vetch.

NOTE See also ⊡ Hairy Vetch (p. 581).

Genus *Vicia* (23 species, 11 native). Similar to *Lathyrus* (p. 244), but stems never winged; leaflets and flowers typically smaller. (Technical feature: *Lathyrus* styles hairy on inner side only; *Vicia* styles hairy on outer side or all around.)

American Vetch
Flowers blue to red-purple. Leaflets 8–16. Trailing, climbing, or sprawling.

Wood Vetch

Flowers white to pale lavender. Leaflets 10–20.

BIGPOD SESBANIA (*Sesbania herbacea*): Summer–fall; open, often moist or wet places. Flowers about ½ in. long. Pods narrow, many-seeded.

BAGPOD (*S. vesicaria*): Flowers about ⁵⁄₁₆ in. long. Pods plump, usually 2-seeded. Also called Bladderpod.

OTHER GENUS INDIAN JOINT-VETCH (*Aeschynomene indica*, no photo): Southeastern; nativity uncertain. Similar; flowers ¼–⅜ in. long; pods conspicuously segmented.

Genus *Sesbania* (7 species, 4 native). Leaves even-pinnate, divided into many leaflets. Flowers in clusters from leaf axils, pealike (p. 224). Pods few- to many-seeded.

Bigpod Sesbania

Bagpod

Flowers yellow, sometimes purple-marked. Leaflets tiny, numerous. HT: 3–12 ft.

Flowers orangish, reddish, or yellowish. HT: 3–12 ft.

FOOTHILL DEER-VETCH (*Lotus humistratus*): Spring–summer; grasslands, shrublands, slopes, deserts. Leaflets 4 or 5, irregularly arranged: 1 at tip, 1 on side, 2 or 3 on other side. Flowers often age reddish. Also called Colchita, Hill Lotus.

WRIGHT'S DEER-VETCH (*L. wrightii*): Open woods. Leaflets 3–6, nearly stalkless.

NOTE See also ⅰ Bird's-foot-trefoil (p. 584).

Genus *Lotus* (41 species, 37 native). Leaves odd-pinnate to nearly palmate, divided into 4–15 (usually 3–5) leaflets. Flowers solitary or in umbels (clusters with individual flower stalks arising from a common point) from leaf axils, pealike (p. 224). Pods variable.

Foothill Deer-vetch

Flowers small, yellow, usually solitary, stalkless. Plants hairy, often mat-forming. HT: 2–12 in.

Wright's Deer-vetch

Leaves appear palmate. HT: 8–16 in.

■ **MEADOW LOTUS** (*Lotus pinnatus*):
Spring–summer; moist or wet places.
Stems often swollen (spongy) at base.
Also called Bog Lotus. **SIMILAR**
■ **STREAMBANK LOTUS** (*L. oblongi-
folius*): Stems usually not swollen; leaflets
5–11 (often 7 or 9); flowers 2-colored
(yellow and white), or mostly all whitish
yellow, sometimes reddish-tinged. Also
called Torrey's Lotus, Narrow-leaf Lotus.

■ **SEASIDE LOTUS** (*L. formosissimus*):
Also similar. Stem bases often swollen.
Leaflets 5 or 7 (often 5). Flowers fade to
yellow and off-white.

Meadow Lotus

Flowers 2-colored:
yellow and white.
Leaflets mostly 5 or 7.
HT: 6–20 in.

Seaside Lotus

Flowers
yellow and
pink-purple.
HT: 6–16 in.

■ **SPANISH LOTUS** (*Lotus unifoliolatus*):
Spring–fall; open woods, grassy places.
Flowers solitary, above single leaflike
bract. Also called Spanish-clover.
Southeastern populations, var. *helleri*
(sometimes treated as a distinct species),
mostly hairless at maturity and with
narrower leaflets.

■ **BIG DEER-VETCH** (*L. crassifolius*): Late
spring–summer; open woods, shrublands.
Flowers in clusters. Also called Broad-leaf
Lotus, Buck Lotus.

Spanish Lotus

Flowers pink-
tinged yellowish
white. Leaflets
usually 3.
HT: 6 in.–3 ft.

Big Deer-vetch

Leaflets 7–17.

Flowers
purple-blotched
greenish yellow. HT: 1–4 ft.

■ **SHOWY PARTRIDGE-PEA**
(*Chamaecrista fasciculata*): Spring–fall; fields, roadsides, open woods. Flowers 1–1½ in. across; petals somewhat unequal in size.

■ **SENSITIVE PARTRIDGE-PEA**
(*C. nictitans*): Flowers ¼–½ in. across; lowest petal much larger than others. Also called Wild Sensitive-plant.

NOTE Species are also called sensitive-pea. Do not confuse with sennas (below), which have mostly wider leaflets (⅝–3 in., vs. mostly ¼–⅝ in. in partridge-peas); upper 3 stamens with reduced anthers (not reduced in partridge-peas); pods sometimes segmented.

Genus *Chamaecrista* (11 species, 9 native). Leaves even-pinnate, divided into several to numerous leaflets. Flowers not pealike; petals 5, sometimes unequal in size; stamens 5–10, often unequal. Pods flattened, elongated.

Showy Partridge-pea
Flowers yellow, purple-red-spotted near center. Leaflets 12–36.
HT: 6 in.–3½ ft.

Sensitive Partridge-pea

Flowers small; petals very unequal in size. HT: 6–30 in.

■ **WILD SENNA** (*Senna marilandica*): Summer; open woods, stream banks, roadsides. Pods flat, with rectangular segments. Also called Maryland Senna, Southern Wild Senna. **SIMILAR NORTHERN WILD SENNA** (*S. hebecarpa*): Eastern. Pod segments nearly square.

■ **LINDHEIMER'S SENNA**
(*S. lindheimeriana*): Dry hills, mesas. Plants velvety-hairy. Pods not segmented. Also called Velvet-leaf Senna.

■ **TWO-LEAF SENNA** (*S. bauhinioides*): Open places. Shrubby; plants gray-hairy.

NOTE See partridge-peas (above); also ⊞ Blunt-leaf Senna (p. 584), with leaflets mostly 6; pods 4-sided, strongly curved.

Genus *Senna* (25 species, 17 native). Leaves even-pinnate, divided into mostly 2–20 leaflets. Flowers not pealike; petals 5, sometimes unequal in size; stamens 10, unequal, upper 3 with much reduced anthers. Pods elongated.

Wild Senna

Flowers yellow; petals slightly unequal in size. Leaflets 12–20.
HT: 3–5 ft.

Lindheimer's Senna

Leaflets mostly 10–12.
HT: 2–5 ft.

Two-leaf Senna

Leaflets 2.
HT: 6–16 in.

■ **WAXY RUSH-PEA** (*Hoffmannseggia glauca*): Spring–fall; desert flats, grasslands, roadsides. Flower clusters and petal bases sticky-hairy (glandular). Also called Indian Rush-pea, Hog-potato. SIMILAR ■ **SICKLE-POD RUSH-PEA** (*H. drepanocarpa*): Flower clusters not sticky-hairy.

RELATED ■ **JAMES' FALSE HOLDBACK** (*Pomaria jamesii*, no photo): Similar to rush-peas. Stems and leaves sprinkled with orange dots (glands) that blacken when dry. Also called James' Rush-pea.

Genus *Hoffmannseggia* (7 native species). Leaves twice pinnately divided into many leaflets. Flowers not pealike; petals 5, somewhat unequal in size, with narrowed base; stamens 10. Pods flat, straight to crescent-shaped.

Waxy Rush-pea — Flowers yellowish to orange, often with reddish markings on uppermost petal. Leaflets small, numerous, bluish gray-green. HT: 4–12 in.

■ **ILLINOIS BUNDLE-FLOWER** (*Desmanthus illinoensis*): Summer; prairies, open woods, roadsides, slopes. Pods crescent-shaped, in ball-shaped clusters, about 1 in. long. Also called Prairie-mimosa.

■ **COOLEY'S BUNDLE-FLOWER** (*D. cooleyi*): Plains, slopes. Bushy. Stamens 10 per flower. Pods few, 1½–2½ in. long.

OTHER GENUS ■ **PRAIRIE ACACIA** (*Acacia angustissima*, no photo): Hillsides, mesas. Resembles Illinois and Cooley's Bundle-flowers; stamens many per flower. Also called White-ball Acacia.

NOTE See also genus *Mimosa* (p. 250).

Genus *Desmanthus* (13 species, 12 native). Leaves twice pinnately divided into many leaflets. Flowers in dense, ball-shaped clusters, tiny, not pealike. Pods variable.

Illinois Bundle-flower

Pods.

Flowers whitish, many, in "puffs"; stamens conspicuous, 5 per flower. Leaflets tiny. HT: 1–3 ft.

Cooley's Bundle-flower

Pods straight or slightly curved. HT: 8–20 in.

■ **CATCLAW SENSITIVE-BRIAR** (*Mimosa nuttallii*): Spring–summer; open woods, prairies, roadsides. Stems prickly, sprawling. Leaflets have visible side veins. Also called Nuttall's Mimosa. **SIMILAR** ■ **LITTLE-LEAF SENSITIVE-BRIAR** (*M. microphylla*): Leaflets lack visible side veins.

OTHER GENERA NEPTUNIA (*Neptunia*): South-central and southeastern. Not prickly. Flowers in "puffs." Also called Puff. **FAIRY-DUSTER** (*Calliandra eriophylla*, no photo): Desert slopes, plains; southwestern, chiefly AZ. Non-prickly shrub with often large, pink or reddish purple "puffs" of 5–10 flowers; stamens many. Also called False Mesquite.

Genus *Mimosa* (20 species, 19 native). Stems sometimes prickly. Flowers pink to white. Pods often prickly. Similar *Desmanthus* species (p. 249) have 1 or more bumps (glands) on leafstalks; stems and pods never prickly.

Catclaw Sensitive-briar

Flowers pink, many, in "puffs"; stamens protruding. HT: to 24 in.

Neptunia
Flowers bright yellow. HT: to 20 in.

FUMARIACEAE
FUMITORY FAMILY

Annual, biennial, or perennial. Leaves alternate or basal; fernlike or lacy, much divided into segments; often bluish gray. Flowers usually in clusters; petals 4: outer pair slightly united at base, inner pair joined at tips; sepals 2, small, often falling early; stamens 6, in 2 sets of 3; pistil 1. Fruits are typically capsules.

■ **GOLDEN CORYDALIS** (*Corydalis aurea*): Spring–summer; rocky or sandy soil. Leaves fernlike. Spur ⅛–¼ in. long, straight or slightly down-curved. Also called Scrambled-eggs.

■ **YELLOW CORYDALIS** (*C. flavula*): Spring; moist soil. Uppermost petal has toothed ridge (crest) at tip; spur about ¹⁄₁₆ in. long, often pointed slightly downward. Also called Short-spur Corydalis.

NOTE Species are also called fumewort.

Genus *Corydalis* (10 species, 9 native). Leaves alternate and basal. Spur (projection) at base of uppermost (outer) petal.

Golden Corydalis

Yellow Corydalis

Flowers yellow. Uppermost petal long-spurred. HT: 6–20 in.

HT: 4–12 in.

■ **PALE CORYDALIS** (*Corydalis sempervirens*): Summer–fall; rocky places, disturbed areas. Flowers in clusters of up to 8. Also called Rock-harlequin.

■ **SCOULER'S CORYDALIS** (*C. scouleri*): Summer; moist woods, stream banks. Flowers in clusters of 15–35. Also called Western Corydalis.

■ **SIERRAN CORYDALIS** (*C. caseana*): Summer; mountain stream banks. Similar to Scouler's Corydalis; flowers 50 or more per cluster, light pink to whitish, with reddish purple inner tips.

NOTE See also ⬛ Fumitory (p. 584).

Pale Corydalis

Flowers pink with yellow tips. Leaf segments narrow. HT: 2–32 in.

Scouler's Corydalis

Flowers pink. Leaf segments egg-shaped. HT: 2–5 ft.

Sierran Corydalis

HT: 1½–3 ft.

■ **DUTCHMAN'S-BREECHES** (*Dicentra cucullaria*): Spring; woods, clearings.

SQUIRREL-CORN (*D. canadensis*): Eastern. Similar to Dutchman's-breeches, but spurs not spread apart.

RELATED ■ **ALLEGHENY-VINE** (*Adlumia fungosa*): Summer–early fall. Climbing or scrambling vine with leaves along stem. Petals united, white to light pink-purple. Also called Climbing Fumitory, Mountain-fringe.

Genus *Dicentra* (7 native species). Leaves basal. Flowers nodding; outer 2 petals have bulge or spur at base, spreading tip.

Dutchman's-breeches

Flowers white to pinkish, with yellowish tips. Spurs pointed, spread apart. HT: 5–10 in.

Squirrel-corn

Spurs rounded. HT: 5–10 in.

Allegheny-vine

Spurs insignificant. Vine.

■ **PACIFIC BLEEDING-HEART** (*Dicentra formosa*): Spring–fall; woods, clearings. Outer petal tips spreading, ¹⁄₁₆–³⁄₁₆ in. long.

■ **EASTERN BLEEDING-HEART** (*D. eximia*): Rocky places. Outer petal tips ³⁄₁₆–⁵⁄₁₆ in. long; flowers rarely white. Also called Fringed or Wild Bleeding-heart.

■ **STEER'S-HEAD** (*D. uniflora*): Spring–summer; slopes, hillsides. Dwarf. Flower solitary; noncurved part of outer petals narrow, shorter than backward-curving tips. SIMILAR **FEW-FLOWER BLEEDING-HEART** (*D. pauciflora*): Mountains of southwestern OR, northern CA, local in southern Sierra Nevada. Flowers 1–3 per cluster; noncurved part of petals broader, longer; plants 3–8 in. tall. Also called Short-horn Steer's-head.

Pacific Bleeding-heart

Flowers rose-purple to pink or cream-colored. Outer petal tips short. HT: 8–18 in.

Eastern Bleeding-heart

Flowers have narrow neck. HT: 10–20 in.

Steer's-head

Outer petal tips long, curved backward. HT: 1–3 in.

■ **GOLDEN-EARDROPS** (*Ehrendorferia chrysantha*): Spring–summer; dry hillsides, disturbed areas, commonly colonizing after fire. Outer petal tips spreading or curved backward to about the middle.

■ **WHITE-EARDROPS** (*E. ochroleuca*): Outer petals spread outward only near tips. Flowers commonly cream-colored, often purple-tipped.

Genus *Ehrendorferia* (2 native species). Similar to *Dicentra* (p. 251), but leaves on stem and at plant base; flowers erect.

Golden-eardrops

Flowers golden yellow. HT: 2–5 ft.

White-eardrops

Flowers whitish to pale yellow. HT: 3–6 ft.

GELSEMIACEAE
JESSAMINE FAMILY
Woody vines, twining or trailing; evergreen. Leaves opposite, simple, and untoothed. Flowers solitary or in clusters, showy; funnel-shaped (petals united) and 5-lobed; sepals 5; stamens 5; pistil 1. Fruits are capsules. Often included in the logania family (Loganiaceae).

■ **YELLOW JESSAMINE** (*Gelsemium sempervirens*): Spring; dry or wet woods, thickets, fencerows. Leaves lance-shaped. Flowers fragrant, funnel-shaped, 1–1½ in. long, in leaf axils. Also called Carolina Jessamine. SIMILAR ■ **RANKIN'S JESSAMINE** (*G. rankinii*): Wet woods, swamps, bogs. Sepal tips long-tapering (broadly pointed, blunt, or rounded in Yellow Jessamine); flowers not fragrant. Also called Swamp Jessamine.

Genus *Gelsemium* (2 native species). With characters of the family. Plants are poisonous.

Yellow Jessamine

Flowers bright yellow; lobes rounded. Twining woody vine.

GENTIANACEAE
GENTIAN FAMILY
Annual, biennial, or perennial. Leaves mostly opposite, less often whorled, basal, or alternate; simple, stalkless, and untoothed. Flowers solitary or in clusters; mostly tubular to funnel- or bell-shaped (petals united), 4- or 5-lobed; sepals united, 4- or 5-lobed; stamens 4 or 5; pistil 1. Fruits are capsules.

■ **WHITISH GENTIAN** (*Gentiana algida*): Late summer–fall; moist or wet mountain meadows. Leaves narrow. Flowers solitary or few, broadly vase-shaped; tissue flaps between lobes irregularly toothed. Also called Arctic Gentian.

■ **NEWBERRY'S GENTIAN** (*G. newberryi*): Basal leaves spoon-shaped; basal and lower leaves wider above middle. Flowers may be pale blue (or deep blue in northern part of range). Also called Alpine Gentian.

Genus *Gentiana* (27 native species). Leaves mostly opposite. Flowers have 5 (or sometimes 4) lobes, alternating with folds or flaps of tissue (plaits), often giving pleated look.

Whitish Gentian

Flowers cream-colored marked with purple or green. Leaves narrow. HT: 2–6 in.

Newberry's Gentian

Flowers blue, or whitish with dark purplish bands. HT: 1½–5 in.

■ **EXPLORER'S GENTIAN** (*Gentiana calycosa*): Late summer–fall; moist or wet places in mountains. Leaf edges and lobes of calyx (united sepals) hairless. Flowers often solitary; tissue flaps between lobes toothed or fringed at tip. Also called Rainier Pleated Gentian, Mountain Bog Gentian.

■ **PLEATED GENTIAN** (*G. affinis*): Moist or wet places in mountains. Leaf edges and calyx lobes fine-hairy. Flowers in clusters. **SIMILAR PARRY'S GENTIAN** (*G. parryi*): Southern Rocky Mountains. Flowers and flower bracts broader.

■ **KING'S-SCEPTER GENTIAN** (*G. sceptrum*): Bogs, wet places. Tissue flaps between flower lobes squared off or rounded. Also called King's Gentian.

Pleated Gentian
HT: 3–30 in.

Explorer's Gentian
Flowers deep blue, often spotted, broadly vase-shaped. HT: 2–18 in.

King's-scepter Gentian
HT: 6–30 in.

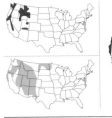

■ **BOTTLE GENTIAN** (*Gentiana andrewsii*): Late summer–fall; moist places. Flowers in clusters; closed, resembling large buds; fringed tissue flaps at tip conspicuously larger than adjacent lobes. Also called Closed Gentian. **SIMILAR** With tissue flaps shorter than or as long as flower lobes. **MEADOW CLOSED GENTIAN** (*G. clausa*): Mostly northeastern. Lobes of calyx (united sepals) roundish. **SOAP-WORT GENTIAN** (*G. saponaria*): Eastern. Calyx lobes narrow; flowers often slightly open at tip.

■ **STRIPED GENTIAN** (*G. villosa*): Open woods. Leaves widest near or above middle. Also called Sampson's Snakeroot. **SIMILAR WHITE PRAIRIE GENTIAN** (*G. alba*): Moist prairies, open woods; mostly midwestern. Leaves mostly widest near base. Also called Pale Gentian.

Bottle Gentian
Flowers deep blue (often whitish below), remain closed. HT: 1–3 ft.

Striped Gentian
Flowers greenish white, often striped or flushed with purple, often partially open at tip. HT: 6–24 in.

■ **NORTHERN-GENTIAN** (*Gentianella amarella*): Summer; moist mountain meadows. Flowers tubular and 4- or 5-lobed; inside base of each lobe has fringelike bristles. Also called Felwort, Autumn Dwarf-gentian.

■ **STIFF-GENTIAN** (*G. quinquefolia*): Moist or wet places. Flower lobes often sharp-tipped, lack fringelike bristles. Also called Agueweed.

Genus *Gentianella* (9 native species). Similar to *Gentiana* (p. 253), but lacks flaps of tissue between flower lobes.

Northern-gentian

Flowers bluish purple to pinkish, fringed within. HT: 4–24 in.

Stiff-gentian

Flowers bluish, lavender, or whitish. HT: 6–30 in.

■ **GREATER FRINGED-GENTIAN** (*Gentianopsis crinita*): Late summer–fall; moist or wet places. Midstem leaves lance- or egg-shaped, ⅜–¾ in. wide. Flowers solitary, on stalks 2–8 in. long.

LESSER FRINGED-GENTIAN (*G. virgata*): Similar range (absent in New England) and habitat. Midstem leaves linear to narrowly lance-shaped, mostly less than ⅜ in. wide. Flower lobes often fringed on sides, with irregularly toothed tip.

■ **ROCKY MOUNTAIN FRINGED-GENTIAN** (*G. thermalis*): Wet mountain meadows, stream banks. Flowers on stalks 1½–6 in. long; lobes irregularly toothed or with short fringe. **SIMILAR PERENNIAL FRINGED-GENTIAN** (*G. barbellata*): Southern and middle Rocky Mountains. Flowers nearly stalkless, windmill-like, with narrow lobes.

Genus *Gentianopsis* (11 native species). Similar to *Gentiana* (p. 253), but lacks flaps of tissue between flower lobes. Flowers always 4-lobed, usually fringed or toothed, sometimes twisted (windmill-like).

Greater Fringed-gentian

Flowers bright blue, long-stalked; lobes deeply fringed. HT: 1–3 ft.

Lesser Fringed-gentian

HT: 6–30 in.

Rocky Mountain Fringed-gentian

HT: 6–24 in.

■ **ONE-FLOWER FRINGED-GENTIAN**
(*Gentianopsis simplex*): Late summer–fall;
wet mountain meadows. Stems
unbranched. Stem leaves in 3–6 pairs.
Flowers solitary; lobes untoothed to
shortly fringed, commonly with jagged-
toothed tip. Also called Hiker's-gentian.

■ **SIERRAN FRINGED-GENTIAN**
(*G. holopetala*): Stems generally branched
at base. Stem leaves in 1–3 pairs. Flowers
solitary; lobes untoothed to unevenly
toothed, often with shallowly toothed tip.
Lobes of calyx (united sepals) often have
dark midrib (lacking in *G. simplex*).

One-flower Fringed-gentian

Flowers
dark blue,
long-stalked.
HT: 2–12 in.

Sierran Fringed-gentian

HT: 2–16 in.

PRAIRIE-GENTIAN (*Eustoma exaltatum*):
Spring–summer; meadows, prairies,
riverbanks, coastal sands. Blue-purple
flowers are most common; variants, most
notably pink or white, are sometimes
found. Also called Catchfly-gentian,
Bluebells. Two subspecies are shown
here: ■ **SHOWY PRAIRIE-GENTIAN**
(ssp. *russellianum*): Leaves gray-green.
Flowers large, 2–4 in. across, often with
whitish inner ring. ■ **TALL PRAIRIE-
GENTIAN** (ssp. *exaltatum*): Flowers 1–2 in.
across, with proportionally narrower lobes.

Genus *Eustoma* (1 native species).
Leaves opposite. Flowers large, solitary
or in clusters; bell-shaped and 5-lobed
(petals appear separate but are united at bases); calyx
(united sepals) tubular, deeply cut into narrow lobes.

Showy Prairie-gentian

Flowers
usually blue-
purple with
darker center.
HT: 10–30 in.

Tall Prairie-gentian

HT: 10–30 in.

■ **MONUMENT-PLANT** (*Frasera speciosa*): Summer; open woods, slopes, mountain meadows. Flowers have 2 fringe-bordered nectar pits per lobe. Also called Green-gentian, Elkweed.
SIMILAR ■ **AMERICAN-COLUMBO** (*F. caroliniensis*): Spring; woods, clearings, meadows. 1 nectar pit per lobe.

OTHERS 1 nectar pit per flower lobe. **WHITE-STEM FRASERA** (*F. albicaulis*, no photo): Flats, slopes; northwestern. Leaves opposite. ■ **CLUSTERED ELKWEED** (*F. fastigiata*): Mountain forests and meadows. Leaves whorled.

RELATED ■ **FELWORT** (*Swertia perennis*): Wet places in mountains. Flowers purplish, 5-lobed.

Genus *Frasera* (13 native species). Flowers in clusters; generally saucer-shaped; 4-lobed, each lobe bearing 1 or 2 nectar pits, these often surrounded by fringed appendages.

Monument-plant
Flowers yellowish green with purple spots, 4-lobed. Leaves whorled. HT: 2–6 ft.

Clustered Elkweed

Flowers usually blue, 4-lobed. HT: 2–5 ft.

Felwort

HT: 8–20 in.

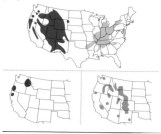

■ **MARSH-FELWORT** (*Lomatogonium rotatum*): Summer–early fall; moist or often wet soil in meadows, marshes, shores; sometimes saline; common in parts of Alaska and Canada. Lobes of calyx (united sepals) slender and conspicuous.

Genus *Lomatogonium* (1 native species). Leaves opposite. Flowers in clusters, saucer-shaped, 4- or 5-lobed, with base of each lobe bearing 2 tiny, fringed, scalelike appendages.

Marsh-felwort

Flowers white to bluish. Stem leaves narrow, stalkless. HT: 4–16 in.

■ **ARIZONA CENTAURY** (*Zeltnera arizonica*): Mostly spring; moist or sometimes wet ground. Basal leaves in clusters. Flowers ¾–1 in. across.

SIMILAR ■ **MONTEREY CENTAURY** (*Z. muehlenbergii*): Late spring–summer. Basal leaves absent or few, not in clusters; flowers ¼–½ in. across.

RELATED Ⅰ **EUROPEAN CENTAURY** (*Centaurium erythraea*, no photo): Open places; mostly northwestern and northeastern; similar Eurasian introduction. Basal leaves in clusters. Flowers ⅜–½ in. across.

NOTE Do not confuse centaury species with *Sabatia* (below).

Genus *Zeltnera* (17 native species). Leaves opposite, sometimes also basal. Flowers have long, slender tube and 5 spreading lobes; calyx (united sepals) tubular, deeply lobed; stamens frequently protruding.

Arizona Centaury

Flowers rose-purple with white or yellowish eye, trumpet-shaped, in loose clusters. HT: 8–20 in.

■ **ROSE-PINK** (*Sabatia angularis*): Summer; moist places. Stems 4-angled. Flowers 5-lobed, rarely white. Also called Rose-gentian, Marsh-pink.

■ **MARSH ROSE-GENTIAN** (*S. dodecandra*): Summer–fall; wet areas. Flowers similar to Rose-pink but with 8–12 lobes. Also called Large Marsh-pink.

■ **SHORT-LEAF ROSE-GENTIAN** (*S. brevifolia*): Spring–fall; wet pinelands. Flowers white with yellowish eye, 5-lobed.

NOTE Several species similar to these, mostly southeastern. Do not confuse *Sabatia* with centaury species (above), which have a flower tube generally as long as or longer than the lobes.

Genus *Sabatia* (21 native species). Leaves opposite, also occasionally basal. Flowers short-tubed, with 5–12 spreading lobes; calyx (united sepals) short-tubed, with slender lobes; style protrudes, the 2 stigmas first entwined, later untwisting.

Rose-pink

Flowers pink with yellow eye. HT: 1–3 ft.

Marsh Rose-gentian

HT: to 2½ ft.

Short-leaf Rose-gentian

HT: to 2 ft.

■ **SPURRED-GENTIAN** (*Halenia deflexa*): Summer; moist places. Flower spurs point downward. Some flowers spurless or with spurs reduced to bumps.

■ **MT. GRAHAM SPURRED-GENTIAN** (*H. rothrockii*): Summer–fall; woods, mountain meadows. Flower spurs spread outward.

Genus *Halenia* (2 native species). Leaves opposite. Flowers tubular and 4-lobed; bases usually have downward- or outward-pointing, hollow projections (spurs).

Spurred-gentian

Flowers purplish or greenish, 4-spurred at base. HT: 6–30 in.

Mt. Graham Spurred-gentian

Flowers yellow. HT: 6–20 in.

■ **PENNYWORT** (*Obolaria virginica*): Spring; woods. Upper leaves broadly spoon- or wedge-shaped; lower leaves scalelike.

NOTE Pennywort is mycotrophic, obtaining some nourishment from soil fungi that are interconnected with the roots of photosynthetic woody plants.

Genus *Obolaria* (1 native species). Plants fleshy. Leaves opposite. Flowers tubular, cut to about the middle into 4 lobes; calyx (united sepals) divided into 2 leaflike segments.

Pennywort

Flowers whitish, nearly stalkless, in leaf axils. HT: 3–6 in.

Plants often purple-tinged.

■ **VIRGINIA BARTONIA** (*Bartonia virginica*): Late summer–fall; swamps, bogs, woods, thickets. Stems wiry. Leaves scalelike; midstem leaves mostly opposite.

■ **SCREWSTEM BARTONIA** (*B. paniculata*): Similar to Virginia Bartonia, but sprawling, with stems frequently twisted; midstem leaves alternate. Flowers whitish or greenish.

■ **SPRING BARTONIA** (*B. verna*): Spring; bogs, wet woods and meadows, ditches. Flowers white. Also called White Bartonia.

NOTE Like Pennywort (p. 259), bartonias are mycotrophic.

Genus *Bartonia* (4 native species). Stems very slender. Leaves opposite or alternate, reduced to scales. Flowers 4-lobed.

Virginia Bartonia

Flowers tiny, greenish yellow to whitish. HT: 4–16 in.

Screwstem Bartonia

HT: 4–16 in.

Spring Bartonia

HT: 2–8 in.

GERANIACEAE   GERANIUM FAMILY

Annual, biennial, or perennial; plants frequently have sticky hairs. Leaves alternate or opposite, sometimes basal; usually lobed or divided. Flowers solitary or in clusters; petals 5; sepals 5; stamens 5, 10, or 15; pistil 1. Fruits 5-segmented, with a long beak formed from the fused styles.

■ **WILD GERANIUM** (*Geranium maculatum*): Spring–early summer; woods. Also called Spotted Crane's-bill.

■ **RICHARDSON'S GERANIUM** (*G. richardsonii*): Spring–fall; woods, moist mountain meadows. Flowers white or pale pink, with purple veins; stalks usually covered with purple- or red-tipped sticky hairs. Also called White Crane's-bill.

■ **STICKY GERANIUM** (*G. viscosissimum*): Spring–summer; woods, mountain meadows. Flowers deep pink with darker veins; stalks may have white- or yellow-tipped sticky hairs. Also called Sticky Purple Crane's-bill.

Genus *Geranium* (25 species, 14 native). Leaves palmately lobed or divided, the divisions usually toothed or lobed. Stamens mostly 10. Mature fruit segments curl up on beak.

Wild Geranium

Flowers purplish pink to lavender. Leaves 3–7-lobed. HT: 1–2 ft.

Richardson's Geranium

HT: 1–3 ft.

Sticky Geranium

HT: 1–2½ ft.

■ **PURPLE GERANIUM** (*Geranium caespitosum*): Summer; open woods, meadows, slopes. Stems often hairy toward base. Leaves 3–5-lobed. Flowers about 1 in. across, sometimes whitish with red-purple veins; petal tips commonly rounded, may be shallowly notched. Also called Wild Geranium, Purple Cluster Crane's-bill.

■ **CAROLINA GERANIUM** (*G. carolinianum*): Woods, clearings, fields, roadsides. Stems often short-hairy. Leaves 5–9-lobed. Flowers ½ in. or less across; petals commonly shallowly notched; sepals minutely spine-tipped. Also called Carolina Crane's-bill. **SIMILAR** ① **DOVE'S-FOOT GERANIUM** (*G. molle*): Mostly eastern and western; native to Eurasia. Stems long-hairy; petals deeply notched; sepals not spine-tipped.

Purple Geranium

Flowers often rose-purple with darker veins, sometimes whitish-streaked. HT: 6–24 in.

Carolina Geranium

Flowers mostly light pink to rose, sometimes whitish. HT: 6–18 in.

■ **HERB-ROBERT** (*Geranium robertianum*): Spring–fall; rocky woods. Plants weedy, with unpleasant odor. Considered by some to be native only to the Old World; possibly also native in Northeast.

RELATED With mature fruit segments spirally twisted. ■ **TEXAS STORK'S-BILL** (*Erodium texanum*): Spring; gravelly or sandy soil. Leaves ⅝–1½ in. long. Also called Desert Heron's-bill.
■ **ROUND-LEAF STORK'S-BILL** (*California macrophylla*, no photo): Similar; leaves round-kidney-shaped, scallop-toothed. Also called Round-leaf Filaree. See also ① Common Stork's-bill (p. 585), with leaves divided into leaflets.

Herb-Robert

Flowers rose-purple. Leaves divided, fernlike. HT: 4–20 in.

Texas Stork's-bill

Flowers reddish purple. Leaves lobed. Stems often lie on ground.

HAEMODORACEAE
BLOODWORT or REDROOT FAMILY

Perennial. Roots reddish. Leaves mostly arise from plant base, simple, narrowly sword-shaped. Flowers in clusters; 6 tepals (3 petals and 3 petal-like sepals); stamens 3; pistil 1. Fruits are capsules.

■ **CAROLINA REDROOT** (*Lachnanthes caroliniana*): Mostly summer; wet ditches, bogs, swamps, pinelands.

Genus *Lachnanthes* (1 native species). With characters of the family. Flowers densely hairy outside; stamens protruding.

Carolina Redroot
Flowers woolly outside, yellow inside. Leaves irislike.
HT: 1–3½ ft.

HYDRANGEACEAE
HYDRANGEA FAMILY

Mostly shrubs and woody vines. Leaves opposite and simple. Flowers in clusters; petals 4–6; sepals 4–6; stamens 8 to many; pistil 1. Fruits are capsules.

■ **MODESTY** (*Whipplea modesta*): Spring–early summer; open woods, clearings, slopes. Often mat-forming; main stem woody and trailing, giving rise to erect, herbaceous flowering shoots. Leaves 3-veined. Also called Yerba de Selva, Whipple-vine, Common Whipplea.

OTHER GENUS *Decumaria* (1 native species). Also with opposite leaves and clusters of small white flowers.
■ **WOOD-VAMP** (*D. barbara*): Wet woods, swamps. Woody vine climbing via small stem rootlets. Stamens 20–30. Also called Climbing-hydrangea.

Genus *Whipplea* (1 native species). Somewhat shrubby. Flowers small, in crowded clusters; petals and sepals each 4–6 (often 5); stamens 8–12; styles 4 or 5.

Modesty

Wood-vamp
Leaves stalked, mostly not hairy.

Flowers white. Leaves nearly stalkless, hairy.

HYDROPHYLLACEAE   WATERLEAF FAMILY

Annual, biennial, or perennial. Leaves alternate, basal, or less often opposite; simple or compound. Flowers in clusters or sometimes solitary; funnel-, bell-, or saucer-shaped (petals united), 5-lobed; sepals 5, united; stamens 5; pistil 1, style 2-lobed (or sometimes styles 2). Fruits are capsules.

■ **VIRGINIA WATERLEAF** (*Hydrophyllum virginianum*): Spring–early summer; woods, ravines, floodplains. Leaves pinnately divided; toothed and sometimes lobed; often mottled. Also called Shawnee-salad. SIMILAR ■ **FENDLER'S WATERLEAF** (*H. fendleri*): Mountain woods. ■ **PACIFIC WATERLEAF** (*H. tenuipes*): Wooded slopes, meadows, stream banks. Leaves as wide as long. Also called Slender-stem Waterleaf.

■ **LARGE-LEAF WATERLEAF** (*H. macrophyllum*): Woods. Upper stems have spreading hairs.

Genus *Hydrophyllum* (9 native species). Leaves lobed or divided. Flowers often in compact, rounded clusters; bell-shaped and 5-lobed; stamens and style protruding.

Virginia Waterleaf

Large-leaf Waterleaf

Flowers white to pale purple. Leaf segments 3–7. HT: 1–3 ft.

Flowers white to pinkish. Leaf segments 7–13. HT: 1–3 ft.

■ **BROAD-LEAF WATERLEAF** (*Hydrophyllum canadense*): Spring–early summer; woods, floodplains, ravines. SIMILAR ■ **GREAT WATERLEAF** (*H. appendiculatum*): Flower stalks bristly-hairy; tiny "teeth" between sepals; stamens short-protruding. Also called Appendaged Waterleaf.

■ **WESTERN WATERLEAF** (*H. occidentale*): Mountain woods, thickets. Leaves pinnate; leaflets toothed on lower edges. Flowers purplish to white; clusters above leaves. Also called California Waterleaf.

■ **BALLHEAD WATERLEAF** (*H. capitatum*): Similar to Western Waterleaf, but lower edges of leaflets untoothed; flower clusters usually shorter than leaves. Also called Dwarf Waterleaf.

Broad-leaf Waterleaf

Western Waterleaf

HT: 6–24 in.

Ballhead Waterleaf

Flowers white to pink-purple; stamens long-protruding. Leaves palmate, maplelike. HT: 1–3 ft.

HT: 4–16 in.

■ **FERN-LEAF PHACELIA** (*Phacelia bipinnatifida*): Spring; woods. Spreading, gland-tipped hairs on branches in flower cluster (hairs shorter, not gland-tipped on Virginia Waterleaf, p. 263). **SIMILAR** ■ **COMMON PHACELIA** (*P. distans*): Slopes, washes. Leaves short-stalked. ■ **THREAD-LEAF PHACELIA** (*P. linearis*): Plains, slopes. Leaves narrow, sometimes 3-lobed.

■ **MIAMI-MIST** (*P. purshii*): Woods. Petals fringed.

DESERT BLUEBELLS (*P. campanularia*): Gravelly or sandy places; southern CA, introduced in southern AZ. Leaves round, toothed. Flowers deep blue, bell- to funnel-shaped.

Genus *Phacelia* (158 native species). Plants usually hairy. Leaves simple or compound, mostly alternate. Flowers typically in coiled clusters, uncoiling as they mature; bell-, saucer-, or funnel-shaped, 5-lobed; stamens and style often protrude, giving "whiskery" appearance. Phacelias are also called scorpionweed.

Fern-leaf Phacelia

Miami-mist
HT: 8–16 in.

Flowers violet-blue. Leaves long-stalked, divided into coarsely toothed segments. HT: 6 in.–3 ft.

Desert Bluebells
HT: 6–24 in.

■ **SILKY PHACELIA** (*Phacelia sericea*): Summer; rocky slopes. Leaves pinnately lobed or divided, silvery-hairy. Also called Purple-fringe.

■ **SILVER-LEAF PHACELIA** (*P. hastata*): Late spring–summer; open places. Leaves lance-shaped, silvery-hairy. **SIMILAR** ■ **VARIABLE-LEAF PHACELIA** (*P. heterophylla*): Some leaves 1- or 2-lobed at base.

Silky Phacelia
Flowers purple, in dense clusters; stamens very long. HT: 4–16 in.

Silver-leaf Phacelia
Flowers white to lavender-pinkish; stamens very long. HT: 1–2 ft.

■ **CATERPILLAR PHACELIA** (*Phacelia cicutaria*): Spring; slopes, shrublands, open woods, grasslands. Plants densely bristly-hairy. Leaves deeply pinnately lobed or divided, toothed. Flowers yellowish white or pale lavender.

■ **STINGING PHACELIA** (*P. malvifolia*): Spring–summer; shrublands, open woods. Leaves broadly triangular, shallowly lobed, coarsely toothed. Flowers cream-colored. Also called Mallow-leaf Phacelia. **DO NOT TOUCH** Plants covered with stinging hairs.

Caterpillar Phacelia

Flower clusters tightly coiled, unfurl into long "fuzzy caterpillars." HT: 6–24 in.

Stinging Phacelia

Plants densely covered with stiff, yellowish, stinging hairs. HT: 6 in.–3 ft.

■ **WASHOE PHACELIA** (*Phacelia curvipes*): Spring; open places. Leaves unlobed. Flowers blue with white center.

■ **FREMONT'S PHACELIA** (*P. fremontii*): Leaves deeply pinnately lobed. Flowers have yellow tube and eye, purplish lobes.

■ **SHORT-LOBE PHACELIA** (*P. brachyloba*): Leaves deeply pinnately lobed. Flowers have yellow tube and eye, white or pink lobes.

■ **GLANDULAR YELLOW PHACELIA** (*P. adenophora*): Leaves deeply pinnately lobed. Flowers usually entirely yellow; lobes occasionally purplish.

NOTE These species lack conspicuous protruding stamens.

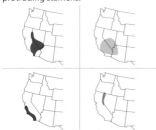

Washoe Phacelia

HT: 2–6 in.

Fremont's Phacelia

HT: 3–12 in.

Short-lobe Phacelia

HT: 6–24 in.

Glandular Yellow Phacelia

HT: 4–16 in.

■ **BRISTLY NAMA** (*Nama hispidum*): Spring–early summer; sandy or gravelly places. Stems upright or spreading. Leaves well distributed on stems. Flowers have 2 styles. Also called Sandbells.

■ **PURPLE-MAT** (*N. demissum*): Spring. Stems trailing. Leaves clustered at stem ends. Flowers have 2 styles. Also called Purple Nama. **SIMILAR** ■ **GROUND NAMA** (*N. aretioides*): Flowers have 1 style (usually divided at tip). Also called Purple Fiddleleaf.

Genus *Nama* (20 native species). Leaves generally alternate and simple. Flowers solitary or in clusters; bell-, funnel-, or trumpet-shaped, 5-lobed; stamens of unequal length.

Bristly Nama

Flowers purplish with yellow eye. HT: 4–20 in.

Purple-mat

Plants often mat-forming. HT: 3–6 in.

■ **POODLE-DOG-BUSH** (*Turricula parryi*): Summer; slopes, shrublands, disturbed places such as after fire. Plants sticky-hairy, have unpleasant odor. Flowers tubular-funnel-shaped, in clusters.

RELATED *Eriodictyon* (8 native species). With similar flowers. ■ **CALIFORNIA YERBA-SANTA** (*E. californicum*): Spring–summer; slopes, woods, shrublands, disturbed places. Pleasantly aromatic evergreen shrub. Leaves leathery, sticky and hairless above, grayish-yellow-felty beneath. Also called Mountain-balm.
■ **HAIRY YERBA-SANTA** (*E. trichocalyx*, no photo): Flowers densely hairy outside.

Genus *Turricula* (1 native species). Shrubby. Leaves alternate and simple. Flowers in clusters, 5-lobed, hairy outside.

Poodle-dog-bush

California Yerba-santa

Flowers whitish to purplish. Leaves thick, short-stalked. HT: 2–8 ft.

Flowers mostly purplish. Leaves thin, stalkless, narrow, crowded on stem. HT: 3–8 ft.

■ **WHISPERING-BELLS** (*Emmenanthe penduliflora*): Spring–early summer; open places, especially after fire or other disturbance. Leaves have many short lobes. Flowers eventually nodding.
■ **ROSE WHISPERING-BELLS** (var. *rosea*) has white to pink flowers.

Genus *Emmenanthe* (1 native species). Plants sticky-hairy, odorous. Leaves alternate and basal, pinnately lobed. Flowers in clusters, bell-shaped, 5-lobed.

Whispering-bells

Flowers yellow to cream-colored. HT: 4–30 in.

Rose Whispering-bells

HT: 4–30 in.

■ **DRAPERIA** (*Draperia systyla*): Late spring–summer; woods, rocky places. Leaves commonly soft-hairy, untoothed. Flowers white, pink, or pale violet.

Genus *Draperia* (1 native species). Leaves opposite and simple. Flowers in clusters, narrowly funnel-shaped, 5-lobed.

Draperia

Flowers often pale violet. Leaves egg-shaped. HT: 4–16 in.

■ **CHRYSANTHEMUM-LEAF EUCRYPTA** (*Eucrypta chrysanthemifolia*): Early spring–early summer; rocky, often sheltered places, shrublands, open woods. Lower leaves somewhat fernlike, commonly 2 or 3 times deeply pinnately divided, the segments often toothed or lobed and sometimes white-blotched. Also called Common Eucrypta, Spotted Hideseed.

■ **SMALL-FLOWER EUCRYPTA** (*E. micrantha*): Lower leaves once pinnately lobed. Also called Dainty Desert Hideseed.

RELATED ■ **AUNT LUCY** (*Ellisia nyctelea*): Woods, disturbed places. Somewhat similar to *Eucrypta*; plants hairy but not sticky or aromatic; flowers bell-shaped. Also called Water-pod.

Genus *Eucrypta* (2 native species). Plants sticky-hairy, aromatic. Leaves alternate, or lower leaves opposite; deeply pinnately lobed or divided. Flowers tiny or small, in clusters, open-bell-shaped and 5-lobed.

Chrysanthemum-leaf Eucrypta

Small-flower Eucrypta
Flowers whitish to blue-purple. HT: 4–10 in.

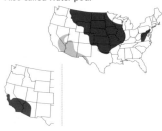
Flowers yellowish white to bluish. Leaves pinnately lobed or divided. HT: 6–24 in.

Aunt Lucy
Flowers white to lavender. HT: 4–16 in.

■ **BABY-BLUE-EYES** (*Nemophila menziesii*): Spring; meadows, open woods. Leaves opposite. Flowers sometimes white. **SIMILAR** ■ **LARGE-FLOWER BABY-BLUE-EYES** (*N. phacelioides*): Sandy soil. Leaves alternate.

FIVESPOT (*N. maculata*): Meadows, woods; chiefly central CA. Leaves opposite. Flowers white with purple-spotted tips.

RELATED ■ **BLUE FIESTA-FLOWER** (*Pholistoma auritum*): Hills, rocky slopes, woods, plains. Leaves opposite toward bottom of stem, alternate toward top; have backward-pointing lobes. Flowers solitary or clustered, dark blue to purplish. Down-curved prickles on stem angles.

Genus *Nemophila* (11 native species). Leaves opposite or alternate, mostly pinnately lobed. Flowers solitary, bell- to saucer-shaped, 5-lobed; sepals usually have tiny, spreading or downturned flaps of tissue in between.

Baby-blue-eyes
Flowers usually bright blue with white center. HT: 4–12 in.

Fivespot
HT: 4–12 in.

Blue Fiesta-flower
HT: 1–3 ft.

■ **SMALL-FLOWER BABY-BLUE-EYES**
(*Nemophila aphylla*): Spring; moist woods.
Leaves cut into broad segments; lower (or
all) leaves alternate. Solitary flowers grow
opposite the leaves.

■ **SMALL-FLOWER NEMOPHILA**
(*N. parviflora*): Spring–summer; slopes,
meadows, woods, roadsides. Similar to
Small-flower Baby-blue-eyes, but lower
(or all) leaves opposite. Also called Small-
flower Baby-blue-eyes, Wood-nymph,
Grove-lover.

RELATED **WHITE FIESTA-FLOWER**
(*Pholistoma membranaceum*): Often
shady places; chiefly central and southern
CA. Flowers white, often with purple mark
near center of each lobe.

Small-flower Baby-blue-eyes

Flowers tiny,
white to pale
blue. HT: 4–16 in.

Small-flower
Nemophila

HT: 6–20 in.

White
Fiesta-
flower

HT: 1–2 ft.

■ **CALIFORNIA HESPEROCHIRON**
(*Hesperochiron californicus*): Spring–
early summer; moist meadows. Leaves
often hairy, untoothed. Flowers white,
sometimes purple-tinged or -veined.

■ **DWARF HESPEROCHIRON**
(*H. pumilus*): Moist meadows and slopes.
Leaves mostly not hairy, at least on lower
surface. Flowers saucer- to shallowly
bowl-shaped; white, sometimes purple-
veined, often with hairy yellow eye.

Genus *Hesperochiron* (2 native species).
Leaves in clusters at plant base, simple
and generally untoothed. Flowers solitary
on leafless stalk; 5-lobed.

California Hesperochiron

Flowers bell- or
funnel-shaped.
HT: 1–4 in.

Dwarf Hesperochiron

Flowers
saucer-shaped.
HT: 1–4 in.

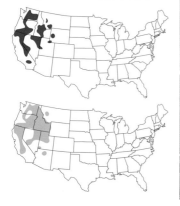

■ **THREE-HEARTS** (*Tricardia watsonii*): Spring; slopes, flats. Leaves mostly near base, untoothed. Calyx 5-lobed, 3 lobes heart-shaped and expanding in fruit.

Genus *Tricardia* (1 native species). Leaves basal and alternate, simple. Flowers in loose clusters, bowl-shaped and 5-lobed; stamens 5; calyx (united sepals) has 5 lobes: 3 broad, 2 narrow.

Three-hearts Flowers cream-colored marked with purple. Conspicuous heart-shaped calyx lobes beneath flowers. HT: 4–16 in.

■ **CALIFORNIA MISTMAIDEN** (*Romanzoffia californica*): Spring; ocean bluffs, wet cliffs, ledges. Plants have tubers at base. Most leaves arise from plant base on long stalks. **SIMILAR** ■ **SITKA MISTMAIDEN** (*R. sitchensis*): Summer; mostly higher elevations. Not tuberous.

NOTE Mistmaiden species resemble members of the saxifrage family (p. 496), but flowers in that family differ in having petals free (not united).

Genus *Romanzoffia* (5 native species). Leaves mostly basal, stem leaves reduced; blades round to kidney-shaped, scalloped-lobed. Flowers in loose clusters, funnel- to bell-shaped and 5-lobed, on nearly leafless stalks.

California Mistmaiden Flowers white with yellow eye. HT: 4–16 in.

■ **OVATE FALSE FIDDLELEAF**
(*Hydrolea ovata*): Summer–fall; wet
ground, shallow water. Upper stems
hairy. Thorns present in leaf axils. Flowers
¾–1 in. across. Also called Blue Waterleaf.
SIMILAR ■ **SKYFLOWER** (*H. corymbosa*):
Usually lacks thorns.

■ **ONE-FLOWER FALSE FIDDLELEAF**
(*H. uniflora*): Upper stems not hairy.
Thorns in leaf axils. Flowers about
½ in. across. **SIMILAR** ■ **WATERPOD**
(*H. quadrivalvis*): Upper stems hairy.

Genus *Hydrolea* (6 species, 5 native).
Plants often have thorns in leaf axils.
Leaves alternate, simple, and untoothed.
Flowers in clusters, bell- to saucer-shaped and deeply
5-lobed. Often treated in its own family, Hydroleaceae.

Ovate False Fiddleleaf

One-flower False
Fiddleleaf

Flowers blue, in
clusters at stem
ends. HT: 8–30 in.

Flowers blue,
in clusters
in leaf axils.
HT: 4–30 in.

HYPERICACEAE
ST.-JOHN'S-WORT FAMILY
Shrubs or annual or perennial herbs. Leaves opposite, simple, and untoothed; surface commonly
sprinkled with tiny, translucent dots (occasionally also black-spotted). Flowers in clusters or sometimes
solitary; petals 4 or 5; sepals 4 or 5; stamens 5 to many; pistil 1. Fruits are capsules.

■ **VIRGINIA MARSH-ST.-JOHN'S-WORT**
(*Triadenum virginicum*): Summer; wet
places.

NOTE The 4 *Triadenum* species are very
similar to one another. Flowers are
purplish pink to yellowish pink.

Genus *Triadenum* (4 native species).
Petals 5; stamens 9, in sets of 3 that
alternate with 3 orange glands near base.

Virginia Marsh-
St.-John's-wort

Flowers
pinkish. Leaves
opposite. HT: 6–24 in.

■ SPOTTED ST.-JOHN'S-WORT (*Hypericum punctatum*): Summer; open woods, fields. Leaves usually black-dotted beneath. Flowers about ½ in. across. **SIMILAR ① COMMON ST.-JOHN'S-WORT** (*H. perforatum*): Widespread; native to Eurasia. Black dots mostly on petal edges. Also called Klamath-weed.

■ SHRUBBY ST.-JOHN'S-WORT (*H. prolificum*): Open woods, pastures, hills, stream banks. Shrub. Flowers golden or orange-yellow, about ¾ in. across, with dense mass of stamens.

■ BOG ST.-JOHN'S-WORT (*H. anagalloides*): Wet places. Mat-forming. Flowers small, about ¼ in. across. Also called Tinker's-penny. **SIMILAR SMALL-FLOWER ST.-JOHN'S-WORT** (*H. mutilum*): Eastern.

Genus *Hypericum* (55 species, 50 native). Most species have yellow, generally 5-petaled flowers with many stamens.

Spotted St.-John's-wort

Shrubby St.-John's-wort

Conspicuous black dots scattered over surface of flowers. HT: 1½–3 ft.

HT: 1–6 ft.

Bog St.-John's-wort

HT: 1–3 in.

■ GREAT ST.-JOHN'S-WORT (*Hypericum ascyron*): Summer; moist or wet places. Flowers 1½–2 in. across; older petals may be somewhat twisted, pinwheel-like.

PINEWEED (*H. gentianoides*): Summer–fall; open places; eastern. Aromatic. Stems wiry. Leaves scalelike. Flowers about ¼ in. across. Also called Orange-grass.

■ ST.-ANDREW'S-CROSS (*H. hypericoides*): Summer–fall; often sandy soil. Shrub. Leaves to 5⁄16 in. wide. Flowers ½–¾ in. across; petals 4; sepals in unequal pairs. **SIMILAR ST.-PETER'S-CROSS** (*H. cruxandreae*): Various habitats; southeastern. Leaves 5⁄16–¾ in. wide; flowers ¾–1 in. across.

Great St.-John's-wort

Flowers large. Leaves broad, stalkless. HT: 2–6 ft.

Pineweed

Flowers small. Leaves scale-like. HT: 4–24 in.

St.-Andrew's-cross

HT: 1–3 ft.

IRIDACEAE
IRIS FAMILY

Perennial, rarely annual. Leaves simple and generally basal (sometimes alternate); usually long and narrow, the base of each typically clasping the next. Flowers solitary or in clusters; 6 tepals (3 petals and 3 petal-like sepals) are similar or dissimilar; stamens 3; pistil 1. Fruits are capsules.

FLOWERS OF THE GENUS *IRIS*

The showy flowers of the genus *Iris* (below) have 3 drooping or spreading, petal-like sepals ("falls") and 3 usually erect petals ("standards"); 3 petal-like style branches are held above the sepals, each covering a single stamen.

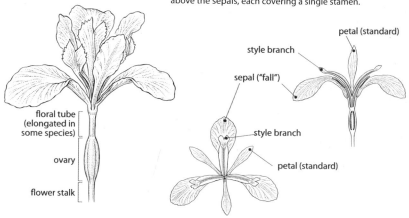

petal (standard)

style branch

sepal ("fall")

style branch

petal (standard)

floral tube (elongated in some species)

ovary

flower stalk

■ **SOUTHERN BLUE FLAG** (*Iris virginica*): Spring–midsummer; wet places. Leaves mostly overtop flowers. **SIMILAR NORTHERN BLUE FLAG** (*I. versicolor*): Northeastern. Flowers mostly overtop leaves; sepal bases have smaller, greenish yellow blotch. ■ **WESTERN BLUE FLAG** (*I. missouriensis*): Leaves usually less than ½ in. wide (½–1¼ in. in Northern and Southern Blue Flags). Also called Rocky Mountain Iris.

■ **DWARF CRESTED IRIS** (*I. cristata*): Spring; woods. Dwarf. Sepals have 3 crinkled, parallel, raised ridges (crests).

DWARF IRIS (*I. verna*): Eastern. Dwarf. Leaves narrow. No crests on sepals.

Genus *Iris* (34 species, 28 native). Leaves arise in a "fan" from plant base; flat, narrowly sword-shaped, folded lengthwise (V-shaped in cross section at base). Flowers showy (see description and illustrations, above).

Southern Blue Flag

Flowers lavender to blue-violet; sepal bases have hairy yellow blotch. HT: 2–3 ft.

Dwarf Crested Iris

HT: 3–9 in.

Dwarf Iris

HT: 2–6 in.

■ **COPPER IRIS** (*Iris fulva*): Spring; wet ground, shallow water. Petals and sepals drooping or spreading. Also called Red Iris.

■ **YELLOW-LEAF IRIS** (*I. chrysophylla*): Open woods. Floral tube (see p. 273) 1¾–4¾ in. long, linear. Also called Slender-tube Iris. **SIMILAR** ■ **SHASTA IRIS** (*I. tenuissima*): Floral tube 1¼–2¼ in. long, narrowly funnel-shaped (slender but expanded abruptly to base of flower). Also called Long-tube Iris.

Copper Iris

Flowers copper, orange, or reddish brown. HT: 1–4 ft.

Yellow-leaf Iris

Flowers cream or pale yellow, with dark veins. HT: 6–12 in.

■ **GROUND IRIS** (*Iris macrosiphon*): Spring; hills, meadows. Floral tube (see p. 273) to 2 in. long; flower stalk (just below ovary) very short. Also called Bowl-tube Iris.

■ **TOUGH-LEAF IRIS** (*I. tenax*): Summer; open woods, fields. Floral tube very short; flower stalk to 1½ in. long. Also called Oregon Iris. **SIMILAR MOUNTAIN IRIS** (*I. douglasiana*): Slopes, open woods, fields; abundant in coastal CA, southern OR. Stems sometimes branched; floral tube intermediate in length between preceding species.

NOTE Iris species can be difficult to tell apart; within a single species, flower colors can range from red-purple, lavender, and grayish blue to yellowish or cream-colored.

Ground Iris

Flowers commonly shades of purple and blue. HT: 6–18 in.

Tough-leaf Iris

Flowers often purplish. HT: 1–2 ft.

■ **PROPELLER-FLOWER** (*Alophia drummondii*): Spring–summer; open woods, grassy areas. Leaves to 1 in. wide. Also called Purple Pleat-leaf.

OTHER GENUS ■ **PRAIRIE-NYMPH** (*Herbertia lahue*): Spring; prairies, meadows, grassy areas. Leaves grasslike, to ¼ in. wide. Inner tepals triangular, much smaller than outer tepals.

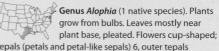

Genus *Alophia* (1 native species). Plants grow from bulbs. Leaves mostly near plant base, pleated. Flowers cup-shaped; tepals (petals and petal-like sepals) 6, outer tepals broader than boat-shaped inner tepals; stamens 3.

Propeller-flower

Flowers purplish; center yellow with dark purple spots. HT: 6–18 in.

Prairie-nymph

Flowers violet-blue; center white with purple spots. HT: 3–9 in.

■ **PRAIRIE-CELESTIAL** (*Nemastylis geminiflora*): Spring; woods, prairies. Leaves somewhat grasslike, pleated. Also called Celestial Ghost-iris, Prairie Pleat-leaf.

Genus *Nemastylis* (4 native species). Plants grow from bulbs. Leaves few, narrowly sword-shaped, pleated. Flowers saucer-shaped; tepals (petals and petal-like sepals) 6, outer tepals slightly larger; stamens 3.

Prairie-celestial

Flowers large, sky blue to lavender-blue, with white center. HT: 5–26 in.

■ **NARROW-LEAF BLUE-EYED-GRASS**
(*Sisyrinchium angustifolium*): Spring–early summer; moist places. Stems winged. Leaves grasslike. Flower clusters on long stalks, 1–4 stalks from axil of leaflike bract (upper stem appears branched). SIMILAR ■ **IDAHO BLUE-EYED-GRASS** (*S. idahoense*): Flower clusters stalkless or nearly so, at end of unbranched stem.

WHITE BLUE-EYED-GRASS (*S. albidum*): Open places; eastern. Stems not branched. Flower clusters paired.

■ **GOLDEN BLUE-EYED-GRASS** (*S. californicum*): Moist places. Leaves sword-shaped. Also called Yellow-eyed-grass.

 Genus *Sisyrinchium* (37 native species). Stems flattened, often 2-winged. Leaves generally grasslike. Flowers commonly blue; tepals (petals and petal-like sepals) 6, spreading, often bristle-tipped; stamens 3.

Narrow-leaf Blue-eyed-grass

Flowers blue to blue-violet, with yellow center. HT: 4–18 in.

White Blue-eyed-grass

Flowers white to bluish. HT: 4–16 in.

Golden Blue-eyed-grass

Flowers yellow. HT: 6–24 in.

■ **GRASS-WIDOW** (*Olsynium douglasii*): Spring; rocky places, open woods, grassy areas. Leaves grasslike, on lower half of stem. Also called Satin-flower. This species has been called Douglas' Blue-eyed-grass or Purple-eyed-grass and placed in the genus *Sisyrinchium* (above); it differs from *Sisyrinchium* species in its round stems and large (to 1½ in. across), pinkish or reddish purple flowers.

Genus *Olsynium* (1 native species). Leaves alternate on stem, grasslike. Flowers saucer- to bowl-shaped; tepals (petals and petal-like sepals) 6; stamens 3.

Grass-widow

Flowers lavender-pink to deep red-purple. HT: 4–16 in.

KRAMERIACEAE · RATANY FAMILY

Shrubs or perennial herbs. Leaves alternate, mostly stalkless, usually simple and untoothed. Flowers solitary in leaf axils, above 2 leaflike bracts; petals 5; sepals 4 or 5; stamens 4; pistil 1. Fruits are round, 1-seeded, nutlike pods covered with prickles and often woolly.

■ **TRAILING RATANY** (*Krameria lanceolata*): Spring–fall; open places. Plants woody-based, silky-hairy. Leaves slender. Flowers superficially resemble orchid flowers. Also called Prairie Sandbur, Rhatany.

NOTE Other ratanies are shrubs; all species are partially parasitic on the roots of nearby plants.

Genus *Krameria* (4 native species). Sepals large, petal-like; true petals small: upper 3 stalked and joined at bases into a fanlike structure, lower 2 reduced to fleshy bumps.

Trailing Ratany

Sepals petal-like, wine red. Trailing or sprawling.

LAMIACEAE or LABIATAE · MINT FAMILY

Annual, biennial, or perennial herbs or shrubs; often aromatic. Stems generally 4-sided (square). Leaves opposite or sometimes basal, simple. Flowers in pairs or clusters, sometimes in whorls that may form larger, headlike to elongated clusters; petals united, typically 2-lipped (sometimes with 4 or 5 nearly equal lobes); sepals 5, united, forming commonly tubular, sometimes 2-lipped calyx; stamens 2 or 4 (often 2 long and 2 short); pistil 1, ovary usually deeply 4-lobed. Fruits are typically nutlets, usually 4.

■ **STONEROOT** (*Collinsonia canadensis*): Late summer–early fall; woods. Leaves large, in several pairs that are scattered along stem. Flowers and crushed leaves have lemonlike fragrance. Also called Horse-balm, Richweed. Do not confuse with ⓘ Perilla (p. 587).

■ **WHORLED STONEROOT** (*C. verticillata*): Spring; chiefly southern Appalachians. Leaf pairs often 2, crowded on upper stem near base of flower cluster and appearing whorled. Flowers whitish, flushed pink or purple. Also called Early Stoneroot, Whorled Horse-balm.

Genus *Collinsonia* (4 native species). Leaves opposite. Flowers 2-lipped, with lower lip fringed.

Stoneroot
Flowers light yellow; 2 protruding stamens. HT: 2–5 ft.

Whorled Stoneroot
Flowers often purplish; 4 protruding stamens. HT: to 1½ ft.

■ **MUSKY-MINT** (*Hyptis alata*): Summer (year-round in Florida); wet places. Plants musky-smelling. Flower clusters rounded, leafy-bracted, on long stalks arising from leaf axils. Also called Clustered Bush-mint.

■ **DESERT-LAVENDER** (*H. emoryi*): Spring; shrublands, canyons, washes. Shrub. Leaves scented, woolly, gray-green.

Genus *Hyptis* (6 species, 2 native). Stems square. Leaves opposite. Flowers in various types of clusters; 2-lipped, middle lobe of lower lip drooping and ending in scoop-like segment; stamens 4.

Musky-mint

Desert-lavender

Flowers white with purple spots. HT: 2–6 ft.

Flowers lavender. HT: 3–9 ft.

■ **DOWNY WOOD-MINT** (*Blephilia ciliata*): Late spring–summer; woods, thickets. Stems short-hairy, usually branched. Upper leaves stalkless or with stalks about ¼ in. long. Also called Downy Pagoda-plant. Do not confuse with Self-heal (p. 279).

■ **HAIRY WOOD-MINT** (*B. hirsuta*): Similar to Downy Wood-mint, but stem hairs longer and spreading; leafstalks ⅜–1½ in. Also called Hairy Pagoda-plant. Do not confuse with Wild-basil (p. 280).

Genus *Blephilia* (3 native species). Aromatic. Stems square. Leaves opposite. Flowers in dense whorls stacked one above the other, with ring of leaflike bracts below each. Flowers 2-lipped; stamens 2, protruding; calyx (united sepals) 2-lipped.

Downy Wood-mint

Hairy Wood-mint

Flowers pale blue, lavender, or whitish, with purple spots; hairy. HT: 1–3 ft.

Flowers whitish or pale lavender, with purplish spots. HT: 1–3 ft.

■ **SELF-HEAL** (*Prunella vulgaris*): Spring–fall; various habitats, often in disturbed places. Leaves (all but upper) usually stalked; stalks ¼–1⅜ in. long. Flowers occasionally pink or white; bracts and sepals sometimes purple-tinged. Also called Heal-all.

NOTE Both native and introduced varieties grow in North America. Do not confuse with Downy Wood-mint (p. 278), which has leaves stalkless or on stalks to ¼ in. long; flowers with 2 protruding stamens.

Genus *Prunella* (2 species, 1 native). Stems square. Leaves opposite. Flowers in crowded clusters on upper stems, with conspicuous, broad, fringed bracts; 2-lipped: upper lip hoodlike, middle lobe of lower lip minutely toothed or fringed; calyx (united sepals) 2-lipped; stamens 4.

Self-heal

Flowers commonly blue-violet. Leaves untoothed or few-toothed. HT: 4–24 in.

■ **BLUNT-SEPAL BRAZOS-MINT** (*Brazoria truncata* var. *truncata*): Spring; sandy soil. Calyx has conspicuous tuft of hairs ("beard") at base; flowers ⅝–¾ in. long. Also called Rattlesnake-flower. **SIMILAR** But with gaps between lower flowers in the cluster; calyx lacking beard. ■ **CENTERVILLE BRAZOS-MINT** (*B. truncata* var. *pulcherrima*): 5–8 pairs of stem leaves below cluster. ■ **SAND BRAZOS-MINT** (*B. arenaria*): 3–5 pairs of stem leaves below cluster.

RELATED ■ **WARNOCK'S-MINT** (*Warnockia scutellarioides*): Limestone soil. Flowers rose, pink, or lavender, ⁵⁄₁₆–½ in. long.

Genus *Brazoria* (2 native species). Stems square. Leaves opposite. Flowers in pairs along stalks and forming elongated clusters, 2-lipped; calyx (united sepals) somewhat inflated, deeply 2-lipped; stamens 4.

Blunt-sepal Brazos-mint

Flowers lavender or pink-lavender, with darker veins and spots; upper lip split in middle. HT: 6–24 in.

Warnock's-mint

Upper lip of flower hoodlike, not split. HT: 6–15 in.

■ AMERICAN DRAGONHEAD

(*Dracocephalum parviflorum*): Late spring–summer; open, often weedy places. Leaves coarsely toothed; teeth often sharp-tipped. Flowers rose, purplish, or light blue.

Genus *Dracocephalum* (3 species, 1 native). Stems square. Leaves opposite. Flowers in dense clusters with conspicuous spine-toothed bracts, 2-lipped; calyx (united sepals) tubular, unequally 5-lobed, the upper lobe much broader, all lobes spine-tipped; stamens 4.

American Dragonhead

Flower clusters have prickly appearance. HT: 6–30 in.

■ WILD-BASIL (*Clinopodium vulgare*):

Summer; woods, thickets, disturbed sites. Leaves short-stalked. Do not confuse with Hairy Wood-mint (p. 278), which has upper leaves long-stalked, stamens 2.

■ **YERBA BUENA** (*C. douglasii*): Spring–summer; shaded woods, shrublands. Plants often mat-forming. Flowers small.

■ LIMESTONE WILD-BASIL

(*C. arkansanum*): Late spring–summer; open rocky places. Leaves slender. Flowers small. Also called Low-calamint.

Genus *Clinopodium* (12 species, 11 native). Strong, minty aroma. Stems usually square. Leaves opposite. Flowers solitary to several in leaf axils; 2-lipped: upper lip erect and 2-lobed, lower lip spreading and 3-lobed; stamens 4.

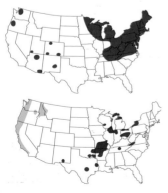

Wild-basil

Flowers rose-purple or pink to whitish, in rounded clusters. Stems erect. HT: 8–20 in.

Yerba Buena

Stems trailing.

Limestone Wild-basil

HT: 10–16 in.

■ **GEORGIA WILD-BASIL** (*Clinopodium georgianum*): Summer; rocky or sandy woods. Shrubby. Leaf edges not rolled under, nearly hairless to sparsely hairy. Also called Georgia-calamint. **SIMILAR FLORIDA WILD-BASIL** (*C. dentatum*): Sandy soil and scrub; FL Panhandle. Leaves widest above middle, nearly stalkless, densely short-hairy. Also called Florida-calamint. **ASHE'S WILD-BASIL** (*C. ashei*): Sandy soil; mostly central FL. Leaf edges strongly rolled under. Also called Lavender-basil, Ashe's-calamint.

Georgia Wild-basil

Flowers pink to lavender, spotted. Leaves widest mostly at or below middle. HT: 10–24 in.

■ **SCARLET WILD-BASIL** (*C. coccineum*): Year-round; sandy soil, scrub. Shrubby. Also called Scarlet-calamint, Red-basil. Do not confuse with Tropical Sage (p. 289), which has flowers with 2 conspicuously protruding stamens.

Scarlet Wild-basil

Flowers large, red. Leaves relatively narrow, widest mostly above middle. HT: 1–3 ft.

■ **FALSE ROSEMARY** (*Conradina canescens*): Spring–fall; sandy soil, scrub. Leaf pairs clustered so that leaves appear whorled. Flowers whitish, pinkish, lavender, or purple; lower lip ³⁄₁₆–⁵⁄₁₆ in. long. Do not confuse with Ashe's Wild-basil (above), which has hairs on underside of leaves erect or spreading (hairs pressed close to leaf surface in False Rosemary). **SIMILAR** ■ **LARGE-FLOWER FALSE ROSEMARY** (*C. grandiflora*): Lower lip of flower ³⁄₈–⁵⁄₈ in. long. ■ **CUMBERLAND FALSE ROSEMARY** (*C. verticillata*): Spring; stream and river banks. Plants to 20 in. tall. Leaves green and hairless on upper surface.

Genus *Conradina* (5 native species). Shrubs; evergreen; strongly aromatic. Stems square. Leaves opposite, narrow; edges strongly curled under. Flowers in clusters from leaf axils; 2-lipped, lower lip 3-lobed; stamens 4.

False Rosemary

Flowers in clusters, spotted, often purplish. Leaves needlelike, densely short-gray-hairy. Shrub. HT: to 20 in.

■ COASTAL-PLAIN DICERANDRA

(*Dicerandra linearifolia*): Summer–fall; sandhills, open pinelands. Minty-aromatic. Leaves linear. Flowers white with purple spots to all purplish red or purple, stalked in whorls along upper stem; overall cluster open. Also called Coastal-plain Balm.

FLORIDA DICERANDRA (*D. densiflora*): Sandhills; northern FL. Flowers pink-purple, in nearly stalkless whorls; overall cluster dense. Also called Florida Balm.

■ ROSE DICERANDRA (*D. odoratissima*):

Sandy soil. Spicy-aromatic. Flowers rose to pink-lavender, spotted; upper lip hoodlike, longer than stamens. Also called Rose Balm.

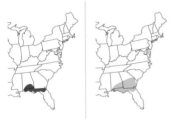

Genus *Dicerandra* (8 native species). Strongly aromatic. Stems square. Leaves opposite. Flowers in clusters from leaf axils; 2-lipped: upper lip 2-lobed, lower lip 3-lobed; calyx (united sepals) tubular, 2-lipped; stamens 4, anthers have minute awns or hornlike projections at tip.

Coastal-plain Dicerandra

Florida Dicerandra

Stamens protruding.
HT: to 20 in.

Stamens protruding.
HT: to 20 in.

Rose Dicerandra

Stamens not protruding.
HT: to 18 in.

■ FLORIDA PENNYROYAL (*Piloblephis rigida*): Year-round; sandy pinelands, oak scrub. Shrubby. Leaves thick, needlelike, ¼–½ in. long. Flowers to ⅜ in. long. Also called Wild Pennyroyal.

OTHER GENUS *Pogogyne* (7 native species). Late spring–summer; vernal pools, moist grasslands. ■ **DOUGLAS' MESA-MINT** (*P. douglasii*): Leaves elliptic; flowers ½–¾ in. long. ■ **SACRAMENTO MESA-MINT** (*P. ziziphoroides*, no photo): Flowers about ¼ in. long.

Genus *Piloblephis* (1 native species). Strongly aromatic. Stems square. Leaves opposite, linear, numerous. Flowers in crowded clusters at stem ends; 2-lipped, lower lip 3-lobed; stamens 4.

Florida Pennyroyal

Flowers lavender or purple-spotted white, in silky clusters.
HT: 6–24 in.

Douglas' Mesa-mint

Flowers lavender or purple, in bristly-hairy clusters.
HT: 4–16 in.

■ **YELLOW GIANT-HYSSOP** (*Agastache nepetoides*): Summer; open woods, thickets, clearings. Also called Catnip Giant-hyssop.

■ **BLUE GIANT-HYSSOP** (*A. foeniculum*): Woods, prairies. Strongly anise-scented. Leaves white beneath. Flowers lavender-blue, scarcely 2-lipped. Also called Anise-hyssop. **SIMILAR PURPLE GIANT-HYSSOP** (*A. scrophulariifolia*): Open woods, thickets; eastern. Leaves green beneath; flowers purplish.

■ **NETTLE-LEAF GIANT-HYSSOP** (*A. urticifolia*): Woods, slopes. Flowers purplish or rose to whitish.

Genus *Agastache* (16 native species). Aromatic. Stems square. Leaves opposite. Flowers in clusters; commonly 2-lipped, middle lobe of lower lip enlarged; stamens 4, protruding. Species are also called horsemint.

Yellow Giant-hyssop

Flowers yellowish white or greenish yellow.
HT: 2–5 ft.

Blue Giant-hyssop

HT: 2–4 ft.

Nettle-leaf Giant-hyssop

HT: 2–5 ft.

■ **MEEHAN'S-MINT** (*Meehania cordata*): Late spring–summer; woods, wooded slopes, ravines, floodplains. Leaves heart-shaped. Flowers showy.

OTHER GENUS ■ **SYNANDRA** (*Synandra hispidula*): Another mint with heart-shaped leaves and showy flowers. Also called Guyandotte-beauty.

Genus *Meehania* (1 native species). Stems square. Leaves opposite. Flowers in clusters at stem ends, 2-lipped; stamens 4.

Meehan's-mint

Flowers purple-blue. Plants trailing.

Synandra

Flowers white to cream-colored.
HT: 8–24 in.

■ **OBEDIENT-PLANT** (*Physostegia virginiana*): Summer–fall; moist or wet, usually open places. Leaves mostly stalkless, toothed. Flowers can be rotated on the stalk and will remain in their new position. Also called False Dragonhead.

RELATED *Macbridea* (2 native species).
■ **CAROLINA BIRDS-IN-A-NEST** (*M. caroliniana*): Summer–fall; moist or usually wet places. Flowers pink to lavender, with white stripes. ■ **WHITE BIRDS-IN-A-NEST** (*M. alba*): Flowers white, lightly purple-marked inside.

Genus *Physostegia* (12 native species). Stems square. Leaves opposite. Flowers showy, in pairs; 2-lipped, upper lip hoodlike and somewhat arching; stamens 4.

Obedient-plant

Flowers whitish to rose or pale pink. HT: 1½–4 ft.

Carolina Birds-in-a-nest

HT: 1–3 ft.

White Birds-in-a-nest

HT: to 1½ ft.

■ **DOWNY SKULLCAP** (*Scutellaria incana*): Summer; woods, thickets. Stems fine-hairy. Leaves long-stalked, lance- to egg-shaped, toothed. Flowers in several clusters from upper part of stem. Hump on calyx characteristic of skullcaps (see inset). Also called Hoary Skullcap.

NOTE *Scutellaria* species are often difficult to tell apart.

Genus *Scutellaria* (43 species, 41 native). Stems square. Leaves opposite. Flowers solitary or in pairs, 2-lipped; stamens 4; calyx (united sepals) tubular and 2-lipped, the tube with a small hump or ridge on top.

Downy Skullcap

Flowers purple with white blotch on lower lip, white tube. HT: 2–3 ft.

■ **MARSH SKULLCAP** (*Scutellaria galericulata*): Late spring–summer; wet places. Flowers solitary in leaf axils, appear paired. Also called Common Skullcap.

■ **CALIFORNIA SKULLCAP** (*S. californica*): Late spring–summer; shrublands, woodlands. Flowers white to pale yellow.

■ **MAD-DOG SKULLCAP** (*S. lateriflora*): Summer–early fall; moist or wet places. Flowers small, in stalked, 1-sided clusters from leaf axils; blue or rarely pink or white.

Marsh Skullcap
Flowers blue to violet-blue, white-blotched. HT: 1–3 ft.

California Skullcap
HT: 6–16 in.

Mad-dog Skullcap
HT: 1–3 ft.

■ **SMOOTH HEDGE-NETTLE** (*Stachys tenuifolia*): Late spring–fall; moist or wet places. Stems hairless or hairy only on angles. SIMILAR ■ **HAIRY HEDGE-NETTLE** (*S. pilosa* var. *pilosa*): Stems hairy on sides as well as angles; leaves stalkless or very short-stalked.

■ **ROUGH HEDGE-NETTLE** (*S. rigida*): Mostly moist places. Stems typically hairy. Lower leaves stalked; blades to 3½ in. long. Also called Rigid Hedge-nettle. SIMILAR **CALIFORNIA HEDGE-NETTLE** (*S. bullata*): Dry coastal slopes; CA. Leaf blades to 7 in. long.

SCARLET HEDGE-NETTLE (*S. coccinea*): Moist places; southwestern mountains.

NOTE Species are also called betony.

Genus *Stachys* (29 species, 25 native). Sometimes odorous. Stems square. Leaves opposite. Flowers at stem ends, commonly with gaps between individual clusters; 2-lipped: upper lip often hoodlike, lower lip with middle lobe longest; stamens 4.

Smooth Hedge-nettle
Flowers rose-pink to lavender, with purple markings. Leaves stalked. HT: 1–3 ft.

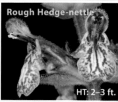
Rough Hedge-nettle
HT: 2–3 ft.

Scarlet Hedge-nettle
HT: 1–2 ft.

■ **COASTAL HEDGE-NETTLE** (*Stachys chamissonis*): Summer–fall; moist or wet places. Populations in CA, often called Chamisso's Hedge-nettle (var. *chamissonis*), have conspicuously hairier leaves and sepals than OR and WA populations, sometimes called Cooley's Hedge-nettle (var. *cooleyae*, pictured).

■ **WHITE-STEM HEDGE-NETTLE** (*S. albens*): Spring–fall; usually wet places. Leaves and stems densely white-woolly with cobwebby hairs. Flowers white to rose-pink, purple-marked, about ½ in. long; calyx (united sepals) white-woolly.

■ **SHADE BETONY** (*S. crenata*): Spring; damp places. Plants hairy. Flowers small, pale lavender or pinkish. Also called Mouse's-ear.

Coastal Hedge-nettle

White stem Hedge-nettle

HT: 1–4 ft.

Flowers rose-red to reddish purple. Leaves and stems hairy. HT: 2–4 ft.

Shade Betony

HT: to 12 in.

■ **AMERICAN GERMANDER** (*Teucrium canadense*): Late spring–early fall; moist or wet places. Leaves toothed. Also called Wood-sage.

■ **CUT-LEAF GERMANDER** (*T. laciniatum*): Prairies, roadsides, hillsides. Dwarf. Leaves "cut" nearly to midrib into slender segments. Flowers white, often with purplish markings.

■ **COASTAL GERMANDER** (*T. cubense*): Open places. Leaves toothed and lobed; midstem leaves irregularly lobed halfway or less to midrib. Flowers white.

Genus *Teucrium* (7 species, 5 native). Sometimes aromatic. Stems square. Leaves opposite. Flowers in clusters; 2-lipped but appearing 1-lipped (upper lip reduced to 2 small lobes), middle lobe of lower lip much larger than others; stamens 4, protruding.

American Germander

Flowers light rose to lavender, with darker markings. HT: 1–3 ft.

Cut-leaf Germander

HT: 3–6 in.

Coastal Germander

HT: 1–2 ft.

■ **FORKED BLUECURLS** (*Trichostema dichotomum*): Summer–fall; open places. Plants somewhat sticky. Stamens arched or curled. Also called Bastard Pennyroyal.

■ **WOOLLY BLUECURLS** (*T. lanatum*): Spring–summer; dry slopes. Shrub. Flower clusters woolly.

■ **VINEGAR-WEED** (*T. lanceolatum*): Spring–fall; open places. Plants strong-smelling. Flower tube bent back at a right angle so stamens face stem.

Genus *Trichostema* (18 native species). Strongly odorous. Stems square. Leaves opposite. Flowers in clusters from leaf axils; 5-lobed, lowest lobe largest, bent downward; stamens 4, typically long-protruding, arched or curled.

Flowers violet-blue; lowest lobe whitish with purple spots. HT: 6–24 in.

Woolly Bluecurls
HT: 2–5 ft.

Vinegar-weed
HT: 6–24 in.

■ **FALSE PENNYROYAL** (*Trichostema brachiatum*): Late summer–fall; open areas. Plants usually fine-hairy. Leaves often 3-veined, untoothed to few-toothed. Flowers have 5 lobes, lowermost slightly longer. Also called Fluxweed.

False Pennyroyal
Flowers small, bluish.
HT: 6–18 in.

■ CALIFORNIA PITCHER-SAGE
(*Lepechinia calycina*): Spring–early summer; grassy or rocky slopes, shrublands, open woods. Leaves broad, 1½–4½ in. long. Calyx swollen in fruit. Also called Woodbalm.

OTHER GENUS ■ **MEXICAN BLADDER-SAGE** (*Salazaria mexicana*): Desert slopes, washes, shrublands. Another shrubby mint with an inflated calyx. Branches twiggy, sharp-tipped. Leaves about ½ in. long, narrow, falling in dry weather. Calyx papery, balloonlike in fruit. Also called Paperbag-bush.

Genus *Lepechinia* (4 native species). Shrubby; aromatic; hairy. Leaves opposite. Flowers in clusters on upper stems; 2-lipped: lower lip longer, upper lip 4-lobed; stamens 4; calyx (united sepals) enlarging in fruit.

California Pitcher-sage
Flowers broadly tubular; white, pale lavender, or pink. HT: 1–4 ft.

Mexican Bladder-sage

Flowers strongly 2-lipped: upper lip pale purple to white, lower lip purple. HT: 1–4 ft.

■ CHIA (*Salvia columbariae*): Spring; dry open places. Leaves mostly at plant base, deeply lobed or divided, crinkled. Flower clusters spiny-bracted, ball-shaped. Also called California Sage.

■ **THISTLE SAGE** (*S. carduacea*): Dry open places. Leaves basal, short-spiny, white-woolly. Flower clusters woolly, spiny. Flowers larger than Chia's; lower lip fringed.

■ **PURPLE SAGE** (*S. dorrii*): Open, often rocky places. Shrub. Leaves opposite or sometimes in tufts, undivided, untoothed. Flower clusters not spiny; bracts rounded, often purplish. Also called Gray Ball Sage.

Genus *Salvia* (59 species, 46 native). Often strongly aromatic. Stems square. Leaves opposite or sometimes basal. Flowers near stem ends, commonly with gaps between individual clusters, 2-lipped; stamens 2, frequently protruding; calyx (united sepals) usually 2-lipped.

Chia
Flowers small, deep blue to purplish, dark-spotted. HT: 6–24 in.

Thistle Sage
HT: 6 in.–3 ft.

Purple Sage
HT: 1–2½ ft.

■ **LYRE-LEAF SAGE** (*Salvia lyrata*):
Spring–early summer; woods, thickets,
roadsides, weedy areas. Leaves mostly
basal, lobed, with end lobe larger.

■ **AZURE BLUE SAGE** (*S. azurea*):
Summer–fall; woods, roadsides, prairies,
fields. Leaves mostly on stem, not lobed.
Flowers ½–1 in. long. Also called Pitcher's
Sage. **SIMILAR** Plants mostly 1–2 ft. tall;
flowers ⅜–½ in. long. **NETTLE-LEAF
SAGE** (*S. urticifolia*): Woods, glades,
thickets; chiefly southeastern. Leaves
conspicuously toothed, 1–2½ in. wide.

■ **LANCE-LEAF SAGE** (*S. reflexa*): Prairies,
open places. Leaves few-toothed to nearly untoothed, ¼–½ in. wide; flowers often
paired. Also called Rocky Mountain Sage.

Lyre-leaf Sage

Flowers blue to
violet, often white-
blotched. HT: 1–2 ft.

Azure Blue Sage

Flowers whorled,
blue; lower lip
prominent,
white-blotched.
HT: 2–5 ft.

■ **TROPICAL SAGE** (*Salvia coccinea*):
Nearly year-round; thickets, open woods.
Also called Scarlet Sage.

■ **CEDAR SAGE** (*S. roemeriana*): Spring–
summer; rocky woods. Similar to Tropical
Sage, but leaves both opposite and at
plant base, the lower ones often with
2 or 3 side leaflets. **SIMILAR AUTUMN
SAGE** (*S. greggii*): Rocky soil; similar range.
Shrubby; leaves opposite, smaller, few-
toothed.

■ **HUMMINGBIRD SAGE** (*S. spathacea*):
Spring–summer; open woods, shrublands. Leaves at plant base and opposite,
triangular. Flowers in bracted clusters.
Also called Crimson Pitcher Sage.

Tropical Sage

Flowers red.
Leaves opposite,
triangular.
HT: 1–3 ft.

Cedar Sage

Leaves large-
toothed,
roundish.
HT: 1–2½ ft.

Hummingbird
Sage

Flowers
purplish
red. HT:
1–2½ ft.

■ HOARY ROSEMARY-MINT

(*Poliomintha incana*): Spring–summer; sandy plains, slopes. Plants closely covered with felty, white hairs. Leaves stalkless, narrow. Flowers occasionally whitish with purple spots; calyx (united sepals) conspicuously long-hairy. Also called Purple-sage. SIMILAR ■ LEAFY ROSEMARY-MINT (*P. glabrescens*): Rocky soil. Mature plants not densely white-hairy; leaves oblong to roundish; calyx short-hairy.

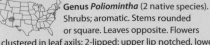

Genus *Poliomintha* (2 native species). Shrubs; aromatic. Stems rounded or square. Leaves opposite. Flowers clustered in leaf axils; 2-lipped: upper lip notched, lower lip 3-lobed; stamens 2.

Hoary Rosemary-mint

Flowers commonly lavender to pink. HT: 6 in.–3 ft.

■ WILD-BERGAMOT (*Monarda fistulosa*):

Mostly summer; woods, thickets, prairies. Single flower cluster at stem end; stamens protruding.

■ **SCARLET BEE-BALM** (*M. didyma*): Woods, thickets. Similar to Wild-bergamot, but flowers scarlet or crimson. Also called Oswego-tea.

■ **WHITE-BERGAMOT** (*M. clinopodia*): Woods, thickets. Also similar, but flowers white. Also called Basil Bee-balm.

Genus *Monarda* (15 native species). Aromatic. Stems square. Leaves opposite. Flowers showy, in dense clusters above circle of conspicuous, leaflike bracts; strongly 2-lipped; stamens 2.

Wild-bergamot

Flowers lavender to pink. HT: 1–4 ft.

Scarlet Bee-balm

HT: 2–5 ft.

White-bergamot

HT: 1–3 ft.

■ **SPOTTED BEE-BALM** (*Monarda punctata*): Late spring–summer; dry, often sandy soil. Flowers in clusters of usually 2–5 per stem; stamens not protruding. Also called Spotted Horsemint.

■ **LEMON BEE-BALM** (*M. citriodora*): Prairies, plains. Similar to Spotted Bee-balm. Calyx teeth bristle-tipped; flowers whitish, pinkish, or purplish. Also called Lemon Horsemint.

Spotted Bee-balm

Flowers pale yellow with dark spots. Leaflike bracts whitish to pinkish purple. HT: 1–3 ft.

Lemon Bee-balm

Flowers whitish to rose-lavender, sometimes spotted. HT: 1–3 ft.

■ **COYOTE-MINT** (*Monardella odoratissima*): Mostly summer; plains, mountain woods, rocky banks and slopes. Leaves short-stalked, untoothed. Flowers sometimes white. Also called Mountain Monardella.

NOTE Most *Monardella* species are native to California. They are also called mountain-balm.

Genus *Monardella* (30 native species). Aromatic. Stems square. Leaves opposite. Flowers showy, in dense clusters above a series of leaflike bracts; not strongly 2-lipped, with 5 narrow lobes; stamens 4.

Coyote-mint

Flowers often pink-purple. HT: 6–24 in.

■ HOARY MOUNTAIN-MINT

(*Pycnanthemum incanum*): Summer; fields, thickets, open woods. Leaves broad, stalked. SIMILAR ■ CALIFORNIA MOUNTAIN-MINT (*P. californicum*): Woods, stream banks, moist meadows, shrublands. Upper leaves less whitish, stalkless. Also called Sierra-mint.

■ NARROW-LEAF MOUNTAIN-MINT

(*P. tenuifolium*): Fields, thickets, meadows, woodland edges, clearings. Stems hairless. Leaves very narrow, stalkless. SIMILAR VIRGINIA MOUNTAIN-MINT (*P. virginianum*): Thickets, wet meadows, marshes; eastern. Stems hairy on angles; leaves broader, narrowly lance-shaped.

Genus *Pycnanthemum* (19 native species). Often strongly aromatic. Stems square. Leaves opposite. Flowers small, in crowded clusters; mostly white, dotted or tinged with pink or purple; 2-lipped or with 5 sometimes equal lobes; stamens 4, protruding.

Hoary Mountain-mint

Upper leaves and bracts conspicuously whitish. HT: 1–3 ft.

Narrow-leaf Mountain-mint

Flowers in small, dense clusters at stem ends. HT: 1–3 ft.

■ DITTANY (*Cunila origanoides*):

Summer–fall; woods, roadsides. Flowers rarely whitish. Also called Stone-mint. Differs from American-pennyroyal (p. 293) in having leaves broader and widest near base; flowers larger, with longer protruding stamens; tubular calyx (united sepals) with nearly equal lobes (not 2-lipped).

Genus *Cunila* (1 native species). Aromatic. Stems square. Leaves opposite. Flowers clustered in leaf axils, weakly 2-lipped; stamens 2, protruding.

Dittany

Flowers small, pinkish or lavender. Leaves stalkless. Stems wiry, reddish. HT: 8–16 in.

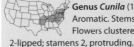

■ **AMERICAN-PENNYROYAL** (*Hedeoma pulegioides*): Summer–fall; woods, fields, roadsides. Strongly aromatic. Leaves short-stalked, elliptic, often with a few teeth. Also called American False Pennyroyal. Compare Dittany (p. 292).

■ **ROUGH FALSE PENNYROYAL** (*H. hispida*): Late spring–summer; prairies, fields, roadsides. Leaves narrow, untoothed. SIMILAR ■ **DRUMMOND'S FALSE PENNYROYAL** (*H. drummondii*): Also has narrow, untoothed leaves; calyx lobes close opening to the calyx tube in fruit.

Genus *Hedeoma* (17 native species). Aromatic. Stems square. Leaves opposite. Flowers clustered in leaf axils, 2-lipped; stamens 2; calyx (united sepals) 2-lipped.

American-pennyroyal

Rough False Pennyroyal

Flowers bluish to pale violet. Stems wiry. HT: 4–18 in.

HT: 4–14 in.

■ **AMERICAN WATER-HOREHOUND** (*Lycopus americanus*): Summer; moist or wet places. Lower leaves deeply pinnately cut or lobed. Flowers 4-lobed. Also called American Bugleweed. SIMILAR ■ **NORTHERN WATER-HOREHOUND** (*L. uniflorus*): Lower leaves toothed but not lobed; flowers 5-lobed. Also called Northern Bugleweed.

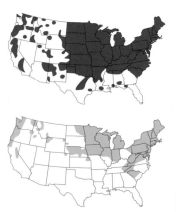

Genus *Lycopus* (9 species, 8 native). Plants sometimes form runners. Stems square. Leaves opposite. Flowers densely clustered in leaf axils, 4- or 5-lobed, not or barely 2-lipped; stamens 2.

American Water-horehound

Flowers small, white. Lower leaves have narrow lobes. HT: 6 in.–3 ft.

■ **AMERICAN WILD MINT** (*Mentha arvensis*): Summer–fall; moist or wet areas. Flowers sometimes white. Also called Field Mint.

NOTE *Mentha* species are the true mints. Several species and hybrids have been introduced, including ⚏ Peppermint and ⚏ Spearmint (both on p. 587), which have flowers in elongated clusters.

Genus *Mentha* (10 species, 1 native). Usually strongly aromatic. Stems square. Leaves opposite. Flowers small, in clusters, usually 4-lobed; stamens 4, protruding.

American Wild Mint

Flowers usually light purple or pink, in clusters in leaf axils. HT: 6–30 in.

■ **COULTER'S WRINKLE-FRUIT** (*Tetraclea coulteri*): Spring–summer; flats, slopes. Leaves gray-green, irregularly few-toothed or untoothed. Flowers may be reddish-tinged outside.

NOTE *Tetraclea* is traditionally included in the vervain family (Verbenaceae).

Genus *Tetraclea* (1 native species). Odorous. Stems square. Leaves opposite. Flowers clustered in leaf axils, trumpet-shaped, with 5 rounded lobes; stamens 4, protruding.

Coulter's Wrinkle-fruit

Flowers cream-colored; stamens and style conspicuous. HT: 6–16 in.

LENNOACEAE   LENNOA FAMILY

Annual or perennial. Plants lack green pigment (chlorophyll); parasitic; stems deeply buried under-ground. Leaves alternate and scalelike. Flowers in clusters; funnel-shaped (petals united), with 4–10 lobes; sepals 4–10; stamens 4–10; pistil 1. Fruits are fleshy capsules.

■ **SCALY-STEM SAND-PLANT** (*Pholisma arenarium*): Spring–midsummer (occasionally also fall); sandy places. Parasitic on the roots of nearby shrubs. Also called Desert Christmas-tree, Purple Pop-ups.

■ **SAND-FOOD** (*P. sonorae*): Plants mushroom-shaped (or mound-shaped if stalk is buried in sand).

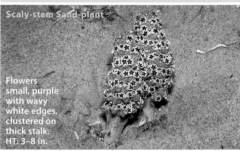

Genus *Pholisma* (2 native species). With characters of the family. Stems buried in sand, attached to roots of host plants.

Scaly-stem Sand-plant

Flowers small, purple with wavy white edges, clustered on thick stalk. HT: 3–8 in.

Sand-food

Plants mushroom- or mound-shaped.

LENTIBULARIACEAE   BLADDERWORT FAMILY

Mostly perennial; carnivorous. Leaves in basal clusters or seemingly absent. Flowers solitary or in clusters; tubular (petals united) and 5-lobed; weakly to strongly 2-lipped, with backward-pointing projection (spur) at base; stamens 2; pistil 1. Fruits are capsules.

■ **COMMON BLADDERWORT** (*Utricularia macrorhiza*): Summer; aquatic. Rootless, free-floating; many underwater bladder-bearing branchlets (see upper photo). Also called Greater Bladderwort.

■ **PURPLE BLADDERWORT** (*U. purpurea*): Spring–fall; aquatic. Flowers pink to violet, with yellow spot; spur short.

■ **FLOATING BLADDERWORT** (*U. inflata*): Spring–fall; aquatic. Free-floating on con-spicuous ring of swollen branchlets. Flowers yellow. Also called Swollen Bladderwort.

Genus *Utricularia* (20 native species). Typical leaves replaced by threadlike branchlets; tiny bladders at tips capture minute aquatic animals. Flowers 2-lipped, spurred.

Common Bladderwort

Purple Bladderwort

HT: 2–6 in.

Floating Bladderwort

Flowers yellow; spur long. HT: 4–16 in.

HT: 4–10 in.

■ **YELLOW-FLOWER BUTTERWORT**
(*Pinguicula lutea*): Spring; moist or wet acid pinelands, bogs. Leaves basal. Flowers yellow; lobes notched.

■ **BLUE-FLOWER BUTTERWORT**
(*P. caerulea*): Spring; moist or wet acid pinelands, bogs. Flowers lavender-blue to whitish; lobes often notched.

■ **COMMON BUTTERWORT**
(*P. vulgaris*): Summer; rocky or gravelly shores, bogs. Flowers violet; lobes not notched. **SIMILAR** ■ **CALIFORNIA BUTTERWORT** (*P. macroceras*): Bogs, wet places. Lower flower lobes wider toward tip. Also called Horned Butterwort.

Genus *Pinguicula* (9 native species). Leaves clustered at plant base, simple, untoothed; upper surfaces sticky-slimy, insect-trapping. Flowers solitary on leafless stalks, tubular and 5-lobed (weakly 2-lipped), spurred.

Yellow-flower Butterwort

Blue-flower Butterwort
HT: to 12 in.

Common Butterwort

HT: 6–16 in.

HT: 2–6 in.

LILIACEAE
LILY FAMILY

Perennial. Leaves basal or alternate (occasionally opposite or whorled), simple, often narrow. Flowers solitary or in clusters; petals and sepals free or sometimes united, 3 each, often similar to one another (and called "tepals"); stamens usually 6 (rarely 3 or 4); pistil 1. Fruits are usually capsules or berries.

■ **FAIRY-WAND** (*Chamaelirium luteum*): Late spring–summer; woods, thickets, meadows, slopes. Leaves stalked, broad and spoon-shaped. Individual plants have either all male flowers (6 stamens each) in drooping clusters or all female flowers (1 pistil each) in erect clusters. Also called Devil's-bit, Blazing-star.

Genus *Chamaelirium* (1 native species). Leaves clustered at plant base, fewer on stems. Flowers small, in elongated clusters; tepals (petals and petal-like sepals) 6. Fruits are capsules.

Fairy-wand

Flowers whitish, aging yellow, in wandlike clusters. HT: female plants 1–2 ft.

HT: male plant 1–2½ ft.

■ **WHITE COLICROOT** (*Aletris farinosa*): Spring–summer; open places. Also called Unicorn-root, White-stargrass. **SIMILAR** ■ **SOUTHERN COLICROOT** (*A. obovata*): Pinewoods, savannas. Flowers short-tubular; lobes pointed inward.

■ **YELLOW COLICROOT** (*A. lutea*): Moist or wet pinewoods, bogs. Flowers yellow, long-tubular; lobes spreading.

■ **GOLDEN COLICROOT** (*A. aurea*): Similar to Yellow Colicroot, but flowers short-tubular; lobes erect.

 **Genus *Aletris*** (5 native species). Leaves clustered at plant base, flat. Flowers small, nearly stalkless, in elongated clusters; tubular and 6-lobed (tepals—petals and sepals—united), outer surface covered with small bumps; stamens 6. Fruits are capsules.

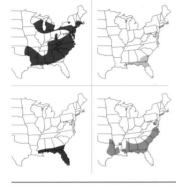

White Colicroot

Flowers white, long-tubular; lobes spreading. HT: 1½–3 ft.

Yellow Colicroot

HT: 1½–3 ft.

Golden Colicroot

HT: 1–3 ft.

■ **GOLDEN-CREST** (*Lophiola aurea*): Early summer; wet pinelands, bogs, ditches. Upper stems and flower clusters white-woolly. Flowers conspicuously yellow-hairy inside (see inset). Tepals triangular, brownish-edged, curved downward at flowering time.

 Genus *Lophiola* (1 native species). Leaves basal and alternate. Flowers in open clusters; tepals (petals and petal-like sepals) 6, abundantly hairy; stamens 6. Fruits are capsules.

Golden-crest

Flowers white-woolly outside, bright yellow within. Leaves long, narrow. HT: 1–3 ft.

■ **CALIFORNIA BOG-ASPHODEL**
(*Narthecium californicum*): Summer;
wet places in mountain meadows.
Stamen tips (anthers) brick red.
SIMILAR ■ **YELLOW-ASPHODEL**
(*N. americanum*): Wet pinelands.
Uncommon. Stamen tips yellow. Also
called Bog-asphodel.

Genus *Narthecium* (3 native species).
Leaves basal, overlapping at base.
Flowers in clusters; tepals (petals and
petal-like sepals) 6; stamens 6, their stalks densely hairy.
Fruits are capsules.

California
Bog-asphodel

Flowers
yellow,
star-shaped,
in elongated
clusters; stamen
stalks woolly.
HT: 8–24 in.

■ **STICKY FALSE ASPHODEL**
(*Triantha glutinosa*): Summer; wetlands.
Midstem often bears 1 bractlike leaf.
SIMILAR Differing in technical characters.
■ **WESTERN FALSE ASPHODEL** (*T.
occidentalis*). ■ **COASTAL FALSE
ASPHODEL** (*T. racemosa*).

OTHER GENERA With stems hairless;
flowers solitary. **WHITE FEATHERLING**
(*Tofieldia glabra*, no photo): Late summer–
fall; NC, SC. Flower stalks to ¼ in. long.
Also called White-false Asphodel. **WHITE
SUNNYBELL** (*Schoenolirion albiflorum*, no
photo): Spring; mostly FL. Flower stalks
¼–½ in. long. ■ **RUSH-FEATHERLING**
(*Pleea tenuifolia*): Late summer–fall.
Stamens mostly 9.

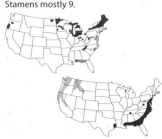

Genus *Triantha* (3 native species). Upper
stem hairy, often sticky. Leaves mostly
at plant base, narrow. Flowers in clusters
of 3–7; tepals (petals and petal-like sepals) 6; stamens 6;
styles 3. Fruits are capsules.

Sticky False Asphodel

Flowers
white to
yellowish
white, in
clusters
of often 3.
Leaves at
plant base
grasslike.
HT: 4–20 in.

Rush-
featherling

Flower
clusters have
sheathing, pointed
bracts. HT: 1–3 ft.

■ **FLY-POISON** (*Amianthium muscitoxicum*): Late spring–summer; woods, meadows, pine savannas. Leaves grasslike. Flowers long-stalked.

NOTE Species are poisonous. Do not confuse with Sticky False Asphodel (p. 298), which has single leaf on midstem, sticky upper stem. Death-camas species (below) have glands at tepal bases. See also Osceola's-plume (p. 300).

Genus *Amianthium* (1 native species). Plants grow from bulbs. Leaves mostly at plant base. Flowers small, in crowded clusters; tepals (petals and petal-like sepals) 6; stamens 6. Fruits are capsules.

Fly-poison

Flowers white, aging greenish. HT: 1–3 ft.

■ **MEADOW DEATH-CAMAS** (*Toxicoscordion venenosum*): Spring–summer; grassy places, open woods, rocky bluffs. Tepals have single gland each, mostly wider toward tip. Also called Grassy Death-camas.

■ **MOUNTAIN DEATH-CAMAS** (*Anticlea elegans*): Summer; moist grasslands, lake-shores, bogs. Tepals have single gland each, 2-lobed at tip.

■ **SANDBOG DEATH-CAMAS** (*Zigadenus glaberrimus*): Summer–early fall; pine savannas, bogs. Tepals have 2 glands each.

NOTE Death-camases are poisonous. Traditionally, they were treated as all belonging to the genus *Zigadenus*.

Death-camas (several genera, 13 native species). Leaves mostly arise from plant base, grasslike; stem leaves alternate, smaller. Flowers in clusters; tepals (petals and petal-like sepals) 6, mostly white, each with 1 or 2 yellowish or greenish glands at base; stamens 6. Fruits are capsules.

Meadow Death-camas

HT: 6–30 in.

Mountain Death-camas

HT: 6–30 in.

Sandbog Death-camas

HT: 2–4 ft.

■ **FEATHER-BELLS** (*Stenanthium gramineum*): Summer–early fall; moist woods, thickets, meadows. Flowers star-shaped, in often large clusters, stalkless or on stalks to ¼ in. long.

OTHER GENUS ■ BRONZE-BELLS (*Anticlea occidentalis*): Late spring–summer; rocky slopes, mountain meadows, stream banks. Flowers narrowly bell-shaped, nodding, on stalks to about 1 in. long; tepals have single 2-lobed gland. This species was traditionally placed in *Stenanthium*.

NOTE Some species are poisonous.

Genus *Stenanthium* (4 native species). Similar to death-camases (p. 299), but glands at base of tepals (petals and petal-like sepals) obscure or absent.

Feather-bells

Bronze-bells

Tepals white to cream-colored, pointed. HT: 2–5 ft.

Tepals greenish to brownish purple; tips curved backward. HT: 6–20 in.

■ **OSCEOLA'S-PLUME** (*Stenanthium densum*): Spring; moist or wet pinelands, bogs. Leaves 1–3, mostly ⅛–¼ in. wide. Gland at base of tepals (petals and petal-like sepals) 1 and obscure, or absent. Fruits elongated, ⅜–¾ in. long, maroonish. Also called Crow-poison, Black-snakeroot.

NOTE Do not confuse with Fly-poison (p. 299), which has leaves 4 or more, mostly ⁵⁄₁₆–⅜ in. wide; tepals turning green in fruit; fruits stout, about ¼ in. long, green.

Osceola's-plume

Flowers usually cream-colored, typically aging pink or rose-purple. HT: 1½–6 ft.

■ **CALIFORNIA FALSE HELLEBORE**
(*Veratrum californicum*): Summer–early fall; wet meadows, clearings in woods. Leaves have pleated appearance. Flower clusters dense, branches erect to spreading. Also called California Corn-lily.

Genus *Veratrum* (9 native species). Leaves alternate; veins conspicuous. Flowers in branched clusters; tepals (petals and petal-like sepals) 6; stamens 6. Fruits are capsules.

California False Hellebore

Flowers cream-white.
HT: 3–6 ft.

■ **GREEN FALSE HELLEBORE** (*V. viride*): Moist or wet ground. Similar to California False Hellebore, but flowers green to yellowish green. Also called Indian-poke, American White-hellebore. Eastern var. *viride* has flower cluster branches mostly spreading to somewhat erect; western var. *eschscholzianum*, sometimes called Indian-hellebore, has flower cluster branches spreading and drooping.

NOTE *Veratrum* species are poisonous.

Green False Hellebore, var. *viride*

HT: 3–6 ft.

var. *eschscholzianum*

HT: 3–6 ft.

■ **VIRGINIA BUNCHFLOWER** (*Veratrum virginicum*): Spring–summer; bogs, marshes, wet woods, meadows. Leaves to 1¼ in. wide. Flower clusters open (not dense). Tepals (petals and sepals) narrow abruptly to stalklike base; 2 glands above narrowed base of each. Do not confuse with Sandbog Death-camas (p. 299), which has hairless (vs. short-hairy) stems.

■ **WOOD'S BUNCHFLOWER** (*V. woodii*): Summer; woods. Similar to Virginia Bunchflower, but leaves to 4 in. wide; flowers brownish, with tepal bases narrowing gradually, glands dark. Also called Wood's False Hellebore.

Virginia Bunchflower

Flowers whitish (aging dark reddish purple).
HT: 2–6 ft.

Wood's Bunchflower

Flowers purple-maroon or chocolate brown (aging green-purple). HT: 2½–5 ft.

■ **BEAR-GRASS** (*Xerophyllum tenax*): Spring–early summer; open woods, clearings, rocky slopes. Leaves grasslike, tough, wiry, in large clump. Buds and blooming flowers clustered at top of long stalk, the flowering and fruiting cluster elongating to 20–30 in. Also called Western Turkey-beard.

■ **EASTERN TURKEY-BEARD** (*X. asphodeloides*, no photo): Open woods. Similar to Bear-grass; flower clusters 6–12 in. long.

Genus *Xerophyllum* (2 native species). Leaves mostly at plant base, long, slender, rigid, arching, toothed; stem leaves smaller. Flowers in dense clusters; tepals (petals and petal-like sepals) 6; stamens 6. Fruits are capsules.

Bear-grass

Flowers small, cream-white, in showy, plumelike clusters. HT: 2–5 ft.

■ **AMERICAN LILY-OF-THE-VALLEY** (*Convallaria majuscula*): Spring; woods. Plants generally scattered but sometimes found in small groups. Leaves broad. Flower lobes spreading or curved backward; tepal midribs greenish. Bract at base of flower stalk commonly ⅜–¾ in. long. **SIMILAR** ① **EUROPEAN LILY-OF-THE-VALLEY** (*C. majalis*): More widespread, frequently in dense populations in disturbed areas; mostly eastern. Bracts on flower stalks mostly ³⁄₁₆–⅜ in. long; tepal midribs white.

NOTE *Convallaria* species are poisonous.

Genus *Convallaria* (2 species, 1 native). Leaves arise from plant base. Flowers in elongated clusters, 6-lobed (tepals— petals and sepals—united); stamens 6. Fruits are berries.

American Lily-of-the-valley

Flowers white, bell-shaped, nodding, in 1-sided clusters. HT: mostly 6–14 in.

■ CANADIAN MAYFLOWER

(*Maianthemum canadense*): Spring; woods, swamps, bogs. Leaves 2 or 3, lowest leaf stalkless or very short-stalked; leaf bases have narrow notch. Also called False Lily-of-the-valley.

■ FALSE LILY-OF-THE-VALLEY

(*M. dilatatum*): Spring; woods, stream banks. Similar to Canadian Mayflower, but lowest leaf has stalk 1½–2½ in. long; leaf bases have broad notch; plants taller. Also called Two-leaf False Solomon's-seal.

■ THREE-LEAF FALSE SOLOMON'S-SEAL

(*M. trifolium*): Spring–early summer; wet woods, bogs. Leaves 2–4 (often 3), taper to sheathing base. Also called False Mayflower.

Genus *Maianthemum* (5 native species). Leaves alternate. Flowers small, in clusters at stem ends; tepals (petals and petal-like sepals) 4 or 6, white; stamens 4 or 6. Fruits are berries, mottled or spotted when young, red when mature.

Canadian Mayflower

Flowers in unbranched clusters; tepals 4. HT: 4–10 in.

False Lily-of-the-valley

HT: 8–18 in.

Three-leaf False Solomon's-seal

Flowers in unbranched clusters; tepals 6. HT: 4–18 in.

■ STARRY FALSE SOLOMON'S-SEAL

(*Maianthemum stellatum*): Spring; woodland edges, meadows, stream banks, sandy shores. Leaves 7–11. Also called Wild Lily-of-the-valley.

■ FEATHERY FALSE SOLOMON'S-SEAL

(*M. racemosum*): Spring–early summer; woods, thickets, floodplains, stream banks. Leaves 7–17. Tepals (petals and sepals) shorter than stamens. Berries red. Also called False Spikenard, Solomon's-plume. Eastern plants (ssp. *racemosum*) have leafstalks to ¼ in. long; western plants (ssp. *amplexicaule*) have stems usually erect, leaves stalkless, clasping.

Starry False Solomon's-seal

Flowers in unbranched clusters of 6–15; tepals 6. HT: 6–24 in.

Feathery False Solomon's-seal

Flowers in branched clusters of 70–250; tepals 6. HT: 1–3½ ft.

■ **SMOOTH SOLOMON'S-SEAL**
(*Polygonatum biflorum*): Spring; woods, fields, roadsides. Leaves hairless. Berries dark blue to blackish. Also called Giant Solomon's-seal. SIMILAR ■ **HAIRY SOLOMON'S-SEAL** (*P. pubescens*): Woods, thickets. Stems to 3 ft. long; veins on lower leaf surface fine-hairy.

Genus *Polygonatum* (3 species, 2 native). Leaves usually alternate. Flowers 1 to several, tubular and 6-lobed (tepals—petals and sepals—united below); stamens 6. Fruits are berries.

Smooth Solomon's-seal

Flowers whitish to greenish yellow, 1 to several dangling from leaf axils. Stems often arching, 1–6 ft. long.

■ **CLASPING-LEAF TWISTED-STALK**
(*Streptopus amplexifolius*): Late spring–midsummer; thickets, stream banks, woods. Stems usually branched. Leaves clasp stem. Tepals spreading or curved backward from about the middle; flower stalks kinked. Berries red or yellow-orange.

■ **ROSY TWISTED-STALK** (*S. lanceolatus*): Stems mostly unbranched. Leaves not clasping stem. Tepals spreading or curved backward near tip; flower stalks curved or bent (not kinked). Berries reddish. SIMILAR ■ **SMALL TWISTED-STALK** (*S. streptopoides*): Flowers saucer-shaped, wine-colored; tepals small, spreading widely, the greenish tip often curved backward.

Genus *Streptopus* (3 native species). Leaves alternate. Flowers solitary or in pairs, dangling underneath leaves from slender stalks; tepals (petals and petal-like sepals) 6; stamens 6. Fruits are berries.

Clasping-leaf Twisted-stalk

Rosy Twisted-stalk

Tepals usually tinged pinkish to purplish. HT: 6–30 in.

Tepals white to greenish yellow. HT: 6 in.–3½ ft.

■ **ROUGH-FRUIT FAIRYBELLS** (*Prosartes trachycarpa*): Spring–summer; woods. Flowers bell-shaped. Berries orange-red to red, covered with tiny bumps, 6–15-seeded.

■ **HOOKER'S FAIRYBELLS** (*P. hookeri*): Similar to Rough-fruit Fairybells. Berries bright red, smooth or hairy, 4–6-seeded.

■ **SMITH'S FAIRYBELLS** (*P. smithii*): Flowers cylindrical; stamens normally not protruding; tepals spreading only at tip. Berries yellow-orange, smooth, elongated, 5–9-seeded. Also called Large-flower Fairybells.

 Genus *Prosartes* (5 native species). Stems commonly arching. Leaves alternate, usually stalkless. Flowers 1 to few, dangling from slender stalks at stem ends; tepals (petals and petal-like sepals) 6; stamens 6. Fruits are berries.

Rough-fruit Fairybells

Tepals broadly spreading, cream to greenish white. HT: 1–3 ft.

Hooker's Fairybells

HT: 1–3 ft.

Smith's Fairybells

HT: 1–3 ft.

■ **YELLOW-MANDARIN** (*Prosartes lanuginosa*): Spring; woods. Leaves soft. Flowers bell-shaped. Berries red, smooth. Also called Yellow Fairybells.

■ **SPOTTED-MANDARIN** (*P. maculata*): Leaves slightly rough. Flowers bell-shaped. Berries straw-colored, hairy. Also called Nodding-mandarin.

Yellow-mandarin

Tepals greenish white to greenish yellow. HT: 1–2½ ft.

Spotted-mandarin

Tepals cream-white spotted with purple. HT: 1–2½ ft.

■ **LARGE-FLOWER BELLWORT** (*Uvularia grandiflora*): Spring–early summer; woods, ravines, floodplains, clearings. Flowers 1–2 in. long. **SIMILAR PERFOLIATE BELLWORT** (*U. perfoliata*): Woods, thickets; eastern. Inside surface of tepals covered with tiny bumps.

■ **SESSILE BELLWORT** (*U. sessilifolia*): Woods, thickets, clearings. Flowers ½–1 in. long. Also called Merrybells, Wild-oats.

Genus *Uvularia* (5 native species). Leaves alternate. Flowers solitary, dangling from slender stalks; tepals (petals and petal-like sepals) 6, usually overlapping; stamens 6. Fruits are capsules.

Large-flower Bellwort — Flowers yellow, nodding. Leaves appear pierced by stem. HT: 8–30 in.

Sessile Bellwort — Leaves stalkless. HT: 4–18 in.

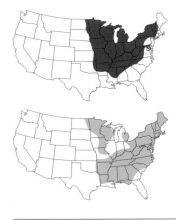

■ **SWAMP-LILY** (*Crinum americanum*): Spring–fall; swamps, marshes. Leaves 2–4 ft. long. Flowers in umbels (with stalks arising from a common point) above 2 papery bracts. Tepals spreading or arched backward; sometimes pink-tinged. Also called String-lily.

Genus *Crinum* (4 species, 1 native). Plants grow from bulbs. Leaves arise from plant base, thick, boat-shaped in cross section (flat near tip). Tepals (petals and petal-like sepals) 6, united at base; stamens 6, their stalks long. Fruits are capsules.

Swamp-lily — Flowers large; tepals white, narrow. Leaves strap-shaped. HT: flowering stalk 2–4 ft.

■ **SPIDER-LILY** (*Hymenocallis occidentalis*): Summer–early fall; woods, floodplains, meadows, swamps. Leaves straplike, wider above middle, often whitish, especially when young. Flowers large, in umbels (stalks arising from a common point); 6 narrow lobes white with green stripe on outside. In var. *eulae*, found mostly in eastern TX, leaves wither before flowers appear. **SIMILAR**

■ **SPRING SPIDER-LILY** (*H. liriosme*): Spring; ditches, marsh edges, pond margins, swamps. Leaves shiny green, leathery, not wider above middle.

Genus *Hymenocallis* (15 native species). Plants grow from bulbs. Leaves arise from plant base. Tepals (petals and petal-like sepals) 6, united at base, the 6 lobes narrow; stamens 6, the stalks joined by a thin membrane into a showy, funnel-shaped cup ("corona"). Fruits are capsules.

Spider-lily
Corona white with yellowish eye; edges toothed.
HT: 1–3 ft.

■ **ATAMASCO-LILY** (*Zephyranthes atamasca*): Midwinter–spring; woods, clearings, meadows. Flowers 2–4 in. long.

■ **EVENING-STAR RAIN-LILY** (*Z. chlorosolen*): Mostly summer–fall; prairies, hills, open woods. Flowers white to pinkish, trumpet-shaped, 3–7 in. long; stamens close together.

■ **COPPER ZEPHYR-LILY** (*Z. longifolia*): Spring–summer; hills, mesas. Flowers yellow, funnel-shaped, 1–1½ in. long.

Genus *Zephyranthes* (16 species, 11 native). Plants grow from bulbs. Leaves arise from plant base. Flowers showy, large, usually solitary on leafless stalk; funnel- or trumpet-shaped, 6-lobed (6 tepals—petals and sepals—united below); stamens 6; stigma 3-lobed. Fruits are capsules.

Atamasco-lily
Flowers white to pinkish, funnel-shaped; stamens separated. Leaves narrow, flat. HT: to 12 in.

Evening-star Rain-lily
HT: to 12 in.

Copper Zephyr-lily
HT: to 12 in.

■ **TORREY'S CRAG-LILY** (*Echeandia flavescens*): Summer–fall; slopes, open woods, grasslands. Flowers star-shaped; outer 3 tepals narrower than inner 3.

OTHER GENERA Also with star-shaped flowers. ■ **LONELY-LILY** (*Eremocrinum albomarginatum*): Spring; sandy flats, dunes. Conspicuous bracts in flower cluster. Tepals of equal width, white with darker, 3-veined midstripe. ■ **MEXICAN-STAR** (*Milla biflora*): Late summer; hillsides, open woods. Flowers in umbrella-like clusters, trumpet-shaped. Tepals united below into slender tube with 6 spreading lobes, green outer midstripes.

Genus *Echeandia* (3 native species). Leaves narrow, arise mostly from plant base. Flowers in clusters; tepals (petals and petal-like sepals) 6; stamens 6. Fruits are capsules.

Torrey's Crag-lily

Tepals orangish yellow with darker, 3-veined midstripe. Leaves grass-like. HT: 6–16 in.

Lonely-lily

Mexican-star

HT: 6–16 in.   HT: 6–18 in.

■ **SAND-LILY** (*Leucocrinum montanum*): Spring; prairies, plains, open mountain woods. Flower clusters at ground level (no aboveground stems). Fruits develop underground. Also called Star-lily, Mountain-lily.

Genus *Leucocrinum* (1 native species). Leaves arise from plant base, narrow. Flowers in clusters, long-tubular and 6-lobed (6 tepals—petals and petal-like sepals—united below); stamens 6. Fruits are capsules.

Sand-lily

Flowers white; tube slender, opening to 6 spreading lobes. Leaves grasslike. HT: 4–8 in.

■ **DESERT-LILY** (*Hesperocallis undulata*):
Spring; desert flats, slopes. Leaves
strongly wavy-margined. Flowers large,
white with silvery green midstripe on
outside of each lobe. Also called Ajo-lily.

Genus *Hesperocallis* (1 native species).
Plants grow from bulbs. Leaves arise
mostly from plant base, long and narrow.
Flowers in unbranched clusters, funnel-shaped, with 6
spreading lobes (6 tepals—petals and sepals—united
below); stamens 6. Fruits are capsules.

Desert-lily

HT: 1–6 ft.

■ **CANADIAN LILY** (*Lilium canadense*):
Summer; moist or wet places. Tepals
spreading, 2–3 in. long; mostly yellow
or orange, less often red; commonly
maroon-spotted but occasionally solid.

Genus *Lilium* (22 species, 21 native).
Plants grow from bulbs. Leaves alternate
or whorled. Flowers large, showy, solitary
or in clusters; tepals (petals and petal-like sepals) 6;
stamens 6. Fruits are capsules.

Canadian Lily

Flowers nodding from
ends of slender stalks.
Leaves whorled. HT: 2–6 ft.

■ **TURK'S-CAP LILY** (*Lilium superbum*): Summer; moist ground. Tepals (petals and sepals) 2¾–4 in. long. Red-flowered forms less common. **SIMILAR** A few of several similar species. **CAROLINA LILY** (*L. michauxii*): Woods, slopes; southeastern. **MICHIGAN LILY** (*L. michiganense*): Moist or wet ground; midwestern. Ⓘ **ASIATIC TIGER LILY** (*L. lancifolium*): Cultivated; sometimes escapes. Leaves all alternate, upper leaves often with dark bulbs in axils.
■ **COLUMBIAN LILY** (*L. columbianum*): Moist woods, meadows, roadsides. Tepals 1½–2½ in. long; anthers yellow. Also called Tiger or Oregon Lily. ■ **LEOPARD LILY** (*L. pardalinum* ssp. *pardalinum*): Streams, rivers, marshes. Tepals 2½–4 in. long; anthers purple to magenta.

Turk's-cap Lily

Flowers nodding from ends of slender stalks; tepals orange or orange-yellow, maroon-spotted, strongly curved backward; stamens protruding. Leaves whorled. HT: 3–8 ft.

■ **KELLEY'S TIGER LILY** (*Lilium kelleyanum*): Summer; wet mountain meadows, thickets, seeps, stream banks. Differs from Leopard Lily (above) in having mildly fragrant (vs. nonfragrant) flowers with shorter tepals (petals and sepals), 1½–2 in. long.

■ **ALPINE LILY** (*L. parvum*): Flowers bell- to funnel-shaped; tepals 1–1½ in. long, orange-red or sometimes yellow-orange, frequently spotted. Also called Sierran Tiger Lily.

Kelley's Tiger Lily

Flowers yellow, spotted, nodding; tepals strongly curved backward. HT: to 6 ft.

Alpine Lily

Flowers spreading or erect; tepals somewhat curved backward. HT: to 5 ft.

■ **WOOD LILY** (*Lilium philadelphicum*): Late spring–summer; prairies, open woods, meadows, thickets. Flowers often 1–3, erect. Tepals (petals and sepals) 2–3 in. long, sometimes with yellowish base; forms with all yellow tepals are uncommon. Appalachian and northeastern populations have mostly whorled leaves; plants farther west tend to have a single whorl, the remaining leaves alternate.

■ **PINE LILY** (*L. catesbaei*): Mostly summer–fall; moist or wet pinelands, seeps. Leaves alternate. Flowers often solitary, erect; tepals 3–4½ in. long, narrowed at base. Also called Catesby's Lily.

Wood Lily

Tepals red to orange, with maroon-spotted, narrowed base. HT: 1–4 ft.

Pine Lily

Tepals red or pink, with maroon-spotted yellow base. HT: 1–3 ft.

■ **WASHINGTON LILY** (*Lilium washingtonianum*): Summer; open woods, shrublands, roadsides. Leaves mostly whorled. Flowers typically face outward, commonly age to light pink, deep pink, or lavender; tepals (petals and sepals) 2½–4 in. long, spreading or often curved backward. Also called Cascade Lily.

■ **CHAPARRAL LILY** (*L. rubescens*): Shrublands, woods. Leaves whorled. Flowers mostly erect, usually age to rose-purple; tepals 1½–2½ in. long, spreading or often curved backward. Also called Redwood Lily.

Washington Lily

Tepals white, often with yellowish and sometimes purple-spotted base. HT: 2–6 ft.

Chaparral Lily

Tepals white with purple spots. HT: 2–6 ft.

■ **YELLOW TROUT-LILY** (*Erythronium americanum*): Spring; woods, ravines. Single yellow flower; tepals strongly curved backward. One-leaved nonflowering plants are common.

■ **GLACIER-LILY** (*E. grandiflorum*): Spring–summer; open woods, slopes, mountain meadows. Flower usually 1 but up to 5, yellow; tepals curved backward. Also called Yellow Avalanche-lily.

Genus *Erythronium* (23 native species). Plants grow from bulbs. Leaves 2, arise from plant base. Flowers solitary or in clusters on leafless stalks; tepals (petals and sepals) 6; stamens 6, protruding. Fruits are capsules. Species are also called dogtooth-violet, adder's-tongue.

Yellow Trout-lily
Leaves mottled.
HT: 4–10 in.

Glacier-lily
Leaves not mottled.
HT: 4–12 in.

■ **PINK FAWN-LILY** (*Erythronium revolutum*): Spring; shady, moist places. Leaves mottled. Flowers 1–3; tepals (petals and sepals) curved backward. Also called Coast Fawn-lily.

■ **HENDERSON'S FAWN-LILY** (*E. hendersonii*): Drier wooded sites. Leaves mottled. Flowers have dark purple center.

NOTE Tepals of some white-flowered species, such as Plainleaf Fawn-lily (p. 313), turn pinkish with age.

Pink Fawn-lily
Flowers pink to violet, with yellow center.
HT: 6–16 in.

Henderson's Fawn-lily

Flowers have dark center.
HT: 4–12 in.

■ **WHITE TROUT-LILY** (*Erythronium albidum*): Spring; woods. Single flower, white with yellow center, often tinged purplish outside. One-leaved nonflowering plants are common.

■ **PRAIRIE TROUT-LILY** (*E. mesochoreum*): Prairies, open woods. Single flower, white with yellow center, often tinged purplish outside. Also called Midland Fawn-lily.

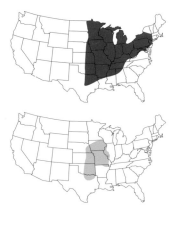

White Trout-lily

Tepals strongly curved backward. Leaves mostly flat, mottled. HT: 2–8 in.

Prairie Trout-lily

Tepals spreading. Leaves somewhat folded lengthwise, usually not mottled. HT: 2–6 in.

■ **AVALANCHE-LILY** (*Erythronium montanum*): Late spring–summer; mountain forests and meadows. Leaves 1½ in. wide, not mottled. Flowers 1–3, often fading pinkish; tepals (petals and sepals) spreading. Also called White Glacier-lily.

■ **PLAINLEAF FAWN-LILY** (*E. purpurascens*): Summer; meadows, woods. Leaves mostly 1 in. or less wide, not mottled. Also called Sierra Nevada Fawn-lily. SIMILAR **SIERRA FOOTHILLS FAWN-LILY** (*E. multiscapideum*): Spring; Sierra Nevada. Leaves mottled.

■ **OREGON FAWN-LILY** (*E. oregonum*): Spring. Leaves mottled.

Avalanche-lily

Flowers white with yellow center. HT: 5–15 in.

Plainleaf Fawn-lily

HT: 2½–8 in.

Oregon Fawn-lily

HT: 6–16 in.

■ **SPOTTED FRITILLARY** (*Fritillaria atropurpurea*): Spring–midsummer; open woods, mountain meadows, grassy slopes. Leaves narrow, to ¼ in. wide; alternate, nearly opposite, or in whorls of 3. Flowers to ¾ in. long. Also called Leopard-lily. **SIMILAR** ■ **CHECKER-LILY** (*F. affinis*): Woodland meadows, grassy areas. Leaves ¼–1 in. wide; flowers ¾–1½ in. long. Several similar species, all sharing common names such as chocolate-lily and mission-bells.

■ **KAMCHATKA FRITILLARY** (*F. camschatcensis*): Rocky beaches, open forests, mountain meadows. Leaves in whorls of 5–10. Also called Black-lily.

Genus *Fritillaria* (20 native species). Plants grow from bulbs. Leaves alternate or whorled. Flowers solitary or in clusters, commonly nodding; tepals (petals and petal-like sepals) 6; stamens 6. Fruits are 6-angled capsules.

Spotted Fritillary

Flowers purplish brown, mottled yellow or white.
HT: 6–24 in.

Kamchatka Fritillary

Flowers usually brownish purple, rarely mottled.
HT: 6–24 in.

■ **YELLOW FRITILLARY** (*Fritillaria pudica*): Spring; open woods, plains, slopes. Leaves mostly alternate. Flowers age reddish or purplish. Also called Yellow-bell.

■ **SCARLET FRITILLARY** (*F. recurva*): Open woods, shrublands. Leaves alternate or in whorls of 2–5. Flowers often yellow-spotted.

Yellow Fritillary

Flowers usually solitary, yellow.
HT: 4–12 in.

Scarlet Fritillary

Flowers red; tips bent backward.
HT: 1–3 ft.

■ **ALP-LILY** (*Lloydia serotina*): Summer; rocky slopes, cliffs, alpine meadows, tundra. Leaves grasslike, shorter on stem. Flowers commonly solitary. Also called Alpine-lily.

Genus *Lloydia* (1 native species). Leaves basal and alternate, narrow. Flowers solitary to few; tepals (petals and petal-like sepals) 6; stamens 6. Fruits are capsules.

Alp-lily

Flowers cream-white with yellowish center, purplish or greenish veins. HT: 2–6 in.

■ **SEGO-LILY** (*Calochortus nuttallii*): Midspring–midsummer; dry open places. Also called Nuttall's Mariposa-lily. SIMILAR **GUNNISON'S MARIPOSA-LILY** (*C. gunnisonii* var. *gunnisonii*): Hills, slopes; similar range. Petals white to purplish; gland patch broad, with purple band just above it extending across petal.

■ **DESERT MARIPOSA-LILY** (*C. kennedyi* var. *kennedyi*): Spring; dry, open or shrubby places. Petals orange to red; gland spot round, dark-splotched.

■ **YELLOW MARIPOSA-LILY** (*C. luteus*): Late spring–midsummer; grasslands, open woods. Petals deep yellow; gland patch broad, marked with red-brown. Also called Gold-nuggets.

Genus *Calochortus* (56 native species). Some species grow from bulbs. Leaves basal and sometimes alternate, narrow. Flowers showy, solitary or in clusters, above 2 leaflike bracts; petals 3, each with often hairy or fringed gland patch or spot at inner base; sepals 3, may be colored; stamens 6. Fruits are capsules. Also called mariposa-tulip.

Sego-lily

Petals white; gland spot round, yellow with purple crescent above. HT: 6–18 in.

Desert Mariposa-lily

HT: 4–8 in.

Yellow Mariposa-lily

HT: 6–18 in.

■ SAGEBRUSH MARIPOSA-LILY
(*Calochortus macrocarpus*): Late spring–
midsummer; plains, slopes, open woods.
Petals have green midstripe beneath;
sepals narrow, equal to or longer than
broad petals.

■ BIG-POD MARIPOSA-LILY
(*C. eurycarpus*): Summer; grasslands, open
woods. Sepals narrow, mostly shorter
than broad petals.

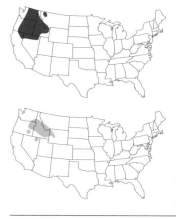

Sagebrush Mariposa-lily

Petals purplish;
gland spot triangular,
often with dark purple
band above. HT: 8–20 in.

Big-pod Mariposa-lily

Petals
white to
lavender; gland
spot triangular,
yellow-green with
red-purple spot
above. HT: 4–20 in.

■ BUTTERFLY MARIPOSA-LILY
(*Calochortus venustus*): Midspring–
midsummer; grasslands, open woods.
Plants 6–24 in. tall. Gland patch hairy,
commonly more or less square. A highly
variable species with a broad range of
colors and patterns, some pictured here.
Also called Square Mariposa-lily.

Butterfly Mariposa-lily

■ **ELEGANT MARIPOSA-LILY**
(*Calochortus elegans*): Late spring–
midsummer; grassy hillsides, open woods.
Also called Elegant Cat's-ear.

■ **LYALL'S MARIPOSA-LILY** (*C. lyallii*):
Late spring–midsummer; dry slopes, open
woods. Petals pointed, fringed on edges;
greenish gland patch has purple crescent
above. Also called Lyall's Star-tulip.

■ **YELLOW-STAR MARIPOSA-LILY**
(*C. monophyllus*): Spring; slopes, open
woods. Petals hairy, often with reddish
brown splotch. Several yellow-flowered
species with hairy petals often marked
with reddish brown, differing in number,
color, and location of hairs.

Elegant Mariposa-lily

Petals whitish, hairy; gland patch purplish above. HT: 2–8 in.

Lyall's Mariposa-lily

Petals white or purple-tinged. HT: 4–20 in.

Yellow-star Mariposa-lily

Petals dark yellow. HT: 3–8 in.

■ **WHITE FAIRY-LANTERN** (*Calochortus albus*): Midspring–midsummer; thickets, open woods, shrublands. Sepals not widely spreading. Also called White Globe-lily.

■ **ROSE FAIRY-LANTERN** (*C. amoenus*): Shaded grassy slopes. Sepals spreading. Also called Purple Fairy-lantern.

■ **GOLDEN FAIRY-LANTERN**
(*C. amabilis*): Shaded places in open woods, shrublands. Sepals spreading; petals densely fringed. Also called Diogenes'-lantern.

White Fairy-lantern

Flowers nodding, remaining more or less closed; petals white to pinkish, lightly fringed. HT: 6–30 in.

Rose Fairy-lantern

Flowers rose. HT: 6–24 in.

Golden Fairy-lantern

Flowers deep yellow. HT: 6–24 in.

■ **LARGE-FLOWER TRILLIUM** (*Trillium grandiflorum*): Spring; woods, floodplains. Flowers stalked, erect or facing outward; petal bases overlap. Also called White Trillium. See also white-flowered forms of Red Trillium (below), which have maroon pistil. SIMILAR ■ **WESTERN WHITE TRILLIUM** (*T. ovatum*): Woods, thickets. Petal bases do not overlap.

■ **PAINTED TRILLIUM** (*T. undulatum*): Woods (mostly acidic soil). Leaves stalked; leaf tips pointed. Flowers white, normally with triangular, red-purple eye.

■ **SNOW TRILLIUM** (*T. nivale*): Early spring; woods, ledges, cliffs (mostly alkaline soil). Dwarf. Leaves bluish green, stalked; leaf tips rounded. Flowers white.

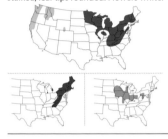

Genus *Trillium* (38 native species). Leaves (actually leaflike bracts) in a whorl of 3. Flowers solitary, showy; petals 3; sepals 3, mostly greenish; stamens 6. Fruits capsulelike or berrylike.

Large-flower Trillium

Painted Trillium

HT: 8–18 in.

Snow Trillium

Flowers white aging pinkish purple. Leaves stalkless; tips pointed. HT: 8–18 in.

HT: 2–4 in.

■ **BENT TRILLIUM** (*Trillium flexipes*): Spring; woods, floodplains. Flowers sometimes held below leaves. Stamen tips (anthers) ¼–½ in., longer than their stalks (filaments). Maroon-flowered forms (see inset) are likely hybrids with Red Trillium.

■ **NODDING TRILLIUM** (*T. cernuum*): Spring–summer; woods, swamps. Similar to Bent Trillium, but anthers typically about as long as filaments, ⅛–¼ in.

■ **RED TRILLIUM** (*T. erectum*): Spring; woods, swamp borders. Flowers held above leaves on erect or curved stalks. Red- or maroon-flowered forms common; white-flowered forms (with maroon pistil) occasional throughout, common at low elevations in southern Appalachians. Also called Purple Trillium, Stinking-benjamin.

Bent Trillium

Flowers white, on "bent-elbow" stalks. Unopened anthers cream-white to yellow. Leaves stalkless. HT: 8–20 in.

Nodding Trillium

Red Trillium

Flowers white, nodding. Unopened anthers pinkish. HT: 6–16 in.

HT: 10–20 in.

■ **SESSILE TRILLIUM** (*Trillium sessile*): Spring; woods. Leaves stalkless, often mottled. Flowers stalkless, occasionally greenish to yellowish. Also called Toadshade. SIMILAR ■ **GIANT TRILLIUM** (*T. chloropetalum*): Woods, slopes. There are also several similar mostly southern species.

■ **YELLOW TRILLIUM** (*T. luteum*): Chiefly southern Appalachians. Flowers have lemon scent.

■ **PRAIRIE TRILLIUM** (*T. recurvatum*): Woods. Leaves stalked. Petals maroon-purple or sometimes yellowish.

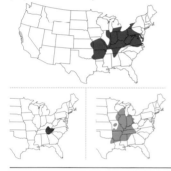

Sessile Trillium

Flowers usually maroon, stalkless; petals erect; sepals spreading. HT: 3–10 in.

Yellow Trillium

Flowers yellow. HT: 8–18 in.

Prairie Trillium

Petals erect; sepals curved downward. HT: 6–20 in.

■ **INDIAN CUCUMBER-ROOT** (*Medeola virginiana*): Spring; woods. Upper whorl of 3 leaves, midstem whorl of 5–11 leaves. Berries dark purple to black.

Genus *Medeola* (1 native species). Leaves in 2 widely spaced whorls. Flowers in clusters; tepals (petals and petal-like sepals) 6, strongly curved backward; stamens 6; styles 3, long, threadlike. Fruits are berries.

Indian Cucumber-root

Flowers yellowish green, dangling from arching stalks. HT: 1–2½ ft.

■ **CALIFORNIA FETID-ADDER'S-TONGUE** (*Scoliopus bigelovii*): Late winter–early spring; shaded slopes. Flowers ill-scented; sepals and petals ½–¾ in. long. Also called Slink-pod. **SIMILAR** ■ **OREGON FETID-ADDER'S-TONGUE** (*S. hallii*): Leaves shorter, usually not mottled; sepals and petals less than ½ in. long.

Genus *Scoliopus* (2 native species). Leaves 2 or 3, arise from plant base. Flowers long-stalked, in clusters; petals 3, very narrow, erect; sepals 3, showy, petal-like, spreading; stamens 3; stigma 3-lobed, arching. Fruits are capsules.

California Fetid-adder's-tongue

Petal-like sepals whitish green, heavily veined purple. Leaves usually 2, broad, commonly mottled. HT: 3–8 in.

■ **SWAMP-PINK** (*Helonias bullata*): Spring–early summer; swamps, bogs. Stems hollow. Basal leaves strap-shaped, growing to 12 in. long, 1½ in. wide. Flowers in dense, egg-shaped clusters.

Genus *Helonias* (1 native species). Leaves mostly arise from plant base (stem leaves much reduced, triangular, bract- or scalelike). Flowers in clusters; tepals (petals and petal-like sepals) 6; stamens 6. Fruits are capsules.

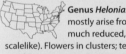

Swamp-pink

Flowers lavender-pink; stamens protruding, anthers bluish. HT: 1–2 ft.

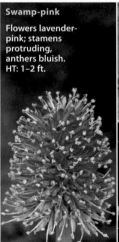

■ **WILD GARLIC** (*Allium canadense*): Spring–summer; roadsides, meadows, fields, open woods. Leaves flat in cross section, solid. Stamens about as long as tepals. Also called Meadow Garlic, Wild Onion. See also ⊞ Field Garlic (p. 587). **SIMILAR** ■ **DRUMMOND'S ONION** (*A. drummondii*): Spring–early summer; prairies, plains, hills. Papery bracts below flower cluster have 1 vein (3–7 veins in Wild Garlic); tiny bulbs in flower clusters only rarely produced.

OTHERS Flower clusters lack tiny bulbs; stamens longer than tepals. ■ **PRAIRIE ONION** (*A. stellatum*): Summer–fall; prairies. ■ **NODDING WILD ONION** (*A. cernuum*): Moist, often rocky or gravelly places.

Genus *Allium* (96 species, 84 native). Plants grow from bulbs; commonly have onion odor. Leaves slender, mostly arise from near plant base, may wither early. Flowers in umbels (stalks arise from a common point) above obvious bracts; tepals (petals and sepals) 6; stamens 6. Fruits are capsules.

Wild Garlic

Flowers white or pinkish, in erect clusters. Clusters often have tiny bulbs that may have a "tail." HT: 6–24 in.

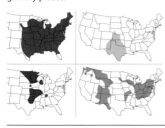

Prairie Onion

Flowers star-shaped; stamens protruding. HT: 6–24 in.

Nodding Wild Onion

Flowers bell-shaped, in nodding clusters. HT: 6–24 in.

■ **SHORT-STYLE ONION** (*Allium brevistylum*): Summer; moist or wet mountain meadows, stream banks.

■ **TALL SWAMP ONION** (*A. validum*): Summer; wet places in mountains. Also called Swamp Onion.

■ **PLAINS ONION** (*A. perdulce*): Spring; prairies, plains, hills. Flowers somewhat urn-shaped, pink.

■ **TEXTILE ONION** (*A. textile*): Spring; plains, hills. Also called White Wild Onion.

Short-style Onion

Flowers rose-pink; stamens not protruding. HT: 8–24 in.

Tall Swamp Onion

Flowers rose-pink; stamens protruding. HT: 1–2½ ft.

Plains Onion

Tepals rose-pink with dark midvein. HT: 4–12 in.

Textile Onion

Tepals white with dark midvein. HT: 4–16 in.

■ **TAPER-TIP ONION** (*Allium acuminatum*): Spring–summer; plains, slopes. Inner 3 tepals (petals and petal-like sepals) smaller. Also called Hooker's Onion.

■ **DESERT ONION** (*A. macropetalum*): Spring; desert plains, hills. Tepals mostly equal in size. Also called Large-petal Onion.

Taper-tip Onion

Flowers rose-purple to pink or whitish. HT: 4–14 in.

Desert Onion

Tepals pink with darker midvein. HT: 2–8 in.

■ **RED SIERRAN ONION** (*Allium obtusum*): Late spring–summer; slopes. Leaves curved. Flowering stalks round.

■ **DWARF ONION** (*A. parvum*): Leaves curved. Flowering stalks flattened. Also called Small Onion.

■ **SCYTHE-LEAF ONION** (*A. falcifolium*): Leaves strongly curved. Flowering stalks very flat. Also called Sickle-leaf Onion, Coast Flat-stem Onion.

■ **FLAT-STEM ONION** (*A. platycaule*): Leaves strongly curved. Tepals (petals and petal-like sepals) narrow. Flowering stalks very flat. Also called Pink-star Onion.

NOTE Species are mostly 1–8 in. tall.

Red Sierran Onion

Tepals whitish or pink, with dark midvein.

Dwarf Onion

Tepals whitish or pinkish, with dark midvein.

Scythe-leaf Onion

Flowers reddish purple.

Flat-stem Onion

Flowers pink; stamens protruding.

■ **RAMP** (*Allium tricoccum*): Summer; woods, floodplains, ravines. Leaves broad, appearing in early to midspring and dying back before the leafless flowering stalks appear. Also called Wild Leek.

Ramp

Flowers white, in ball-shaped clusters. Leaves broad. HT: 4–16 in.

■ **FALSE GARLIC** (*Nothoscordum bivalve*): Spring–fall; open woods, prairies, disturbed areas. Leaves grasslike. Flowers about 1 in. across; lobes have darker midvein beneath. Also called Crow-poison. False Garlic has no strong odor. Do not confuse with *Allium* species (pp. 321–323), which have an onion or garlic odor; tepals not joined at their bases.

OTHER GENUS ■ **COMMON MUILLA** (*Muilla maritima*): Spring; coastal scrub, grasslands, woods. Also has umbels of white flowers, no onion odor. Flowers to ½ in. across; tepals free or united only at very base.

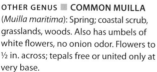

Genus *Nothoscordum* (2 species, 1 native). Plants grow from bulbs. Leaves basal. Flowers in umbels (stalks arising from a common point); tepals (petals and sepals) 6, united at base into short tube; stamens 6. Fruits are capsules.

False Garlic

Flowers white with yellowish center. HT: 8–16 in.

Common Muilla

HT: 4–20 in.

■ **ELEGANT BRODIAEA** (*Brodiaea elegans*): Spring–summer; open woods, meadows, grasslands. Leaves narrow, elongated, rounded on underside, often withering early. Near flower center are 3 antherless stamens, these whitish, mostly flat, about as long as the 3 anther-bearing stamens.

■ **CROWN BRODIAEA** (*B. coronaria*): Spring; grasslands. Similar to Elegant Brodiaea, but antherless stamens hornlike, rolled inward, longer than anther-bearing stamens.

NOTE Both of these species have been called Harvest Brodiaea. *Brodiaea* species are also called cluster-lily.

 Genus *Brodiaea* (14 native species). Plants grow from bulblike corms. Leaves arise from plant base, crescent-shaped in cross section. Flowers in open umbels above leaflike bracts; tepals (petals and petal-like sepals) 6, united at base; 3 anther-bearing (fertile) stamens and 3 antherless (sterile) stamens. Fruits are capsules.

Elegant Brodiaea

Crown Brodiaea

Flowers blue-purple to violet. HT: 4–20 in.

HT: 2–10 in.

■ **BLUE-DICKS** (*Dichelostemma capitatum*): Mostly spring; open woods, grasslands, deserts. Flowers have 6 anther-bearing (fertile) stamens of 2 sizes. Also called Wild-hyacinth.

■ **OOKOW** (*D. multiflorum*): Flowers pink to blue-purple; stamens 3, all fertile. **SIMILAR FORK-TOOTH OOKOW** (*D. congestum*): Central CA to WA. Also with 3 fertile stamens, but has 2-lobed corona tips (as in Blue-dicks).

Genus *Dichelostemma* (5 native species). Similar to *Brodiaea* (above), but leaves keeled on underside; flower clusters often denser; stamens usually 3 (antherless ones mostly absent); ring ("corona") of flaplike appendages attached to inside of flower near base of lobes.

Blue-dicks

Ookow

Flowers mostly blue to purple; corona whitish, its tips deeply 2-lobed. HT: 1–2 ft.

Corona tips not 2-lobed. HT: 1–2½ ft.

■ **SNAKE-LILY** (*Dichelostemma volubile*):
Spring; woods, shrublands. Flowers have
3 anther-bearing (fertile) and 3 sterile
stamens.

■ **FIRECRACKER-FLOWER** (*D. ida-maia*):
Spring–summer; woodland borders,
grasslands. Flowers have 3 stamens,
all fertile.

Snake-lily

Flowers usually pink;
corona whitish.
Stems twining.

Firecracker-flower

Flowers have
red tube, yellow-
green lobes; corona
whitish. HT: 1–3 ft.

■ **LARGE-FLOWER TRITELEIA** (*Triteleia
grandiflora*): Spring–summer; open
woods, prairies, plains. Leaves few,
grasslike. Flower base tubular; lobes
spreading, dark bluish purple to nearly
white; inner 3 tepals (petals and petal-like
sepals) commonly have ruffled edges;
filaments (stamen stalks) thick. Also
called Douglas'-brodiaea. A variant with
wide, flat filaments, found from northern
CA to southwestern British Columbia, is
treated by some as **HOWELL'S TRITELEIA**
(*T. grandiflora* var. *howellii*), also called
Howell's-brodiaea.

NOTE *Triteleia* species are also called wild-
hyacinth, triplet-lily.

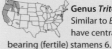

Genus *Triteleia* (14 native species).
Similar to *Brodiaea* (p. 324), but leaves
have central ridge on underside; anther-
bearing (fertile) stamens 6.

Large-flower
Triteleia

Tepals usually
lavender-blue
with darker
midstripe.
HT: 8–30 in.

Howell's Triteleia

Tepals often pale blue
to whitish, with darker
midstripe. HT: 8–20 in.

■ **FOOL'S ONION** (*Triteleia hyacinthina*): Spring–summer; stream banks. Flower base bowl-shaped. Also called Hyacinth-brodiaea, White-brodiaea.

■ **PRETTY-FACE** (*T. ixioides*): Spring–summer; grasslands, woods. Flower base funnel-shaped; filaments (stamen stalks) flattened, forked. Also called Golden-brodiaea.

RELATED ■ COMMON GOLDEN-STARS (*Bloomeria crocea*): Spring; hills, woods, shrublands, grasslands. Tepals (petals and petal-like sepals) free or barely united at base.

Fool's Onion

Tepals white or lilac-blue, with darker midstripe. HT: 6–24 in.

Pretty-face

Tepals yellow with darker midstripe. HT: 4–32 in.

Common Golden-stars

HT: 6–24 in.

■ **PINK FUNNEL-LILY** (*Androstephium breviflorum*): Spring; plains, slopes. Leaves grasslike. Flower lobes longer than tube.

■ **BLUE FUNNEL-LILY** (*A. coeruleum*): Prairies, grassy slopes, rocky areas. Flower tube as long as or longer than lobes.

Genus *Androstephium* (2 native species). Plants grow from corms. Leaves arise from plant base, few. Flowers in umbels; 6 spreading lobes (tepals—petals and sepals—united below); stamens 6, their filaments (stalks) joined to form tubular "crown" in flower center. Fruits are capsules.

Pink Funnel-lily

Flowers whitish to red-purple, with darker midstripe on lobes. HT: 4–12 in.

Blue Funnel-lily

Flowers pale blue to violet. HT: 3–8 in.

■ **BLUE BEAD-LILY** (*Clintonia borealis*): Spring–early summer; woods. Flowers in clusters of 3–8. Berries blue. Also called Yellow Clintonia.

■ **SPECKLED WOOD-LILY** (*C. umbellulata*): Flowers in clusters of 10–25; tepals often speckled with purple. Berries black. Also called White Clintonia.

Genus *Clintonia* (4 native species). Leaves mostly arise from plant base, conspicuously wide; stem leaves much smaller. Flowers solitary or in clusters; tepals (petals and petal-like sepals) 6; stamens 6. Fruits are berries.

Blue Bead-lily

Speckled Wood-lily

Flowers yellow, often nodding. HT: 8–20 in.

Flowers white to greenish white, mostly erect. HT: 10–24 in.

■ **QUEEN'S-CUP** (*Clintonia uniflora*): Late spring–summer; woods. Flowers solitary. Berries blue. Also called Bride's-bonnet.

■ **RED CLINTONIA** (*C. andrewsiana*): Spring–early summer; coastal redwood forests. Flowers in clusters of 20–45. Berries blue to blue-black.

Queen's-cup
Flowers white. HT: 6–10 in.

Red Clintonia
Flowers rose-purple to red. HT: 10–30 in.

■ **COMMON CAMAS** (*Camassia quamash*): Spring; meadows, fields. Flowers 1–2 in. across, slightly irregular, with 1 tepal curving downward, the rest upward; many flowers open at one time. Also called Blue Camas, Small Camas. SIMILAR **LEICHTLIN'S CAMAS** (*C. leichtlinii*): Wet meadows; Pacific states. All tepals alike; 1–3 flowers open at one time. Also called Large Camas.

■ **EASTERN CAMAS** (*C. scilloides*): Prairies, open woods, stream banks. Flowers ½–¾ in. across; clusters to 18 in. long, with 7–50 flowers. Also called Wild Hyacinth. SIMILAR ■ **PRAIRIE CAMAS** (*C. angusta*): Prairies. Flower clusters 11–35 in. long, with 50–100 flowers.

Genus *Camassia* (6 native species). Plants grow from bulbs. Leaves arise from plant base, strap-shaped. Flowers in clusters; tepals (petals and petal-like sepals) 6, often twisting upon drying; stamens 6; style 1. Fruits are capsules.

Common Camas

Eastern Camas

Flowers blue to blue-violet. HT: 6 in.–3 ft.

Flowers lavender to pale blue. HT: to 2½ ft.

■ **WAVY-LEAF SOAP-PLANT** (*Chlorogalum pomeridianum*): Spring–summer; open woods, shrublands, fields. Leaves strongly wavy-margined. Flowers in large clusters; tepals twist together above the growing fruit after flowering. Also called Amole. SIMILAR ■ **NARROW-LEAF SOAP-PLANT** (*C. angustifolium*): Grasslands, woods. Leaves not strongly wavy-margined; plants shorter (1–2 ft.).

RELATED *Odontostomum* (1 native species). ■ **HARTWEG'S DOLL'S-LILY** (*O. hartwegii*): Spring; grassy hillsides. Flowers small; tepals 3–7-veined; 6 minute sterile stamens alternate with the larger fertile ones. Also called Hartweg's Odontostomum.

Genus *Chlorogalum* (5 native species). Plants grow from bulbs. Leaves arise from plant base. Flowers in elongated, branching clusters; tepals (petals and petal-like sepals) 6; stamens 6. Fruits are capsules.

Wavy-leaf Soap-plant

Hartweg's Doll's-lily

Tepals small, downturned, cream-colored to yellowish; stamens short. HT: 6–18 in.

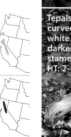

Tepals narrow, often curved backward, white with darker midvein; stamens long. HT: 2–7 ft.

■ **YELLOW STAR-GRASS** (*Hypoxis hirsuta*): Mostly spring–summer; woods, prairies, meadows. Leaves soft, flexible, about ¼ in. wide. Also called Common Goldstar. SIMILAR ■ **FRINGED YELLOW STAR-GRASS** (*H. juncea*): Year-round (mostly spring); moist or often wet woods. Leaves wiry, threadlike.

Genus *Hypoxis* (7 native species). Leaves arise from plant base. Flowers in clusters; tepals (petals and petal-like sepals) 6; stamens 6. Fruits are capsules.

Yellow Star-grass

Flowers yellow, hairy outside. Leaves grasslike, usually hairy. HT: 2–10 in.

LIMNANTHACEAE   MEADOWFOAM FAMILY

Annual. Leaves alternate and pinnately lobed or divided. Flowers solitary, long-stalked; petals 3–5; sepals 3–5; stamens 3–10; pistils 2–5. Fruits are tiny nutlets.

■ **DOUGLAS' MEADOWFOAM** (*Limnanthes douglasii*): Spring; moist low places, vernal pools. There are four subspecies: **DOUGLAS' MEADOWFOAM** (ssp. *douglasii*): Leaves divided into 5–13 leaflets. **PALE MEADOWFOAM** (ssp. *rosea*): Petals white with darker, often pinkish veins; leaflets often very narrow; nutlets warty; also called Rosy Meadowfoam. **SNOWY MEADOWFOAM** (ssp. *nivea*, no photo): Petals white with darker veins; nutlets mostly smooth. **POINT REYES MEADOWFOAM** (ssp. *sulphurea*): Petals yellow. SIMILAR ■ **WHITE MEADOWFOAM** (*L. alba* ssp. *alba*): Petals white; sepals densely hairy.

Genus *Limnanthes* (9 native species). Leaves pinnately lobed or divided into leaflets. Flowers bowl- to bell-shaped; petals 5 (or rarely 4), often notched at tip; stamens 10 (or rarely 8).

Douglas' Meadowfoam
Petals yellow with white tip. HT: 4–16 in.

Pale Meadowfoam
HT: 4–16 in.

Point Reyes Meadowfoam
HT: 4–16 in.

■ **FALSE MERMAID-WEED** (*Floerkea proserpinacoides*): Spring–early summer; moist woods, floodplains. Stems weak. Leaves pinnate, with generally 3–5 segments. Petals white, shorter than sepals (top, left). Fruits minutely warty (top, right). Also called False Mermaid.

Genus *Floerkea* (1 native species). Leaves deeply pinnately lobed or divided into segments. Flowers very small; petals 3; sepals 3; stamens 6 or sometimes 3.

False Mermaid-weed

Flowers solitary on threadlike stalks. HT: mostly 4–8 in.

LINACEAE   FLAX FAMILY

Annual or perennial. Leaves alternate or occasionally opposite; simple and untoothed. Flowers in clusters; petals 5; sepals 5; stamens 5, filaments (stalks) united; 5 minute, toothlike sterile (antherless) stamens sometimes alternate with 5 fertile stamens; pistil 1. Fruits are capsules.

■ **WESTERN BLUE FLAX** (*Linum lewisii*): Spring–summer; slopes, open woods, meadows, grasslands. Flowers ¾–1½ in. across, rarely white. Also called Lewis' Flax, Prairie Flax. **SIMILAR ▣ COMMON FLAX** (*L. usitatissimum*): Widespread; native to Old World. Inner sepals minutely fringed. ■ **MEADOW FLAX** (*L. pratense*): Prairies, plains. Flowers ½–¾ in. across.

■ **STIFF YELLOW FLAX** (*L. medium*): Summer; open places. Flowers about ½ in. across. Several similar eastern and western yellow-flowered species.

Genus *Linum* (34 species, 29 native). Leaves mostly narrow, stalkless. Flowers in often open clusters; petals frequently fall early; styles 5.

Western Blue Flax

Flowers blue. Leaves narrow. HT: 6–30 in.

Stiff Yellow Flax

Flowers yellow. HT: 6–30 in.

LOASACEAE
BLAZING-STAR or STICKLEAF FAMILY

Annual, biennial, or perennial; sometimes shrubby; plants bristly-hairy. Leaves mostly alternate; simple but often deeply lobed. Flowers solitary or in clusters, often showy; petals 5; sepals 5; stamens 5 to many; pistil 1. Fruits are capsules.

■ **GIANT BLAZING-STAR** (*Mentzelia laevicaulis*): Summer–fall; slopes, road-sides, washes. Leaves ragged-toothed to deeply wavy-lobed. Flowers large; outer-most stamens sometimes flattened.

■ **SAN JOAQUIN BLAZING-STAR** (*M. pectinata*): Spring–early summer; slopes, grasslands, open woods. Leaves pinnate, with narrow lobes. Flowers yellowish orange with copper-red eye.

■ **TEN-PETAL BLAZING-STAR** (*M. decapetala*): Summer; plains, slopes, roadsides. Flowers large, cream-colored to pale yellow; 5 petals and 5 petal-like stamens. Also called Giant Evening-star.

Genus *Mentzelia* (71 native species). Leaves alternate, or sometimes in basal clusters, covered with barbed hairs that adhere to clothing. Petals 5; stamens usually many, conspicuous. Species are also called stickleaf.

Giant Blazing-star
Flowers lemon yellow, star-shaped; stamens numerous. HT: 1–3 ft.

San Joaquin Blazing-star
HT: 6–20 in.

Ten-petal Blazing-star
HT: 1–3 ft.

■ **LINDLEY'S BLAZING-STAR** (*Mentzelia lindleyi*): Spring–summer; rocky slopes, coastal scrub. Leaves deeply lobed.

■ **SAND BLAZING-STAR** (*M. involucrata*): Late winter–spring; desert slopes, washes, flats. Leaves toothed. Also called White-bract Blazing-star. See Desert Rock-nettle (p. 332), which lacks jagged-edged bracts, and Ghost-flower (p. 520).

■ **WHITE-STEM BLAZING-STAR** (*M. albicaulis*): Spring–summer; open woods, shrublands, washes. Stems whitish. Leaves often deeply lobed.

■ **UNITED BLAZING-STAR** (*M. congesta*): Spring–summer; mostly open places. Also called Ventana Blazing-star.

Lindley's Blazing-star
Flowers golden yellow; petal tips pointed. HT: 6–24 in.

Sand Blazing-star
Flowers cream-colored to pale yellow, with light orange veins; petal tips pointed. HT: 6–18 in.

White-stem Blazing-star
Flowers small, bright yellow. HT: 4–16 in.

United Blazing-star
Flowers small, yellow, partly hidden by bracts. HT: 4–16 in.

■ **DESERT ROCK-NETTLE** (*Eucnide urens*): Spring–summer; cliffs, washes, rocky slopes, plains. Plants bushy, covered with stinging hairs. Leaves coarsely toothed. Also called Desert Stingbush. Compare Sand Blazing-star (p. 331).

■ **YELLOW ROCK-NETTLE** (*E. bartonioides*): Spring–summer; ledges, slopes. Leaves shallowly lobed and jagged-toothed. Also called Warnock's Rock-nettle, Yellow Stingbush.

OTHER GENUS ■ **STINGING CEVALLIA** (*Cevallia sinuata*): Summer–fall; open areas. Leaves pinnately wavy-lobed. Petals narrow, hairy; stamens 5. Also called Stinging-serpent.

Genus *Eucnide* (3 native species). Leaves broadly egg-shaped to round; edges toothed or lobed. Petals 5; stamens many, conspicuous. **DO NOT TOUCH** Plants bristly with hairs, some barbed, some needlelike and stinging.

Desert Rock-nettle

Yellow Rock-nettle

Flowers large, bright yellow. HT: 1–3 ft.

Stinging Cevallia

Flowers large, cream-colored to pale yellow. HT: 1–3 ft.

Flowers small, yellow to orangish, in clusters. HT: to 2 ft.

■ **THURBER'S SANDPAPER-PLANT** (*Petalonyx thurberi*): Spring–summer; desert plains, hills, washes. Plants shrubby at base, spreading. Leaves ⅛–5⁄16 in. wide, becoming smaller toward plant tip. Petals ⅛–¼ in. long; stamens conspicuous.

■ **SHINY-LEAF SANDPAPER-PLANT** (*P. nitidus*): Slopes, canyons. Leaves ⅜–1 in. wide, not becoming reduced upward. Petals ¼–⅜ in. long.

Genus *Petalonyx* (4 native species). Leaves alternate. Flowers in clusters; petals 5, with narrow, stalklike bases ("claws"), often partially united; stamens 5, protruding.

Thurber's Sandpaper-plant

Shiny-leaf Sandpaper-plant

Flowers cream-colored. Leaves stalk-less, thick, grayish green. HT: 1–3 ft.

Leaves short-stalked, green. HT: 6–18 in.

LOGANIACEAE

LOGANIA or PINKROOT FAMILY

Woody plants or annual or perennial herbs. Leaves opposite and simple, often with tiny membranes (stipules) at their base. Flowers solitary or in clusters; tubular below (petals united) and 5-lobed; sepals 5; stamens 5; pistil 1. Fruits are usually capsules.

■ **INDIAN-PINK** (*Spigelia marilandica*): Spring–summer; woods, thickets. Leaves mostly stalkless. Flowers tubular, 1½–2 in. long, in 1-sided clusters at stem ends; style long-protruding. Also called Pinkroot.

NOTE *Spigelia* species are poisonous. Flowers of the remaining 5 species, all uncommon, outwardly do not resemble those of Indian-pink.

Genus *Spigelia* (6 native species). Flowers red, pink, purplish, whitish, or yellowish; lobes of calyx (united sepals) narrow. Fruits are capsules.

Indian-pink

Flowers bright red outside, yellow-green inside; lobes pointed. HT: 6–30 in.

■ **LAX HORNPOD** (*Mitreola petiolata*): Summer–fall; marshes, pond margins, ditches, moist or wet woods. Leaves ¾–3 in. long, opposite, generally short-stalked. Flowers 5-lobed. Also called Stalked Miterwort. **SIMILAR SWAMP HORNPOD** (*M. sessilifolia*): Wet places; southeastern. Leaves to 1½ in. long, stalkless. Also called Sessile Miterwort, Small-leaf Miterwort.

Genus *Mitreola* (2 native species). Flowers tiny, in clusters, 5-lobed. Fruits are tiny, 2-lobed ("2-horned") capsules.

Lax Hornpod

Flowers tiny, white, in 1-sided clusters. HT: 8–20 in.

LYTHRACEAE   LOOSESTRIFE FAMILY

Annual, biennial, or perennial herbs, or sometimes shrubs or trees. Leaves opposite, whorled, or sometimes alternate; simple and untoothed. Flowers solitary or in clusters; each flower has bowl-shaped or tubular green base (seemingly formed by united sepals); petals 4–8, usually crumpled in bud; sepals 4–8; stamens 4 to many; pistil 1. Fruits are capsules.

■ **SWAMP LOOSESTRIFE** (*Decodon verticillatus*): Summer; shallow water, mucky edges of swamps, marshes, lakes, ponds. Stems often arching. Leaves opposite or whorled. Also called Water-willow.

Genus *Decodon* (1 native species). Plants woody at base. Stems slender, often arching, rooting at tips. Leaves opposite or whorled. Flowers clustered in axils of upper leaves; petals 4 or 5; stamens 8 or 10; style elongated.

Swamp Loosestrife
Petals magenta, crinkle-margined; bases narrowed. HT: 2–8 ft.

■ **WINGED LOOSESTRIFE** (*Lythrum alatum*): Mostly summer; wet places. Flowers short-stalked in axils of upper leaves. SIMILAR ■ **CALIFORNIA LOOSESTRIFE** (*L. californicum*): Spring–fall.
■ **SALTMARSH LOOSESTRIFE** (*L. lineare*): Summer–fall; brackish marshes, shores. Leaves narrow; flowers white to pale lilac. Also called Narrow-leaf Loosestrife.
Ⓘ **HYSSOP LOOSESTRIFE** (*L. hyssopifolia*): Mainly Pacific states; from Eurasia. Flowers stalkless, light pink to lavender.

NOTE See also Ⓘ Purple Loosestrife (p. 588).

RELATED ■ **CLAMMY CUPHEA** (*Cuphea viscosissima*): Summer–fall; open areas. Plants sticky-hairy. Upper 2 petals larger. Also called Blue Waxweed.

Genus *Lythrum* (12 species, 6 native). Stems sometimes 4-angled. Petals usually 6, often wrinkled; stamens 4–12 (often 6).

Winged Loosestrife   **Clammy Cuphea**

Petals purplish, often wrinkled. Leaves alternate toward top, opposite toward bottom. HT: 1–4 ft.

Petals red-purple, often wrinkled, unequal in size. HT: 6–24 in.

MALPIGHIACEAE   MALPIGHIA or BARBADOS-CHERRY FAMILY

Trees, shrubs, woody vines, or rarely perennial herbs. Leaves simple and usually opposite. Flowers in clusters or sometimes solitary; petals 5, their bases narrow and stalklike, their blades often conspicuously crinkled, toothed, or fringed; sepals 5; stamens 5–10 (rarely fewer); pistil 1. Fruits dry or fleshy.

■ **DESERT-VINE** (*Cottsia gracilis*):
Spring–fall; desert slopes, washes, flats.
Climbing or scrambling vine. Leaves
opposite, narrow, with silky hairs. Flowers
yellow to orange-yellow, aging reddish.
Fruits 2- or 3-winged, resembling maple
fruits. Also called Slender Janusia.

Genus *Cottsia* (1 native species). With
characters of the family. A somewhat
woody vine. Fruits dry.

RELATED ■ **NARROW-LEAF
GOLDSHOWER** (*Galphimia angustifolia*):
Rocky hillsides, prairies. Shrubby. Flowers
yellow or orangish, aging reddish. Fruits
are 3-lobed capsules. Also called Narrow-
leaf Thryallis.

Desert-vine

Petal
blades
broadly
rounded.

Narrow-leaf Goldshower

Petal blades
triangular-
egg-shaped.
HT: mostly
6–24 in.

MALVACEAE   MALLOW FAMILY

Annual, biennial, or perennial herbs or shrubs; frequently with star-shaped hairs. Leaves alternate; mostly palmately veined; unlobed, shallowly to deeply lobed, or divided into segments. Flowers solitary or in clusters; petals 5; sepals 5, united below, sometimes with sepal-like bracts beneath; stamens many, their stalks united to form a conspicuous tube around pistil; style branched, with several separate stigmas. Fruits are capsules, or ringlike and breaking into disk- or wedge-shaped segments.

PARTS OF A *HIBISCUS* FLOWER

A distinctive feature of flowers of the
mallow family is the often prominent
central "tube" of stamens that
surrounds the pistil.

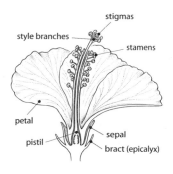

stigmas

style branches

stamens

petal

pistil

sepal

bract (epicalyx)

FRUITS OF THE MALLOW FAMILY

**HALBERD-LEAF
ROSE-MALLOW**
Many-seeded capsules,
egg-shaped to round-
egg-shaped (p. 337).

TURK'S-CAP
Pulpy (p. 338).

SEASHORE-MALLOW
Flattened, hairy, 5-angled,
5-seeded capsules (p. 339).

ROSE PAVONIA
Separating into 5 rounded,
1-seeded segments (p. 339).

PURPLE POPPY-MALLOW
A ring, breaking into 1-seeded, usually beaked segments (p. 340).

DESERT FIVE-SPOT
A ring, breaking into 1-seeded segments (p. 340).

WILD-HOLLYHOCK
A ring, breaking into 1–3-seeded, bristly-hairy segments that split open when ripe (p. 341).

WHITE CHECKER-MALLOW
A ring, tardily breaking into 1-seeded, often beaked segments (p. 342).

GLADE-MALLOW
A ring, breaking into 1-seeded segments (p. 343).

ALKALI-MALLOW
A ring, breaking into 1-seeded segments (p. 343).

SIDA
A ring, breaking into usually 2-beaked segments with 2 chambers (p. 344).

BUFFPETAL
Surrounded by a bladderlike calyx (p. 344).

HISPID FALSE MALLOW
Surrounded by a bladderlike, 5-winged calyx (p. 344).

SHRUBBY INDIAN-MALLOW
A 5-part false capsule opening at tips (p. 344).

NARROW-LEAF GLOBE-MALLOW
A ring, breaking into 2-chambered segments (p. 345).

CAROLINA BRISTLE-MALLOW
A ring, breaking into bristly-hairy, 2-beaked segments (p. 346).

■ **COMMON ROSE-MALLOW** (*Hibiscus moscheutos*): Mostly summer; marshes, wet places. Leaves hairy beneath; sometimes 3-lobed. Flowers large, white or pink, usually with red or red-purple center; petals 2½–4 in. long. Also called Swamp-mallow, Crimson-eyed Rose-mallow. Ssp. *lasiocarpos*, mostly west of the Mississippi River, has leaves hairy also on upper surface; sometimes called Hairy or Woolly Rose-mallow.

Genus *Hibiscus* (20 species, 13 native). Flowers often solitary in leaf axils; sepallike bracts beneath true sepals 6–20, usually narrow; stigmas ball-shaped or knobby. Fruits are many-seeded, usually egg- to round-egg-shaped capsules.

■ **SAVANNA ROSE-MALLOW** (*H. aculeatus*): Spring–summer; mostly pinelands, wet places. Flowers creamcolored to cream-yellow, with maroon center; fade to pinkish. Also called Pineland Hibiscus, Comfort-root.

Common Rose-mallow

Savanna Rose-mallow

Leaves mostly lance- or egg-shaped. HT: 3–7 ft.

Leaves deeply lobed, with rough surface. HT: about 3 ft.

■ **HALBERD-LEAF ROSE-MALLOW**
(*Hibiscus laevis*): Summer; marshes,
wet places. Leaves triangular, generally
hairless. Flowers large, pink or sometimes
white; petals 2–3 in. long, often overlapping. Also called Smooth Rose-mallow.
Compare similar Common Rose-mallow
(p. 336), which has leaves hairy, mostly
unlobed, and with typically rounded
base; flowers sometimes without darker
center and with petals 2½–4 in. long. See
also Seashore-mallow (p. 339).

■ **GREAT ROSE-MALLOW**
(*H. grandiflorus*): Spring–summer.
Shrubby. Leaves conspicuously hairy,
broadly triangular-egg-shaped, often
3-lobed, with heart-shaped base. Petals
4½–6 in. long. Also called Large-flower
Hibiscus, Swamp Hibiscus.

Halberd-leaf Rose-mallow

Leaves often arrowhead-shaped. HT: 3–6 ft.

Flowers have reddish or purple-red center.

Great Rose-mallow

Flowers large; petals not or scarcely overlapping. HT: 3–6 ft.

■ **PALEFACE ROSE-MALLOW** (*Hibiscus
denudatus*): Late winter–fall; slopes,
washes, flats. Shrubby. Leaves unlobed,
often egg-shaped to roundish. Flowers
sometimes nearly white. Also called Rock
Hibiscus, Naked Hibiscus.

■ **DESERT ROSE-MALLOW** (*H. coulteri*):
Spring–fall (mostly summer); slopes,
canyons. Shrubby. Upper leaves deeply
3-lobed, lower leaves egg-shaped.
Flowers sometimes whitish. Also called
Coulter's Hibiscus. Compare ⊞ Flower-
of-an-hour (p. 589).

Paleface Rose-mallow

Flowers mostly lavender-pink; dark reddish streaks at petal bases. HT: 1–3 ft.

Desert Rose-mallow

Flowers mostly pale yellow; dark streaks at petal bases. HT: 1–3 ft.

■ **SCARLET ROSE-MALLOW** (*Hibiscus coccineus*): Mostly summer; swampy places. Leaves mostly deeply 3–5-lobed. Petals 3–4 in. long.

■ **HEART-LEAF ROSE-MALLOW** (*H. martianus*): Spring–fall; gravelly hills, scrub. Leaves broadly egg-shaped, with heart-shaped base. Petals 1–1½ in. long. Also called Tulipan del Monte.

■ **POEPPIG'S ROSE-MALLOW** (*H. poeppigii*): Year-round; hammocks. Shrubby. Leaves egg-shaped. Petals ¾–1 in. long.

Scarlet Rose-mallow

Flowers bright red; petals not overlapping. HT: to 8 ft.

Heart-leaf Rose-mallow

Flowers crimson to dark rose-red; petals overlapping. HT: 1–3 ft.

Poeppig's Rose-mallow

Flowers red, pendant. HT: 1–4 ft.

■ **TURK'S-CAP** (*Malvaviscus arboreus* var. *drummondii*): Spring–fall; open woods, thickets, stream banks. Shrubby. Leaves hairy, about as wide as long, toothed and often shallowly 3-lobed, with heart-shaped base. Flowers mostly ¾–1½ in. long, never fully opening; petals twisted and partially wrapped around each other. Fruits red. Also called Drummond's Wax-mallow, Texas-mallow.

NOTE Do not confuse with Poeppig's Rose-mallow (above), which does not have twisted petals.

Genus *Malvaviscus* (2 species, 1 native). Shrubby. Flowers solitary in leaf axils or in clusters near stem ends; petals 5, contorted; sepal-like bracts beneath true sepals 7–12, narrow; stigmas ball-shaped or knobby. Fruits pulpy.

Turk's-cap

Flowers red, remain partially closed; stamen column and style long-protruding. Leaves somewhat maplelike. HT: 2–4 ft.

■ **SEASHORE-MALLOW** (*Kosteletzkya virginica*): Spring–fall; marshes, shores, wet places. Flowers sometimes lavender, rarely whitish, mostly 1½–3 in. across. Also called Virginia Saltmarsh-mallow, Virginia Fen-rose. Do not confuse with Halberd-leaf Rose-mallow (p. 337), which has leaves hairless; flowers larger with darker center. See also Common Rose-mallow (p. 336), which sometimes has flowers pink but larger, 5–8 in. across.

RELATED ■ **ROSE PAVONIA** (*Pavonia lasiopetala*, no photo): Rocky open woods. Shrubby. Leaves velvety-hairy, coarsely toothed. Flowers rose-pink, 1–1½ in. across; styles 10 (5 in Seashore-mallow). Fruits separate into 5 rounded, 1-seeded segments. Also called Wright's Pavonia, Rock-rose.

Genus *Kosteletzkya* (2 native species). Similar to *Hibiscus* (p. 336), but fruits are flattened, hairy, 5-angled, 5-seeded capsules. Flowers solitary in leaf axils or sometimes in clusters near stem ends.

Seashore-mallow

Flowers mostly pinkish. Leaves hairy, triangular-egg-shaped or sometimes arrowhead-shaped. HT: 1½–4 ft.

■ **PLAINS POPPY-MALLOW** (*Callirhoe alcaeoides*): Spring–summer; plains, prairies. Lower leaves typically triangular and scallop-toothed, upper leaves typically deeply palmately lobed. Petal tips minutely fringed or unevenly cut. Also called Light, Pale, or Pink Poppy-mallow.

■ **FRINGED POPPY-MALLOW** (*C. digitata*): Plains, prairies, glades, rocky woods. Leaves cut into segments often ¼ in. or less wide. Petal tips irregularly toothed (similar to Plains Poppy-mallow). Also called Finger Poppy-mallow, Winecup. **SIMILAR** ■ **TALL POPPY-MALLOW** (*C. leiocarpa*): Very similar.

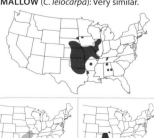

Genus *Callirhoe* (9 native species). Flowers solitary in leaf axils or sometimes in clusters near stem ends; sepal-like bracts beneath true sepals 0 or 3; stigmas threadlike. Fruits in a ring, breaking into 1-seeded, usually beaked segments.

Plains Poppy-mallow

Flowers pale pink to nearly white; no bracts beneath sepals. HT: 6–24 in.

Fringed Poppy-mallow

Flowers wine-red to purplish; no bracts beneath sepals. HT: 1–4 ft.

■ **PURPLE POPPY-MALLOW** (*Callirhoe involucrata*): Spring–fall; plains, prairies, open woods. Leaves palmately lobed. Flowers solitary; 3 sepal-like bracts immediately beneath true sepals. Also called Winecup. Variants have petals white (White Winecup) or white with broad, purplish midstripe (Variegated Winecup). **SIMILAR** ■ **WOODLAND POPPY-MALLOW** (*C. papaver*): Spring–summer; woods, glades, roadsides. Visible gap between bracts and sepals.

■ **CLUSTERED POPPY-MALLOW** (*C. triangulata*): Summer; prairies, sandy soil. Also similar to Purple Poppy-mallow, but lower leaves triangular, upper leaves often 3–5-lobed; flowers in clusters.

Purple Poppy-mallow

Clustered Poppy-mallow

Flowers usually red-rose to reddish purple, with whitish center. HT: 6–18 in.

Lower leaves triangular. HT: 1–2½ ft.

■ **DESERT FIVE-SPOT** (*Eremalche rotundifolia*): Spring; desert plains, washes, mesas. Leaves scallop-toothed with heart-shaped base, commonly tinged reddish or purplish. Petal bases whitish with conspicuous reddish spot.

Genus *Eremalche* (3 native species). Flowers solitary in leaf axils or in clusters near stem ends; sepal-like bracts beneath true sepals 3, very narrow; stigmas ball-shaped or knobby. Fruits in a ring, breaking into 1-seeded segments.

Desert Five-spot

Flowers globe-shaped, pink to rose-lilac. Leaves round or kidney-shaped. HT: 6–24 in.

■ **WHITE-MALLOW** (*Eremalche exilis*):
Spring; dry places. Stems mostly trailing
or spreading. Leaves generally palmately
3–5-lobed. Petals about ¼ in. long. Also
called Trailing-mallow.

■ **PARRY'S-MALLOW** (*E. parryi* ssp.
parryi): Hills, grasslands, open woods.
Leaves deeply 3–5-lobed. Petals ⅝–1 in.
long.

White-mallow

Flowers
small, white or
pale lavender.
HT: 4–16 in.

Parry's-mallow

Flowers pink-lavender
to purple. HT: 4–20 in.

■ **WILD-HOLLYHOCK** (*Iliamna rivularis*):
Summer–fall; mountain meadows, stream
banks, woodland borders, clearings,
disturbed places. Leaves palmately
3–7-lobed, maplelike. Flowers pink to
lavender or sometimes white, mostly
1¼–2⅜ in. across. Also called Streambank
Wild-hollyhock, Mountain-hollyhock.

Genus *Iliamna* (7 native species). Flowers
solitary in leaf axils or in clusters; sepal-
like bracts beneath true sepals 3; stigmas
ball-shaped or knobby. Fruits in a ring, breaking into 1–3-
seeded, bristly-hairy segments, splitting when ripe.

Wild-hollyhock

Flowers commonly
large, in clusters near
stem ends. HT: 2–6 ft.

■ **CHECKERBLOOM** (*Sidalcea malviflora*): Spring–summer; grassy slopes, meadows, open woods. Leaves round in outline; palmately lobed, basal leaves shallowly, stem leaves deeply. Petals have unevenly toothed, sometimes shallowly notched tip. Also called Dwarf Checker-mallow.

■ **OREGON CHECKER-MALLOW** (*S. oregana*): Moist or wet meadows, stream banks, marshes. Flowers not white-veined, in denser clusters than in Checkerbloom; sepals have short, star-shaped hairs. Also called Bog-mallow. SIMILAR ■ **ROCKY MOUNTAIN CHECKER-MALLOW** (*S. neomexicana*): Sepal hairs long. Also called New Mexico Checker-mallow.

NOTE *Sidalcea* species are often difficult to tell apart.

Genus *Sidalcea* (24 native species). Flowers in elongated clusters; stigmas threadlike. Fruits in a ring, tardily breaking into 1-seeded, often beaked segments.

Checkerbloom

Oregon Checker-mallow

Flowers bright to dark pink, often with white veins, in elongated clusters. HT: 6–24 in.

Flowers rose-pink to lavender, in crowded clusters. HT: 1½–5 ft.

■ **WHITE CHECKER-MALLOW** (*Sidalcea candida*): Late spring–summer; wet meadows, stream banks, marshes. Basal and lowermost leaves round, shallowly lobed; stem leaves deeply palmately lobed. Flowers white or cream-colored, occasionally pale pink, sometimes drying to light yellow.

■ **MAPLE-LEAF CHECKER-MALLOW** (*S. malachroides*): Woods, clearings, roadsides, canyons. All leaves shallowly lobed, maplelike. Flowers in crowded clusters, white or occasionally purple-tinged.

White Checker-mallow

Petal tips unevenly toothed or shallowly notched. HT: 1–3 ft.

Maple-leaf Checker-mallow

Petal tips typically notched. HT: 1½–5 ft.

■ **GLADE-MALLOW** (*Napaea dioica*): Summer; moist woods and borders, meadows, river and stream banks. Leaves palmately lobed, lower ones more deeply lobed than upper ones, with 7–11 jagged-toothed lobes.

OTHER GENUS ■ **VIRGINIA-MALLOW** (*Sida hermaphrodita*): Moist roadsides, river and stream banks, glades, floodplains. Outwardly similar to Glade-mallow, especially in upper part of plant, but flowers bisexual (containing both stamens and pistil); stigmas knobby.

 Genus *Napaea* (1 native species). Flowers in clusters, unisexual, males and females on separate plants; stigmas threadlike. Fruits in a ring, breaking into 1-seeded segments.

Glade-mallow

Flowers white, in clusters. Leaves palmately lobed. HT: 3–8 ft.

Male flower. | Female flower.

Virginia-mallow

HT: 3–10 ft.

■ **ALKALI-MALLOW** (*Malvella leprosa*): Spring–fall; moist, usually alkaline places. Plants densely covered with star-shaped hairs. Leaves as wide as or wider than long, with often asymmetrical base, scalloped or toothed edges. Flowers sometimes rose- or lavender-tinged. Also called Dollar-weed, Whiteweed. Do not confuse with ⬛ Common Mallow (p. 589), which has petal tips often conspicuously notched; stigmas threadlike.

■ **SCURFY-MALLOW** (*M. lepidota*): Plains, hillsides, fields, roadsides. Leaves dotted with scales, triangular; edges irregularly toothed or notched. Flowers yellowish, or sometimes whitish or pinkish.

■ **ARROW-LEAF-MALLOW** (*M. sagittifolia*): Leaves somewhat arrowhead-shaped, with small side lobes at base, untoothed.

Genus *Malvella* (3 native species). Leaves palmately veined from base. Flowers 1–3 from leaf axils; sepal-like bracts beneath true sepals 0 or 3, narrow; stigmas ball-shaped or knobby. Fruits in a ring, breaking into 1-seeded segments.

Alkali-mallow

Flowers commonly white to cream-yellow. Leaves grayish-hairy, shell-shaped. Trailing.

Scurfy-mallow

Trailing or sprawling.

Arrow-leaf-mallow

Trailing or sprawling.

■ **SIDA** (*Sida*): Spring–fall; various habitats. Flowers lack sepal-like bracts. Also called Fanpetals. Most native species are southern; the eastern Prickly Sida (*S. spinosa*, not pictured), introduced over much of its range, has pale yellow flowers. A *Sida* species not similar to these, Virginia-mallow, is covered on p. 343 with Glade-mallow, which it resembles.

RELATED (No photos.) Once classified in *Sida*; flowers yellow; calyx enlarges to form bladderlike covering around fruits (see p. 336). ■ **BUFFPETAL** (*Rhynchosida physocalyx*): Slopes, plains, washes. Sepal-like bracts absent. ■ **HISPID FALSE MALLOW** (*Malvastrum hispidum*): Prairies, rocky places. Sepal-like bracts beneath true sepals 3, narrow.

Genus *Sida* (15 species, 12 native). Sometimes shrubby. Flowers solitary or in clusters; petals usually notched, with 1 of the 2 lobes larger; stigmas ball-shaped or knobby. Fruits in a ring, breaking into 2-beaked (or sometimes 1-beaked) segments with 2 chambers (1 upper, 1 lower).

Sida

Flowers sometimes white.

Flowers sometimes salmon or purplish.

Flowers often yellow; petals generally notched, unequally lobed. Leaves typically have toothed or scalloped edges. HT: 6 in.–5 ft.

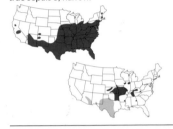

■ **TEXAS INDIAN-MALLOW** (*Abutilon fruticosum*): Late spring–fall; prairies, shrublands, open woods, slopes. Leaves heart-shaped to triangular. Several similar species with yellow to orange flowers. Do not confuse with ⊞ Velvetleaf (p. 588), which has 10–15 fruit segments (vs. 6–9).

■ **SHRUBBY INDIAN-MALLOW** (*A. incanum*): Slopes, hills, plains. Shrub. Plants velvety-hairy. Flowers orangish with maroon center; petals become somewhat swept back with age. Fruit segments 5. Also called Pelotazo.

■ **DWARF INDIAN-MALLOW** (*A. parvulum*): Slopes, hills, plains. Flowers pinkish to brick red, or rarely orange or yellowish. Fruit segments 5.

Genus *Abutilon* (18 species, 16 native). Plants often conspicuously covered with star-shaped hairs. Leaves often heart-shaped, palmately veined. Flower stigmas ball-shaped or knobby. Fruits in a ring, not or tardily breaking into beakless to prominently beaked segments, opening when ripe.

Texas Indian-mallow

Flowers yellow. Leaves gray-hairy, toothed. HT: mostly 1–3 ft.

Shrubby Indian-mallow

HT: 3–5 ft.

Dwarf Indian-mallow

HT: 8–24 in.

■ **SCARLET GLOBE-MALLOW**
(*Sphaeralcea coccinea*): Spring–fall; open
woods, shrublands, plains, hills, valleys.
Leaves deeply palmately divided into
narrow, usually toothed or lobed segments. Flowers occasionally pinkish; petal
tips often notched and lobed; usually
lacks slender bracts below sepals (rarely
1–3). Also called Common Globe-mallow.

■ **NARROW-LEAF GLOBE-MALLOW**
(*S. angustifolia*): Desert scrub, roadsides,
slopes, fields. Leaves have 2 short lobes
near base. Also called Copper Globe-
mallow.

NOTE Many *Sphaeralcea* species are
difficult to tell apart.

 Genus *Sphaeralcea* (27 native species).
Sometimes shrubby. Flowers solitary
in leaf axils or in clusters; sepal-like
bracts beneath true sepals small, slender, 0–3 (mostly 3);
stigmas ball-shaped or knobby. Fruits in a ring, breaking
into beaked or beakless, 2-chambered segments: upper
chamber smooth-sided, lower one patterned.

Scarlet Globe-mallow

Narrow-leaf Globe-mallow

Flowers
red to orange. Leaves
gray-green. HT: 4–12 in.

Flowers
reddish
orange to
pink. Leaves
gray-green.
HT: 10–30 in.

■ **DESERT GLOBE-MALLOW**
(*Sphaeralcea ambigua*): Spring–fall; desert
slopes and flats. Flowers reddish orange,
apricot, pink, rose, lavender, or whitish;
petals ⅝–1 in. long. Also called Apricot
Globe-mallow, Desert-hollyhock.

OTHERS With leaves not conspicuously
grayish or yellowish; petals 5⁄16–½ in.
long. ■ **MUNRO'S GLOBE-MALLOW**
(*S. munroana*, no photo): Spring–fall;
open places. Flowers reddish orange.
Also called White-stem Globe-mallow.

■ **COULTER'S GLOBE-MALLOW**
(*S. coulteri*): Late winter–spring; desert
slopes and flats. Flowers salmon-orange
to orange.

Desert Globe-mallow
Leaves grayish or yellowish
green, egg-shaped to nearly
round, usually shallowly
3-lobed. HT: 1–3 ft.

Coulter's
Globe-mallow

Leaves
bright green
to slightly grayish.
HT: mostly 6–12 in.

■ CAROLINA BRISTLE-MALLOW

(*Modiola caroliniana*): Mostly spring–early summer; roadsides, lawns, disturbed places. Flowers reddish, orange-red, orangish, salmon-pink, or purplish red. Introduced in western part of its range. Also called Carolina-mallow, Bristly-mallow.

Genus *Modiola* (1 native species). Flowers solitary in leaf axils; 3 sepal-like bracts beneath true sepals; stigmas ball-shaped or knobby. Fruits in a ring, breaking into bristly-hairy, 2-beaked segments.

Carolina Bristle-mallow

Flowers often orange-red to salmon-pink, with darker center. Leaves toothed, typically shallowly to deeply palmately lobed. Trailing, spreading, or reclining.

MARANTACEAE   ARROWROOT FAMILY

Perennial. Leaves basal or alternate, simple, and untoothed; side veins parallel, curving upward near edges. Flowers in bracted clusters; petals 3; sepals 3; fertile stamen 1, sterile stamens petal-like; pistil 1. Fruits capsulelike.

■ ALLIGATOR-FLAG (*Thalia geniculata*):

Summer–fall; shallow water, ponds, wet ditches, marshes, swamps, stream margins. Leaves long-stalked, the blades broadly lance-shaped and diverging from stalk at an angle. Flowers purple, in uncrowded, nodding or sometimes spreading clusters. Also called Fire-flag.

■ POWDERY THALIA (*T. dealbata*):

Flower clusters crowded, mostly erect. Plants usually strongly coated with white powder.

Genus *Thalia* (2 native species). Aquatic. Leaves arise from plant base. Flowers in pairs on zigzag stalks; showy parts consist of petals and petal-like sterile stamens.

Alligator-flag

Flower clusters mostly nodding. HT: 2–9 ft.

Powdery Thalia

Flower clusters mostly erect. HT: 2–6 ft.

MAYACACEAE

BOGMOSS or MAYACA FAMILY

Perennial, aquatic. Leaves alternate, simple, and untoothed. Flowers solitary; petals 3; sepals 3; stamens 3; pistil 1. Fruits are capsules.

■ **BOGMOSS** (*Mayaca fluviatilis*): Spring–summer; wet shores or quiet water. Plants mosslike in appearance. Flowers often have whitish center, rarely all whitish.

Genus *Mayaca* (1 native species). With characters of the family. Leaves spirally arranged.

Bogmoss

Flowers pink to rose-violet, stalked. Leaves narrow, crowded on stems. Creeping or floating. HT: to 8 in.

MELASTOMATACEAE

MELASTOME FAMILY

Annual or perennial herbs or woody plants. Leaves opposite and simple; typically with 1–4 pairs of curved, conspicuous side veins running from base to tip. Flowers generally in clusters, infrequently solitary; petals and sepals each 4 or 5; stamens 8 or 10; pistil 1. Fruits are capsules or berries.

■ **VIRGINIA MEADOW-BEAUTY** (*Rhexia virginica*): Summer–fall; open, moist or wet places. Midstem 4-angled, the angles winged and sparsely hairy. Leaves 3-veined, mostly lance-shaped. Anthers about ¼ in. long, hornlike and bent to one side. Also called Handsome-Harry.

■ **MARYLAND MEADOW-BEAUTY** (*R. mariana* var. *mariana*): Spring–fall. Stems unequally 4-sided, conspicuously hairy. Also called Pale Meadow-beauty.

NOTE Several similar species. Do not confuse with Fireweed (p. 362) or Showy Evening-primrose (p. 365), both having flowers with a 4-lobed stigma.

Genus *Rhexia* (11 native species). Leaves mostly 3-veined. Flowers in clusters, showy; petals 4; stamens 8, conspicuous; style elongated. Fruits are urn- or flask-shaped capsules.

Virginia Meadow-beauty

Flowers rose-lavender with bright yellow anthers. HT: 6 in.–3 ft.

Maryland Meadow-beauty

Flowers pale pink to white. HT: 6 in.–3 ft.

■ **FRINGED MEADOW-BEAUTY** (*Rhexia petiolata*): Spring–summer; moist or usually wet places. Stems not hairy. Leaves 3-veined; edges conspicuously hairy. Anthers about 1/16 in. long. Also called Ciliate Meadow-beauty. **SIMILAR** ■ **NUTTALL'S MEADOW-BEAUTY** (*R. nuttallii*): Leaf edges not conspicuously hairy; sepals and flower bases have gland-tipped hairs.

■ **YELLOW MEADOW-BEAUTY** (*R. lutea*): Plants bushy-branched. Stems hairy. Leaves relatively narrow. Do not confuse with evening-primroses (pp. 364–365), which have a 4-lobed stigma.

Fringed Meadow-beauty

Flowers pink to rose-lavender. HT: 6–30 in.

Yellow Meadow-beauty

Flowers yellow. HT: 6–18 in.

MENYANTHACEAE

BUCK-BEAN or BOG-BEAN FAMILY

Perennial. Leaves basal or alternate, simple or compound. Flowers mostly in clusters; saucer-, bell-, or funnel-shaped (petals united), 5-lobed; sepals 5, united; stamens 5; pistil 1. Fruits are usually capsules.

■ **BUCK-BEAN** (*Menyanthes trifoliata*): Spring–summer; wet places. Leaves arise from plant base, long-stalked, divided into 3 leaflets. Flowers mostly white, can be pinkish or purple-tinged; lobes hairy on upper surface. Also called Bog-bean.

RELATED ■ **DEER-CABBAGE** (*Nephrophyllidium crista-galli*): Wetlands. Leaves undivided; round to kidney-shaped (resembling those of marsh-marigolds, p. 463). Flower lobes have raised midveins.

Genus *Menyanthes* (1 native species). Aquatic. Leaves basal. Flowers funnel-shaped, with spreading lobes.

Buck-bean

Deer-cabbage

Flower lobes form a star shape. HT: 4–15 in.

Flower lobes wavy-edged. HT: 4–20 in.

■ **BIG FLOATING-HEART** (*Nymphoides aquatica*): Spring–summer; quiet water. Leaves floating, 2–6 in. wide, rough-surfaced beneath. Flower stalks red-dotted. Late-season plants may have banana-like clusters of thick, blunt-tipped, fleshy roots near base of flower stalk. Also called Banana-plant.

SIMILAR ■ **LITTLE FLOATING-HEART** (*N. cordata*): Summer–fall. Leaves heart-shaped, 1–2½ in. wide, smooth beneath; flower stalks rarely red-dotted; late-season fleshy roots slender, taper-tipped.

NOTE ⊡ Yellow Floating-heart (p. 590) has yellow flowers and lacks late-season fleshy roots. The leaves of water-lilies (p. 357) have sharper lobes.

Genus *Nymphoides* (5 species, 2 native). Aquatic. Leaves long-stalked, floating; blades deeply notched, with rounded lobes. Flowers in umbels, saucer- to bell-shaped, 5-lobed.

Big Floating-heart

Flowers white. Leaves nearly round, with heart-shaped base.

MONOTROPACEAE
INDIAN-PIPE FAMILY

Perennial. Plants lack green pigment (chlorophyll). Stalks often fleshy, with scaly bracts. Flowers solitary or in clusters; petals 3–6; sepals 0–5; stamens 8–10 (usually twice petal number); pistil 1. Fruits are capsules or berries. Usually included in the heath family (Ericaceae). Plants are mycotrophic, obtaining nourishment through fungi that are interconnected with the roots of oaks or conifers.

■ **SNOWPLANT** (*Sarcodes sanguinea*): Late spring–summer; mountain woods, especially coniferous. Stalks covered with tiny glands.

Genus *Sarcodes* (1 native species). Plants lack green color. Petals 5, united; stamens 10. Fruits are capsules.

Snowplant

Flowers red, urn-shaped. Stalks fleshy, bright red. HT: 6–15 in.

■ **FRINGED-PINESAP** (*Pleuricospora fimbriolata*): Summer; woods, especially coniferous. Stalks fleshy. Flowers small, cream-colored to yellowish; petal edges jagged or fringed.

RELATED With petal edges not fringed, petals hairy on inner surface.
■ **CALIFORNIA PINEFOOT** (*Pityopus californicus*): Late spring–summer; woods. Flowers cream-colored to yellowish.
■ **GNOMEPLANT** (*Hemitomes congestum*): Late spring–summer; woods. Flowers cream-colored to pink or reddish; petals united below. Also called Coneplant.

Genus *Pleuricospora* (1 native species). Plants lack green color. Petals usually 4; stamens usually 8. Fruits are berries.

Fringed-pinesap
HT: 2½–6 in.

California Pinefoot
HT: 1–4 in.

Gnomeplant
HT: 1–4 in.

■ **INDIAN-PIPE** (*Monotropa uniflora*): Summer–fall; woods. Stalks fleshy. Flowers solitary, tubular, nodding; erect in fruit.

■ **PINESAP** (*M. hypopitys*): Summer–fall. Stalks fine-hairy above. Flowers several; cream-colored, yellowish, orange, or reddish. Also called Yellow Bird's-nest.

RELATED ■ **SWEET-PINESAP** (*Monotropsis odorata*): Late winter–spring (some in fall). Plants aromatic. Flowers several, small, purplish to maroon; petals united below. Fruits are purplish berries. Also called Pygmy-pipes.

Genus *Monotropa* (2 native species). Plants lack green color. Petals mostly 4 or 5; stamens 8–10. Fruits are capsules.

Indian-pipe
Flowers and stalks white or pinkish, aging blackish.
HT: 3–10 in.

Pinesap
HT: 2–12 in.

Sweet-pinesap
HT: 1½–5 in.

■ **CANDYSTICK** (*Allotropa virgata*):
Summer; woods, often among conifers.
Stalks vertically striped. Also called
Sugarstick.

Genus *Allotropa* (1 native species). Plants
lack green color. Flowers small; petals 5;
stamens 10. Fruits are capsules.

Candystick

Flowers whitish, bowl-
shaped. Stalks striped red
and white. HT: 6–18 in.

■ **PINEDROPS** (*Pterospora andromedea*):
Summer; various habitats, but most
common in western coniferous woods.
Stalks yellowish, reddish, or brownish.
Also called Giant-bird's-nest.

Genus *Pterospora* (1 native species).
Plants lack green color. Stalks densely
covered with sticky hairs. Flowers small,
dangling on stalks from upper part of plant; petals 5,
united; stamens 10. Fruits are capsules.

Pinedrops

Flowers cream-
colored or yellowish,
urn-shaped. Stalks
wandlike. HT: 1–4 ft.

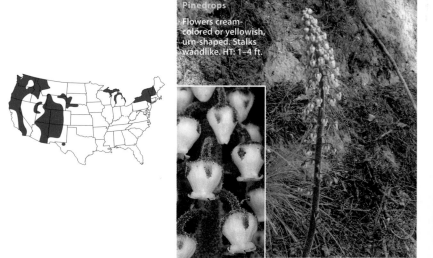

NELUMBONACEAE — LOTUS FAMILY

Perennial; aquatic. Leaves simple, large, and long-stalked. Flowers solitary; tepals (petals and petal-like sepals) numerous, the outer ones more sepal-like, grading into larger, petal-like ones; stamens numerous; pistils many, individually sunken in a broad, spongy, flat-topped receptacle. Fruits are nutlets, loosely embedded in the hardened receptacle.

■ **AMERICAN LOTUS** (*Nelumbo lutea*): Mostly summer; quiet water. Leaves 1–2½ ft. wide. Flowers large, 6–10 in. across. Also called Water-chinquapin, Yellow Lotus.

Genus *Nelumbo* (2 species, 1 native). With characters of the family. Leaves floating or raised above the water.

American Lotus

Flowers light yellow, on long stalks. Leafstalk attached near center of circular blade.

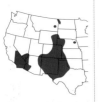

NYCTAGINACEAE — FOUR-O'CLOCK FAMILY

Annual or perennial; sometimes shrubby. Leaves mostly opposite; simple and usually untoothed. Flowers typically in clusters, frequently above sepal-like bracts; true petals absent; sepals (showy part of flower) united, mostly bell-, funnel-, or trumpet-shaped; stamens 1 to many; pistil 1. Fruits 1-seeded.

■ **SNOWBALL SAND-VERBENA** (*Abronia fragrans*): Spring–fall; sandy soil. Leaves opposite. Flowers usually white. Also called Sweet Sand-verbena. **SIMILAR** ■ **FRAGRANT WHITE SAND-VERBENA** (*A. elliptica*): Sandy or gravelly soil. Snowball Sand-verbena sometimes shares this species' common name.

■ **DESERT SAND-VERBENA** (*A. villosa*): Late winter–summer; sandy soil. Plants densely sticky-hairy. Flowers pink to magenta, with whitish eye. Several other species have similarly colored flowers.

Genus *Abronia* (18 native species). Stems often prostrate, commonly sticky-hairy. Flowers trumpet-shaped, the lobes frequently notched; in long-stalked, rounded or headlike clusters above sepal-like bracts; stamens 5–9.

Snowball Sand-verbena

Flowers in roundish clusters. Stems prostrate to erect.

Desert Sand-verbena

Sprawling, often mat-forming.

■ **YELLOW SAND-VERBENA**
(*Abronia latifolia*): Spring–fall; beaches, dunes. Leaves opposite, thick and succulent. Plants often form large patches.

OTHERS Also with prostrate stems and found on beaches. ■ **RED SAND-VERBENA** (*A. maritima*): Flowers dark red to red-purple. ■ **PINK SAND-VERBENA** (*A. umbellata*): Flowers pink to magenta, with whitish or yellowish eye.

Yellow Sand-verbena

Flowers yellow. Stems prostrate.

Red Sand-verbena

Pink Sand-verbena

■ **TRAILING-WINDMILLS** (*Allionia incarnata*): Early spring–late fall; dry open places. Leaves in pairs of 1 small, 1 larger. Flowers in clusters of 3 that resemble a single flower. Also called Trailing-four-o'clock. **SIMILAR** ■ **ANNUAL-WINDMILLS** (*A. choisyi*): Fruits edged with 4–8 slender, often gland-tipped teeth (teeth 0–4 and triangular in Trailing-windmills).

OTHER GENUS Also trailing, with flowers similarly colored and leaves in each pair unequal. ■ **BURROWING-FOUR-O'CLOCK** (*Okenia hypogaea*): Beaches. Flowers solitary, funnel-shaped, with 5 notched lobes; stamens 5–18. Fruits buried, maturing under the sand. Also called Beach-peanut.

Genus *Allionia* (2 native species). Plants usually sticky-hairy. Leaves opposite, those in a pair usually unequal in size. Flowers fan-shaped, with 3 notched lobes; in clusters of 3 that together resemble a single flower; sepal-like bracts beneath; stamens 12 per cluster, conspicuous.

Trailing-windmills

Flowers pink to rose-purple. Trailing or sprawling.

Burrowing-four-o'clock

Flowers rose-purple. Trailing.

■ **WILD FOUR-O'CLOCK** (*Mirabilis nyctaginea*): Late spring–early fall; fields, roadsides, disturbed places. Flowers in clusters of 3; green, 5-lobed "cup" (involucre) resembles sepals. Also called Heart-leaf Four-o'clock.

OTHERS With leaves very narrow, stalk-less. ■ **NARROW-LEAF FOUR-O'CLOCK** (*M. linearis*): Late spring–summer; open woods, prairies, plains, hillsides. Flowers deep to light pink or white, less than ½ in. long. Also called Ribbon Four-o'clock.

■ **SCARLET FOUR-O'CLOCK** (*M. coccinea*): Late spring–fall; open woods, grassy or rocky slopes. Flowers red, ½–¾ in. long; stamens long-protruding.

NOTE *Mirabilis* species are also called umbrella-wort.

Genus *Mirabilis* (21 species, 20 native). Flowers mostly bell- or funnel-shaped, the lobes sometimes notched; in clusters of 1–16 borne within a green cup (involucre) formed from united, sepal-like bracts; stamens 3–5, protruding.

Wild Four-o'clock

Flowers pink to red-purple. Leaves egg-shaped to triangular, stalked. HT: 1–4 ft.

Narrow-leaf Four-o'clock
HT: 6 in.–3 ft.

Scarlet Four-o'clock
HT: 6 in.–3 ft.

■ **COLORADO FOUR-O'CLOCK** (*Mirabilis multiflora*): Late spring–early fall; open woods, shrublands, rocky places, desert scrub. Leaves 1½–3 in. wide. Flowers in a cluster of 6, with conspicuous, green, 5-lobed, sepal-like "cup" (involucre). Also called Desert or Giant Four-o'clock.

■ **BIGELOW'S DESERT FOUR-O'CLOCK** (*M. laevis* var. *villosa*): Mostly spring–fall; canyons, rocky places, desert washes. Leaves ¾–1½ in. wide. Flowers mostly solitary, with small green "cup" below. Also called Desert Wishbone-bush.

Colorado Four-o'clock
Flowers large, magenta. Bushy. HT: 1–2½ ft.

Bigelow's Desert Four-o'clock
Flowers usually white to pink-tinged. Bushy. HT: 1–3 ft.

■ **SWEET FOUR-O'CLOCK** (*Mirabilis longiflora*): Summer–early fall; slopes, rocky canyons. Leaf blades 2–5½ in. long, with heart-shaped base. Flowers 3–6 in. long, with slender tube, 5 flaring lobes; stamens 5, purplish; style long-protruding. Also called Maravilla.

OTHER GENERA ■ **ANGEL-TRUMPETS** (*Acleisanthes longiflora*): Mostly spring–fall; rocky or sandy soil. Flowers resemble Sweet Four-o'clock. Leaves opposite, triangular-lance-shaped, short-stalked; blades to 1¾ in. long.

■ **SOUTHWESTERN RINGSTEM** (*Anulocaulis leiosolenus*): Late spring–early fall; rocky soil. Leaves basal, nearly round. Flowers 1–1½ in. long; stamens 3, purplish; style long-protruding.

Sweet Four-o'clock

Flowers whitish with red-purple eye; hairy outside. Leaves opposite, long-stalked. HT: 2–4 ft.

Angel-trumpets

Trailing or sprawling.

Southwestern Ringstem

Flowers whitish to pinkish. HT: 1½–3 ft.

■ **SCARLET MUSK-FLOWER** (*Nyctaginia capitata*): Late spring–early fall; roadsides, fields, shrublands. Leaves opposite, triangular, with smooth or wavy edges. Also called Devil's-bouquet.

OTHER GENERA Also with protruding stamens and style. ■ **RED CYPHOMERIS** (*Cyphomeris gypsophiloides*): Summer–fall; plains, rocky slopes, open woods, desert scrub. Sticky bands on stem. Flowers small, in elongated clusters; stamens 5.

■ **CLIMBING-WARTCLUB** (*Commicarpus scandens*): Late spring–fall; thickets, canyons, hillsides, roadsides. Plants commonly reclining or scrambling. Flowers tiny, in umbels (stalks arising from a common point); stamens 2.

Genus *Nyctaginia* (1 native species). Plants often sticky-hairy, ill-scented. Leaves opposite, fleshy. Flowers narrowly funnel-shaped, with slender tube, 5 flaring lobes; several in a cluster above 6–20 sepal-like bracts; stamens 5–8.

Scarlet Musk-flower

Flowers red or red-orange, sometimes marked with yellow; stamens and style long-protruding. HT: 6–30 in.

Red Cyphomeris

Flowers dark pink to purple-red. HT: mostly 16–32 in.

Climbing-wartclub

Flowers greenish white or greenish yellow.

■ **SCARLET SPIDERLING** (*Boerhavia coccinea*): Spring–winter; open, often disturbed places. Also called Wineflower. **SIMILAR** ■ **RED SPIDERLING** (*B. diffusa*): Leaves mostly on lower half of plant.

■ **COULTER'S SPIDERLING** (*B. coulteri*): Late spring–early fall; roadsides, plains, deserts. Bracts beneath flowers short, deciduous (falling off). **SIMILAR LARGE-BRACT SPIDERLING** (*B. wrightii*): Summer; southwestern. Bracts beneath flowers persistent, more than half as long as fruit.

Genus *Boerhavia* (15 native species). Stems repeatedly forked, sometimes with sticky bands. Leaves opposite, those in a pair usually unequal in size. Flowers in clusters, bell- to widely funnel-shaped, mostly 5-lobed; sepal-like bracts 1–3; stamens 2–8.

Scarlet Spiderling

Coulter's Spiderling

Flowers tiny, pink to whitish, in elongated clusters. HT: 8–32 in.

Flowers tiny, purple-red, in headlike clusters. Trailing or sprawling.

NYMPHAEACEAE   WATER-LILY FAMILY

Perennial; aquatic. Leaves simple; below, at, or above water surface. Flowers solitary; petals mostly numerous; sepals commonly 3–9; stamens many; pistil usually 1. Fruits berrylike, leathery. (*Brasenia* and *Cabomba*, often placed in a separate family, Cabombaceae, have 3 petals, more than 1 pistil.)

■ **YELLOW POND-LILY** (*Nuphar advena*): Spring–fall; quiet water. Leaf blades 5–16 in. long; leafstalks round. Flowers to 1½ in. across; sepals mostly 6, with green patch at base inside. **SIMILAR** Spring–summer-blooming; leaf blades mostly floating.
■ **INDIAN POND-LILY** (*N. polysepala*): Flowers 2–4 in. across; sepals mostly 9.
■ **BULL-HEAD POND-LILY** (*N. variegata*): Leafstalks flattened above, usually winged; flowers 1–2 in. across; sepals usually 6, each with reddish patch.

Genus *Nuphar* (8 native species). Aquatic. Leaf veins mostly arise from along midrib ("pinnate"). Sepals mostly 5–9, showy, petal-like, yellow or sometimes tinged greenish or reddish (true petals resemble the stamens).

Yellow Pond-lily

Flowers globe-shaped, yellow. Leaf blades usually held above the water, broadly egg- to heart-shaped, notched at base.

■ **AMERICAN WHITE WATER-LILY**
(*Nymphaea odorata*): Spring–fall; quiet
water. Leaves mostly 4–12 in. wide.
Flowers commonly floating, to 8 in.
across. Also called Fragrant Water-lily.

■ **YELLOW WATER-LILY** (*N. mexicana*):
Flowers floating or held above water. Also
called Banana Water-lily.

RELATED ■ **WATERSHIELD** (*Brasenia
schreberi*): Summer. Leafstalk attached
near center of gelatinous underside of
blade. Flowers small; petals 3; sepals 3.

Genus *Nymphaea* (8 species, 6 native).
Aquatic. Leaves usually floating;
most veins arise from base of midrib
("palmate"; compare *Nuphar*, p. 356). Petals numerous,
showy; sepals 4, mostly greenish; stamens numerous.

American White Water-lily

Flowers white (or rarely pink). Leaves nearly circular, notched at base.

Yellow Water-lily

Flowers yellow.

Watershield

Flowers purplish to maroon.

■ **CAROLINA FANWORT** (*Cabomba
caroliniana*): Summer; quiet water.
Floating leaves few, mostly ½–1 in. long,
narrowly elliptic to elongated-diamond-
shaped; leafstalk attached near center of
underside of blade. Flowers ⁵⁄₁₆–⁵⁄₈ in.
across, sometimes tinged pinkish or
purplish.

NOTE Do not confuse with White Water
Buttercup (p. 466), which has underwater
leaves alternate; petals 5.

Genus *Cabomba* (2 species, 1 native).
Aquatic. Floating leaves (present at flowering time) alternate, undivided, narrow;
underwater leaves (always present) opposite (or rarely
whorled), finely divided. Petals 3; sepals 3, petal-like;
stamens 3–6 (often 6); pistils commonly 2–4.

Carolina Fanwort

Flowers white with yellowish center. Underwater leaves opposite, fan-shaped, finely divided.

OLEACEAE   OLIVE FAMILY

Trees, shrubs, or rarely perennial herbs. Leaves usually opposite, rarely alternate; simple or compound. Flowers in clusters or sometimes solitary; often 4-lobed (petals united), or petals absent; sepals often 4, united; stamens 2; pistil 1. Fruits various.

■ **ROUGH MENODORA** (*Menodora scabra*): Spring–summer; mesas, rocky or grassy slopes, open woods. Leaves undivided. Buds reddish orange. Also called Twinberry. **SIMILAR** ■ **LOW MENODORA** (*M. heterophylla*): Rocky or sandy ground. Some leaves deeply cut into 3–7 lobes or segments; buds bright red. Also called Redbud Menodora.

■ **SHOWY MENODORA** (*M. longiflora*): Rocky soil. Flowers have slender tube.

Genus *Menodora* (5 native species). Flowers bowl-, funnel-, or trumpet-shaped, 5- or sometimes 6-lobed; calyx (united sepals) has 5–15 narrow lobes. Fruits are capsules with paired, round lobes.

Rough Menodora

Flowers yellow, shallowly funnel-shaped; stamens protruding. HT: 6–24 in.

Showy Menodora

Flowers trumpet-shaped; stamens hidden. HT: 1–2 ft.

ONAGRACEAE   EVENING-PRIMROSE FAMILY

Mostly annual, biennial, or perennial herbs. Leaves alternate, opposite, whorled, or basal; simple but sometimes deeply lobed. Flowers solitary or in clusters; petals usually 4; sepals usually 4 (2–7); stamens mostly 4 or 8 (2–10); pistil 1. Fruits are capsules or occasionally seedlike or nutlike.

FLOWERS OF THE ONAGRACEAE

In species of the family Onagraceae, the "stalk" beneath each flower consists of the tubular or cylindrical ovary, usually a floral tube (hypanthium) that is often prolonged beyond the top of the ovary, and sometimes a true flower stalk extending below the ovary. The floral tube, when present, bears the petals, sepals, and stamens at or near its rim. Flowers of the genus *Oenothera* (illustrated here) have a long floral tube and lack a true stalk. In *Oenothera* and some other genera, the stigma is 4-lobed. Several genera have unlobed stigmas, these often knobby or ball- to button-shaped.

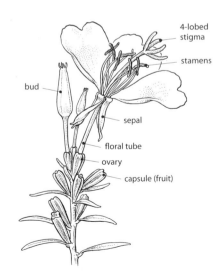

4-lobed stigma

stamens

bud

sepal

floral tube

ovary

capsule (fruit)

- **DEERHORN CLARKIA** (*Clarkia pulchella*): Late spring–early summer; grassy hillsides, open places. Petal bases narrow, stalklike, with pair of teeth near base; petal tips 3-lobed, middle lobe largest; stamens 4. Also called Pink-fairies, Beautiful or Elkhorn Clarkia, Ragged-robin.

- **LOVELY CLARKIA** (*C. concinna*): Open woods, grassy places, road banks. Petal bases lack teeth; tips have 3 nearly equal lobes; stamens 4. Also called Red-ribbons.

- **GUNSIGHT CLARKIA** (*C. xantiana*): Slopes. Petals sometimes spotted, tips have 2 lobes with tiny tooth in between; stamens 8.

NOTE Clarkias are also called fairyfans.

Genus *Clarkia* (41 native species). Leaves mostly alternate. Flowers solitary or in leafy-bracted clusters; petals 4, their tips often minutely toothed to deeply lobed; sepals 4, sometimes joined at their tips and turned to one side; stamens usually 8; stigma 4-lobed. Fruits are capsules.

Deerhorn Clarkia

Flowers lavender to rose-purple. Leaves narrow. HT: 6–18 in.

Lovely Clarkia

Flowers pink, often streaked. HT: 6–18 in.

Gunsight Clarkia

Flowers lavender to red-purple. HT: 6–30 in.

- **FAREWELL-TO-SPRING** (*Clarkia amoena*): Summer; slopes, coastal bluffs. Flowers rarely whitish. Also called Herald-of-summer.

- **SPECKLED CLARKIA** (*C. cylindrica*): Spring–summer; slopes, flats. Petal bases often dark red-purple.

- **WINECUP CLARKIA** (*C. purpurea* ssp. *quadrivulnera*): Spring–summer; grassy places, shrublands. Flowers sometimes entirely deep red-purple. Also called Purple Clarkia, Fourspot.

- **RUBY CHALICE CLARKIA** (*C. rubicunda*): Spring–summer; open woods, shrublands.

Farewell-to-spring

Flowers usually pink or lavender, with reddish central blotches. HT: 1–3 ft.

Speckled Clarkia

Flowers pink-lavender, speckled dark red-purple. HT: 6–18 in.

Winecup Clarkia

Flowers often lavender with purple spot toward petal tips. HT: 6–24 in.

Ruby Chalice Clarkia

Flowers rose-pink to lavender, with bright red center. HT: 1–3 ft.

■ **SLENDER CLARKIA** (*Clarkia gracilis*): Spring–summer; open places. Petals sometimes dark-spotted toward base.

■ **WILLOW-HERB CLARKIA** (*C. epilobioides*): Spring; shrublands, woods. Flowers age pinkish.

■ **ELEGANT CLARKIA** (*C. unguiculata*): Mostly spring; slopes, woods. Flowers sometimes salmon or dark red-purple; petal bases very narrow, stalklike.

■ **TONGUE CLARKIA** (*C. rhomboidea*): Spring–summer; slopes, open woods, shrublands. Flowers often spotted; petals have 2 tiny, blunt teeth near base. Also called Diamond Clarkia.

Slender Clarkia

Willow-herb Clarkia

Flowers pink or lavender. HT: 1–3 ft.

Flowers whitish. HT: 6–24 in.

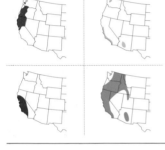

Elegant Clarkia

Flowers commonly rose-lavender. HT: 1–3 ft.

Tongue Clarkia

Flowers pink-lavender to rose. HT: 1–3 ft.

■ **ROCK-FRINGE** (*Epilobium obcordatum*): Summer; rocky places in mountains. Plants commonly mat-forming. Leaves ¼–¾ in. long. Flowers 1–2 in. across; stigma 4-lobed. Also called Heart or Rose Willow-herb.

■ **AMERICAN WILLOW-HERB** (*E. ciliatum*): Moist or wet places. Variable. Leaves 1½–4½ in. long, lance- to egg-shaped, alternate above, opposite below. Flowers ¼–1 in. across, white, pink, or rose-purple; stigma not lobed. Also called Northern or Fringed Willow-herb.

■ **WHITE-FLOWER WILLOW-HERB** (*E. lactiflorum*, no photo): Plants 6–20 in. tall. Leaves ¾–2 in. long. Flowers mostly white (occasionally pink-tinged), ¼–½ in. across.

Genus *Epilobium* (39 species, 36 native). Flowers in clusters; petals 4, tips notched; sepals 4; stamens 8, in 2 unequal-length sets; stigma knobby, club-shaped, or 4-lobed. Fruits are slender capsules; seeds usually have a tuft of hairs at tip. Species are also called willow-weed.

Rock-fringe

American Willow-herb

Flowers showy, rose or rose-purple; petals notched. Leaves opposite, elliptic to round-egg-shaped. HT: 2–6 in.

HT: 1–4 ft.

■ **TALL ANNUAL WILLOW-HERB**
(*Epilobium brachycarpum*): Summer–fall;
open woods, hills, roadsides. Lower stems
often peeling. Leaves alternate, narrow.
Flowers ¼–1 in. across, sometimes white;
petals notched. Also called Panicled
Willow-herb, Parched-fireweed.

■ **DENSE-FLOWER WILLOW-HERB**
(*E. densiflorum*): Summer; moist or wet
places. Leaves mostly alternate. Flowers
¼–⅝ in. across, sometimes white; petals
notched. Seeds lack tuft of hairs. Also
called Dense Spike-primrose.

SIMILAR ■ **SMOOTH WILLOW-HERB**
(*E. campestre*): Flowers pink, ¹⁄₁₆–³⁄₁₆ in.
across. Also called Pygmy Willow-herb,
Smooth Spike primrose.

Tall Annual Willow-herb

Dense-flower Willow-herb

Flowers mostly rose-
purple to pink, in narrow,
leafy-bracted spikes.
HT: 1–3 ft.

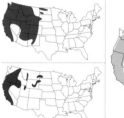
Flowers
rose-pink, in
open, branched
clusters. HT: 1–4 ft.

■ **HUMMINGBIRD-TRUMPET** (*Epilobium
canum*): Summer–late fall; rocky slopes,
canyons, flats. Herbaceous or shrubby,
commonly sprawling. Leaves grayish
green to green, mostly opposite. Flowers
¾–1¼ in. across; stamens and style long-
protruding; stigma 4-lobed. Also called
California-fuchsia, Zauschneria.

■ **YELLOW WILLOW-HERB** (*E. luteum*):
Summer; mountain meadows and
stream banks. Leaves opposite, lance-
to egg-shaped. Flowers 1–1½ in. across;
style protruding; stigma 4-lobed. Do not
confuse with yellow-flowered evening-
primroses (p. 364), which have sepals
spreading or usually back-curved (erect
in Yellow Willow-herb).

Hummingbird-trumpet

Flowers orange-red
to scarlet, tubular,
with 4 notched
lobes. HT: 6–30 in.

Yellow Willow-herb

Flowers cream-yellow;
petals partly over-
lapping, notched.
HT: 6–24 in.

■ **FIREWEED** (*Chamerion angustifolium*): Summer; open places, slopes, disturbed areas (such as after fire). Leaves 2½–7 in. long, 5–10 times as long as wide, narrowly lance-shaped. Flowers mostly 15 or more, each ¾–1¼ in. across, rarely white. Also called Great Willow-herb, Narrow-leaf Fireweed. Do not confuse with meadow-beauties (p. 347).

■ **BROAD-LEAF WILLOW-HERB** (*C. latifolium*): Slopes, gravelly and rocky places, stream banks. Leaves 1–3 in. long, 2½–5 times as long as wide, elliptic to broadly lance-shaped. Flowers mostly 12 or fewer, each 1–2¼ in. across, rarely white. Also called River-beauty, Broad-leaf Fireweed.

Genus *Chamerion* (2 native species). Similar to *Epilobium* (p. 360), but main leaves always alternate; flowers slightly asymmetrical; petals not notched; sepals very narrow, commonly somewhat similar to petals in color; stamens in a single, equal-length set; stigma always 4-lobed.

Fireweed
Flowers mostly pink-purple. Style usually longer than stamens. HT: 2–8 ft.

Broad-leaf Willow-herb
Flowers mostly pink to rose-purple. Style shorter than stamens. HT: 6–24 in.

■ **LARGE-FLOWER GAURA** (*Gaura longiflora*): Summer–fall; prairies, hill-sides, roadsides, open woods. Hairs on stems pressed close, sometimes curled. Flowers ½–1 in. across; petals all on one side; style and stamens conspicuous; stigma 4-lobed. Also called Long-flower Beeblossom, Tall Gaura. **SIMILAR**
■ **BIENNIAL GAURA** (*G. biennis*): Stem hairs mostly spreading, straight. Also called Biennial Beeblossom.

■ **SOUTHERN GAURA** (*G. angustifolia*): Late winter–fall; open woods, sandy places. Leaves narrow, toothed. Flowers ½ in. or less across; petals sometimes only 3. Also called Southern Beeblossom.

NOTE See similar False Gaura (p. 363).

Genus *Gaura* (20 native species). Leaves alternate, sometimes also basal. Flowers in clusters; petals 4, commonly all on one side of flower, their bases narrowed, stalklike; sepals 4, narrow, bent backward; stamens 8; stigma 4-lobed. Fruits nutlike.

Large-flower Gaura
Flowers white, becoming pinkish. Leaves mostly narrowly elliptic. HT: 2–7 ft.

Southern Gaura

HT: 3–6 ft.

■ **SCARLET GAURA** (*Gaura coccinea*):
Spring–fall; plains, slopes, open woods.
Leaves ⅜–1½ in. long. Flowers to ½ in.
across; petals on one side of flower;
style and stamens conspicuous; stigma
4-lobed. Also called Scarlet Beeblossom,
Wild-honeysuckle, Butterfly-weed. Do not
confuse with *Chamerion* species (p. 362),
which have flowers larger, with sepals not
bent back; capsules long.

■ **SMALL-FLOWER GAURA**
(*G. parviflora*): Plains, prairies, hillsides,
open woods, roadsides. Stems sticky-
hairy. Leaves 1½–4 in. long, hairy; basal
leaves often wither early. Flowers very
small, about ³⁄₁₆ in. across, mostly pale
pink to rose. Also called Lizard-tail,
Velvetweed, Midget Beeblossom.

Scarlet Gaura

Small-flower Gaura

Flowers whitish, becoming pink to dark red, in elongated clusters. HT: 6–24 in.

Flowers crowded in slender, often nodding clusters. HT: 1–6 ft.

■ **FALSE GAURA** (*Stenosiphon linifolius*):
Spring–fall; rocky hillsides, cliffs, prairies,
roadsides. Basal leaves wither early; stem
leaves become gradually smaller toward
top of stem. Petals rounded to diamond-
shaped; sepals whitish, bent backward;
style and stamens conspicuous; stigma
4-lobed. Plants often drop leaves in
times of drought. Also called Flax-leaf
Stenosiphon.

NOTE False Gaura differs from white-
flowered species of *Gaura* (p. 362) by its
threadlike floral tube (see illustration,
p. 358), which is narrower than the
ovary just beneath it (in *Gaura*, tube is
cylindrical, about as wide as the ovary),
and by its evenly distributed petals (all on
one side in *Gaura*).

Genus *Stenosiphon* (1 native species).
Leaves alternate and basal, becoming
reduced toward top of stem. Flowers in
elongated clusters; petals 4, with narrow, stalklike base;
sepals 4; stamens 8; stigma 4-lobed. Fruits seedlike.

False Gaura

Flowers white, crowded in wandlike clusters. Stem leaves many, linear to narrowly lance-shaped. HT: 2–8 ft.

■ **COMMON EVENING-PRIMROSE** (*Oenothera biennis*): Summer–fall; fields, roadsides, disturbed places. Flowers yellow, mostly ¾–1½ in. across (up to 2 in.), open in the evening; petals rounded to shallowly notched; stamens nearly equal in length. Fruits cylindrical. Several similar species.

■ **COMMON SUNDROPS** (*O. fruticosa*): Summer; open woods, fields, disturbed places. Flowers 1–2 in. across, open on sunny days; petals rounded or often shallowly notched; stamens unequal in length. Fruits club-shaped, 4-winged above, narrowed toward base.

Genus *Oenothera* (62 species, 59 native). Leaves alternate and often basal. Flowers (see illustration, p. 358) in upper leaf axils or distinct clusters; petals 4, their tips notched or toothed; sepals 4, first joined and turned to one side, later bent backward; stamens 8; stigma 4-lobed. Fruits are capsules.

Common Evening-primrose

Common Sundrops

Stigma 4-lobed. Stem leaves lance-shaped. HT: 1–5 ft.

Flowers yellow with darker veins; stigma 4-lobed. HT: 1–3 ft.

■ **CUT-LEAF EVENING-PRIMROSE** (*Oenothera laciniata*): Spring–fall; open places. Leaves basal and alternate. Flowers ½–1½ in. across, yellow or cream-yellow, aging reddish.

■ **THREAD-LEAF SUNDROPS** (*O. linifolia*): Spring–summer; open places. Flowers less than ½ in. across, yellow.

■ **HOOKER'S EVENING-PRIMROSE** (*O. elata*): Summer–fall; open places. Flowers 2–4 in. across, yellow, often aging pinkish purple. Also called Tall Evening-primrose.

■ **YELLOW DESERT EVENING-PRIMROSE** (*O. primiveris*): Spring; washes, sandy hills, desert plains. Flowers 1–3 in. across, yellow, aging purplish or orangish red. Also called Bottle Evening-primrose.

Cut-leaf Evening-primrose

Stigma 4-lobed. Stem leaves toothed to deeply pinnately lobed. HT: 6–30 in.

Thread-leaf Sundrops

Stigma 4-lobed. Stem leaves thread-like. HT: 6–18 in.

Hooker's Evening-primrose

Stigma 4-lobed. HT: 1–5 ft.

Yellow Desert Evening-primrose

Stigma 4-lobed. Leaves in a basal cluster. HT: 4 in. or less.

■ **MISSOURI EVENING-PRIMROSE**
(*Oenothera macrocarpa*): Spring–summer;
rocky prairies, glades, hillsides, road cuts.
Leaves crowded, narrowly lance-shaped,
green to silvery. Flowers large, 2–5 in.
across; petals rounded to shallowly
toothed or notched, aging orangish or
reddish. Also called Ozark Sundrops.

■ **SHOWY EVENING-PRIMROSE**
(*O. speciosa*): Prairies, plains, open woods,
roadsides, disturbed places. Leaves
elliptic-lance-shaped, often few-lobed
near base, untoothed or toothed. Flowers
large, 1½–3½ in. across; petals rounded or
shallowly notched. Also called Pink-ladies,
White or Pink Evening-primrose.

Missouri Evening-primrose

Flowers yellow; stigma
4-lobed. Leaves untoothed
or inconspicuously
toothed. HT: 6–18 in.

Showy Evening-primrose

Flowers commonly
pale pink to rose-
pink, with yellowish
eye; often opening
white; stigma
4-lobed.
HT: 6–18 in.

■ **DUNE EVENING-PRIMROSE**
(*Oenothera deltoides*): Late winter–spring;
sandy places. Leaves basal and alternate.
Flower buds nodding. Flowers large,
1½–3½ in. across; petals rounded or
notched, aging pink or lavender. Mature
stems peeling, on older plants typically
curving to form a "birdcage" or "basket"
(see inset). Also called Basket Evening-
primrose, Devil's-lantern.

■ **TUFTED EVENING-PRIMROSE**
(*O. caespitosa*): Spring–summer; slopes,
canyons, clearings, roadsides. Plants
short-stemmed or stemless. Leaves in a
basal cluster. Flower buds mostly erect.
Flowers large, 1½–4 in. across; petals
notched, aging pink to rose-lavender.
Also called Stemless or Desert Evening-
primrose, Sand-lily.

Dune Evening-primrose

Flowers white
with yellowish
eye; stigma
4-lobed.
HT: to 18 in.

Tufted Evening-primrose

Flowers white;
stigma 4-lobed.
HT: to 12 in.

■ LAVENDER-LEAF SUNDROPS
(*Calylophus lavandulifolius*): Spring–summer; prairies, plains, hills, roadsides. Leaves untoothed, gray-hairy. Flowers 1–2 in. across; petals rounded to ruffle-edged. Also called Lavender-leaf Evening-primrose. SIMILAR With leaves not grayish, often toothed; sepals distinctly keeled (midrib raised); stamens of 2 lengths.

■ SERRATE-LEAF SUNDROPS
(*C. serrulatus*): Stigma does not protrude beyond stamen tips. Also called Yellow Sundrops, Plains Yellow Evening-primrose. ■ BERLANDIER'S SUNDROPS (*C. berlandieri*): Stigma protrudes beyond stamen tips (stigma and sometimes center of flower black in one variety). Also called Berlandier's Evening-primrose, Square-bud Day-primrose.

Genus *Calylophus* (6 native species). Similar to *Oenothera* (p. 364), but leaves alternate; stigma disk- or button-shaped (instead of 4-lobed).

Lavender-leaf Sundrops

Flowers yellow, aging orangish or purplish; stigma disk-shaped. Leaves alternate, crowded, narrow. HT: 3–12 in.

■ CALIFORNIA SUNCUP (*Camissonia californica*): Late winter–spring; dry open places. Stem leaves slender, jagged-toothed to sharply lobed; basal leaves pinnately lobed, generally withering early. Flowers ½–1 in. across, aging pinkish or salmon, each on a "stalk" that is actually the narrow, elongated ovary. Fruits very narrow, downward-pointing. Also called Mustard-evening-primrose and superficially resembles some members of the mustard family (Brassicaceae, p. 164).

Genus *Camissonia* (57 native species). Leaves alternate or basal. Flowers in clusters or solitary in leaf axils; petals 4; sepals 4; stamens 8; stigma ball-shaped or knobby. Fruits are capsules.

California Suncup

Flowers yellow, often red-spotted at petal bases; stigma ball-shaped. HT: 6 in.–3 ft.

■ **TANSY-LEAF SUNCUP** (*Camissonia tanacetifolia*): Spring–summer; meadows, fields. Leaves basal, commonly hairy. Flowers 1–1½ in. across; petals rounded to minutely toothed, aging orangish or apricot.

■ **LONG-LEAF SUNCUP** (*C. subacaulis*): Meadows, moist places. Leaves basal, mostly hairless, lance-shaped to narrowly elliptic, often wavy-edged and sometimes few-lobed at base. Also called Northern Suncup. **SIMILAR** ■ **COAST SUNCUP** (*C. ovata*): Grassy slopes, fields. Leaves narrowly elliptic to egg-shaped, short-hairy along edges and veins. Also called Golden-eggs.

Tansy-leaf Suncup

Flowers yellow. Leaves irregularly pinnately lobed. HT: about 4 in.

Long-leaf Suncup

Flowers yellow. Leaves mostly, unlobed. HT: about 4 in.

■ **BEACH SUNCUP** (*Camissonia cheiranthifolia*): Spring–summer; beaches, dunes, coastal strand. Stems mostly prostrate and spreading. Leaves alternate and basal, thick-textured, gray-hairy, commonly blunt. Flowers ½–1¼ in. across, occasionally red-spotted, aging pinkish to orange-red. Fruits stalkless, very narrow, bent or curved. Plants become shrubby in southern part of range. Also called Beach-primrose, Beach Evening-primrose.

■ **MINIATURE SUNCUP** (*C. micrantha*): Dunes, beaches, desert flats, washes. Leaves mostly narrow, wavy-edged, pointed. Flowers ⅛–½ in. across. Also called Small Suncup.

Beach Suncup

Stigma ball-shaped.

Flowers bright yellow. HT: to 6 in.

Miniature Suncup

HT: 4–24 in.

■ **BOOTH'S SUNCUP** (*Camissonia boothii*): Spring–summer; open places. Variable, with several named varieties. Stems sometimes peeling. Leaves elliptic to lance- or spoon-shaped, may be dark-spotted. Flowers 5/16–5/8 in. across; petals rounded, aging pink or reddish. Fruits very narrow, stalkless, generally bent or curved. Also called Bottle-washer, Shredding Suncup.

Booth's Suncup

Flowers white; clusters often nodding at tip. HT: 2–16 in.

Leaves sometimes in a basal cluster.

Stigma ball-shaped.

■ **BROWN-EYES** (*Camissonia claviformis*): Mostly spring–early summer; sandy plains, desert washes, rocky flats, slopes. Several named varieties. Leaves mostly at or near plant base, sometimes along stem; variable, from unlobed to pinnately lobed with large end segment. Flowers 1/4–3/4 in. across; white or sometimes yellow, with brownish red eye; aging pink to reddish purple. Fruits stalked, club-shaped. Also called Brown-eyed-primrose, Clavate-fruited-primrose.

Brown-eyes

Flower clusters nodding at tip. HT: 6–18 in.

Stigma ball-shaped.

Flowers sometimes yellow.

■ **SPREADING GROUNDSMOKE**
(*Gayophytum diffusum*): Late spring–
summer; slopes, open woods, shrublands,
grasslands. Stems wiry, branched, often
reddish. Flowers 3/16–1/2 in. across, white
with yellowish eye, commonly aging pink
or rose. Also called Diffuse Gayophytum.

NOTE Several similar species, most with
flowers 1/8–1/4 in. across.

Genus *Gayophytum* (8 native species).
Leaves alternate or occasionally opposite
below. Flowers in leaf axils; petals 4;
sepals 4; stamens 8; stigma ball-shaped or knobby. Fruits
are capsules, sometimes constricted between seeds.

Spreading Groundsmoke

Flowers in leaf axils. Leaves
very narrow, stalkless.
Stems slender.
HT: 6–24 in.

■ **SHRUBBY WATER-PRIMROSE**
(*Ludwigia octovalvis*): Year-round;
marshes, swamps, wet places. Flowers
1–1½ in. across; stamens 8. Fruits
cylindrical, narrow. Also called Long-fruit
or Mexican Primrose-willow.

■ **WING-STEM WATER-PRIMROSE**
(*L. decurrens*): Spring–fall. Stems winged.
Flowers ½–1 in. across. Also called Erect
or Upright Primrose-willow.

■ **SEEDBOX** (*L. alternifolia*): Spring–fall.
Flowers ½–¾ in. across; stamens 4. Also
called Square-pod Water-primrose,
Rattlebox.

NOTE Water-primroses are also called
false loosestrife. There are several species,
native and introduced, similar to these.

Genus *Ludwigia* (31 species, 27 native).
Sometimes shrubby. Leaves alternate or
sometimes opposite. Flowers in leaf axils;
petals and sepals usually 4 or 5; stamens 4, or less often 8
or 10; stigma knobby or lobed. Fruits are capsules.

Shrubby Water-primrose

Petals 4,
yellow. Leaves
alternate, often
lance-shaped,
nearly stalkless.
HT: to 6 ft.

Wing-stem
Water-primrose

Stems 4-angled,
winged. HT: to 6 ft.

Seedbox

Fruits
squarish.
HT: 1–3 ft.

■ CREEPING WATER-PRIMROSE

(*Ludwigia peploides*): Spring–fall; ponds, streams, swamps, ditches. Plants hairless. Leaves alternate, stalked; lower leaves spoon-shaped to nearly round, upper leaves lance-shaped to elliptic. Flowers ¾–1¼ in. across; stamens 10. Also called Floating Primrose-willow. **SIMILAR LARGE-FLOWER WATER-PRIMROSE** (*L. grandiflora*): Mostly southeastern; introduced in part from American tropics. Plants hairy; flowers 1–2 in. across; petals 5 or sometimes 6. Also called Uruguayan or Hairy Water-primrose.

■ ANGLE-STEM WATER-PRIMROSE

(*L. leptocarpa*): Petals occasionally 6 or 7. Also called Angle-stem Primrose-willow.

Creeping Water-primrose

Flowers on erect stems. Main stems creeping or floating.

Angle-stem Water-primrose

Petals usually 5. Stems erect. HT: 6 in.–5 ft.

■ SMALL ENCHANTER'S-NIGHTSHADE

(*Circaea alpina*): Late spring–summer; woods, seeps, swamps, bogs. Leaves 1–2½ in. long, opposite, stalked, egg-shaped, conspicuously toothed. Flowers bloom before clusters have elongated. Fruit stalks spreading or partly down-turned. Also called Alpine Enchanter's-nightshade.

■ LARGE ENCHANTER'S-NIGHTSHADE

(*C. canadensis*): Woods. Leaves 2½–5½ in. long, shallowly toothed. Flowers bloom after clusters have elongated (flowers appear more spread out). Fruit stalks sharply downturned. Also called Broad-leaf Enchanter's-nightshade.

Genus *Circaea* (2 native species). Leaves opposite. Flowers tiny, in clusters; petals 2, notched; sepals 2, lance-shaped, petal-like; stamens 2. Fruits seedlike, densely covered with hooked bristles.

Small Enchanter's-nightshade

Flowers white, tiny, on hairless stalks. HT: 2–10 in.

Large Enchanter's-nightshade

Flower stalks hairy. HT: 8–30 in.

ORCHIDACEAE   ORCHID FAMILY

Perennial. Leaves basal or alternate, rarely opposite or whorled; simple, sometimes reduced to bracts. Flowers solitary or in clusters, often showy; petals 3: 2 typical, a 3rd, the lip, usually conspicuously different in shape and color and sometimes with an elongated tubular projection (spur); sepals 3 (1 middle, 2 side), usually petal-like; stamens and pistil occur together on a modified central structure, the column; ovary stalklike, beneath rest of flower. Fruits are capsules. Most North American species are terrestrial (growing in soil). The majority of orchids worldwide are from tropical regions, where they generally live as epiphytes ("air plants"), growing on trees but obtaining minerals from rainwater and surface water.

FLOWERS OF THE ORCHIDACEAE

The diverse appearance of orchid flowers derives from the varied presentation of their parts, including the sepals, petals, and lip. Illustrated here are flowers of the genera *Platanthera* (p. 384), *Corallorhiza* (p. 372), and *Cypripedium* (p. 378). The flowers of most orchids twist in a semicircle (180°) as they develop; by maturity the lip has moved into the lowermost position.

PLATANTHERA SPECIES

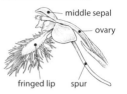

middle sepal
ovary
fringed lip
spur

CORALLORHIZA SPECIES

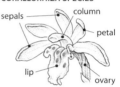

sepals
column
petal
lip
ovary

CYPRIPEDIUM SPECIES

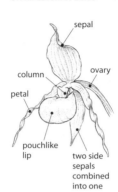

sepal
column
ovary
petal
pouchlike lip
two side sepals combined into one

■ **PHANTOM ORCHID** (*Cephalanthera austiniae*): Spring–summer; woods, stream banks. Flowers up to 25 per cluster; side sepals spreading or forward-pointing, middle sepal and petals arching forward; lip has yellow blotch. Plants darken in age. Also called Snow Orchid.

NOTE These plants lack the green pigment chlorophyll, necessary for photosynthesis. They are mycotrophic, obtaining nutrients through an association with a soil fungus.

Genus *Cephalanthera* (1 native species). Plants lack green pigment. Leaves reduced to bracts. Flowers in elongated clusters; tip of lip bent downward.

Phantom Orchid

Flowers white. Stems white, with narrow, sometimes leaflike, sheathing bracts. HT: 8–25 in.

■ **ROUND-LEAF ORCHIS** (*Amerorchis rotundifolia*): Late spring–summer; wet woods, swamps, boggy ground, fens, tundra. Solitary basal leaf broadly egg-shaped to nearly round. Side sepals spreading, middle sepal and petals arching and hoodlike. Small, narrow, leaflike bracts in flower cluster. Also called Small Round-leaf Orchid, One-leaf Orchis.

Genus *Amerorchis* (1 native species). Leaves basal. Flowers in a loose cluster of 4–15; lip 3-lobed, with middle lobe longer and often notched, tubular spur at base.

Round-leaf Orchis

Flowers white, pinkish, or pale purple; lip purple-spotted, with conspicuous spur. HT: 3–12 in.

■ **STRIPED CORALROOT** (*Corallorhiza striata*): Spring–summer; woods, stream banks, swamps. Stems yellowish, tan, or purplish. Leaves absent (stem bases usually bear tubular, sheathing bracts). Flowers 3–30 per stem; sepals and petals arch forward; lip unlobed. Also called Hooded Coralroot.

■ **SPRING CORALROOT** (*C. wisteriana*): Early spring–midsummer; woods. Sepals and petals about ¼ in. long, not striped, frequently arching forward but sometimes spreading; lip sometimes plain white. Also called Wister's Coralroot.

SIMILAR ■ **AUTUMN CORALROOT** (*C. odontorhiza*): Late summer–fall; woods. Flowers not usually fully opened; sepals and petals ⅛–³⁄₁₆ in. long.

Genus *Corallorhiza* (7 native species). Plants normally lack green pigment (some species show occasional green traces); mycotrophic. Leaves absent. Flowers sometimes small, in elongated clusters; lip unlobed to 3-lobed.

Striped Coralroot

Spring Coralroot

Flowers pale tan, salmon-yellow, or whitish, with purple or reddish brown stripes. HT: 4–20 in.

Lip often purple-spotted. HT: to 15 in.

■ **SPOTTED CORALROOT** (*Corallorhiza maculata*): Spring–summer; woods. Stems tan, yellow, or reddish purple. Lip 3-lobed, with side lobes much smaller than down-curved middle lobe, a tiny swelling often on underside near base. Also called Summer Coralroot.

■ **PACIFIC CORALROOT** (*C. mertensiana*): Woods. Stems often pinkish. Lip, some-times white or purple and white, has toothlike, inconspicuous side lobes and prominent, chinlike swelling on underside of base. Also called Western Coralroot.

■ **NORTHERN CORALROOT** (*C. trifida*): Woods, swamps. Stems pale yellow or greenish. Lip sometimes spotted and lobed, lacks conspicuous swelling at base. Also called Early, Pale, or Yellow Coralroot.

Spotted Coralroot

Pacific Coralroot

Flowers tan, yellowish, or reddish purple; lip typically purple-spotted. HT: 6–24 in.

Lip typically bright pink-purple. HT: 1–2 ft.

Northern Coralroot

Lip typically white. HT: 4–12 in.

■ **CRESTED-CORALROOT** (*Hexalectris spicata*): Spring–summer; woods, glades. Stems tan to purplish. Leaves absent. Flowers up to 25 per stem, yellowish tan, sometimes flushed with purple; sepals spreading, their tips curved backward; petals mostly pointing forward, their tips often curved backward; lip shallowly 3-lobed, white with bright purple ridges.

GIANT-CORALROOT (*H. grandiflora*): Summer–fall; wooded slopes, canyons; southwestern TX. Flowers pink to purple-red; lip has straight, white ridges. Also called Greenman's Hexalectris.

■ **PURPLE-SPIKE CRESTED-CORALROOT** (*H. warnockii*): Summer; woods. Flowers dark purple to maroon; lip white with yellowish, wavy or ruffled ridges. Also called Texas Purple-spike.

Genus *Hexalectris* (5 native species). Plants lack green pigment; mycotrophic. Leaves absent. Flowers in elongated clusters; lip 3-lobed, with conspicuous longitudinal ridges on middle lobe.

Crested-coralroot

Giant-coralroot

Sepals and petals appear striped. HT: 10–32 in.

HT: 6–16 in.

Purple-spike Crested-coralroot

HT: 6–16 in.

■ **PUTTY-ROOT** (*Aplectrum hyemale*): Spring; woods. Solitary leaf appears in late summer or fall, persists through winter, withers in spring as plant comes into bloom; blade 4–8 in. long, gray-green with numerous whitish veins above, greenish purple beneath. Flowers mostly 7–15 per stem; sepals spreading; petals forward-pointing. Also called Adam-and-Eve.

NOTE The flower's lip, ⅜–½ in., is longer than Spotted Coralroot's (about ¼ in., p. 373) and generally shorter than Crested-coralroot's (½–¾ in., p. 373). Do not confuse with Cranefly Orchid (below).

Genus *Aplectrum* (1 native species). Leaf solitary, basal, absent at flowering time. Flowers in loose clusters; lip 3-lobed, with middle lobe wavy-edged.

Putty-root

Flowers greenish or yellowish, tinged with purple or brown. Flowering stalk leafless. HT: 8–18 in.

■ **CRANEFLY ORCHID** (*Tipularia discolor*): Summer; woods. Solitary leaf appears in late summer or early fall, persists through winter, withers in spring before plant blooms. Leaf stalked; blade 2–4 in. long, smooth or often pleated, dark green above (sometimes purple-marked), wine-purple beneath. Flowers up to 40 per stem; sepals and petals spreading; one petal partially overlaps the middle sepal, giving flower a lopsided look. Also called Crippled-cranefly.

NOTE Do not confuse with the spring-blooming Putty-root (above), which has leaves longer, with numerous whitish veins; flowers lacking a spur.

Genus *Tipularia* (1 native species). Leaf solitary, basal, absent at flowering time. Flowers in slender, elongated clusters; lip 3-lobed, with side lobes small, middle lobe long, and narrow, conspicuous spur at base.

Cranefly Orchid

Lip has slender, curved spur.

Flowers dangling and delicate, greenish or yellowish, often marked with purple or brown. Flowering stalk leafless. HT: 6–24 in.

Leaf egg-shaped, prominently veined.

■ **FAIRY-SLIPPER** (*Calypso bulbosa* var. *americana*): Spring–early summer; moist or wet woods. Solitary leaf appears in late summer or early fall, persists through winter, withers after plant has bloomed. Leaf stalked; blade pleated lengthwise, broadly egg-shaped to elliptic, 1–2½ in. long. Flower solitary, nodding; sepals and petals narrow, spreading or frequently forward-pointing, occasionally white; lip slipper-shaped, white or sometimes purplish, with purple spots and conspicuous yellow splotch. Narrow, lance-shaped bract at flower base.

■ **PACIFIC FAIRY-SLIPPER** (*C. bulbosa* var. *occidentalis*): Woods. Similar to var. *americana*; lip typically has reddish purple markings, small white blotch. Also called Western Fairy-slipper.

Genus *Calypso* (1 native species). Leaf solitary, basal. Flower solitary; lip inflated, slipper- or shoe-shaped.

Fairy-slipper

Pacific Fairy-slipper

Lip has sparse tuft of whitish bristles. HT: 4–8 in.

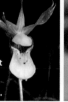

Flower usually pink. Lip has dense tuft of yellow bristles. HT: 4–8 in.

■ **DRAGON'S-MOUTH** (*Arethusa bulbosa*): Late spring–summer; bogs, fens, swamps, wet meadows. Solitary, grasslike leaf appears just after plant has bloomed, 4–8 in. long when mature; flowering stem leafless. Sepals erect; petals arching forward; flower occasionally white. Also called Wild-pink, Bog-rose.

Genus *Arethusa* (1 native species). Leaf solitary, low on stem; 2 or 3 sheathing bracts beneath. Flower solitary (or rarely 2); lip drooping and wavy-edged, with 3 fringed, longitudinal ridges.

Dragon's-mouth

Flower large, usually pink to magenta. Lip purplish-spotted, yellow-splotched, "bearded" along middle. HT: 2–16 in.

■ **SPREADING-POGONIA** (*Cleistes divaricata*): Spring–early summer; pinewoods, swampy woods. Leaf solitary, partway up stem. Sepals unlike petals: slender, purplish or maroon, erect to widely spreading, with tip often back-curved; petals broader, rose-pink or sometimes whitish, forward-pointing and overlapping, curled back at tip; lip yellowish green with purple veins, 1⅜–2¼ in. long. Also called Rosebud Orchid.

■ **SMALL SPREADING-POGONIA** (*C. bifaria*): Pinelands, open woods, meadows, hills. Similar; lip ¾–1⅜ in. long. Also called Small Rosebud Orchid.

NOTE Spreading-pogonias are sometimes placed in *Pogonia* (below).

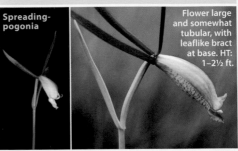

Genus *Cleistes* (2 native species). Leaf solitary, about midstem; smaller, leaflike bract at top of stem. Flower usually solitary; lip wavy-edged or minutely toothed.

Spreading-pogonia

Flower large and somewhat tubular, with leaflike bract at base. HT: 1–2½ ft.

Small Spreading-pogonia

Petals light pink to white. HT: 6–18 in.

■ **ROSE POGONIA** (*Pogonia ophioglossoides*): Spring–summer; moist or wet meadows, bogs, pine-woods, seeps, ditches. Leaf usually solitary and at midstem, lance-shaped to elliptic; occasionally a second, basal leaf. Sepals spreading or somewhat forward-pointing; petals strongly forward-pointing; lip fringed, with greenish or yellowish patch. Flowers rarely white. Also called Snake-mouth Orchid.

Genus *Pogonia* (1 native species). Leaves 1 or 2, basal or on stem. Flowers 1 or 2; lip spoon-shaped, heavily fringed.

Rose Pogonia

Flowers pink, often solitary. Leaflike bract beneath flower. HT: 6–18 in.

■ **THREE-BIRDS ORCHID** (*Triphora trianthophora*): Summer–fall; woods, thickets, swamps. Leaves clasp stem, widely spreading and broadly egg-shaped. Flowers mostly 3–6 per stem; sepals spreading or slightly forward-pointing, side sepals somewhat curved; petals arched forward, hoodlike; lip has slightly ruffled edges, round middle lobe with greenish ridges. Flowers in a population generally bloom simultaneously in response to a decrease in temperature. Also called Nodding-pogonia.

■ **GENTIAN NODDINGCAPS** (*T. gentianoides*): Summer; pinelands, woods, lawns. Leaves held close to stem, not spreading. Flowers mostly 3–10, greenish, sometimes brownish-tinged, not twisted 180° (see p. 371); lip faces stem. Also called Least Noddingcaps.

Genus *Triphora* (5 native species). Leaves alternate. Flowers solitary or in clusters; lip 3-lobed, with side lobes turned upward, middle lobe curved downward and with 3 longitudinal ridges.

Three-birds Orchid
Flowers white to pink, with leaflike bracts beneath.
HT: 3–10 in.

Gentian Noddingcaps
Flowers greenish, not fully opening.
HT: 3–10 in.

■ **GRASS-PINK** (*Calopogon tuberosus*): Early spring–fall; moist or wet meadows, bogs, swamps, pinelands. Leaf generally solitary, grasslike, to 20 in. long. Flowers up to about 15 per stem, with typically 1–3 open at any one time; sepals and petals spreading, pink to magenta, or sometimes white; side sepals ⅝–1 in. long; lip ½–¾ in. long, widened at tip and bearing stamenlike bristles. Also called Tuberous Grass-pink.

■ **PALE GRASS-PINK** (*C. pallidus*): Flowers pink to white; side sepals to ½ in. long, commonly sickle-shaped and frequently bent backward; lip ⁵⁄₁₆–½ in. long.

Genus *Calopogon* (5 native species). Leaves 1–3 on lower stem. Flowers in a loose cluster; not twisted 180° (see p. 371), thus lip uppermost, its surface covered with slender, club-tipped bristles that resemble stamens; column in flower center curves upward, mimicking a lip.

Grass-pink
Flowers usually pink to magenta; lip at top of flower, bristly. HT: 1–3 ft.

Pale Grass-pink

HT: 6–18 in.

■ **PINK LADY'S-SLIPPER** (*Cypripedium acaule*): Spring–early summer; woods, swamps, boggy places. Middle sepal curved forward; 2 petals narrow, spreading, purplish, slightly twisted; lip hanging, with longitudinal opening, occasionally white. Also called Pink Moccasin-flower.

■ **SHOWY LADY'S-SLIPPER** (*C. reginae*): Wet woods and meadows, fens, seeps. Stems leafy. Flowers 1 or 2; middle sepal and 2 petals broad and spreading, white, not twisted; lip white tinged with rose-pink (or rarely all white), horizontal, with opening above. Also called Queen's Lady's-slipper.

SPOTTED LADY'S-SLIPPER (*C. guttatum*): Open woods, meadows; Alaska, Canada. Leaves basal, 2. Flowers solitary; lip cream-colored with pink-purple blotches, pitcherlike, with wide opening above.

Genus *Cypripedium* (12 native species). Plants commonly hairy. Leaves basal or alternate, pleated. Flowers usually 1 or 2, in most species with the 2 side sepals united and somewhat hidden behind a pouchlike or slipperlike lip (thus displaying 2 petals, an often similar middle sepal, and an inflated lip); leaflike bract at flower base.

Pink Lady's-slipper

Flowers solitary; lip mostly pink or magenta. Leaflike bract at flower base. Pair of broad basal leaves. HT: 6–24 in.

Showy Lady's-slipper

HT: 1–3 ft.

Spotted Lady's-slipper

HT: 4–12 in.

■ **YELLOW LADY'S-SLIPPER** (*Cypripedium parviflorum*): Spring–summer; woods, meadows, ravines, fens. Variable, with 3 named varieties. Stems leafy. Sepals and petals yellowish green or sometimes deep purple or maroon, the middle sepal ⅝–1¼ in. wide and spreading or arching forward, the 2 petals spreading or drooping and twisted; lip ⅝–2 in. long, its opening ¼–½ in. long, sometimes purple-lined or -spotted. Also called Yellow Moccasin-flower.

■ **KENTUCKY LADY'S-SLIPPER** (*C. kentuckiense*): Spring; woods, ravines, seeps. Flowers 1 or 2; middle sepal (1⅜–2 in. wide) and 2 petals purplish brown; lip 2–2½ in. long, its opening 1–1¾ in. long. The largest of our lady's-slippers. Also called Southern Lady's-slipper.

Yellow Lady's-slipper

Flowers 1 or 2. Lip bright yellow, with small opening. HT: 6–30 in.

Kentucky Lady's-slipper

Lip cream-colored to light yellow, with large opening. HT: 1–3 ft.

■ **LESSER PURPLE FRINGED ORCHID** (*Platanthera psycodes*): Summer; wet places. Leaves lance-shaped to elliptic. Middle sepal cupped forward, side sepals often back-angled; petals have toothed edges; lip has conspicuously fringed lobes, spur at base ½–¾ in. long. **SIMILAR**
■ **LARGE PURPLE FRINGED ORCHID** (*P. grandiflora*): Flowers larger; fringes of lip mostly cut ⅓–½ way to base of lobes (⅓ or less in *P. psycodes*); spur ¾–1 in. long, with round opening (figure-eight- or dumbbell-shaped in *P. psycodes*). Also called Greater Purple Fringed Orchid.

■ **PURPLE FRINGELESS ORCHID** (*P. peramoena*): Lip 3-lobed with middle lobe notched, spur ¾–1¼ in. long.

Lesser Purple Fringed Orchid

Purple Fringeless Orchid

Flowers lavender to rose-purple; lip deeply 3-lobed, with prominent tubular spur at base. HT: 1–3 ft.

Lip has toothed lobes, conspicuous spur. HT: 1–3 ft.

■ **RAGGED FRINGED ORCHID** (*Platanthera lacera*): Mostly summer; bogs, swamps, meadows, fields, ditches. Middle sepal and slender petals arched forward, side sepals back-angled; petals less than ⅛ in. wide, untoothed; lip spur ½–⅞ in. long. Also called Green Fringed Orchid.

■ **EASTERN PRAIRIE FRINGED ORCHID** (*P. leucophaea*): Wet prairies, fens, marshes. Side sepals cupped forward; petals broadly wedge-shaped, ¼–½ in. wide, minutely toothed; lip spur 1¼–1¾ in. long. Also called Prairie Fringed Orchid.

■ **WHITE FRINGED ORCHID** (*P. blephariglottis*): Wet woods and meadows. Side sepals back-curved; lip spur in northern populations ⅝–1 in. long, in most southern populations 1¼–2 in. long.

Ragged Fringed Orchid

Lip greenish white or pale cream-colored, deeply 3-lobed. HT: 6–30 in.

Lobes of lip cut into narrow, fringed segments; spur tubular, prominent.

Eastern Prairie Fringed Orchid

White Fringed Orchid

Lip white or cream-colored, fringed, 3-lobed; spur long, slender. HT: 1–3½ ft.

Lip white, unlobed, fringed; spur conspicuous. HT: 1–3 ft.

■ **WHITE BOG ORCHID** (*Platanthera dilatata*): Late spring–summer; wet places. Leaves several, narrowly lance-shaped. Middle sepal and petals strongly arched forward and hoodlike, side sepals spreading or back-angled; lip spur tubular, ⅛–¾ in. long. Also called Leafy White Orchid, Bog-candle, Scentbottle.

■ **CLUB-SPUR ORCHID** (*P. clavellata*): Wet places. Leaf solitary (or occasionally 2). Flowers pale cream-colored, often tinged greenish or yellowish; lip rectangular or broadly wedge-shaped, with squared-off or 3-toothed tip, spur ⁵⁄₁₆–½ in. long. Also called Green Woodland Orchid.

■ **SNOWY ORCHID** (*P. nivea*): Wet places. Flowers not twisted 180° (see p. 371), thus lip uppermost; lip spur ⁷⁄₁₆–⅝ in. long. Sometimes placed in *Habenaria* (p. 384).

White Bog Orchid

Club-spur Orchid

Flowers often whitish green; lip relatively broad and short. HT: 6–18 in.

Snowy Orchid

Flowers white; lip at top, distinctly bent backward. HT: 1–2½ ft.

Flowers white; lip has widened base, narrow, elongated tip. HT: 6 in.–3 ft.

■ **LESSER ROUND-LEAF ORCHID** (*Platanthera orbiculata*): Late spring–summer; moist or wet woods, bogs. Leaves 2, nearly round, at ground level. Flowers more than 12 per stem; middle sepal erect, side sepals back-angled; petals spreading; lip spur slender, ½–1 in. long. Small, leaflike bracts along flower stalk. **SIMILAR** ■ **GREATER ROUND-LEAF ORCHID** (*P. macrophylla*): Flowers to 25 per stem; lip spur 1–1¾ in. long.

■ **HOOKER'S ORCHID** (*P. hookeri*): Woods, thickets. Flowers to 25 per stem; no leaflike bracts on flower stalk; greenish middle sepal and petals arched forward and hoodlike, side sepals sharply bent backward; lip spur tubular, ½–1 in. long.

Lesser Round-leaf Orchid

Hooker's Orchid

Flowers white or greenish white; lip narrowly strap-shaped and usually pointed downward. HT: 6–24 in.

Lip yellowish green, triangular-lance-shaped, with typically up-curved tip. HT: 8–16 in.

■ **GREEN BOG ORCHID** (*Platanthera aquilonis*): Late spring–summer; moist or wet places. Stems leafy. Flowers up to 45 per stem; middle sepal and petals strongly arched forward and hoodlike, side sepals spreading or back-angled; lip spur ¹⁄₁₆–³⁄₁₆ in. long. Also called Tall Northern Bog Orchid.

■ **BLUNT-LEAF ORCHID** (*P. obtusata*): Late spring–summer. Usually 1 basal leaf. Flowers more than 12 per stem.

■ **PALE GREEN ORCHID** (*P. flava*): Spring–fall. Leaves usually 2 or 3. Flowers up to 45 per stem; base of lip has earlike lobe on either side, spur ³⁄₁₆–⁵⁄₁₆ in. long. Also called Tubercled Orchid. Do not confuse with Bracted Orchid (p. 383).

Green Bog Orchid

Blunt-leaf Orchid

Flowers greenish; lip yellow-ish green, narrowly lance-shaped.
HT: 6–24 in.

Lip narrow, linear.
HT: 2–12 in.

Pale Green Orchid

Lip short, strap-shaped, downturned or bent backward.
HT: 6–24 in.

■ **DOWNY RATTLESNAKE-PLANTAIN** (*Goodyera pubescens*): Summer–fall; woods. Leaves evergreen, with conspicuous network of whitish veins. Flowers roundish, up to 60 per cluster; middle sepal and petals strongly arched forward and hoodlike, side sepals egg-shaped and concave; lip a somewhat 2-lobed pouch ending in a blunt, beaklike tip. Small, leaflike bracts in flower cluster.

Genus *Goodyera* (4 native species). Leaves evergreen, in basal clusters. Flowers whitish, in hairy, spikelike clusters; lip short, swollen or pouchlike, with prominent beak.

Downy Rattlesnake-plantain

Flowers small, whitish, in a crowded, cylindrical, spikelike cluster.
HT: 6–18 in.

■ **DWARF RATTLESNAKE-PLANTAIN**
(*Goodyera repens*): Summer; woods, bogs,
swamps. Leaves evergreen; blades ³⁄₈–³⁄₄
in. long, plain green or patterned with
whitish or silver. Sepals and petals similar
to Downy Rattlesnake-plantain (p. 387),
but lip a single (not 2-lobed) pouch with
down-curved, spoutlike tip. **SIMILAR**
■ **CHECKERED RATTLESNAKE-
PLANTAIN** (*G. tesselata*): Mostly woods.
Leaf blades mostly ³⁄₄–2 in. long; lip has
horizontal to slightly curved tip.

■ **GIANT RATTLESNAKE-PLANTAIN**
(*G. oblongifolia*): Mostly woods. Leaves
evergreen; blades 1¹⁄₂–2³⁄₈ in. long, usually
with pale central vein and fainter side
veins, occasionally nearly white-netted
throughout. Lip has tonguelike tip.

Dwarf
Rattlesnake-
plantain

Flowers
very small,
white,
in open
spirals of
up to 30.
HT: 4–7 in.

Leaves
sometimes
white-veined.

Giant Rattlesnake-plantain

Leaves often
have prominent
pale midvein. HT: 8–20 in.

■ **NODDING LADIES'-TRESSES**
(*Spiranthes cernua*): Late summer–fall;
open moist places. Leaves narrow.
Flowers often more than 50 per stem,
more or less tubular; sepals and petals
close together and strongly forward-
pointing; lip somewhat narrowed in
middle, often with toothed or wavy-
edged tip; sometimes tinged pale
yellowish green in center.

■ **GREAT PLAINS LADIES'-TRESSES**
(*S. magnicamporum*): Prairies, fens. Basal
leaves wither well before plants bloom.
Flowers up to 50 per stem; lip usually
not narrowed in middle, often tinged
light yellow in center. Also called Prairie
Ladies'-tresses.

Genus *Spiranthes* (23 native species).
Leaves chiefly basal, sometimes shorter
and sheathing on stem. Flowers in often
spiraling, spikelike clusters; lip has often wavy-edged or
toothed tip, minute bump or tooth on either side at base.
Species are often difficult to tell apart.

Nodding
Ladies'-
tresses

Flowers
white, in
a dense
spiral.
HT: 6–18 in.

Great
Plains
Ladies'-
tresses

Side
sepals
conspic-
uously
spreading.
HT: 6–24 in.

■ **HOODED LADIES'-TRESSES**
(*Spiranthes romanzoffiana*): Summer;
wet places, bluffs, dunes. Leaves narrow.
Flowers up to 60, in 3 parallel, spiraling
rows; often with greenish veins in
center; sepals and petals arched forward,
hoodlike; lip distinctly narrowed in
middle, with toothed tip.

OTHERS With lip not narrowed in middle.
■ **SHINING LADIES'-TRESSES**
(*S. lucida*): Mostly spring–summer; moist
or wet places. Basal leaves 1¼–4¾ in.
long; flowers up to 30, held horizontally
in loose spirals. ■ **SLENDER LADIES'-**
TRESSES (*S. lacera*): Summer; open
woods, meadows, roadsides. Basal leaves
¾–2 in. long; flowers up to 35, in a single,
loose to moderately dense spiral.

Hooded Ladies'-tresses

Shining Ladies'-tresses
Lip yellow-
blotched.
HT: 4–12 in.

Slender
Ladies'-tresses
Lip greenish-
blotched.
HT: 6–18 in.

Flowers
white,
tubular.
Lip violin
shaped,
unblotched.
HT: 6–18 in.

■ **LEAFLESS BEAKED ORCHID** (*Sacoila*
lanceolata var. *lanceolata*): Spring–early
summer; open woods, meadows, pinewoods, ditches. Large basal leaves absent
when plants bloom. Flowers usually
pinkish red, orange-red, or brick-red;
plants with greenish or yellowish green
flowers known as forma *albidaviridis*
(right photo). Also called Leafless Beaked
Lady Orchid, Scarlet-ladies'-tresses.

RELATED *Dichromanthus* (2 native
species). Blooming summer–fall.
■ **CINNABAR-LADIES'-TRESSES**
(*D. cinnabarinus*): Slopes, stream banks
wooded canyons. Leaves present when
plants bloom, chiefly basal. Flowers bright
red or orange. Also called Scarlet-ladies'-
tresses. ■ **MICHUACAN LADY ORCHID**
(*D. michuacanus*): Woods, grassy slopes.
Flowers in 1-sided spike.

Genus *Sacoila* (2 native species).
Formerly included in *Spiranthes* (p. 388),
differing in part by the lip lacking minute
bumps or teeth at base.

Leafless Beaked Orchid

Flowers
tubular.
HT: 1–2 ft.

Cinnabar-
ladies'-
tresses

Sepal
and petal
tips curved
backward.
HT: 1–3 ft.

Michuacan
Lady Orchid

Flowers
cream-
colored
with green
stripes. HT: to 2 ft.

■ **GIANT ORCHID** (*Pteroglossaspis ecristata*): Summer–early fall; pinewoods, sandy scrub, fields. Leaves elongated, to about 2½ ft. Flowers about 12, in a spikelike cluster with a twisted appearance; typically yellowish or pale green, sometimes tinged brownish purple; sepals and petals curved forward, hoodlike; lip (lower right photo) marked with brown or dark purple. Also called Noncrested-eulophia, Spiked-medusa.

Genus *Pteroglossaspis* (1 native species). Leaves basal or on lower stem. Flowers in loose, spikelike clusters; lip 3-lobed: side lobes curved upward, middle lobe broad, rounded, down-curved.

Giant Orchid

Leaves narrow, pleated. Conspicuous, narrow, leaflike bracts in flower cluster. HT: 1–4 ft.

■ **SHADOW-WITCH** (*Ponthieva racemosa*): Fall–winter; swamps, seeps, stream banks, moist woods, ravines. Flowers up to 35 per cluster; sepals and petals whitish with green veins; sepals lance-shaped and spreading, the middle one hidden by petals; petals nearly triangular, with stalklike base, the 2 petals together mimicking a lip; lip at top of flower. Also called Hairy Shadow-witch.

Genus *Ponthieva* (2 native species). Leaves basal. Flowers in elongated clusters; not twisted 180° (see p. 371), thus the lip uppermost, its sides folded to form a pouch, its tip conspicuously elongated.

Shadow-witch

Flowers somewhat flat, held horizontally. Leaves in a basal cluster of 3–8. HT: 6–24 in.

Tip of lip prominent.

Sepals and petals appear striped.

■ **GIANT HELLEBORINE** (*Epipactis gigantea*): Spring–summer; stream banks, wet places. Leaves egg-lance-shaped, clasping stem. Flowers commonly 4–18; sepals ⅝–¾ in. long, egg-lance-shaped, spreading or curved forward; petals similar but smaller; end lobe of lip elongated, with 2 prominent humps. Also called Chatterbox, Stream Orchid.

NOTE Do not confuse with Ⓘ Helleborine (p. 590), generally found in dry or moist sites.

Genus *Epipactis* (3 species, 1 native). Leaves alternate, strongly ribbed or pleated. Flowers in elongated clusters; lip narrowed and "hinged" near middle, in 2 parts: a cup, or "boat," and a horizontal or downward-pointing lobe.

Giant Helleborine
Flowers green or yellowish green, tinged and veined with rose, reddish purple, or maroon. Conspicuous, narrowly lance-shaped bracts in flower cluster. HT: mostly 1–3 ft.

■ **WILD COCO** (*Eulophia alta*): Summer–fall; swamps, marshy places, ditches. Leaves to about 3 ft. long. Flowers up to about 50 per stem; sepals erect or somewhat curved forward; petals arched forward; lip wavy-edged, its surface "bearded."

Genus *Eulophia* (1 native species). Leaves basal or on lower stem. Flowers in elongated clusters; lip 3-lobed: side lobes curved upward, middle lobe curved downward and minutely bristly on surface.

Wild Coco

Flowers green to purplish or maroon. Leaves elongated, pleated. HT: 2–5 ft.

■ **FLORIDA BUTTERFLY ORCHID**
(*Encyclia tampensis*): Mostly spring–
summer; on branches and trunks. Plants
perch on trees. Leaves rigid, narrowly
sword-shaped. Flowers up to 40 per
plant; sepals and petals alike, somewhat
spoon-shaped, spreading. Also called
Tampa Butterfly Orchid. This orchid is an
epiphyte (see p. 371).

Genus *Encyclia* (1 native species). Leaves
grow from tops of bulblike base. Flowers
in a loose cluster; lip deeply 3-lobed: side
lobes smaller and curved upward, middle lobe rounded.

Florida Butterfly Orchid

Flowers greenish or
yellowish, often tinged
brownish or purplish;
lip white with purple
blotch. HT: to about
20 in.

■ **GREEN FLY ORCHID** (*Epidendrum
magnoliae*): Summer–fall; on branches
and trunks. Flowers up to 15 per stem;
sepals slenderly spoon-shaped, their
edges commonly rolled backward; petals
similar but conspicuously narrower; lip
3-lobed, with 2 prominent bumps above.
This orchid is an epiphyte (see p. 371).

Genus *Epidendrum* (7 native species).
Leaves alternate. Flowers in elongated
clusters; lip has unlobed to deeply
3-lobed tip.

Green Fly Orchid

Flowers yellowish green or
green, sometimes purple-
tinged. Leaves leathery,
narrowly elliptic, pointed.
HT: to about
15 in.

ORCHIDS OF SOUTHERN FLORIDA

Numerous orchids, often epiphytic (see p. 371), are found in the subtropical climate of Florida's southern tip. A few are featured here.

LEAFY VANILLA (*Vanilla phaeantha*): Spring–midsummer; on trunks and branches in hammocks and swamps. Plants leafy. Stems green, typically zigzagging. Sepals and petals narrowly spoon-shaped, about 3½ in. long; lip tubular.

□ **VANILLA** (*V. planifolia*, no photo): The vanilla of commerce, introduced into southern FL centuries ago. Differs from Leafy Vanilla in smaller sepals and petals (to 2¼ in. long); longer fruits or "beans" (6–10 in. vs. 4 in.).

GHOST ORCHID (*Dendrophylax lindenii*): Spring–summer. Plants lack leaves; the many fleshy roots contain chlorophyll and carry on photosynthesis. Sepals and petals narrow, greenish white; lip 3-lobed, the middle lobe with 2 elongated, dangling lobes; lip spur 4½–7 in. long. Also called Frog Orchid, Palm-polly.

Leafy Vanilla

Flowers large, greenish; lip whitish with yellow lines, wavy-edged tip.

Ghost Orchid

Flowers large, whitish; lip white, with 2 conspicuous, arching, twisted lobes; spur very long, slender.

ORCHIDS OF SOUTHERN FLORIDA

PINE-PINK (*Bletia purpurea*): Winter–spring; hammocks, swamps. Plants to 5 ft. tall. Leaves pleated, narrowly lance-shaped. Flowers pink to purple (or sometimes whitish); petals hoodlike; lip has yellow ridges.

DELICATE IONOPSIS (*Ionopsis utricularioides*): Spring; on branches. Leaves thick. Flowers pinkish; sepals and petals small; lip broad, conspicuous, 2-lobed, with darker veins. Also called Delicate Violet Orchid.

DINGY-FLOWER STAR ORCHID (*Epidendrum amphistomum*): Winter–midsummer; on trunks and branches. Stems leafy, sometimes reddish. Flowers small, in ball-shaped clusters, greenish yellow to reddish brown. Also called Big-mouth Star Orchid.

NIGHT-SCENTED ORCHID (*E. nocturnum*): Midsummer–winter; on trunks and branches. Fragrant at night. Stems leafy. Sepals and petals long, slender, pale yellow; lip white, with bright yellow in center, 3-lobed, the middle lobe narrow.

Pine-pink

Delicate Ionopsis

Dingy-flower Star Orchid

Night-scented Orchid

ORCHIDS OF SOUTHERN FLORIDA

COW-HORN ORCHID (*Cyrtopodium punctatum*): Winter–early spring; on trunks and branches. Leaves narrow, pleated. Sepals and petals broad, wavy-edged, yellowish with brownish purple mottling; lip 3-lobed. Also called Cigar or Bee-swarm Orchid.

FLORIDA DANCING LADY ORCHID (*Oncidium ensatum*): Year-round; woods, slopes. Leaves long, narrow. Sepals and petals elliptic, greenish yellow with brownish spots; lip 3-lobed, bright yellow.

FLORIDA DOLLAR ORCHID (*Prosthechea boothiana* var. *erythronioides*): Midsummer–fall; on trunks and branches. Leaves narrowly lance-shaped, shiny. Sepals and petals spoon-shaped, greenish yellow with brown-purple spots; lip obscurely 3-lobed.

FLORIDA CLAMSHELL ORCHID (*P. cochleata* var. *triandra*): Fall–spring; on trees and rocks. Sepals and petals narrow, greenish yellow, pointing downward, away from the purplish, shell-shaped lip (lip at top of flower).

Cow-horn Orchid

Florida Dancing Lady Orchid

Florida Dollar Orchid

Florida Clamshell Orchid

OROBANCHACEAE   BROOMRAPE FAMILY

Annual or perennial. Plants lack green color (chlorophyll). Leaves reduced to scales. Flowers in clusters, infrequently solitary; tubular (5 petals united), often bent, usually 2-lipped; sepals united; stamens 4; pistil 1. Fruits are capsules. Members of this family are attached to and parasitic on the roots of green plants, from which they obtain nourishment.

■ **DESERT BROOMRAPE** (*Orobanche cooperi*): Mostly late winter–early summer; deserts. Plants mostly purplish or purplish brown. Flowers ¾–1¼ in. long, generally stalkless in dense clusters; lips ¼–⅜ in. long. Parasitic on roots of plants in the aster family (Asteraceae). Also called Cooper's Broomrape.

■ **CALIFORNIA BROOMRAPE** (*O. californica*): Late spring–early fall; slopes, flats, meadows. Flowers ¾–2 in. long; lips commonly widely flaring, ⅜–½ in. long. Several subspecies. Parasitic on roots of plants in the aster family (Asteraceae).

Genus *Orobanche* (15 species, 12 native). Plants commonly finely sticky-hairy. Flowers tubular, 2-lipped: upper lip generally 2-lobed, lower lip 3-lobed.

Desert Broomrape
Flowers purplish. HT: 4–16 in.

California Broomrape
Flowers purplish, pinkish, whitish, or yellowish. HT: 1½–14 in.

■ **CLUSTERED BROOMRAPE** (*Orobanche fasciculata*): Spring–summer; slopes, plains, prairies, dunes. Stems partly aboveground. Flowers 4–20 per plant, long-stalked; lobes of calyx (united sepals) equal to or shorter than calyx tube. Parasitic on sagebrush or wormwood (*Artemisia*), wild-buckwheat (*Eriogonum*), and stonecrop (*Sedum*).

■ **NAKED BROOMRAPE** (*O. uniflora*): Woods, thickets, seeps. Stems nearly entirely belowground. Flowers 1–3 per plant, long-stalked; calyx lobes slender, longer than calyx tube. Parasitic on several kinds of plants. Also called One-flower Broomrape, Cancer-root.

Clustered Broomrape
Flowers yellowish to purple-tinged.
HT: 3–8 in.

Naked Broomrape
Flowers mostly purplish or bluish to cream-white, with yellow bands inside.
HT: 2–8 in.

■ **CALIFORNIA GROUNDCONE** (*Boschniakia strobilacea*): Spring–summer; woods, shrublands. Flower clusters 1½–2 in. thick. Parasitic on roots of manzanita (*Arctostaphylos*) and madrone (*Arbutus*).
SIMILAR ■ **SMALL GROUNDCONE** (*B. hookeri*): Clusters to 1¼ in. thick; parasitic on Salal (p. 218). Also called Vancouver Groundcone. **NORTHERN GROUNDCONE** (*B. rossica*): British Columbia to AK. Bracts fringed; parasitic on roots of alder (*Alnus*).

RELATED ■ **SQUAWROOT** (*Conopholis americana*): Woods. Flower clusters about 1 in. thick. Parasitic on roots of oak (*Quercus*). Also called Cancer-root.
■ **ALPINE SQUAWROOT** (*C. alpina* var. *mexicana*, no photo): Southwestern mountains. Similar. Also called Mexican Squawroot.

Genus *Boschniakia* (3 native species). Plants club-shaped, fleshy, covered with overlapping scales and bracts; older plants resemble slender pine cones. Flowers 2-lipped: upper lip hoodlike, lower lip 3-lobed.

California Groundcone
Plants yellowish, brownish, red, or purple. Flowers purple-tinged to reddish brown. HT: 4–10 in.

Squawroot
Flowers yellowish or cream-colored.

Plants yellowish or straw-colored, aging brownish. HT: 2–10 in.

■ **BEECHDROPS** (*Epifagus virginiana*): Late summer–fall; woods. Flowers pale brown or whitish, with purple-red to brownish purple streaks or spots. Only the lower, unopened, self-pollinating flowers produce seeds. Parasitic on roots of beech (*Fagus*).

Genus *Epifagus* (1 native species). Upper flowers tubular, somewhat 2-lipped, 4-lobed; lower flowers budlike, not opening.

Beechdrops

Stems commonly branched; tan or brownish, sometimes purplish. HT: 6–18 in.

OXALIDACEAE

WOOD-SORREL FAMILY

Mostly perennial or sometimes annual. Leaves alternate or at plant base; usually compound, often divided into 3 heart-shaped leaflets. Flowers in clusters or solitary; petals 5; sepals 5; stamens united by their stalks, mostly 10 and in 2 sets of unequal length; pistil 1. Fruits are typically capsules.

■ **COMMON YELLOW WOOD-SORREL** (*Oxalis stricta*): Spring–fall; various habitats, especially disturbed sites. Leaflets to ¾ in. wide. Flowers ¼–½ in. across. A few similar, widespread species, some apparently introduced.

■ **GREAT YELLOW WOOD-SORREL** (*O. grandis*): Spring–early summer; woods. Leaflets 1–1½ in. wide. Flowers about 1 in. across. **SIMILAR WESTERN YELLOW WOOD-SORREL** (*O. suksdorfii*): Western.

NOTE See also ⚑ Bermuda-buttercup (p. 591), which has leaves all basal.

Genus *Oxalis* (28 species, 20 native). With characters of the family. Plants have sour juice.

Common Yellow Wood-sorrel

Flowers yellow. Leaves alternate. HT: 2–20 in.

Great Yellow Wood-sorrel

Flowers yellow. Leaves alternate; leaflet edges lined with brown-purple. HT: 1–2½ ft.

■ **VIOLET WOOD-SORREL** (*Oxalis violacea*): Spring–early summer (sometimes again in fall); woods, prairies. Leaves all basal, often reddish purple beneath; leaflets about ¾ in. wide. Flowers about ¾ in. across, in clusters.

■ **TEN-LEAF WOOD-SORREL** (*O. decaphylla*): Summer; woods, clearings, canyons. Leaflets 4–7, wedge-shaped.

■ **MOUNTAIN WOOD-SORREL** (*O. montana*): Spring–summer; woods. Leaves all basal, green beneath. Flowers solitary. Also called Common or Northern Wood-sorrel. **SIMILAR** ■ **REDWOOD-SORREL** (*O. oregana*): Spring.

Violet Wood-sorrel

Ten-leaf Wood-sorrel

HT: 2–10 in.

Mountain Wood-sorrel

Flowers lavender to dull rose-purple (rarely white). HT: 4–12 in.

Flowers white to pinkish, with dark rose veins, yellow spot at petal bases. HT: 2–6 in.

PAEONIACEAE
PEONY FAMILY

Mostly shrubby perennial herbs. Leaves at plant base and alternate on stem; compound. Flowers solitary or few, showy; petals mostly 5–10; sepals 5 or 6, persistent, somewhat leathery; stamens many; pistils 2–8. Fruits are pods (follicles).

■ **BROWN'S PEONY** (*Paeonia brownii*): Spring–early summer; slopes, open woods, plains, thickets. Plants somewhat fleshy. Leaves bluish gray, fernlike, 5–8 per stem; tips of segments mostly blunt or rounded. Flowers to 1½ in. across. Also called Western Peony. **SIMILAR** ■ **CALIFORNIA PEONY** (*P. californica*): Late winter–early spring; shrublands, coastal scrub. Plants 14–30 in. tall. Leaves 7–12 per stem; tips of segments somewhat sharp; flowers dark red or maroon; petal edges sometimes paler or pinkish.

Genus *Paeonia* (2 native species). Leaves commonly divided into lobed segments.

Brown's Peony

Flowers round, solitary, frequently nodding, maroon to bronze; petal edges often yellowish. HT: 8–18 in.

PAPAVERACEAE   POPPY FAMILY

Annual or perennial (rarely woody); frequently with whitish or colored sap. Leaves basal, alternate, opposite, or whorled; simple, but sometimes lobed or dissected. Flowers showy, solitary or in clusters; petals 4–12, commonly crumpled (rarely absent); sepals 2 or 3, usually falling early; stamens often many; pistil 1. Fruits are capsules.

■ **BLOODROOT** (*Sanguinaria canadensis*): Early spring; woods, floodplains. Leaf long-stalked; blade almost circular in outline, deeply notched at base, palmately lobed, bluish green and conspicuously veiny beneath. Leaf smaller and partially surrounds flower stalk at flowering time, later expands to up to 10 in. wide. Flower often large.

NOTE Do not confuse with the less common Twinleaf (p. 155), which has its leaf divided into 2 segments.

Genus *Sanguinaria* (1 native species). Plants have orange-red sap. Single leaf arises from plant base. Single flower; petals mostly 8–12, unequal; stamens many. Capsules podlike, narrow.

Bloodroot

Petals white; stamens orange-yellow. Leaf lobed and bluntly toothed. HT: mostly 4–12 in.

■ **COULTER'S MATILIJA-POPPY** (*Romneya coulteri*): Spring–summer; canyons, shrublands, washes. Leaves 2–8 in. long, pinnately lobed or divided into segments. Flowers large, 4–7 in. across. Buds not hairy. **SIMILAR** ■ **BRISTLY MATILIJA-POPPY** (*R. trichocalyx*): Leaves 1–4 in. long; flowers 2½–5½ in. across; buds hairy. Also called Hairy Matilija-poppy.

Genus *Romneya* (2 native species). Plants shrubby, woody-based. Leaves alternate, deeply 3–5-lobed. Flowers solitary, large; petals 6, thin, crinkled (resembling crepe paper); stamens many. Capsules bristly.

Coulter's Matilija-poppy

Petals white; stamens yellow. Leaves grayish green. HT: 3–8 ft.

■ **WHITE PRICKLY-POPPY** (*Argemone albiflora*): Mostly spring–summer; roadsides, fields. Leaves pinnately lobed. Flowers large.

OTHERS (No photos.) Sometimes also called White Prickly-poppy, some flowering through fall; mainly differ from *A. albiflora* and each other in technical characters. ■ **PRAIRIE WHITE PRICKLY-POPPY** (*A. polyanthemos*): Prairies, roadsides. ■ **SOUTHWESTERN PRICKLY-POPPY** (*A. pleiacantha*): Slopes, hills, plains, washes. ■ **FLAT-BUD PRICKLY-POPPY** (*A. munita*): Slopes, hills, shrublands.

Genus *Argemone* (15 species, 14 native). Plants sometimes shrubby; have whitish, yellow, or orange sap; commonly prickly. Leaves basal and alternate, generally pinnately lobed, often mottled. Petals 6, thin, crinkled (resembling crepe paper); sepals 2 or 3, each with conspicuous "horn" near tip; stamens 20 to numerous.

White Prickly-poppy

Petals white; stamens yellow. Leaves wavy-edged, prickly, thistlelike. HT: 1–3 ft.

■ **MEXICAN PRICKLY-POPPY** (*Argemone mexicana*): Spring–fall; roadsides, fields, disturbed places. Flowers large, 1½–2¾ in. across; stamens 30–50. Also called Yellow Prickly-poppy. **SIMILAR** ■ **GOLDEN PRICKLY-POPPY** (*A. aenea*): Spring–summer; plains, roadsides. Flowers 2¾–4¾ in. across; petals yellow, golden yellow, or bronze; stamens about 150.

■ **ROSE PRICKLY-POPPY** (*A. sanguinea*): Early spring–summer; fields, disturbed places. Flowers large. Also called Red Prickly-poppy. **SIMILAR** ■ **CHISOS PRICKLY-POPPY** (*A. chisosensis*): Mostly spring–early summer; plains, slopes. Stems more densely prickly.

Mexican Prickly-poppy

Flowers yellow. Leaves pinnately lobed, wavy-edged, prickly. HT: 10–32 in.

Rose Prickly-poppy

Flowers rose to lavender or white. HT: 16–32 in.

■ **WHITE BEAR-POPPY** (*Arctomecon merriamii*): Spring; rocky soil, desert hills and slopes. Leaves 3–7-lobed at tip. Flowers large; petals 6. Buds hairy. Also called Great Bear-claw-poppy.

■ **LAS VEGAS BEAR-POPPY** (*A. californica*): Similar to White Bear-poppy, but flowers yellow; buds not hairy. Also called Golden Bear-claw-poppy.

DWARF BEAR-POPPY (*A. humilis*, no photo): Known only from southwestern UT. Flowers white, 4-petaled. Plants 4–10 in. tall. Also called Dwarf Bear-claw-poppy.

NOTE Bear-poppies are also called bear-paw-poppy.

Genus *Arctomecon* (3 native species). Leaves mostly clustered at plant base; blades wedge-shaped (narrow at base, wide at tip), covered with long hairs. Flowers solitary or in clusters; petals 6 (or sometimes 4); stamens many.

White Bear-poppy

Petals white; stamens yellow. Leaves basal, densely hairy. HT: 8–20 in.

Las Vegas Bear-poppy

Flowers yellow. HT: 8–20 in.

■ **WHITE PYGMY-POPPY** (*Canbya candida*): Spring; sandy soil. Leaves narrow, fleshy, clustered near plant base.

■ **YELLOW PYGMY-POPPY** (*C. aurea*): Spring–early summer. Similar to White Pygmy-poppy, but flowers yellow. Also called Golden Pygmy-poppy.

Genus *Canbya* (2 native species). Plants very small. Leaves crowded near plant base, undivided, unlobed, stalkless. Flowers solitary; petals 6; stamens 6–15.

White Pygmy-poppy

Flowers white. HT: about 1 in.

Yellow Pygmy-poppy

Flowers yellow. HT: to 2½ in.

■ **CREAM-CUPS** (*Platystemon californicus*): Spring; grassy areas, rocky slopes, dunes. Leaves narrow, hairy. Petals white or cream-colored, sometimes with yellow at tip or base or occasionally all yellow.

Genus *Platystemon* (1 native species). Leaves opposite or whorled, mostly on lower half of plant, unlobed. Flowers solitary, long-stalked; petals 6; stamens many. Capsules break into narrow segments at maturity.

Cream-cups
Flowers solitary on hairy stalks.
HT: 4–12 in.

■ **NARROW-LEAF QUEEN-POPPY** (*Hesperomecon linearis*): Spring; grassy places, open woods. Leaves mostly near plant base, narrow, hairy, stalkless. Flowers on hairy stalks; white or cream-colored, sometimes marked with yellow, or occasionally 3 yellow and 3 white petals.

RELATED *Meconella* (3 native species).
■ **CALIFORNIA FAIRY-POPPY** (*M. californica*): Late winter–spring; rocky or grassy places, open woods. Plants not hairy. Leaves basal and on stems: basal leaves spoon-shaped and stalked, stem leaves opposite or whorled, not hairy.

Genus *Hesperomecon* (1 native species). Similar to *Platystemon* (above), but pistil has 3 stigmas (6 to many in *Platystemon*); stems branch from plant base (vs. branching above base); capsules do not break into segments.

Narrow-Leaf Queen-poppy
Petals sometimes blotched with yellow.
HT: 4–14 in.

California Fairy-poppy
Petals white, or some yellowish.
HT: 2–7 in.

■ **WOOD-POPPY** (*Stylophorum diphyllum*): Spring; woods, thickets. Leaves pale beneath; mostly arise from plant base, but single pair of opposite leaves on upper stem. Flowers 1½–2 in. across. Also called Celandine-poppy.

NOTE Easily confused with ⊞ Greater Celandine (p. 591), which has stem leaves alternate; flowers smaller (about ¾ in. across); capsules narrow, erect, hairless.

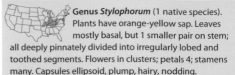

Genus *Stylophorum* (1 native species). Plants have orange-yellow sap. Leaves mostly basal, but 1 smaller pair on stem; all deeply pinnately divided into irregularly lobed and toothed segments. Flowers in clusters; petals 4; stamens many. Capsules ellipsoid, plump, hairy, nodding.

Wood-poppy
Petals and stamens yellow. Leaves long-stalked, deeply divided.
HT: 12–20 in.

■ **CALIFORNIA-POPPY** (*Eschscholzia californica* ssp. *californica*): Midwinter–late summer; grassy areas, shrublands, open woods. Flowers solitary or in clusters; 2–3 in. across; orange, golden yellow, light yellow, or rarely cream-colored, commonly with orange spot at petal bases. Flower sits above conspicuous, disklike rim. **SIMILAR** ■ **MEXICAN GOLD-POPPY** (ssp. *mexicana*): Open, sandy or rocky desert areas. Circular rim narrower or greatly reduced.

RELATED BUSH-POPPY (*Dendromecon rigida*, no photo): Spring–early summer; dry slopes, shrublands; CA. Evergreen shrub or small tree. Leaves lance-shaped, grayish green. Flowers similar, yellow. Seedlings can be numerous after disturbances such as fire. Also called Tree-poppy.

Genus *Eschscholzia* (10 native species). Plants have colorless or orange sap. Leaves basal or alternate, finely divided into narrow segments. Petals usually 4; sepals 2, united into a conelike cap, shedding as petals expand; stamens 12 to many. Capsules elongated.

California-poppy

Flowers large, commonly orange. Leaves lacy or fernlike. HT: 6–24 in.

Disklike rim often pinkish or purplish.

■ **LITTLE GOLD-POPPY** (*Eschscholzia minutiflora*): Spring; desert slopes, washes, flats. Leaves grayish or bluish green; end lobes widened at tip, blunt. Flowers usually ½–¾ in. across (less often to 1½ in.). **SIMILAR PARISH'S GOLD-POPPY** (*E. parishii*): Southern CA. Leaves green; end lobes slender (not widened at tip). Also called Pygmy-poppy.

■ **DESERT GOLD-POPPY** (*E. glyptosperma*): Spring; desert washes, flats, slopes. Flowers mostly 1–2 in. across, solitary on leafless stalks. **SIMILAR** ■ **FRYING-PANS** (*E. lobbii*): Late winter–spring; grassy fields. Flowers ½–1 in. across. Also called Lobb's Gold-poppy.

Little Gold-poppy

Flowers in clusters or solitary, yellow or yellow-orange. Leaves fernlike, arising from plant base and typically also on stem. HT: 4–18 in.

Desert Gold-poppy

Flowers solitary, yellow. Leaves fernlike, all arising from plant base. HT: 4–14 in.

■ **KLUANE ARCTIC POPPY** (*Papaver radicatum* ssp. *kluanense*): Summer; alpine rocky places. Sap whitish. Leaves arise from plant base, pinnately lobed, grayish or bluish green and densely hairy on both surfaces. Flowers rarely pink-tinged or brick-red.

■ **ALPINE POPPY** (*P. pygmaeum*, no photo): Plants 2–4½ in. high. Leaves sparsely hairy above, essentially hairless beneath. Flowers yellow-orange or yellow, drying pinkish; petals have yellow spot at base. Also called Dwarf Poppy.

NOTE Several native poppies similar to these are found mostly in Alaska and northern Canada.

Genus *Papaver* (16 species, 10 native). Plants have whitish or colored sap. Leaves mostly basal. Petals usually 4; stamens many; pistil thick, capped by "disk" with 4–20 velvety stigmatic lines radiating from center like wheel spokes. Capsules open by tiny holes (pores) beneath disk.

Kluane Arctic Poppy

Flowers usually yellow, on bristly-haired, leafless stalks. HT: 3–6 in.

■ **FIRE POPPY** (*Papaver californicum*):
Spring; clearings and grassy places in
shrublands and woods, especially after
fire or other disturbance. Sap white.
Leaves basal and on stem, deeply
pinnately divided into toothed or lobed
segments. Flower style absent. Also called
Western Poppy.

NOTE See introduced poppies (p. 591).

RELATED *Stylomecon* (1 native species).
■ **WIND-POPPY** (*S. heterophylla*): Spring;
grassy places, openings in shrublands.
Similar in appearance to Fire Poppy, but
sap yellow; flowers have dark purple spot
at petal bases; style present.

Fire Poppy

Flowers large,
orange to
orange-red,
with greenish
spot at petal
bases. HT: 1–2 ft.

Stigmas radiate.

Wind-poppy

Stigma
ball-like.
HT: 1–2 ft.

PARNASSIACEAE · GRASS-OF-PARNASSUS FAMILY

Perennial. Leaves mostly arise from plant base; simple, typically palmately veined and untoothed.
Flowers solitary on slender stalks; petals 5; sepals 5; fertile (anther-bearing) stamens 5, alternating with
sterile stamens that are united into bundles, each usually divided above; pistil 1. Fruits are capsules.

■ **AMERICAN GRASS-OF-PARNASSUS**
(*Parnassia glauca*): Summer–fall; wet
places. Leaf blades thick, broadly egg-
shaped. Each sterile stamen bundle has 3
ball-shape-tipped, threadlike stalks. Also
called Fen Grass-of-Parnassus. **SIMILAR**
■ **MARSH GRASS-OF-PARNASSUS**
(*P. palustris*): Threadlike stalks 6 to many.
Also called Arctic Grass-of-Parnassus.

■ **FRINGED GRASS-OF-PARNASSUS**
(*P. fimbriata*): Sterile stamen bundles end
in 5–8 minute, yellowish projections.

Genus *Parnassia* (9 native species). Petals
cream-colored or white, with grayish,
greenish, or yellowish veins.

American Grass-of-
Parnassus

Fringed Grass-
of-Parnassus

Lower
half of
petals
fringed.
HT: 4–14 in.

Flowers
solitary.
Stem leaf 1;
basal leaves in a cluster,
long-stalked. HT: 6–18 in.

PASSIFLORACEAE
PASSION-FLOWER FAMILY

Chiefly herbaceous perennial or woody vines, trailing or climbing by tendrils. Leaves alternate and usually simple, often palmately lobed. Flowers solitary or in clusters; petals usually 5; sepals 5; stamens 5, elevated on stalk with 1 pistil, 3 styles. Fruits are mostly berries.

■ **PURPLE PASSION-FLOWER** (*Passiflora incarnata*): Spring–summer; open woods, thickets, fields, fencerows. Leaves deeply 3-lobed, toothed. Flowers 2–3 in. across. Also called Maypop.

■ **YELLOW PASSION-FLOWER** (*P. lutea*): Summer; woods, thickets, moist places. Leaves shallowly 3-lobed, untoothed. Flowers ½–1 in. across.

■ **MEXICAN PASSION-FLOWER** (*P. mexicana*): Summer; climbing over woody plants, especially along streams. Leaves 2-lobed. Flowers 1–1½ in. wide.

Genus *Passiflora* (19 species, 13 native). Flowers often showy; central "crown" (corona) usually conspicuously fringed.

Purple Passion-flower

Flowers white or pale lavender, with purplish fringe. Vine, climbing or trailing.

Yellow Passion-flower

Flowers mostly yellowish green.

Mexican Passion-flower

Flowers greenish with reddish fringe.

PEDALIACEAE
SESAME FAMILY

Annual or perennial. Leaves opposite (or upper ones alternate), simple. Flowers solitary or in clusters; petals 5, united; sepals 5; stamens usually 4. Fruits are usually capsules with horns, hooks, or prickles.

■ **UNICORN-PLANT** (*Proboscidea louisianica*): Summer; open places. Flowers in clusters of mostly 8–25, each 1½–2 in. long, with yellow lines and dark spots inside. Also called Devil's-claw, Ram's-horn. **SIMILAR** ■ **DOUBLE-CLAW** (*P. parviflora*): Flowers 10 or fewer, to 1⅜ in. long. Also called Red Devil's-claw.

■ **DESERT UNICORN-PLANT** (*P. althaeifolia*): Flowers few to many, yellow or copper-colored, with darker streaks and spots within. Also called Devil's-claw.

Genus *Proboscidea* (5 native species). Plants sticky-hairy, ill-smelling. Leaves heart-shaped to nearly round. Flowers in clusters, tubular and 2-lipped: upper lip has 2 erect lobes, lower lip has 3 spreading lobes. Fruits have beak splitting lengthwise into 2 long-curved hooks or claws.

Unicorn-plant
Dried fruits 4–8 in. long.

Flowers white to pinkish or purplish. HT: 1–2½ ft.

Desert Unicorn-plant

Flowers mostly yellow. HT: 1–2 ft.

PENTHORACEAE   DITCH-STONECROP FAMILY

Perennial. Leaves alternate and simple. Flowers in clusters; petals absent; sepals 5; stamens 10; pistils 5, united to about middle. Fruits are small clusters of 5 pods joined at their bases.

■ **DITCH-STONECROP** (*Penthorum sedoides*): Summer–fall; wet, moist, or muddy places. Flowers borne along upper side of curved stalks. Fruits become reddish in age.

Genus *Penthorum* (1 native species). Fruiting cluster looks like an angular, 5-lobed, crownlike capsule.

Ditch-stonecrop

Flowers small, cream-colored to greenish. Leaves toothed. HT: 6–30 in.

PHRYMACEAE   LOPSEED FAMILY

Perennial. Leaves opposite and simple. Flowers in slender, elongated clusters; tubular (petals united) and 2-lipped; sepals 5, united; stamens 4; pistil 1. Fruits seedlike, developing inside bristle-tipped calyx (united sepals) that is bent down against flower stalk.

■ **LOPSEED** (*Phryma leptostachya*): Summer; open woods, thickets. Flowers whitish, pinkish, or purplish. Do not confuse with Jumpseed (p. 432), which has leaves alternate; flowers and fruits not paired.

Genus *Phryma* (1 native species). Flowers have shallowly 2-lobed upper lip, larger 3-lobed lower lip.

Lopseed

Leaves opposite, egg-shaped, toothed. HT: 1–3 ft.

Flowers paired, spreading horizontally. Fruits hang downward.

PHYTOLACCACEAE   POKEWEED FAMILY

Annual or perennial herbs or woody plants. Leaves simple, usually alternate and untoothed. Flowers in clusters; petals absent; sepals 4–8; stamens 4–30; pistils 1–12. Fruits are often berries or seedlike.

■ **POKEWEED** (*Phytolacca americana* var. *americana*): Mostly spring–fall; roadsides, clearings, thickets, open woods. Stems commonly purplish red. Leaves 4–14 in. long. Mature flower clusters elongated, 5–12 in. long, often drooping; stamens 10. Individual fruit stalks longer than the purple-black berries. Also called Poke, Pokeberry. **SIMILAR** ■ **MARITIME POKEWEED** (*P. americana* var. *rigida*): Coastal sands, tidal marsh edges, roadsides. Clusters erect, to 3½ in. long; fruit stalks shorter than berries.

NOTE Species are potentially poisonous.

Genus *Phytolacca* (6 species, 1 native). Sepals usually 5, petal-like (true petals absent); stamens 8–25; pistils 6–12, in a ring, usually united at base. Fruits are berries.

Pokeweed

Flowers small, whitish to pink-tinged. Leaves untoothed. HT: 3–10 ft.

Berries.

■ **ROUGE-PLANT** (*Rivina humilis*): Mostly spring–fall; open woods, hammocks, thickets, hillsides, roadsides. Leaves 1–6 in. long; edges smooth to wavy. Flowers small, in elongated clusters. Berries red or orange. Also called Pigeon-berry, Bloodberry, Inkberry.

Genus *Rivina* (1 native species). Sepals 4, petal-like (true petals absent); stamens 4; pistil 1. Fruits are berries.

Rouge-plant

Flowers pink to whitish. Berries mostly bright red. Erect to sprawling or vinelike. HT: 1–5 ft.

PLUMBAGINACEAE

LEADWORT FAMILY

Perennial (or rarely annual) herbs, sometimes shrubby. Leaves often basal; simple and untoothed. Flowers in clusters; petals 5, usually united (at least at very base); sepals 5, united and forming a tubular, 5- or 10-ribbed calyx that is often papery, sometimes colored; stamens 5, each opposite (in front of) a petal; pistil 1. Fruits small, capsulelike.

■ **CAROLINA SEA-LAVENDER** (*Limonium carolinianum*): Mostly summer–fall; salt marshes, salt flats. Leaves fleshy to somewhat leathery. Flowers in much-branched, fan-shaped sprays. Also called Marsh-rosemary. SIMILAR ■ **WESTERN MARSH-ROSEMARY** (*L. californicum*): Summer–late fall; salt marshes, beaches, coastal strand. ■ **TRANS-PECOS SEA-LAVENDER** (*L. limbatum*): Summer; inland alkaline flats, playas, wet meadows.

Genus *Limonium* (8 species, 3 native). Leaves basal. Flowers along 1 side of branch; branches form large open clusters; petals nearly separate; calyx (united sepals) pleated, papery, often funnel-shaped; tiny bracts below flowers.

Carolina Sea-lavender

Leaves lance- to spoon-shaped. HT: 6–30 in.

Flowers tiny, mostly purplish.

■ **THRIFT** (*Armeria maritima*): Spring–summer; coastal bluffs, beaches, gravelly tundra, lakeshores. Leaves grasslike, somewhat fleshy, densely crowded at plant base. Flowers in headlike clusters; beneath bracted cluster is a downward-pointing tubular sheath. Also called Sea Thrift, Sea-pink.

Genus *Armeria* (1 native species). Leaves basal, parallel-veined. Flowers in clusters above conspicuous, overlapping, papery bracts; petals nearly separate; calyx (united sepals) pleated, papery, funnel-shaped.

Thrift

Flowers small, rose-pink to white. Leaves grasslike. HT: 2–20 in.

POLEMONIACEAE
PHLOX FAMILY

Mostly annual or perennial. Leaves basal, alternate, or opposite; simple or compound. Flowers usually in clusters; funnel- or trumpet-shaped, or less often bell- or bowl-shaped (petals united), usually 5-lobed; sepals 5, united; stamens 5, attached to flower tube; pistil 1, stigmas normally 3. Fruits are capsules.

■ WILD BLUE PHLOX (*Phlox divaricata*): Spring–early summer; woods. Flowers sometimes reddish purple or whitish; lobes sometimes notched at tip (those with unnotched lobes more common in western part of range). Also called Forest or Woodland Phlox, Wild-sweet-William.

■ SHOWY PHLOX (*P. speciosa*): Open woods, brushy flats. Flowers sometimes whitish; lobes notched at tip. Also called Bush Phlox.

Genus *Phlox* (64 native species). Leaves opposite (rarely alternate on upper stem). Flowers often showy, trumpet-shaped, 5-lobed; stamens short-stalked, attached at different levels.

Wild Blue Phlox — Flowers usually blue-purple. Leaves mostly lance-shaped. HT: 10–20 in.

Showy Phlox — Flowers mostly pink. HT: 6–18 in.

SMOOTH PHLOX (*Phlox glaberrima*): Summer; moist or wet places; eastern. Plants generally hairless. Leaves narrow, not veiny. **SIMILAR ■ GARDEN PHLOX** (*P. paniculata*): Summer–early fall. Leaves broader, minutely hairy-edged, with conspicuous side veins; flower tube sparsely hairy. Also called Fall or Summer Phlox.

■ DOWNY PHLOX (*P. pilosa*): Spring–early summer; prairies, woods. Plants typically hairy and sticky. Leaves narrow. Also called Prairie Phlox.

ANNUAL PHLOX (*P. drummondii*): Spring–early summer; open places; Southeast; TX native. Upper leaves alternate. Flowers red, pink, purple, or white, often with dark eye. Also called Drummond's Phlox.

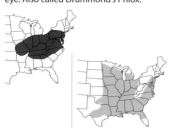

Smooth Phlox — Flowers rose-purple to white, hairless; stamen tips visible. Leaves narrowly lance-shaped. HT: 2–5 ft.

Downy Phlox — Flower tube often hairy; stamen tips not visible. HT: 1–2 ft.

Annual Phlox — Flowers sometimes red. HT: 6–20 in.

■ **LONG-LEAF PHLOX** (*Phlox longifolia*): Spring–summer; open places. Leaves narrow. Flowers ⁷⁄₁₆–⁵⁄₈ in. long, with lobes ⁵⁄₁₆–½ in. long.

■ **STANSBURY'S PHLOX** (*P. stansburyi*): Resembles Long-leaf Phlox; flowers mostly ¾–1¼ in. long, with lobes about ¼ in. long. Also called Cold Desert or Inch-tube Phlox.

■ **DESERT PHLOX** (*P. tenuifolia*): Mostly spring; desert slopes and washes. Stems vinelike, supported by surrounding vegetation. Leaves narrow. Also called Santa Catalina Mountain or Vine Phlox.

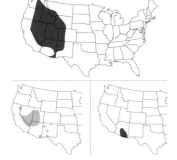

Long-leaf Phlox

Flowers pink to lavender, or sometimes white; tube short, lobes long. HT: 8–16 in.

Stansbury's Phlox

Flower tube long, lobes short. HT: 4–12 in.

Desert Phlox

Flowers white with yellow center. Sprawling.

■ **HOOD'S PHLOX** (*Phlox hoodii*): Spring–early summer; open places. Plants compact, cushion- or mat-forming. Leaves in tufts, stiff, sharp, ³⁄₁₆–³⁄₈ in. long; edges usually cobwebby-hairy, rarely nearly hairless. Flowers sometimes pink or lilac. Also called Carpet Phlox.

■ **SPREADING PHLOX** (*P. diffusa*): Leaves not stiff, ¼–¾ in. long, hairy only at base. Flowers sometimes white. Do not confuse this and Hood's Phlox with Moss Campion (p. 196), or with dwarf-primroses (p. 446).

■ **MOSS PHLOX** (*P. subulata*): Spring; open places, cliffs. Leaves crowded, stiff, sharp, ¼–¾ in. long; edges minutely hairy. Flowers pink or rose-purple, or sometimes white. Also called Moss-pink. Do not confuse with Wild-pink (p. 196).

Hood's Phlox

Flowers often white. Leaves crowded, needlelike. HT: to 6 in.

Spreading Phlox

Flowers often pink to lavender. HT: to 4 in.

Moss Phlox

Flower lobes notched at tip. HT: to 8 in.

■ **SLENDER-PHLOX** (*Microsteris gracilis*): Spring–early summer; open places. Plants commonly sticky-hairy; stems vary from unbranched to much-branched. Leaves narrow. Flowers ¼–½ in. long, ⅛–¼ in. across; tube yellowish; lobes pink, lavender, or white, with tip notched or occasionally squared off. Also called Annual-phlox, Midget-phlox, Pink-twink.

NOTE Differs from *Collomia* (below) in having a thin membrane that unites the 5 pointed lobes of the tubular calyx.

Genus *Microsteris* (1 native species). Technical features similar to *Phlox* (p. 409). Upper leaves alternate, lower ones opposite. Flowers not showy. Seeds slimy when wet.

Slender-phlox

Flowers small; lobes usually notched at tip. HT: 3–10 in.

■ **LARGE-FLOWER COLLOMIA** (*Collomia grandiflora*): Spring–summer; open places. Leaves stalkless, mostly lance-shaped. Flowers ¾–1¼ in. long, ⅜–¾ in. across, in dense, leafy-bracted clusters at stem ends. Also called Grand Collomia.

■ **NARROW-LEAF COLLOMIA** (*C. linearis*): Flowers ⁵⁄₁₆–⅝ in. long, about ¼ in. across, in dense clusters at stem ends. Also called Tiny-trumpet. **SIMILAR** ■ **STAINING COLLOMIA** (*C. tinctoria*): Flowers similar, but borne in small clusters of 2–4 in forks of much-branched stems.

NOTE Collomias are also called mountain-trumpet.

Genus *Collomia* (13 native species). Stems often finely sticky-hairy. Leaves alternate (occasionally opposite below). Flowers in clusters, funnel- to trumpet-shaped, 5-lobed.

Large-flower Collomia

Flowers often pale yellow. HT: 6 in.–3 ft.

Flowers sometimes peach-colored.

Narrow-leaf Collomia

Flowers often pink to pale lavender. HT: mostly 4–16 in.

Flowers sometimes whitish.

■ **VARIABLE-LEAF COLLOMIA** (*Collomia heterophylla*): Spring–summer; open places. Leaves untoothed to lobed, usually hairy. Flowers about ½ in. long, in clusters above leafy bracts at stem and branch tips, sometimes white. Also called Vari-leaf Collomia.

■ **ALPINE COLLOMIA** (*C. debilis*): Summer; rocky alpine slopes. Plants clump- or mat-forming. Stems slender, spreading. Flowers ½–1½ in. long, in leafy-bracted clusters at ends of upturned branches.

Variable-leaf Collomia

Flowers mostly rose-colored. Lower leaves deeply lobed. HT: 2–8 in.

Alpine Collomia

Flowers lavender to pink. Leaves untoothed or sometimes lobed. HT: to 4 in.

Flowers sometimes whitish.

■ **SHOWY JACOB'S-LADDER** (*Polemonium pulcherrimum*): Summer; open woods, meadows, slopes. Leaves chiefly basal; leaflets 9–25, mostly ¼–¾ in. long. Flowers bell- to shallowly bowl-shaped, commonly with yellow (or whitish) eye. Also called Pretty Jacob's-ladder, Showy Polemonium.

SIMILAR WESTERN JACOB'S-LADDER (*P. occidentale*): Moist or often wet places; chiefly western. Plants 1–3 ft. tall; leaves mostly along stems; leaflets ⅜–1½ in. long. Also called Western Polemonium.

■ **SPREADING JACOB'S-LADDER** (*P. reptans*): Spring; woods, clearings, thickets. Leaves mostly basal; leaflets 7–17, commonly ½–1½ in. long. Also called Greek-valerian.

Genus *Polemonium* (20 species, 19 native). Plants commonly sticky-hairy; sometimes ill-scented. Leaves alternate or basal, pinnately divided into leaflets. Flowers in clusters, funnel-, bell-, or bowl-shaped and 5-lobed.

Showy Jacob's-ladder

Spreading Jacob's-ladder

Flowers blue-violet, in relatively crowded clusters. HT: mostly 4–14 in.

Flowers lavender-blue, in relatively open clusters. HT: 8–20 in.

■ **TOWERING JACOB'S-LADDER**
(*Polemonium foliosissimum*): Summer;
woods, meadows, slopes. Leaves along
stems; leaflets 11–25, mostly ⅜–1⅜ in.
long. Flowers bell- to shallowly bowl-
shaped, sometimes have yellowish eye.
Flowers white or cream-colored in var.
alpinum, yellowish in var. *flavum*. Also
called Leafy Jacob's-ladder, Towering
Polemonium.

NOTE Do not confuse with Showy Jacob's-
ladder, which is shorter, with leaves
mostly basal; or Western Jacob's-ladder,
which has flower clusters longer than
wide overall (both on p. 412).

Towering Jacob's-ladder

Flowers usually
blue-violet,
in relatively
short, wide
clusters.
HT: mostly
16 in.–3 ft.

Flowers
sometimes
whitish.

Flowers
occasionally
yellowish.

■ **SKY-PILOT** (*Polemonium viscosum*):
Summer; alpine slopes and meadows.
Plants sticky-hairy. Leaves chiefly basal,
a few on stems; leaflets many, typically
deeply divided into smaller segments
(¹⁄₁₆–¼ in. long) that appear to be whorled.
Flowers ⅝–1 in. long, in more or less
compact clusters; occasionally white.
Also called Sticky Jacob's-ladder, Skunkweed. **SIMILAR** ■ **SIERRAN SKY-PILOT**
(*P. eximium*): Flowers ½–⅝ in. long.

■ **HONEY SKY-PILOT** (*P. brandegeei*):
Rocky places in mountains. Leaflets less
crowded than in Sky-pilot, with many
(not all) divided into smaller segments.
Flowers ¾–1½ in. long. Also called Pale or
Yellow Sky-pilot, Brandegee's Jacob's-ladder.

Sky-pilot

Flowers usually
violet-blue, narrowly
funnel-shaped. HT: 3–15 in.

Honey Sky-pilot

Flowers pale
yellow or
cream-colored.
HT: 3–15 in.

■ **GREAT POLEMONIUM** (*Polemonium carneum*): Spring–summer; open woods, clearings, thickets, grassy places. Leaves mostly on stems; leaflets mostly 9–19, generally ¾–1½ in. long. Flowers pale peach, salmon, yellowish, lavender, or less often blue or white, usually with yellow eye; tube ⅝–1 in. long, spreading lobes ⅜–½ in. long. Also called Royal Jacob's-ladder.

■ **ANNUAL POLEMONIUM** (*P. micranthum*): Spring; open places. Leaves mostly on stems; leaflets 7–15, each ¹⁄₁₆–⁵⁄₁₆ in. long. Flowers typically solitary, sometimes bluish; tube and lobes both less than ¼ in. long. Also called Little Bells Polemonium, Annual Jacob's-ladder.

Great Polemonium

Flowers in open clusters. HT: 1–3 ft.

Annual Polemonium

Flowers tiny, mostly white with yellow eye. HT: 2–10 in.

■ **DENSE FALSE GILY-FLOWER** (*Allophyllum gilioides*): Spring–early summer; open places. Plants hairy, often sticky above. Leaves alternate and sometimes also basal; some pinnate, with 5–11 lobes ⅛ in. or less wide. Flowers ³⁄₁₆–⅜ in. long. Also called Blue False Gilia, Straggling-gilia.

SIMILAR With wider leaf lobes (³⁄₁₆–½ in.).
■ **PURPLE FALSE GILY-FLOWER** (*A. divaricatum*): Spring–early summer. Also called Pink False Gilia, Straggling Volcanic-gilia. ■ **WHITE FALSE GILY-FLOWER** (*A. integrifolium*): Summer. Also called White False Gilia.

NOTE Plants are sometimes ill-scented.

Genus *Allophyllum* (about 8 native species). Leaves mostly alternate or basal; untoothed, toothed, or pinnately lobed; top leaves commonly palmately 3- or 5-lobed. Flowers in clusters of 2–8 above bractlike leaf; funnel- to trumpet-shaped, 5-lobed; calyx (united sepals) often sticky-hairy.

Dense False Gily-flower

Flowers small, blue-violet. Leaf lobes narrow. HT: 4–16 in.

Purple False Gily-flower

Flower tube red-purple, lobes pinkish. HT: 8–24 in.

White False Gily-flower

Flowers small, white. HT: 3–10 in.

■ **MINIATURE-GILIA** (*Allophyllum capillare*): Summer; slopes, meadows, open woods. Flowers narrowly funnel- to somewhat trumpet-shaped, ³⁄₁₆–⁵⁄₁₆ in. long; calyx (united sepals) sticky-hairy; flowers sometimes white. Also called Smooth-leaf-gilia.

BRIDGES'-GILIA (*A. leptaleum*): Similar to Miniature-gilia. Flowers have yellow tube, pink lobes; calyx usually hairless. ■ Ssp. *leptaleum* has flowers ½–¾ in. long, with a purple throat. ■ Ssp. *bicolor* has flowers ⁵⁄₁₆–½ in. long, with a yellow throat and sometimes purple-streaked.

NOTE These two species, once in *Gilia*, are often treated in *Navarretia* (below), even though they lack the conspicuous prickly bracts characteristic of that genus.

Miniature-gilia

Flowers very small, often pink-lavender or bluish. Leaves narrow. HT: 2–10 in.

Bridges'-gilia

Flowers pink; style conspicuously protruding. HT: 2–14 in.

■ **NEEDLE-LEAF NAVARRETIA** (*Navarretia intertexta*): Late spring–summer; drying pools, meadows, slopes. Flower clusters may be densely white-hairy.

■ **DOWNY NAVARRETIA** (*N. pubescens*): Open slopes. Flower clusters sticky-hairy; stamens and style protruding. **SIMILAR SKUNKWEED** (*N. squarrosa*): Chiefly West Coast. Plants have skunklike odor; stamens and style not protruding.

■ **BREWER'S NAVARRETIA** (*N. breweri*): Meadows, slopes. Flowers very small. Also called Yellow Navarretia.

NOTE Navarretias are also called pincushion-plant.

Genus *Navarretia* (about 30 native species). Stems slender or wiry. Leaves mostly alternate, pinnately divided into narrow, firm, spine-tipped segments. Flowers in dense, spiny-bracted clusters, funnel- or trumpet-shaped and 5-lobed; sepals united below, often spine-tipped.

Needle-leaf Navarretia

Flowers small, commonly whitish, in dense, spiny clusters. HT: 2–8 in.

Flowers may be light lavender or pale blue.

Downy Navarretia

Flowers blue, often dark purple-marked near center. HT: 4–12 in.

Brewer's Navarretia

Flowers yellow. HT: 1½–3½ in.

■ **GIANT WOOLLY-STAR** (*Eriastrum densifolium*): Late spring–fall; slopes, washes, dunes. Stems woody at base. Leaves have 2–16 slender segments. Flowers mostly ½–¾ in. long, sometimes whitish. Also called Dense Eriastrum.

■ **SAPPHIRE WOOLLY-STAR** (*E. sapphirinum*): Late spring–summer; dry places. Leaves have 2 slender segments near base. Flowers about ½ in. long.

■ **DESERT WOOLLY-STAR** (*E. eremicum*): Spring; open, often sandy places. Leaves have 2–6 slender segments. Flowers about ⅝ in. long, slightly to distinctly asymmetrical, upper 3 lobes yellowish-spotted at base.

Genus *Eriastrum* (13 native species). Similar to *Navarretia* (p. 415), but leaves often sharp-pointed and soft-prickly but not rigidly spine-tipped; flower clusters typically densely covered with cobwebby hairs.

Giant Woolly-star

Flowers often blue with darker veins. Leaves grayish green. HT: 6–18 in.

Sapphire Woolly-star

Flowers sapphire blue with yellow center. HT: 3–12 in.

Desert Woolly-star

Flowers blue-lavender; lobes unequal. HT: 2–10 in.

■ **MINIATURE WOOLLY-STAR** (*Eriastrum diffusum*): Spring; open, often sandy places. Plants spreading, commonly wider than tall. Flowers in clusters of 3–20, each ¼–⅜ in. long, typically light blue-lavender, sometimes with yellowish center; lobes occasionally cream-colored. Also called Spreading or Diffuse Eriastrum. **SIMILAR** ■ **GREAT BASIN WOOLLY-STAR** (*E. sparsiflorum*): Late spring–summer; slopes, hills, plains, washes. Plants erect, commonly taller than wide; leaves typically needlelike, usually without 2 slender segments near base; flowers in clusters of 2–5. Also called Few-flower Eriastrum. ■ **WILCOX'S WOOLLY-STAR** (*E. wilcoxii*): Leaves often have 2–6 slender segments.

Miniature Woolly-star

Flowers small, in dense, spiny clusters. Leaves often have 2 slender segments near base. HT: mostly 2–6 in.

■ **BRISTLY CALICO** (*Langloisia setosissima* ssp. *setosissima*): Spring; desert slopes, flats, washes. Teeth or lobes toward leaf tip have 1 bristle, lower teeth often have 2 or 3 bristles. Flower lobes nearly equal, about ³⁄₁₆ in. long, sometimes streaked (not spotted) with purple. Also called Bristly Langloisia, Bristly-gilia.

■ **SPOTTED BRISTLY CALICO** (*L. setosissima* ssp. *punctata*): Deserts, plains, hills, valleys. Similar to Bristly Calico; flower lobes ¼–³⁄₈ in. long, each commonly with 2 yellowish spots. Also called Spotted Langloisia, Lilac-sunbonnet.

Genus *Langloisia* (3 native species). Leaves alternate, with conspicuously bristle-tipped teeth or lobes. Flowers in leafy-bracted clusters, tubular-funnel- to trumpet-shaped, 5-lobed; calyx (united sepals) has bristle-tipped lobes.

Bristly Calico
Flowers lavender. Leaves bristly. HT: 1–3 in.

Spotted Bristly Calico
Flowers often lavender with purple spots. HT: 1–6 in.

Flowers sometimes white with purple spots.

■ **DESERT CALICO** (*Langloisia matthewsii*): Spring; desert slopes, flats, washes. Leaves bear single bristle on all teeth. Flowers often deep rose-lavender, sometimes pale pink or whitish; ½–¾ in. long; lobes toothed, notched, or squared-off at tip, upper 3 each with irregular maroon arch above whitish splotch toward base (sometimes yellowish at very base).

■ **SCHOTT'S CALICO** (*L. schottii*): Flowers white, pale pink, or light lavender, ¼–½ in. long; lobes often pointed, upper 3 maroon-marked at base. Also called Little Sunbonnets, Schott's-gilia.

NOTE These two species are often placed in their own genus, *Loeseliastrum*.

Desert Calico
Flowers distinctly 2-lipped. Leaves bristly. HT: 1–6 in.

Schott's Calico
Flowers often white. HT: 1–4 in.

■ **BLUE-HEAD GILIA** (*Gilia capitata*):
Spring–early summer; open woods,
meadows, slopes. Several subspecies.
Leaves pinnately divided into narrow
segments. Flowers ¼–⅜ in. long, 50–100
per cluster. Also called Globe Gilia.

■ **CALIFORNIA GILIA** (*G. achilleifolia* ssp.
achilleifolia): Open places. Leaves in basal
clusters, fernlike, the narrow segments
often curved. Flowers ⅜–¾ in. long,
nearly stalkless, in hemispherical clusters
of 8–25. Also called Yarrow-leaf Gilia.

■ **MANY-STEM CALIFORNIA GILIA**
(*G. achilleifolia* ssp. *multicaulis*): Flowers
¼–⅜ in. long, often stalked, 1–7 per cluster,
sometimes whitish.

NOTE Gilias are also called gily-flower.

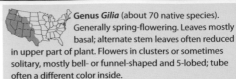

Genus *Gilia* (about 70 native species).
Generally spring-flowering. Leaves mostly
basal; alternate stem leaves often reduced
in upper part of plant. Flowers in clusters or sometimes
solitary, mostly bell- or funnel-shaped and 5-lobed; tube
often a different color inside.

Blue-head Gilia

California Gilia

Flowers
blue-
lavender.
HT: 6–24 in.

Flowers
blue-violet,
in ball-shaped
clusters.
HT: 6 in.–3 ft.

Many-stem
California Gilia

HT: 6–24 in.

■ **SHOWY GILIA** (*Gilia cana*): Spring;
slopes, desert flats. Leaves in basal
clusters, cobwebby-hairy. Flowers ⅝–1 in.
long; tube purple at base, yellow-banded
above. Also called Banded or Mojave
Gilia. **SIMILAR BROAD-FLOWER GILIA**
(*G. latiflora*): Chiefly southern CA. Stems
not cobwebby-hairy near base in most
varieties. Also called Mojave Gilia.

■ **ROSY GILIA** (*G. sinuata*): Spring–early
summer; plains, slopes. Leaves (but not
stem bases) cobwebby-hairy. Flowers ¼–
½ in. long. Also called Shy Gilia. **SIMILAR**
■ **NEVADA GILIA** (*G. brecciarum*): Spring;
open woods, shrublands, slopes, desert
flats. Stem bases (and sometimes leaves)
cobwebby-hairy. Also called Argus Gilia.

Showy Gilia

Flower lobes
pinkish to
violet. Leaf
lobes toothed.
Stems cobwebby-
hairy near base.
HT: 4–12 in.

Rosy Gilia

Flower lobes lavender,
pinkish, or nearly
whitish. Stems hairless
below. HT: 4–15 in.

■ **BIRD'S-EYE GILIA** (*Gilia tricolor*):
Spring; grassy plains and slopes. Leaves
basal and on stems; leaf segments
very slender. Flowers ¼–¾ in. long;
tube yellow below, with purple ring or
purple spots near rim (above); flowers
sometimes pale or whitish.

■ **ROCK GILIA** (*G. scopulorum*): Spring;
rocky desert slopes and washes. Plants
sticky-hairy. Leaves mostly basal, pinnately
lobed. Flowers narrowly funnel- to
trumpet-shaped, ⅜–⅝ in. long, to ¼ in.
across, commonly yellow or yellow-
banded in throat.

Bird's-eye Gilia

Flower lobes pink or blue-
violet, paler at base.
HT: 4–12 in.

Rock Gilia

Flower lobes
pink-lavender.
HT: 4–15 in.

■ **NEEDLE-LEAF BLUE GILIA** (*Gilia
acerosa*): Spring–early summer; open
places. Plants finely sticky-hairy. Flowers
to ¾ in. across, blue, violet-blue, or purple,
with white-edged yellow eye.

■ **BLUEBOWLS** (*G. rigidula*): Leaf
segments broader, not needlelike. Also
called Blue Gilia.

■ **SPLIT-LEAF GILIA** (*G. incisa*): Leaves
on lower stem distinctly stalked, their
segments sharply and irregularly toothed.
Flowers mostly lavender, ¼–⅜ in. across.
Also called Cut-leaf Gilia.

NOTE These 3 species are often placed
in *Giliastrum*.

Needle-leaf Blue Gilia

Bluebowls

Leaf segments
needlelike, HT: 2–6 in.

Flowers
shallowly
bowl- or
saucer-shaped.
HT: 3–12 in.

Split-leaf Gilia

Lower leaf segments
jagged-toothed.
HT: 10–20 in.

■ **SAND GILIA** (*Gilia leptomeria*): Spring; open places. Flowers narrowly funnel- to trumpet-shaped, very small, about ¼ in. long; lobes sometimes toothed or short-pointed; stamens attached between lobes. Also called Great Basin Gilia.

■ **BROAD-LEAF GILIA** (*G. latifolia*): Rocky desert hills and washes. Plants commonly sticky-hairy. Leaves typically on lower half of plant, with spine-tipped teeth or lobes. Flowers funnel- to somewhat trumpet-shaped, small, ¼–⅞ in. long; stamens attached in tube.

NOTE These 2 species are often placed in *Aliciella*.

Sand Gilia

Broad-leaf Gilia

Flowers whitish, often pink-lavender-flushed, with yellow center. Leaves mostly basal, pinnately toothed or lobed. HT: 3–10 in.

Flowers pink with pale center. Leaves hollylike. HT: 4–12 in.

■ **SKYROCKET** (*Ipomopsis aggregata*): Late spring–early fall; open woods, fields, slopes. Leaves narrowly pinnately lobed. Flowers sometimes salmon, pinkish, or whitish; common form (shown, called Scarlet Skyrocket or Scarlet-gilia) has red flowers about ⅝–1¼ in. long; flower lobes sharply pointed.

■ **SLENDER-TUBE SKYROCKET** (*I. tenuituba* ssp. *tenuituba*): Similar to Skyrocket; flowers 1–1¾ in. long, may be white or lavender. Also called Lavender-gilia.

■ **STANDING-CYPRESS** (*I. rubra*): Summer–fall; pastures, fields, sandhills, woodland borders. Leaves feathery, the segments threadlike. Flowers ¾–1 in. long; lobes not sharp-pointed. Also called Texas-plume, Red-gilia.

Genus *Ipomopsis* (24 native species). Similar to *Gilia* (p. 418), but mostly summer-flowering; leaves on upper stem often not notably reduced; flowers typically trumpet-shaped, with tube similarly colored outside and inside.

Skyrocket
Flowers red, sometimes speckled. HT: 1–3 ft.

Slender-tube Skyrocket
Flowers usually pinkish. HT: 1–2 ft.

Standing-cypress
Flowers red; lobes speckled. HT: 2–5 ft.

■ **PALE-FLOWER SKYROCKET**
(*Ipomopsis longiflora*): Spring–fall; plains, sandhills, mesas, slopes. Flowers in open, branched clusters; each mostly 1¼–2 in. long. Also called White-flower Skyrocket, Blue-gilia.

■ **MANY-FLOWER IPOMOPSIS**
(*I. multiflora*): Summer–fall; open woods, slopes. Flowers in elongated clusters; each ⁵⁄₁₆–⁵⁄₈ in. long, with lobes somewhat unequal, stamens conspicuous; flowers sometimes pale. Also called Many-flower-gilia, Many-flower Skyrocket.

Pale-flower Skyrocket

Flowers pale blue-lavender to whitish. Leaves and leaf segments threadlike. HT: 6–24 in.

Many-flower Ipomopsis

Flowers violet or violet-blue. Leaves and leaf segments narrow, often hairy. HT: 6–24 in.

■ **BALL-HEAD IPOMOPSIS** (*Ipomopsis congesta*): Summer; open places. Several varieties, differing especially in their leaves: nearly hairless to densely white-hairy; alternate or predominately basal; unlobed to palmately or pinnately lobed or segmented. Flowers very small, sometimes purple-flecked; anther stalks visible. Also called Ball-head-gilia, Globe-gilia, Ball-head Skyrocket.

■ **SPIKED IPOMOPSIS** (*I. spicata*): Late spring–early summer; open places. Plants commonly white-hairy. Leaves basal and on stems, unlobed or few-lobed, generally narrow. Flowers small; anther stalks hidden; clusters headlike in some forms. Also called Spiked-gilia, Spiked Skyrocket.

Ball-head Ipomopsis

Flowers white, in ball-shaped clusters. Leaf segments generally narrow. HT: 4–16 in.

Spiked Ipomopsis

Flowers white, in generally elongated clusters. HT: 4–16 in.

■ **LOW LINANTHUS** (*Linanthus demissus*): Spring; open flats and slopes. Plants mat-forming. Flowers ¼–½ in. across; white with yellow center, purplish markings at base of each lobe. Also called Mat Linanthus, Desert-snow, Humble-gilia.

■ **PARRY'S LINANTHUS** (*L. parryae*): Leaves divided into 3–7 slender segments. Flowers ½–1 in. across; white or blue-purple, with dark purple marks at base of lobes. Also called Sand Blossoms.

■ **FRINGED LINANTHUS** (*L. dianthiflorus*): Leaves slender. Flowers ½–1 in. across, pink with yellowish center; lobes conspicuously toothed, base whitish with dark purple splotch. Also called Ground-pink.

Genus *Linanthus* (49 native species). Leaves opposite or sometimes alternate, undivided or more often palmately divided into 3–9 narrow segments. Flowers usually in clusters; bell-, funnel-, or trumpet-shaped, with usually 5 (4–6) lobes. Many species are often placed in *Leptosiphon*.

Low Linanthus

Flowers bell-shaped. Leaves palmately divided. HT: 1–4 in.

Parry's Linanthus

Flowers funnel-shaped. HT: 1–4 in.

Fringed Linanthus

Flowers funnel-shaped. HT: 1–4 in.

■ **EVENING-SNOW** (*Linanthus dichotomus*): Spring; open places. Leaves opposite, often palmately divided. Flowers ¾–1¼ in. across; white, sometimes with brownish or purplish tinge on outside of lobes. **SIMILAR**

■ **BIGELOW'S LINANTHUS** (*L. bigelovii*): Leaves only infrequently divided into segments; flowers to ½ in. across.

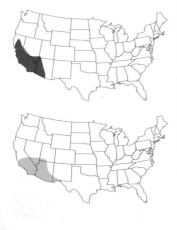

Evening-snow

Flowers funnel-shaped. Leaves commonly divided into 3 or 5 threadlike segments. HT: 2–8 in.

■ **VARIABLE LINANTHUS** (*Linanthus parviflorus*): Spring; open places, woods. Leaves appear whorled or clustered. Flowers ¾–1⅜ in. long, about ⁷⁄₁₆ in. across, in headlike clusters; variable in color, lobes may have reddish dots at base. Also called False Babystars. **SIMILAR** ■ **PINK-LOBE LINANTHUS** (*L. androsaceus*): Woods, shrublands, grassy places. Flowers pink; lobes of calyx (united sepals) hairy-edged (calyx hairy overall in Variable Linanthus). Also called False Babystars. ■ **BICOLOR LINANTHUS** (*L. bicolor*): Grassy places, open woods, shrublands. Flowers only ¼ in. across; pink or white, with yellow eye. Also called True Babystars, Bicolor Leptosiphon.

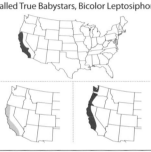

Variable Linanthus

Flowers may be yellow.

Flowers trumpet-shaped, often white. Leaves palmately divided into narrow segments. HT: 2–10 in.

Flowers may be pink or purple.

■ **MUSTANG-CLOVER** (*Linanthus montanus*): Late spring–summer; open woods, dry slopes. Leaves divided into narrow segments that appear whorled or clustered. Flowers 1–1¼ in. long, about ½ in. across, with yellow eye. Bracts beneath flowers slender, conspicuously white-hairy-edged. Also called Mustang Linanthus. **SIMILAR** ■ **WHISKER-BRUSH** (*L. ciliatus*): Spring–early summer. Plants 4–12 in. tall; flowers ½–1 in. long, about ¼ in. across; lobes pink with reddish spot at base. Also called Bristly-leaf Linanthus, Bristly-bract Leptosiphon.

Mustang-clover

Flowers trumpet-shaped, in clusters. HT: 6–24 in.

Lobes sometimes white with purple spot at base.

Lobes often pink with purple spot at base.

■ **NUTTALL'S LINANTHUS** (*Linanthus nuttallii*): Mostly summer; open woods, slopes. Stems woody at base. Leaf segments about ½ in. long. Flowers funnel-shaped, in clusters, stalkless, about ⅜ in. across. Also called Bushy Linanthus.

■ **DESERT-GOLD** (*L. aureus*): Spring; plains, mesas, slopes, washes. Stems wiry. Leaf segments mostly ⅛–¼ in. long. Flowers stalked, funnel-shaped, ⅜–⅝ in. across, typically yellow with darker eye; flowers of less common ssp. *decorus* white with dark eye. Also called Golden Linanthus, Golden-gilia. Do not confuse with yellow-flowered forms of Variable Linanthus (p. 423), which have flowers stalkless and trumpet-shaped.

Nuttall's Linanthus

Flowers white with yellow eye. Leaves divided into narrow segments that appear whorled or clustered. HT: 4–12 in.

Desert-gold

Flowers bright yellow, solitary. Leaves divided into needlelike segments that appear whorled. HT: 2–6 in.

ssp. *decorus*

■ **CALIFORNIA PRICKLY-PHLOX** (*Linanthus californicus*): Spring; slopes, brushy hills, sandhills. Shrubby. Leaves mostly alternate, palmately divided into 5–9 needlelike segments. Flowers ¾–1 in. across, occasionally whitish.

California Prickly-phlox

Flowers generally pink to rose-lilac, trumpet-shaped. Leaves crowded, prickly. HT: 1–3 ft.

■ **GRANITE PRICKLY-PHLOX** (*Linanthus pungens*): Late spring–summer; open places on mountain slopes, rocky alpine regions. Similar to California Prickly-phlox (p. 424), but plants generally shorter; leaf segments 3–7; flowers funnel- (vs. trumpet-) shaped, ½–¾ in. across, usually whitish (sometimes lavender-tinted), or occasionally pale yellow or pinkish. Also called Granite-gilia, Mountain Prickly-phlox.

Granite Prickly-phlox

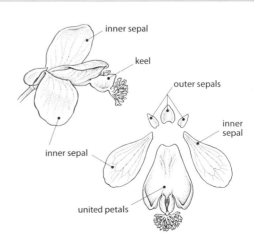

Flowers commonly whitish, funnel-shaped. Leaves crowded, prickly. HT: 4–12 in.

POLYGALACEAE · MILKWORT FAMILY

Annual, biennial, or perennial herbs or woody plants; without milky juice. Leaves usually alternate, sometimes whorled or basal; simple and untoothed. Flowers in clusters or occasionally solitary; flower structure unusual: petals 3, joined below with stamen tube; lower petal boat-shaped (the "keel"), its tip often fringed or lobed; sepals 5, inner 2 (side sepals) largest, petal-like ("wings"); stamens 6–8, their stalks united into a tube split along upper side; pistil 1. Fruits are typically capsules. **NOTE** Do not confuse with legumes bearing typical pealike flowers (p. 224), which have 10 stamens and usually green sepals. Also compare with orchids (p. 371).

MILKWORT FLOWERS

In flowers of the genus *Polygala* (p. 426), the two inner (side) sepals are petal-like, and the three true petals are united below. The lower petal (the "keel") is boat-shaped, with its tip sometimes beaked or fringed.

inner sepal

keel

outer sepals

inner sepal

inner sepal

united petals

■ **WHITE MILKWORT** (*Polygala alba*): Spring–fall; prairies, plains, slopes, roadsides. Leaves alternate. Flowers tiny, white, in slender, tapering clusters.

■ **SENECA-SNAKEROOT** (*P. senega*): Spring–summer; open woods, prairies, swamps. Similar to White Milkwort, but stems sticky-hairy; leaves broader, the upper ones lance-shaped.

■ **WHORLED MILKWORT** (*P. verticillata*): Summer–fall; prairies, open woods. Most leaves whorled. Flowers tiny, white or greenish white, occasionally tinged pinkish or purplish.

Genus *Polygala* (55 species, 54 native). Mostly herbs. Leaves usually alternate. Although called "milkworts," these plants do not have milky juice.

White Milkwort

Leaves linear, very narrow. Stems hairless, wiry. HT: 8–16 in.

Seneca-snakeroot

HT: 4–20 in.

Whorled Milkwort

HT: 4–16 in.

■ **PURPLE MILKWORT** (*Polygala sanguinea*): Spring–fall; open places. Leaves alternate. Flowers tiny, in dense clusters. Also called Blood or Field Milkwort. SIMILAR **CROSS-LEAF MILKWORT** (*P. cruciata*): Pinelands, wet places; eastern. Lower leaves whorled. Also called Drum-heads.

■ **ORANGE MILKWORT** (*P. lutea*): Pinelands, wet places. Leaves alternate.

DWARF MILKWORT (*P. nana*): Pinelands, wet places. Leaves mostly basal. Also called Candyroot.

■ **SHORT PINE BARREN MILKWORT** (*P. ramosa*): Pinelands, wet places. Leaves chiefly alternate. Flowers in branched clusters. Also called Yellow Milkwort.

Purple Milkwort

Flowers often pinkish. HT: 4–16 in.

Orange Milkwort

Flowers orange. HT: 4–16 in.

Dwarf Milkwort

Flowers yellow. HT: to 6 in.

Short Pine Barren Milkwort

Flowers yellow. HT: 4–16 in.

■ **PINK MILKWORT** (*Polygala incarnata*): Summer–fall; woods, fields, meadows, pine savannas. Stems slender. Leaves alternate, sparse, short, very narrow. Flowers many, in crowded clusters. Also called Procession-flower.

■ **GAYWINGS** (*P. paucifolia*): Spring–summer; woods. Leaves few, near stem ends. Flowers 1–4, pale to dark rose-purple (or rarely white); stamens 6. Also called Fringed Milkwort, Flowering-wintergreen.

■ **CALIFORNIA MILKWORT** (*P. californica*): Mostly spring; slopes, shrublands, woods. Stems leafy. Flowers 3–10, rose to pale pink (or rarely white).

Pink Milkwort

Flowers pink to purplish; keel tip (p. 425) conspicuously fringed.
HT: 8–18 in.

Gaywings

Flower wings large, wide-spreading; keel tip conspicuously fringed. HT: 3–6 in.

California Milkwort

Flower wings large, spreading; keel tip mostly blunt.
HT: 2–14 in.

■ **VELVET-SEED MILKWORT** (*Polygala obscura*): Mostly summer; hills, slopes. Leaves alternate, ½–1½ in. long. Flowers purplish; keel tip (see p. 425) blunt.

SIMILAR Flowering spring–fall in similar habitats; also with alternate leaves and purplish flowers; somewhat shrubby at base. ■ **GLAND-LEAF MILKWORT** (*P. macradenia*, no photo): Leaves less than ½ in. long, hairy, conspicuously gland-dotted; flowers 1 or 2 in upper leaf axils. ■ **LINDHEIMER'S MILKWORT** (*P. lindheimeri*): Leaves hairy, ¼–¾ in. long; flower clusters short, loose, with noticeable beak on keel.

Velvet-seed Milkwort

Flowers small, in loose clusters.
HT: 6–18 in.

Lindheimer's Milkwort

Keel tip beaked.
HT: 4–10 in.

POLYGONACEAE   BUCKWHEAT, SMARTWEED, or KNOTWEED FAMILY

Mostly annual, biennial, or perennial herbs, occasionally woody plants. Stems commonly have swollen joints. Leaves usually basal or alternate, less often opposite or whorled; simple. Flowers mostly tiny or small, in clusters; petals and sepals generally alike (and called "tepals"), mostly 4–6; stamens 2–9; pistil 1. Fruits seedlike, 2- or 3-sided, often enclosed in "fruiting flowers" (formed by the persistent, sometimes enlarged tepals) that are sometimes winged.

FLOWERS OF THE GENUS *ERIOGONUM*

A characteristic feature of the genus *Eriogonum* (p. 434) is the presence of an involucre (a conspicuous set of bracts) that surrounds a group of 6–100 flowers; formed of united bracts, each involucre typically has 5–10 teeth or sepal-like lobes.

STIPULAR SHEATHS

In many genera, stipules are present, these typically expanded into a sheath ("ocrea") that wraps around the stem at each node.

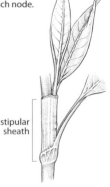

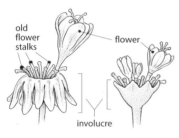

old flower stalks

flower

involucre

fringed stipular sheath

stipular sheath

■ **CANAIGRE** (*Rumex hymenosepalus*): Spring; open, sandy or gravelly places. Leaves mostly near plant base, 5–12 in. long, often twisted or conspicuously wavy. Fruiting flowers (right photo) typically ⁵⁄₁₆–⅝ in. long, winged, reddish to reddish brown. Also called Arizona Dock, Wild-rhubarb, Desert-rhubarb.

■ **VEINY DOCK** (*R. venosus*): Spring–early summer; open, often sandy places. Leaves distributed along stems, mostly 1–6 in. long, flat or somewhat wavy. Fruiting flowers (right photo) typically ⅝–1½ in. long; broadly winged; salmon, red, or deep rose. Also called Winged Dock, Wild-begonia.

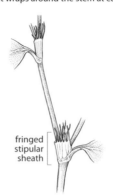

Genus *Rumex* (63 species, 40 native). Leaves alternate, sometimes basal; stipular sheaths (see above) present. Flowers in bunches or whorls along stalks; tepals (petals and similar sepals) usually 6; stamens 6. Fruits seedlike, 3-sided, in enlarged fruiting flowers that are usually 3-winged, sometimes with 1–3 grainlike bumps.

Canaigre

HT: mostly 1–3 ft.

Veiny Dock

HT: 6–18 in.

■ **SWAMP DOCK** (*Rumex verticillatus*): Spring–early summer; wet places. Leaves alternate. Clusters show conspicuous gaps between whorls of flowers. Fruiting flowers winged. Also called Water Dock. Compare introduced docks (p. 592).

■ **HEART-WING SORREL** (*R. hastatulus*): Spring–summer; open places, often sandy soil. Leaves chiefly basal, usually with 2 narrow lobes. Flowers unisexual (plants male or female). Also called Sour Dock, Wild Sorrel. **SIMILAR ①** **SHEEP SORREL** (*R. acetosella*): Widespread; from Eurasia. Fruiting flowers wingless. ■ **ALPINE SHEEP SORREL** (*R. paucifolius*): Spring–fall; mountain meadows. Leaves normally unlobed, lance- to egg-shaped.

Swamp Dock

Flowers greenish, long-stalked. Leaves often lance-shaped. HT: 1–4 ft.

Heart-wing Sorrel

Fruiting flowers reddish, winged. HT: 6 in.–3 ft.

■ **MOUNTAIN-SORREL** (*Oxyria digyna*): Summer; rocky or gravelly places in high mountains, tundra. Leaves basal, long-stalked; blades kidney-shaped to nearly round, somewhat fleshy, palmately veined, green or reddish. Flowers tiny, in dense, elongated clusters; yellowish, green, or reddish. Fruits round, winged, notched at tip; commonly red-tinged or reddish.

Genus *Oxyria* (1 native species). Leaves mostly basal; stipular sheaths (see p. 428) present. Flowers in clusters; tepals (petals and similar sepals) 4; stamens often 6. Fruits seedlike, 2-sided, flattened, broadly winged.

Mountain-sorrel
Fruiting plant. HT: 2–16 in.

■ **COASTAL JOINTWEED** (*Polygonella articulata*): Late summer–fall; sandy places. Stems wiry. Leaves very narrow, sometimes fall early. Flowers whitish, pinkish, or occasionally reddish, often nodding in fruit. Also called Sand or Northern Jointweed. SIMILAR ■ **LARGE-FLOWER JOINTWEED** (*P. robusta*): Edges of inner tepals deeply fringed.

■ **OCTOBER-FLOWER** (*P. polygama*): Pinelands. Wider leaves wedge- or spoon-shaped. Flowers may age yellow; 2 outer tepals become back-bent.

Genus *Polygonella* (11 native species). Stems slender, often look jointed. Leaves alternate. Flowers emerge from axils of papery sheaths; tepals (petals and similar sepals) 5; stamens 8. Fruits seedlike, mostly 3-sided.

Coastal Jointweed

Flowers many, very small. HT: 4–20 in.

October-flower

Flowers whitish or pinkish. HT: 6–24 in.

■ **BEACH KNOTWEED** (*Polygonum paronychia*): Spring–summer; coastal strand, beaches, dunes. Shrubby, commonly spreading. Leaves narrow, 1-veined, with edges curled under; frayed remains of stipular sheaths conspicuous on older stems. Flowers ¼–⅜ in. long; tepals white or pink, with darker midvein. Also called Dune or Black Knotweed.

■ **DOUGLAS' KNOTWEED** (*P. douglasii*): Summer–fall; open, often disturbed places. Leaves narrow; stipular sheaths frayed. Flowers about ⅛ in. long; tepals greenish with whitish or pinkish edges.

NOTE *Polygonum* species are often difficult to tell apart.

Genus *Polygonum* (33 species, 28 native). Leaves usually alternate; stipular sheaths (see p. 428) typically conspicuous, thin, silvery or whitish, not hairy. Flowers generally very small, mostly clustered in leaf axils; tepals (petals and similar sepals) 5; stamens 3–8. Fruits seedlike, mostly 3-sided, partly or wholly enclosed in unwinged fruiting flowers.

Beach Knotweed

Stipular sheath.

Douglas' Knotweed

Flowers and leaves crowded near stem tips. HT: 2–10 in.

Flowers and leaves uncrowded along stems. HT: 4–20 in.

■ **WATER SMARTWEED** (*Persicaria amphibia*): Summer; shallow water, wet shores, moist meadows. Aquatic and terrestrial forms are commonly found. Stipular sheaths (see p. 428) variable: hairy or not, bristle-fringed or not, sometimes with conspicuous horizontal flange on usually nonflowering shoots. Flowers very small, pink, rose, or red; clusters solitary or sometimes 2. Seedlike fruits 2-sided (disk-shaped). **SIMILAR** ⊡ **PRINCE'S-FEATHER** (*P. orientalis*): Moist places; scattered but mostly eastern; from southern Asia. Plants to 8 ft. tall; leaves egg-shaped; flower clusters often drooping.

Genus *Persicaria* (26 species, 15 native). Similar to *Polygonum* (p. 430). Stipular sheaths papery, often tinged brownish, may be hairy or bristle-fringed. Flowers generally in spikelike clusters; tepals (petals and similar sepals) 4 or 5; stamens 5–8. Fruits seedlike, 2- or 3-sided.

Water Smartweed

Floating leaves (aquatic form) elliptic, not hairy.

Flowers in dense, often thickish, spikelike clusters at stem ends. Leaves (land form) lance-shaped, often hairy. HT: mostly 1–3 ft.

■ **PENNSYLVANIA SMARTWEED** (*Persicaria pensylvanica*): Spring–fall; moist or wet places. Leaves lance-shaped, may have dark blotch; stipular sheaths (see p. 428) papery, not fringed. Seedlike fruits mostly 2-sided (disk-shaped). **SIMILAR** ⊡ **LADY'S-THUMB** (*P. maculosa*): Widespread; from Eurasia. Stipular sheaths minutely fringed.

PALE SMARTWEED (*P. lapathifolia*): Spring–fall; widespread. Flowers whitish to pink; veins of outer tepals (petals and sepals) end in anchor-shaped fork.

■ **DOTTED SMARTWEED** (*P. punctata*): Summer–fall. Stipular sheaths fringed with bristles. Flowers whitish, covered with minute dots. Fruits usually 3-sided.

Pennsylvania Smartweed

Flowers whitish to rose-pink; clusters spike-like, usually erect. HT: mostly 6 in.–4 ft.

Pale Smartweed

Flower clusters usually nodding. HT: 6 in.–3 ft.

Dotted Smartweed

Clusters typically show noticeable gaps between flowers. HT: 6 in.–3 ft.

■ **JUMPSEED** (*Persicaria virginiana*):
Summer–fall; woods, thickets. Leaves
broadly lance- to egg-shaped. Early
leaves sometimes have dark blotch on
upper surface; stipular sheaths (see
p. 428) fine-hairy with bristle-fringed
edges, often turn brownish. Flowers
whitish or greenish white, rarely pink-
tinged. Fruiting flowers have 2 persistent,
downward-pointing, hook-tipped styles;
seedlike fruits 2-sided (disk-shaped). Also
called Virginia or Woodland Knotweed.

NOTE Do not confuse with Lopseed
(p. 406).

Jumpseed

Flowers
become
widely spaced
along slender stalks.
HT: mostly 1½–3 ft.

Fruiting
flowers
hook-tipped,
drooping.

■ **ARROW-LEAF TEARTHUMB** (*Persicaria
sagittata*): Summer–fall; moist or often
wet places. Stems 4-angled, weak, leaning
on or intertwined with other plants.
Stipular sheaths (see p. 428) papery, often
tinged brownish. Midvein on underside
of leaf prickly. Flowers tiny, white or pink-
tinged. Seedlike fruits 3-sided. Also called
Arrow-vine.

■ **HALBERD-LEAF TEARTHUMB**
(*P. arifolia*): Midvein on underside of leaf
hairy, not prickly. Seedlike fruits 2-sided
(disk-shaped). **SIMILAR** ▣ **ASIATIC
TEARTHUMB** (*P. perfoliata*): Mostly
eastern; from Asia. Leaves triangular;
stipular sheaths leafy, often cup- or
saucer-shaped; flowers become fleshy
and blue in fruit. Also called Mile-a-
minute-weed.

Arrow-leaf Tearthumb

Flowers in
long-stalked,
headlike clusters.
Stems densely
covered with backward- or
downward-pointing prickles.

Leaves
have
downward-
pointing,
parallel
lobes at base.

Halberd-leaf
Tearthumb

Leaves have
outward-pointing,
spreading lobes at base.

■ **CLIMBING FALSE BUCKWHEAT**
(*Fallopia scandens*): Late summer–fall;
disturbed places, thickets, woods. Stipular
sheaths (see p. 428) papery, smooth
(not bristly). Flowers tiny, in elongated
clusters, greenish or whitish (occasionally
pinkish), becoming strongly 3-winged in
fruit; seedlike fruits dark, smooth, shiny.

■ **FRINGED BLACK-BINDWEED**
(*F. cilinodis*): Late spring–fall. Similar to
Climbing False Buckwheat; stipular sheaths
have downturned bristles at base. Also
called Fringed False Buckwheat. **SIMILAR**
① **BLACK-BINDWEED** (*F. convolvulus*):
Widespread Eurasian introduction.
Stipular sheath bases not bristly; fruiting
flowers keeled (not winged); seedlike
fruits dark, finely granular, dull. Also
called False Buckwheat.

Genus *Fallopia* (8 species, 2 native).
Similar to *Persicaria* (p. 431). Flowers
have 5 tepals (petals and similar sepals).
Fruits seedlike, 3-sided, enclosed in enlarged fruiting
flowers that are either 3-keeled or 3-winged.

Climbing False Buckwheat

Leaves heart-shaped. Twining vine.

Fruiting flowers have smooth-edged or frilly wings.

Fringed Black-bindweed

Fruiting flowers narrowly keeled (ridged).

■ **AMERICAN BISTORT** (*Bistorta
bistortoides*): Summer; moist mountain
meadows and stream banks, alpine
slopes. Leaves chiefly basal, lance-shaped
to elliptic, long-stalked; stem leaves
smaller, stalkless. Flower clusters ⅜–1 in.
thick, 3 times or less as long as wide; flowers very small, occasionally pale pink;
stamens conspicuous. Also called Western
Bistort. Do not confuse with Diamond-
leaf Saxifrage (p. 507), which has leaves all
basal, without sheaths, diamond-shaped,
toothed; flowering stalk hairy.

■ **ALPINE BISTORT** (*B. vivipara*): Summer;
woods, meadows, slopes, tundra. Flowers
white or pinkish, in clusters 3⁄16–⅜ in. thick,
more than 3 times as long as wide; lower
flowers often replaced by tiny, pinkish
to purplish bulbs. Also called Viviparous
Knotweed, Serpent-grass.

Genus *Bistorta* (4 species, 3 native).
Similar to *Persicaria* (p. 431). Leaves
mostly basal, the leafstalk bases long-
sheathing (wrapping around stem), with the (often
darker) stipular sheath above them. Flowers have 5 tepals
(petals and similar sepals). Fruits seedlike, 3-sided.

American Bistort

Alpine Bistort

Flowers usually white, in dense, short-cylindric to ball-shaped clusters.
HT: 6–24 in.

Flowers in more slender clusters.
HT: 4–12 in.

■ **ALPINE KNOTWEED** (*Aconogonon phytolaccifolium*): Summer; mountain meadows and woods, rocky slopes. Leaves 2–6 in. long, elliptic to triangular-egg-shaped, mostly pointed; stipular sheaths (see p. 428) reddish brown. Flowers tiny, whitish. Also called Poke Knotweed, Alpine Fleece-flower.

■ **DAVIS' KNOTWEED** (*A. davisiae*): Rocky slopes. Leaves ¾–3 in. long, mostly lance-shaped and blunt; stipular sheaths reddish brown. Flowers tiny or very small, greenish white to pinkish white. Also called Newberry's Knotweed.

Genus *Aconogonon* (3 native species). Similar to *Persicaria* (p. 431). Flowers distinctly stalked, in clusters; tepals (petals and similar sepals) 5; stamens 8. Fruits seedlike, 3-sided.

Alpine Knotweed

Davis' Knotweed

Flowers in open, branched clusters along upper stems. HT: mostly 2–6 ft.

Flowers in small clusters in leaf axils. HT: 6–18 in.

■ **SANDHILL WILD-BUCKWHEAT** (*Eriogonum tomentosum*): Summer–fall; sandhills, sandy pinelands, open woods. Leaves basal and whorled, elliptic to spoon-shaped, light brown-hairy to white-hairy beneath. Flowers brownish-hairy outside. Also called Southern Wild-buckwheat, Dog-tongue.

■ **ANNUAL WILD-BUCKWHEAT** (*E. annuum*): Spring–fall; open, often grassy places. Stems hairy. Basal leaves often wither early; stem leaves alternate, conspicuously soft-white-hairy, especially beneath. Flowers tiny, in open, sometimes flat-topped sprays; white but occasionally pinkish, drying reddish brown.

Genus *Eriogonum* (224 native species). Herbs or shrubs. Stipular sheaths (see p. 428) absent. Flowers surrounded by an involucre (p. 428), the overall "cluster" comprised of usually many involucres; tepals (petals and similar sepals) typically 6; stamens 9. Fruits seedlike, 2- or 3-sided.

Sandhill Wild-buckwheat

Annual Wild-buckwheat

Flowers cream-colored to pinkish, in open clusters. HT: 1–3 ft.

HT: 1½–4 ft.

■ **CUSHION WILD-BUCKWHEAT** (*Eriogonum ovalifolium*): Spring–summer; deserts, plains, shrublands, woods, rocky slopes. Plants generally mound-forming. A variable species. Leaves in a dense basal cluster, often long-stalked; blades relatively small, elliptic, spoon-shaped, or rounded. Flowers white to pinkish or purplish or yellowish. Also called Oval-leaf Wild-buckwheat.

Cushion Wild-buckwheat

Flowers small, in ball-like clusters on leafless stalks. HT: 2–12 in.

Leaves typically densely silvery or white-woolly.

■ **SULPHUR-FLOWER WILD-BUCKWHEAT** (*Eriogonum umbellatum*): Spring–fall; open woods, shrublands, grasslands, slopes. A highly variable species with more than 3 dozen named varieties, some dwarf and mat-forming, others erect shrubs. Leaves basal; egg-shaped, elliptic, or spoon-shaped; often whitish-hairy beneath. Leafless stalks end in whorl of leafy bracts, above them several tight clusters of small flowers in umbrella-like arrangement (umbel). Flowers not hairy outside, sometimes age rose, reddish, or orange.

SIMILAR ■ **YELLOW WILD-BUCKWHEAT** (*E. flavum*): Summer; plains, hills, slopes. Flowers densely hairy outside. Also called Alpine Golden Wild-buckwheat.

Sulphur-flower Wild-buckwheat

Flower clusters above a whorl of leaflike bracts on leafless stalks. Flowers usually yellow. HT: mostly 6–18 in.

Leaves in basal clusters.

Flowers may be cream-colored.

■ **DESERT-TRUMPET** (*Eriogonum inflatum*): Year-round; desert slopes, washes, flats. Stems grayish or bluish green, commonly (but not always) conspicuously inflated. Leaves basal, stalked; blades oval to kidney-shaped, often wrinkly. Flowers yellow, hairy outside. Also called Indian-pipeweed, Bladderstem.

Desert-trumpet

Flowers tiny, in open clusters. Main branches attached umbrella-like to stem. HT: mostly 6 in.–3 ft.

■ **THYME-LEAF WILD-BUCKWHEAT** (*Eriogonum thymoides*): Spring–early summer; slopes, shrublands, open woods. Somewhat shrubby. Leaves mostly in tufts toward plant base; very small and narrow; hairy, especially beneath. Flowers small; pale yellow or cream-colored, aging pinkish; hairy outside.

■ **MATTED WILD-BUCKWHEAT** (*E. caespitosum*): Slopes, grasslands, shrublands, open woods. Leaves basal and densely matted, very small, conspicuously white-hairy. Flowers small, yellow or reddish, densely hairy outside.

Thyme-leaf Wild-buckwheat

Flowers in compact clusters. Whorl of leaflike bracts on midstem. HT: 3–10 in.

Matted Wild-buckwheat

Flowers in compact clusters on bractless stalks. HT: to 4 in.

■ **PINK SPINEFLOWER** (*Chorizanthe membranacea*): Spring–early summer; slopes, grassy places, shrublands, open woods. Leaves alternate and basal, hairy beneath. Flowers tiny, hairy; surrounding funnel-shaped membranous cup (involucre) has 6 teeth with hook-tipped bristles. Also called Clustered Spineflower.

■ **TURKISH-RUGGING** (*C. staticoides*): Rocky and grassy hills, shrublands, open woods. Leaves mostly basal. Flowers tiny, rose to reddish; surrounding reddish tube (involucre) has 6 bristle-tipped teeth.

■ **FRINGED SPINEFLOWER** (*C. fimbriata*): Similar to Turkish-rugging, including season and habitat. Flowers small, fringed, with yellow at base and white to rose above, darkening in age.

Genus *Chorizanthe* (33 native species). Leaves basal or alternate. Similar to *Eriogonum* (p. 434), but teeth of involucre tipped with slender bristles or spines; flowers single (rarely 2) in each involucre (which thus mimics a narrow-lobed calyx); stamens 3–9.

Pink Spineflower

Flowers white to rose. Leaves narrow. HT: mostly 6–24 in.

Turkish-rugging

HT: 2–24 in.

Fringed Spineflower
HT: 4–14 in.

■ **ROUND-LEAF PUNCTUREBRACT** (*Oxytheca perfoliata*): Spring–summer; desert slopes, flats, washes. Plants sometimes reddish or purplish. Leaves spoon-shaped, hairless except on edges. Leaflike bracts circular to broadly triangular, with 3 bristles, appear pierced by stem. Flowers tiny, sometimes yellowish green or pinkish; surrounding cuplike involucre has 4 slender spines. Also called Saucer-plant.

■ **TREE-LIKE PUNCTUREBRACT** (*O. dendroidea*): Summer–fall; slopes, shrublands, open woods. Leaves hairy, very narrow. Bracts scalelike to leaflike, linear to triangular.

Genus *Oxytheca* (3 native species). Leaves basal. Differs from *Eriogonum* (p. 434) in that lobes of involucre are bristle- or spine-tipped; differs from *Chorizanthe* (above) in having 2–10 flowers per involucre (vs. 1 or rarely 2).

Round-leaf Puncturebract
Flowers often whitish. Conspicuous, saucer-shaped, leaflike bracts. HT: 3–8 in.

Flowers 5–10 per involucre.

Tree-like Puncturebract

Flowers whitish or pinkish. HT: 2–16 in.

PONTEDERIACEAE
PICKEREL-WEED FAMILY

Annual or perennial; aquatic, free-floating or rooted in mud. Leaves mostly basal or alternate; simple and untoothed. Flowers solitary or in clusters; 6 tepals (3 petals and 3 petal-like sepals), mostly united below; stamens 3 or 6; pistil 1. Fruits are generally capsules or nutlets.

■ **BLUE MUD-PLANTAIN** (*Heteranthera limosa*): Spring–fall; muddy pond or lake edges, ditches, shallow water. Leaves egg-shaped to elliptic. Flowers solitary.

■ **KIDNEY-LEAF MUD-PLANTAIN** (*H. reniformis*): Summer–fall. Leaves round-kidney-shaped. Flowers in clusters of 3–10, white to pale blue.

■ **WATER STAR-GRASS** (*H. dubia*): Spring–fall. Stems floating or creeping. Leaves ribbonlike. Flowers solitary, yellow. Also called Grass-leaf Mud-plantain.

Genus *Heteranthera* (7 native species). Underwater and floating leaves stalkless, ribbon- or grasslike; above-water leaves stalked, with broad blade. Flowers have slender tube, 6 equal or unequal lobes; stamens 3.

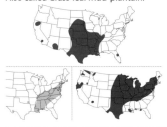

Blue Mud-plantain

Flowers commonly purple-blue, sometimes white. HT: 1–9 in.

Kidney-leaf Mud-plantain

HT: 1–4 in.

Water Star-grass

■ **PICKEREL-WEED** (*Pontederia cordata*): Spring–fall; marsh, pond, and lake margins, shallow water. Leaves vary from broadly heart-shaped (4½ in. wide) to narrowly lance-shaped (¾ in. wide); leafstalks very long. Flowers in dense clusters; upper middle lobe spotted greenish yellow.

NOTE See also Ⅰ Water-hyacinth (p. 592), a free-floating plant with inflated leafstalks. When not in flower, the often heart-shaped, blunt-lobed leaf bases distinguish Pickerel-weed from arrow-arums (p. 74) and arrowheads (p. 52), which have generally sharper-lobed leaves and different vein patterns.

Genus *Pontederia* (1 native species). Leaves mostly arise from plant base. Flowers in clusters; tubular at base and 2-lipped: upper lip with 3 partially united lobes, lower lip with 3 free lobes; stamens 6.

Pickerel-weed

Flowers violet-blue (or rarely whitish). Leaves heart-, arrow-, or lance-shaped. HT: 1–3 ft.

PORTULACACEAE
PURSLANE FAMILY

Annual, biennial, or perennial; frequently succulent. Leaves basal, opposite, or alternate; simple. Flowers solitary or in clusters; petals 2–19 (mostly 4–6); sepals 2–9 (often 2); stamens 1 to many; pistil 1. Fruits are capsules. **NOTE** Many species have 2 sepals, a useful identification feature for the family.

■ **SPRING-BEAUTY** (*Claytonia virginica*): Spring; woods, thickets, clearings, roadsides, lawns. Basal leaves usually 0–2; stem leaves ¹⁄₁₆–³⁄₈ in. wide. Petals white or pink, often with darker veins.

■ **CAROLINA SPRING-BEAUTY** (*C. caroliniana*): Woods. Basal leaves 6–21; stem leaves ⁷⁄₁₆–1 in. wide. **SIMILAR**
■ **WESTERN SPRING-BEAUTY** (*C. lanceolata*): Moist open places, slopes. Basal leaves 1–6, often wither early; stem leaves stalkless. Flowers rarely yellow to orange. Also called Lance-leaf Spring-beauty.

Genus *Claytonia* (25 native species). Often succulent. Leaves mostly basal; a single opposite pair (occasionally fused) on stem. Flowers in clusters; petals 5; stamens 5; sepals 2.

Spring-beauty

Carolina Spring-beauty

Stem leaves narrow, tapering gradually to base. HT: mostly 3–10 in.

Stem leaves broader, distinctly stalked. HT: 3–8 in.

■ **CANDY-FLOWER** (*Claytonia sibirica*): Early spring–summer; moist woods, meadows, thickets, stream banks. Basal leaves stalked, lance-shaped to elliptic; stem leaves stalkless. Mature flower clusters have small leaflike bracts at base of each flower stalk; petals usually notched, white or pink with darker pink veins. Also called Siberian Spring-beauty, Siberian Miner's-lettuce.

■ **HEART-LEAF SPRING-BEAUTY** (*C. cordifolia*): Late spring–summer; wet meadows, stream banks, seeps. Basal leaves stalked, broadly heart-shaped to nearly round; stem leaves stalkless. Flower clusters lack bracts; petals commonly notched. Also called Cordate-leaf Spring-beauty.

Candy-flower

Petals have pink veins. HT: 5–16 in.

Heart-leaf Spring-beauty

Petals white. HT: 4–12 in.

■ **ALPINE SPRING-BEAUTY** (*Claytonia megarhiza*): Summer; gravelly and rocky high slopes. Basal leaves to 1 in. wide. Petals commonly notched, white to deep pink. Also called Fell-fields Claytonia.

■ **SERPENTINE SPRING-BEAUTY** (*C. exigua*): Spring; woods, shrublands, bluffs, slopes. Basal leaves ¼ in. or less wide; stem leaves 2, stalkless, united around stem as a round to squarish disk (ssp. *glauca*), or free or joined at base and appearing 2-lobed (ssp. *exigua*, pictured). Petals ¹⁄₁₆–¼ in. long, commonly notched. Also called Pale Claytonia, Big-root Spring-beauty. **SIMILAR** ■ **GYPSUM SPRING-BEAUTY** (*C. gypsophiloides*): Petals pink or white, ¼–³⁄₈ in. long. Also called Coast Range Claytonia.

Alpine Spring-beauty

Petals mostly white to pale pink. Basal leaves fleshy, spoon-shaped. HT: 2–10 in.

Serpentine Spring-beauty

Petals white to pale pink, sometimes rose-tinged. Basal leaves grayish, fleshy, narrow. HT: 2–5 in.

■ **MINER'S-LETTUCE** (*Claytonia perfoliata*): Spring; woods, shrublands, roadsides. Basal leaves long-stalked; blades triangular, elliptic, or kidney-shaped, ¼–2 in. wide, very broad at base (abruptly contracting to leafstalk). Flowers white or sometimes pinkish; petals sometimes notched. **SIMILAR** ■ **NARROW-LEAF MINER'S-LETTUCE** (*C. parviflora* ssp. *parviflora*): Woods, rocky areas, disturbed places. Basal leaves ribbonlike to very narrowly spoon-shaped, about ⅛ in. wide, gradually tapering to leafstalk. Also called Stream-bank Spring-beauty, Indian-lettuce.

Miner's-lettuce

Flowers small, in clusters. Stem leaves (inset) united into a "cup" or "saucer" that appears to be pierced by stem. HT: 3–16 in.

■ **CHAMISSO'S MONTIA** (*Montia chamissoi*): Late spring–summer; wet places. Leaves opposite, fleshy. Flowers white to pinkish, small; petals about ⅛ in. long. Also called Toad-lily.

■ **SMALL-LEAF MONTIA** (*M. parvifolia*): Late spring–midsummer; moist slopes, seeps, woods, stream banks. Leaves spoon-shaped, fleshy, basal and alternate. Flowers pink or white; petals ¼–½ in. long. Also called Little-leaf Montia.

■ **NARROW-LEAF MONTIA** (*M. linearis*): Spring; woods, shrublands, meadows. Leaves narrow, fleshy, stalkless, alternate. Flowers white; petals about ¼ in. long.

Genus *Montia* (8 native species). Similar to *Claytonia* (p. 439); differs most obviously in having more than 2 stem leaves that are always free (not fused into a disk). Sepals 2.

Chamisso's Montia

Leaves lance-, egg-, or spoon-shaped. HT: 2–12 in.

Small-leaf Montia

HT: 4–12 in.

Narrow-leaf Montia

HT: 2–12 in.

■ **RED-MAIDS** (*Calandrinia ciliata*): Spring; open places. Leaves somewhat fleshy, linear to spoon-shaped. Flowers in axils of leaflike bracts; petals ³⁄₁₆–½ in. long; stamens 3–15. Capsules nearly enclosed by fruiting calyx (sepals). Also called Fringed Red-maids. **SIMILAR BREWER'S RED-MAIDS** (*C. breweri*): Chiefly coastal CA. Petals ⅛–¼ in. long; stamens 3–6. Capsules longer than fruiting calyx.

Genus *Calandrinia* (2 native species). Plants more or less succulent. Leaves alternate. Flowers in loose, elongated clusters (usually only 1 per stalk in bloom at a time); petals 5; sepals 2; stamens 3–15.

Red-maids

Flowers occasionally pale or white.

Flowers usually rose-violet to rose-red. HT: to 6 in.

■ **LARGE-FLOWER FAMEFLOWER**
(*Phemeranthus calycinus*): Spring–fall; rock
outcrops, rocky soil. Leaves fleshy, narrow,
cylindrical, crowded near plant base.
Petals about ½ in. long; stamens 25–45.
Also called Rock-pink Fameflower.

■ **SUNBRIGHT** (*P. parviflorus*): Open
woods, shrublands, grasslands, slopes.
Petals about ¼ in. long; stamens 4–8.
Also called Prairie Fameflower. SIMILAR
■ **QUILL FAMEFLOWER** (*P. teretifolius*):
Rocky places. Plants to 15 in. tall; flowers
deep pink; stamens mostly 12–20. Also
called Appalachian Fameflower, Rock-
portulaca.

NOTE *Phemeranthus* species are also
called flameflower and false fameflower.

Genus *Phemeranthus* (16 native species).
Plants succulent. Leaves alternate or
nearly opposite, sometimes crowded
near plant base, usually round in cross section (rarely flat).
Flowers solitary or in clusters; petals mostly 5; sepals 2
(often fall early); stamens 4 to many.

Large-flower Fameflower

Sunbright

Flowers light pink to
purplish, rarely nearly
whitish. HT: to 8 in.

Flowers
rose-pink
to magenta,
clustered at ends
of wiry, leafless
stalks. HT: to 15 in.

■ **PYGMY FAMEFLOWER** (*Phemeranthus
brevifolius*): Summer–fall; hills, ledges,
slopes. Leaves ¼–½ in. long. Flowers 1–3
in leaf axils; petals ¼–⅜ in. long, rarely
whitish; stamens 20–25; stigmas 3. Also
called Club-leaf Fameflower.
SIMILAR ■ **SHOWY FAMEFLOWER**
(*P. brevicaulis*): Spring–summer; ridges,
canyons, slopes. Leaves ½–1 in. long;
petals about ½ in. long, rose-pink to
purple-red; stigma solitary. Also called
Dwarf Fameflower.

Pygmy Fameflower

Flowers
mostly rose-
pink to lavender,
on short stalks.
Leaves crowded
near plant base, fleshy,
cylindrical. HT: 1–3 in.

ORANGE FAMEFLOWER
(*Phemeranthus aurantiacus*): Spring–fall;
slopes, plains, desert washes and flats.
Leaves alternate, fleshy, linear to narrowly
lance-shaped; the flat leaves are unusual
for the genus. Flowers 1–3 in leaf axils,
showy, commonly orange or red-tinged
orange, but sometimes yellow-orange or
yellow; stamens many.

Orange Fameflower
Flowers frequently orange.
Leaves along stems, nearly
stalkless, the wider ones
flat. HT: 4–20 in.

COPPER PURSLANE (*Portulaca
suffrutescens*): Spring–summer; slopes,
flats, roadsides. Leaf axils sometimes
conspicuously hairy. Flowers ¾–1 in.
across; petals notched; stamens 25–35.
Also called Shrubby Purslane.

PINK PURSLANE (*P. pilosa*): Spring–fall;
open places. Stems often trailing, with
upturned branches. Leaves cylindrical
to somewhat flattened; leaf axils often
hairy. Flowers ¼–½ in. across; petals
notched to short-tipped; stamens
5–35 (mostly 5–12). Also called Shaggy
Purslane, Kiss-me-quick. SIMILAR South
American introductions. ⊞ ROSE-MOSS
(*P. grandiflora*): Eastern. Flowers 1–2 in.
across. ⊞ BROAD-LEAF PINK PURSLANE
(*P. amilis*): FL and adjacent Southeast.
Leaves flattened, spoon-shaped. Also
called Paraguayan Purslane.

Genus *Portulaca* (10 species, 6 native).
Plants succulent. Leaves alternate or
nearly opposite, some crowded just
beneath flowers. Flowers in clusters or sometimes solitary,
stalkless; petals 5–7; sepals 2; stamens mostly 6–40.

Copper Purslane

Flowers orange or coppery.
Leaves fleshy, very narrow,
cylindrical. HT: 6–12 in.

Pink Purslane

Flowers deep
pink to purplish.
Leaves fleshy,
very narrow.
HT: 2–8 in.

■ **SILK-COTTON PURSLANE** (*Portulaca halimoides*): Spring–early fall; sandy places. Leaf axils sometimes distinctly hairy. Flowers about ¼ in. across; stamens 4–18. Also called Sinker-leaf Purslane, Desert Portulaca.

■ **WING-POD PURSLANE** (*P. umbraticola* ssp. *lanceolata*): Late spring–early fall; prairies, plains, thickets, rocky slopes, roadsides. Leaf axils usually inconspicuously hairy. Flowers ⁵⁄₁₆–½ in. across; stamens 7–30. Fruits (see inset) have circular wing. Also called Crown-pod Purslane, Chinese-hat.

NOTE See also ① Common Purslane (p. 593).

Silk-cotton Purslane

Flowers small, yellow. Leaves very narrow, fleshy, cylindrical. HT: 2–5 in.

Wing-pod Purslane

Flowers rose or orange-red, with yellowish center. Leaves fleshy, flattened, often spoon-shaped. HT: 3–8 in.

■ **BITTERROOT** (*Lewisia rediviva*): Early spring–early summer; open, rocky or gravelly places. Flowers solitary, mostly 1½–2½ in. across; sepals 6–9; stamens 20–50; stigmas 4–9. Whorl of small bracts on flower stalks. Also called Oregon Bitterroot.

■ **ALPINE LEWISIA** (*L. pygmaea*): Late spring–late summer; slopes. Flowers solitary or in clusters of 2–4, to ¾ in. across; sepals 2; stamens 5–8; stigmas 3–6. Pair of small bracts on flower stalks. Also called Least Lewisia, Pygmy Bitterroot. **SIMILAR** ■ **NEVADA LEWISIA** (*L. nevadensis*): Sepal edges mostly untoothed (vs. usually toothed). Also called Nevada Bitterroot.

Genus *Lewisia* (16 native species). Plants fleshy. Leaves mostly basal. Flowers solitary or in clusters, on stalks with 2–9 small bracts; petals 5–19; sepals 2–9; stamens 1–50. Sepals usually 2 but often appear to be more because of bracts.

Bitterroot

Flowers sometimes white.

Flowers larger; petals 10–19, mostly rose-pink. Leaves basal, fleshy, cylindrical. HT: 1–3 in.

Alpine Lewisia

Flowers small; petals 5–9, pink or white. Leaves basal, fleshy, somewhat flattened. HT: 1–3 in.

■ **SISKIYOU LEWISIA** (*Lewisia cotyledon*): Spring–summer; slopes, rock crevices. Leaves basal, fleshy, spoon-shaped. Petals 7–10, each ½–¾ in. long; stamens 5–12. Also called Cliff-maids. **SIMILAR**

■ **COLUMBIAN LEWISIA** (*L. columbiana*): Petals ¼–½ in. long; stamens 5 or 6.

■ **SHORT-SEPAL LEWISIA** (*L. brachycalyx*): Mountain meadows. Flowers solitary, stalkless; petals ½–1 in. long; stamens 9–15.

■ **THREE-LEAF LEWISIA** (*L. triphylla*): Slopes, meadows, open woods. Basal leaves wither early; stem leaves narrow, 2 or 3. Petals to ¼ in. long; stamens 3–5.

NOTE Lewisias are also called bitterroot.

Siskiyou Lewisia

Flowers in clusters, pinkish with white edges, or sometimes mostly whitish. HT: mostly 4–10 in.

Short-sepal Lewisia
HT: 1–3 in.

Three-leaf Lewisia
HT: 1–4 in.

■ **PUSSYPAWS** (*Cistanthe umbellata*): Spring–fall; open places. Stems prostrate to nearly erect. Leaves basal, spoon-shaped, somewhat fleshy. Petals 4, very small, withering. The pinkish or whitish, papery sepals persist and conspicuously enlarge. Also called Mt. Hood Pussypaws.

Genus *Cistanthe* (11 native species). Leaves basal or alternate. Flower clusters generally 1-sided, above often unequal, papery bracts; petals 2–4; sepals 2, papery along edges or throughout; stamens mostly 1–3.

Pussypaws

Flower clusters dense, pinkish or whitish. HT: 3–15 in.

PRIMULACEAE   PRIMROSE FAMILY

Annual or perennial. Leaves mostly opposite or basal (occasionally whorled or alternate); simple. Flowers solitary or in clusters; petals usually 5 (rarely 0), united (at least at very base); sepals 5, united below; stamens usually 5, each directly opposite (in front of) a petal lobe; pistil 1. Fruits are capsules.

■ **ROCKY MOUNTAIN DWARF-PRIMROSE** (*Douglasia montana*): Spring–summer; rocky places in mountains. Also called Mountain Douglasia.

■ **CLIFF DWARF-PRIMROSE** (*D. laevigata*): Leaves generally hairless. Flowers nearly stalkless. Also called Smooth-leaf Douglasia. **SIMILAR** ■ **SNOW DWARF-PRIMROSE** (*D. nivalis*): Leaves finely gray-hairy; flowers stalked.

NOTE See also Moss Campion (p. 196), with stamens and style protruding; and cushion-forming phlox species (p. 410), normally with (opposite) stem leaves.

Genus *Douglasia* (9 native species). Plants cushion-forming. Leaves crowded. Flowers narrowly funnel-shaped, 5-lobed.

Rocky Mountain Dwarf-primrose
Flowers pink to rose-violet, with yellow eye, usually solitary. Leaves narrowly lance-shaped. HT: to 2 in.

Cliff Dwarf-primrose
Flowers pink, deep rose, or reddish, in clusters of 2–10, nearly stalkless. HT: to 3 in.

■ **PARRY'S PRIMROSE** (*Primula parryi*): Summer; mountain meadows, stream banks. Plants ill-scented. Flowers in clusters; lobes broad. Several similar western species.

■ **LAKE MISTASSINI PRIMROSE** (*P. mistassinica*): Midspring–early summer; meadows, fens, rocks, cliffs, shores. Flower lobes narrower. Also called Bird's-eye Primrose.

■ **SIERRAN PRIMROSE** (*P. suffrutescens*): Summer; rocky cliffs, crevices. Leaves spatula-shaped, with toothed tip. Flowers 2 to several, magenta with yellow eye.

Genus *Primula* (20 species, 19 native). Leaves clustered at plant base. Flowers in often umbrella-like clusters (umbels); narrowly funnel- to trumpet-shaped, with 5 often notched lobes; mostly pink, violet, or white.

Parry's Primrose

Lake Mistassini Primrose
Flowers lilac to pink, with yellow eye. HT: to 10 in.

Flowers magenta with yellow eye. Leaves basal, elongated. HT: 4–20 in.

Sierran Primrose

HT: to 5 in.

■ **SWEET-FLOWER ROCK-JASMINE**
(*Androsace chamaejasme*): Mostly
summer; rocky places at high elevations.
Usually 1 conspicuously hairy flowering
stem per leaf cluster. Flower clusters
crowded. Also called Alpine Rock-jasmine.

■ **PYGMY-FLOWER ROCK-JASMINE**
(*A. septentrionalis*): Spring–summer;
slopes, meadows, open woods. Several
flowering stems per leaf cluster. Flower
clusters more open.

SIMILAR ■ **WESTERN ROCK-JASMINE**
(*A. occidentalis*): Tiny bracts at base of
flower cluster egg-shaped (vs. narrow).

NOTE Some rock-jasmines are also called
fairy-candelabra.

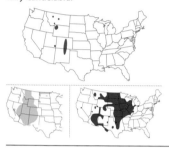

 Genus *Androsace* (5 native species).
Leaves clustered at plant base. Flowers
in umbrella-like clusters (umbels),
tubular-bell- to trumpet-shaped, 5-lobed.

Sweet-flower Rock-jasmine

Flowers small, cream-colored with yellow eye that ages pinkish. Leaves basal; edges hairy-fringed. HT: to 4 in.

Pygmy-flower Rock-jasmine

Flowers tiny, white. Leaves basal; edges irregularly toothed. HT: to 10 in.

■ **EASTERN SHOOTING-STAR**
(*Dodecatheon meadia*): Spring–summer;
open woods, prairies, meadows. Leaves
basal, elliptic to spoon-shaped. Flower
lobes swept back. Capsule (fruit) walls
thick.

■ **WESTERN SHOOTING-STAR**
(*D. pulchellum*): Meadows, open woods,
slopes. Capsule walls thin, flexible. Also
called Few-flower Shooting-star.

NOTE Several similar species.

 Genus *Dodecatheon* (17 native species).
Leaves arise from plant base. Flowers in
umbrella-like clusters (umbels); parts in
4s or 5s; lobes strongly curved backward; stamens and
style protruding.

Eastern Shooting-star

Flowers nodding, white to lavender or pink. HT: to 2 ft.

Western Shooting-star

Flowers magenta to lavender. HT: to 2 ft.

■ **STARFLOWER** (*Trientalis borealis* ssp. *borealis*): Spring–summer; woods, bogs, swamps. Leaves clustered in a whorl at top of stem; stem nearly leafless below. Flower stalks mostly shorter than leaves. Also called Maystar.

■ **WESTERN STARFLOWER** (*T. borealis* ssp. *latifolia*): Woods, prairies. Similar to Starflower, but flowers generally pink to rose, sometimes pale. Also called Broadleaf Starflower.

■ **ARCTIC STARFLOWER** (*T. europaea* ssp. *arctica*, no photo): Bogs, swamps. A few small leaves on stem below main whorl. Flowers white, on stalks mostly longer than main leaves.

 Genus *Trientalis* (2 native species). Leaves in a whorl of 3–10 at stem top. Flowers 1 to few on slender stalks above leaves, saucer-shaped and 6- or 7-lobed; stamens 6 or 7.

Starflower

Flowers white. Leaves lance-shaped, in single whorl. HT: 4–8 in.

Western Starflower

Flowers usually pink. Leaves egg-shaped, in single whorl. HT: 4–10 in.

■ **WATER-PIMPERNEL** (*Samolus valerandi* ssp. *parviflorus*): Spring–fall; wet soil, shallow water, stream banks, brackish marshes. Flowers tiny, white; lobes longer than tube. Also called Brookweed.

■ **COAST WATER-PIMPERNEL** (*S. ebracteatus*): Flowers small, white or pinkish; lobes shorter than tube. Also called Limewater Brookweed.

Genus *Samolus* (3 native species). Leaves basal and alternate, commonly spoon-shaped with rounded tip. Flowers in elongated clusters, somewhat bell-shaped, 5-lobed; stamens 5.

Water-pimpernel

Some stem leaves extend into flower cluster. HT: 6–24 in.

Coast Water-pimpernel

Leaves mostly on lower half of plant. HT: 6–24 in.

■ **SEA-MILKWORT** (*Glaux maritima*): Mostly summer; salt marshes, alkaline or saline soil. Leaves short, fleshy, narrow. Flowers solitary in leaf axils.

Genus *Glaux* (1 native species). Plants fleshy. Leaves opposite (or upper leaves alternate). Petals absent; sepals united, forming bell-shaped calyx with 5 petal-like lobes.

Sea-milkwort
Flowers small, reddish or pinkish to white. HT: to 16 in.

■ **FEATHERFOIL** (*Hottonia inflata*): Spring–summer; quiet water. Leaves mostly near water surface. Flowers in tiered whorls around constrictions on stalk; flowering stalk elongated, hollow, swollen. Also called Water-violet.

Genus *Hottonia* (1 native species). Aquatic; main plant body floating. Leaves pinnately divided into threadlike segments. Flowers above sepal-like bracts; sepals 5, united at base, longer than the 5 petals.

Featherfoil
Flowers small, white. Leaves feathery. HT: to 12 in.

■ **FRINGED LOOSESTRIFE** (*Lysimachia ciliata*): Late spring–summer; moist or wet ground. Leaves egg-shaped; leafstalk edges have minute fringe of hairs.
SIMILAR LANCE-LEAF LOOSESTRIFE (*L. lanceolata*): Meadows, prairies, woods; eastern. Leaves lance-shaped, tapering to short-stalked or stalkless base.

■ **NARROW-LEAF LOOSESTRIFE** (*L. quadriflora*): Summer; wet places. Leaves opposite, narrow, stalkless; 1 main vein; edges often rolled inward.

■ **WHORLED LOOSESTRIFE** (*L. quadrifolia*): Summer; open woods, thickets. Leaves lance-shaped, in whorls of 3–7.

NOTE Loosestrifes are also called yellow-loosestrife.

 Genus *Lysimachia* (18 species, 13 native). Leaves usually opposite or whorled. Flowers solitary or in clusters, saucer- or star-shaped, mostly yellow, often with reddish eye. Some species have reddish to dark purple spots or streaks on flowers and leaves.

Fringed Loosestrife

Narrow-leaf Loosestrife
HT: 1–3 ft.

Whorled Loosestrife
HT: 1–3 ft.

Flowers arching or nodding on long stalks from leaf axils. Leaves opposite, broad, stalked. HT: 1–3 ft.

■ **TUFTED LOOSESTRIFE** (*Lysimachia thyrsiflora*): Late spring–summer; swamps, boggy places. Leaves opposite. Flowers have narrow lobes, conspicuous stamens.

■ **SWAMP-CANDLES** (*L. terrestris*): Swamps, wet shores. Leaves opposite. Late-season plants may have red bulblets in leaf axils. Also called Bulbil-loosestrife.

NOTE See also introduced yellow loosestrifes (p. 593).

Tufted Loosestrife
Flowers in short, dense, stalked clusters from leaf axils.
HT: 1–2½ ft.

Swamp-candles
Flowers in elongated clusters at stem ends.
HT: 1–3 ft.

PYROLACEAE
SHINLEAF or WINTERGREEN FAMILY

Perennial; usually evergreen. Leaves basal, alternate, opposite, or whorled; simple, frequently shiny. Flowers solitary or in clusters; petals 5, commonly waxy; sepals 5; stamens 10, opening by small pores at anther tips; pistil 1. Fruits are capsules. Usually included in the heath family (Ericaceae).

■ ONE-FLOWER WINTERGREEN

(*Moneses uniflora*): Late spring–summer; woods, swamps, boggy places. Leaves roundish, in 2s or 3s near plant base. Flower parts normally in 5s, occasionally in 4s. Stalks become erect in fruit. Also called Wood-nymph, Wax Flower, Single-delight.

Genus *Moneses* (1 native species). Leaves near plant base. Flowers solitary; stigma crownlike, 5-lobed.

One-flower Wintergreen

Flowers white to pale pinkish, nodding, solitary. HT: 1½–6 in.

■ PIPSISSEWA (*Chimaphila umbellata*):
Summer; woods. Leaves often whorled, shiny, somewhat leathery, widest above middle. Also called Prince's-pine.

■ SPOTTED PIPSISSEWA (*C. maculata*):
Leaves widest below middle, whitish or pale green along veins. Flowers white, in clusters of 2–5. Also called Striped Wintergreen, Striped Prince's-pine. **SIMILAR ■ LITTLE PIPSISSEWA** (*C. menziesii*): Plants 2–6 in. tall; leaf veins white or not; flowers 1–3, white to pink. Also called Little Prince's-pine.

Genus *Chimaphila* (3 native species). Leaves on stems; opposite, whorled, or nearly whorled. Flowers loosely clustered; stamen stalks conspicuously widened below. Fruits erect.

Pipsissewa

Flowers pinkish to white, nodding, in clusters of 4–8. HT: 4–12 in.

Spotted Pipsissewa

Leaves whitish or pale green along veins. HT: 4–12 in.

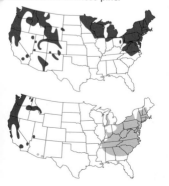

■ ROUND-LEAF SHINLEAF
(*Pyrola americana*): Summer; woods, swamps, bogs. Also called American Wintergreen. **SIMILAR** Differ in technical characters. **GREENFLOWER SHINLEAF** (*P. chlorantha*): Woods; northeastern, western. Also called Greenflower Wintergreen. **WAXFLOWER SHINLEAF** (*P. elliptica*): Northern, southwestern.

■ PINK SHINLEAF (*P. asarifolia*): Woods, swamps, bogs. Also called Pink or Bog Wintergreen.

■ WHITE-VEIN SHINLEAF (*P. picta*):
Woods. Leaves egg-shaped to elliptic, often purple below, white-veined above. Flowers greenish, whitish, or pinkish. Also called White-vein Wintergreen.

Genus *Pyrola* (7 native species). Leaves basal or on lower part of stem. Flowers in elongated clusters. Fruits nodding.

Round-leaf Shinleaf

Flowers white, nodding; style bent, protruding. Leaves basal, firm, shiny, nearly round.
HT: 6–18 in.

Pink Shinleaf

Flowers pink to purplish or reddish.
HT: 6–18 in.

White-vein Shinleaf

HT: 4–12 in.

■ LITTLE SHINLEAF (*Pyrola minor*):
Mostly summer; usually moist woods. Flowers small, white to pinkish, remain more or less closed; style tiny, straight, not protruding. Also called Lesser Wintergreen.

RELATED ■ **SIDEBELLS** (*Orthilia secunda*): Flowers small, white to greenish; style straight; arching stalk becomes upright as plants go to fruit (fruit remains pendant). Also called One-sided-shinleaf, One-sided Wintergreen.

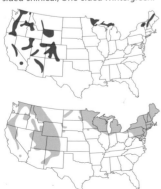

Little Shinleaf

Flowers nodding.
HT: 2–10 in.

Sidebells

Flowers dangle from 1 side of arching stalk. HT: 2–10 in.

RANUNCULACEAE

BUTTERCUP FAMILY

Perennial or annual herbs, rarely shrubby. Leaves usually basal or alternate, simple or compound. Flowers solitary or in clusters; petals 0 to many; sepals generally 3–12, sometimes petal-like; stamens 5 to many; pistils 1 to many. Fruits mostly seedlike or podlike (follicles), infrequently berries.

■ **MOUSE-TAIL** (*Myosurus minimus*): Spring; moist or wet fields, woodland borders, rocky woods, stream banks, vernal pools. Leaves grasslike, fleshy. Sepals greenish white, petal-like; slender receptacle ("mouse tail") elongates in fruit. Fruit clusters held above leaves.

■ **VERNAL-POOL MOUSE-TAIL** (*M. sessilis*): Vernal pools, alkaline meadows. Fruit clusters overtopped by some leaves.

Genus *Myosurus* (5 native species). Leaves basal, linear. Flowers solitary; sepals 3–8, tiny, petal-like; petals 5, narrow, blending in with the 5–25 stamens; pistils many, all on slender, tapering receptacle. Fruits seedlike.

Mouse-tail

Flowers long-stalked; ring of sepals at base of tail-like central column (receptacle). HT: 2–6 in.

Vernal-pool Mouse-tail

Flowers essentially stalkless. HT: 1½–4 in.

■ **GOLDENSEAL** (*Hydrastis canadensis*): Spring; woods. Rootstock yellow. Leaves appear wrinkled at flowering time, expand considerably after flowering. Fruits (see inset) red, raspberry-like, appear to be borne directly from leaf base.

NOTE Do not confuse with False Bugbane (p. 454), which has flowers in clusters; fruits seedlike.

Genus *Hydrastis* (1 native species). Single leaf arises from plant base, 2 alternate leaves on stem; all leaves palmately 3–9-lobed, the lobes toothed. Flowers solitary; sepals 3, petal-like (true petals absent), falling early; stamens many; pistils several. Fruits a cluster of fused berries.

Goldenseal

Flowers solitary, greenish white to white; stamens numerous. Leaves palmately lobed. HT: 6–20 in.

■ **FALSE BUGBANE** (*Trautvetteria caroliniensis*): Summer; woods, seeps, stream banks, mountain meadows. Seedlike fruits in clusters. Also called Tassel-rue.

NOTE Do not confuse with Goldenseal (p. 453), which has solitary flowers and berries (vs. seedlike fruits). The palmately lobed leaves of False Bugbane distinguish it from baneberries (below), bugbanes (p. 455), and meadow-rues (p. 457), all of which have compound leaves.

Genus *Trautvetteria* (1 native species). Leaves basal and alternate, 5–11-lobed, the lobes cut or toothed. Flowers in clusters; sepals 3–5, petal-like (true petals absent), falling early; stamens many; pistils several. Fruits seedlike.

False Bugbane

Flowers in a spreading cluster; stamens numerous, showy, white. Leaves deeply palmately lobed. HT: 1½–3 ft.

■ **RED BANEBERRY** (*Actaea rubra*): Spring–early summer; woods, stream banks, swampy places. Berries usually red (sometimes white), with dark "eye" spot; fruit stalks slender, greenish or brownish.

■ **WHITE BANEBERRY** (*A. pachypoda*): Woods. Similar to Red Baneberry, but leaflets typically hairless beneath (often hairy on veins in Red Baneberry); berries usually white (rarely red), with larger "eye" spot, on thick, reddish stalk.

NOTE Species are difficult to tell apart in flower. White Baneberry has stigma mostly wider than ovary (narrower in Red Baneberry); petal tips often "squared off" (vs. round to somewhat pointed). Baneberries are also called doll's-eyes.

Genus *Actaea* (2 native species). Leaves alternate, 1 or more times divided into leaflets. Flowers white, in clusters; petals 4–10, often spoon-shaped; sepals 3–5, petal-like, falling early; stamens many; pistil 1. Fruits are berries. Poisonous.

Red Baneberry

Stamens conspicuous. Leaflets toothed or lobed. Fruit stalks slender. HT: 1–3 ft.

White Baneberry

Fruit stalks thick. HT: 1–3 ft.

■ **BLACK COHOSH** (*Cimicifuga racemosa*): Summer; woods, thickets. Leaves divided into numerous leaflets. Flowers small, white; petals mostly 4; pistil stalkless, usually 1 per flower. Also called Black Bugbane, Black-snakeroot. **SIMILAR**
■ **MOUNTAIN BUGBANE** (*C. americana*): Late summer–fall; woods, coves. Petals commonly 2; pistils stalked, 3–8 per flower. Also called American Bugbane.
■ **TALL BUGBANE** (*C. elata*): Summer; woods, stream banks, slopes. Petals absent.

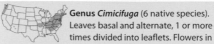

Genus *Cimicifuga* (6 native species). Leaves basal and alternate, 1 or more times divided into leaflets. Flowers in elongated clusters; petals 0–8, their tips often 2-lobed; sepals 4 or 5, petal-like, commonly falling early; stamens many; pistils 1–8. Fruits small, podlike.

Black Cohosh

Flowers in wandlike, often branched clusters. Leaflets sharply toothed. HT: 2½–8 ft.

■ **GOLDTHREAD** (*Coptis trifolia*): Late spring–summer; wet or moist woods, bogs. Rootstock yellow-orange. Flowers erect, solitary; sepals showy, petal-like (true petals narrow, club-shaped).

OTHERS With rootstock brown; leaflets stalked; flowers in clusters, whitish or greenish white, with very slender sepals and petals bulging at base, slender at tip.
■ **IDAHO GOLDTHREAD** (*C. occidentalis*, no photo): Spring. Leaflets toothed, few-lobed. Flowers erect. ■ **OREGON GOLD-THREAD** (*C. laciniata*): Spring–summer. Leaflets toothed, deeply lobed. Flowers nodding. Also called Cut-leaf Goldthread.

Genus *Coptis* (4 native species). Evergreen. Leaves arise from plant base, divided into usually 3 leaflets. Sepals 5–7, petal-like, wider or longer than the 5–7 petals; stamens 10 to many; pistils 4–15. Fruits small, podlike.

Goldthread

Sepals white; petals yellow-tipped.

Leaflets 3, toothed. HT: 2–6 in.

Oregon Goldthread

Sepals and petals slender. HT: 2–10 in.

■ **FALSE RUE-ANEMONE**
(*Enemion biternatum*): Spring; woods.
Leaflets irregularly and often deeply
lobed. Flowers 1–4 per cluster. Do not
confuse with Rue-anemone (below).
SIMILAR ■ **WESTERN FALSE RUE-
ANEMONE** (*E. occidentale*): Woods,
shrublands. Flowers 1–3.

■ **WILLAMETTE FALSE RUE-ANEMONE**
(*E. hallii*): Late spring–early summer;
moist woods, stream banks. Leaflets hairy
beneath. Flowers 3–10.

Genus *Enemion* (5 native species). Leaves
basal and alternate, often 2 or 3 times
divided into leaflets. Flowers usually in
clusters; sepals usually 5, petal-like (true petals absent);
stamens many; pistils 2–10. Fruits podlike, veiny.

False Rue-anemone

**Willamette False
Rue-anemone**

Flowers white, with
usually 5 petal-like
sepals. HT: 4–16 in.

Stamens in a
dense, conspicuous
cluster. HT: 1–2½ ft.

■ **RUE-ANEMONE** (*Anemonella
thalictroides*): Spring; woods, thickets.
Basal leaves long-stalked; stem leaves 2
(opposite) or 3 (whorled); leaflets have
3 rounded or blunt lobes. Flowers in
umbels; sepals petal-like, typically 5–10.
Fruits in clusters, ribbed.

NOTE Very similar to and often included
in *Thalictrum* (p. 457), which does not
have flowers in umbels. Do not confuse
with False Rue-anemone (above), which
has stem leaves alternate; leaflets often
deeply lobed; petal-like sepals normally
only 5.

Genus *Anemonella* (1 native species).
Leaves 1 or 2 times divided into leaflets.
Flowers in umbrella-like clusters (umbels)
of 3–6, or rarely solitary; sepals 5–10, petal-like (true
petals absent); stamens many; pistils 8–12. Fruits seedlike.

Rue-anemone

Flowers typically
white, sometimes pink.
Leaves divided into 3 shallowly
lobed leaflets. HT: 4–12 in.

■ **EARLY MEADOW-RUE** (*Thalictrum dioicum*): Spring; woods, thickets. This species blooms before leaves are fully expanded. Leaves divided into many leaflets. **SIMILAR** Summer-blooming.
■ **VEINY-LEAF MEADOW-RUE** (*T. venulosum*): Prairies, woods.
■ **WESTERN MEADOW-RUE** (*T. occidentale*): Open woods, meadows.
■ **FENDLER'S MEADOW-RUE** (*T. fendleri*): Woods, stream banks.

NOTE *Thalictrum* species are difficult to tell apart. Flowers are often unisexual, the individual plants commonly bearing either all male (stamens only) or all female (pistils only) flowers.

Genus *Thalictrum* (21 native species). Leaves basal and alternate, divided into many leaflets. Flowers in clusters; sepals 4–10, petal-like (true petals absent); stamens 7–30; pistils 1–16. Fruits seedlike, frequently ribbed, often in clusters.

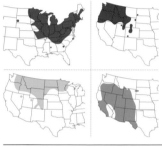

Early Meadow-rue

Male flowers drooping; anthers yellowish. Leaflets have 3–12 scallop-edged lobes. HT: 1–3 ft.

■ **WAXY-LEAF MEADOW-RUE** (*Thalictrum revolutum*): Spring–summer; open woods, thickets. Leaves divided into many leaflets. **SIMILAR** ■ **PURPLE MEADOW-RUE** (*T. dasycarpum*): Woods, thickets, swamps, wet meadows, prairies. Differs in technical characters.

Waxy-leaf Meadow-rue

Male flowers whitish, drooping. Leaflets unlobed to 3-lobed. HT: 2½–5 ft.

■ **ROUND-LOBE HEPATICA** (*Hepatica americana*): Spring; woods. Leaves have 3 blunt or rounded lobes; occasionally mottled above, often purplish beneath. Flowers solitary on hairy stalks; color varies from blue-violet and lavender to pinkish or white.

■ **SHARP-LOBE HEPATICA** (*H. acutiloba*): Similar to Round-lobe Hepatica, but lobes of leaves more pointed.

NOTE Species are also called liverleaf. Sometimes included in *Anemone* (below).

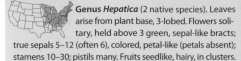

Genus *Hepatica* (2 native species). Leaves arise from plant base, 3-lobed. Flowers solitary, held above 3 green, sepal-like bracts; true sepals 5–12 (often 6), colored, petal-like (petals absent); stamens 10–30; pistils many. Fruits seedlike, hairy, in clusters.

Round-lobe Hepatica

Leaves blunt-lobed. HT: 2–7 in.

Sharp-lobe Hepatica

Leaves have somewhat pointed lobes. HT: 2–7 in.

■ **CANADIAN ANEMONE** (*Anemone canadensis*): Spring–summer; moist places. Basal leaves 1–5, deeply divided. Flowers white, 1–2 in. across, with usually 5 petal-like sepals. Fruits in ball-like clusters.

■ **COLUMBIAN ANEMONE** (*A. deltoidea*): Woods. Basal leaf usually 1 (sometimes 2 or absent), divided into 3 toothed leaflets. Flowers 1½–2¼ in. across.

NOTE Anemones are also called windflower.

Genus *Anemone* (21 native species). Basal leaves often lobed or divided, may be absent at flowering time. Flowers 1 to several, mostly long-stalked, above 2–7 usually whorled, leaflike bracts (here called stem leaves); sepals 4–20, petal-like (true petals absent); stamens and pistils many. Fruits seedlike, often beaked.

Canadian Anemone

Flowers solitary. Stem leaves 3, stalkless, deeply cut into coarsely toothed segments. HT: 6–30 in.

Columbian Anemone

Flowers solitary. Stem leaves 3, stalkless, undivided. HT: 4–12 in.

■ **WOOD ANEMONE** (*Anemone quinquefolia*): Spring–early summer; woods, thickets, stream banks. Basal leaf 1 (or absent); stem leaves 3; leaflets 5 (or 3 and outer pair commonly deeply lobed). Petal-like sepals mostly 5.

■ **OREGON ANEMONE** (*A. oregana*): Spring; woods, open slopes. Basal leaf 1 (or absent); stem leaves 3. Petal-like sepals 5–7, each ⅜–¾ in. long; stamens generally 30–75. Also called Blue Anemone. SIMILAR ■ **LYALL'S ANEMONE** (*A. lyallii*): Spring–summer. Flowers white to pale blue-purple; petal-like sepals narrow and shorter (to ⁵⁄₁₆ in. long); stamens mostly 10–25. Also called Little Mountain Anemone.

Wood Anemone

Flowers white, solitary. Stem leaves stalked, each divided into 3 or 5 toothed leaflets. HT: 3–10 in.

Oregon Anemone

Flowers blue to purple, solitary. Stem leaves stalked, each divided into 3 irregularly toothed or lobed leaflets. HT: 4–12 in.

■ **TALL ANEMONE** (*A. virginiana*): Late spring–summer; woods, fields, riverbanks. Basal leaves 1–5; stem leaves 3, stalked. Flowers often greenish white; petal-like sepals usually 5. Fruits woolly, in dense clusters to ⅝ in. thick. SIMILAR ■ **LONG-HEAD ANEMONE** (*A. cylindrica*): Prairies, open woods, roadsides. Fruiting clusters more cylindrical, to ⅜ in. thick. Both species also called Thimbleweed.

■ **CUT-LEAF ANEMONE** (*A. multifida*): Spring–summer; open woods, slopes, meadows. Basal leaves 3–6; stem leaves 3–5, divided into narrow segments. Flowers 1 to several; yellowish, whitish, bluish, purplish, reddish, or maroon; petal-like sepals 5–9. Also called Red Anemone.

Tall Anemone

Fruiting heads.

Stem leaves divided into 3–5 toothed segments. HT: 1–3 ft.

Cut-leaf Anemone

Stem leaves divided into narrow segments. HT: 6–24 in.

■ **DESERT ANEMONE** (*Anemone tuberosa*): Spring; slopes, ledges, stream banks. Basal leaves 1–3; stem leaves in 1 or 2 whorls of 3, deeply divided into small segments. Flowers 1–5; petal-like sepals 8–10.

■ **TEN-PETAL ANEMONE** (*A. berlandieri*): Late winter–spring; grasslands, hillsides, open woods. Single whorl of leaves above middle of stem, with segments conspicuously narrower than those of the 3–6 basal leaves. Flowers solitary; petal-like sepals 10–20, typically whitish inside, blue-lavender to purple outside.

■ **CAROLINA ANEMONE** (*A. caroliniana*): Similar to Ten-petal Anemone, including season and habitat, but stem leaves at or below midstem; basal leaves 1 or more and also divided into narrow segments. Flowers blue, purple, pink, or whitish.

Desert Anemone

Flowers white to pinkish purple. Stem leaves whorled, dissected. HT: 4–12 in.

Ten-petal Anemone

HT: 12–20 in.

Carolina Anemone

Flowers solitary. HT: 4–14 in.

■ **AMERICAN PASQUEFLOWER** (*Pulsatilla patens* ssp. *multifida*): Spring–summer; prairies, slopes, open woods. Plants normally silky-hairy. Stem leaves whorled, divided into slender segments. Flowers solitary, large; petal-like sepals 5–8, rarely whitish. Also called Prairie-crocus. Do not confuse with Hairy Clematis (p. 462), which looks similar in fruit but has several opposite stem leaves; see also Prairie-smoke (p. 485), which has similar fruit clusters.

■ **WESTERN PASQUEFLOWER** (*P. occidentalis*): Slopes, mountain meadows. Stem leaves fernlike, pinnately dissected into numerous segments. Fruit clusters resemble upside-down mops. Also called Mountain Pasqueflower.

Genus *Pulsatilla* (2 native species). Sometimes included in *Anemone* (p. 458), but fruits have long, feathery tails.

American Pasqueflower

Flowers usually purple or blue. Fruit clusters feathery. HT: 4–16 in.

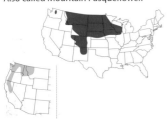

Western Pasqueflower

Flowers white or purple-tinged. HT: 6–24 in.

Fruit clusters shaggy.

PURPLE CLEMATIS (*Clematis occidentalis*): Spring–early summer; slopes, cliffs, rocky woods. Leaflets 3. The eastern ■ var. *occidentalis* has reddish violet or rose-colored flowers; the western ■ var. *grosseserrata* has usually violet or violet-blue flowers.
SIMILAR ■ **ROCKY MOUNTAIN CLEMATIS** (*C. columbiana*): Also has violet or violet-blue flowers, but leaves divided into 6 or 9 leaflets. Also called Columbian Clematis.

NOTE Unlike other *Clematis*, these species have conspicuous, flattened, sterile stamens surrounding the fertile ones.

 Genus *Clematis* (32 species, 26 native). Mostly vines, herbaceous or somewhat woody, climbing via tendril-like leafstalks or leaf tips. Leaves opposite, simple or compound. Flowers solitary or in clusters; sepals usually 4, petal-like (true petals absent); stamens and pistils many. Fruits seedlike, with long "tails," in clusters.

Purple Clematis (eastern)
Flowers large, rose-colored, usually solitary. Climbing or trailing.
Fruits have elongated tails.

Purple Clematis (western)
Flowers violet.

■ **VIRGIN'S-BOWER** (*Clematis virginiana*): Summer; various habitats, often moist places. Flowers unisexual, plants either male (flowers with stamens only) or female (with pistils only).

■ **WESTERN VIRGIN'S-BOWER** (*C. ligusticifolia*): Summer; various, often moist habitats. Leaflets often 5 (or 9–15).
SIMILAR ■ **TEXAS VIRGIN'S-BOWER** (*C. drummondii*): Spring–fall; shrublands, slopes, grasslands. Leaflets 5, mostly 3-lobed. Also called Old-man's-beard.

■ **CHAPARRAL CLEMATIS** (*C. lasiantha*): Winter–spring; shrublands, open woods. Leaflets 3 (or 5). Also called Pipestem Clematis.

Virgin's-bower
Flowers white or cream-colored, in clusters. Leaves divided into 3 usually toothed leaflets. Climbing.

Fruits.

Western Virgin's-bower (female)
Leaflets commonly 5 or 7.
(male)

Chaparral Clematis
Flowers large, mostly solitary.

■ **LEATHER-FLOWER** (*Clematis viorna*):
Spring–summer; woods, thickets, cliffs.
Leaves mostly divided into 3–8 leaflets,
or sometimes undivided. Flowers 1 to
several, usually nodding. Fruits have
feathery tails. Also called Vasevine.
SIMILAR One of several similar species.
PITCHER'S LEATHER-FLOWER
(*C. pitcheri*): Spring–fall; rock outcrops;
southern TX to northern IL. Upper leaf
surface has prominent network of veins;
tails of fruits not feathery.

■ **SCARLET LEATHER-FLOWER**
(*C. texensis*): Spring–summer; woods, cliffs,
stream banks. Also called Scarlet Clematis.

■ **SWAMP LEATHER-FLOWER** (*C. crispa*):
Spring–summer; wet woods, swamps.

Leather-flower

Flowers red-
purple, fleshy,
urn-shaped,
with recurved
tips. Climbing.

Swamp Leather-flower

Vine.

Scarlet Leather-flower

Flowers rose-red to scarlet.

Flowers violet-blue,
large and bell-shaped,
with wavy-edged tips.

■ **CURLYHEADS** (*Clematis ochroleuca*):
Spring; woods, woodland borders,
roadsides. Plants mostly erect. Leaves
undivided. Flowers usually nodding.

■ **PINE-WOODS CLEMATIS**
(*C. baldwinii*): Year-round; pinewoods.
Leaves undivided. Flowers mostly violet-
blue, on long stalks (4–12 in.).

■ **HAIRY CLEMATIS** (*C. hirsutissima*):
Spring–summer; mountain meadows,
grasslands, open woods. Also called
Sugarbowls. Do not confuse with
American Pasqueflower (p. 460).

■ **BIGELOW'S CLEMATIS** (*C. bigelovii*):
Spring–fall; slopes, canyons. Plants erect
or sprawling. Flowers purple or brownish
purple.

Curlyheads

Flowers
pale purple
to yellowish,
urn-shaped.
HT: 8–24 in.

Pine-woods Clematis

Flower tips
wavy-edged.
HT: 8–24 in.

Hairy Clematis

Flowers
mostly dark
violet-blue.
Leaf segments
narrow. HT: 6–25 in.

Bigelow's Clematis

Leaflets
lobed.
HT: 4–24 in.

■ **YELLOW MARSH-MARIGOLD** (*Caltha palustris*): Spring; swamps, bogs, marshes, wet woods. Leaves arise from plant base and also on stem, toothed to untoothed. Do not confuse with ⊞ Lesser Celandine (p. 594), which has flowers with both petals (yellow) and sepals (green); fruits seedlike.

■ **WHITE MARSH-MARIGOLD** (*C. leptosepala*): Wet mountain meadows, seeps, pond margins, stream banks. Leaves usually only arising from plant base. See White Globe-flower (below).

NOTE Marsh-marigolds are also called cowslip.

Genus *Caltha* (3 native species). Leaves undivided and deeply notched at base. Flowers in clusters or solitary; sepals 5–12, petal-like (true petals absent); stamens 10 to many; pistils 4 to many. Fruits small, podlike, in clusters.

Yellow Marsh-marigold

Flowers bright yellow to orange-yellow. Leaves round to kidney-shaped. HT: 8–24 in.

White Marsh-marigold

Flowers normally white with yellow stamens. HT: 6–14 in.

■ **WHITE GLOBE-FLOWER** (*Trollius albiflorus*): Summer; wet mountain meadows, stream banks, wet slopes. Stem leaves nearly stalkless. Do not confuse with White Marsh-marigold (above), which has leaves round to kidney-shaped.

■ **YELLOW GLOBE-FLOWER** (*T. laxus*): Wet ground. Similar to White Globe-flower, but flowers yellow. Also called Spreading Globe-flower.

Genus *Trollius* (4 species, 3 native). Leaves basal and alternate, deeply palmately divided into segments that are 3-lobed and toothed. Flowers usually solitary; sepals 5–9, showy, petal-like (true petals resemble stamens); stamens many; pistils 5 to many. Fruits podlike, in clusters.

White Globe-flower

Flowers white with yellow stamens. Leaves palmately cut and lobed. HT: 6–18 in.

Yellow Globe-flower

Flowers yellow. HT: 6–18 in.

■ **HISPID BUTTERCUP** (*Ranunculus hispidus*): Early spring–fall; woods, grasslands, swamps, marshes. Main leaves as wide as long. Petals 5, widest mostly above middle. Also called Swamp Buttercup. **SIMILAR** ■ **EARLY BUTTERCUP** (*R. fascicularis*): Winter–spring; woods, grasslands. Main leaves longer than wide. Petals widest mostly at or below middle.

■ **STRAIGHT-BEAK BUTTERCUP** (*R. orthorhynchus*): Spring–summer; meadows, wet ground. Leaves typically divided into 3 or 5 (sometimes 7) coarsely toothed leaflets. Petals mostly 5 or 6. Also called Western Swamp Buttercup.

NOTE See introduced buttercups (p. 594).

Genus *Ranunculus* (77 species, 65 native). Leaves basal and alternate, simple or compound. Flowers solitary or in clusters; petals 0 to many (often 5); sepals 3–5; stamens 10 to many; pistils 4 to many. Fruits seedlike, in clusters. Species are also called crowfoot.

Hispid Buttercup
Flowers yellow. Leaves toothed, 3-lobed or divided into 3 leaflets. HT: 6 in.–3 ft.

Straight-beak Buttercup

HT: 6–30 in.

■ **SAGEBRUSH BUTTERCUP** (*Ranunculus glaberrimus*): Spring–summer; shrublands, plains, open woods. Plants somewhat fleshy. Leaves basal and alternate. Petals mostly 5. In var. *ellipticus* (see inset), basal leaves unlobed, elliptic.

■ **ESCHSCHOLTZ'S BUTTERCUP** (*R. eschscholtzii*): Late spring–summer; slopes, mountain meadows. A variable species with several varieties. Basal leaf lobes often round-toothed. Also called Subalpine Buttercup.

■ **ALPINE BUTTERCUP** (*R. adoneus*): Spring–summer; mountain meadows. Also called Snow Buttercup.

Sagebrush Buttercup

Flowers yellow. Basal leaves typically have 3 broad, rounded lobes. HT: 2–10 in.

Eschscholtz's Buttercup

Basal leaves commonly deeply 3-lobed. HT: 2–8 in.

Alpine Buttercup

Leaves divided into narrow segments. HT: 4–8 in.

■ **HOOKED BUTTERCUP** (*Ranunculus recurvatus*): Spring; woods, swampy areas. Petals 5, very small. Seedlike fruits have prominent hooked beak. **SIMILAR** ■ **WOODLAND BUTTERCUP** (*R. uncinatus*): Spring–summer; shady moist soil.

■ **KIDNEY-LEAF BUTTERCUP**: (*R. abortivus*): Early spring–summer; woods, meadows, disturbed places. Stems not hairy. Basal leaves long-stalked, kidney-shaped to round, undivided. Petals 5, tiny.

GRACEFUL BUTTERCUP (*R. inamoenus*): Late winter–summer; slopes, mountain meadows; Rocky Mountain region. Similar to Kidney-leaf Buttercup. Midstem leafless.

Hooked Buttercup

Flowers pale yellow; petals as long as to somewhat shorter than sepals. Leaves deeply divided. HT: 1–2 ft.

Kidney-leaf Buttercup

Petals shorter than sepals. Stem leaves stalkless, deeply divided. HT: 8–20 in.

Graceful Buttercup

Petals longer than sepals. HT: to 12 in.

■ **CALIFORNIA BUTTERCUP** (*Ranunculus californicus*): Winter–summer; open woods, slopes, grassy places. Petals 9–20. Similar species occur elsewhere, including AZ and TX.

■ **WATER-PLANTAIN BUTTERCUP** (*R. alismifolius*): Spring–summer; wet or moist places. Leaves linear to lance-shaped, undivided and untoothed. Petals 5–12. **SIMILAR** ■ **CREEPING SPEARWORT** (*R. flammula*): Wet places, shallow water. Stems rooting at nodes; leaves threadlike to narrowly spear-shaped, to ⅜ in. wide; petals 5 or 6.

WATER-PLANTAIN SPEARWORT (*R. ambigens*): Northeastern. Similar to Creeping Spearwort, but leaves larger (⅜–1 in. wide).

California Buttercup

Flowers have many yellow petals. Leaves divided into 3 or 5 toothed leaflets. HT: 7–28 in.

Water-plantain Buttercup

Flowers yellow. HT: 2–20 in.

■ **CURSED BUTTERCUP** (*Ranunculus sceleratus*): Early spring–summer; wet ground, shallow water. Petals 3–5, each 1/16–3/16 in. long. A chiefly western variety, *multifidus*, has leaves more deeply divided; fruits smooth (vs. wrinkled).

■ **GREATER YELLOW WATER BUTTERCUP** (*R. flabellaris*): Spring–summer; shallow water, damp shores. Petals 5 or 6 (to 14), each 1/4–1/2 in. long.

■ **LESSER YELLOW WATER BUTTERCUP** (*R. gmelinii*): Similar to Greater; petals 4–14, each 1/8–1/4 in. long.

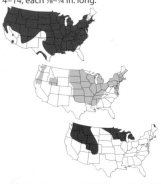

Cursed Buttercup

Flowers yellow. Leaves divided into lobed segments. HT: 6–20 in.

Greater Yellow Water Buttercup

Lesser Yellow Water Buttercup

Leaves deeply lobed to dissected.

■ **WHITE WATER BUTTERCUP** (*Ranunculus aquatilis*): Spring–summer; lakes, ponds, streams. Aquatic, often mat-forming. Leaves usually all divided into threadlike segments; in some western populations, some leaves kidney-shaped and deeply lobed (see inset).

■ **WATERFALL BUTTERCUP** (*R. hystriculus*): Winter–summer; shaded streams, rock faces near waterfalls. Leaves often shallowly lobed or toothed. Sepals petal-like, white or sometimes pale yellow; true petals tiny.

■ **ANDERSON'S BUTTERCUP** (*R. andersonii*): Spring; shrublands, rocky slopes. Leaves parsleylike. Also called Pink Buttercup.

White Water Buttercup

Flowers white with yellow center. Leaves finely dissected.

Waterfall Buttercup

Leaves basal, long-stalked, kidney-shaped to round. HT: 6–16 in.

Anderson's Buttercup

Flowers white or reddish-tinged. HT: 2–10 in.

■ **WESTERN MONKSHOOD** (*Aconitum columbianum*): Summer; seeps, stream banks, woods, mountain meadows. Stems erect to leaning. Flowers in elongated clusters, mostly blue to purple, or sometimes whitish. Also called Columbian Monkshood. SIMILAR ■ **SOUTHERN BLUE MONKSHOOD** (*A. uncinatum*): Late summer–early fall; swamps, seeps, woods.

■ **WHITE MONKSHOOD** (*A. reclinatum*): Late spring–summer; woods (mostly in mountains). Flowers white to creamcolored or yellowish.

NOTE Monkshoods, also called aconite and wolfsbane, are poisonous. Do not confuse with larkspurs (below), which have flowers spurred, not hooded.

Genus *Aconitum* (5 native species). Leaves basal and alternate, palmately divided into 3–7 segments. Flowers in elongated clusters; petals 2, hidden by petal-like sepals; sepals 5: 2 lower, 2 side, 1 usually hoodlike or helmetshaped upper; stamens many; pistils 3–5. Fruits podlike.

Western Monkshood

White Monkshood

Hood elongated, mostly horizontal. HT: to 3 ft.

Hood arching, helmet-shaped. Leaves palmately divided into toothed segments. HT: to 7 ft.

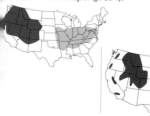

■ **NELSON'S LARKSPUR** (*Delphinium nuttallianum*): Spring–midsummer; plains, open woods, hillsides. Leaves round in outline, divided into narrow segments. Also called Two-lobe or Nuttall's Larkspur. SIMILAR ■ **DWARF LARKSPUR** (*D. tricorne*): Spring; woods, thickets, prairies.

■ **TALL LARKSPUR** (*D. glaucum*): Summer; meadows, woods, wet places. Leaves cut into 5–9 broad, sharply and coarsely toothed segments. Also called Tower Larkspur.

NOTE There are numerous very similar purple- or blue-flowered larkspurs. Leaves vary from few to many and from shallowly to deeply lobed. Do not confuse larkspurs with monkshoods (above). See also ⊞ Rocket-larkspur (p. 594).

Genus *Delphinium* (61 species, 60 native). Leaves as described in *Aconitum* (above). Petals 4; sepals 5, showy, petallike; upper 2 petals each have projection (spur) fitting into similar projection on uppermost sepal; stamens many; pistils 3 (or rarely 5). Fruits podlike, usually 3 in a cluster.

Nelson's Larkspur

Tall Larkspur

Flowers blue-purple to lavender. HT: to 6 ft.

Flowers commonly blue-purple, spurred. HT: to 2 ft.

■ **PLAINS LARKSPUR** (*Delphinium carolinianum* ssp. *virescens*): Early spring–early summer; grassy plains, prairies, fields. Leaf segments narrow. Also called Prairie or White Larkspur.

■ **SCARLET LARKSPUR** (*D. cardinale*): Late spring–midsummer; dry shrublands, open woods. Basal leaves absent at bloom time; leaf segments narrow. Also called Cardinal Larkspur. **SIMILAR** ■ **RED LARKSPUR** (*D. nudicaule*): Spring; shady woods, rocky slopes. Basal leaves present at bloom time; leaf segments broad; flowers sometimes red-orange.

■ **YELLOW LARKSPUR** (*D. luteum*): Spring; coastal bluffs.

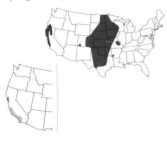

Plains Larkspur

Flowers spurred, white or faintly tinged with blue or lavender. HT: 1–2½ ft.

Scarlet Larkspur

Flowers red (upper petals yellow). HT: 2–5 ft.

Yellow Larkspur

Flowers yellow. HT: 8–16 in.

■ **EASTERN RED COLUMBINE** (*Aquilegia canadensis*): Spring–summer; woods, thickets, ledges, cliffs. Spur tips close together; sepals longer than petal blades. Also called Wild or Canadian Columbine. **SIMILAR** ■ **ROCKY MOUNTAIN RED COLUMBINE** (*A. elegantula*): Open woods, slopes. Spur tips spread apart.

■ **WESTERN RED COLUMBINE** (*A. formosa*): Woods, stream banks, meadows. Opening (mouth) to each spur equal-sided. Also called Crimson or Sitka Columbine. **SIMILAR VAN HOUTTE'S COLUMBINE** (*A. eximia*): CA coast ranges. Opening to each spur angled (lower toward outside).

Genus *Aquilegia* (21 species, 20 native). Leaves basal and alternate, divided into fan- or wedge-shaped leaflets. Flowers 1 to several, large; petals 5, each has long, tubular spur with swollen tip; sepals 5, showy, petal-like, alternating with petals; stamens many, often protruding; pistils 5–10. Fruits podlike, in clusters.

Eastern Red Columbine

Flowers yellow at face, otherwise red, longer than wide, nodding; petal-like sepals point forward. HT: 1–3 ft.

Western Red Columbine

Flowers as wide as long; petal-like sepals horizontally spreading. HT: 1–3 ft.

■ **YELLOW COLUMBINE** (*Aquilegia flavescens*): Summer; woods, mountain meadows, rocky slopes. Flower spurs ½–¾ in. long.

■ **GOLDEN COLUMBINE** (*A. chrysantha*): Spring–summer; moist slopes, canyons. Flower spurs 1½–2½ in. long.

■ **LONG-SPUR COLUMBINE** (*A. longissima*): Summer; moist places in canyons. Flower spurs 2½–7 in. long.

Yellow Columbine

Flowers yellow, nodding. HT: 6–30 in.

Golden Columbine

Flowers erect; spurs long. HT: 1–4 ft.

Long-spur Columbine

Flowers erect; spurs very long. HT: 1–3 ft.

■ **COLORADO COLUMBINE** (*Aquilegia coerulea* var. *coerulea*): Summer; woods, wet mountain meadows, rocky slopes. Leaves divided into leaflets. Flower spurs 1–2¾ in. long. Also called Blue Columbine.

■ **JONES' COLUMBINE** (*A. jonesii*): Limestone regions in high mountains. Dwarf. Basal leaves small. Flower spurs to ½ in. long. Also called Limestone Columbine.

■ **SMALL-FLOWER COLUMBINE** (*A. brevistyla*): Open woods, meadows. Basal leaves shorter than stems. Flowers blue; spurs ¼–⅜ in. long. **SIMILAR** ■ **ROCKY MOUNTAIN COLUMBINE** (*A. saximontana*): Rocky slopes. Basal leaves as long as stems.

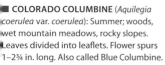

Colorado Columbine

Flowers erect, often deep blue to purplish, with white petal blades. HT: 6–30 in.

Jones' Columbine

Flowers erect, usually solitary, above crowded basal leaves. HT: 1½–5 in.

Small-flower Columbine

Flowers nodding; spurs short, hooked. HT: 8–32 in.

■ **COVILLE'S COLUMBINE** (*Aquilegia pubescens*): Summer; open rocky places in alpine regions. Flowers may be tinged yellow, pink, or blue; spurs 1–1½ in. long. Also called Alpine or Sierran Columbine.

■ **WHITE COLORADO COLUMBINE** (*A. coerulea* var. *ochroleuca*): A variety of Colorado Columbine (p. 469); spurs 1⅜–2¼ in. long.

■ **LARAMIE COLUMBINE** (*A. laramiensis*): Summer; rock crevices. Spurs about ¼ in. long, hooked.

Coville's Columbine
Flowers erect, often cream-colored to yellowish. HT: 6–20 in.

White Colorado Columbine
Flowers erect, white to pale blue. HT: 6–30 in.

Laramie Columbine
Flowers nodding, cream-colored or lavender-tinged. HT: 2–10 in.

RHAMNACEAE   BUCKTHORN FAMILY

Woody plants. Leaves alternate or opposite, simple. Flowers in clusters; petals 4 or 5, usually with narrowed base, hoodlike tip; sepals 4 or 5; stamens 4 or 5; pistil 1. Fruits berrylike or capsulelike.

■ **NEW JERSEY-TEA** (*Ceanothus americanus*): Spring–early summer; open places. Flower clusters on long stalks from leaf axils. **SIMILAR PRAIRIE REDROOT** (*C. herbaceus*): Chiefly central N. America. Flower clusters at stem ends.

■ **MAHALA-MAT** (*C. prostratus*): Open woods, flats. Usually mat-forming. Leaves evergreen, with 3–9 stiff teeth. Flowers blue to lavender, aging whitish or pinkish. Also called Squaw-carpet, Prostrate Ceanothus.

SISKIYOU-MAT (*C. pumilus*): Open places; northern CA, southwestern OR. Flowers similar to Mahala-mat.

Genus *Ceanothus* (51 native species). Shrubs or small trees. Flower parts in 5s. Most species western, especially in CA.

New Jersey-tea

Mahala-mat
Leaves opposite, hollylike. HT: mostly 2–6 in.

Flowers white. Leaves alternate; 3 main veins from base. HT: 1½–3½ ft.

Siskiyou-mat
Leaves untoothed or 3-toothed at tip.

ROSACEAE
ROSE FAMILY

Trees, shrubs, or annual or perennial herbs. Leaves alternate or basal, simple or compound; often with 2 sometimes prominent leaflike appendages (stipules) at leafstalk base. Flowers solitary or in clusters; petals usually 5; sepals 5, united at base; stamens generally 10 to many; pistils 1 to many. Petals, sepals, and stamens attached at or near rim of a saucer-, cup-, or urn-shaped structure (hypanthium) that surrounds pistil(s). Fruits vary from seedlike to large and fleshy.

■ **MOUNTAIN-MISERY** (*Chamaebatia foliolosa*): Late spring–summer; wooded slopes. Low shrub, evergreen, often mat-forming. Leaves strong-smelling. Fruits solitary, seedlike. Also called Sierran Mountain-misery, Bear-clover.

OTHER GENUS ■ **FERNBUSH** (*Chamaebatiaria millefolium*): Summer; dry, often rocky slopes. Similar to Mountain-misery, but taller; leaves mostly 2 times divided; fruits small pods, in a cluster of usually 5. Also called Desert-sweet, Tansy-bush.

Genus *Chamaebatia* (2 native species). Leaves alternate, 2 or 3 times pinnately divided into leaflets. Petals 5; stamens many; pistil 1. Fruits seedlike, leathery.

Mountain-misery
Flowers white, in loose clusters at stem ends. Leaves fernlike, sticky. HT: 6–24 in.

Fernbush
Pods leathery, usually 5 per cluster. HT: 2–6 ft.

■ **BOWMAN'S-ROOT** (*Gillenia trifoliata*): Spring–summer; woods, woodland borders. Leaves nearly stalkless; leaflets 3, taper-tipped, sharply toothed. Stipules (paired appendages at leaf base) slender, inconspicuous, usually falling early. Flowers white or sometimes pale pink, often with reddish base; petals narrow, frequently twisted. Fruits hairy. Also called Mountain Indian-physic.

■ **AMERICAN-IPECAC** (*G. stipulata*): Similar to Bowman's-root, but leaflets of lower leaves may be deeply toothed or divided; stipules conspicuous, persistent, leafletlike; fruits mostly hairless. Also called Midwestern Indian-physic.

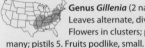
Genus *Gillenia* (2 native species). Leaves alternate, divided into 3 leaflets. Flowers in clusters; petals 5; stamens many; pistils 5. Fruits podlike, small.

Bowman's-root
Flowers star-shaped, in loose clusters. HT: 1½–3 ft.

American-ipecac

Leaves appear to have 5 leaflets. HT: 1½–3 ft.

■ **MEADOWSWEET** (*Spiraea alba*): Summer; woodland borders, meadows, swampy places, shores. Flowers white. Also called White Meadowsweet.

■ **BIRCH-LEAF SPIREA** (*S. betulifolia*): Woods, slopes. Flowers white. Also called Shiny-leaf Meadowsweet.

■ **STEEPLEBUSH** (*S. tomentosa*): Wet places. Leaves densely felty beneath. Flowers usually pink. Also called Hardhack. SIMILAR ■ **DOUGLAS' SPIREA** (*S. douglasii*): Also called Douglas' Meadowsweet.

MOUNTAIN SPIREA (*S. splendens*): Moist places; chiefly northwestern. Flowers pink; clusters broader than long. Also called Rose Meadowsweet.

Genus *Spiraea* (12 species, 8 native). Shrubs. Leaves alternate. Flowers small, in clusters; petals 5; stamens many; pistils 3–7 (often 5). Fruits podlike, usually tiny.

Meadowsweet

Clusters narrowly pyramid-shaped (longer than broad). HT: 1½–6 ft.

Birch-leaf Spirea

Clusters flat-topped. HT: 6–24 in.

Steeplebush

Clusters steeplelike. HT: 6–24 in.

Mountain Spirea

Clusters flat-topped. HT: 1–3 ft.

■ **QUEEN-OF-THE-PRAIRIE** (*Filipendula rubra*): Summer; moist or wet prairies and meadows. Small leaflets intermingle with much larger leaflets; side leaflets typically 3–5-lobed; end leaflet largest, deeply lobed. Lower leaves large. Crushed leaves have a mild wintergreen aroma.

NOTE ① Queen-of-the-meadow (p. 594) is a whitish-flowered relative with side leaflets coarsely toothed but not lobed.

Genus *Filipendula* (4 species, 2 native). Leaves basal and alternate, pinnately divided into toothed or lobed leaflets of different sizes, with end leaflet commonly largest. Flowers in clusters; petals usually 5; stamens many; pistils 5–15. Fruits seedlike, in clusters.

Queen-of-the-prairie

Flowers small, pink, in large clusters; stamens conspicuous. HT: 3–7 ft.

■ **GOAT'S-BEARD** (*Aruncus dioicus*): Late spring–early summer; woods, stream banks. Leaflets double-toothed. Male flowers have conspicuous stamens. Mature fruits on downward-pointing stalks. Also called White Goat's-beard, Bride's-feathers.

NOTE Do not confuse with False Goat's-beard (p. 511).

Genus *Aruncus* (1 native species). Leaves alternate, divided into several leaflets. Flowers in plumelike clusters; petals 5; male flowers (15–30 stamens) and female flowers (usually 3 pistils) on separate plants. Fruits seedlike.

Goat's-beard

**Flowers cream-colored, tiny, in showy sprays.
HT: 3–7 ft.**

Male flowers.

■ **CANADIAN BURNET** (*Sanguisorba canadensis*): Summer; moist or wet places. Flower clusters 1¼–5 in. long; stamens 4 per flower.

■ **GREAT BURNET** (*S. officinalis*): Summer; wet places. Flower clusters ¾–1¼ in. long; stamens 4 per flower. **SIMILAR ☐ SALAD BURNET** (*S. minor*): Disturbed places; western, northeastern; native to Eurasia. Flowers green or purple-tinged; stamens many per flower.

■ **WESTERN BURNET** (*S. annua*): Spring–summer; open places. Leaflets deeply pinnate, with narrow segments. Stamens usually 2 per flower. Also called Annual or Prairie Burnet.

Genus *Sanguisorba* (5 species, 4 native). Leaves alternate and basal, pinnately divided into leaflets. Flowers in dense clusters; sepals 4, petal-like (true petals absent); stamens 2 to many; pistils 1 or 2. Fruits seedlike.

Canadian Burnet

**Flowers white. Leaflets coarsely toothed.
HT: 1–5 ft.**

Great Burnet

**Flowers maroon.
HT: 1–5 ft.**

Western Burnet

**Flowers greenish.
HT: 8–32 in.**

■ ROCKY MOUNTAIN ROCKMAT
(*Petrophyton caespitosum*): Summer–early fall; rocky crevices, ledges. Plants mat-forming. Leaves spatula-shaped, frequently gray-silky-hairy. Flowers small, in dense, spikelike clusters, occasionally light pink; stamens showy, longer than the minute petals. Also called Tufted Rockmat, Rock-spirea.

Genus *Petrophyton* (4 native species). Dwarf shrubs; evergreen. Leaves alternate, mostly crowded at plant base. Flowers in closely packed clusters; petals 5; stamens many; pistils 3–7 (often 5). Fruits podlike, minute.

Rocky Mountain Rockmat

Flowers whitish. Leaves in basal tufts. HT: 1–6 in.

■ PARTRIDGE-FOOT (*Luetkea pectinata*):
Summer; rocky slopes, moist meadows. Plants have runners, often mat-forming. Leaves in basal tufts and fewer on stem, fan-shaped with narrow lobes at tips. Flowers small.

Genus *Luetkea* (1 native species). Dwarf shrub; evergreen. Leaves mostly basal; tips deeply lobed. Flowers in clusters; petals 5; stamens about 20; pistils usually 5. Fruits podlike, small.

Partridge-foot

Flowers in clusters; petals white, stamens yellow. HT: 2–7 in.

■ **ONE-FLOWER KELSEYA** (*Kelseya uniflora*): Spring–early summer; mountain rock crevices. Plants form mosslike patches on limestone cliff faces. Leaves densely crowded, silky-hairy.

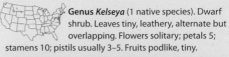

Genus *Kelseya* (1 native species). Dwarf shrub. Leaves tiny, leathery, alternate but overlapping. Flowers solitary; petals 5; stamens 10; pistils usually 3–5. Fruits podlike, tiny.

One-flower Kelseya

Flowers tiny, pinkish white to pinkish purple. HT: 2–3 in.

■ **PINEWOODS HORKELIA** (*Horkelia fusca*): Late spring–summer; open woods, meadows. A variable species. Leaflets several-toothed or lobed, nearly hairless to densely hairy. Petals white to pinkish, as long as to longer than sepals. Also called Dusky Horkelia.

■ **THREE-TOOTH HORKELIA** (*H. tridentata*): Leaflets usually 3-toothed at tip, silky-hairy at least on lower surface. Petals about as long as sepals. Also called Clustered Horkelia.

NOTE Horkelias are also called honeydew.

Genus *Horkelia* (19 native species). Often aromatic. Leaves mostly basal, also alternate, pinnately divided into toothed or lobed leaflets. Flowers in clusters; petals 5; stamens 10; pistils 5 to many. Fruits seedlike.

Pinewoods Horkelia

Petals broadened and sometimes notched at tip. HT: 6–24 in.

Three-tooth Horkelia

Petals mostly narrow. HT: 6–18 in.

■ **GORDON'S IVESIA** (*Ivesia gordonii*): Summer; rocky slopes, alpine meadows. Leaflets numerous, 4–8-lobed. Flowers in dense clusters; petals narrow, yellow; stamens 5; pistils mostly 1–4. Also called Alpine Ivesia.

■ **CLUBMOSS IVESIA** (*I. lycopodioides*): Similar to Gordon's Ivesia, but leaflets 4–10-lobed; flowers with broader petals and mostly 5–15 pistils.

NOTE Ivesias are also called mousetail. Do not confuse yellow-flowered *Ivesia* species with Alpine Avens (p. 485), which has flowers not densely clustered, stamens many.

Genus *Ivesia* (29 native species). Similar to *Horkelia* (p. 475), but leaflets commonly numerous, tiny, and situated around a central axis, the whole leaf resembling a tail (leaves rarely mostly flat); stamens 5–35 (frequently 5 or 20). Flowers yellow, white, or pinkish.

Gordon's Ivesia

Clubmoss Ivesia

HT: 2–8 in.

HT: 2–12 in.

■ **MOUSETAIL IVESIA** (*Ivesia santolinoides*): Summer; slopes. Flowers in open clusters; stamens 15.

RELATED ■ **CONGDON'S FALSE HORKELIA** (*Horkeliella congdonis*): Sagebrush meadows. Similar to Mousetail Ivesia in having white flowers. Leaves somewhat like those of Clubmoss Ivesia (above). Flowers differ from *Horkelia* (p. 475) in having 20 stamens (vs. 10). Also called Sagebrush-honeydew.

Mousetail Ivesia

Leaves silvery-hairy, cylindrical, tail-like, with many crowded leaflets. HT: 6–18 in.

Petals white, broad.

Congdon's False Horkelia

Petals relatively narrow. HT: 6–24 in.

■ **VIRGINIA STRAWBERRY** (*Fragaria virginiana*): Spring–summer; meadows, open woods. Terminal tooth on leaflets usually shorter than teeth on either side. Flowers ½–¾ in. across. Seedlike fruits deeply embedded in fleshy receptacle. Also called Mountain or Wild Strawberry. **SIMILAR WOOD STRAWBERRY** (*F. vesca*): Widespread. Terminal tooth of leaflets as long as or longer than teeth on either side; flowers ½ in. or less across; seedlike fruits shallowly embedded in receptacle. Also called Wild or Woodland Strawberry.

■ **BEACH STRAWBERRY** (*F. chiloensis*): Coastal beaches, dunes, bluffs. Flowers ¾–1½ in. across. Also called Sand or Coast Strawberry.

Genus *Fragaria* (3 native species). Leaves basal, divided into 3 leaflets. Flowers in clusters; petals 5; sepals 5, with 5 sepal-like bracts; stamens many; pistils many. Fruits numerous, seedlike, borne on the outside of a swollen receptacle.

Virginia Strawberry

Beach Strawberry

Flowers white. Leaves long-stalked; leaflets 3, toothed. Plants creep via runners. HT: 3–6 in.

Leaves somewhat leathery, shiny above. HT: 3–8 in.

CINQUEFOILS

■ **COMMON CINQUEFOIL** (*Potentilla simplex*): Spring–early summer; open woods, fields, roadsides. Plants at first erect, later arching and then trailing. Leaves palmately divided into 5 leaflets. Flowers yellow, solitary on long stalks from leaf axils. First (lowest) flower usually arises from the second leaf-bearing node on stem. Also called Oldfield Five-fingers.

■ **DWARF CINQUEFOIL** (*P. canadensis*): Similar to Common Cinquefoil. Leaflets strongly wedge-shaped at base. First (lowest) flower usually arises from the first leaf-bearing node on stem. Also called Canadian Cinquefoil, Running Five-fingers.

Genus *Potentilla* (69 species, 65 native). Leaves basal and alternate, pinnately or palmately divided into leaflets. Flowers most often in clusters; petals usually 5; sepals 5, alternating with 5 tiny or small sepal-like bracts; stamens many (often 20); pistils many. Fruits seedlike.

Common Cinquefoil

Dwarf Cinquefoil

Leaflets toothed mostly along upper half. HT: 2–6 in.

Leaflets toothed along upper ⅔–¾. HT: 8–12 in.

CINQUEFOILS

■ **ROUGH CINQUEFOIL** (*Potentilla norvegica*): Late spring–early fall; open places. Stems usually soft-hairy. Mature flower clusters prominently leafy-bracted; flowers ¼–½ in. across. Also called Norwegian Cinquefoil.

■ **FAN-LEAF CINQUEFOIL** (*P. flabellifolia*): Summer; mountain meadows, slopes. Stems sparsely hairy to nearly hairless. Mature flower clusters only sparingly leafy-bracted; flowers ½–¾ in. across.

■ **SNOW CINQUEFOIL** (*P. nivea*, no photo): Mountain meadows, alpine slopes, tundra. Plants 1½–6 in. tall. Leaflets 3, typically densely white-hairy beneath. Flowers yellow, about ½ in. across.

Rough Cinquefoil

Petals yellow, as long as or shorter than sepals. Leaves palmately divided into 3 leaflets. HT: 1–2 ft.

Fan-leaf Cinquefoil

Petals yellow, longer than sepals. Leaflets 3. HT: 4–12 in.

CINQUEFOILS

■ **SLENDER CINQUEFOIL** (*Potentilla gracilis*): Mostly summer; meadows, open woods. Plants sparingly to densely hairy. Leaflets 1–3 in. long, commonly hairy, toothed to narrowly lobed. Also called Graceful Cinquefoil. **SIMILAR MOUNTAIN-MEADOW CINQUEFOIL** (*P. diversifolia*): Meadows, slopes; western. Leaflets ⁵⁄₁₆–1 in. long, not hairy, toothed mostly along upper half. Also called Varileaf or Diverse-leaf Cinquefoil.

NOTE Leaves mostly basal in these two species. Species with plentiful stem leaves include Ⅱ Sulphur Cinquefoil, which has paler yellow flowers; and Ⅱ Silvery Cinquefoil, with leaflets densely white-hairy beneath; flowers bright yellow. (Both species shown on p. 595.)

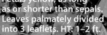
Slender Cinquefoil

Flowers yellow. Leaves palmately divided into 5 or 7 (or 9) toothed leaflets. HT: 8–32 in.

CINQUEFOILS

■ PENNSYLVANIA CINQUEFOIL
(*Potentilla pensylvanica*): Summer; alpine slopes and meadows, prairies. Leaves pinnately divided; leaflets cut halfway or more to midrib. Flowers yellow.

WOOLLY CINQUEFOIL (*P. hippiana*): Range similar to Pennsylvania Cinquefoil. Leaflets cut mostly less than halfway to midrib. Also called Hipp's Cinquefoil.

OTHERS Found in western mountains. **■ SHORT-LEAF CINQUEFOIL** (*P. brevifolia*): Leaves finely sticky-hairy. **■ SHEEP CINQUEFOIL** (*P. ovina*): Leaves hairy.

NOTE Do not confuse pinnate-leaved cinquefoils with Alpine Avens (p. 485) or *Ivesia* (p. 476).

Pennsylvania Cinquefoil

Leaflets mostly 5–11, upper 3 largest. HT: 2–8 in.

Woolly Cinquefoil

Leaflets 5–13, densely white-hairy beneath. HT: 2½–14 in.

Short-leaf Cinquefoil

Leaflets 3–7, parsleylike, blunt-toothed. HT: 2–6 in.

Sheep Cinquefoil

Leaflets mostly 9–17, deeply cut into slender segments. HT: 2–8 in.

CINQUEFOILS

■ STICKY CINQUEFOIL (*Potentilla glandulosa*): Late spring–summer; open woods, mountain meadows, alpine tundra. Stems and leafstalks usually sticky-hairy. Flower clusters commonly have somewhat spreading branches, appearing relatively open. Plants are variable in petal length and color, leaflet length, and type and degree of hairiness. Also called Glandular Cinquefoil. **SIMILAR**
■ TALL CINQUEFOIL (*P. arguta*): Open woods, meadows, prairies, roadsides. Stem hairs brownish; flowers usually white or cream-colored, in clusters with erect, crowded branches, appearing more dense. Also called White Cinquefoil.

Sticky Cinquefoil

Flowers often deep yellow, sometimes cream-colored or pale yellow. Basal leaves pinnately divided into 5, 7, or 9 deeply toothed leaflets. HT: 6–30 in.

CINQUEFOILS

■ **SCARLET CINQUEFOIL** (*Potentilla thurberi*): Summer–early fall; mountain meadows, stream banks. Leaves palmately divided into 5 or 7 leaflets, dark green above, pale and hairy beneath. Also called Red or Thurber's Cinquefoil.

OTHER CINQUEFOILS Several other genera, once included in *Potentilla*, differ in technical characters. ■ **MARSH-CINQUEFOIL** (*Comarum palustre*): Mostly summer; swampy or boggy places. Stems trailing, rooted in wet soil or in mud in shallow water. Leaflets sharply toothed, blue-green above, pale beneath. Petals red-purple; sepals red- or purple-tinged, pointed, petal-like. Also called Purple Marshlocks.

Scarlet Cinquefoil
Petals longer than sepals.
HT: 1–2 ft.

Marsh-cinquefoil
Petals shorter than sepals.

Leaves pinnately divided into 5 or 7 leaflets.
HT: to 12 in.

CINQUEFOILS

■ **THREE-TOOTH-CINQUEFOIL** (*Sibbaldiopsis tridentata*): Late spring–summer; open woods, rock outcrops, balds, gravelly shores. Leaflets have 2–5 (usually 3) large teeth at tip. The evergreen leaves commonly turn red in winter. Also called Wine-leaf-cinquefoil, Mountain-cinquefoil, Shrubby-fivefingers.

Three-tooth-cinquefoil

Flowers white. Leaves palmately divided into 3 wedge-shaped leaflets. HT: 4–12 in.

CINQUEFOILS

■ **SILVERWEED** (*Argentina anserina*):
spring–early fall; lake shores, marshy
places, meadows, roadsides. Spreads by
runners, these often reddish. Runners,
leafstalks, and flower stalks usually
conspicuously hairy. Leaves have smaller
leaflets mixed in with larger ones. Also
called Common Silverweed. **SIMILAR**
■ **PACIFIC SILVERWEED** (*A. egedii*):
Beaches, sandy bluffs, coastal marshes,
damp places. Runners, leafstalks, and
flower stalks hairless or only sparsely
hairy. Also called Coastal Silverweed.

Silverweed

Flowers yellow,
solitary, long-stalked.
Leaves pinnately divided
into many toothed leaflets;
silvery-hairy beneath. HT: to 6 in.

CINQUEFOILS

■ **SHRUBBY-CINQUEFOIL** (*Dasiphora
fruticosa*): Mostly summer; meadows,
boggy or swampy places, rocky shores,
slopes. Shrub. Leaflets 3–7 (usually 5).
Flowers solitary or few in a cluster; petals
broad, rounded. Also called Bush-
cinquefoil, Golden-hardhack.

Shrubby-cinquefoil

Flowers yellow.
Leaves pinnately
divided into narrow
leaflets. Shrub.
HT: 6 in.–3½ ft.

■ **CREEPING SIBBALDIA** (*Sibbaldia procumbens*): Summer; mountain meadows, alpine slopes. Stems creeping; plants mat- or cushion-forming. Leaflets have 2–5 (usually 3) teeth at tip. Flowers about ¼ in. across; 5 sepal-like bracts alternate with 5 sepals. Also called Prostrate Sibbaldia.

Genus *Sibbaldia* (1 native species). Leaves mostly basal, divided into 3 leaflets. Flowers usually in clusters; petals 5; stamens 5; pistils 5–15. Fruits seedlike, minute.

Creeping Sibbaldia

Petals yellow, minute, shorter than sepals. Leaflets 3, wedge-shaped. HT: 1–4 in.

■ **BARREN-STRAWBERRY** (*Waldsteinia fragarioides*): Spring; woods, thickets, fields. Leaflets toothed, sometimes shallowly lobed.

OTHERS With shallowly 3–5-lobed leaves (no leaflets). ■ **PIEDMONT BARREN-STRAWBERRY** (*W. lobata*): Spring; woods, stream banks. Petals shorter than sepals. Also called Lobed Barren-strawberry. ■ **IDAHO BARREN-STRAWBERRY** (*W. idahoensis*, no photo): Early summer; mountain woods and meadows. Petals as long as or slightly longer than sepals.

NOTE Do not confuse *Waldsteinia* with ⌧ Mock Strawberry (p. 595), which has solitary flowers with conspicuous 3-toothed bracts.

Genus *Waldsteinia* (3 native species). Leaves mostly basal, lobed or more often divided into 3 leaflets. Flowers in loose clusters; petals 5; stamens many; pistils 2–6. Fruits seedlike, tiny.

Barren-strawberry

Flowers yellow. Leaves long-stalked, divided into 3 leaflets. HT: 3–7 in.

Piedmont Barren-strawberry

Petals short. Leaves undivided. HT: to 6 in.

■ **COMMON AGRIMONY** (*Agrimonia gryposepala*): Summer; open woods, thickets, roadsides, marshy places. Leaves divided, with 3–9 major (larger) leaflets. Fruits top-shaped, grooved at base, bristly above. Also called Tall Agrimony.

NOTE *Agrimonia* species, also called groovebur, differ chiefly in number of major leaflets and type and degree of hairiness of various parts. Do not confuse with yellow-flowered avens (pp. 484–485), which have flowers large and not in narrow clusters.

Genus *Agrimonia* (7 native species). Leaves alternate, pinnately divided into leaflets, these mainly of 2 sizes. Flowers in elongated clusters; petals 5; stamens 5–20; pistils 2. Fruits nutlike, the rim bearing hooked bristles.

Common Agrimony

Flowers small, yellow, in long, narrow clusters. Leaves have both large and small leaflets. HT: 1–6 ft.

Fruits.

■ **WHITE AVENS** (*Geum canadense*): Late spring–summer; woods, woodland borders, stream banks, swamps. Lower leaves typically divided into 3 leaflets. Petals as long as to slightly longer than sepals; tiny sepal-like bracts alternate with sepals. Fruits in headlike clusters, with sepals downturned. **SIMILAR** With petals shorter than sepals. ■ **ROUGH AVENS** (*G. laciniatum*): Flowers white, on conspicuously long-hairy stalks.
■ **VIRGINIA AVENS** (*G. virginianum*): Flowers yellowish white to pale yellow, on minutely hairy stalks. Also called Cream Avens.

Genus *Geum* (15 species, 14 native). Leaves usually pinnately divided into leaflets. Flowers solitary or in clusters; petals 5; stamens many; pistils many. Fruits seedlike, in dense clusters. Styles persist, becoming much elongated and often kinked near tip.

White Avens

Fruits have hooked bristles.

Flowers white, solitary or few. Uppermost leaves toothed or lobed. HT: 1–3 ft.

■ **SPRING AVENS** (*Geum vernum*):
Spring; woods, thickets, disturbed places.
Leaves quite variable, even on the same
plant: may be long- or short-stalked,
simple or divided into 3 or more leaflets.
Flowers lack tiny sepal-like bracts
between sepals. Fruits have hooked
bristles, occur in dense cluster on slender
stalk raised above downturned sepals.

NOTE Do not confuse flowering
specimens with Kidney-leaf Buttercup
or Hooked Buttercup (p. 465), which lack
the stipules (paired leaflike appendages
at base of leafstalk) characteristic of the
stem leaves of many members of the rose
family, including Spring Avens.

Spring Avens

Flowers yellow
or cream-colored;
petals minute, as
long as sepals. Leaves
variable, toothed or
lobed. HT: 6–24 in.

■ **YELLOW AVENS** (*Geum aleppicum*):
Late spring–summer; meadows, stream
banks, woods, marshy or swampy places.
End leaflet of basal leaf 3–5-lobed and
toothed; main side leaflets moderately
smaller. Flower stalks often have long
hairs; petals as long as to slightly longer
than sepals; tiny sepal-like bracts
alternate with sepals. Fruits in headlike
clusters, with hooked bristles and downturned sepals. Also called Aleppo Avens.

■ **LARGE-LEAF AVENS** (*G. macrophyllum*):
Similar to Yellow Avens, but side leaflets
of basal leaf much smaller than end
leaflet; flower stalks mostly minutely
hairy, with few or no long hairs. Also
called Big-leaf Avens.

Yellow Avens

Large-leaf Avens

Fruits.

Flowers
yellow.
HT: 1–3 ft.

End leaflet round to
kidney-shaped. HT: 4–12 in.

■ **ALPINE AVENS** (*Geum rossii*): Summer; alpine meadows and slopes. Tiny, sepal-like bracts alternate with often purple-tinged sepals. Fruits seedlike, hairy, with persistent style as long as fruit, which lacks the kink found in fruits of most avens. Also called Ross' Avens.

NOTE Do not confuse with pinnate-leaved *Potentilla* species such as Sheep Cinquefoil (p. 479), which has a nearly flat, green flower base (cup- to funnel-shaped in Alpine Avens); fruits that are not hairy and with a style that arises from just below tip and breaks off at maturity. See also *Ivesia* (p. 476).

Alpine Avens
Flowers bright yellow. Leaves mostly basal, pinnately divided into toothed leaflets. HT: 3–9 in.

■ **PRAIRIE-SMOKE** (*Geum triflorum*): Spring–summer; meadows, slopes, prairies, plains, open woods. Leaves mostly basal, fernlike. Flowers several (often 3) per cluster, urn-shaped; sepals and long, narrow bracts more conspicuous than pinkish, yellowish, or whitish petals. Fruiting clusters erect; styles of fruits feathery, elongated, 1–2 in. long. Also called Old-man's-whiskers, Three-flower Avens, Pink-plumes.

■ **WATER AVENS** (*G. rivale*): Wet places. Lower leaves resemble those of Yellow Avens (p. 484). Flowers have bracts much shorter than sepals. Styles of fruits to ⁵⁄₁₆ in. long. Also called Purple Avens.

Prairie-smoke

Flowers reddish or purplish, nodding. HT: 6–24 in.

Styles of fruits not kinked.

Water Avens

Styles of fruits prominently kinked. HT: 1–3 ft.

■ **WHITE MOUNTAIN-AVENS** (*Dryas octopetala*): Summer; rocky places in mostly high mountains, tundra. Stems creeping; plants mat-forming. Leaves wrinkled above, mostly white-woolly beneath; edges scalloped, often curling under. Also called Eight-petal Mountain-avens. **SIMILAR** Same common name. **WHITE MOUNTAIN-AVENS** (*D. integrifolia*): Alaska and northern Canada, local in central and western MT. Leaves untoothed or few-toothed; upper surface smooth or only slightly wrinkled. Also called Entire-leaf Mountain-avens.

■ **YELLOW MOUNTAIN-AVENS** (*D. drummondii*): Late spring–summer. Leaves resemble those of *D. octopetala*. Also called Drummond's Mountain-avens.

Genus *Dryas* (3 native species). Shrubby; evergreen. Leaves alternate, leathery. Flowers solitary; petals 8–10; stamens many; pistils many. Fruits seedlike, with feathery styles.

White Mountain-avens

Fruits have long, feathery "tails" (styles).

Flowers long-stalked; petals white, stamens yellow. HT: 2–6 in.

Yellow Mountain-avens

Flowers yellow. HT: 4–9 in.

■ **ROSE** (*Rosa*): Late spring–summer; various habitats. Stems usually prickly; erect, or sometimes climbing or trailing. Leaves divided into 3–11 leaflets. Flowers solitary or in clusters. The seedlike fruits are enclosed in a fleshy, generally red or orange, round to pear- or urn-shaped matured hypanthium (see p. 471), sometimes topped by persistent sepals, and called a "hip."

NOTE "Wild-growing" roses include both native species and species escaped from cultivation. Native roses most often have flowers with 5 light or dark pink petals. Introduced roses occur in several colors and sometimes have many petals.

Genus *Rosa* (about 32 species, 21 native). Shrubs. Stems generally prickly. Leaves alternate, pinnately divided into leaflets; stipules (paired appendages at base of leafstalk) may be conspicuous. Flowers frequently large; petals often 5; stamens many; pistils many. Fruits seedlike.

Rose

Flowers showy; petals commonly pink. HT: mostly 1–6 ft.

Rose hips.

■ **DEWBERRY** (*Rubus flagellaris*): Spring–early summer; woods, thickets, fields, bluffs. Plants woody, prostrate or low-arching, with broad-based prickles. Fruits red when young, turning black. Also called Northern Dewberry.

■ **BRISTLY DEWBERRY** (*R. hispidus*): Summer; moist or wet places. Stems have both slender, narrow-based prickles and stiff, pointed bristles.

■ **TRAILING BLACKBERRY** (*R. ursinus*, no photo): Spring–summer; open woods, thickets, meadows. Stems have sharp prickles. Flowers white, unisexual (plants either male or female). Also called Pacific or California Blackberry, California Dewberry.

Genus *Rubus* (about 200 species, most native). Mostly shrubs, often called brambles. Stems may be prickly. Leaves simple or compound. Petals 5; stamens many; pistils several to many. Fruits juicy, tiny, clustered around a central axis (receptacle) and forming the "berry."

Dewberry

Bristly Dewberry

Flowers white.

Stems bristly. HT: to 12 in.

Stems have curved prickles. Leaflets commonly 3. HT: to 12 in.

■ **THIMBLEBERRY** (*Rubus parviflorus*): Late spring–summer; thickets, woods, woodland borders. Shrubby. Stems lack prickles. Sepals bear very short, sticky, yellow-orange hairs. Fruits raspberry-like, bright red.

■ **FLOWERING RASPBERRY** (*R. odoratus*): Summer; woodland borders. Similar to Thimbleberry. Sepals densely covered with sticky, purple hairs. Fruits dull red. Also called Purple-flowering Raspberry.

Thimbleberry

Flowers large, white, several. Leaves large, maplelike. HT: 2–6 ft.

Flowering Raspberry

Flowers pink to purple. HT: 1½–5 ft.

■ **HAIRY-FRUIT DWARF BRAMBLE**
(*Rubus lasiococcus*): Summer; thickets,
woods. Stems lack prickles, creeping.
Leaves 3-lobed or divided into 3 leaflets.
Fruits red, short-hairy.

STRAWBERRY BRAMBLE (*R. pedatus*):
Late spring–early summer; woods, stream
banks; northwestern. Similar to Hairy-fruit
Dwarf Bramble, but side leaflets usually
deeply cleft; fruits not hairy.

■ **DWARF RED RASPBERRY** (*R. pubescens*):
Midspring–midsummer; wet places. Stems
trailing or creeping. Leaves have 3 leaflets.
Petals erect, white.

■ **NAGOONBERRY** (*R. arcticus*): Summer;
moist or wet soil. Stems not creeping.
Leaflets 3. Fruits dark red or purplish.

Hairy-fruit Dwarf
Bramble

Petals spreading,
white. HT: to 4 in.

Strawberry Bramble

Leaflets appear
to be 5. HT: to 4 in.

Dwarf Red Raspberry

Fruits
dark red.
HT: 4–12 in.

Nagoonberry

Petals
pink to deep
rose. HT: 2–6 in.

■ **FALSE VIOLET** (*Dalibarda repens*):
Mostly summer; woods, swampy places.
Stems creeping. The showy flowers are
usually sterile; fruits form in shorter-
stalked, smaller, less conspicuous flowers
without petals. Also called Dewdrop,
Robin-run-away.

Genus *Dalibarda* (1 native species).
Evergreen. Leaves basal, heart-shaped.
Flowers solitary; petals 5; stamens many;
pistils 5–10. Fruits seedlike, in clusters.

False Violet

Flowers white, at
ends of long stalks;
stamens conspicuous.
Leaves on downy
stalks, violet-like;
edges scalloped.
HT: 2–6 in.

RUBIACEAE

MADDER or COFFEE FAMILY

Trees, shrubs, or woody vines; sometimes annual or perennial herbs. Leaves generally opposite or whorled; simple and commonly untoothed. Flowers frequently in clusters; usually 4-lobed (petals united); sepals mostly 4, united; stamens mostly 4; pistil 1. Fruits various. Interpetiolar stipules—small membranes at the stem junctions where 2 leaf, or leafstalk, bases meet—are a characteristic feature of the family, often present but not always easy to observe.

■ **SCARLET BOUVARDIA** (*Bouvardia ternifolia*): Spring–fall; canyons, slopes. Plants woody-based, herbaceous above. Flowers in clusters, ¾–1½ in. long, 4- or occasionally 5-lobed, finely hairy outside; flowers rarely pink or white. Also called Firecracker-bush, Trompetilla.

Genus *Bouvardia* (1 native species). Mostly shrubs. Leaves opposite or whorled. Flowers tubular or trumpet-shaped, usually 4-lobed; stamens 4 or 5. Fruits are capsules.

Scarlet Bouvardia

Flowers usually red-orange to scarlet, narrowly trumpet-shaped. Leaves mostly in whorls of 3 or 4. HT: 1–3 ft.

■ **PARTRIDGE-BERRY** (*Mitchella repens*): Late spring–midsummer; woods. Plants trailing or creeping, often mat-forming. Leaves glossy dark green with lighter midvein. Flowers in pairs at stem ends. Each berry is formed from the united ovaries of a flower pair.

Genus *Mitchella* (1 native species). Evergreen. Stems prostrate. Leaves opposite. Flowers in pairs, funnel- to trumpet-shaped and 4-lobed; stamens 4. Fruits are red (or rarely white), solitary berries derived from both flowers.

Partridge-berry

Flowers white or pink-tinged. Leaves roundish.

Berries red.

Flowers fuzzy inside.

■ **BLUETS** (*Houstonia caerulea*): Mostly spring–summer; woods, meadows, disturbed places. Leaves mostly basal, spoon-shaped. Flowers solitary, stalked, ⅜–½ in. across. Also called Quaker-ladies.

■ **SMALL BLUETS** (*H. pusilla*): Early spring; woods, meadows, disturbed places. Similar to Bluets; flowers about ¼ in. across. Also called Tiny Bluets.

■ **ROUND-LEAF BLUETS** (*H. procumbens*): Spring–fall; sandy places. Leaves opposite, broadly egg-shaped to nearly round. Also called Innocence.

■ **RED BLUETS** (*H. rubra*): Spring–summer; plains, hillsides. Leaves mostly opposite, narrow, fleshy. Flowers stalkless in leaf axils. Also called Desert Innocence.

Genus *Houstonia* (18 native species). Leaves mostly opposite, sometimes basal. Flowers funnel- to trumpet-shaped and generally 4-lobed; stamens 4. Fruits are capsules.

Bluets
Flowers pale blue with yellow eye. HT: 2–6 in.

Small Bluets
Flowers blue-violet with reddish eye. HT: 2–6 in.

Round-leaf Bluets
Flowers white. Plants creeping.

Red Bluets
Flowers bright pink to reddish, with light eye. HT: to 4 in.

■ **LONG-LEAF BLUETS** (*Houstonia longifolia*): Summer; open woods, hillsides. Leaves opposite, tapering at base. Flowers in clusters. See similar Prairie-bluets (p. 491). SIMILAR ■ **CANADIAN BLUETS** (*H. canadensis*): Spring; rocky woods, slopes. Basal leaf cluster prominent; leaf edges fringed with hairs. Also called Fringed Bluets.

■ **BROAD-LEAF BLUETS** (*H. purpurea*): Spring–midsummer; woods, rock outcrops. Leaves opposite, rounded at base. Also called Woodland Bluets.

■ **NEEDLE-LEAF BLUETS** (*H. acerosa*): Spring–summer; sandy or rocky places. Leaves opposite or whorled, very narrow, pointed. Flowers solitary.

Long-leaf Bluets
Flowers purplish to white. Leaves narrow, 1-veined. HT: 4–10 in.

Broad-leaf Bluets
Leaves broad, 3- or 5-veined. HT: 6–20 in.

Needle-leaf Bluets
Leaves stiff, needlelike. HT: 2–12 in.

■ **PRAIRIE-BLUETS** (*Stenaria nigricans*): Spring–fall; prairies, rocky hillsides, open woods. Plants grow from taproot. Flowers clustered at stem ends. Differs from Long-leaf Bluets (p. 490) by often having clusters of smaller leaves in leaf axils; some stalkless flowers. Also called Narrow-leaf-bluets, Diamond-flowers.

OTHER GENERA ■ **CLUSTERED-BLUETS** (*Oldenlandia uniflora*): Summer–fall; wet soil. Stems hairy. Leaves ¼–⅜ in. wide. Flowers clustered in leaf axils. Also called Clustered Mille-graines. ■ **KELLOGGIA** (*Kelloggia galioides*): Summer; open woods, meadow borders, slopes. Leaves narrowly lance-shaped. Few-flowered clusters at stem ends. Resembles some *Galium* (below).

Genus *Stenaria* (4 native species). Differs from *Houstonia* (p. 490) in technical characters, such as features of the seeds. Only *S. nigricans* is common.

Prairie-bluets

Flowers purplish or pink to white. Leaves opposite, narrow, 1-veined. HT: 2–20 in.

Clustered-bluets

Flowers tiny, white, stalkless. HT: 4–20 in.

Kelloggia

Fruits bristly. HT: 2–20 in.

■ **CLEAVERS** (*Galium aparine*): Spring–summer; various habitats. Plants often leaning or sprawling. Downward-pointing hairs along stem angles and leaf edges. Fruits covered with hooked bristles. Also called Catchweed Bedstraw.

SWEET-SCENTED BEDSTRAW (*G. triflorum*): Various habitats; widespread. Stem angles hairless or hairy. Leaf edges have upward-pointing hairs. Also called Fragrant Bedstraw.

■ **LICORICE BEDSTRAW** (*G. circaezans*): Woods, thickets. Leaves 3- or 5-veined, broad, widest near middle. Flowers greenish, hairy outside. Also called Forest Bedstraw, Wild-licorice. Do not confuse with Lance-leaf Bedstraw (p. 492).

Genus *Galium* (74 species, 66 native). Stems usually 4-sided. Leaves whorled. Flowers in clusters, small, 4-lobed (a few 3-lobed). Fruits usually nutlets with 2 round lobes; smooth, hairy, or with hooked bristles. Many similar species.

Cleavers

Flowers greenish white to white. Leaves 1-veined, in whorls of 8 (or 6), narrow. Fruits bristly. HT: 6 in.–3 ft.

Sweet-scented Bedstraw

Leaves in whorls of 6 (or 4). HT: 6–30 in.

Licorice Bedstraw

Leaves in whorls of 4. HT: 6–24 in.

■ **NORTHERN BEDSTRAW** (*Galium boreale*): Summer; open woods, meadows, fields, wet places. Leaves 3-veined (or 5-veined), narrowly lance-shaped, ⅝–1¾ in. long. Fruits hairless to short-hairy (lacking hooked bristles).

■ **PHLOX-LEAF BEDSTRAW** (*G. andrewsii*): Spring–summer; slopes, open woods, shrublands. Often mat-forming. Leaves narrow, about ⅜ in. long. Fruits dark, somewhat berrylike, hairless. Also called Andrews' Bedstraw.

Northern Bedstraw

Phlox-leaf Bedstraw

Flowers white. Leaves in whorls of 4, blunt-tipped. HT: 1–2½ ft.

Flowers greenish yellow. Leaves in whorls of 4, stiff and sharp-pointed. HT: 2–6 in.

■ **PURPLE BEDSTRAW** (*Galium latifolium*): Summer; woods. Leaves 3-veined, broadly lance-shaped, widest below middle. Also called Wide-leaf Bedstraw. **SIMILAR LANCE-LEAF BEDSTRAW** (*G. lanceolatum*): Northeastern, Great Lakes, Appalachian region. Leaves 3-veined (or 5-veined). Flowers yellowish green, aging purple or maroon. Fruits bristly. Also called Lance-leaf Wild-licorice. Similar Licorice Bedstraw (p. 491) has leaves widest near middle; flowers hairy outside.

NOTE See introduced bedstraws and also Ⅰ Field-madder (all shown on p. 595).

Purple Bedstraw

Flowers purple to maroon. Leaves in whorls of 4, pointed at tip. Fruits hairless. HT: 6–24 in.

■ **ROUGH BUTTONWEED** (*Diodia teres*): Summer; open woods, fields, roadsides, disturbed areas. Leaves narrow. Membranes (stipules) "connecting" a pair of leaf bases have 5–9 slender bristles. Flowers small, pinkish purple or sometimes white, hairy outside; calyx (united sepals) 4-lobed. Also called Poor-joe.

■ **VIRGINIA BUTTONWEED** (*D. virginiana*): Moist or wet places. Stipules have 3–5 bristles. Flowers white or pink-tinged, hairy inside; calyx 2-lobed.

NOTE Do not confuse *Diodia* with *Oldenlandia* (p. 491), which has stipular bristles absent; flowers tiny.

Genus *Diodia* (3 species, 2 native). Leaves opposite, stalkless. Flowers solitary or few in leaf axils; tubular below, 4-lobed; stamens 4. Fruits split into two 1-seeded nutlets.

Rough Buttonweed

Virginia Buttonweed

Flowers mostly pinkish purple, funnel-shaped; stamens short. HT: 6–30 in.

Flowers mostly white, trumpet-shaped; stamens long. HT: 6–30 in.

SANTALACEAE
SANDALWOOD FAMILY

Woody plants or perennial herbs. Partially parasitic; plants are green but obtain some nutrients through an attachment to other plants. Leaves alternate or sometimes opposite; simple and untoothed. Flowers in clusters; sepals usually 4 or 5, petal-like (true petals absent); stamens 4 or 5, opposite (in front of) sepals; pistil 1. Fruits usually berrylike.

■ **BASTARD TOADFLAX** (*Comandra umbellata*): Spring–summer; various habitats. Flowers small, clustered at stem ends. Fruits bluish, purplish, or brownish; dry to somewhat fleshy.

RELATED ■ **FALSE TOADFLAX** (*Geocaulon lividum*): Flowers small, few on stalks from leaf axils. Fruits orange to red, juicy. Also called Northern-comandra.

Genus *Comandra* (1 native species). Leaves alternate. Sepals mostly 5, triangular, each with tuft of hairs on inner surface.

Bastard Toadflax

False Toadflax

Flowers whitish with yellow-green center. HT: 4–16 in.

Flowers greenish brown to purplish. HT: 4–12 in.

SARRACENIACEAE   PITCHER-PLANT FAMILY

Perennial. Leaves hollow, tubular and opening at top to form a "pitcher" modified for trapping prey; inside, nectar production and areas of "slippery" surfaces and downward-pointing hairs direct insects deeper into the tube and hinder their escape. Flowers solitary on leafless stalks; petals 5; sepals 5; stamens many; pistil 1. Fruits are capsules.

■ **CALIFORNIA PITCHER-PLANT** (*Darlingtonia californica*): Spring–summer; boggy places with streams, seeps. Flowers have slender, greenish sepals longer than the dark red-purple petals. Also called Cobra-lily, Cobra-plant.

NOTE Insects attracted by the pitcher's aroma may land on the "fangs" and move inward, seeking the abundant nectar. They venture down—or tumble in after flying into the windowlike areas—to the pitcher base, where they are digested, primarily by bacteria.

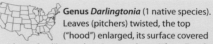
Genus *Darlingtonia* (1 native species). Leaves (pitchers) twisted, the top ("hood") enlarged, its surface covered with windowlike patches; 2 appendages ("fangs") at front. Stamens in a ring around enlarged, bell-shaped pistil.

California Pitcher-plant

Flowers large, nodding. Pitcher suggestive of a cobra with hooded head and fangs. HT: pitchers to 2 ft.

■ **YELLOW PITCHER-PLANT** (*Sarracenia flava*): Spring; wet pinelands, bogs. Base or stalk of lid narrow, often purplish, its edges bent backward (reflexed). **SIMILAR** ■ **PALE PITCHER-PLANT** (*S. alata*): Lid base shorter, its edges not reflexed.

■ **WHITE PITCHER-PLANT** (*S. leucophylla*): Pitchers have whitish and clear patches above, sometimes purple-veined; lid edge ruffled. Flowers red to maroon.

■ **SWEET PITCHER-PLANT** (*S. rubra*): Pitchers green, often red-veined above. Flowers red to maroon.

NOTE Prey-trapping mechanism is similar to California Pitcher-plant (above); prey are digested by enzymes produced by the plant.

Genus *Sarracenia* (11 native species). Leaves (pitchers) vertically winged along one side, the top bearing a hood or flaplike lid usually more or less horizontally above the opening. Petals drooping, falling early; sepals often colored, petal-like; style greatly enlarged, umbrella-like.

Yellow Pitcher-plant

Flowers large, nodding, yellow. Pitchers pale green to yellowish, sometimes purplish-tinged. HT: pitchers 1–3 ft.

White Pitcher-plant

HT: pitchers to 3 ft.

Sweet Pitcher-plant

HT: pitchers 4–24 in.

PURPLE PITCHER-PLANT (*Sarracenia purpurea*): Spring–summer; wet pinelands, swampy places, bogs. Pitchers often reclining, commonly flushed with red or purple; hood vertical, wavy-edged. Flowers burgundy red to maroon. **SIMILAR** **ROSE PITCHER-PLANT** (*S. rosea*): Flowers pink.

PARROT PITCHER-PLANT (*S. psittacina*): Spring. Pitchers reclining, broadly winged; hood round, often reddish, with whitish and clear patches. Flowers red to maroon.

HOODED PITCHER-PLANT (*S. minor*): Spring. Pitchers erect, with small vertical wing; hood strongly arching, with whitish and clear patches. Flowers yellow.

Purple Pitcher-plant

Parrot Pitcher-plant
HT: pitchers 4–10 in.

Pitchers have large, vertical wing. HT: pitchers 4–12 in.

Hooded Pitcher-plant
HT: pitchers 6–15 in.

SAURURACEAE
LIZARD'S-TAIL FAMILY

Perennial; aromatic. Leaves alternate or basal; simple and untoothed. Flowers individually tiny, in clusters; petals and sepals absent; stamens usually 6 or 8; pistils 1–5. Fruits seedlike or capsules.

YERBA-MANSA (*Anemopsis californica*): Spring–summer; moist or wet, alkaline or saline places. Leaves mostly arise from plant base, broad, fleshy, long-stalked; stem leaves few. The dense, cone-shaped cluster of 75–150 tiny flowers surrounded by 4–9 prominent, petal-like bracts resembles a single, large flower.

Genus *Anemopsis* (1 native species). Flowers in a dense cluster atop a whorl of petal-like bracts; each has 6 stamens and 1 pistil (no petals or sepals) above a small (about ¼ in.), white bract. Fruits are small capsules.

Yerba-mansa
Flowers tiny, in a conelike cluster above a ring of white (to reddish), petal-like bracts. HT: 6–30 in.

■ **LIZARD'S-TAIL** (*Saururus cernuus*): Spring–summer; wet soil, shallow water. Leaves heart-shaped. Flowers tiny, white; stamens, with their threadlike stalks (filaments), form showy part of the curved, nodding cluster. Clusters become erect in fruit. Also called Water-dragon.

Genus *Saururus* (1 native species). Leaves alternate, long-stalked, palmately veined. Flowers tiny, many, in a long, narrow cluster; pistils 3–5 per flower, joined at their bases; stamens 6 or 8 (no petals or sepals). Fruits seedlike, wrinkled.

Lizard's-tail

Slender, tail-like flower cluster tapers to a nodding tip. HT: 6 in.–4 ft.

SAXIFRAGACEAE
SAXIFRAGE FAMILY

Perennial, or rarely annual. Leaves basal and sometimes alternate; simple and usually palmately veined. Flowers commonly small, mostly in clusters; petals usually 5 (rarely 0); sepals 5; stamens 3–10; pistils usually 2 and united at base (frequently appearing as a single 2-beaked pistil). Fruits are capsules or small pods, occasionally seedlike. The flowers generally have a hypanthium (see rose family, p. 471).

■ **ELMERA** (*Elmera racemosa*): Summer; ledges, cliffs, rock crevices. Plants usually short- or long-hairy. Leaves kidney-shaped, with scalloped edges; stem leaves generally 2 or 3; basal leaves long-stalked, wider than long; stipules (paired appendages at leaf base) conspicuous. Flowers very small, sticky-hairy outside. Also called Yellow-coralbells.

NOTE Do not confuse with alumroots (pp. 499–500), all with unlobed petals; Three-toothed Miterwort (p. 497), with only basal leaves; or Fringecups or woodland-stars (p. 498), both with 10 stamens.

Genus *Elmera* (1 native species). Leaves basal and alternate, palmately veined. Flowers in clusters; petals 5, typically 3–7-lobed at tip; stamens 5.

Elmera

Flowers cream-colored to greenish yellow, tubular-cup-shaped. HT: 4–10 in.

Petals narrow, with fingerlike lobes.

■ **BREWER'S MITERWORT** (*Mitella breweri*): Late spring–summer; woods, meadows, stream banks. Stem leaves absent. Flowers small, greenish yellow; sepals spreading or back-curved; petals appear feathery or fringed; stamens 5. Also called Feathery Bishop's-cap.

SIMILAR ■ **NAKED MITERWORT** (*M. nuda*): Woods, swamps, bogs. Plants to 8 in. tall. Stem leaf 1 or absent. Flowers yellowish green; stamens 10. Also called Small or Bare-stem Bishop's-cap.

■ **FIVE-STAMEN MITERWORT** (*M. pentandra*): Moist woods, stream banks, wet meadows. Stamens 5, opposite the feathery petals (alternate with the petals in other *Mitella* species). Also called Five-point Bishop's-cap.

Genus *Mitella* (9 native species). Leaves mostly basal, palmately veined. Flowers in sometimes 1-sided clusters; petals 5, each often divided into 3–10 segments; sepals usually triangular, often petal-like, sometimes back-curved; stamens 5 (or 10). Do not confuse with *Tellima* (p. 498).

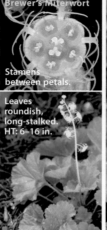

Brewer's Miterwort

Stamens between petals.

Leaves roundish, long-stalked. HT: 6–16 in.

Five-stamen Miterwort

Stamens opposite petals. HT: 6–16 in.

■ **TWO-LEAF MITERWORT** (*Mitella diphylla*): Spring; woods. Basal leaves round-egg-shaped, long-stalked. Petals divided into several threadlike segments, appearing fringed; stamens 10.

■ **SIDE-FLOWER MITERWORT** (*M. stauropetala*): Late spring–early summer; woods. Flowers white or purplish; petals have usually 3 (rarely 2 or 0) threadlike segments; sepals petal-like; stamens 5.

■ **THREE-TOOTHED MITERWORT** (*M. trifida*): Late spring–early summer; woods. Petals have 3 fingerlike (not threadlike) lobes; sepals petal-like; stamens 5.

NOTE Miterworts are also called bishop's-cap. Do not confuse with woodland-stars (p. 498), which have 10 stamens; or Elmera (p. 496).

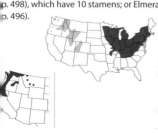

Two-leaf Miterwort

Flowers small, white. Single, opposite pair of stalkless stem leaves. HT: 6–16 in.

Side-flower Miterwort

HT: 10–20 in.

Three-toothed Miterwort

HT: 6–16 in.

■ **FRINGECUPS** (*Tellima grandiflora*): Spring–early summer; woods, thickets, stream banks. Leaves mostly basal, with long, hairy stalks; blades round-heart- to kidney-shaped, shallowly lobed and toothed. Petals fringed and often back-curved, greenish white, commonly aging reddish. Also called False Alumroot, Fragrant Fringecup.

NOTE Do not confuse with Elmera (p. 496), which has 5 stamens; miterworts (p. 497), often with only basal leaves and usually 5 stamens; or woodland-stars (below), with often deeply lobed leaves and pistils with 3 styles (styles 2 in Fringecups).

Genus *Tellima* (1 native species). Plants hairy. Leaves chiefly basal, a few alternate on stem, palmately lobed. Flowers in nearly 1-sided, elongated clusters; petals 5, fringed; stamens 10.

Fringecups

Flowers have cup-shaped base, in narrow clusters. HT: 1–3 ft.

■ **BULBOUS WOODLAND-STAR** (*Lithophragma glabrum*): Spring–early summer; open places. Basal leaves deeply divided. Small bulbs often in axils of leaves and floral bracts. Flowers pink or white.

SMALL-FLOWER WOODLAND-STAR (*L. parviflorum*): Open places; similar range. Bulbs absent. Flowers generally white.

■ **BOLANDER'S WOODLAND-STAR** (*L. bolanderi*): Slopes. Leaves shallowly lobed. Bulbs often present. Flowers white.

NOTE Several species are also called prairie-star. Do not confuse with western white-flowered miterworts (p. 497) or Elmera (p. 496), both with 5 stamens; or with Fringecups (above).

Genus *Lithophragma* (10 native species). Leaves chiefly basal, a few often alternate on stem; palmately lobed or divided. Flowers normally in clusters; petals 5, frequently toothed to deeply lobed, their bases narrow; stamens usually 10.

Bulbous Woodland-star

Petals deeply 5- (or 3-) lobed, appearing as many narrow petals. HT: 4–10 in.

Small-flower Woodland-star

Petals deeply 3- (or 5-) lobed. HT: 4–12 in.

Bolander's Woodland-star

Petals often untoothed. HT: 1–2 ft.

■ **POKER ALUMROOT** (*Heuchera cylindrica*): Spring–summer; open rocky places. Leaves basal, kidney- to heart-egg-shaped, with rounded, toothed lobes. Flowers tubular-bell-shaped; sepals showy, petal-like, cream-colored to greenish yellow (true petals much smaller or often absent). Also called Round-leaf or Lava Alumroot. Several similar species, some with greenish flowers.

■ **CORALBELLS** (*H. sanguinea*): Spring–fall; rocky canyons, shaded cliffs. Flower clusters open; sepals showy, deep pink to deep red (true petals half as long as sepals).

Genus *Heuchera* (32 native species). Leaves basal and sometimes a few on stem, palmately lobed. Flowers commonly in relatively narrow, branched clusters; saucer-shaped to tubular (often bell-shaped); petals 5 (or rarely 0), stamens 5. Species can be difficult to tell apart.

Poker Alumroot
Flowers in crowded clusters.
HT: 6–30 in.

Coralbells
Flowers reddish, bell-shaped.
HT: 1–2 ft.

■ **AMERICAN ALUMROOT** (*Heuchera americana*): Spring–early summer; open, often rocky woods, bluffs. Leaves mostly basal, roundish with toothed lobes, sometimes white-mottled. Flower clusters open; flowers greenish, whitish, or pinkish, symmetrical to slightly asymmetrical, ⅛–¼ in. long (to sepal tips); stamen tips (anthers) orange. Also called Common Alumroot.

■ **PRAIRIE ALUMROOT** (*H. richardsonii*): Open, often rocky woods, prairies, hillsides. Similar to American Alumroot, but flowers often asymmetrical, ¼–⅜ in. long; stamens and style not or typically only moderately protruding. Also called Richardson's Alumroot.

American Alumroot
Flowers very small, drooping; stamens and style long-protruding.
HT: 1–4 ft.

Prairie Alumroot
Stamens and style somewhat protruding.
HT: 6–30 in.

■ **CREVICE ALUMROOT** (*Heuchera micrantha*): Late spring–summer; cliffs, rock crevices. Leaves chiefly basal, usually longer than wide; leafstalks hairy. Petals tiny, narrow, white or occasionally pinkish; sepals hairy; stamens protruding. Also called Small-flower Alumroot. **SIMILAR** ■ **SMOOTH ALUMROOT** (*H. glabra*): Leaves usually as wide as or wider than long, with pointed teeth; leafstalks hairless. Also called Alpine Alumroot.

OTHERS Also with hairy sepals. ■ **HAIRY ALUMROOT** (*H. villosa*): Summer–early fall. Petals often coiled. Also called Maple-leaf Alumroot, Rock Alumroot. ■ **LITTLE-FLOWER ALUMROOT** (*H. parviflora*): Petals bent backward. Also called Small-flower or Cave Alumroot.

Crevice Alumroot

Leaves lobed, with small, rounded teeth. HT: mostly 6–24 in.

Hairy Alumroot — Leaves have angular lobes, pointed teeth. HT: mostly 1–3 ft.

Little-flower Alumroot — Leaves have rounded lobes and teeth. HT: mostly 6–24 in.

■ **FOAMFLOWER** (*Tiarella cordifolia*): Spring–early summer; woods. Leaves arise from plant base, heart- or egg-shaped. Flowers white or sometimes pink-tinged; stamens conspicuous; 5 petal-like sepals alternate with 5 petals that each have a narrow, stalklike base. Also called Heart-leaf Foamflower.

Genus *Tiarella* (2 native species). Leaves basal and sometimes alternate, palmately lobed or divided. Flowers in clusters; petals 5, narrow; sepals petal-like; stamens 10, prominent.

Foamflower

Flowers small, in delicate clusters. Leaves long-stalked, shallowly lobed or toothed. HT: 8–20 in.

■ **THREE-LEAF FOAMFLOWER** (*Tiarella trifoliata* var. *trifoliata*): Late spring–summer; woods, meadows, stream banks. Leaves mostly arise from plant base (stem leaves 1–3), divided into 3 leaflets, each irregularly (not deeply) lobed and toothed. Flowers have petal-like sepals; true petals threadlike, similar to the conspicuous stamen stalks (filaments), sometimes curved. Also called Western or Trefoil Foamflower. SIMILAR ■ **CUTLEAF FOAMFLOWER** (*T. trifoliata* var. *laciniata*): Leaflets deeply cut into jagged-toothed segments.

■ **ONE-LEAF FOAMFLOWER** (*T. trifoliata* var. *unifoliata*): Leaves normally not divided into leaflets, but with 3–5 toothed lobes.

Three-leaf Foamflower

One-leaf Foamflower

Flowers very small, white, in clusters. Leaves divided into 3 leaflets. HT: 8–20 in.

Leaves somewhat maplelike. HT: 8–20 in.

■ **PIGGYBACK-PLANT** (*Tolmiea menziesii*): Late spring–summer; woods, thickets, stream banks. Leaves toothed, shallowly lobed. Flowers tubular, greenish to brownish purple. Buds at the base of some leaf blades can give rise to new plants. Also called Youth-on-age.

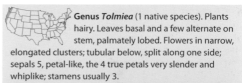

Genus *Tolmiea* (1 native species). Plants hairy. Leaves basal and a few alternate on stem, palmately lobed. Flowers in narrow, elongated clusters; tubular below, split along one side; sepals 5, petal-like, the 4 true petals very slender and whiplike; stamens usually 3.

Piggyback-plant

HT: 1–2½ ft.

■ **OREGON BOLANDRA** (*Bolandra oregana*): Late spring–early summer; moist rocks, wet cliffs. Sepals prominent, ¼–⅜ in. long, narrow, spreading. Also called Northern False Coolwort. **SIMILAR** ■ **SIERRAN BOLANDRA** (*B. californica*): Leaves have mostly blunt lobes and teeth. Sepals about ³⁄₁₆ in. long; petals greenish or purplish. Also called Sierran False Coolwort.

Genus *Bolandra* (2 native species). Leaves palmately veined, mostly basal; stem leaves alternate, those on midstem with conspicuous stipules (leaflike appendages at base of leafstalk). Petals 5, slender-tipped; stamens 5.

Oregon Bolandra

Flowers vase-shaped, in clusters; petals very narrow, purplish. Basal leaves long-stalked, roundish, with sharply toothed lobes. HT: 6–24 in.

■ **BUTTERCUP-LEAF SUKSDORFIA** (*Suksdorfia ranunculifolia*): Late spring–summer; moist or wet cliffs, ledges, rock outcrops. Basal leaves long-stalked, round or kidney-shaped, deeply 3-lobed or cut into segments; edges have round lobes or teeth. Flowers in somewhat flat-topped clusters; petal bases sometimes purplish-tinged. Also called Buttercup-leaf Mock Brookfoam. Do not confuse with boykinias (p. 503), which have basal leaves with pointed or triangular teeth.

■ **VIOLET SUKSDORFIA** (*S. violacea*): Spring. Stem leaves bear toothed, leaflike stipules at base; basal leaves undivided, with scallop-lobed edges. Also called Violet Mock Brookfoam.

Genus *Suksdorfia* (2 native species). Plants sticky-hairy above. Leaves basal and alternate, palmately lobed to divided; stem leaves fewer, their bases enlarged or bearing conspicuous leaflike appendages (stipules). Flowers in clusters; petals 5; stamens 5.

Buttercup-leaf Suksdorfia

Violet Suksdorfia

Flowers white. Stem leaves enlarged at base. HT: 4–14 in.

Flowers violet. HT: 4–10 in.

■ SULLIVANT'S SULLIVANTIA

(*Sullivantia sullivantii*): Late spring–summer; rocks, cliffs. Leaves mostly basal, long-stalked, shallowly lobed and toothed. **SIMILAR** Differing in range and technical characters. ■ **HAPEMAN'S SULLIVANTIA** (*S. hapemanii*). ■ **OREGON SULLIVANTIA** (*S. oregana*).

NOTE Sullivantias are also called coolwort. Do not confuse with boykinias (below), which have leaves of some species cut more than halfway to base; petals ³⁄₁₆–¼ in. long, falling after flowering (in sullivantias, ⅛ in. or less long and persisting even after withering).

Genus *Sullivantia* (3 native species). Leaves chiefly basal, with a few sometimes on stems, palmately veined or lobed. Flowers in clusters; petals 5; stamens 5.

Sullivant's Sullivantia

Flowers very small, white, in clusters. Leaves round-kidney-shaped. HT: 4–14 in.

■ COAST BOYKINIA (*Boykinia*

occidentalis): Summer; moist woods, stream banks. Midstem leaves commonly bear brownish, bristlelike stipules. Petals spoon-shaped to elliptic, white, about ³⁄₁₆ in. long. Also called Coastal Brookfoam.

■ **MOUNTAIN BOYKINIA** (*B. major*): Stream banks, wet meadows. Midstem leaves bear conspicuous, leafy stipules. Petals round, white, about ¼ in. long. Also called Mountain Brookfoam.

■ **EASTERN BOYKINIA** (*B. aconitifolia*, no photo): Moist woods, cliffs, stream banks. Leaves similar to Mountain Boykinia. Flowers and stipules similar to Coast Boykinia. Also called Allegheny Brookfoam, Brook-saxifrage.

Genus *Boykinia* (6 native species). Plants often sticky-hairy. Leaves basal and alternate, palmately lobed, the lobes toothed; commonly with stipules (appendages at base of leafstalk). Flowers in clusters, bell- or urn-shaped below; petals 5, often falling early; stamens 5.

Coast Boykinia

Mountain Boykinia

Leaves deeply lobed. HT: 1–3 ft.

Flowers in open clusters. Leaves shallowly lobed. HT: 6–18 in.

Flowers in relatively dense clusters.

■ **ROUND-LEAF BOYKINIA** (*Boykinia rotundifolia*): Summer; stream banks, seeps. Leaves kidney-shaped to nearly circular, with inconspicuous, bristlelike stipules (appendages at base). Petals white, about ¹⁄₁₆ in., barely longer than the green sepals. Also called Round-leaf Brookfoam.

ALASKA BOYKINIA (*B. richardsonii*): High mountain meadows, tundra, heathlands; Alaska, Yukon Territory. Leaf shape similar to Round-leaf Boykinia. Petals white or pinkish, about ½ in., conspicuously longer than the often purplish sepals. Also called Bear-flower, Richardson's Boykinia, Richardson's Brookfoam.

Round-leaf Boykinia

Flowers urn-shaped. Leaves shallowly round-lobed, toothed. HT: mostly 1–2½ ft.

Alaska Boykinia

Flowers bell-shaped. HT: mostly 12–20 in.

■ **TELESONIX** (*Telesonix heucheriformis*): Summer; rock crevices, ledges, outcrops. Sepals often reddish. Flowers have bell-shaped base; petals (including "stalk") ⅛–¼ in. long, with narrow blade.

■ **JAMES' TELESONIX** (*T. jamesii*): Very similar to and frequently treated as a variety of *T. heucheriformis*. Petals ¼–⅜ in. long, with nearly circular blade. Also called James' False Saxifrage.

NOTE Do not confuse with Purple Mountain Saxifrage (p. 509), which has opposite, stalkless, very small stem leaves.

Genus *Telesonix* (2 native species). Plants generally sticky-hairy. Leaves basal and alternate, palmately veined. Flowers in clusters; petals 5, with narrow, stalklike base; stamens 10.

Telesonix

James' Telesonix

Flowers in clusters, pink to magenta. Leaves stalked, kidney-shaped, toothed. HT: 3–8 in.

HT: 3–8 in.

■ **MERTEN'S SAXIFRAGE** (*Saxifraga mertensiana*): Spring–summer; stream banks, ledges, rock outcrops. Leaves basal, kidney-shaped to nearly round. Flowers very small. Small pinkish bulbs often in leaf axils or flower clusters.

■ **BROOK SAXIFRAGE** (*S. odontoloma*): Summer; moist or wet places. Leaves round-kidney-shaped. Also called Stream Saxifrage. **SIMILAR RED-STEM SAXIFRAGE** (*S. lyallii*): Northwestern MT to AK. Leaves fan-shaped, toothed along broad tip. Also called Lyall's Saxifrage.

OTHER ■ **HEART-LEAF SAXIFRAGE** (*S. nelsoniana*, no photo): Leaves regularly toothed; bulbs absent.

Genus *Saxifraga* (66 native species). Leaves usually basal. Flowers usually in clusters; petals usually 5; stamens 10, often conspicuous, sometimes with flattened stalks and resembling narrow petals; paired pistil tips in flower center generally conspicuous.

Merten's Saxifrage

Brook Saxifrage

Leaves have shallow, typically 3-toothed lobes.

Leaves regularly toothed.

Petals egg-shaped, white, not spotted. HT: 6–16 in.

Petals roundish, stalked, white with 2 yellowish spots at base. HT: 8–24 in.

■ **RUSTY SAXIFRAGE** (*Saxifraga ferruginea*): Summer; stream banks, rock outcrops, seeps, open woods. Leaves basal, toothed. Flowers small. **SIMILAR** ■ **MICHAUX'S SAXIFRAGE** (*S. michauxii*): Appalachian region. Also called Mountain or Cliff Saxifrage.

■ **BUD SAXIFRAGE** (*S. bryophora*): Summer; mountain meadows, ledges. Leaves untoothed or few-toothed. Flowers often replaced by small bulbs.

■ **LETTUCE-LEAF SAXIFRAGE** (*S. micranthidifolia*): Spring–early summer; wet cliffs, stream banks, rocky woods. Basal leaves numerous, sharply and prominently toothed. Also called Mountain-lettuce.

Rusty Saxifrage

Flowers white; 3 larger petals yellow-spotted at base. Pinkish bulbs sometimes present in clusters. HT: 6–18 in.

Bud Saxifrage

Lettuce-leaf Saxifrage

All petals yellow-spotted at base. HT: 2–10 in.

HT: 12–30 in.

■ **OREGON SAXIFRAGE** (*Saxifraga oregana*): Spring–summer; bogs, marshes, wet meadows. Leaves widest above middle, untoothed or wavy-toothed. Flower clusters initially dense, more open in age; petals often fall early. Also called Bog Saxifrage.

■ **SWAMP SAXIFRAGE** (*S. pensylvanica*): Late spring–early summer. Similar to Oregon Saxifrage. Leaves untoothed to obscurely toothed. Also called Eastern Saxifrage.

Oregon Saxifrage
Petals tiny, white or greenish white. Leaves basal.
HT: 1–3½ ft.

Swamp Saxifrage
Petals tiny, greenish white or purplish.
HT: 1–3½ ft.

■ **EARLY SAXIFRAGE** (*Saxifraga virginiensis*): Spring; rock outcrops, ledges, rocky woods, stream banks. Flowering stems hairy. Leaves usually shallowly toothed. Flower clusters compact when young, become open in age.

■ **CALIFORNIA SAXIFRAGE** (*S. californica*): Shaded, often grassy places. Petals relatively broad. **SIMILAR** ■ **RED-FUZZ SAXIFRAGE** (*S. eriophora*): Moist slopes. Leaves reddish-hairy beneath.

NOTE There are several western species similar to the ones shown here.

Early Saxifrage

California Saxifrage
Petals broader.
HT: 6–12 in.

Petals white. Leaves basal, egg-shaped to elliptic. HT: 4–14 in.

DIAMOND-LEAF SAXIFRAGE
(*Saxifraga rhomboidea*): Spring–summer;
slopes, mountain meadows. Plants sticky-
hairy above. Leaves usually toothed;
leafstalks winged. Also called Snowball
Saxifrage. Do not confuse with American
Bistort (p. 433). SIMILAR **GRASSLAND
SAXIFRAGE** (*S. integrifolia*): Spring; grassy
slopes, mountain meadows. Upper stems
and leaves hairy, mostly untoothed; leaf
edges often minutely hairy-fringed. Also
called Columbian Saxifrage.

Diamond-leaf Saxifrage

Flowers small, white, in
close clusters. Leaves basal,
triangular-egg- to diamond-
shaped. HT: 4–12 in.

SPOTTED SAXIFRAGE (*Saxifraga
bronchialis*): Late spring–summer; rocky
slopes, crevices, cliffs. Plants cushion-
or mat-forming. Leaves mostly in basal
tufts (a few on stem), bristly-edged,
narrowly bayonet-shaped, stiff, ¼–½ in.
long. Petals sometimes appear yellowish.
Also called Matted or Dotted Saxifrage.
SIMILAR **THREE-TOOTH SAXIFRAGE**
(*S. tricuspidata*): Alaska, Canada. Leaves
wedge-shaped, with sharply 3-toothed
tip. Also called Prickly Saxifrage.

Spotted
Saxifrage

Petals white or
cream-colored,
spotted yellowish
and purplish; stamen
stalks threadlike.
HT: 2–6 in.

TOLMIE'S SAXIFRAGE (*S. tolmiei*):
Summer; high mountain meadows, stream
banks, rock crevices. Basal leaves crowded,
fleshy, club- to narrowly spoon-shaped,
round-tipped, smooth-edged, ⅛–⅜ in. long.

Tolmie's Saxifrage

Petals white,
unspotted; stamen
stalks wide, resemble
narrow petals. HT: 1–4 in.

■ **TUFTED SAXIFRAGE** (*Saxifraga caespitosa*): Late spring–summer; rocky places in high mountains. Plants often mat-forming, sticky-hairy above. Leaves chiefly basal (1 or 2 reduced leaves on stem), 2–7-lobed (commonly 3-lobed) at tip. Flowers 1 to few, sometimes pale yellow; petals not stalked. Also called Tufted Alpine Saxifrage.

SIMILAR ■ **WEDGE-LEAF SAXIFRAGE** (*S. adscendens*): Plants generally in single clumps rather than mat-forming; leaves basal and 3–8 on stem, typically shallowly 3-toothed at tip; petals short-stalked.

Tufted Saxifrage

Flowers small, often white. Basal leaves crowded, mostly 3-lobed at tip. HT: mostly 1–6 in.

■ **WEAK SAXIFRAGE** (*Saxifraga rivularis*): Summer; rocky places in high mountains. Leaves basal and on stem, round-kidney-shaped, 3–7-lobed. Flowers 3/16–3/8 in. across; petals occasionally pinkish-veined. Also called Pygmy or Alpine Saxifrage.

■ **NODDING SAXIFRAGE** (*S. cernua*): Similar to Weak Saxifrage, but flowers usually solitary, 3/8–3/4 in. across; clusters of small bulbs in leaf axils, replacing all but uppermost flowers. Also called Drooping Saxifrage.

Weak Saxifrage

Flowers small, white, in clusters of 2–5. Leaves ivylike. HT: 1–4 in.

Nodding Saxifrage

Stems bear red or purplish bulbs. HT: to 6 in.

■ **WHIPLASH SAXIFRAGE** (*Saxifraga flagellaris*): Summer; high rocky places, alpine meadows. Plants spread by whiplike runners (stolons). Leaves hairy-edged. Sepals more or less erect. Also called Spider-plant, Stoloniferous Saxifrage. **SIMILAR** ■ **GOLDBLOOM SAXIFRAGE** (*S. chrysantha*): Runners absent; leaves nearly hairless; sepals bent downward.

OTHERS Chiefly in Alaska and Canada; similar height. ■ **YELLOW MARSH SAXIFRAGE** (*S. hirculus*): Wet meadows, tundra. Sepals downturned, their edges fringed. ■ **YELLOW MOUNTAIN SAXIFRAGE** (*S. aizoides*): Stream banks, moist rocks. Sepals spreading, hairless.

Whiplash Saxifrage

Yellow Marsh Saxifrage
Petals often spotted.
HT: 2–10 in.

Flowers yellow, solitary to 3. Basal leaves in dense clusters. Runners slender, reddish. HT: 2–5 in.

Yellow Mountain Saxifrage

Sepals visible between petals. HT: 2–5 in.

■ **PURPLE MOUNTAIN SAXIFRAGE** (*Saxifraga oppositifolia*): Spring–summer; rocky alpine places, heathlands, tundra. Plants cushion- or mat-forming. Leaves opposite (unusual for a saxifrage), commonly oval. Flowers solitary, showy; sepal edges hairy-fringed. Also called Purple or Twinleaf Saxifrage.

NOTE Do not confuse with Moss Campion (p. 196), which has leaves very narrow and petals sometimes notched; or with James' Telesonix (p. 504).

Purple Mountain Saxifrage

Flowers magenta to purple. Leaves very small, conspicuously hairy-fringed. HT: 1–2 in.

■ LEATHERLEAF-SAXIFRAGE

(*Leptarrhena pyrolifolia*): Summer; moist or wet mountain meadows, stream banks. Leaves mostly basal, hairless, 1–6 in. long, generally widest at or above middle. Stamens conspicuous (top right photo); petals sometimes pinkish. Fruits (bottom right photo) turn red or reddish purple. Also called Pearleaf, False Saxifrage.

Genus *Leptarrhena* (1 native species). Similar to *Saxifraga* (p. 505), differing in technical characters. The dark green, deeply veined, leathery leaves easily distinguish it from look-alike species such as Oregon Saxifrage (p. 506).

Leatherleaf-saxifrage

Flowers small, white, in crowded clusters. Leaves leathery, glossy, scallop-toothed. HT: 6–18 in.

■ UMBRELLA-PLANT (*Darmera peltata*):

Spring–early summer; mountain streams and stream banks. Leaves nearly circular, mostly 8–16 in. across, lobed and toothed; leafstalk attached near middle of underside. Flowers often pink, sometimes white, in clusters on long, hairy stalks; flowers bloom before the large leaves appear. Also called Indian-rhubarb, Great Shield-leaf.

Genus *Darmera* (1 native species). Leaves basal, long-stalked, circular, depressed in center. Flowers in clusters; petals 5; stamens 10.

Umbrella-plant

HT: 1–5 ft.

■ **FALSE GOAT'S-BEARD** (*Astilbe biternata*): Late spring–early summer; woods, slopes. Upper stems finely sticky-hairy. Leaves divided; end leaflets commonly 3-lobed. Petals greenish white, white, or yellowish white (female flowers sometimes petal-less). Seedlike fruits about ⅛ in. long, erect. Also called Appalachian False Goat's-beard.

NOTE Do not confuse with the similar but more widespread Goat's-beard (p. 473), which has end leaflets usually not lobed; flowers with 15–30 stamens (male) or with usually 3 pistils (female); fruits about ⅟₁₆ in. long, downward-pointing.

Genus *Astilbe* (2 species, 1 native). Leaves alternate, divided into large leaflets. Flowers in showy, feathery clusters; petals 5; frequently (but not always) unisexual, the male flowers (with 10 stamens) and female flowers (with 2 pistils joined at bases) on separate plants.

False Goat's-beard
Flowers tiny, in plumelike sprays. Leaflets sharply toothed. HT: 3–6 ft.

Male flowers.

■ **AMERICAN GOLDEN-SAXIFRAGE** (*Chrysosplenium americanum*): Spring; mud, seeps, springy places. Plants mat-forming. Leaves mostly opposite. Flowers very small, stalkless; stamens typically 8. Also called Water-mat, Water-carpet. **SIMILAR** ■ **PACIFIC GOLDEN-SAXIFRAGE** (*C. glechomifolium*): Leaves scallop-edged; flowers short-stalked. Also called Western Golden-saxifrage.

■ **NORTHERN GOLDEN-SAXIFRAGE** (*C. tetrandrum*): Late spring–early summer. Stamens 4.

Genus *Chrysosplenium* (6 native species). Leaves opposite or alternate. Petals absent; sepals 4; stamens 4–8, attached along the edge of an 8-lobed fleshy central disk that surrounds the paired pistil tips. Opened fruits cuplike, with plump seeds, resembling eggs in a nest.

American Golden-saxifrage

Flowers commonly green or greenish yellow, with red- or orange-tipped stamens. Leaves untoothed or few-toothed.

Northern Golden-saxifrage

Plants often yellowish green; seeds reddish.

SCROPHULARIACEAE   FIGWORT or SNAPDRAGON FAMILY

Annual or perennial herbs, sometimes shrubs. Leaves variously arranged, simple to dissected. Flowers solitary or in clusters; petals 4 or usually 5 (or rarely 0), united, frequently 2-lipped; sepals mostly 4 or 5; stamens typically 4 in 2 unequal-length pairs, occasionally 2 or 5; sterile (antherless) stamen sometimes present; pistil 1. Fruits are capsules. Do not confuse with the mint family (Lamiaceae, p. 277).

YELLOW MONKEY-FLOWER (*Mimulus guttatus*): Spring–summer; wet places; western. Leaves mostly palmately veined. Flowers yellow, ½–1½ in. long; long-stalked; uppermost calyx lobe larger. SIMILAR ■ ROUND-LEAF MONKEY-FLOWER (*M. glabratus*): Flowers ⅝–¾ in.

■ **MUSK MONKEY-FLOWER**
(*M. moschatus*): Summer. Leaves pinnately veined. Flowers ⅝–1¼ in. long. SIMILAR **FLORIFEROUS MONKEY-FLOWER** (*M. floribundus*): Western. Flowers smaller.

Genus *Mimulus* (about 90 native species). Leaves opposite. Flowers usually solitary in upper leaf axils; funnel- or trumpet-shaped and 2-lipped, lower lip with 2 often hairy ridges; calyx (united sepals) tubular and 5-angled; stamens 4.

Yellow Monkey-flower

Flowers strongly 2-lipped; ridges on lower lip nearly close throat. HT: mostly 6 in.–3 ft.

Musk Monkey-flower

Flowers weakly 2-lipped; throat usually open, hairy; calyx lobes mostly equal. HT: 2–12 in.

■ **PRIMROSE MONKEY-FLOWER**
(*Mimulus primuloides*): Summer; moist slopes, wet meadows. Plants creeping, mat-forming. Leaves mostly crowded near plant base. Flowers weakly 2-lipped, ½–¾ in. long, often red-spotted; throat open; lobes rounded or often notched. Also called Yellow Creeping or Meadow Monkey-flower.

■ **LITTLE RED-STEM MONKEY-FLOWER**
(*M. rubellus*): Spring–early summer; washes and moist, often sandy places. Plants commonly sticky-hairy; stems frequently reddish. Leaves along stem. Flowers stalked, ¼–⁵⁄₁₆ in. long; ribs of calyx (united sepals) often reddish.

Primrose Monkey-flower

Flowers yellow, on long, slender stalks. HT: 1–5 in.

Little Red-stem Monkey-flower

Flowers often yellow. HT: 1–8 in.

Flowers sometimes pink to purplish.

■ **LEWIS' MONKEY-FLOWER** (*Mimulus lewisii*): Summer; moist or wet places in mountains. Plants sticky-hairy. Leaves opposite, mostly 1½–3 in. long, egg- or lance-shaped, usually toothed. Flowers ¼–2 in. long, long-stalked. Also called Great Purple Monkey-flower.

OTHERS With similarly colored but smaller, nearly stalkless flowers.
■ **BIGELOW'S MONKEY-FLOWER** (*M. bigelovii*): Spring; washes, desert plains and slopes. Leaves ⅝–1⅜ in. long, mostly untoothed. Flowers ¾–1 in. long. Also called Desert or Yellow-throat Monkey-flower. ■ **DWARF PURPLE MONKEY-FLOWER** (*M. nanus*): Late spring–early summer; shrublands, open woods, slopes. Leaves generally ½–¾ in. long, untoothed. Flowers ⅜–⅝ in. long; style slightly protruding.

Lewis' Monkey-flower
Flowers pink to purple, with hairy yellow throat.
HT: 1–3 ft.

Bigelow's Monkey-flower
HT: 1–10 in.

Dwarf Purple Monkey-flower
HT: 1–4 in.

■ **SCARLET MONKEY-FLOWER** (*Mimulus cardinalis*): Spring–fall; seeps, wet canyons, stream banks. Plants sticky-hairy. Leaves opposite, toothed. Flowers ½–2 in. long, on stalks 1¼–4 in. long; strongly 2-lipped: upper lip erect and arching, with lobes sometimes swept back, lower lip spreading or downturned. Also called Crimson or Cardinal Monkey-flower. **SIMILAR** ■ **EASTWOOD'S MONKEY-FLOWER** (*M. eastwoodiae*): Late spring–summer; moist crevices, cliffs. Stems trailing or hanging. Flowers about 1 in. long, on stalks mostly ⅜–1¼ in. long. Also called Scarlet Monkey-flower.

Scarlet Monkey-flower

Flowers large, scarlet to orange-red, with hairy yellow throat; stamens and style protruding.
HT: 1–3 ft.

■ **YELLOW-AND-WHITE MONKEY-FLOWER** (*Mimulus bicolor*): Spring; moist places. Flowers mostly ⅝–1 in. long.

■ **NARROW-LEAF PANSY MONKEY-FLOWER** (*M. angustatus*): Vernal pools, grassy depressions. Leaves narrow. Flowers 1–2 in. long. Also called Purple-lip Pansy Monkey-flower.

■ **DEATH VALLEY MONKEY-FLOWER** (*M. rupicola*): Crevices. Flowers about 1 in. long. Also call Rock-midget.

■ **DOUGLAS' MONKEY-FLOWER** (*M. douglasii*): Slopes. Flowers 1–2 in. long; upper lip 2-lobed, lower lip minute. Also called Chinless Monkey-flower, Purple Mouse-ears, Brownies.

Yellow-and-white Monkey-flower

Flowers white and yellow, usually red-spotted. HT: 4–12 in.

Narrow-leaf Pansy Monkey-flower

Flowers pink-purple with purple spots, yellow throat. HT: 2–4 in.

Death Valley Monkey-flower

Flowers pink or whitish, with purple spots, yellow center. HT: 1–6 in.

Douglas' Monkey-flower

Flowers magenta with yellow and purple mottling within. HT: 2–3 in.

■ **BUSH MONKEY-FLOWERS** (*Mimulus aurantiacus* and related species): Spring–summer; rocky places, hills, canyons, shrublands, open woods. Plants typically are much-branched shrubs. Leaves often somewhat sticky; edges commonly rolled under. Flowers 1–2½ in. long, variably colored white, cream, light yellow, golden yellow, yellow-orange, orange, salmon, brick-red, or crimson.

NOTE These differ from other *Mimulus* in being woody, at least at the plant base. They are sometimes placed in their own genus, *Diplacus*.

Bush Monkey-flower

Leaves opposite. Plants shrubby. HT: 6 in.–5 ft.

■ **DOWNY MONKEY-FLOWER** (*Mimulus pilosus*): Spring–summer; moist, gravelly or sandy places. Leaves relatively narrow. Flowers ¼–⅜ in. long.

NOTE This species differs from other *Mimulus* in having a more deeply lobed calyx (united sepals) that is not 5-angled. It is sometimes placed in its own genus, *Mimetanthe*, and called False Monkey-flower.

Downy Monkey-flower

Flowers small, yellow with 2 maroon dots. Leaves opposite. Plants densely soft-hairy. HT: 2–12 in.

■ **ALLEGHENY MONKEY-FLOWER** (*Mimulus ringens*): Summer; wet places. Stems 4-angled. Leaves stalkless, lance-shaped, toothed. Flowers ¾–1¼ in. long, on stalks ¾–1½ in. long, purplish (or occasionally pinkish to whitish) with yellowish or whitish center. Also called Square-stem Monkey-flower.

■ **SHARP-WING MONKEY-FLOWER** (*M. alatus*): Similar to Allegheny Monkey-flower. Leafstalks narrowly winged, ⅛–¾ in. long. Flowers similar in color to *M. ringens*, nearly stalkless or on stalks to ⅛ in. long (to ⅝ in. long in fruit).

Allegheny Monkey-flower

Flowers violet-blue to lavender, conspicuously stalked. Leaves stalkless. HT: 1–4 ft.

Sharp-wing Monkey-flower

Flowers not notably stalked. Leaves distinctly stalked. HT: 1–3 ft.

■ **STICKY CHINESE-HOUSES** (*Collinsia tinctoria*): Late spring–summer; rocky areas, open woods. Leaves opposite. Flowers in dense, sticky-hairy whorls, nearly stalkless; upper lip much smaller than "bearded" (short-haired) lower lip. Also called Tincture-plant.

SIMILAR With upper and lower lips nearly equal in size. ■ **CHINESE-HOUSES** (*C. heterophylla*): Spring–midsummer; shady places. Upper lip white to pale lavender, lower lip violet to rose-purple. Also called Innocence, Purple Chinese-houses.
■ **SOUTHERN CHINESE-HOUSES** (*C. concolor*): Spring; open woods, shrublands. Flowers bluish purple; upper lip mostly the same shade as lower lip.

 Genus *Collinsia* (19 native species). Leaves opposite. Flowers solitary or in clusters, 2-lipped: upper lip erect and 2-lobed, lower lip appears 2-lobed, with middle (3rd) lobe folded lengthwise and hidden beneath side lobes; fertile stamens 4, enclosed in hidden middle lobe of lower lip.

Sticky Chinese-houses
Flowers yellowish, whitish, or lavender, with purple spots or lines. HT: 6–24 in.

Chinese-houses
HT: 6–24 in.

Southern Chinese-houses
HT: 6–24 in.

■ **LARGE-FLOWER BLUE-EYED MARY** (*Collinsia grandiflora*): Spring–early summer; open places. Leaves opposite. Flower stalks to ¾ in. long. Do not confuse with Chinese-houses (above), which has dense whorls of short-stalked flowers with violet lower lip.

■ **SMALL-FLOWER BLUE-EYED MARY** (*C. parviflora*): Spring–early summer; shady places. Flowers small, in loose whorls above but often opposite below.

OTHERS Eastern woodland species.
■ **EASTERN BLUE-EYED MARY** (*C. verna*, no photo): Spring. Similar to Large-flower Blue-eyed Mary. ■ **VIOLET BLUE-EYED MARY** (*C. violacea*): Flowers typically white and violet, with lobes more deeply notched than Eastern Blue-eyed Mary.

Large-flower Blue-eyed Mary
Flowers in loose whorls; upper lip white to light blue, lower lip deep blue. HT: 4–16 in.

Small-flower Blue-eyed Mary
HT: 4–16 in.

Violet Blue-eyed Mary
HT: 8–15 in.

■ **SPINSTER'S BLUE-EYED MARY**
(*Collinsia sparsiflora*): Spring; grassy places, shrublands. Leaves opposite, narrow. Flowers long-stalked, solitary in axils of bracts, or occasionally 2 or 3 together; flowers sometimes whitish. Also called Few-flower Blue-eyed Mary.

■ **RATTAN'S BLUE-EYED MARY**
(*C. rattanii*): Spring; open woods. Flowers small. Also called Sticky Blue-eyed Mary.
SIMILAR ■ **TORREY'S BLUE-EYED MARY**
(*C. torreyi*): Spring–summer; open woods. Flowers in axils of much reduced bracts; upper lip pale, lower lip mostly violet-blue; stalks strongly downturned in fruit.

Spinster's Blue-eyed Mary

Upper stems nearly hairless.

Flowers usually lavender or purple; lower lip often darker. HT: 3–12 in.

Rattan's Blue-eyed Mary

Upper stems finely sticky-hairy. HT: 3–15 in.

■ **LARGE-FLOWER TONELLA** (*Tonella floribunda*): Spring; rocky slopes, grassy hills. Main leaves deeply cut into 3 segments, lowermost and uppermost sometimes undivided. Flowers ¼–½ in. across, in loose whorls. Also called Beautiful or Giant Tonella, Greater Baby-innocence.

■ **SMALL-FLOWER TONELLA** (*T. tenella*): Open woods, slopes. Flowers ³⁄₁₆ in. or less across. Also called Lesser Baby-innocence.

Genus *Tonella* (2 native species). Leaves opposite. Flowers in axils of upper leaves, 2-lipped or with 5 unequal lobes; stamens 4.

Large-flower Tonella

Small-flower Tonella

Flowers tiny. HT: 2–10 in.

Flowers light blue-lavender and whitish, with purple marks. HT: 5–15 in.

■ **BLUE TOADFLAX** (*Nuttallanthus canadensis*): Spring–early summer; open woods, fields, roadsides. Leaves very narrow; alternate on erect stems, opposite on nonflowering prostrate stems. Flowers ¼–⅜ in. long, bluish to purple (rarely white), with 2 white bumps near center; spur ¹⁄₁₆–¼ in. long; stalk hairless, short (¹⁄₁₆–¼ in. long). Also called Oldfield Toadflax. SIMILAR ■ **TEXAS TOADFLAX** (*N. texanus*): Flowers about ½ in. long; spur ³⁄₁₆–⅜ in. long.

■ **FLORIDA TOADFLAX** (*N. floridanus*): Spring; sandy places. Flowers ³⁄₁₆–¼ in. long; spur minute; stalk sticky-hairy, ³⁄₁₆–½ in. long. Also called Apalachicola Toadflax.

Genus *Nuttallanthus* (3 native species). Leaves alternate or opposite. Flowers in clusters, 2-lipped: upper lip 2-lobed, lower lip 3-lobed; slender downward projection (spur) at base; stamens 4.

Blue Toadflax

Florida Toadflax

Flower spur slender, often curved. HT: 4–26 in.

Flower spur inconspicuous. HT: 4–16 in.

■ **NUTTALL'S-SNAPDRAGON** (*Sairocarpus nuttallianus*): Spring–early summer; rocky places, canyons, dunes. Stems weak, clinging via twining branchlets. Also called Violet Toad's-mouth.

■ **COULTER'S-SNAPDRAGON** (*S. coulterianus*): Disturbed places, such as after fire. Also weak-stemmed. Flowers white or lavender-tinged, with white or yellowish hump. Also called White-snapdragon, Chaparral Toad's-mouth.

■ **WITHERED-SNAPDRAGON** (*S. multiflorus*): Disturbed places. Stems erect, stout. Flowers rose-pink with cream-colored or tan-yellow, wrinkled hump. Also called Sticky-snapdragon, Sierran Toad's-mouth.

Genus *Sairocarpus* (12 native species). Plants often hairy. Leaves mostly opposite below, alternate above. Flowers usually in clusters, 2-lipped: upper lip has 2 erect earlike lobes, lower lip has 3 spreading lobes and prominent hump in middle that closes throat opening; stamens 4.

Nuttall's-snapdragon
Flowers violet with whitish, purple-veined hump. HT: 1–3 ft.

Coulter's-snapdragon
HT: 1–4 ft.

Withered-snapdragon
HT: 2–5 ft.

■ **YELLOW TWINING-SNAPDRAGON**
(*Neogaerrhinum filipes*): Late winter–
spring; washes, desert slopes. Commonly
climbing or twining among desert shrubs.
Leaves opposite, linear or narrowly lance-
or egg-shaped. Flowers on stalks 1–4 in.
long; lower lip has dark-spotted, hairy
hump. Also called Filipes-snapdragon.

■ **LAX TWINING-SNAPDRAGON**
(*N. strictum*): Spring; rocky slopes, grassy
hills, shrublands, especially after fire.
Climbing on other plants or trailing. Lower
lip of flower has purple-veined, hairy
hump. Also called Kellogg-snapdragon.

NOTE Twining-snapdragons are also
called climbing-snapdragon.

 Genus *Neogaerrhinum* (2 native species).
Twining, vinelike. Leaves opposite, sometimes alternate above. Flowers solitary in
leaf axils, 2-lipped: upper lip 2-lobed, lower lip 3-lobed;
stamens 4.

 Yellow Twining-snapdragon

 Flowers
yellow, on
very slender,
twining
stalks.

 Lax Twining-snapdragon

 Flowers
lavender
to blue-violet.

■ **SNAPDRAGON-VINE** (*Maurandella
antirrhiniflora*): Spring–fall; climbing or
sprawling over rocks, sand, or shrubs.
Vine. Leaves arrowhead-shaped. Flowers
on stalks ½–1½ in. long; lower lip has
hairy, dark-lined, cream-colored or
yellowish hump partially closing throat.
Also called Violet Twining-snapdragon,
Roving-sailor.

RELATED ■ **DUNE SNAPDRAGON-
VINE** (*Epixiphium wislezeni*): Similar vine.
Flowers on stalks ⅜ in. or less long; hairy
hump on lower lip does not close throat.
Calyx (united sepals) becomes net-veined
and inflated in fruit. Also called Net-cup
Snapdragon-vine, Balloon-shrub.

 Genus *Maurandella* (1 native species).
Prostrate or twining. Leaves alternate
to nearly opposite, palmately veined.
Flowers solitary in leaf axils, 2-lipped: upper lip 2-lobed,
lower lip 3-lobed; stamens 4.

 Snapdragon-vine
Flowers
sometimes
rose-red.

 Flowers
commonly
violet, typically
long-stalked.

 Dune Snapdragon-vine

Flowers lavender,
on short stalks.

■ **GHOST-FLOWER** (*Mohavea confertiflora*): Spring; gravelly slopes, sandy washes. Leaves narrow. Flowers somewhat cuplike, abundantly maroon-spotted within, 1–1⅜ in. long; lobe edges ragged. Superficially similar to Sand Blazing-star (p. 331) and Desert Rock-nettle (p. 332), both of which have flowers with separate petals and many stamens.

■ **GOLDEN DESERT-SNAPDRAGON** (*M. breviflora*): Leaves lance- to egg-shaped. Flowers ⅝–¾ in. long, sparingly maroon-spotted within. Also called Lesser Mohavea.

Genus *Mohavea* (2 native species). Plants sticky-hairy. Leaves alternate. Flowers in axils of upper leaves; tube short, lobes spreading; 2-lipped (best seen in profile), lower lip with hairy, maroon-splotched hump at base; stamens 2.

Ghost-flower

Flowers pale cream-yellow. HT: 4–16 in.

Golden Desert-snapdragon

Flowers deep lemon-yellow. HT: 2–8 in.

■ **LANCE-LEAF FIGWORT** (*Scrophularia lanceolata*): Spring–midsummer; open woods, thickets, stream banks. Stems 4-angled. Leaves opposite, lance-shaped, sharply toothed. Flowers small, ⁵⁄₁₆–½ in. long; sterile stamen usually wider than long, somewhat fan-shaped. Also called American, Early, or Hare Figwort.

■ **LATE FIGWORT** (*S. marilandica*): Midsummer–fall; open woods, thickets, stream banks. Flowers ³⁄₁₆–⁵⁄₁₆ in. long; sterile stamen typically longer than wide, dark. Also called Maryland Figwort, Carpenter's-square. **SIMILAR**
■ **CALIFORNIA FIGWORT** (*S. californica*): Spring–summer; moist thickets, shrub-lands, roadsides. Flowers ⁵⁄₁₆–½ in. long.

Genus *Scrophularia* (12 species, 11 native). Leaves opposite. Flowers in large, branched clusters, strongly 2-lipped: upper lip 2-lobed and erect, lower lip 3-lobed, with middle lobe bent downward; fertile stamens 4, a 5th, sterile stamen attached near base of upper lip.

Lance-leaf Figwort

Flowers reddish, greenish, or brownish. HT: 2–6 ft.

Sterile stamen typically yellowish green.

Late Figwort

Sterile stamen dark purple or brown. HT: to 8 ft.

■ **FOXGLOVE BEARDTONGUE** (*Penstemon digitalis*): Spring–early summer; open places. Lower half of stem nearly hairless. Flowers ⅝–1¼ in. long; white or faintly violet-tinged, with pale purple lines within; strongly 2-lipped, the lower lip equal to or somewhat smaller than the upper; sterile stamen sparsely to moderately hairy. Also called Smooth Beardtongue, Tall White Beardtongue.

■ **PALE BEARDTONGUE** (*P. pallidus*): Lower half of stem conspicuously hairy. Flowers ⅝–⅞ in. long, the lower lip usually distinctly longer than the upper; sterile stamen generally densely hairy. Also called Eastern White Beardtongue. Do not confuse with Slender Beardtongue (p. 526).

 Genus *Penstemon* (about 240 native species). Leaves usually opposite; upper leaves lance-shaped and stalkless, lower ones spoon-shaped and stalked. Flowers in elongated clusters, tubular or trumpet-shaped, 2-lipped; stamens 5, sterile one sometimes conspicuously hairy ("bearded").

Foxglove Beardtongue

Pale Beardtongue

HT: mostly 1–3½ ft.

Flower tube narrow at base, greatly expanded above.

Flower tube narrow at base, moderately expanded above. HT: 1–2½ ft.

■ **TUBE BEARDTONGUE** (*Penstemon tubiflorus*): Spring–early summer; open woods, prairies, roadsides. Stems mostly hairless. Leaves opposite. Flowers ¾–1 in. long, somewhat 2-lipped; tube expands gradually (expands rapidly at the throat in many beardtongues); lobes spreading; sterile stamen short-hairy. Also called White Wand Beardtongue. Do not confuse with Foxglove and Pale Beardtongues (above), which have flowers strongly 2-lipped, with purple lines within.

■ **WHITE BEARDTONGUE** (*P. albidus*): Stems typically hairy on upper and lower part of plant. Flowers white or pale pink to lavender. Also called Red-line Beardtongue, Prairie White Beardtongue.

Tube Beardtongue
Flowers white.
HT: 1–3 ft.

Flower tube gradually enlarges from base; white within.

White Beardtongue

Flower tube gradually enlarges from base; reddish purple lines within. HT: 6–18 in.

■ **HOT-ROCK BEARDTONGUE**
(*Penstemon deustus*): Late spring–early summer; slopes, rocky places. Leaves opposite. Flowers ⅜–¾ in. long, 2-lipped, the upper lip short. Also called Scabland Beardtongue.

■ **YELLOW BEARDTONGUE** (*P. confertus*): Spring–summer; slopes, moist meadows, open woods. Flowers ⅜–½ in. long. Also called Lesser Yellow Beardtongue. **SIMILAR** ■ **HIGH MOUNTAIN BEARDTONGUE** (*P. flavescens*): High slopes. Leaves thicker; flowers ½–⅝ in. long. Also called Greater Yellow Beardtongue.

Hot-rock Beardtongue

Flowers white or cream-colored; dark lines within. Leaves usually prominently toothed. HT: 6–24 in.

Yellow Beardtongue

Flowers pale yellow or yellowish white. Leaves untoothed. HT: 6–24 in.

■ **FIRECRACKER BEARDTONGUE**
(*Penstemon eatonii*): Spring–early summer; desert slopes, plains, open woods. Leaves opposite. Flowers 1–1¼ in. long. Also called Eaton's-firecracker. **SIMILAR** ■ **SCARLET-BUGLER** (*P. centranthifolius*): Grassy hills, shrublands. Leaves waxy, bluish or whitish green; flowers 1–1⅜ in. long.

■ **UTAH BEARDTONGUE** (*P. utahensis*): Spring–early summer; canyons. Flowers ¾–1 in. long; crimson, purple-red, or pink-purple; lobes widely spreading.

■ **BEARDLIP BEARDTONGUE**
(*P. barbatus*): Early summer; slopes, open woods. Flowers 1–1¼ in. long, orange-red to scarlet, strongly 2-lipped.

Firecracker Beardtongue

Utah Beardtongue

Flower lobes spreading. HT: 6–24 in.

Flowers scarlet, narrowly tubular; lobes not widely spreading. HT: 1–3 ft.

Beardlip Beardtongue

Lobes of lower lip back-curved. HT: 1–3 ft.

PARRY'S BEARDTONGUE (*Penstemon parryi*): Spring; canyons, slopes. Leaves bluish green, untoothed; stem leaves opposite (not joined). Flowers ½–¾ in. long, 2-lipped.

ARIZONA BEARDTONGUE (*P. pseudospectabilis*): Slopes, washes. Stem leaves grayish green, toothed; pairs of upper leaves united at base and encircling stem (so that stem appears to pierce them). Flowers ¾–1 in. long, 2-lipped. Also called Rosy Desert Beardtongue.

Parry's Beardtongue

Flowers magenta or lavender-rose. HT: mostly 1½–3 ft.

Arizona Beardtongue

Flowers purple-pink or rose-purple. HT: mostly 1½–4 ft.

PALMER'S BEARDTONGUE (*Penstemon palmeri*): Spring–summer; slopes, canyons, washes. Pairs of upper leaves often united at base (appearing pierced by stem). Flowers 1–1⅜ in. long, strongly 2-lipped; pale pink to rose, with red-violet lines on lower lip. Also called Scented Beardtongue.

SHOWY BEARDTONGUE (*P. spectabilis*): Spring; slopes, shrublands. Upper leaf pairs united at base, forming a "cup" that appears pierced by stem. Flowers 1–1⅜ in. long; strongly 2-lipped and somewhat inflated; mostly rose-purple or lavender-purple, the lobes similar in color or often blue to violet-blue. Also called Royal Beardtongue.

Palmer's Beardtongue

Sterile stamen conspicuous, yellow-hairy.

Flowers pinkish, inflated. Leaves gray-green. HT: 1½–5 ft.

Showy Beardtongue

Flowers often rose-purple with bluish lobes. Leaves green. HT: 2–4 ft.

■ **COBAEA BEARDTONGUE** (*Penstemon cobaea*): Spring; prairies, pastures, open woods, roadsides. Flowers 1½–2½ in. long, strongly 2-lipped; violet, pale lavender, rose-purple, pink, or white, usually with purple lines within; sterile stamen prominently hairy. Also called Foxglove Beardtongue.

Cobaea Beardtongue

Flowers large, inflated, sometimes white. HT: 6 in.–3½ ft.

Flowers sometimes purplish.

Flowers sometimes pinkish. Leaves opposite.

■ **LARGE BEARDTONGUE** (*Penstemon grandiflorus*): Spring–early summer; prairies, plains, hills. Flowers 1½–2 in. long, strongly 2-lipped; pink to deep lavender, with magenta lines within; sterile stamen short-hairy. Also called Shell-leaf or Large-flower Beardtongue.

■ **FUZZY-TONGUE BEARDTONGUE** (*P. eriantherus*): Slopes, plains. Plants variable, often sticky-hairy. Flowers ⅝–1½ in. long, strongly 2-lipped; pale lavender, violet, red-purple, or dark blue-purple, often with purple lines within; sterile stamen frequently long-hairy. Also called Crested Beardtongue.

Large Beardtongue

Flowers large, inflated. Leaves opposite. HT: 1½–3½ ft.

Fuzzy-tongue Beardtongue

Flowers inflated, commonly hairy inside. HT: 6–18 in.

■ SAWSEPAL BEARDTONGUE

(*Penstemon glaber*): Late spring–summer; plains, slopes, roadsides. Leaves opposite; upper stem leaves ½–1⅜ in. wide. Flowers ¾–1½ in. long, strongly 2-lipped, somewhat inflated. Also called Western Smooth Beardtongue. Differs from Fuzzy-tongue Beardtongue (p. 524) in having short-hairy (vs. hairless) anthers on fertile stamens, and the sterile stamen sparsely short-hairy at tip.

■ ROYAL BEARDTONGUE (*P. speciosus*):

Slopes. Similar to Sawsepal Beardtongue. Upper stem leaves mostly ⅛–½ in. wide. Fertile stamens usually have hairless anthers. Also called Showy Beardtongue. See also Wasatch Beardtongue (below).

NOTE Both of these species resemble Blue Beardtongue (below), differing in technical characters.

Sawsepal Beardtongue

Flowers in shades of blue-violet and blue; typically paler and with reddish purple lines within.
HT: 1½–2½ ft.

Royal Beardtongue

Flowers typically whitish within.
HT: 6 in.–3 ft.

■ WASATCH BEARDTONGUE

(*Penstemon cyananthus*): Late spring–summer; hills, slopes. Leaves opposite. Flowers mostly ¾–1 in. long, strongly 2-lipped, somewhat inflated; lobes of calyx (united sepals) lance-shaped, noticeably longer than wide; anthers on fertile stamens have short, usually straight hairs (usually hairless on Royal Beardtongue, above). Also called Blue Beardtongue.

■ BLUE BEARDTONGUE (*P. cyaneus*):

Flowers about 1 in. long; calyx lobes as long as or barely longer than wide.
SIMILAR ■ ROCKY MOUNTAIN BEARDTONGUE (*P. strictus*): Anthers on fertile stamens have long, tangled hairs. Also called Porch Beardtongue.

Wasatch Beardtongue

Flowers have violet tube, blue lobes; clusters relatively symmetrical.
HT: 1–2½ ft.

Blue Beardtongue

Flower clusters tend to be 1-sided.
HT: 1–2½ ft.

■ **HAIRY BEARDTONGUE** (*Penstemon hirsutus*): Late spring–early summer; woods, fields, roadsides, prairies. Stems commonly short-hairy, with some longer hairs. Flowers about 1 in. long, strongly 2-lipped, somewhat inflated. Also called Northeastern Beardtongue.

■ **SLENDER BEARDTONGUE** (*P. gracilis*): Stems fine-hairy. Leaves hairless to sparsely hairy. Flowers mostly ⅝–¾ in. long, strongly 2-lipped. Also called Lilac Beardtongue. Pale Beardtongue (p. 521) has leaves conspicuously hairy and sometimes velvety; white flowers with purple lines within.

Hairy Beardtongue
Flowers pale violet with whitish lobes; hump on lower lip nearly closes throat. Leaves opposite. HT: 1½–3 ft.

Slender Beardtongue
Lower lip has purple lines, lacks hump. HT: 1½–2 ft.

■ **RYDBERG'S BEARDTONGUE** (*Penstemon rydbergii*): Summer; slopes, meadows. Leaves opposite. Flowers mostly ⁷⁄₁₆–¾ in. long, 2-lipped; tube moderately expanded above. Also called Meadow Beardtongue.

■ **SMALL-FLOWER BEARDTONGUE** (*P. procerus*): Similar to Rydberg's Beardtongue, but flowers smaller, ¼–⅜ in. long; tube barely expanded above. Also called Pincushion Beardtongue.

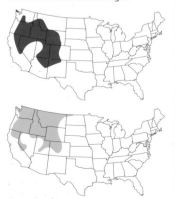

Rydberg's Beardtongue

Flowers typically blue-purple; lower lip has hairy, whitish or yellowish patch. HT: 8–30 in.

Small-flower Beardtongue
Flowers small. HT: 2–18 in.

WHIPPLE'S BEARDTONGUE

Penstemon whippleanus): Summer; slopes, high mountain meadows. Plants typically sticky-hairy above. Stem leaves opposite, basal leaves usually well developed. Flowers generally nodding, ¾–1 in. long, strongly 2-lipped, moderately inflated; colors either light (white, whitish yellow, or lavender), often with purplish branching veins, or dark shades of violet, maroon, or brownish purple); sterile stamen prominent, hairy. Also called Dark or Dusky Beardtongue.

Whipple's Beardtongue

Lower lip of flower hairy, longer than upper lip. HT: 1–2 ft.

SHRUBBY BEARDTONGUE (*Penstemon fruticosus*): Late spring–summer; slopes, rocky places. Leaves opposite, mostly ¾–1½ in. long. Flowers generally 1–2 in. long, 2-lipped; tips of fertile stamens woolly, tip of sterile stamen hairy. Also called Bush Beardtongue.

DAVIDSON'S BEARDTONGUE
(*P. davidsonii*): Leaves mostly ⅜–¾ in. long. Stems creeping. Flowers ¾–1⅜ in. long. Also called Timberline Beardtongue.

ROCK BEARDTONGUE (*P. rupicola*):
Leaves somewhat bluish green, sometimes hairy. Flowers 1–1⅜ in. long; pink, red-rose, or rose-purple; lower lip hairless or with a few long hairs; sterile stamen sparsely hairy or hairless. Also called Cliff Beardtongue.

Shrubby Beardtongue

Flowers blue-lavender to light purple; lower lip has white-hairy patch. Shrubby. HT: 6–16 in.

Davidson's Beardtongue

Flowers blue-lavender to blue-purple. Mat-forming. HT: 2–5 in.

Rock Beardtongue

Flowers often deep pink. Stems creeping. HT: 2–6 in.

■ WOODLAND-BEARDTONGUE

(*Nothochelone nemorosa*): Summer; rocky slopes, woods. Plants sticky-hairy above. Leaves opposite, coarsely toothed. Flowers 1–1⅜ in. long, 2-lipped; pink, rose-purple, or pale maroon; finely sticky-hairy outside, hairless within; all stamens hairy.

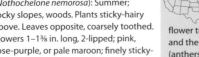

Genus *Nothochelone* (1 native species). Similar to *Penstemon* (p. 521), but fertile stamens are attached at one level in the flower tube (attached at different levels in *Penstemon*), and the bases of their stalks are conspicuously hairy (anthers are also hairy, as in some *Penstemon*).

Woodland-beardtongue

Flowers typically pink-purple.
HT: 1–3 ft.

■ YELLOW BUSH-BEARDTONGUE

(*Keckiella antirrhinoides*): Spring; slopes, shrublands. Leaves opposite. Flowers ⅝–1 in. long; upper lip arching; sterile stamen conspicuously hairy.

■ GAPING BUSH-BEARDTONGUE

(*K. breviflora*): Summer; slopes, shrublands. Flowers ½–⅝ in. long; sterile stamen hairless.

■ HEART-LEAF BUSH-BEARDTONGUE

(*K. cordifolia*): Spring–summer; slopes, shrublands, open woods. Flowers 1¼–1½ in. long, red or orange-red. **SIMILAR**

■ REDWOOD BUSH-BEARDTONGUE

(*K. corymbosa*): Summer–fall; slopes, open woods. Flowers 1–1¼ in. long, pink to red.

Genus *Keckiella* (7 native species). Similar to *Penstemon* (p. 521), but plants are shrubs; flower stamens attached, as in *Nothochelone* (above). Similar *Lonicera* species (p. 191) have unlobed lower lip (3-lobed in *Keckiella*).

Yellow Bush-beardtongue

Flowers yellow, short-tubular. HT: 2–8 ft.

Gaping Bush-beardtongue

Flowers cream-colored, rose-tinged. HT: 2–6 ft.

Heart-leaf Bush-beardtongue

Flowers reddish, long-tubular. HT: 3–9 ft.

WHITE TURTLEHEAD (*Chelone glabra*): Summer–fall; moist or often wet places. Leaves short-stalked or stalkless, toothed. Flowers mostly cream-white, sometimes tinged with green or pink.

OTHERS With pink, purple, or red-purple flowers. ■ **LYON'S TURTLEHEAD** (*C. lyonii*): Mountain woods, coves, stream banks. Leaves on stalks ½–1½ in. long. Also called Pink Turtlehead. **CUTHBERT'S TURTLEHEAD** (*C. cuthbertii*, no photo): Bogs, swamps; chiefly southeastern VA, western NC. Leaves rounded at base, stalkless. ■ **PURPLE TURTLEHEAD** (*C. obliqua*, no photo): Wet woods, stream banks. Leaf blades taper to wedge-shaped base; leafstalks ¼–½ in. long. Also called Red Turtlehead.

Genus *Chelone* (4 native species). Leaves opposite. Flowers in clusters, 2-lipped, the lower lip hairy ("bearded") in throat; fertile stamens 4, hairy; a 5th stamen sterile, tiny, hairless.

White Turtlehead
Upper lip arches over lower lip.

Lyon's Turtlehead
Leaves rounded at base. HT: 1–3 ft.

Leaves opposite, narrowly lance-shaped. HT: 1–3 ft.

■ **AMERICAN-BROOKLIME** (*Veronica americana*): Late spring–summer; moist or wet places. Leaves lance- to egg-shaped, to 1¼ in. wide, distinctly stalked. Flowers ¼–⅜ in. across, in elongated clusters. Also called American Speedwell. **SIMILAR WATER SPEEDWELL** (*V. anagallis-aquatica*): Widespread; considered by some to be introduced from Eurasia. At least the middle and upper leaves stalkless, their bases frequently clasping the stem.

■ **MARSH SPEEDWELL** (*V. scutellata*): Leaves linear to narrowly lance-shaped, mostly ⅜ in. or less wide, their bases not clasping the stem. Also called Narrow-leaf or Grass-leaf Speedwell.

NOTE See introduced speedwells (p. 596).

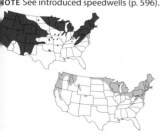

Genus *Veronica* (26 species, 10 native). Leaves opposite (but leaflike bracts beneath flowers may be alternate). Flowers solitary or in clusters, saucer-shaped and 4-lobed, the lobes generally of unequal width; stamens 2, conspicuous. Fruits heart-shaped in some species.

American-brooklime

Marsh Speedwell
Leaves stalkless, narrow, willowlike. HT: 4–16 in.

Flowers small, blue to violet-blue. Leaves opposite, short-stalked. HT: 6 in.–3 ft.

■ **CUSICK'S SPEEDWELL** (*Veronica cusickii*): Summer; rocky slopes, high mountain meadows, stream banks. Leaves stalkless, egg-shaped to elliptic. Flowers ⁵⁄₁₆–½ in. across, in clusters.

■ **AMERICAN ALPINE SPEEDWELL** (*V. wormskjoldii*): Similar to Cusick's Speedwell; flowers ¼–⅜ in. across.

NOTE See introduced speedwells (p. 596).

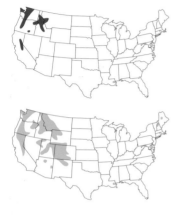

Cusick's Speedwell
Flowers deep blue to blue-violet. Leaves opposite.
HT: 3–8 in.

American Alpine Speedwell

Style ¼–⅜ in. long.

Style ⅛ in. or less long.
HT: 4–10 in.

■ **THYME-LEAF SPEEDWELL** (*Veronica serpyllifolia* ssp. *humifusa*): Spring–summer; moist places. Plants often creeping at base. Leaves ⁵⁄₁₆–⅝ in. wide. Flowers ¼–⁵⁄₁₆ in. across, on stalks to ¼ in. long, in elongated clusters. See also 𝕀 ssp. *serpyllifolia* (p. 596).

■ **PURSLANE SPEEDWELL** (*V. peregrina*): Leaves linear to narrowly spoon-shaped, mostly less than ⁵⁄₁₆ in. wide. Flowers to ⅛ in. across, nearly stalkless in axils of alternate, leaflike bracts. Western populations are typically hairy, eastern ones mostly hairless. Also called Neckweed.

NOTE See introduced speedwells (p. 596).

Thyme-leaf Speedwell

Flowers small, bright blue. Midstem leaves opposite, elliptic to broadly egg-shaped.
HT: 3–12 in.

Purslane Speedwell

Flowers tiny, whitish. Midstem leaves opposite, mostly relatively narrow.
HT: 2–12 in.

CULVER'S-ROOT (*Veronicastrum virginicum*): Summer; woods, prairies, meadows, stream banks. Leaves narrowly lance-shaped, sharply toothed. Flowers small; stamens conspicuous.

Genus *Veronicastrum* (1 native species). Leaves whorled. Flowers in clusters, tubular, 4-lobed; stamens 2, protruding.

Culver's-root

Flowers white to pinkish, in spikelike clusters. Leaves in whorls of 3–7. HT: 2–6 ft.

FEATHER-LEAF KITTENTAILS (*Synthyris pinnatifida*): Summer; rocky slopes, alpine tundra. Basal leaves pinnate, parsley- or fern-like, stem leaves bractlike. Also called Cut-leaf Kittentails.

WESTERN MOUNTAIN KITTENTAILS (*S. missurica*): Spring–early summer; slopes, woods. Basal leaves roundish, hairless, toothed and shallowly lobed. Flowers in somewhat crowded clusters; lobes distinctly longer than tubular base.

ROUND-LEAF KITTENTAILS (*S. reniformis*): Spring; woods. Leaves similar to Western Mountain Kittentails but hairy. Flowers in loose clusters; lobes equal to or slightly shorter than tubular base. Also called Snow-queen, Spring-queen.

Genus *Synthyris* (9 native species). Leaves chiefly basal, often shallowly lobed to divided. Flowers in elongated clusters, 4-lobed (1 lobe typically larger); stamens 2, conspicuous. Do not confuse with *Besseya* (p. 532).

Feather-leaf Kittentails
Flowers blue-violet or purple, in dense clusters. HT: 2–9 in.

Western Mountain Kittentails
HT: 4–16 in.

Round-leaf Kittentails
HT: 2–6 in.

■ **FOOTHILL KITTENTAILS** (*Besseya plantaginea*): Summer; meadows, slopes. Main leaves basal, broad, 2–6 in. long. Flowers 2-lipped, in dense clusters.

■ **BULL'S KITTENTAILS** (*B. bullii*): Late spring–early summer; sandy grasslands, gravelly stream banks.

■ **ALPINE KITTENTAILS** (*B. alpina*): Late spring–summer; high mountain meadows, alpine tundra. Basal leaves 1–2 in. long. Petals purple, united into a snout-shaped flower.

■ **WYOMING KITTENTAILS** (*B. wyomingensis*): Spring; plains, hills, slopes. Flowers lack petals; stamens purple.

Genus *Besseya* (8 native species). Leaves basal and alternate. Flowers in spikelike clusters, 2-lipped, petals sometimes absent or only partly developed; calyx (united sepals) 2- or 4-lobed; stamens 2, conspicuous. Do not confuse with *Synthyris* (p. 531). Species are also called coraldrops.

Foothill Kittentails — Flowers whitish, often tinged pinkish or purplish. HT: 8–16 in.

Bull's Kittentails — Flowers yellowish. HT: 8–16 in.

Alpine Kittentails — HT: 2–8 in.

Wyoming Kittentails — HT: 4–10 in.

■ **CLAMMY HEDGE-HYSSOP** (*Gratiola neglecta*): Spring–summer; muddy or wet places. Plants sticky-hairy. Leaves opposite. Flowers ⅜ in. long; 2 sepal-like bracts beneath 5 sepals (sepals appear to be 7). Also called Common Hedge-hyssop, Mud-hyssop. **SIMILAR** But with sepal-like bracts absent. ■ **BRACTLESS HEDGE-HYSSOP** (*G. ebracteata*): Flowers ¼ in. long, nearly hidden by sepals. ■ **BRANCHED HEDGE-HYSSOP** (*G. ramosa*): Leaves narrow, with rounded, clasping base; flowers ½ in. long.

■ **GOLDEN HEDGE-HYSSOP** (*G. aurea*): Flowers ½ in. long, rarely white; 2 sepal-like bracts beneath flowers. Also called Yellow Hedge-hyssop, Golden-pert.

Genus *Gratiola* (12 native species). Leaves opposite. Flowers solitary in leaf axils, weakly 2-lipped, appearing 4- or 5-lobed; fertile stamens 2 (sterile stamens 2 and minute, or 0).

Clammy Hedge-hyssop

Golden Hedge-hyssop

Flower tube yellowish, lobes whitish. Leaves narrowed toward base, not clasping. HT: 4–12 in.

Flowers yellow. HT: 4–12 in.

■ **FALSE PIMPERNEL** (*Lindernia dubia*): Summer–fall; wet places, especially muddy or sandy shores. Leaves opposite, mostly stalkless, elliptic. Flower stalk shorter than or equal to the leaf beneath it in var. *dubia*, conspicuously longer in var. *anagallidea*. Flowers often darker at edges of lobes. Also called Yellow-seed False Pimpernel. Do not confuse with Clammy Hedge-hyssop (p. 532), which appears to have 7 sepals; or with White-flower Mecardonia (below).

■ **SAVANNAH FALSE PIMPERNEL** (*L. grandiflora*): Year-round; wetlands. Plants creeping, mat-forming. Leaves broadly egg-shaped to nearly round, mostly stalkless. Flower stalk longer than leaf beneath it. Also called Blue-moneywort.

Genus *Lindernia* (8 species, 5 native). Leaves opposite. Flowers solitary in leaf axils, 2-lipped: upper lip short and notched, lower lip 3-lobed; fertile stamens usually 2.

False Pimpernel, var. *dubia*

var. *anagallidea*

Flowers small, pale lavender, bluish, or whitish. HT: 3–10 in.

Savannah False Pimpernel

Flowers small, purple-mottled or -spotted. HT: 8–16 in.

■ **WHITE-FLOWER MECARDONIA** (*Mecardonia acuminata*): Summer–fall; moist or wet places. Leaves toothed mostly above middle. Flowers small, tubular; outer 3 sepals slightly wider than inner 2. Also called Purple Mecardonia, Axil-flower. Do not confuse with Clammy Hedge-hyssop (p. 532) or False Pimpernel (above), both with 2 stamens and without pair of bracts at base of flower stalk.

■ **YELLOW-FLOWER MECARDONIA** (*M. procumbens*): Similar to White-flower Mecardonia; outer 3 sepals distinctly wider than inner 2. Also called Prostrate Mecardonia, Baby-jump-up.

NOTE Mecardonias are also called water-hyssop.

Genus *Mecardonia* (2 native species). Stems 4-angled. Leaves opposite. Flowers solitary in leaf axils, each on long stalk with 2 small, leaflike bracts at stalk base; 2-lipped: upper lip has 2 united lobes, lower lip 3-lobed and hairy inside; sepals relatively long, unequal in width; stamens 4.

White-flower Mecardonia

Yellow-flower Mecardonia

Flowers white, often purple-marked. Leaves opposite. HT: 6–24 in.

Flowers yellow with darker veins. HT: 6–18 in.

■ **NARROW-LEAF PALESEED**
(*Leucospora multifida*): Late spring–fall; moist or wet places, especially stream banks and shores. Plants conspicuously short-hairy, sometimes sticky. Flowers whitish, pinkish, or lavender. Also called Narrow-leaf-conobea.

OTHER GENUS ■ **BLUE-STREAMWORT**
(*Stemodia durantifolia*): Early spring–fall; wet places. Plants sticky-hairy. Leaves undivided, toothed. Each flower has 2 sepal-like bracts beneath. Also called White-woolly Twintip.

Genus *Leucospora* (1 native species). Leaves opposite, occasionally whorled. Flowers solitary (or sometimes paired) on stalks from leaf axils, tubular, 5-lobed, 2-lipped, the lips short; stamens 4.

Narrow-leaf Paleseed

Leaves opposite, fernlike.

Flowers very small, commonly pale lavender. HT: 4–8 in.

Blue-streamwort

Flowers blue-violet. HT: to 3 ft.

■ **ROUND-LEAF WATER-HYSSOP**
(*Bacopa rotundifolia*): Mostly summer; shallow water, mud. Plants creeping, often mat-forming. Leaves palmately veined; veins several. Flowers 5-lobed. Also called Disk Water-hyssop.

■ **BLUE WATER-HYSSOP** (*B. caroliniana*): Plants mat-forming. Leaves have lemon-like odor when crushed. Flowers 4- or 5-lobed, bright blue to violet-blue. Also called Lemon or Carolina Water-hyssop.

■ **COASTAL WATER-HYSSOP** (*B. monnieri*): Plants mat-forming. Leaves mostly 1-veined. Flowers 5-lobed, white to pale blue or lilac; center greenish yellow with dark ring. Also called Herb-of-grace.

Genus *Bacopa* (7 species, 6 native). Leaves opposite. Flowers solitary (or paired) from leaf axils, tubular-bell-shaped, with 4 or usually 5 lobes; sepals conspicuously unequal in width; stamens usually 4.

Round-leaf Water-hyssop

Flowers small, white with bright yellow center. Leaves round, clasping stem.

Blue Water-hyssop

Leaves egg-shaped, clasping stem.

Coastal Water-hyssop

Leaves spoon- or wedge-shaped, not clasping stem.

■ **BLUEHEARTS** (*Buchnera americana*): Spring–fall; open woods, prairies, meadows, roadsides. Leaves opposite, lance-shaped, few-toothed or untoothed. Flowers hairy outside and especially inside, deep purple to lavender-pink, occasionally white; lobes rounded, sometimes shallowly notched. Also called American Bluehearts.

NOTE Do not confuse with *Phlox* (p. 409), which has flowers with 5 stamens inserted at different levels within the tubular base; or with *Glandularia* (p. 556), which has leaves often lobed and flowers in crowded, often rounded clusters, the lobes commonly conspicuously notched.

Genus *Buchnera* (3 native species). Flowers in clusters, tubular and 5-lobed; stamens 4. Partially parasitic.

Bluehearts

Flowers trumpet-shaped, usually purplish. HT: 1–3 ft.

Flowers occasionally white.

■ **PURPLE-GERARDIA** (*Agalinis purpurea*): Summer–fall; roadsides, open moist areas. Stems commonly 4-angled, not hairy. Flowers hairy, on stalks to ³⁄₁₆ in. long, rarely white. **SIMILAR** ■ **FASCICLED-GERARDIA** (*A. fasciculata*): Sandy soil. Stems short-hairy, rough; tufts of leaves present in some leaf axils. ■ **SLENDER-LEAF-GERARDIA** (*A. tenuifolia*): Open places. Stems not hairy; flowers on slender stalks ³⁄₈–³⁄₄ in. long.

■ **AURICLED-GERARDIA** (*A. auriculata*): Prairies, open woods. Stems covered with downward-pointing hairs. Some leaves lobed at base. Flower stalks to ³⁄₁₆ in. long.

Genus *Agalinis* (35 native species). Leaves chiefly opposite. Flowers in clusters near stem ends, funnel-shaped, somewhat 2-lipped, 5-lobed; stamens 4. Partially parasitic. Species are also called false foxglove.

Purple-gerardia

Auricled-gerardia

Flowers purple to rose, with yellowish lines and purple spots inside. Leaves opposite, very narrow. HT: 1–3 ft.

Leaves lance-shaped. HT: 1–3 ft.

■ **YAUPON BLACK-SENNA** (*Seymeria cassioides*): Late summer–fall; open woods, pinelands, sandhills. Leaves opposite, small, mostly ¼–⅝ in. long, finely divided. Flowers ⁵⁄₁₆–⅜ in. long. Also called Senna Seymeria.

■ **PIEDMONT BLACK-SENNA** (*S. pectinata*): Similar to Yaupon Black-senna; leaves mostly ⅝–1¼ in. long. Also called Comb Seymeria.

OTHER GENUS ■ **MULLEIN-FOXGLOVE** (*Dasistoma macrophylla*): Summer; woods. Lowest leaves fernlike, upper ones lance-shaped. Flowers about ⅝ in. long; tube longer than lobes. Similar yellow false foxgloves (below) have flowers funnel- to trumpet-shaped, 1–2 in. long.

Genus *Seymeria* (5 native species). Leaves chiefly opposite, divided into leaflets or narrow segments. Flowers in elongated clusters; tube shorter than the 5 spreading lobes, 2 of which are partially fused; stamens 4. Partially parasitic.

Yaupon Black-senna

Piedmont Black-senna

Flowers hairy outside. HT: 6–24 in.

Flowers yellow, often purple-marked inside, hairless outside. HT: 1½–3 ft.

Mullein-foxglove

Flowers densely hairy inside, hairless outside. HT: 3–6 ft.

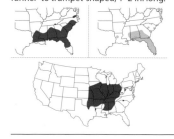

■ **SMOOTH YELLOW FALSE FOX-GLOVE** (*Aureolaria flava*): Summer–fall; open woods. Upper stems hairless. Flowers 1⅜–2 in. long. **SIMILAR** ■ **APPALACHIAN YELLOW FALSE FOXGLOVE** (*A. laevigata*): Lower leaves lance-egg-shaped, unlobed or rarely shallowly lobed at base. Also called Entire-leaf Yellow False Foxglove.

■ **FERN-LEAF YELLOW FALSE FOXGLOVE** (*A. pedicularia*): Flowers 1–1½ in. long. Also called Annual Yellow False Foxglove. **SIMILAR** ■ **LARGE-FLOWER YELLOW FALSE FOXGLOVE** (*A. grandiflora*): Flowers 1½–2 in. long, on minutely hairy stalks.

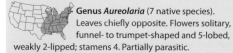

Genus *Aureolaria* (7 native species). Leaves chiefly opposite. Flowers solitary, funnel- to trumpet-shaped and 5-lobed, weakly 2-lipped; stamens 4. Partially parasitic.

Smooth Yellow False Foxglove

Flowers yellow. Leaves opposite; upper leaves unlobed, lower ones (at left) deeply lobed. HT: 2–6 ft.

Fern-leaf Yellow False Foxglove

Flowers on finely sticky-hairy stalks. All leaves lobed. Upper stems hairy. HT: 1–3 ft.

■ **LEMON PRAIRIE INDIAN-PAINTBRUSH** (*Castilleja purpurea* var. *citrina*): Spring; prairies, hills. Plants grayish green, soft-hairy. Leaves typically 3- or 5-lobed. Sepals and the usually 3-lobed bracts yellowish; corollas (united petals) 1–1½ in. long, greenish or pale yellow, mostly hidden by the colorful bracts. Also called Yellow Prairie Indian-paintbrush.

NOTE Several other yellowish-flowered species and varieties are found throughout the range of the genus.

Genus *Castilleja* (about 107 native species). Leaves alternate. Flowers in clusters, interspersed with leaflike bracts that typically have colored tips; tubular and 2-lipped: upper lip beaklike, arching, hooded, usually longer than the 3-toothed, -lobed, or -pouched lower lip; calyx (united sepals) usually green; stamens 4. Partially parasitic.

Lemon Prairie Indian-paintbrush

Flowering clusters yellow.
HT: 6–18 in.

■ **SULPHUR INDIAN-PAINTBRUSH** (*Castilleja sulphurea*): Summer; slopes, meadows, woods. Bracts broad and unlobed, finely sticky-hairy, bright or pale yellow, or sometimes cream-yellow; corollas (united petals) greenish, ¾–1¼ in. long, only their slender tips visible among the bracts and sepals.

■ **DOWNY INDIAN-PAINTBRUSH** (*C. sessiliflora*): Spring–early summer; prairies, plains, hills. Plants soft-hairy. Bracts 3-lobed, greenish- or pinkish-tinged; corollas yellowish, sometimes purplish-tinged or cream-colored, 1⅜–2¼ in. long, prominently visible among the bracts and sepals. Also called Great Plains Indian-paintbrush.

Sulphur Indian-paintbrush

Flowering clusters commonly light yellow.
HT: 6–20 in.

Downy Indian-paintbrush

Flowering clusters commonly greenish and cream-yellow.
HT: 4–12 in.

■ SCARLET INDIAN-PAINTBRUSH

(*Castilleja coccinea*): Late spring–summer; meadows, prairies, roadsides; moist or wet places. Plants often hairy. Upper stem leaves commonly 3- or 5-lobed. Bracts 3- or 5-lobed, with brightly colored tips; corollas (united petals) about 1 in. long, greenish yellow. Also called Eastern Indian-paintbrush.

■ WOOLLY INDIAN-PAINTBRUSH

(*C. foliolosa*): Spring; slopes, shrublands. Colorful bracts unlobed or 3-lobed; corollas ⅝–¾ in. long, greenish. Also called Felt Indian-paintbrush.

Scarlet Indian-paintbrush

Flowering clusters usually scarlet or orange-red. HT: 6–24 in.

Woolly Indian-paintbrush

Clusters sometimes yellow or cream-colored.

Plants gray- or white-woolly, bushy. HT: 1–2 ft.

■ GIANT RED INDIAN-PAINTBRUSH

(*Castilleja miniata*): Summer; moist slopes, meadows, stream banks. Stems often branched above. Calyx (united sepals) as well as the 3- or 5-lobed bracts red or red-orange; corollas (united petals) 1–1¾ in. long, yellowish green, commonly red-edged. Also called Scarlet or Great Red Indian-paintbrush.

■ ANNUAL INDIAN-PAINTBRUSH

(*C. minor* ssp. *minor*): Wet places, often in alkaline soil. Plants finely sticky-hairy. Stems usually unbranched. Bracts red or red-orange, unlobed; calyx green; corollas greenish yellow, ⅝–1 in. long. Also called Lesser or Alkali Indian-paintbrush.

NOTE There are many similar western species with red or red-orange flowers.

Giant Red Indian-paintbrush

Flowers plainly visible among the colorful, lobed upper bracts. HT: 1–3 ft.

Annual Indian-paintbrush

Flowers nearly hidden among the colorful, slender, unlobed upper bracts. HT: 1–3 ft.

■ **LEMMON'S INDIAN-PAINTBRUSH**
(*Castilleja lemmonii*): Summer; moist or
wet mountain meadows. Plants sticky-
hairy. Leaves linear to lance-shaped, the
uppermost sometimes 3-lobed. Bracts
colorful, 3- or 5-lobed; flowers ⅝–¾ in.
long, yellowish to greenish.

SIMILAR Among several species with
rose, magenta, lilac, or purple clusters.
■ **HAYDEN'S INDIAN-PAINTBRUSH**
(*C. haydenii*): Summer; alpine meadows.
Flowers ¾–1 in. long. ■ **PURPLE
PRAIRIE INDIAN-PAINTBRUSH**
(*C. purpurea* var. *purpurea*): Spring;
prairies, hills. Flowers 1–1½ in. long.

Lemmon's Indian-
paintbrush

Flowering
clusters
magenta
or purplish.
HT: 4–8 in.

Hayden's Indian-
paintbrush

HT: 4–8 in.

Purple Prairie Indian-
paintbrush

HT: 6–18 in.

■ **PURPLE OWL-CLOVER** (*Castilleja
exserta* ssp. *exserta*): Spring; slopes, fields,
grasslands. Plants sticky-hairy. Leaves
divided into 5–9 threadlike segments.
Bracts purplish or sometimes cream-
colored, with 5–9 slender lobes; flowers
similarly colored, ½–1¼ in. long; lower lip
3-pouched, with yellow or whitish tips.
Also called Exserted Indian-paintbrush,
Escobita.

■ **DENSE-FLOWER OWL-CLOVER**
(*C. densiflora*): Grassy places. Leaves
slender, unlobed or 3-lobed. Bracts 3- or
sometimes 5-lobed. Also called Grassland
Indian-paintbrush.

Purple Owl-clover

Flowering
clusters
typically
pink-purple
or purple.
HT: 6–18 in.

Beak of
upper lip
densely
hairy, with
hooklike tip.

Dense-flower Owl-clover

Beak of
upper lip
straight,
minutely
hairy.
HT: 6–18 in.

■ **NARROW-LEAF OWL-CLOVER**
(*Castilleja attenuata*): Spring; meadows,
grassy slopes. Plants fine-hairy. Leaves
slender, the uppermost often 3-lobed.
Bracts have 3 slender lobes, the
uppermost tipped whitish or pale yellow;
flowers ⅜–1 in. long, whitish or purple-
tinged, tips of lower lip yellowish with
purple dots. Also called Attenuate Indian-
paintbrush, Valley-tassel.

■ **PALE OWL-CLOVER** (*C. lineariiloba*):
Plants prominently hairy. Leaves slender,
the uppermost commonly 5–7-lobed.
Bracts 5–7-lobed; flowers ⅝–1¼ in. long,
whitish, yellowish, or occasionally pinkish
purple. Also called Pallid Owl-clover,
Sagebrush Indian-paintbrush.

Narrow-leaf Owl-clover

Flowering clusters
typically greenish
and whitish.
Lower lip
only slightly
3-pouched.
HT: 6–18 in.

Pale Owl-clover

Lower lip
3-pouched.
HT: 6–18 in.

INDIAN-PAINTBRUSH RELATIVES

■ **BROAD-SCALE OWL-CLOVER**
(*Orthocarpus cuspidatus*): Summer; slopes.
Bracts 3-lobed, middle lobe prominently
widest; flowers ⅜–1 in. long; upper lip
ends in straight or slightly curved beak,
lower lip pouched. Three subspecies:
Copeland's Owl-clover, Siskiyou Mountain
Owl-clover, Short-flower Owl-clover.

■ **THIN-LEAF OWL-CLOVER**
(*O. tenuifolius*): Slopes. Upper lip of flower
ends in sharply hooked beak.

ROSY OWL-CLOVER (*O. bracteosus*):
Meadows; chiefly OR, northern CA.
Bracts lack the very wide middle lobe.
SIMILAR ■ **PURPLE-WHITE OWL-
CLOVER** (*O. purpureoalbus*): Woods,
meadows. Flowers 2-colored.

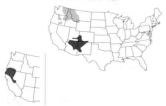

Broad-scale Owl-clover

Flowers purple-pink
and white; bracts
rose-tipped.
HT: 4–16 in.

Thin-leaf Owl-clover

Flowers
yellow; bracts
rose-tipped.
HT: 4–16 in.

Rosy Owl-clover

Flowers rose;
bracts green or
purple-tinged.
HT: 4–16 in.

INDIAN-PAINTBRUSH RELATIVES

◀ **YELLOW OWL-CLOVER** (*Orthocarpus luteus*): Summer; slopes, open woods, meadows, prairies. Stems hairy, hairs often spreading. Leaves narrowly lance-shaped, the uppermost sometimes 3-lobed. Flowers ⅜–½ in. long, upper lip about equal in length to lower lip. SIMILAR ■ **TOLMIE'S OWL-CLOVER** (*O. tolmiei*): Stem hairs minute, mostly downward-pointing; flowers yellow (or occasionally purplish), upper lip hook-tipped and slightly longer than lower lip.

Yellow Owl-clover
Flowers yellow; bracts 3-lobed. HT: 4–16 in.

INDIAN-PAINTBRUSH RELATIVES

■ **FIELD OWL-CLOVER** (*Castilleja campestris* ssp. *campestris*): Spring–early summer; vernal pools, moist grassy areas. Bracts and leaves unlobed. Also called Vernal Pool Indian-paintbrush.

■ **CREAMSACS** (*C. rubicundula* ssp. *rhospermoides*): Spring; grassy places. Stems hairy. Bracts and upper leaves several-lobed. Lower lip of flower typically has 2 purple spots at base. Also called Cromwell Indian-paintbrush.

■ **HAIRY OWL-CLOVER** (*C. tenuis*): Late spring–summer; grassy meadows. Stems prominently hairy. Bracts and upper leaves several-lobed. Flowers white to light yellow. Also called Hairy Indian-paintbrush.

Field Owl-clover
Flowers yellow, lower lip conspicuously 3-pouched; bracts green, narrowly lance-shaped. HT: 4–12 in.

Creamsacs
Flowers yellow; bracts 5–9-lobed. HT: 6–25 in.

Hairy Owl-clover
Flowers commonly whitish; bracts 3–7-lobed. HT: 4–18 in.

INDIAN-PAINTBRUSH RELATIVES

■ **JOHNNYTUCK** (*Triphysaria eriantha*):
Spring; grassy places. Stems purplish,
fine-hairy below. Leaves 3–7-lobed.
Bracts 3–5-lobed. Flowers mostly ½–1 in.
long; upper lip purple-beaked, lower lip
strongly 3-pouched; flowers may be all
yellow (Yellow Johnnytuck), yellow and
white (Butter-and-eggs), or, in coastal CA,
white aging rose-pink (Rose Johnnytuck).
SIMILAR ■ **YELLOW-BEAK OWL-CLOVER**
(*T. versicolor*): Stems greenish, hairless
below; beak of upper lip of flower yellow
or whitish. Also called Smooth Owl-clover,
Yellow-beak False Owl-clover.

NOTE Technically, these differ from Field
Owl-clover and related species (p. 541) by
the anthers having 1 pollen sac (vs. 2).

Johnnytuck

Butter-and-eggs

HT: 3–14 in.

Yellow Johnnytuck

Rose Johnnytuck

■ **ALKALI BIRD'S-BEAK** (*Cordylanthus
maritimus*): Summer–fall; alkaline
meadows, salt marshes. Leaves narrowly
lance-shaped. Flowers whitish; often
yellow-tipped on inland plants, purple
tipped on coastal plants (and called
Saltmarsh Bird's-beak). **SIMILAR**
■ **SLENDER BIRD'S-BEAK** (*C. tenuis*):
Woods, slopes. Leaves slender; flowers
cream-colored with maroon blotch.

■ **WRIGHT'S BIRD'S-BEAK** (*C. wrightii*):
Open woods, mesas. Leaves divided into
3 or more threadlike segments.

■ **PURPLE BIRD'S-BEAK** (*C. parviflorus*):
Open woods, rocky slopes, mesas. Leaves
linear or divided into 3 slender segments.

Genus *Cordylanthus* (18 native species).
Leaves alternate. Flowers tubular (5
united petals), 2-lipped, the upper lip
hooded and beaklike; calyx (united sepals) bractlike,
lance-shaped; bracts among flowers resemble either
leaves or calyx; stamens generally 4. Partially parasitic.

Alkali Bird's-beak

Saltmarsh Bird's-beak

HT: mostly 4–12 in.

HT: mostly 4–12 in.

Wright's Bird's-beak

Flowers yellowish or lavender.
HT: mostly 6–18 in.

Purple Bird's-beak

Flowers pink to lavender, yellow-tipped.
HT: mostly 6–18 in.

AMERICAN COW-WHEAT

Melampyrum lineare): Summer; woods, meadows, peat lands. Leaves mostly ¼ in wide or less in var. *lineare*, typically ⅛–1¼ in. wide in var. *latifolium*. Leaflike bracts beneath flowers sometimes have triangular lobes or pointed teeth at base; flowers sometimes tinged or aging pink or purple-rose.

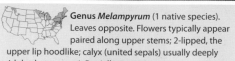

Genus *Melampyrum* (1 native species). Leaves opposite. Flowers typically appear paired along upper stems; 2-lipped, the upper lip hoodlike; calyx (united sepals) usually deeply 4-lobed; stamens 4. Partially parasitic.

American Cow-wheat

Flowers white, with yellow on lower lip.

Flowers small, tubular. Leaves opposite. HT: 4–16 in.

Leaves sometimes lance- or egg-shaped.

YELLOW-RATTLE (*Rhinanthus minor*):

Summer; meadows, fields, thickets, roadsides. Stems somewhat 4-angled. Leaves linear to lance-shaped. Flowers stalkless in axils of leaflike bracts; upper lip usually has 2 tiny teeth near tip; calyx inflated and nearly round in fruit. Also called Little Yellow-rattle.

Genus *Rhinanthus* (2 species, 1 native). Leaves opposite. Flowers in clusters, 2-lipped: upper lip arching and hoodlike, lower lip 3-lobed; calyx (united sepals) urnlike, more or less flattened, 4-lobed; stamens 4. Partially parasitic.

Yellow-rattle

Flowers yellow, in leafy-bracted clusters. Leaves opposite, stalkless, prominently toothed. HT: 6–30 in.

■ **BRACTED LOUSEWORT** (*Pedicularis bracteosa*): Summer; slopes, mountain meadows, woods. Leaves mostly alternate on stem, the larger ones fernlike. Conspicuous lance-shaped bracts in flower cluster. Flowers ¾–1 in. long, sometimes all reddish or purple; lower lip about ¼ in. long, upper lip hoodlike. Also called Towering Lousewort.

■ **GIANT LOUSEWORT** (*P. procera*): Similar to Bracted Lousewort. Leaves basal and alternate. Flowers yellow, sometimes tinged with reddish or purplish, 1–1⅜ in. long; lower lip ⁵⁄₁₆–½ in. long, upper lip has 2 tiny teeth just below tip. Also called Gray's Lousewort.

Genus *Pedicularis* (36 species, 35 native). Leaves basal or alternate (rarely opposite). Flowers in usually dense, leafy-bracted clusters, 2-lipped: upper lip arched and usually hoodlike, lower lip 3-lobed; stamens 4, enclosed in upper lip; tip of style generally protruding. Partially parasitic.

Bracted Lousewort

Giant Lousewort

Flowers usually yellowish, sometimes red-tinged. HT: 1–3 ft.

Lower lip very small.

Lower lip prominent. HT: 2–4 ft.

■ **CANADIAN LOUSEWORT** (*Pedicularis canadensis*): Spring–early summer; woods, prairies, meadows, stream banks. Upper stems typically prominently hairy. Leaves mostly basal; stem leaves alternate, deeply lobed. Flowers ⅝–1 in. long, colored all cream to yellow, all reddish or maroon, or with reddish upper lip and yellowish lower lip (2-colored); upper lip hoodlike, with 2 tiny but conspicuous teeth just below tip. Also called Forest Lousewort, Wood-betony.

■ **SWAMP LOUSEWORT** (*P. lanceolata*): Late summer–fall; moist or wet places. Upper stems typically nearly hairless. Leaves mostly opposite, toothed or lobed. Upper lip of flower lacks teeth but may be shallowly notched; each half of calyx (united sepals) has prominent, leaflike appendage. Also called Swamp-betony.

Canadian Lousewort

Flowers often yellowish, sometimes reddish. HT: 6–24 in.

Swamp Lousewort

Flowers cream-colored or pale yellow. HT: 1–3 ft.

INDIAN-WARRIOR (*Pedicularis densiflora*): Late winter–spring; shrublands, open woods. Plants hairy. Leaves mostly basal, fernlike. Toothed bracts in flower cluster. Flowers 1–1⅜ in. long, with tube mostly straight, upper lip hoodlike; flowers rarely orangish or yellowish. Also called Red-flower Lousewort.

FERNLEAF LOUSEWORT (*P. cystopteridifolia*): Summer; slopes, mountain meadows. Like Indian-warrior, plants hairy, with mostly basal, fernlike leaves. Slender-tipped bracts in flower cluster. Flowers mostly ¾–1 in. long. Do not confuse with Parry's Lousewort (p. 546), which has a tiny, straight beak on upper lip (do not mistake protruding tip of style for a beak in Fernleaf Lousewort).

Indian-warrior

Flowers straight, deep red to purple; lower lip tiny. HT: 6–24 in.

Fernleaf Lousewort

Flowers curved, purple or reddish purple; lower lip prominent. HT: 6–18 in.

JUNIPER LOUSEWORT (*Pedicularis centranthera*): Spring–early summer; slopes, open woods. Leaves basal, fernlike, with toothed and ruffled edges. Flowers 1¼–1¾ in. long, with upper lip hoodlike. Also called Wood-betony, Dwarf Lousewort.

PINEWOODS LOUSEWORT (*P. semibarbata*): Flowers ⅝–1 in. long. Also called Pine or Dwarf Lousewort.

Juniper Lousewort

Flowers pale violet or cream-colored, with purplish tip. HT: 2–6 in.

Pinewoods Lousewort

Flowers yellow, commonly with reddish or purplish tip. HT: 2–6 in.

■ **PARRY'S LOUSEWORT** (*Pedicularis parryi*): Summer; slopes, meadows. Leaves mostly basal, fernlike. Flowers ⅝–¾ in. long; cream-colored to yellow in ssp. *parryi*; pink or rose in ssp. *purpurea*; hooded upper lip has a straight beak about ¹⁄₁₆ in. long. Do not confuse with Canadian Lousewort (p. 544), which has upper lip with 2 teeth but not beaked; or with Fernleaf Lousewort (p. 545).

■ **BIRD'S-BEAK LOUSEWORT** (*P. ornithorhyncha*): Flowers mostly ⅜–⅝ in. long, pink to reddish purple; prominently hooded upper lip has beak to ³⁄₁₆ in. long. Also called Duck's-bill.

Parry's Lousewort, ssp. *parryi*

Parry's Lousewort, ssp. *purpurea*

Flowers often cream-colored to yellow; beak tiny. HT: 4–20 in.

Flowers sometimes pink or rose

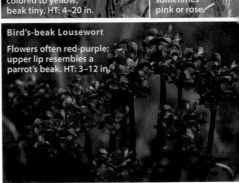

Bird's-beak Lousewort

Flowers often red-purple; upper lip resembles a parrot's beak. HT: 3–12 in.

■ **ELEPHANT'S-HEAD LOUSEWORT** (*Pedicularis groenlandica*): Summer; wet meadows, woods, stream banks. Leaves mostly basal, fernlike. Flower clusters hairless. Flowers resemble an elephant's head, with the swollen upper lip ("head") tapering to a long, upcurved beak ("trunk"), and flaring side lobes ("ears") on the lower lip.

■ **LITTLE ELEPHANT'S-HEAD LOUSE-WORT** (*P. attollens*): Wet meadows, woods, stream banks. Flower clusters hairy.

■ **LEAFY LOUSEWORT** (*P. racemosa*): Slopes, woods. Leaves all on stem, narrowly lance-shaped, toothed. Flowers sometimes pink. SIMILAR ■ **COILED LOUSEWORT** (*P. contorta*): Slopes, meadows. Leaves mostly basal, fernlike.

Elephant's-head Lousewort

Flowers pink to red-purple; elephant's-head-shaped; beak long. HT: 6–24 in.

Little Elephant's-head Lousewort

Flowers pink to whitish; beak shorter. HT: 6–18 in.

Leafy Lousewort

Flowers often white or pale yellow; beak downturned. HT: 6–18 in.

SMILACACEAE — GREENBRIER or CATBRIER FAMILY

Herbaceous or woody vines, usually with tendrils. Stems sometimes prickly. Leaves alternate (or appearing whorled) and simple. Flowers in umbrella-like clusters (umbels), unisexual (plants either male or female); 6 tepals (3 petals and 3 petal-like sepals) mostly greenish, yellowish, or brownish; stamens 6; pistil 1. Fruits are berries, mostly dark blue or dark purple to blackish (less often red).

GREENBRIER (*Smilax*): Spring–early summer (rarely fall); mostly woods, thickets (a few in wetlands). Vines. Stems sometimes prickly. Fruits usually dark blue or dark purple, sometimes red. Also called Catbrier.

Genus *Smilax* (21 native species). Leaves have 3–9 prominent longitudinal veins arching from base and meeting at tip.

Greenbrier

Flowers in umbels.

SOLANACEAE — NIGHTSHADE or POTATO FAMILY

Annual or perennial herbs or shrubs. Leaves mostly alternate and simple. Flowers solitary or in clusters; 5-lobed (petals united); sepals 5, united; stamens usually 5; pistil 1. Fruits are capsules or berries.

SACRED THORN-APPLE (*Datura wrightii*): Mostly spring–fall; sandy or gravelly, open places. Leaves ill-smelling, egg-shaped, untoothed to coarsely lobed. Flowers 6–8 in. long. Fruits round, stiff-prickly, nodding (upper photo). Also called Western Jimsonweed.

DESERT THORN-APPLE (*D. discolor*): Similar to Sacred Thorn-apple; flowers 3–6 in. long, purple inside.

NOTE See also ⓘ Jimsonweed (p. 599), which has flowers to 4 in. long; fruits erect.

Genus *Datura* (4 species, 2 native). Plants often have disagreeable odor. Leaves alternate. Flowers solitary, large, funnel- to trumpet-shaped, with 5 slender teeth on rim; stamens 5. Fruits are prickly capsules. Poisonous.

Sacred Thorn-apple

Flowers large, white or lavender-tinted. HT: 1–5 ft.

Desert Thorn-apple

Flowers white with purplish center. HT: 6 in.–3 ft.

■ **COYOTE TOBACCO** (*Nicotiana attenuata*): Spring–fall; dry open ground. Leaves mostly stalked, lance- to egg-shaped, unpleasant smelling. Flowers 1–1⅜ in. long, about ⅜ in. across, occasionally pink-tinged.

■ **INDIAN TOBACCO** (*N. quadrivalvis*): Spring–fall. Flowers 1½–2 in. long, ¾–2 in. across.

■ **DESERT TOBACCO** (*N. obtusifolia*): Nearly year-round. Stem leaves stalkless, with clasping base. Flowers ½–1 in. long, about ⅜ in. across, white to greenish white.

Genus ***Nicotiana*** (10 species, 5 native). Plants usually ill-scented. Leaves alternate and basal, untoothed. Flowers in clusters, tubular (commonly trumpet-shaped) and 5-lobed; stamens 5. Fruits are capsules. Poisonous.

Coyote Tobacco

Indian Tobacco

Flower tube and lobes both long. HT: 1–5 ft.

Flowers greenish white to white; tube long, lobes short. Plants sticky-hairy. HT: 1–4 ft.

Desert Tobacco

Flower tube and lobes both short. HT: 1–3 ft.

■ **CLAMMY GROUND-CHERRY** (*Physalis heterophylla*): Spring–fall; open woods, fields, prairies, roadsides. Plants soft-hairy, often sticky. Leaves untoothed to irregularly toothed. Several similar species, difficult to tell apart. **SIMILAR** ■ **THICK-LEAF GROUND-CHERRY** (*P. crassifolia*): Spring; open, sandy and rocky places. Flowers yellow, without dark center, saucer- or wheel-shaped, borne on long, slender stalks. Also called Yellow Nightshade Ground-cherry.

RELATED ■ **PURPLE-GROUND-CHERRY** (*Quincula lobata*): Spring–fall; prairies, plains, roadsides. Similar papery-husk-covered berries, but flowers purple, erect.

Genus ***Physalis*** (27 species, 25 native). Leaves alternate or appearing opposite. Flowers commonly solitary, bell- to saucer- or wheel-shaped; stamens 5. Fruiting calyx (united sepals) greatly inflated, often 5-angled, wholly (but loosely) enclosing the fleshy, many-seeded berry.

Clammy Ground-cherry

Berries yellow, enclosed in a papery husk.

Flowers yellowish with brownish to purplish center, bell-shaped, nodding. HT: 1–3 ft.

Purple-ground-cherry

Flowers purple, wheel- or saucer-shaped, upright. HT: 2–6 in.

■ **GREEN-LEAF FIVE-EYES**
(*Chamaesaracha coronopus*): Mostly
spring–summer; open places. Leaves
¼–½ in. wide. Flowers pale yellow to
greenish white. **SIMILAR HAIRY FIVE-
EYES** (*C. sordida*): Southwestern. Leaves
to 1¾ in. wide, sticky-hairy. Also called
Dingy Chamaesaracha.

RELATED ■ **DWARF FALSE GROUND-
CHERRY** (*Leucophysalis nana*): Spring–
summer; open places. Flowers about
¾ in. across. Berries fleshy, many-seeded,
wrapped in calyx. Also called Dwarf-
chamaesaracha. ■ **LARGE FALSE
GROUND-CHERRY** (*L. grandiflora*, no
photo): Summer; disturbed areas. Similar;
taller (to 3 ft.); flowers 1¼–1½ in. across.
Also called White-flower-ground-cherry.

Genus *Chamaesaracha* (7 native species).
Leaves alternate. Flowers 1–4 in leaf
axils, shallowly bowl- to wheel-shaped,
with cushionlike pads near center; stamens 5. Fruiting
calyx (united sepals) closely wraps around the whitish to
yellowish, few-seeded berry (only its top exposed).

Green-leaf Five-eyes

Flower center has darker starlike pattern. HT: to 10 in.

Dwarf False Ground-cherry

Flowers whitish with greenish yellow center. HT: 2–10 in.

■ **CAROLINA HORSE-NETTLE** (*Solanum
carolinense*): Spring–fall; fields, roadsides,
disturbed places. Stems, leafstalks, and
lower leaf surface prickly.

■ **EASTERN BLACK NIGHTSHADE**
(*S. ptycanthum*): Spring–fall; fields,
roadsides, disturbed places. Not prickly.
SIMILAR ☐ **GROUND-CHERRY
NIGHTSHADE** (*S. physalifolium*): Chiefly
western; from South America. Plants
sticky-hairy; calyx covers base of greenish
or yellowish berry. Also called Hairy
Nightshade. ■ **CUT-LEAF NIGHTSHADE**
(*S. triflorum*): Leaves deeply pinnately
lobed; berries green. **WILD POTATO**
(*S. jamesii*): Summer; wooded slopes;
southwestern. Leaves pinnately divided
into leaflets.

Genus *Solanum* (54 species, 35 native).
Leaves alternate. Flowers typically loosely
clustered, often star-shaped, with 5
triangular lobes; stamens 5, prominent in flower center,
opening by small pores at anther tips. Fruits are berries,
sometimes wrapped in calyx (united sepals). Poisonous.

Carolina Horse-nettle

Flowers pale violet or white. Leaves untoothed to wavy-lobed. Berries yellowish. HT: 1–3 ft.

Eastern Black Nightshade

Flowers white. Berries shiny, black. HT: 1–2½ ft.

■ **BUFFALO-BUR** (*Solanum rostratum*): Spring–fall; prairies, plains, roadsides, disturbed places. Plants covered with stiff, yellowish prickles. Berries have prickly covering. Also called Horned Nightshade.

■ **SILVER-LEAF NIGHTSHADE** (*S. elaeagnifolium*): Spring–fall; fields, prairies, roadsides, disturbed places. Plants with or without prickles. Fruits not prickly; orange or yellowish, eventually aging blackish. Also called White Horsenettle. **SIMILAR PURPLE NIGHTSHADE** (*S. xanti*): Rocky slopes; chiefly AZ, CA. Plants never prickly; leaves green.

NOTE See also ⧉ Bittersweet Nightshade (p. 599), which has stems climbing or twining.

Buffalo-bur
Flowers yellow. Leaves deeply lobed, prickly. HT: 6–30 in.

Fruits prickly.

Silver-leaf Nightshade

Flowers lavender to violet-blue. Leaves untoothed to wavy-edged; silvery-hairy. HT: 1–3 ft.

SPARGANIACEAE   BUR-REED FAMILY

Perennial; generally aquatic. Leaves basal and alternate, simple, and untoothed; usually erect but sometimes floating and ribbonlike. Flowers small, with scalelike "petals," unisexual, densely crowded into several separate male and female ball-like clusters, the males above the females. Fruits small, 1-seeded, somewhat spongy, with hard beak, borne in burlike balls.

■ **GIANT BUR-REED** (*Sparganium eurycarpum*): Spring–fall; muddy shores, shallow water. Flower clusters borne along zigzag stalk above leaflike bracts; stigmas 2. Also called Broad-fruit Bur-reed. **SIMILAR** With stigma 1; fruits spindle-shaped. ■ **AMERICAN BUR-REED** (*S. americanum*): Female or fruiting clusters from axils of leaflike bracts. ■ **SIMPLE-STEM BUR-REED** (*S. emersum*): Some female clusters above axils.

Genus *Sparganium* (9 native species). With characters of the family. Leaves elongated; bases wrap around stem.

Giant Bur-reed

Leaves long, narrow. Fruits broadly wedge-shaped, widest at top below beak, in burlike balls. HT: 2–5 ft.

TETRACHONDRACEAE   TETRACHONDRA FAMILY

Annual or perennial. Leaves opposite, simple, and usually untoothed. Flowers solitary, 4-lobed (petals united); sepals 4; stamens 4; pistil 1. Fruits are capsules or nutlets. Sometimes placed in Loganiaceae or Buddlejaceae.

■ **JUNIPER-LEAF** (*Polypremum procumbens*): Spring–fall; open places. Plants bushy-branched, often spreading, leaning to erect. Leaves narrow, mostly ½–1 in. long. Flowers solitary in leaf axils; sepals slender, pointed. Also called Rustweed, Polly-prim.

Genus *Polypremum* (1 native species). With characters of the family. Flowers hairy in center. Fruits are tiny capsules.

Juniper-leaf

Flowers tiny, white, 4-lobed. Leaves linear, stalkless. HT: 8–12 in.

TURNERACEAE   TURNERA FAMILY

Perennial herbs or shrubs. Leaves alternate and simple. Flowers solitary or in clusters; petals 5; sepals 5; stamens 5; pistil 1; styles 3 and with conspicuously divided, fringed stigmas. Fruits are capsules.

■ **PITTED STRIPESEED** (*Piriqueta cistoides* ssp. *caroliniana*): Nearly year-round; pinelands, sandy roadsides. Leaf edges usually toothed or wavy. Flowers have tiny fringe of hairs at petal bases.

NOTE Do not confuse with frostweeds (p. 197), which have flowers with unequal sepals and many stamens.

Genus *Piriqueta* (1 native species). With characters of the family. The 3 styles are somewhat brushlike in appearance.

Pitted Stripeseed

Flowers yellow. HT: 6–16 in.

TYPHACEAE   CAT-TAIL FAMILY

Perennial. Leaves mostly basal; simple and untoothed. Flowers tiny, unisexual, with no obvious petals; densely crowded (on the same stalk) into separate male and female spikes, the male above the female; female spike becomes the familiar cat-tail. Fruits minute, 1-seeded.

BROAD-LEAF CAT-TAIL (*Typha latifolia*): Spring–summer; wet places; widespread, except extreme Southwest. Leaves long, narrow. Flowers in spikelike clusters; female spike ¾–1⅜ in. thick; no gap between male and female spikes.

■ **NARROW-LEAF CAT-TAIL** (*T. angustifolia*): Female spike ⅜–¾ in. thick, with gap of ⅝–4 in. separating male spike.

■ **SOUTHERN CAT-TAIL** (*T. domingensis*): Female spike ½–1 in. thick, with gap of ½–3 in. separating male spike.

Genus *Typha* (3 native species). Leaves elongated, somewhat twisted; bases wrap around stem.

Broad-leaf Cat-tail

Female (lower) spike dark brown. HT: 3–9 ft.

Narrow-leaf Cat-tail

Female spike dark brown. HT: to 9 ft.

Southern Cat-tail

Female spike light brown or yellowish. HT: 13 ft.

URTICACEAE   NETTLE FAMILY

Annual or perennial. Leaves opposite or alternate, simple. Flowers typically in clusters in leaf axils; minute or tiny, unisexual, greenish or whitish. Fruits seedlike.

■ **STINGING NETTLE** (*Urtica dioica*): Mostly late spring–summer; roadsides, fields, thickets, woods. Stems generally 4-sided. Leaves opposite, toothed, 2½–8 in. long.

■ **WESTERN STINGING-NETTLE** (*Hesperocnide tenella*): Spring–early summer; moist places. Base of stinging hairs may be dark. Leaves opposite, mostly ¾–3 in. long.

■ **WOOD-NETTLE** (*Laportea canadensis*): Mostly summer; woods. Leaves alternate.

Nettles (several related genera; 7 species, 5 native). **NOTE** Plants are covered with stinging hairs; do not touch.

Stinging Nettle

Flowers in slender clusters. HT: 1–6 ft.

Stinging hairs.

Western Stinging-nettle

Flowers in rounded clusters. HT: 6–24 in.

Wood-nettle

Flowers in feathery clusters. HT: mostly 1–3½ ft.

FALSE NETTLE (*Boehmeria cylindrica*): Summer–fall; moist or often wet places. Plants barely to prominently hairy. Leaves long-stalked; blades elliptic or lance- or egg-shaped, toothed, 3-veined from base. Flower clusters unbranched, generally erect, their stalks sometimes leafy at tip. Also called Bog-hemp.

OTHER GENUS *Pilea* (5 species, 4 native).
CLEARWEED (*P. pumila*): Moist, often shaded places. Plants hairless, smooth and somewhat shiny. Stems translucent. Flower clusters branched, mostly spreading or a bit drooping. Also called Richweed.

Genus *Boehmeria* (2 species, 1 native). With characters of the family. Plants lack stinging hairs.

False Nettle

Clearweed

Flowers in elongated clusters from leaf axils. Leaves opposite. HT: mostly 1–3 ft.

Flowers in short sprays. Leaves opposite. HT: mostly 6–24 in.

VALERIANACEAE — VALERIAN FAMILY

Annual or perennial. Leaves opposite and sometimes basal; simple or compound. Flowers in clusters; mostly 5-lobed (petals united), funnel- or trumpet-shaped, often with a projection (spur) or bulge at base; sepals present or not; stamens mostly 3, often protruding; pistil 1. Fruits dry, 1-seeded.

SITKA VALERIAN (*Valeriana sitchensis*): Mostly summer; mountain meadows, open wooded slopes. Basal leaves few. SIMILAR **EDIBLE VALERIAN** (*V. edulis*): Summer, meadows, slopes. Leaves mostly basal; flowers tiny, white. Also called Tobacco-root.

LARGE-FLOWER VALERIAN (*V. pauciflora*): Spring–early summer; woods. Flowers have slender tubes. SIMILAR **ARIZONA VALERIAN** (*V. arizonica*): Woods; southwestern mountains.

Genus *Valeriana* (16 species, 15 native). Stem leaves opposite, often pinnately lobed. Flowers tubular, 5-lobed; calyx (united sepals) has 5–20 inward coiled lobes that become feathery bristles in fruit.

Sitka Valerian

Flowers small, white or pinkish. Leaves mostly opposite, pinnately lobed. HT: 1–3 ft.

Large-flower Valerian

Flowers light pink, slenderly tubular. HT: 1–3 ft.

■ SHORT-SPUR PLECTRITIS

(*Plectritis congesta*): Spring; bluffs, slopes, meadows. Flowers pale to dark pink (or rarely white), tubular, 2-lipped; short projection (spur) near base. Also called Rosy Plectritis, Sea-blush.

■ LONG-SPUR PLECTRITIS (*P. ciliosa*):

Slopes, meadows. Flowers pink with 2 darker spots on lower lip; spur slender, elongated.

■ WHITE PLECTRITIS (*P. macrocera*):

Moist places. Flowers scarcely 2-lipped, white to pale pink; spur thick, blunt. Also called Rotund Plectritis.

Genus *Plectritis* (3 native species). Leaves opposite and undivided. Flowers tubular, 5-lobed, spurred; sepals absent; stamens 3. Fruits commonly winged.

Short-spur Plectritis

Flowers small, pink, in rounded clusters; spur relatively short. HT: 4–24 in.

Long-spur Plectritis

Spur long, slender. HT: 4–20 in.

White Plectritis

Spur stout, blunt. HT: 4–24 in.

■ BEAKED CORNSALAD (*Valerianella radiata*): Spring; fields, woodland edges, roadsides. Flowers in dense, flat-topped, squarish or rectangular clusters. Species are difficult to tell apart. SIMILAR

Ⅱ **EUROPEAN CORNSALAD** (*V. locusta*): Chiefly eastern and northwestern; from Eurasia. Flower lobes bluish or blue-tinged. Also called Lamb's-lettuce.

Genus *Valerianella* (14 species, 11 native). Stems have forked branching. Leaves opposite and undivided. Flowers tiny, funnel-shaped, in clusters that occur in 2s or 4s; stamens 3, commonly protruding. Fruits seedlike.

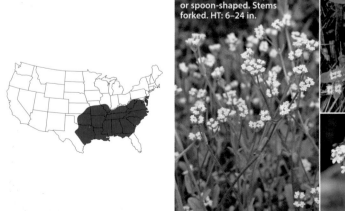

Beaked Cornsalad

Flowers tiny, white. Leaves stalkless, strap- or spoon-shaped. Stems forked. HT: 6–24 in.

VERBENACEAE · VERVAIN FAMILY

Annual, biennial, or perennial herbs or woody shrubs or trees. Stems often 4-angled. Leaves opposite and simple. Flowers in clusters; 4- or 5-lobed (petals united below); sepals 4 or 5, united; stamens 4, in 2 pairs; pistil 1, ovary not or only shallowly 4-lobed. Fruits are nutlets.

WHITE VERVAIN (*Verbena urticifolia*): summer–fall; fields, meadows, open woods, roadsides. Flowers tiny, in very narrow clusters and mostly not overlapping. Also called Nettle-leaf Vervain.

PROSTRATE VERVAIN (*V. bracteata*): spring–fall; fields, prairies, plains, roadsides. Stems commonly lying on the ground. Leaves often 3-lobed, middle lobe largest and deeply toothed. Also called Large-bracted Vervain.

Genus *Verbena* (29 species, 23 native). Stems commonly 4-angled. Leaves opposite. Flowers in spikelike clusters, mostly funnel-shaped and 5-lobed; stamens 4.

White Vervain. Flowers white, in wandlike clusters. Leaves opposite. HT: 1½–5 ft.

Prostrate Vervain. Flowers blue-purple to purple, in clusters with many leaflike bracts.

BLUE VERVAIN (*Verbena hastata*): summer–fall; usually moist places. Leaves opposite, stalked, lance-shaped; lower leaves sometimes arrowhead-shaped. Flower clusters dense, crowded, narrow, with tiny bracts. Several similar species.

NEW MEXICO VERVAIN (*V. macdougallii*): Summer; mountain meadows. Flower clusters relatively thick, with conspicuous bracts to ⁵⁄₁₆ in. long.

HILLSIDE VERVAIN (*V. neomexicana*): spring–fall; canyons, plains, slopes. Flowers in cluster mostly not overlapping.

NOTE See introduced vervains (p. 600).

Blue Vervain. Flowers mostly bluish purple to violet, in slender clusters arranged candelabra-like at stem tops. HT: 2–5 ft.

New Mexico Vervain. Flower clusters thicker. HT: 1–3 ft.

Hillside Vervain. Gaps between flowers in cluster. HT: 1–2½ ft.

■ **ROSE-VERVAIN** (*Glandularia canadensis*): Spring–fall; open places. Flowers ¾–1 in. long, pink to purple, or rarely white, in rounded clusters (elongating in age).

■ **DAKOTA-VERVAIN** (*G. bipinnatifida*): Leaves typically deeply divided. Flowers about ½ in. long. Also called Prairie-vervain. **SIMILAR** □ **MOSS-VERVAIN** (*G. pulchella*): Southern; from South America. Leaves deeply dissected into linear segments. Tube of calyx (united sepals) has scattered black glands among the hairs. Also called South America-vervain.

NOTE Species are also called mock vervain.

Genus *Glandularia* (13 species, 12 native). Similar to *Verbena* (p. 555), but flowers trumpet-shaped, in often broader, denser clusters; styles longer, ¼–¾ in. (mostly ⅛ in. or less in *Verbena*).

Rose-vervain

Flower lobes notched. Leaves opposite, lobed or coarsely toothed. HT: 1–2 ft.

Dakota-vervain

Some leaves twice divided into narrow segments. HT: 6–18 in.

■ **NORTHERN FOG-FRUIT** (*Phyla lanceolata*): Spring–fall; open places, moist or wet ground. Leaves widest at or below middle, toothed from tip to below middle. Flowers pale blue, purplish, pink, or white, often with yellowish center.

■ **TURKEY-TANGLE FOG-FRUIT** (*P. nodiflora*): Leaves widest toward tip, 3/16–1 in. wide, toothed only above middle. **SIMILAR** ■ **WEDGE-LEAF FOG-FRUIT** (*P. cuneifolia*): Leaves 1/16–5/16 in. wide.

NOTE Fog-fruits are also called frog-fruit.

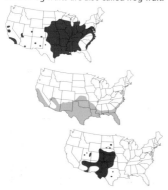

Genus *Phyla* (5 species, 4 native). Stems sometimes 4-angled. Leaves opposite. Flowers in rounded clusters that become cylindrical in age, 4-lobed, somewhat 2-lipped; stamens 4.

Northern Fog-fruit

Flowers tiny, in long-stalked, rounded clusters. Leaves opposite, lance-shaped. Trailing.

Turkey-tangle Fog-fruit

Leaves widest toward tip. Trailing.

VIOLACEAE
VIOLET FAMILY

Annual or perennial. Leaves mostly alternate or basal; simple, sometimes deeply lobed. Flowers solitary or in clusters; petals 5, the lowermost usually wider and with projection (spur) or bulge at base; sepals 5; stamens 5, in a ring around ovary; pistil 1, style club-shaped, bent at base. Fruits are capsules.

CANADIAN VIOLET (*Viola canadensis*): spring–early summer; woods. Stipules appendages at base of leafstalk) untoothed. Side petals bearded. **SIMILAR CREAM VIOLET** (*V. striata*): eastern. Stipules large, fringed.

SWEET WHITE VIOLET (*V. blanda*, no photo): Woods; eastern. Stemless. Petals beardless. **SIMILAR WILD WHITE VIOLET** (*V. macloskeyi*): Wet soil; eastern, western.

BOG WHITE VIOLET (*V. lanceolata*): Open, usually wet places; eastern. Side petals beardless. Also called Lance-leaf Violet.

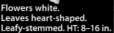

Genus *Viola* (71 species, 68 native). Flowers solitary; in many species, small hairs form "beards" near center. "Stemless" violets have underground stems from which basal leaves and flower stalks arise separately; "leafy-stemmed" violets have aboveground stems bearing leaves and flowers.

Canadian Violet
Flowers white. Leaves heart-shaped. Leafy-stemmed. HT: 8–16 in.

Bog White Violet
Leaves elongated, tapering at base. Stemless. HT: 2–6 in.

YELLOW FOREST VIOLET (*Viola pubescens*): Spring–early summer; woods, meadows. Plants hairy to sometimes nearly hairless. Side petals bearded. **SIMILAR STREAM VIOLET** (*V. glabella*): stream banks, moist woods; CA, Northwest. Also called Pioneer Violet.

WESTERN ROUND-LEAF VIOLET (*V. orbiculata*): Spring–early summer; mountain woods. Leaves thin, sometimes remain green over winter. **SIMILAR EVERGREEN VIOLET** (*V. sempervirens*): spring; woods. Plants spread via runners; leaves evergreen, often purple-marked. Also called Redwood Violet. **ROUND-LEAF VIOLET** (*V. rotundifolia*): Spring; woods. Stemless; leaves not evergreen.

Yellow Forest Violet
Flowers yellow. Leaves heart-shaped, with short-pointed tip. Leafy-stemmed. HT: 4–16 in.

Western Round-leaf Violet
Leaves round with blunt tip. Leafy-stemmed but typically appearing stemless. HT: mostly 1–2 in.

■ **NUTTALL'S VIOLET** (*Viola nuttallii*): Spring–early summer; plains, hills, woods. Leaf blades 1–4 in. long, elliptic to lance-shaped. Outside of upper petals yellow or sometimes purple-tinged; side petals bearded. Also called Yellow Prairie Violet.

■ **GOOSE-FOOT VIOLET** (*V. purpurea*): Spring–early summer; slopes, hills. Similar to Nuttall's Violet. Leaf blades to 1½ in. long, round to egg-shaped, often with purplish veins (especially beneath). Outside of upper petals usually purple-tinged. Also called Mountain Violet.

■ **HALBERD-LEAF VIOLET** (*V. hastata*): Spring; woods. Upper leaf surface commonly silver-mottled. Side petals slightly bearded. Also called Spear-leaf Violet.

Nuttall's Violet
Flowers yellow. Leaves untoothed, wavy, or with widely spaced teeth. Leafy-stemmed. HT: 2–6 in.

Goose-foot Violet
Leaves often bear a few large teeth or shallow lobes. Leafy-stemmed. HT: 2–6 in.

Halberd-leaf Violet
Leaves triangular or arrowhead-shaped. Leafy-stemmed. HT: 3–9 in.

■ **THREE-PART VIOLET** (*Viola tripartita*): Spring; woods. Leaves wedge- to lance-shaped or 3-lobed.

■ **MOOSE-HORN VIOLET** (*V. lobata*): Spring–early summer; woods. Leaves frequently palmately lobed or divided into segments. Also called Pine Violet.

SHELTON'S VIOLET (*V. sheltonii*): Spring–early summer; mountain woods; chiefly Pacific states. Leaves as wide as or wider than long. Also called Fan Violet.

■ **DOUGLAS' VIOLET** (*V. douglasii*): Spring; grassy places. Leaves usually longer than wide. Also called Douglas' Golden Violet.

NOTE The species shown here are leafy-stemmed and have bearded side petals.

Three-part Violet
Some leaves deeply 3-lobed. HT: 4–12 in.

Moose-horn Violet
Leaves palmately divided into 3–12 broad segments. HT: 4–12 in.

Shelton's Violet
Leaves divided into 3 deeply lobed segments. HT: 2–6 in.

Douglas' Violet
Leaves dissected into many slender segments. HT: 2–6 in.

■ **COMMON BLUE VIOLET** (*Viola sororia*): spring–early summer; woods, meadows, roadsides, lawns. Leaves heart-shaped, usually hairy. Side petals bearded. **SIMILAR** ■ **WESTERN DOG VIOLET** (*V. adunca*): Leafy-stemmed; stipules appendages at leafstalk base) conspicuous. Also called Early Blue Violet.

■ **NORTHERN BOG VIOLET** (*V. nephrophylla*): Wet places; all regions except Southeast. Leaves hairless, egg-heart-shaped. Side (and often lowermost) petals bearded. Also called Kidney-leaf Violet.

■ **LONG-SPUR VIOLET** (*V. rostrata*): Woods. Stipules conspicuous. Flowers often light blue-violet with darker center; all petals beardless.

Common Blue Violet

Flowers typically blue-violet with whitish center. Stemless. HT: 2–6 in.

Northern Bog Violet

Side petals somewhat forward-pointing. Stemless. HT: 2–6 in.

Long-spur Violet

Flowers have prominent spur. Leafy-stemmed. HT: 4–8 in.

■ **MISSOURI VIOLET** (*Viola missouriensis*): spring–early summer; woods. Similar to Common Blue Violet (above), but leaves at flowering time are mostly longer than wide (vs. as wide as long). The two species hybridize, and intermediate plants are common.

■ **ARROW-LEAF VIOLET** (*V. sagittata*): Woods, fields. Base of leaf may bear 4–6 large teeth or small lobes (some leaves, especially early ones, may be heart-shaped). Side and lowermost petals bearded. Also called Arrowhead Violet.

Missouri Violet

Flowers blue-violet with light-colored center. Leaves triangular, hairless. Stemless. HT: 2–6 in.

Arrow-leaf Violet

Leaves commonly arrowhead-shaped. Stemless. HT: 3–6 in.

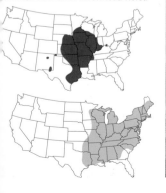

■ **PRAIRIE VIOLET** (*Viola pedatifida*): Spring; prairies, woods. Leaves divided into narrow segments (or may be deeply palmately lobed). Also called Larkspur Violet. See also Bird-foot Violet (below).

■ **THREE-LOBE VIOLET** (*V. triloba*): Woods. Leaves variably heart-shaped to 3- or 5-lobed.

■ **FIELD PANSY** (*V. bicolor*): Open woods, fields, prairies, roadsides. Stipules (appendages at base of leafstalk) large, leaflike, cut into slender segments; end lobe spoon-shaped. Flowers bluish white or blue. Also called Wild Pansy. See ⓘ Johnny-jump-up and ⓘ European Field Pansy (p. 600), both having end lobe of stipules toothed or scalloped.

Prairie Violet
Flowers violet. Side (and often lowermost) petals bearded. Stemless. HT: 2–8 in.

Three-lobe Violet
Side and lowermost petals bearded. Stemless. HT: 3–8 in.

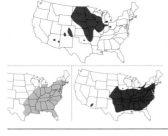

Field Pansy

Side petals bearded.

Stipules conspicuous. Leafy-stemmed. HT: 2–16 in.

■ **BIRD-FOOT VIOLET** (*Viola pedata*): Spring–early summer; woods, fields, roadsides. All petals beardless. Two-colored flowers (upper 2 petals dark purple) are sometimes called Pansy Violet. Do not confuse with Prairie Violet (above), which has side (and often lowermost) petals bearded.

■ **BECKWITH'S VIOLET** (*V. beckwithii*): Spring; prairies, woods. Leaves divided into narrow segments. Side petals bearded, lower petals may be whitish. Also called Great Basin Violet, Western Pansy.

Bird-foot Violet

Flowers blue-lilac; stamens orange, protruding. Leaves divided into narrow segments. Stemless. HT: 4–10 in.

Beckwith's Violet
Flowers commonly have upper petals dark violet, lower petals lavender, center yellow. Leafy-stemmed. HT: 1–3 in.

GREEN-VIOLET (*Hybanthus concolor*): pring–early summer; woods. Flowers n drooping stalks. Leaves alternate, ntoothed or sparsely toothed.

NODDING GREEN-VIOLET *H. verticillatus*): Prairies, open places. eaves narrow, commonly opposite elow and alternate above.

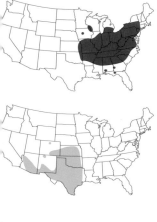

Genus *Hybanthus* (4 species, 3 native). With characters of the family. Flowers 1 to few on stalks from leaf axils.

Green-violet

Nodding Green-violet

Flowers small, green or greenish white. HT: 1–3 ft.

Flowers may be purple-tinged. HT: 4–14 in.

XYRIDACEAE   **YELLOW-EYED-GRASS FAMILY**

Annual or perennial. Leaves arise from plant base, linear. Flower clusters have tightly overlapping scales from which 3-petaled, yellow (or rarely whitish) flowers protrude. Fruits are capsules.

SLENDER YELLOW-EYED-GRASS *Xyris torta*): Summer; wet places. Plant ase bulblike. Leaves and flowering stem nore or less spirally twisted. Flowers merge 1 or 2 at a time from cluster at nd of leafless stalk. Also called Twisted ellow-eyed-grass.

OTE Species are difficult to tell apart; owering stems are short (2–8 in.) on ome species, tall (to 4½ ft.) on others.

Genus *Xyris* (22 native species). With characters of the family. Flower cluster resembles a small pinecone.

Slender Yellow-eyed-grass

Flowers small, bright yellow, in solitary, conelike cluster. Leaves grasslike. HT: 6 in.–3 ft.

ZYGOPHYLLACEAE

CALTROP or CREOSOTE-BUSH FAMILY

Annual or perennial herbs or shrubs. Leaves usually opposite and compound. Flowers often solitary; petals 5; sepals 5; stamens 10; pistil 1. Fruits are capsules or break into nutlets.

■ **SMOOTH-STEM FAGONIA** (*Fagonia laevis*): Mostly late winter–spring; rocky slopes, mesas, washes. Leaflets narrowly lance-shaped. Spines at base of leafstalk somewhat curved, to ⅛ in. long. Also called California Fagonbush.
SIMILAR ■ **SPINY-STEM FAGONIA** (*F. pachyacantha*): Stems mostly prostrate, commonly gland-covered; leaflets broader, elliptic to egg-shaped; stipular spines straight, ³⁄₁₆–½ in. long. Also called Sticky Fagonbush.

Genus *Fagonia* (2 native species). Stems grooved, with forked branching. Leaves opposite, divided into 3 spine-tipped leaflets; pair of spines (stipules) at base of leafstalk. Flowers solitary in leaf axils; petals 5; stamens 10. Fruits are capsules.

Smooth-stem Fagonia

Petals dark pink to purplish, their bases narrowed, stalklike, often twisted. Leaflets spine-tipped. HT: 4–24 in.

■ **ORANGE CALTROP** (*Kallstroemia grandiflora*): Spring–fall; drylands, plains, slopes, roadsides. Plants sprawling. Stems hairy. Flowers 1–2 in. across. Also called Arizona-poppy, Summer-poppy. Not related to poppies. Do not confuse with California-poppy (p. 402), which has leaves dissected; flowers 4-petaled.

■ **CALIFORNIA CALTROP** (*K. californica*): Flowers yellow, sometimes fading to nearly white, ¼–½ in. across. **SIMILAR** ■ **WARTY CALTROP** (*K. parviflora*): Flowers orange to yellow-orange, also often fading, ½–1 in. across.

NOTE See also ⊞ Puncture-vine (p. 600), which has flowers small, yellow; fruits hard-spiny, breaking into 5 nutlets.

Genus *Kallstroemia* (6 native species). Leaves opposite, even-pinnate. Flowers solitary; petals 5; stamens 10. Fruits beaked, often bumpy or warty, breaking into 10 nutlets.

Orange Caltrop

Flowers large, orange with reddish center. Leaves divided into 5–9 pairs of leaflets.

California Caltrop

Flowers smaller, yellow.

ntroduced Species

ntroduced plants, also referred to as exotic, lien, non-native, and non-indigenous, are pecies that are not native to the particular egion in which they are found. Most ıon-North American plants found here re Eurasian in origin, either brought ver intentionally for their ornamental or ıseful qualities, or imported accidentally hrough agricultural enterprises. Once ere, many non-native species have ound it easy to "hitchhike" by means f interstate transportation and further xpand their range.

It is not necessarily easy to tell a native vildflower from an exotic one. Well-ntentioned highway plantings of "mixed" vildflowers frequently include some ıon-native species, and attractive displays n Websites advertising wildflower walks nay show images of Dames'-rocket and ther non-native plants. Also, not all ıon-natives are restricted to roadsides nd open places; for example, woodlands re home to the introduced Greater elandine, which can give the impression f being a native wildflower. While many ntroduced plants are attractive and have he appearance of being native, they may be weedy or potentially invasive. People may dig up introduced Ox-eye Daisies from a roadside—perhaps confusing them with the cultivated Shasta Daisy—and transplant them on their property with calamitous results, for the ill-behaved Ox-eye spreads quickly, intruding into areas where it may be unwelcome and rendering itself unsuitable for most gardens.

Plant introductions may be relatively neutral with respect to the consequences they have on their new surroundings. Some, however, have a negative impact through disruption of the complex balance among plants and animals in a native community. (See Conservation, page 13, for a discussion of how introduced species may negatively affect natural plant communities.)

In an effort to promote conservation, the majority of the introduced species covered in this guide are described and illustrated here, so that readers may recognize these "wildflowers" as non-natives that are potentially invasive. Some look-alike exotics are included in the main section of the guide, alongside their native counterparts, and noted with a I symbol.

SEA-FIG (*Carpobrotus chilensis*): Year-round; dunes, sandy places; West Coast (native southern Africa). Stems trailing, mat-forming. Leaves opposite, succulent. Flowers 1–2 in. across, solitary; petals many, narrow, rose-magenta. Also called Fig Marigold.

HOTTENTOT-FIG (*C. edulis*): Flowers 3–4 in. across, pink or yellowish.

AIZOACEAE, p. 51 · FIG-MARIGOLD FAMILY

Sea-fig

Hottentot-fig

CRYSTALLINE ICE-PLANT (*Mesembryanthemum crystallinum*): Spring–fall; coastal bluffs, sandy places; mostly southern CA, southern AZ (native southern Africa). Stems trailing. Leaves succulent, flat, wavy-edged, covered with glistening, colorless, tiny projections. Flowers solitary or in clusters; petals many, narrow, white aging pinkish. Also called Common Ice-plant.

SLENDER-LEAF ICE-PLANT (*M. nodiflorum*, no photo): Leaves cylindrical, narrow. Flowers age yellow.

AIZOACEAE, p. 51 · FIG-MARIGOLD FAMILY

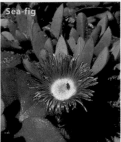
Crystalline Ice-plant

ALLIGATOR-WEED (*Alternanthera philoxeroides*): Spring–fall; wet places; Southeast (native South America). Sprawling and mat-forming, often in extensive colonies. Leaves opposite, stalkless, elliptic, untoothed. Flowers small, white, in dense, headlike clusters. Silverhead (p. 53) differs in having leaves succulent, some immediately below most flower clusters.

AMARANTHACEAE, p. 52 · AMARANTH FAMILY

Alligator-weed

ROUND-LEAF THOROUGH-WAX (*Bupleurum rotundifolium*): Spring–summer; disturbed places; scattered (native Eurasia). HT: 1–2 ft. Leaves alternate, broadly egg-shaped, the upper ones appearing pierced by stem. Flowers tiny, in small clusters above a ring of yellow or greenish yellow, leaflike bracts. Also called Hare's-ear.

See native *Bupleurum* species (p. 57).

APIACEAE, p. 54 · PARSLEY FAMILY

Round-leaf Thorough-wax

WILD PARSNIP (*Pastinaca sativa*):
Summer; disturbed places; widespread
(native Europe). HT: 1–4 ft. Leaves
alternate and basal, the lower ones large
and pinnately divided into coarsely
toothed leaflets. Flowers tiny, yellow, in
umbrella-like clusters. Fruits seedlike,
¼ in. long, elliptic, flattened.

NOTE Sap may cause blisters.

APIACEAE, p. 54   PARSLEY FAMILY

FENNEL (*Foeniculum vulgare*): Spring–
fall; disturbed places; scattered (native
Eurasia). HT: 3–6 ft. Anise-scented. Leaves
alternate and basal, finely divided into
threadlike segments. Flowers tiny, yellow,
in umbrella-like clusters.

APIACEAE, p. 54   PARSLEY FAMILY

POISON-HEMLOCK (*Conium maculatum*):
Early summer; disturbed places; widespread (native Eurasia). HT: 2–7 ft. Stems,
especially lower ones, often splotched
with red-purple. Leaves large, alternate,
fernlike, divided into many leaflets. Flowers tiny, white, in umbrella-like clusters.
Fruits seedlike, ⅛ in. long, broadly elliptic,
the ribs often wavy-edged.

NOTE Poisonous.

The often red-spotted stems distinguish
this species from *Ligusticum* (p. 63).

APIACEAE, p. 54   PARSLEY FAMILY

QUEEN-ANNE'S-LACE (*Daucus carota*):
Spring–fall; disturbed places; widespread
(native Eurasia). HT: 1–4 ft. Plants hairy.
Leaves alternate and basal, fernlike, cut
into narrow segments. Flowers tiny, white,
in umbrella-like clusters; central-most
flower usually dark red-purple. Ring of
finely divided bracts below main cluster.
Fruits seedlike, minutely prickly. Also
called Wild-carrot.

APIACEAE, p. 54   PARSLEY FAMILY

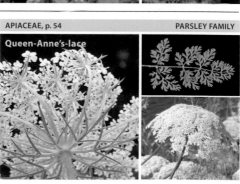

GIANT HOGWEED (*Heracleum mantegazzianum*): Summer; disturbed places; mostly Northwest, Northeast (native Southwest Asia). HT: 8–15 ft. Leaves alternate and basal, to 8 ft. long, divided into coarsely toothed and lobed segments. Flowers small, white, in very large, umbrella-like clusters.

NOTE Sap may cause blisters.

See the native *Heracleum* species Cow-parsnip (p. 62).

APIACEAE, p. 54 · PARSLEY FAMILY

PERIWINKLE (*Vinca minor*): Spring–summer; roadsides, woods; mostly East (native Europe). Stems trailing; plants sometimes shrubby. Sap milky. Leaves opposite, evergreen, broadest near middle. Flowers solitary; somewhat funnel-shaped, with 5 flaring lobes; lavender-blue to blue-violet. Also called Lesser Periwinkle.

GREATER PERIWINKLE (*V. major*): Mostly West, South. Leaves broadest near base.

APOCYNACEAE, p. 71 · DOGBANE FAMILY

WATER-LETTUCE (*Pistia stratiotes*): Year-round; lakes, ponds, rivers, streams, canals, marshes, swamps; FL, Gulf coast (origin uncertain). Aquatic and floating; forms extensive colonies. Leaves spirally arranged, spongy, broadly wedge-shaped, parallel-veined, soft-hairy. Flowers inconspicuous.

ARACEAE, p. 73 · ARUM FAMILY

COMMON BURDOCK (*Arctium minus*): Mostly summer; disturbed places; widespread (native Eurasia). HT: 3–6 ft. Leaves basal and alternate, large, thinly gray-hairy beneath. Flower heads reddish purple, in burlike structures covered with slender, hook-tipped, spinelike bracts.

GREATER BURDOCK (*A. lappa*, no photo): Flower heads larger, on longer stalks.

The large, spineless leaves and flower heads with hook-tipped bracts distinguish burdocks from thistles (pp. 100, 567).

ASTERACEAE, p. 83 · ASTER FAMILY

BULL THISTLE (*Cirsium vulgare*): Summer; disturbed places; widespread (native Eurasia). HT: mostly 2–5 ft. Stems spiny-winged, often hairy. Leaves toothed to deeply lobed, with spiny or prickly edges. Flower heads solitary, red-purple to rose, surrounded by spine-tipped bracts. Also called Spear Thistle.

CANADIAN THISTLE (*C. arvense*): Plants less spiny; stems not winged. Flower heads smaller, in clusters.

See native *Cirsium* species (pp. 100–101).

ARTICHOKE-THISTLE (*Cynara cardunculus*): Spring–summer; disturbed places; CA (native Mediterranean). HT: mostly 2–6 ft. Leaves pinnately lobed and divided, often with stout, yellowish spines along edges; basal leaves larger than stem leaves. Flower heads very large, blue-violet to purplish, surrounded by broad, pointed or spine-tipped bracts.

MUSK-THISTLE (*Carduus nutans*): Summer; disturbed places; widespread (native Eurasia). HT: 1½–6 ft. Stems spiny-winged. Leaves deeply lobed, spiny-toothed. Flower heads pink to purplish red, often nodding; outer spine-tipped bracts spreading or bent backward. Also called Nodding-thistle.

SCOTCH-THISTLE (*Onopordum acanthium*): Spiny-winged stems white-woolly.

BLESSED MILK-THISTLE (*Silybum marianum*): Leaves mottled with white.

YELLOW STAR-THISTLE (*Centaurea solstitialis*): Summer–fall; disturbed places; mostly West (native Eurasia). HT: to 3 ft. Flower heads yellow; bracts have stout spines.

WOOLLY DISTAFF-THISTLE (*Carthamus lanatus*): Mostly West Coast. Bracts narrow, with spine-tipped lobes.

BLESSED-THISTLE (*Centaurea benedicta*): West, East. Outer bracts leaflike; inner bracts spiny.

CORNFLOWER (*Centaurea cyanus*): Spring–summer; disturbed places; widespread (native Eurasia). HT: mostly 1–3 ft. Leaves alternate, grayish-hairy, narrow. Flower heads showy, usually blue but sometimes whitish, pink, or purple; outer flowers much larger; sepal-like bracts surrounding flower head conspicuously toothed. Also called Bachelor's-button.

See also American Basket-flower (p. 101).

ASTERACEAE, p. 83   ASTER FAMILY

Cornflower

SPOTTED KNAPWEED (*Centaurea stoebe* ssp. *micranthos*): Summer; disturbed places; widespread (native Eurasia). HT: 1–5 ft. Plants gray-hairy. Leaves alternate, pinnately divided into narrow segments. Flower heads pink or purplish; outer flowers larger; sepal-like bracts surrounding flower head have comblike fringe.

DIFFUSE KNAPWEED (*C. diffusa*): Mostly West. Flower heads whitish. Also called White Knapweed.

ASTERACEAE, p. 83   ASTER FAMILY

Spotted Knapweed   Diffuse Knapweed

RUSSIAN KNAPWEED (*Acroptilon repens*): Late spring–summer; disturbed places; mostly West (native Eurasia). HT: to 3 ft. Stems have cobwebby hairs. Leaves basal and alternate, the lower ones often few-lobed. Flower heads pink, purplish, or whitish; sepal-like bracts surrounding flower head round or oval, with broad, papery edges. Also called Hardheads.

ASTERACEAE, p. 83   ASTER FAMILY

Russian Knapweed

FLORIDA TASSELFLOWER (*Emilia fosbergii*): Year-round; disturbed places; mostly FL (native tropical Asia). HT: to 3 ft. Leaves alternate and stalkless, the upper ones typically clasping stem. Flower heads in clusters; cylindrical to narrowly urn-shaped; pinkish, purplish, or reddish. Also called Fosberg's Pualele.

ASTERACEAE, p. 83   ASTER FAMILY

Florida Tasselflower

ORANGE HAWKWEED (*Hieracium auranticaum*): Summer; disturbed places; East, Northwest (native Europe). HT: 6–18 in. Plants have milky juice. Leaves basal, spoon-shaped, hairy. Flower heads in clusters, orange; black hairs on stalks and bracts. Also called Devil's-paintbrush.

MEADOW HAWKWEED (*H. caespitosum*): Similar, but flowers yellow. Also called Field Hawkweed, King-devil.

See also Orange Agoseris (p. 90) and native *Hieracium* species (p. 91).

ASTERACEAE, p. 83 — ASTER FAMILY

Orange Hawkweed

Meadow Hawkweed

COMMON DANDELION (*Taraxacum officinale*): Year-round; disturbed places; widespread (native Eurasia). HT: 2–16 in. Plants have milky juice. Leaves in a basal cluster, with mostly backward-pointing lobes or teeth. Flower heads solitary, yellow. Fruiting heads ball-shaped, fluffy. Drooping, sepal-like bracts distinguish Common Dandelion from look-alikes such as Hairy Cat's-ear (*Hypochaeris radicata*, not included in this guide).

ASTERACEAE, p. 83 — ASTER FAMILY

Common Dandelion

PRICKLY LETTUCE (*Lactuca serriola*): Summer; disturbed places; widespread (native Eurasia). HT: to 2½ ft. Plants have milky juice. Flower heads in clusters, yellow. See native *Lactuca* (pp. 88–89).

SPINY-LEAF SOW-THISTLE (*Sonchus asper*): Leaves clasp stem; rounded lobes at leaf base down-curved or coiled.

SMOOTH HAWK'S-BEARD (*Crepis capillaris*): Dandelion-like, but leaves both basal and on stem; flower heads in clusters. See native *Crepis* species (p. 89).

ASTERACEAE, p. 83 — ASTER FAMILY

Prickly Lettuce

Spiny-leaf Sow-thistle

Smooth Hawk's-beard

YELLOW SALSIFY (*Tragopogon dubius*): Summer; disturbed places; widespread (native Europe). HT: 1–3 ft. Plants have milky juice. Leaves grasslike, alternate and basal. Flower heads solitary, yellow; green sepal-like bracts longer than flowers. Also called Yellow Goat's-beard. See Lindley's Silver-puffs (p. 90), with leaves all basal.

MEADOW SALSIFY (*T. pratensis*): Sepal-like bracts shorter than to as long as the yellow flowers.

SALSIFY (*T. porrifolius*): Flowers purple.

ASTERACEAE, p. 83 — ASTER FAMILY

Yellow Salsify

Meadow Salsify

Salsify

CHICORY (*Cichorium intybus*): Spring–summer; disturbed places; widespread (native Eurasia). HT: 1–3 ft. Plants have milky juice. Leaves mostly clustered at plant base, dandelion-like; stem leaves reduced. Flower heads blue (or occasionally whitish or pinkish).

See also *Lygodesmia* species (p. 86).

ASTERACEAE, p. 83   ASTER FAMILY

Chicory

OX-EYE DAISY (*Leucanthemum vulgare*): Late spring–summer; disturbed places; widespread (native Europe). HT: mostly 6–30 in. Basal leaves spoon-shaped, with narrow stalk and coarsely round-toothed to lobed blade. Flower heads solitary and large, with yellow center, white rays. The cultivated (not weedy) Shasta Daisy (*L.* × *superbum*) has similar flower heads, but basal leaves oblong and with pointed teeth.

See also False Aster (p. 147).

ASTERACEAE, p. 83   ASTER FAMILY

Ox-eye Daisy

ENGLISH DAISY (*Bellis perennis*): Spring–summer; roadsides, lawns; East, West (native Eurasia). HT: mostly 4–10 in. Leaves in clusters at plant base, spoon-shaped. Flower heads solitary on leafless stalks, with yellow center, white rays (sometimes tinged pink or purple). Also called Lawn Daisy.

ASTERACEAE, p. 83   ASTER FAMILY

English Daisy

MAYWEED (*Anthemis cotula*): Late spring–summer; disturbed places; widespread (native Eurasia). HT: 6–24 in. Ill-scented. Leaves alternate, fernlike. Flower heads have yellow center, white rays (the rays sterile). Also called Stinking Chamomile, Dog-fennel.

OTHERS With rays fertile (no photos). **GERMAN CHAMOMILE** (*Matricaria chamomilla*): Pleasantly aromatic. **CORN CHAMOMILE** (*Anthemis arvensis*) and **SCENTLESS MAYWEED** (*Tripleurospermum inodorum*): Not aromatic.

ASTERACEAE, p. 83   ASTER FAMILY

Mayweed

FEVERFEW (*Tanacetum parthenium*):
Summer–fall; disturbed places; mostly
East, West (native Eurasia). HT: 1–2 ft.
Aromatic. Leaves alternate, deeply
divided into coarsely toothed segments.
Flower heads have yellow center, white
rays.

COSTMARY (*T. balsamita*): Leaves sweetly
fragrant, undivided, scallop-toothed;
leaf bases often few-lobed. Flower heads
similar or rays absent. Also called Alecost.

ASTERACEAE, p. 83   ASTER FAMILY

Feverfew

Costmary

COMMON TANSY (*Tanacetum vulgare*):
Summer; disturbed places; widespread
(native Eurasia). HT: 1–4 ft. Aromatic.
Leaves fernlike, deeply pinnately divided
into lobed and toothed segments. Flower
heads in dense clusters, golden yellow,
buttonlike. Similar to Dune Tansy (p. 107),
but flower heads smaller and generally
more numerous.

ASTERACEAE, p. 83   ASTER FAMILY

Common Tansy

BRASS-BUTTONS (*Cotula coronopifolia*):
Spring–winter; marshy areas; West
Coast; (native southern Africa, Australia).
HT: 2–8 in. Plants somewhat fleshy,
aromatic. Leaves alternate, untoothed to
coarsely toothed or few-lobed. Flower
heads solitary on long stalks, yellow,
buttonlike.

AUSTRALIAN BRASS-BUTTONS
(*C. australis*): Leaves fernlike. Flower heads
tiny, cream-colored to yellow.

ASTERACEAE, p. 83   ASTER FAMILY

Brass-buttons

Australian Brass-buttons

TANSY RAGWORT (*Senecio jacobaea*):
Spring–summer; disturbed places; mostly
Northwest (native Eurasia). HT: mostly
1–4 ft. Leaves fernlike, pinnately divided.
Flower heads in dense clusters, all yellow.
Also called Tansy Butterweed.

COMMON GROUNDSEL (*S. vulgaris*):
HT: to 20 in. Leaves coarsely toothed or
lobed. Flower heads lack rays; sepal-like
bracts often black-tipped.

See native *Senecio* species (p. 140).

ASTERACEAE, p. 83   ASTER FAMILY

Tansy Ragwort

Common Groundsel

ELECAMPANE (*Inula helenium*): Summer; disturbed places; West, East (native Eurasia). HT: mostly 2–5 ft. Basal leaves (often withered by flowering time) to 18 in. long; stem leaves to 12 in. long. Flower heads yellow, with many, very narrow rays; sepal-like bracts surrounding flower head broad, egg-shaped.

ASTERACEAE, p. 83 ASTER FAMILY

Elecampane

COLT'S-FOOT (*Tussilago farfara*): Spring–early summer; disturbed places; Northeast (native Eurasia). HT: to 20 in. Basal leaves (developing after plants have bloomed) roundish, long-stalked, white-hairy beneath. Flower heads solitary, yellow, with narrow rays; flowering stalks have small, scalelike leaves.

ASTERACEAE, p. 83 ASTER FAMILY

Colt's-foot

POLICEMAN'S-HELMET (*Impatiens glandulifera*): Summer; moist places; Northwest, Northeast (native Himalayas). HT: 3–6 ft. Leaves typically whorled. Flowers in clusters, each dangling from a slender stalk; cornucopia-shaped, with short, tail-like spur at base; pink, red, purple, or white. Also called Himalayan Balsam.

See native *Impatiens* species (p. 153).

BALSAMINACEAE, p. 153 TOUCH-ME-NOT FAMILY

Policeman's-helmet

COMMON HOUND'S-TONGUE (*Cynoglossum officinale*): Spring–summer; disturbed places; widespread (native Eurasia). HT: 1–4 ft. Leaves basal and alternate, untoothed, hairy. Flowers small, in clusters, trumpet-shaped and 5-lobed, reddish purple. The several individual flower clusters from axils of conspicuous leaflike bracts distinguish this from native species (p. 158), which have a single branched flower cluster at the stem end.

BORAGINACEAE, p. 157 BORAGE FAMILY

Common Hound's-tongue

YELLOW-AND-BLUE FORGET-ME-NOT (*Myosotis discolor*): Spring–summer; disturbed places; East, West (native Europe). HT: 4–20 in. Leaves relatively narrow, untoothed, hairy. Flowers tiny, in coiled clusters; trumpet-shaped and 5-lobed; opening yellowish, turning bluish.

See native forget-me-nots (pp. 158–159).

BORAGINACEAE, p. 157 — BORAGE FAMILY

Yellow-and-blue Forget-me-not

CORN-GROMWELL (*Buglossoides arvensis*): Spring–summer; disturbed places; widespread (native Eurasia). HT: 6–30 in. Leaves mostly alternate, stalkless, untoothed, hairy. Flowers small, solitary in upper leaf axils, funnel-shaped and 5-lobed, whitish.

See also Spring and Large-seed Forget-me-nots (p. 159), which have flowers with tiny toothlike projections in the throat and a 2-lipped calyx (united sepals).

BORAGINACEAE, p. 157 — BORAGE FAMILY

Corn-gromwell

VIPER'S-BUGLOSS (*Echium vulgare*): Summer–fall; disturbed places; scattered (native Eurasia). HT: 1–3 ft. Plants bristly-hairy. Leaves relatively narrow. Flowers in clusters; funnel-shaped and 5-lobed; pink in bud, opening blue (or sometimes rose-pink or whitish); style and stamens conspicuously protruding. Also called Blueweed.

BORAGINACEAE, p. 157 — BORAGE FAMILY

Viper's-bugloss

INDIAN HELIOTROPE (*Heliotropium indicum*): Spring–fall; disturbed places; Southeast (native tropical America). HT: 1–2½ ft. Leaves egg-shaped, untoothed, hairy. Flowers tiny, in coiled clusters, trumpet-shaped and 5-lobed, light blue to violet. Also called Turnsole.

See native *Heliotropium* species (p. 163).

BORAGINACEAE, p. 157 — BORAGE FAMILY

Indian Heliotrope

HOARY-ALYSSUM (*Berteroa incana*): Summer; disturbed places; widespread (native Eurasia). HT: to 2 ft. Plants finely gray-hairy. Leaves alternate, narrow. Petals white, deeply notched. Pods inflated.

SHEPHERD'S-PURSE (*Capsella bursa-pastoris*): Basal leaves pinnate. Pods triangular.

FIELD PENNYCRESS (*Thlaspi arvense*): Upper leaves have arrowhead-shaped base. Pods circular, winged, notched.

BRASSICACEAE, p. 164   MUSTARD FAMILY

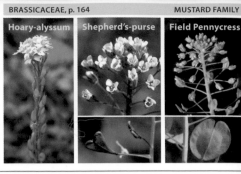

Hoary-alyssum   Shepherd's-purse   Field Pennycress

GARLIC-MUSTARD (*Alliaria petiolata*): Spring–early summer; woods, thickets; East (native Eurasia). HT: 6 in.–3½ ft. Garlic odor. Leaves coarsely toothed, the basal leaves kidney-shaped, the stem leaves alternate and triangular-heart-shaped. Flowers small, in clusters; petals 4, white. Pods narrow.

BRASSICACEAE, p. 164   MUSTARD FAMILY

Garlic-mustard

WATERCRESS (*Nasturtium officinale*): Summer; wet places; widespread (native Eurasia). Floating or trailing. Leaves pinnately divided into 3–9 leaflets, the end leaflet often largest and round. Flowers tiny, in clusters; petals 4, white. Pods shortly elongated.

BRASSICACEAE, p. 164   MUSTARD FAMILY

Watercress

EARLY WHITLOW-GRASS (*Draba verna*): Spring; disturbed places; East, West (native Eurasia). HT: 2–6 in. Leaves small, in a basal cluster. Flowers tiny, in clusters; petals 4, white, each deeply notched. Pods small, flat.

See native *Draba* species (pp. 171–172).

BRASSICACEAE, p. 164   MUSTARD FAMILY

Early Whitlow-grass

BROAD-LEAF PEPPERWEED (*Lepidium latifolium*): Summer; disturbed places; West (native Eurasia). HT: 1½–5 ft. Basal leaves long. Flowers tiny, white. Pods tiny.

FIELD PEPPERGRASS (*L. campestre*): Widespread (native Eurasia). HT: to 20 in. Stem leaves arrowhead-shaped at base.

SHIELD PEPPERGRASS (*L. perfoliatum*): West (native Eurasia). HT: to 18 in. Lower leaves fernlike; upper heart-shaped, clasp stem. Flowers yellow or cream-colored.

See native *Lepidium* species (p. 168).

BRASSICACEAE, p. 164 MUSTARD FAMILY

Broad-leaf Pepper-weed

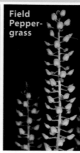
Field Pepper-grass

Shield Pepper-grass

BLACK MUSTARD (*Brassica nigra*): Summer; disturbed places; widespread native Eurasia. HT: 1–5 ft. Flowers yellow. Pods narrow, erect, held close to stem.

COMMON WINTERCRESS (*Barbarea vulgaris*): HT: 8–30 in. Lower leaves have short side lobes, broad end lobe. See additional *Barbarea* species (p. 173).

FLIXWEED (*Descurainia sophia*): Mostly West. HT: 8–30 in. Leaves fernlike. Pods slender. See native *Descurainia* species p. 173).

BRASSICACEAE, p. 164 MUSTARD FAMILY

Black Mustard

Common Winter-cress

Flixweed

WILD RADISH (*Raphanus raphanistrum*): Summer; disturbed places; widespread native Eurasia. HT: 1–2½ ft. Leaves alternate, coarsely toothed and lobed. Flowers in clusters; petals 4, pale yellow to whitish, usually dark-veined. Pods constricted between seeds, long-beaked at tip. Also called Jointed Charlock.

RADISH (*R. sativus*, see photo below): Similar, but flowers mostly pink-purple or white.

BRASSICACEAE, p. 164 MUSTARD FAMILY

Wild Radish

BLUE MUSTARD (*Chorispora tenella*): Summer; disturbed places; West (native Eurasia). HT: 6–18 in. Leaves alternate, many-toothed. Flowers pinkish purple. Pods slender, 1–1¾ in. long. Also called Purple Mustard.

AFRICAN MUSTARD (*Strigosella africana*): West (native Mediterranean). HT: 4–16 in. Flowers similar. Some hairs on plant branched. Pods 1½–2½ in. long.

BRASSICACEAE, p. 164 MUSTARD FAMILY

Blue Mustard

African Mustard

Radish

HONESTY (*Lunaria annua*): Late spring–summer; disturbed places; scattered (native Europe). HT: 1½–3 ft. Flowers in clusters; petals 4, pinkish purple (or rarely white). Pods large, circular, slender-beaked at tip; outer walls separate at maturity and leave a persistent silvery white membrane. Also called Money-plant.

BRASSICACEAE, p. 164   **MUSTARD FAMILY**

Honesty

DAME'S-ROCKET (*Hesperis matronalis*): Spring–early summer; roadsides, open woods; widespread (native Europe). HT: 1½–3½ ft. Leaves alternate, lance-shaped, toothed. Flowers in clusters; petals 4, purple, pink, or sometimes whitish. Pods slender.

See also Purple-rocket (p. 178).

BRASSICACEAE, p. 164   **MUSTARD FAMILY**

Dame's-rocket

CREEPING BELLFLOWER (*Campanula rapunculoides*): Summer; disturbed places; widespread (native Eurasia). HT: 1–3 ft. Leaves alternate, lance-shaped. Flowers somewhat nodding, in elongated, mostly 1-sided clusters; open-bell-shaped and 5-lobed; violet-blue.

See also native bellflowers (pp. 184–185).

CAMPANULACEAE, p. 184   **BELLFLOWER FAMILY**

Creeping Bellflower

SPIDER-FLOWER (*Cleome hassleriana*): Summer–fall; disturbed places; East (native South America). HT: to 5 ft. Plants sticky-hairy, ill-scented. Leaves alternate, palmate, with 5–7 leaflets. Flowers in clusters; petals 4, pink to whitish, stalked, all grouped on one side; stamens long-protruding. Pods stalked, slender.

See native *Cleome* species (p. 189).

CAPPARACEAE, p. 189   **CAPER FAMILY**

Spider-flower

JAPANESE HONEYSUCKLE (*Lonicera japonica*): Spring–fall; roadsides, woods; East (native eastern Asia). Woody vine, trailing or twining. Leaves opposite. Flowers in pairs in leaf axils, 2-lipped, white aging yellowish; stamens protruding.

See native *Lonicera* species (p. 191).

CAPRIFOLIACEAE, p. 190   HONEYSUCKLE FAMILY

Japanese Honeysuckle

COMMON CHICKWEED (*Stellaria media*): Spring–fall; disturbed places; widespread (native Eurasia). HT: 4–16 in. Leaves opposite, egg-shaped to elliptic, untoothed. Flowers small, solitary or in clusters; petals 5, deeply notched (often look like 10), white, commonly shorter than the green sepals.

See also Star Chickweed (p. 193).

CARYOPHYLLACEAE, p. 192   PINK FAMILY

Common Chickweed

BABY'S-BREATH (*Gypsophila paniculata*): Summer; disturbed places; widespread (native Eurasia). HT: 1½–3 ft. Plants much branched. Leaves opposite, narrow. Flowers tiny, in large, delicately branched clusters; petals 5, white or occasionally light pink; stamens protruding.

CARYOPHYLLACEAE, p. 192   PINK FAMILY

Baby's-breath

CORNCOCKLE (*Agrostemma githago*): Spring–summer; disturbed places; widespread but uncommon (native Eurasia). HT: 1–3 ft. Leaves opposite, slender. Flowers mostly solitary; petals 5, deep pink to purplish; calyx (united sepals) tubular, its slender green lobes conspicuous beneath the petals.

CARYOPHYLLACEAE, p. 192   PINK FAMILY

Corncockle

DEPTFORD PINK (*Dianthus armeria*): Spring–summer; disturbed places; widespread (native Eurasia). HT: 6–24 in. Leaves opposite, slender. Flowers small, often in clusters; petals 5, white-dotted rose or pink, toothed; sepals joined to form a tube.

CARYOPHYLLACEAE, p. 192   PINK FAMILY

Deptford Pink

BOUNCING-BET (*Saponaria officinalis*): Spring–fall; disturbed places; widespread (native Eurasia). HT: 1–3 ft. Leaves opposite. Flowers in clusters; petals 5, pink to whitish, long-stalked; sepals joined to form a tube; stamens protruding. Distinguished from *Silene* (below and pp. 195–196) in having 2 (vs. 3 or 5) styles.

CARYOPHYLLACEAE, p. 192   PINK FAMILY

Bouncing-bet

WHITE CAMPION (*Silene latifolia*): Summer; disturbed places; widespread (native Eurasia). HT: 1–2½ ft. Leaves opposite. Flowers unisexual, in clusters; petals 5, white, deeply notched; sepals (calyx) joined into a tube; styles 3.

NIGHT-FLOWERING CATCHFLY (*S. noctiflora*, no photo): Similar to White Campion, but flowers bisexual, styles 5.

BLADDER CAMPION (*S. vulgaris*): Flowers bisexual; stamens protruding; calyx swollen.

See native *Silene* species (pp. 195–196).

CARYOPHYLLACEAE, p. 192   PINK FAMILY

White Campion

Bladder Campion

ROSE CAMPION (*Silene coronaria*): Summer; disturbed places; East, West (native Eurasia). HT: 6–30 in. Plants white-hairy. Leaves opposite. Flowers typically magenta; styles 5.

RAGGED-ROBIN (*S. flos-cuculi*): Northeast. Flowers rose-pink; petals deeply 4-lobed.

MALTESE-CROSS (*S. chalcedonica*): Northeast. Flowers usually red; petals deeply notched.

CARYOPHYLLACEAE, p. 192   PINK FAMILY

Rose Campion

Maltese-cross

Ragged-robin

FIELD BINDWEED (*Convolvulus arvensis*): spring–fall; disturbed places; widespread (native Eurasia). Trailing or climbing. Leaf bases somewhat pointed. Flowers to 1 in. long, solitary, funnel-shaped, white to pink; ³⁄₁₆–¾ in. gap between flower base and pair of small bracts below. Hedge False Bindweed (p. 201) has leaf bases square-lobed; flowers 1½–3 in. long, with a pair of bracts actually surrounding the base (sepals). See also Texas Bindweed (p. 202).

CONVOLVULACEAE, p. 199 — MORNING-GLORY FAMILY

Field Bindweed

ALAMO-VINE (*Merremia dissecta*): spring–fall; disturbed places; Gulf coast (native tropical America, possibly also southern U.S.). Twining vine. Leaves alternate, deeply palmately 5–9-lobed, the lobes themselves coarsely toothed and lobed. Flowers large, usually solitary, funnel-shaped, white with purplish or reddish center. Also called Noyau-vine, Cut-leaf-morning-glory.

Alamo-vine is told from *Convolvulus* and *Ipomoea* species (p. 202) by its leaves.

CONVOLVULACEAE, p. 199 — MORNING-GLORY FAMILY

Alamo-vine

IVY-LEAF MORNING-GLORY (*Ipomoea hederacea*): Summer; disturbed places; East, South (native tropical America and probably southern U.S.). Twining vine. Stems have spreading hairs. Leaves alternate, mostly 3-lobed (some unlobed or 5-lobed). Flowers funnel-shaped, purple or blue. Similar species (p. 203) have stems hairless or with hairs not spreading.

COMMON MORNING-GLORY (*I. purpurea*): Widespread (native tropical America). Leaves broadly heart-shaped.

CONVOLVULACEAE, p. 199 — MORNING-GLORY FAMILY

Ivy-leaf Morning-glory / Common Morning-glory

CYPRESS-VINE (*Ipomoea quamoclit*): summer–fall; disturbed places; Southeast (native tropical America). Twining vine. Leaves alternate, pinnately divided into many narrow segments. Flowers 1 to few, trumpet-shaped and 5-lobed, red; stamens and style protruding.

See additional red-flowered *Ipomoea* species (p. 204).

CONVOLVULACEAE, p. 199 — MORNING-GLORY FAMILY

Cypress-vine

MOSSY STONECROP (*Sedum acre*): Summer; disturbed places; East, Northwest (native Eurasia). Mat-forming. Leaves overlapping, succulent, tiny, ovoid. Flowers small, in clusters; petals 5, yellow. Also called Golden-carpet, Wallpepper.

See native stonecrops (p. 205).

CRASSULACEAE, p. 205 **STONECROP FAMILY**

Mossy Stonecrop

ORPINE (*Hylotelephium telephium*): Summer–fall; disturbed places; East (native Eurasia). HT: 10–24 in. Plants fleshy. Leaves alternate or occasionally opposite, becoming smaller toward top of stem. Flowers in clusters; petals 5, deep pink to purple-red.

See also Allegheny Stonecrop (p. 207), which has leaves little reduced upward; petals paler.

CRASSULACEAE, p. 205 **STONECROP FAMILY**

Orpine

BALSAM-PEAR (*Momordica charantia*): Year-round; disturbed places; chiefly FL (native Old World tropics). Vine, creeping or climbing by tendrils; ill-scented. Leaves alternate, deeply palmately 5–9-lobed. Flowers unisexual, mostly solitary, 5-lobed, yellow. Fruits are yellow to orange, warty-skinned gourds, splitting open to expose seeds with a red, sticky covering.

CUCURBITACEAE, p. 207 **CUCUMBER FAMILY**

Balsam-pear

TEASEL (*Dipsacus fullonum*): Summer; disturbed places; widespread (native Eurasia). HT: 1½–6 ft. Stems prickly. Leaves opposite, coarsely toothed; midrib prickly beneath. Flowers small, in a prickly-bracted, columnar head; tubular and 4-lobed; lavender, pink, or whitish.

CUT-LEAF TEASEL (*D. laciniata*, no photo): East. Main leaves deeply pinnately cut or lobed.

See also thistles (pp. 100–101, 567), which have alternate stem leaves.

DIPSACACEAE **TEASEL FAMILY**

Teasel

CYPRESS SPURGE (*Euphorbia cyparissias*): Spring–summer; disturbed places; widespread (native Europe). HT: 6–12 in. Plants have milky juice. Leaves very narrow (to ⅛ in. wide). Flowers less conspicuous than the bright green or yellowish, saucer-shaped bracts just beneath them.

LEAFY SPURGE (*E. esula*): Leaves ¹⁄₁₆–⁵⁄₁₆ in. wide.

See native *Euphorbia* species (p. 222).

EUPHORBIACEAE, p. 221 SPURGE FAMILY

ROSARY-PEA (*Abrus precatorius*): Summer; disturbed places; FL (native Old World tropics). Twining vine, more or less woody. Leaves alternate, pinnately divided into 10–30 leaflets. Flowers in clusters, pealike (p. 224), lavender-pink or light reddish purple. Pods open to reveal black-tipped, bright red seeds. Also called Crab's-eye.

NOTE Poisonous.

FABACEAE, p. 224 LEGUME FAMILY

CROWN-VETCH (*Securigera varia*): Late spring–summer; disturbed places; widespread (native Eurasia). HT: 1–3 ft. Leaves alternate, pinnately divided into 11–25 leaflets. Flowers in rounded clusters, pealike (p. 224), pink and white. Pods narrow. Also called Axseed.

FABACEAE, p. 224 LEGUME FAMILY

HAIRY VETCH (*Vicia villosa*): Spring–summer; disturbed places; widespread (native Eurasia). Trailing, climbing, or sprawling. Stems often hairy. Leaves alternate, pinnately divided into 14–18 leaflets; tendril at tip of leaf. Flowers ½–⅝ in. long; in elongated, 1-sided clusters; pealike (p. 224); blue-purple or purple and white.

See also American Vetch (p. 245), which has flowers ⅝–1 in. long, in loose clusters; stipules often sharply toothed.

FABACEAE, p. 224 LEGUME FAMILY

EVERLASTING-PEA (*Lathyrus latifolius*): Summer; disturbed places; widespread (native Europe). Trailing or climbing via tendrils. Stems winged. Leaves alternate, divided into 2 lance-shaped leaflets; stipules (paired appendages at leaf stalk base) conspicuous. Flowers in clusters, pealike (p. 224), rose or whitish. Pods beanlike. Also called Perennial Sweet-pea.

See native *Lathyrus* species (pp. 244–245).

FABACEAE, p. 224 — **LEGUME FAMILY**

Everlasting-pea

KUDZU (*Pueraria montana* var. *lobata*): Summer–fall; disturbed places; Southeast (native eastern Asia). Woody-based vine, trailing or climbing, often covering shrubs, trees, and even buildings. Plants hairy. Leaves alternate, divided into 3 egg-shaped leaflets, these often lobed. Flowers in elongated clusters, pealike (p. 224), reddish purple. Pods flat, hairy.

FABACEAE, p. 224 — **LEGUME FAMILY**

Kudzu

JAPANESE-CLOVER (*Kummerowia striata*): Summer–fall; disturbed places; East (native eastern Asia). Mostly trailing. Leaves alternate, nearly stalkless, clover-like, divided into 3 leaflets. Flowers small, solitary or few from leaf axils, pealike (p. 224), pink or purple.

KOREAN-CLOVER (*K. stipulacea*, no photo): Similar. Leaves stalked.

Lance-shaped, papery, brownish stipules (appendages at leaf base) distinguish these species from *Lespedeza* (p. 231).

FABACEAE, p. 224 — **LEGUME FAMILY**

Japanese-clover

ALFALFA (*Medicago sativa*): Spring–fall; disturbed places; widespread (native Eurasia). HT: 6–30 in. Leaves alternate, divided into 3 relatively narrow leaflets, each toothed at tip. Flowers small, in crowded, round to short-cylindrical clusters; pealike (p. 224); pink, blue, violet, yellowish, or whitish. Pods coiled in 2 or 3 turns.

FABACEAE, p. 224 — **LEGUME FAMILY**

Alfalfa

BLACK MEDICK (*Medicago lupulina*): Spring–fall; disturbed places; widespread (native Eurasia). HT: prostrate or to 30 in. Stems 4-angled. Leaves alternate, cloverlike, divided into 3 leaflets. Flowers tiny, in headlike clusters, pealike (p. 224), yellow. Pods tiny, kidney-shaped, veiny, coiled, single-seeded, turning blackish. The pods distinguish this species from yellow clovers such as Large Hop Clover (below).

FABACEAE, p. 224   **LEGUME FAMILY**

Black Medick

WHITE CLOVER (*Trifolium repens*): Spring–fall; lawns, open places; widespread (native Eurasia). HT: 4–10 in. Leaves divided into 3 leaflets, often with V-shaped mark. Flowers small, in dense, ball-shaped clusters, pealike (p. 224), white or pink-tinged. Leaves and flower stalk arise separately from creeping stem.

RED CLOVER (*T. pratense*): HT: 6–24 in. Flowering stalks leafy; flowers pink-purple to whitish.

See native *Trifolium* species (p. 232).

FABACEAE, p. 224   **LEGUME FAMILY**

White Clover

Red Clover

RABBIT-FOOT CLOVER (*Trifolium arvense*): Spring–summer; disturbed places; East, West (native Eurasia). HT: 4–12 in. Leaflets 3. Flowers pealike (p. 224), in cylindrical, light pink to whitish, feathery-hairy clusters.

CRIMSON CLOVER (*T. incarnatum*): HT: 1–2 ft. Flowers crimson.

LARGE HOP CLOVER (*T. aureum*): HT: 8–20 in. This and other yellow-flowered clovers resemble Black Medick (above). Also called Greater Hop Clover.

FABACEAE, p. 224   **LEGUME FAMILY**

Rabbit-foot Clover   Crimson Clover   Large Hop Clover

YELLOW SWEET-CLOVER (*Melilotus officinalis*): Spring–fall; disturbed places; widespread (native Eurasia). HT: 1–6 ft. Leaves alternate, divided into 3 elliptic leaflets. Flowers ³⁄₁₆–¹⁄₄ in. long, in elongated clusters, pealike (p. 224).

ANNUAL YELLOW SWEET-CLOVER (*M. indicus*, no photo): Western, southern (native Eurasia). Flowers yellow, ¹⁄₈ in. or less long. Also called Sour-clover.

WHITE SWEET-CLOVER (*M. albus*): Flowers white.

FABACEAE, p. 224   **LEGUME FAMILY**

Yellow Sweet-clover

White Sweet-clover

BIRD'S-FOOT-TREFOIL (*Lotus corniculatus***):** Summer; disturbed places; widespread (native Eurasia). HT: 2–16 in. Leaves alternate, divided into 5 leaflets (3 terminal and 2 near leafstalk base). Flowers in clusters, pealike (p. 224), bright yellow (orangish or red-marked in age). Pods slender, tipped with persistent style.

See native *Lotus* species (pp. 246–247).

FABACEAE, p. 224   LEGUME FAMILY

SHOWY RATTLEBOX (*Crotalaria spectabilis***):** Summer–fall; disturbed places; Southeast (native southern Asia). HT: 1½–4 ft. Leaves alternate, undivided, untoothed, widest near tip. Flowers in elongated clusters, pealike (p. 224), yellow. Pods inflated.

See native *Crotalaria* species (p. 234).

FABACEAE, p. 224   LEGUME FAMILY

BLUNT-LEAF SENNA (*Senna obtusifolia***):** Summer–fall; disturbed places; Southeast (native tropical America). HT: to 4 ft. Leaves alternate, pinnately divided into 6 (or 4) broad leaflets. Flowers solitary or in pairs; petals 5, yellow. Pods 4-sided, long, narrow, strongly curved. Also called Sicklepod, Coffee-weed.

See native *Senna* species (p. 248).

FABACEAE, p. 224   LEGUME FAMILY

FUMITORY (*Fumaria officinalis***):** Spring–summer; disturbed places; scattered (native Eurasia). HT: 8–30 in. Leaves fernlike, much divided into lobed segments. Flowers pink with dark tips, in elongated clusters, similar to pink-flowered *Corydalis* (p. 251). Fruits round (elongated in *Corydalis*). Also called Earth-smoke.

FUMARIACEAE, p. 250   FUMITORY FAMILY

COMMON STORK'S-BILL (*Erodium cicutarium*): Spring–fall; disturbed places; widespread (native Eurasia). HT: to 18 in. Stems hairy. Leaves pinnately divided into lobed and toothed leaflets. Flowers small, in clusters; petals 5, pink or purplish pink. Fruits seedlike, each with a long "tail," united into a beaklike structure before separating at maturity. Also called Redstem Filaree.

See native stork's-bills (p. 261).

GERANIACEAE, p. 260 — GERANIUM FAMILY

BLACKBERRY-LILY (*Belamcanda chinensis*): Summer; disturbed places; East (native eastern Asia). HT: 2–3 ft. Leaves sword-shaped, their bases overlapping. Flowers in clusters; tepals 6 (3 petals, 3 sepals, all alike), orangish (or rarely yellowish), red-spotted. Fruits open to reveal shiny, black seeds.

IRIDACEAE, p. 273 — IRIS FAMILY

YELLOW FLAG (*Iris pseudacorus*): Spring–early summer; wet places; widespread (native Eurasia). HT: 2–4 ft. Leaves sword-shaped, their bases overlapping. Flowers bright yellow (see p. 273 for the *Iris* flower structure).

See native *Iris* species (pp. 273–274).

IRIDACEAE, p. 273 — IRIS FAMILY

BUGLEWEED (*Ajuga reptans*): Spring–early summer; lawns, disturbed places; scattered (native Eurasia). HT: 4–12 in.; mat-forming. Flowering stems square. Leaves basal and opposite, sometimes flushed purplish or bronze. Flowers in leafy-bracted whorls along upper stem, violet-blue, 2-lipped but upper lip very short (Self-heal, p. 279, has a prominent upper lip). Also called Carpet Bugle.

LAMIACEAE, p. 277 — MINT FAMILY

GROUND-IVY (*Glechoma hederacea*): Spring–midsummer; lawns, disturbed places; widespread (native Eurasia). HT: 4–12 in.; creeping. Flowering stems square. Leaves opposite, kidney-shaped to round, scallop-edged. Flowers in whorls in leaf axils, 2-lipped, blue-violet with purple-spotted lower lip. Also called Gill-over-the-ground.

LAMIACEAE, p. 277   MINT FAMILY

Ground-ivy

CATNIP (*Nepeta cataria*): Summer–fall; disturbed places; widespread (native Eurasia). HT: 1–3 ft. Aromatic, finely white-hairy. Stems square. Leaves opposite, triangular-egg-shaped, coarsely round-toothed. Flowers in crowded clusters; 2-lipped; white or pale pink, with purplish spots.

LAMIACEAE, p. 277   MINT FAMILY

Catnip

PURPLE DEAD-NETTLE (*Lamium purpureum*): Spring–fall; disturbed places; widespread (native Eurasia). HT: 4–14 in. Stems square. Leaves opposite, stalked, egg-shaped; upper leaves crowded, angled downward, sometimes tinged reddish or purple. Flowers in upper leaf axils, 2-lipped, pink-purple with purple-spotted lower lip.

HENBIT (*L. amplexicaule*): Similar, but upper leaves stalkless, about as wide as long, not down-bent.

LAMIACEAE, p. 277   MINT FAMILY

Purple Dead-nettle   Henbit

MOTHERWORT (*Leonurus cardiaca*): Summer; disturbed places; widespread (native Eurasia). HT: 1½–4 ft. Stems square. Leaves opposite, palmately lobed, toothed; those on upper stems have 3 lance-shaped lobes. Flowers in dense clusters in leaf axils, 2-lipped, light pink to whitish or purple-tinged; upper lip hairy; calyx (united sepals) has spine-tipped lobes.

LAMIACEAE, p. 277   MINT FAMILY

Motherwort

COMMON HOREHOUND (*Marrubium vulgare*): Summer; disturbed places; widespread (native Eurasia). HT: 1–2½ ft. Plants white-woolly. Stems square. Leaves opposite, scallop-toothed, prominently wrinkled above, often white-hairy beneath. Flowers small, in dense clusters in leaf axils, 2-lipped, whitish; calyx (united sepals) has hook-tipped teeth.

LAMIACEAE, p. 277   MINT FAMILY

SPEARMINT (*Mentha spicata*): Summer–fall; moist or wet places; widespread (native Eurasia). HT: 1–3 ft. Aromatic. Stems square. Leaves opposite, mostly stalkless, toothed. Flowers tiny, in dense clusters mostly at stem ends; 2-lipped; pale purple, pink, or white; stamens protruding.

PEPPERMINT (*M. × piperita*, no photo): Main leaves stalked; leaves have peppermint odor.

See also American Wild Mint (p. 294).

LAMIACEAE, p. 277   MINT FAMILY

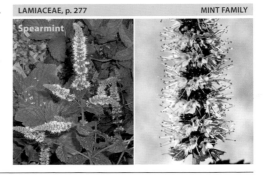

PERILLA (*Perilla frutescens*): Late summer–fall; disturbed places; East (native eastern Asia). HT: 1–3 ft. Aromatic. Stems square. Leaves opposite, long-stalked, broadly egg-shaped, blunt-toothed, sometimes reddish purple. Flowers tiny, in elongated clusters, 5-lobed (slightly 2-lipped), whitish tinged with lavender-pink. Also called Beefsteak-plant. Do not confuse with stoneroots (p. 277), which have flowers with conspicuously protruding stamens.

LAMIACEAE, p. 277   MINT FAMILY

FIELD GARLIC (*Allium vineale*): Summer; disturbed places; East, West (native Eurasia). HT: 1–3 ft. Onion odor. Leaves partway up stem, slender, round in cross section, hollow. Flowers in clusters; tepals 6 (3 petals, 3 sepals, all alike), purplish or pink, or sometimes whitish or greenish. Some or all of the flowers may be replaced by tiny bulbs with "tails." See also Wild Garlic (p. 321), which has flat, solid leaves and often 2–4 (vs. 1) papery bracts beneath flower cluster.

LILIACEAE, p. 296   LILY FAMILY

ORANGE DAYLILY (*Hemerocallis fulva*): Late spring–early summer; roadsides, disturbed places; East (native eastern Asia). HT: 2½–4 ft. Leaves arise from plant base, narrowly sword-shaped. Flowers large, in clusters, funnel-shaped, orange with yellow center. True lilies (pp. 309–311) have stem leaves.

LILIACEAE, p. 296   LILY FAMILY

Orange Daylily

STAR-OF-BETHLEHEM (*Ornithogalum umbellatum*): Spring; roadsides, open woods; East (native Eurasia). HT: 6–12 in. Leaves grasslike. Flowers in clusters; tepals 6 (3 petals, 3 sepals, all alike), white, each with green midstripe on the outside.

LILIACEAE, p. 296   LILY FAMILY

Star-of-Bethlehem

PURPLE LOOSESTRIFE (*Lythrum salicaria*): Summer; wet places; widespread (native Eurasia). HT: 2–5 ft. Stems 4-angled. Leaves opposite or sometimes in whorls of 3, stalkless, lance-shaped. Flowers in elongated clusters; petals typically 6, magenta-purple, wrinkled.

See additional *Lythrum* species (p. 334).

LYTHRACEAE, p. 334   LOOSESTRIFE FAMILY

Purple Loosestrife

VELVETLEAF (*Abutilon theophrasti*): Summer–fall; disturbed places; widespread (native Eurasia). HT: 3–5 ft. Leaves alternate, heart-shaped, velvety-hairy. Flowers solitary; petals 5, yellow. Fruit a ring of 10–15 conspicuously beaked segments.

See native *Abutilon* species (p. 344).

MALVACEAE, p. 335   MALLOW FAMILY

Velvetleaf

HOLLYHOCK (*Alcea rosea*): Summer; disturbed places; widespread (native Old World). HT: to 10 ft. Plants hairy. Leaves alternate, long-stalked, large, nearly round, palmately 3–7-lobed. Flowers very large, in elongated clusters; petals 5, commonly pink or white but sometimes purplish, reddish, or whitish.

MALVACEAE, p. 335　　　MALLOW FAMILY

FLOWER-OF-AN-HOUR (*Hibiscus trionum*): Summer; disturbed places; widespread (native Eurasia). HT: 12–20 in. Plants hairy. Leaves alternate, long-stalked, palmately divided into 3 often toothed or lobed segments. Flowers solitary, above a whorl of slender bracts; petals 5, cream-colored or pale yellow, with dark red-purple blotches at base. Mature calyx (united sepals) inflated, dark-veined. Also called Venice Mallow.

See native *Hibiscus* species (pp. 336–337).

MALVACEAE, p. 335　　　MALLOW FAMILY

MUSK MALLOW (*Malva moschata*): Summer; disturbed places; Northwest, Northeast (native Eurasia). HT: 1–3 ft. Leaves alternate, deeply divided into several segments. Flowers large, solitary or in clusters; petals 5, rose, pink, or whitish, sometimes darker-veined, their tips squared off and shallowly notched.

HIGH MALLOW (*M. sylvestris*): Leaves shallowly 5–7-lobed, toothed. Flowers often rose-purple with darker stripes.

MALVACEAE, p. 335　　　MALLOW FAMILY

COMMON MALLOW (*Malva neglecta*): Late spring–fall; disturbed places; widespread (native Eurasia). HT: 6–18 in. Leaves kidney-shaped to round, shallowly 5–7-lobed, scallop-toothed. Flowers 1 to few in leaf axils; petals 5, small, white or tinged and veined pinkish or lavender. Fruit segments arranged in a button-shaped disk. Also called Dwarf Mallow, Cheeses.

See also Alkali-mallow (p. 343).

MALVACEAE, p. 335　　　MALLOW FAMILY

CAESAR-WEED (*Urena lobata*): Year-round; disturbed places; FL (native Old World tropics). HT: 1–9 ft. Sometimes shrubby. Leaves alternate, broadly egg-shaped to nearly round, toothed and often shallowly lobed, covered with star-shaped hairs. Flowers solitary or in clusters; petals 5, pink with darker base; conspicuous, tubular pistil-stamen column in center. Fruits burlike.

MALVACEAE, p. 335   MALLOW FAMILY

YELLOW FLOATING-HEART (*Nymphoides peltata*): Summer; quiet water; scattered (native Eurasia). Aquatic. Leaves floating, 2½–6 in. wide, nearly round with heart-shaped base. Flowers yellow, 5-lobed, the lobe edges fringed. Also called Water-fringe, Fringed-water-lily.

See native *Nymphoides* species (p. 349).

MENYANTHACEAE, p. 348   BUCK-BEAN FAMILY

HELLEBORINE (*Epipactis helleborine*): Summer–fall; disturbed places; scattered (native Eurasia). HT: to 3 ft. Similar to Giant Helleborine (p. 391), but flowers have smaller sepals (⅜–½ in. long) and the end lobe of the lip is as wide as or wider than long (the lip of the Giant Helleborine flower is 3-lobed, with the end lobe elongated). Flower parts variously greenish, greenish white, pinkish, purplish, or purplish brown.

ORCHIDACEAE, p. 371   ORCHID FAMILY

LAWN ORCHID (*Zeuxine strateumatica*): Fall–winter; moist, often grassy places; Gulf coast, FL (native tropical Asia). HT: 2–10 in. Leaves alternate, stalkless. Flowers in dense clusters, white; lip yellowish with 2 rounded lobes at tip. Also called Soldier's Orchid.

Do not confuse with ladies'-tresses (pp. 388–389), which have leaves chiefly basal; flowers with an egg-shaped lip, its tip often wavy-edged or toothed.

ORCHIDACEAE, p. 371   ORCHID FAMILY

BERMUDA-BUTTERCUP (*Oxalis pes-caprae*): Late fall–spring; disturbed places; CA (native southern Africa). HT: to 14 in. Leaves arise from plant base, each divided into 3 heart-shaped, sometimes purple-dotted leaflets. Flowers large, in clusters; petals 5, bright yellow.

See native yellow-flowered *Oxalis* species (p. 396).

OXALIDACEAE, p. 396 — WOOD-SORREL FAMILY
Bermuda-buttercup

GREATER CELANDINE (*Chelidonium majus*): Spring–summer; woods, disturbed places; East (native Eurasia). HT: 1–2½ ft. Plants have orange-yellow juice. Leaves alternate, deeply pinnately divided into irregularly toothed segments. Flowers in clusters; petals 4, yellow.

Do not confuse with Wood-poppy (p. 402).

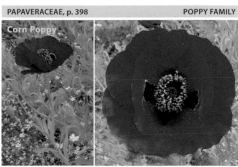

PAPAVERACEAE, p. 398 — POPPY FAMILY
Greater Celandine

CORN POPPY (*Papaver rhoeas*): Late spring–summer; disturbed places; scattered (native Eurasia). HT: 1–3 ft. Plants have milky juice; bristly-hairy. Leaves alternate and basal, pinnately divided, toothed. Flowers large, solitary; petals 4, usually red with dark blotch at base; stigmatic lines 8–14 (see p. 403).

LONG-HEAD POPPY (*P. dubium*, no photo): Similar. Petals orange to red, may be unblotched; stigmatic lines 5–9.

See native *Papaver* species (pp. 403–404).

PAPAVERACEAE, p. 398 — POPPY FAMILY
Corn Poppy

ENGLISH PLANTAIN (*Plantago lanceolata*): Summer; disturbed places; widespread (native Eurasia). HT: 6–24 in. Leaves arise from plant base, narrowly elliptic. Flowers tiny, in densely crowded, short-cylindrical clusters; petals 4, papery; stamens protruding.

COMMON PLANTAIN (*P. major*): Basal leaves broad. Flowers in slender, elongated clusters.

PLANTAGINACEAE — PLANTAIN FAMILY
English Plantain
Common Plantain

CORAL-VINE (*Antigonon leptopus*): Spring–fall; disturbed places; Gulf coast (native Mexico, Central America). Woody-based vine, spreading or climbing via tendrils. Leaves alternate, triangular or egg- or heart-shaped, conspicuously veiny. Flowers in nodding clusters; tepals (petals and petal-like sepals) 5, usually rose-pink to purplish.

POLYGONACEAE, p. 428   BUCKWHEAT FAMILY

JAPANESE KNOTWEED (*Fallopia japonica*): Summer; disturbed places; East, West (native eastern Asia). HT: 3–6 ft. Stems bamboolike. Leaves alternate, large, with squared-off base. Flowers small, in clusters, white or greenish white. Also called Mexican-bamboo.

GIANT KNOTWEED (*F. sachalinensis*, no photo): Leaf bases heart-shaped.

See additional *Fallopia* species (p. 433).

POLYGONACEAE, p. 428   BUCKWHEAT FAMILY

CURLY DOCK (*Rumex crispus*): Spring–fall; disturbed places; widespread (native Eurasia). HT: 1½–4 ft. Plants sometimes red-tinged. Leaves alternate, strongly curled or wavy-edged. Flowers tiny, in whorls along elongated stalks, greenish.

BROAD-LEAF DOCK (*R. obtusifolius*): Leaves broader, not strongly wavy-edged. Flower edges minutely spiny-toothed (untoothed in Curly Dock). Also called Bitter Dock.

See additional *Rumex* (pp. 428–429).

POLYGONACEAE, p. 428   BUCKWHEAT FAMILY

WATER-HYACINTH (*Eichhornia crassipes*): Spring–fall; ponds, ditches; Gulf coast, southern CA (native tropical regions). Aquatic, floating, flowering stalk to 10 in. Leaves egg-shaped to round; leafstalks spongy-inflated. Flowers in clusters, slightly 2-lipped, blue or bluish purple, with purple-rimmed yellow blotch in middle of upper lobe.

See also Pickerel-weed (p. 438).

PONTEDERIACEAE, p. 438   PICKEREL-WEED FAMILY

COMMON PURSLANE (*Portulaca oleracea*): Spring–fall; disturbed places; widespread (native Eurasia). Often prostrate, sometimes mat-forming. Leaves alternate, spoon- or wedge-shaped, flat, succulent. Flowers solitary or in clusters; petals usually 5, yellow, notched at tip.

See additional *Portulaca* species (pp. 443–444).

Common Purslane

SCARLET PIMPERNEL (*Anagallis arvensis*): Spring–summer; disturbed places; widespread (native Eurasia). HT: 4–12 in. Stems 4-angled. Leaves opposite (rarely whorled), stalkless, dark-dotted beneath. Flowers small, solitary in leaf axils; petals 5, usually red-orange or salmon-colored; a blue-flowered variant uncommonly encountered.

Scarlet Pimpernel

GARDEN YELLOW LOOSESTRIFE (*Lysimachia vulgaris*): Summer; disturbed places; Northeast (native Eurasia). HT: mostly 2–3 ft. Leaves opposite or in whorls of 3 or 4, dotted. Flowers mostly in clusters at stem ends; petals 5, yellow; sepal edges red-orange.

LARGE YELLOW LOOSESTRIFE (*L. punctata*): Flowers 1–3 in leaf axils; sepal edges green.

Whorled Loosestrife and Swamp-candles (p. 450) have petals streaked or spotted.

Garden Yellow Loosestrife   Large Yellow Loosestrife

MONEYWORT (*Lysimachia nummularia*): Summer; moist places; East, Northwest (native Eurasia). Stems creeping, often mat-forming. Leaves opposite, round, dotted. Flowers solitary, yellow. Also called Creeping-jenny.

Moneywort

ROCKET-LARKSPUR (*Consolida ajacis*): Summer; disturbed places; widespread (native Eurasia). HT: 1–2½ ft. Similar to larkspurs of the genus *Delphinium* (pp. 467–468), but the 4 petals in the flower center are united into a single, hairless, 4-lobed structure (in *Delphinium*, each flaplike lower petal is 2-lobed, often hairy). Flowers blue, purple, pink, or white; pistil and fruit each 1, commonly hairy. Also called Annual-larkspur.

RANUNCULACEAE, p. 453   BUTTERCUP FAMILY

CREEPING BUTTERCUP (*Ranunculus repens*): Spring–summer; disturbed places; East, West (native Eurasia). HT: 6–18 in.; often creeping. Leaves often mottled, divided into 3 deeply lobed and toothed segments, middle segment stalked. Petals 5, yellow.

BULBOUS BUTTERCUP (*R. bulbosus*, no photo): Not creeping. Sepals bent down.

MEADOW BUTTERCUP (*R. acris*): Middle leaf segment not stalked. Also called Tall Buttercup.

RANUNCULACEAE, p. 453   BUTTERCUP FAMILY

LESSER CELANDINE (*Ranunculus ficaria*): Spring; moist places; East, Northwest (native Eurasia). HT: 2–6 in. Leaves basal and alternate, heart-shaped. Flowers solitary; petals 7–10, yellow. Seedlike fruits in rounded clusters. Also called Pilewort, Fig Buttercup. Do not confuse with Yellow Marsh-marigold (p. 463).

BUR BUTTERCUP (*R. testiculatus*): Leaves divided into narrow segments. Seedlike fruits pointy-beaked, in cylindrical heads. Also called Hornseed Buttercup.

RANUNCULACEAE, p. 453   BUTTERCUP FAMILY

QUEEN-OF-THE-MEADOW (*Filipendula ulmaria*): Summer; disturbed places; Northeast (native Eurasia). HT: mostly 2–4 ft. Leaves basal and alternate, pinnately divided into coarsely and sharply toothed leaflets, some of these large and some tiny. Flowers in clusters; petals usually 5, cream-white; stamens protruding.

See also Queen-of-the-prairie (p. 472).

ROSACEAE, p. 471   ROSE FAMILY

SULPHUR CINQUEFOIL (*Potentilla recta*): Late spring–summer; disturbed places; widespread (native Eurasia). HT: 1–2 ft. Plants hairy. Stems abundantly leafy. Leaves palmately divided into 5–7 coarsely toothed leaflets. Flowers in clusters; petals 5, pale yellow, notched.

SILVERY CINQUEFOIL (*P. argentea*): HT: 5–16 in. Plants woolly. Leaves divided into 5 leaflets, densely silvery-hairy beneath. Flowers yellow.

See native cinquefoils (pp. 477–481).

ROSACEAE, p. 471 — ROSE FAMILY

MOCK STRAWBERRY (*Duchesnea indica*): spring–summer; disturbed places; East, West (native Asia). Trailing, spreading by runners; flowering stalks 1–4 in. tall. Leaves alternate, divided into 3 leaflets. Flowers solitary; petals 5, yellow; whorl of 3-toothed, leaflike bracts just beneath flower. Fruits strawberry-like but tasteless. Also called Indian-strawberry.

See also *Waldsteinia* species (p. 482).

ROSACEAE, p. 471 — ROSE FAMILY

YELLOW BEDSTRAW (*Galium verum*): summer; disturbed places; scattered (native Eurasia). HT: 6 in.–3 ft. Stems bluntly 4-angled. Leaves in whorls of 8–12, very narrow, 1-veined. Flowers tiny, in large clusters, 4-lobed, bright yellow. Fruits smooth.

HEDGE BEDSTRAW (*G. mollugo*): HT: 1–4 ft. Leaves in whorls of 6–8, 1-veined. Flowers white. Fruits smooth. Also called Wild-madder.

See native *Galium* species (pp. 491–492).

RUBIACEAE, p. 489 — MADDER FAMILY

FIELD-MADDER (*Sherardia arvensis*): spring–summer; disturbed places; East, West (native Eurasia). HT: 4–15 in. Stems 4-angled. Leaves in whorls of 4–6 (mostly 6), sharp-tipped. Flowers tiny, in clusters at stem ends, trumpet-shaped and 4-lobed, pink or lilac; whorl of leaflike bracts beneath cluster. Also called Blue Field-madder.

See purple-flowered bedstraws (p. 492), which lack whorl of bracts.

RUBIACEAE, p. 489 — MADDER FAMILY

ROUGH MEXICAN-CLOVER (*Richardia scabra*): Spring–fall; disturbed places; Gulf coast (native tropical America and possibly southeastern U.S.). HT: 6–24 in. Leaves opposite, nearly stalkless. Flowers small, in clusters at stem ends, funnel-shaped and 6- (or 5-) lobed, white. Fruits minutely warty. Also called Florida Pusley.

TROPICAL MEXICAN-CLOVER (*R. brasiliensis*, no photo): Similar. Fruits hairy. Also called Brazilian Pusley.

RUBIACEAE, p. 489 — MADDER FAMILY

Rough Mexican-clover

COMMON SPEEDWELL (*Veronica officinalis*): Spring–summer; disturbed places; East, West (native Europe). HT: 2–10 in. Leaves opposite (upper often alternate). Flowers small, in elongated clusters, saucer-shaped and 4-lobed, light blue or lilac.

THYME-LEAF SPEEDWELL (*V. serpyllifolia* ssp. *serpyllifolia*): Flowers white or pale blue with violet-blue veins.

CORN SPEEDWELL (*V. arvensis*): Flowers blue-violet.

See native *Veronica* species (pp. 529–530).

SCROPHULARIACEAE, p. 512 — FIGWORT FAMILY

Common Speedwell

Thyme-leaf Speedwell

Corn Speedwell

FOXGLOVE (*Digitalis purpurea*): Late spring–summer; disturbed places; Northeast, Northwest (native Europe). HT: 2–5 ft. Plants hairy. Leaves basal and alternate, the lower ones often gray-hairy beneath. Flowers large and somewhat drooping, in mostly 1-sided, elongated clusters; tubular and 5-lobed; usually pink-purple (occasionally lavender or whitish), spotted within.

NOTE Poisonous.

SCROPHULARIACEAE, p. 512 — FIGWORT FAMILY

Foxglove

KENILWORTH-IVY (*Cymbalaria muralis*): Summer; crevices, rock walls; scattered (native Europe). Trailing. Leaves alternate, kidney-shaped to round, shallowly palmately lobed. Flowers solitary; 2-lipped, with short projection (spur) at base; purplish with yellow patch.

SCROPHULARIACEAE, p. 512 — FIGWORT FAMILY

Kenilworth-Ivy

EYEBRIGHT (*Euphrasia stricta*): Summer–fall; disturbed places; Northeast (native Europe). HT: 4–15 in. Leaves opposite (or alternate above), palmately veined, coarsely and sharply toothed. Flowers small, in axils of leaflike upper bracts; 2-lipped; pale lavender or whitish, with dark purple stripes, yellow-blotched lower lip. Several similar native and introduced species found in northern North America.

SCROPHULARIACEAE, p. 512   FIGWORT FAMILY

Eyebright

JAPANESE MAZUS (*Mazus pumilus*): Spring–fall; disturbed places; East, Northwest (native eastern Asia). Creeping. Leaves opposite (or alternate above). Flowers small, in clusters, mostly blue-violet, 2-lipped: upper lip short, lower lip spreading and 3-lobed, with 2 yellow-spotted white humps.

SCROPHULARIACEAE, p. 512   FIGWORT FAMILY

Japanese Mazus

SHARP-LEAF CANCERWORT (*Kickxia elatine*): Summer; disturbed places; East, West (native Eurasia). Prostrate or trailing. Leaves mostly alternate, the upper ones 2-lobed at base. Flowers small, solitary, 2-lipped: upper lip dark purple, lower lip yellow; tail-like spur at base.

ROUND-LEAF CANCERWORT (*K. spuria*, no photo): Leaves nearly round.

DWARF-SNAPDRAGON (*Chaenorrhinum minus*): HT: to 10 in. Plants erect. Flowers lavender and white; spur short.

SCROPHULARIACEAE, p. 512   FIGWORT FAMILY

Sharp-leaf Cancerwort

Dwarf-snapdragon

YELLOW TOADFLAX (*Linaria vulgaris*): Spring–fall; disturbed places; widespread (native Eurasia). HT: 1–2½ ft. Leaves alternate, narrow. Flowers in clusters, 2-lipped, yellow with orange-yellow center; tail-like spur at base. Also called butter-and-eggs.

DALMATIAN TOADFLAX (*L. dalmatica*): Leaves broad-based.

SCROPHULARIACEAE, p. 512   FIGWORT FAMILY

Yellow Toadflax

Dalmatian Toadflax

YELLOW GLANDWEED (*Parentucellia viscosa*): Spring–summer; moist places; Northwest (native Eurasia). HT: 4–24 in. Leaves mostly opposite. Flowers in clusters, yellow, 2-lipped: upper lip hoodlike, lower lip 3-lobed. Partially parasitic.

SCROPHULARIACEAE, p. 512 — FIGWORT FAMILY

Yellow Glandweed

COMMON MULLEIN (*Verbascum thapsus*): Summer–fall; disturbed places; widespread (native Eurasia). HT: 2–6 ft. Plants densely gray-hairy. First-year plants form a cluster of large, velvety leaves; second-year plants have spikelike clusters of flowers with 5 yellow petals. Also called Great Mullein.

SCROPHULARIACEAE, p. 512 — FIGWORT FAMILY

Common Mullein

MOTH MULLEIN (*Verbascum blattaria*): Summer–fall; disturbed places; widespread (native Eurasia). HT: 1–4 ft. Leaves basal and alternate. Flowers in elongated clusters, 5-lobed, yellow or white, often with red-purple center.

SCROPHULARIACEAE, p. 512 — FIGWORT FAMILY

Moth Mullein

HENBANE (*Hyoscyamus niger*): Summer; disturbed places; West, North (native Eurasia). HT: to 3 ft. Ill-scented. Leaves alternate (or nearly opposite). Flowers in 1-sided clusters; funnel-shaped, with 5 unequal lobes; greenish yellow, with purple veins, dark purple center. Seed capsule held within urn-shaped calyx (sepals).

NOTE Poisonous.

SOLANACEAE, p. 547 — NIGHTSHADE FAMILY

Henbane

JIMSONWEED (*Datura stramonium*): Summer; disturbed places; widespread (native tropical America). HT: 1–4 ft. Ill-scented. Leaves alternate, wavy-toothed or -lobed. Flowers large, solitary; funnel-shaped and shallowly 5-lobed, with 5 slender teeth on rim; white or tinged pink to violet. Seed capsule sharply prickly. Also called Thorn-apple.

NOTE Poisonous.

See native *Datura* species (p. 547).

SOLANACEAE, p. 547   NIGHTSHADE FAMILY

Jimsonweed

BITTERSWEET NIGHTSHADE (*Solanum dulcamara*): Summer–fall; disturbed places; mostly North (native Eurasia). Somewhat shrubby vine; climbing, trailing, or sometimes erect. Leaves alternate, with 1–4 (often 2) basal lobes. Flowers in clusters, each with 5 purple, swept-back lobes and cone-shaped, yellow, united anthers. Berries red at maturity. Also called Climbing Nightshade.

NOTE Poisonous.

See additional *Solanum* (pp. 549–550).

SOLANACEAE, p. 547   NIGHTSHADE FAMILY

Bittersweet Nightshade

APPLE-OF-PERU (*Nicandra physalodes*): Summer; disturbed places; East (native tropical America). HT: 1–4 ft. Leaves alternate, irregularly toothed or lobed. Flowers nodding, solitary, broadly bell-shaped, blue; sepals have arrowhead-shaped base. Sepals swollen at maturity, surrounding the fruit (lower right photo). Also called Shoo-fly.

See also ground-cherries, Purple-ground-cherry (p. 548).

SOLANACEAE, p. 547   NIGHTSHADE FAMILY

Apple-of-Peru

LANTANA (*Lantana camara*): Year-round; disturbed places; Southeast (native West Indies). HT: 1–5 ft. Shrub. Leaves opposite, conspicuously veiny above. Flowers small, in clusters; trumpet-shaped and unequally 4-lobed; orange, pink, yellow, lavender, or cream-colored (often aging different shades). Also called Shrub-verbena.

VERBENACEAE, p. 555   VERVAIN FAMILY

Lantana

BRAZILIAN VERVAIN (*Verbena brasiliensis*): Summer–fall; disturbed places; Southeast (native tropical America). HT: to 5 ft. Stems 4-angled. Leaves opposite; bases narrowed. Flowers in slender spikes, funnel-shaped and 5-lobed, blue-purple.

PURPLE-TOP VERVAIN (*V. bonariensis*, no photo): Similar; leaf bases clasping.

EUROPEAN VERVAIN (*V. officinalis*): Scattered (native Eurasia). HT: to 2 ft. Flower spikes slender.

See native *Verbena* species (p. 555).

VERBENACEAE, p. 555 — **VERVAIN FAMILY**

Brazilian Vervain

European Vervain

EUROPEAN FIELD PANSY (*Viola arvensis*): Spring–summer; disturbed places; widespread (native Eurasia). HT: to 12 in. Leaves alternate, variable; stipules (appendages at leafstalk base) leaflike, pinnately lobed, with large end lobe. Flowers solitary; petals 5, cream-colored or yellow (upper may be purple-tipped), often shorter than sepals. Sepals shorter than petals in **JOHNNY-JUMP-UP** (*V. tricolor*) and Field Pansy (p. 560).

VIOLACEAE, p. 557 — **VIOLET FAMILY**

European Field Pansy

Johnny-jump-up

SYRIAN-RUE (*Peganum harmala*): Late spring–fall; disturbed places; West (native Mediterranean). HT: to 2½ ft. Bushy. Leaves alternate, somewhat fleshy, dissected into many linear segments. Flowers solitary; petals 5, white. Fruits roundish, 3-lobed. Also called African-rue, Harmal.

ZYGOPHYLLACEAE, p. 562 — **CALTROP FAMILY**

Syrian-rue

PUNCTURE-VINE (*Tribulus terrestris*): Spring–fall; disturbed places; widespread (native Eurasia). Prostrate, mat-forming. Leaves mostly opposite (those of a pair often unequal in size), pinnately divided into leaflets. Flowers solitary; petals 5, bright yellow. Fruits burlike, breaking into 5 sections, each section with paired, stout spines. Also called Caltrop.

See also *Kallstroemia* species (p. 562).

ZYGOPHYLLACEAE, p. 562 — **CALTROP FAMILY**

Puncture-vine

Acknowledgments

This book was a challenge to put together, and the staff at Andrew Stewart Publishing, Inc., worked hard to keep it moving forward. I am grateful to Andrew Stewart for going the distance with me. Arthur Riscen, executive editor, oversaw every aspect of the project. I worked closely with two assiduous and energetic editors, Pamela Nelson and Amy Hughes (Amy also wrote text for the section "What Is a Wildflower?"); and with the talented art director, Joanne Larson. Consultants Richard Spellenberg and Gil Nelson reviewed everything from text to photographs and prepared "A Key to Colors and Shapes."

To The Dawes Arboretum, thank you. The board of trustees, as well as the director, Luke Messinger, allowed me the time to pursue this endeavor. Mike Ecker, Lori Totman, and the rest of the staff likewise were accommodating. Greg Payton gave welcome technical support.

Assistance from Barnes & Noble came from Andrea Rotondo, Michael Vagnetti, Maria Spano, and Betsy Beier. George Scott, past editor-in-chief of Andrew Stewart Publishing and originator of the series, and Alicia Mills, former associate publisher at Andrew Stewart, gave early input. Craig Tufts of the National Wildlife Federation was also instrumental in the development of the series.

Drew Stevens and Charles Nix created the elegant book design. The beautiful line drawings are the work of Bobbi Angell. Jessie M. Harris, Dan Tenaglia, Ben Legler, Charles Schurch Lewallen, and a host of other accomplished photographers are responsible for the thousands of superb images that make up the book. Thanks to copy editor and indexer Jennifer Dixon; photo editor Laura Russo Epstein; and Jessica Peralta, Sylvia Masa-Booth, Valerie Kenyon, and Sumi Sin, who were involved in map production. Additional help came from Patricia Fogarty, Linda Patterson Eger, Lois Safrani, Lisa Jean Humphrey, and Griffin Hanna.

I benefited from the expertise of those individuals kind enough to critique family or generic accounts: Ihsan Al-Shehbaz, Daniel F. Austin, Paul E. Berry, Harvey E. Ballard, Jr., Philip Cantino, Frederick W. Case, Jr., Ronald A. Coleman, Alison Colwell, Tom Daniel, Carolyn Ferguson, Diane M. Ferguson, Peggy Fiedler, Craig C. Freeman, Paul A. Fryxell, Verne Grant, Richard R. Halse, Neil A. Harriman, Ronald L. Hartman, Peter C. Hoch, Larry Hufford, Denis M. Kearns, Tass Kelso, Robert W. Kiger, Alexander Krings, Thomas G. Lammers, Deborah Lewis, Tim Lowrey, Dale McNeal, Richard Patrick McNeil, Larry Mellichamp, David Morgan, J. K. Morton, Robin O'Quinn, James S. Pringle, George Rogers, Heidi H. Schmidt, David M. Sutherland, Sue Thompson, Gary Wallace, Elizabeth Fortson Wells, Tom Wendt, Justin Williams, Martin F. Wojciechowski, and Wendy B. Zomlefer. A few of their evaluations arrived too late for me to incorporate their suggestions into the text, but I have added changes in nomenclature to the synonym list. The decision to retain traditional families for this field guide was my own.

Many other reviewers looked over the maps, photos, and portions of the text and made valuable corrections: Drake Barton, Bill Carr, John Game, Philip Jenkins, Nick Jensen, Robert B. Kaul, Gary E. Larson, Patrick McMillan, Richard Old, H. Wayne Phillips, Zachary A. Principe, Jon Rebman, Fred Roberts, Al Schneider, Jason R. Singhurst, Bruce A. Sorrie, Dan Spaulding, Sue Vrilakas, and Stanley L. Welsh. Also helpful were Robert J. (Bob) O'Kennon, Barney Lipscomb, Jim Morefield, Guy Nesom, Alfred Schotz, John L. Strother, and Kay & George Yatskievych.

My children, Michelle and Brian, patiently endured the arduous writing process. Michelle turned my barely legible handwriting into a typed manuscript.

Lastly, my heartfelt appreciation goes to John Kartesz for his unflagging support and friendship. John generously allowed me access to prepublication copies of BONAP's comprehensive *Floristic Synthesis of North America*; this versatile CD provided the county-level data used to generate the base maps for the guide. In addition, John and his associate Misako Nishino were invaluable in helping to procure many of the photos.

References

Identification Guides

Books on wildflowers are published nearly every year. An excellent way to keep up with the latest publications and to find guides for your area or for an area you plan to visit is through the Internet. Search the Website of Barnes & Noble or other large book dealer, using keywords in your search criteria that will bring up titles for a specific area (for example, "plants, Mojave Desert" or "wildflowers, Great Lakes"). There are also search engines designed specifically for locating books, such as Bookfinder.com or Google Books; these provide broader (and more exhaustive) searches. A small sampling of regional guides is given here.

GENERAL

Flora of North America Editorial Committee, eds. 1993+. *Flora of North America North of Mexico*. 14+ vols. New York: Oxford University Press.

Rickett, Harold W. 1966–1975. *Wild Flowers of the United States*. Edited by William C. Steere et al. 6 vols. New York: New York Botanical Garden and McGraw-Hill.

EASTERN AND CENTRAL

Bell, C. Ritchie, and Bryan J. Taylor. 1982. *Florida Wild Flowers and Roadside Plants*. Chapel Hill, NC: Laurel Hill Press.

Bessette, Alan E., et al. 2000. *Wildflowers of Maine, New Hampshire, and Vermont in Color*. Syracuse, NY: Syracuse University Press.

Freeman, Craig C., and Eileen K. Schofield. 1991. *Roadside Wildflowers of the Southern Great Plains*. Lawrence: University Press of Kansas.

Horn, Dennis, and Tavia Cathcart. 2005. *Wildflowers of Tennessee, the Ohio Valley, and the Southern Appalachians*. Edmonton, AB: Lone Pine Publishing.

Ladd, Doug. 2001. *North Woods Wildflowers*. A Falcon Guide. Guilford, CT: Globe Pequot Press.

Nelson, Gil. 2005. *East Gulf Coastal Plain Wildflowers*. A Falcon Guide. Guilford, CT: Globe Pequot Press.

Newcomb, Lawrence. 1989. *Newcomb's Wildflower Guide*. Boston: Little, Brown.

Porcher, Richard Dwight, and Douglas Alan Rayner. 2001. *A Guide to the Wildflowers of South Carolina*. Columbia: University of South Carolina Press.

Thieret, John W. 2001. *National Audubon Society Field Guide to North American Wildflowers, Eastern Region*, rev. ed. First edition by William A. Niering and Nancy C. Olmstead. New York: Alfred A. Knopf.

Wharton, Mary E., and Roger W. Barbour. 1971. *A Guide to the Wildflowers and Ferns of Kentucky*. Lexington: University Press of Kentucky.

Yatskievych, Kay. 2000. *Field Guide to Indiana Wildflowers*. Bloomington: Indiana University Press.

WESTERN

Ajilvsgi, Geyata. 2003. *Wildflowers of Texas*, rev. ed. Fredericksburg, TX: Shearer Publishing.

Blackwell, Laird R. 2006. *Great Basin Wildflowers: A Guide to Common Wildflowers of the High Deserts of Nevada, Utah, and Oregon*. A Falcon Guide. Guilford, CT: Globe Pequot Press.

Epple, Anne Orth, and Lewis E. Epple. 1997. *A Field Guide to the Plants of Arizona*, 2nd ed. A Falcon Guide. Guilford, CT: Globe Pequot Press.

Kershaw, Linda J., Jim Pojar, and Andy MacKinnon. 1998. *Plants of the Rocky Mountains*. Edmonton, AB: Lone Pine Publishing.

Kozloff, Eugene N. 2005. *Plants of Western Oregon, Washington, and British Columbia*. Portland, OR: Timber Press.

MacKay, Pam. 2003. *Mojave Desert Wildflowers*. A Falcon Guide. Guilford, CT: Globe Pequot Press.

Niehaus, Theodore F., Charles L. Ripper, and Virginia Savage. 1998. *A Field Guide to Southwestern and Texas Wildflowers*. Peterson Field Guides. Boston: Houghton Mifflin.

Niehaus, Theodore F., and Charles L. Ripper. 1976. *A Field Guide to Pacific States Wildflowers*, 2nd ed. Peterson Field Guides. Boston: Houghton Mifflin.

Phillips, H. Wayne. 1999. *Central Rocky Mountain Wildflowers*. A Falcon Guide. Guilford, CT: Globe Pequot Press. (Guides to both the southern and northern Rockies are available from this same author/publisher.)

Pojar, Jim, and Andy MacKinnon. 2004. *Plants of the Pacific Northwest Coast: Washington, Oregon, British Columbia, and Alaska*, rev. ed. Edmonton, AB: Lone Pine Publishing.

Pratt, Verna E. 1991. *Wildflowers Along the Alaska Highway*. Anchorage: Alaskakrafts Publishing.

Spellenberg, Richard. 2001. *National Audubon Society Field Guide to North American Wildflowers, Western Region*, rev. ed. New York: Alfred A. Knopf.

Spellenberg, Richard. 2003. *Sonoran Desert Wildflowers*. A Falcon Guide. Guilford, CT: Globe Pequot Press.

Wiese, Karen. 2000. *Sierra Nevada Wildflowers*. A Falcon Guide. Guilford, CT: Globe Pequot Press.

Conservation and Wildflower Societies

Groups concerned with the preservation of our native flora and fauna exist at all levels, state through federal. The Websites of state natural heritage programs typically have facts about threatened and endangered species, listings of nature preserves, and contact information for staff members who can answer specific queries. In addition, many U.S. states and Canadian provinces have native plant societies, and these institutions can be excellent sources of information. Websites of some of the more prominent conservation organizations and wildflower societies are listed here.

California Native Plant Society. http://www.cnps.org

Center for Plant Conservation. http://centerforplantconservation.org

Georgia Native Plant Society. http://www.gnps.org

Lady Bird Johnson Wildflower Center. http://www.wildflower.org

National Wildlife Federation. http://www.nwf.org

NatureServe. http://www.natureserve.org

New England Wild Flower Society. http://www.newfs.org

Plant Nomenclature

The Biota of North America Program (BONAP), directed by John Kartesz, publishes the CD *Floristic Synthesis of North America* (2009), a comprehensive assessment of the plants of North America, with geography, nomenclature, ecology, and much more. The voluminous data in the *Synthesis* served as the basis for the core information contained within the Plants National Database (http://plants.usda.gov). BONAP is located at 9319 Bracken Lane, Chapel Hill, NC 27516. The BONAP Website (http://www.bonap.org) provides updated nomenclature and further links to explore.

Weeds and Invasive Species

Bryson, Charles T., and Michael S. DeFelice, eds. 2009. *Weeds of the South*. Athens: University of Georgia Press.

Center for Invasive Species and Ecosystem Health. http://www.invasive.org

DiTomaso, Joseph M., and Evelyn A. Healy. 2007. *Weeds of California and Other Western States*. 2 vols. Oakland: University of California Agriculture and Natural Resources Communication Services.

Lorenzi, Harri J., and Larry S. Jeffery. 1987. *Weeds of the United States and Their Control*. New York: Van Nostrand Reinhold.

Old, Richard. 2008. *1200 Weeds of the 48 States & Adjacent Canada: An Interactive Identification Guide*, DVD. Pullman, WA: XID Services.

Uva, Richard H., Joseph C. Neal, and Joseph M. DiTomaso. 1997. *Weeds of the Northeast*. Ithaca, NY: Cornell University Press.

Synonyms of Scientific Names

Ongoing research continues to lead to reevaluations in how wildflowers are classified, often resulting in changes in scientific names. New names replace the ones in use, and the latter become synonyms. The accounts in *Flora of North America North of Mexico* (see the Bibliography) reflect these revisions. Botanists make their own judgments about whether the results of a particular research project warrant a change in classification; hence, there can be more than one scientific name in use for the same plant species. This list cross-references some names used in other references and field guides with the names used in this guide. (A genus name repeated in the cross-reference indicates the original name is still in use for some species.)

Acetosella=Rumex

Acmispon helleri=Lotus unifoliolatus

Acomastylis rossii=Geum rossii

Acrolasia albicaulis=Mentzelia albicaulis

Actaea alba=Actaea pachypoda

Actaea elata=Cimicifuga elata

Actaea podocarpa=Cimicifuga americana

Actaea racemosa=Cimicifuga racemosa

Actinomeris alternifolia=Verbesina alternifolia

Adenolinum=Linum

Agaloma marginata=Euphorbia marginata

Aliciella latifolia=Gilia latifolia

Aliciella leptomeria=Gilia leptomeria

Althaea rosea=Alcea rosea

Amerosedum lanceolatum=Sedum lanceolatum

Ampelamus albidus=Cynanchum laeve

Anemone=Anemone, Hepatica, Pulsatilla

Anemonidium canadense=Anemone canadensis

Anthericum=Echeandia

Antheropeas=Eriophyllum

*Antirrhinum=Neogaerrhinum, Sairocarpus

Aphyllon=Orobanche

Arabis=Arabis, Arabidopsis, Boechera, Turritis

Arabis drummondii=Boechera stricta

Arabis hirsuta ssp. *pycnocarpa=Arabis pycnocarpa*

Arabis holboellii var. *retrofracta=Boechera retrofracta*

Arenaria=Arenaria, Eremogone, Minuartia, Moehringia

Asarum arifolium=Hexastylis arifolia

Asarum virginicum=Hexastylis virginica

Ascyrum hypericoides=Hypericum hypericoides

Ascyrum stans=Hypericum crux-andreae

Aster=Aster, Doellingeria, Eucephalus, Eurybia, Ionactis, Oclemena, Oreostemma, Sericocarpus, Symphyotrichum

Atragene=Clematis

Batrachium aquatile=Ranunculus aquatilis

Beloperone californica=Justicia californica

*Bonamia=Stylisma

Boykinia=Boykinia, Telesonix

Brodiaea=Brodiaea, Dichelostemma, Triteleia

Brodiaea douglasii=Triteleia grandiflora

Brodiaea lutea=Triteleia ixioides

Cacalia atriplicifolia=Arnoglossum atriplicifolium

Cacalia lanceolata=Arnoglossum ovatum

Cacalia muehlenbergii=Arnoglossum reniforme

Cacalia suaveolens=Hasteola suaveolens

Cacalia tuberosa=Arnoglossum plantagineum

Caesalpinia jamesii=Pomaria jamesii

Calamintha–Clinopodium

*Callisia=Cuthbertia

Camissoniopsis=Camissonia

Campanula americana=Campanulastrum americanum

Campanula prenanthoides=Asyneuma prenanthoides

Capnoides sempervirens=Corydalis sempervirens

Caraxeron vermiculare=Blutaparon vermiculare

Cardamine integrifolia=Cardamine californica

Cardamine rhomboidea=Cardamine bulbosa

Carex fraseri=Cymophyllus fraserianus

*Cassia=Chamaecrista, Senna

Centaurea americana=Plectocephalus americanus

Centaurea maculosa=Centaurea stoebe ssp. *micranthos*

*Original genus name is still in use, but there is no representative species in this wildflower guide.

Centaurea repens=Acroptilon repens

Centaurium=Centaurium, Zeltnera

Ceratocephala testiculata=Ranunculus testiculatus

Chamaepericlymenum canadense=Cornus canadensis

Chamaesaracha=Chamaesaracha, Leucophysalis

Chlorocrepis=Hieracium

Chrysanthemum balsamita=Tanacetum balsamita

Chrysanthemum leucanthemum= Leucanthemum vulgare

Chrysanthemum parthenium=Tanacetum parthenium

Chrysopsis graminifolia=Pityopsis graminifolia

Chrysopsis villosa=Heterotheca villosa

Chrysopsis villosa var. camporum=Heterotheca camporum

Chrysothamnus nauseosus=Ericameria nauseosa

Chylismia=Camissonia

Ciliaria austromontana=Saxifraga bronchialis

Cladothrix lanuginosa=Tidestromia lanuginosa

Clementsia rhodantha=Rhodiola rhodantha

Cleome isomeris=Isomeris arborea

Cnicus benedictus=Centaurea benedicta

Coldenia=Tiquilia

Comandra livida=Geocaulon lividum

Convolvulus=Calystegia, Convolvulus

Cooperia drummondii=Zephyranthes chlorosolen

Coronilla varia=Securigera varia

Crocanthemum=Helianthemum

Crunocallis chamissoi=Montia chamissoi

Cylactis=Rubus

Cymopterus lemmonii=Pseudocymopterus montanus

Cypripedium calceolus=Cypripedium parviflorum

Dactylorhiza viridis=Coeloglossum viride

Datura meteloides=Datura wrightii

Delphinium ajacis=Consolida ajacis

Dentaria californica=Cardamine californica

Dentaria diphylla=Cardamine diphylla

Dentaria heterophylla=Cardamine angustata

Dentaria laciniata=Cardamine concatenata

Dentaria multifida=Cardamine dissecta

Dicentra=Dicentra, Ehrendorferia

Dichromena=Rhynchospora

Disporum=Prosartes

Dithyrea wislizeni=Dimorphocarpa wislizeni

Dracopis amplexicaulis=Rudbeckia amplexicaulis

Drymocallis=Potentilla

Dugaldia hoopesii=Hymenoxys hoopesii

Dyssodia=Dyssodia, Thymophylla

Endodeca serpentaria−Aristolochia serpentaria

Engelmannia pinnatifida=Engelmannia peristenia

Epilobium=Chamerion, Epilobium

Eremothera=Camissonia

Erigeron canadensis=Conyza canadensis

Erocallis triphylla=Lewisia triphylla

Erodium macrophyllum=California macrophylla

Erophila verna=Draba verna

Erythrocoma triflora=Geum triflorum

Eulobus=Camissonia

Eulophia ecristata=Pteroglossaspis ecristata

Eupatoriadelphus=Eutrochium

Eupatorium=Ageratina, Conoclinium, Eupatorium, Eutrochium, Fleischmannia

Eupatorium rugosum=Ageratina altissima

Euphorbia albomarginata=Chamaesyce albomarginata

Euploca convolvulacea=Heliotropium convolvulaceum

Eustylis purpurea=Alophia drummondii

Evolvulus pilosus=Evolvulus nuttallianus

Fauria crista-galli=Nephrophyllidium crista-galli

Fritillaria lanceolata=Fritillaria affinis

Gentiana=Gentiana, Gentianella, Gentianopsis

Gentiana detonsa var. elegans=Gentianopsis thermalis

Gentiana procera=Gentianopsis virgata

Gentianodes algida=Gentiana algida

Geum=Geum, Waldsteinia

Gilia capillaris=Allophyllum capillare

Gilia leptalea=Allophyllum leptaleum

Giliastrum acerosum=Gilia acerosa

Giliastrum rigidulum=Gilia rigidula

Glottidium vesicarium=Sesbania vesicaria

Gnaphalium obtusifolium=Pseudognaphalium obtusifolium

Greggia=Nerisyrenia

Gutierrezia dracunculoides=Amphiachyris dracunculoides

Habenaria=Coeloglossum, Habenaria, Piperia, Platanthera

Halenia recurva=Halenia rothrockii

Haplopappus divaricatus=Croptilon divaricatum

Haplopappus macronema=Ericameria discoidea

Haplopappus nuttallii=Xanthisma grindelioides

Haplopappus spinulosus=Xanthisma spinulosum

Haplopappus validus=Croptilon hookerianum

Hecatonia scelerata=Ranunculus sceleratus

*Hedyotis=Houstonia, Oldenlandia, Stenaria

Hedyotis crassifolia=Houstonia pusilla

Helenium hoopesii=Hymenoxys hoopesii

Hemizonia pungens=Centromadia pungens

Hesperoscordum maritimum=Muilla maritima

Heterotheca graminifolia=Pityopsis graminifolia

Heterotheca mariana=Chrysopsis mariana

Hirculus platysepalus ssp. crandallii= Saxifraga flagellaris

Hirculus prorepens=Saxifraga hirculus

Hirculus serpyllifolius ssp. chrysanthus= Saxifraga chrysantha

Hoffmannseggia jamesii=Pomaria jamesii

Houstonia nigricans=Stenaria nigricans

Hylodesmum pauciflorum=Desmodium pauciflorum

Hymenocallis caroliniana=Hymenocallis occidentalis

Hymenoxys acaulis=Tetraneuris acaulis

Hypericum pyramidatum=Hypericum ascyron

Hypericum stans=Hypericum crux-andreae

Hypericum virginicum=Triadenum virginicum

Hypopitys monotropa=Monotropa hypopitys

Ipomoea stolonifera=Ipomoea imperati

Ipomoea trichocarpa=Ipomoea cordatotriloba

Iris domestica=Belamcanda chinensis

Isanthus brachiatus=Trichostema brachiatum

Isopyrum=Enemion

Isotrema=Aristolochia

Janusia gracilis=Cottsia gracilis

Kalmia buxifolia=Leiophyllum buxifolium

Kalmia procumbens=Loiseleuria procumbens

Kumlienia hystricula=Ranunculus hystriculus

Lactuca tatarica ssp. pulchella=Mulgedium pulchellum

Lathyrus maritimus=Lathyrus japonicus

Lepidotheca suaveolens=Matricaria discoidea

Leptodactylon californicum=Linanthus californicus

Leptodactylon pungens=Linanthus pungens

Leptosiphon androsaceus=Linanthus androsaceus

Leptosiphon aureus=Linanthus aureus

Leptosiphon bicolor=Linanthus bicolor

Leptosiphon ciliatus=Linanthus ciliatus

Leptosiphon montanus=Linanthus montanus

Leptosiphon nuttallii=Linanthus nuttallii

Leptosiphon parviflorus=Linanthus parviflorus

Lespedeza=Kummerowia, Lespedeza

Lesquerella=Physaria

Leucelene ericoides=Chaetopappa ericoides

Ligularia=Senecio

Lilium andinum=Lilium philadelphicum

Lilium tigrinum=Lilium lancifolium

Limnorchis hyperborea=Platanthera aquilonis (in part)

Linanthastrum nuttallii=Linanthus nuttallii

Linaria=Linaria, Nuttallanthus

Linum perenne var. lewisii=Linum lewisii

*Lippia=Phyla

Lithospermum arvense=Buglossoides arvensis

Loeseliastrum matthewsii=Langloisia matthewsii

Loeseliastrum schottii=Langloisia schottii

Lophotocarpus calycinus=Sagittaria montevidensis ssp. calycina

Lotus helleri=Lotus unifoliolatus

Lotus purshianus=Lotus unifoliolatus

Lychnis=Silene

Lychnis alba=Silene latifolia

Lygodesmia=Lygodesmia, Pleiacanthus, Stephanomeria

Machaeranthera canescens=Dieteria canescens

Machaeranthera grindelioides=Xanthisma grindelioides

Machaeranthera pinnatifida=Xanthisma spinulosum

Machaeranthera tortifolia=Xylorhiza tortifolia

Machaerocarpus californicus=Damasonium californicum

Macrosiphonia=Mandevilla

Malcolmia africana=Strigosella africana

Malvastrum=Eremalche, Malvastrum

Matelea gonocarpos=Gonolobus suberosus

Matricaria inodora=Tripleurospermum inodorum

Matricaria maritima ssp. inodora= Tripleurospermum inodorum

Matricaria matricarioides=Matricaria discoidea

Matricaria perforata=Tripleurospermum inodorum

Matricaria recutita=Matricaria chamomilla

Maurandya=Epixiphium, Maurandella

Meconella linearis=Hesperomecon linearis

Megalodonta beckii=Bidens beckii

Melandrium album=Silene latifolia

Melanthium=Veratrum

Mentha canadensis=Mentha arvensis

Mesembryanthemum=Mesembryanthemum, Carpobrotus

Micranthes=Saxifraga

Microseris=Microseris, Nothocalais, Uropappus

Montia=Claytonia, Montia

Muscaria=Saxifraga

Myosotis alpestris=Myosotis asiatica

Myosotis sylvatica var. alpestris=Myosotis asiatica

Naumburgia thyrsiflora=Lysimachia thyrsiflora

Navarretia capillaris=Allophyllum capillare

Navarretia leptalea=Allophyllum leptaleum

Nemastylis purpurea=Alophia drummondii

Nicotiana trigonophylla=Nicotiana obtusifolia

Nuttallia decapetala=Mentzelia decapetala

Oenothera=Calylophus, Gaura, Oenothera, Stenosiphon

Oenothera missouriensis=Oenothera macrocarpa

Oligoneuron album=Solidago ptarmicoides

Oligoneuron rigidum=Solidago rigida

Oncidium floridanum=Oncidium ensatum

Orchis rotundifolia=Amerorchis rotundifolia

Orchis spectabilis=Galearis spectabilis

Oreobroma=Lewisia

Oreocarya flava=Cryptantha flava

Orthocarpus=Castilleja, Orthocarpus, Triphysaria

Orthocarpus faucibarbatus=Triphysaria versicolor

Orthocarpus hispidus=Castilleja tenuis

Orthocarpus purpurascens=Castilleja exserta ssp. exserta

Osmorhiza chilensis=Osmorhiza berteroi

Oxalis acetosella=Oxalis montana

Oxybaphus=Mirabilis

Parnassia parviflora=Parnassia palustris

Penstemon=Keckiella, Nothochelone, Penstemon

Petalostemon=Dalea

Philoxerus vermicularis=Blutaparon vermiculare

Phlox gracilis=Microsteris gracilis

Phoenicaulis eurycarpa=Anelsonia eurycarpa

Physalis lobata=Quincula lobata

Picradenia=Hymenoxys

Platystigma linearis=Hesperomecon linearis

Pneumonanthe affinis=Gentiana affinis

Poinsettia=Euphorbia

Polygonum=Aconogonon, Bistorta, Fallopia, Persicaria, Polygonum

Polygonum cuspidatum=Fallopia japonica

Polymnia uvedalia=Smallanthus uvedalius

Polyrrhiza lindenii=Dendrophylax lindenii

Porteranthus=Gillenia

Portulaca mundula=Portulaca pilosa

Portulaca parvula=Portulaca halimoides

Potentilla=Argentina, Comarum, Dasiphora, Potentilla, Sibbaldiopsis

Poteridium annuum=Sanguisorba annua

Primula=Dodecatheon, Primula

Pseudotaenidia montana=Taenidia montana

Psilochenia=Crepis

Psoralea=Hoita, Orbexilum, Pediomelum, Psoralidium, Rupertia

Psoralea psoralioides=Orbexilum pedunculatum

Psychrophila leptosepala=Caltha leptosepala

Pyrola secunda=Orthilia secunda

Quamoclit coccinea=Ipomoea coccinea

Quamoclit vulgaris=Ipomoea quamoclit

Ramischia secunda=Orthilia secunda

Reynoutria=Fallopia

Rhaponticum repens=Acroptilon repens

Rhododendron=Ledum, Rhododendron

Rhus diversiloba=Toxicodendron diversilobum

Rhus radicans=Toxicodendron radicans

Rorippa nasturtium-aquaticum=Nasturtium officinale

Rubacer=Rubus

Rydbergia grandiflora=Hymenoxys grandiflora

Salvia pitcheri=Salvia azurea

Samolus floribundus=Samolus valerandi ssp. parviflorus

Sanguisorba occidentalis=Sanguisorba annua

Sarcostemma cynanchoides=Funastrum cynanchoides ssp. cynanchoides

Sarracenia purpurea var. burkii=Sarracenia rosea

*Satureja=Clinopodium, Piloblephis

Schoenocrambe linearifolia=Hesperidanthus linearifolius

Schoenocrambe linifolia=Sisymbrium linifolium

Schrankia=Mimosa

Scutellaria mexicana=Salazaria mexicana

Sedum=Diamorpha, Hylotelephium, Rhodiola, Sedum

Senecio=Packera, Senecio

Sida=Malvastrum, Malvella, Rhynchosida, Sida

Silene cucubalus=Silene vulgaris

Siphonoglossa=Justicia

Sisymbrium linearifolium=Hesperidanthus linearifolius

Sisyrinchium douglasii=Olsynium douglasii

Smilacina=Maianthemum

Solanum americanum (in part)=Solanum ptycanthum

Solanum nigrum (in part)=Solanum ptycanthum

Solanum sarrachoides=Solanum physalifolium

Solidago=Euthamia, Solidago

Specularia=Heterocodon, Triodanis

Spergulastrum lanuginosum ssp. saxosum= Arenaria lanuginosa var. saxosa

Sphaeralcea angusta=Malvastrum hispidum

Spiraea latifolia=Spiraea alba

Spiranthes=Dichromanthus, Sacoila, Spiranthes

Steironema=Lysimachia

Stellaria jamesiana=Pseudostellaria jamesiana

Stenanthella occidentalis=Anticlea occidentalis

Stenanthium occidentale=Anticlea occidentalis

Stenorrhynchos=Dichromanthus, Sacoila

Stephanomeria spinosa=Pleiacanthus spinosus

Streptopus roseus=Streptopus lanceolatus

Swertia=Frasera, Swertia

*Talinum=Phemeranthus

Taraxia=Camissonia

Telosiphonia=Mandevilla

Tetraneuris grandiflora=Hymenoxys grandiflora

Thalictrum thalictroides=Anemonella thalictroides

Thlaspi=Noccaea, Thlaspi

Tithymalus=Euphorbia

*Tofieldia=Triantha

Tolmachevia integrifolia=Rhodiola integrifolia

Tovara virginiana=Persicaria virginiana

Trachelospermum difforme=Thyrsanthella difformis

Tradescantia=Cuthbertia, Tradescantia

Trifurcia lahue=Herbertia lahue

Trilisa=Carphephorus

Tripleurospermum perforatum= Tripleurospermum inodorum

Truellum sagittatum=Persicaria sagittata

Utricularia vulgaris=Utricularia macrorhiza

Valerianella olitoria=Valerianella locusta

Verbena=Glandularia, Verbena

Veronicastrum serpyllifolium ssp. humifusum= Veronica serpyllifolia ssp. humifusa

Vexibia nuttalliana=Sophora nuttalliana

Viguiera multiflora=Heliomeris multiflora

Viguiera parishii=Bahiopsis parishii

Vincetoxicum gonocarpos=Gonolobus suberosus

Viola kitaibeliana=Viola bicolor

Viola papilionacea=Viola sororia

Viola pensylvanica=Viola pubescens

Viola rafinesquii=Viola bicolor

Wyethia scabra=Scabrethia scabra

Ximenesia encelioides=Verbesina encelioides

Zauschneria californica=Epilobium canum

Zigadenus densus=Stenanthium densum

Zigadenus elegans=Anticlea elegans

Zigadenus venenosus=Toxicoscordion venenosum

Zosterella dubia=Heteranthera dubia

Photo Credits

The photographs in the species accounts are credited clockwise, starting from the top left image; inset photos are indicated by *(ins)*. Other photos are credited left to right, top to bottom (lr/tb). Photos that appear in the table of contents and the key to colors and shapes are credited to the page on which they appear in the species accounts. Photographers and companies listed here hold copyright to the individual photos.

d Charles Schurch Lewallen **Bottom: a** Daniel Mathews; **b** Gary A. Monroe @ National Plants Database; **c** Dave Powell, USDA Forest Service, Bugwood. org; **d** Craig C. Freeman

322 Top: a Ben Legler; **b** William R. Gray, cyberflora@xmission. com **Bottom: a** Steve Matson; **b** Dianne Fristrom; **c** Vernon H. Oswald; **d** Doreen Smith, Marin CNPS

323 Top: a Sparky Stensaas, Pink Guppy; **b** http:// stanmalcolmphoto.com; **c** Dan Mullen **Bottom: a** Charles Schurch Lewallen; **b** Dan Tenaglia, http://missouriplants. com; **c**, **d** Michael Charters, http://calflora.net

324 Top: a Robert E. Preston; **b**, **c** Ben Legler; **d** Gerald & Buff Corsi, Focus on Nature, Inc. **Bottom: a** Steve Matson; **b** Michael Charters, http:// calflora.net; **c** Vernon H. Oswald; **d** Christopher L. Christie

325 Top: a Dan Suzio, Photo Researchers, Inc.; **b** Vernon H. Oswald; **c** R. Spellenberg **Bottom: a** Christopher L. Christie; **b** Jerry Murray

326 Top: a Ben Legler; **b** Jessie M. Harris; **c** Bob Gibbons, Photo Researchers, Inc. **Bottom: a** Al Schneider, http:// swcoloradowildflowers.com; **b** Charles Schurch Lewallen

327 Top: a Doris Hawrelluk; **b**, **c** Jessie M. Harris **Bottom: a** Ben Legler; **b***(ins)* Gerald D. Carr; **c** George W. Hartwell

328 Top: a Christopher L. Christie; **b**, **c***(ins)* Charles Schurch Lewallen **Bottom: a** Vince Scheidt; **b** Mark S. Brunell, University of the Pacific; **c** Vernon H. Oswald; **d** Ken Gilliland

329 Top: a Merel R. Black, http:// wisplants.uwsp.edu **Bottom: a** Jessie M. Harris; **b** Vernon H. Oswald; **c** Jessie M. Harris

330 Top: a Steve Matson; **b** Ben Legler; **c** David G. Smith, http://delawarewildflowers. org **Bottom: a** Jessie M. Harris; **b** Christopher L. Christie; **c** Dan Tenaglia, http:// missouriplants.com

331 Top: a William R. Gray, cyberflora@xmission.com; **b** Keir Morse; **c** Christopher L.

Christie **Bottom: a** Janell Hillman; **b** Michael Charters, http://calflora.net; **c** Christopher L. Christie; **d** Mark Turner; **e***(ins)* Ben Legler

332 Top: a Steve Matson; **b** Stephen J. Krasemann, Photo Researchers, Inc.; **c** R. Spellenberg **Bottom: a** Michael G. Simpson; **b** R. Spellenberg; **c** Michael G. Simpson

333 Top: a Charles Schurch Lewallen **Bottom: a** Shirley Denton; **b**, **c** Dan Tenaglia, http://missouriplants.com

334 Top: a Gary P. Fleming **Bottom: a**, **b** Charles Schurch Lewallen; **c** Jessie M. Harris; **d** Dan Tenaglia, http:// missouriplants.com

335 Top: a http://fireflyforest. com; **b** R. Spellenberg; **c** Bob Harms; **d** Bill Carr, The Nature Conservancy of Texas

336 Bottom: a David Liebman, Pink Guppy; **b** Gil Nelson, http://www.gilnelson.com/ stockimages; **c** http:// southeasternflora.com; **d** Jessie M. Harris

337 Top: a Jessie M. Harris; **b** Charles Schurch Lewallen; **c** Jessie M. Harris **Bottom: a** Charles R. Hutchins; **b***(ins)* Saint Mary's College of California; **c** http://fireflyforest. com; **d***(ins)* Melissa A. Carr

338 Top: a Jessie M. Harris; **b** T. Ann Williams, Atlas of Florida Vascular Plants, http://florida.plantatlas.usf.edu; **c** Charles R. Hutchins **Bottom: a** Alfred Schotz

339 Top: a Jessie M. Harris **Bottom: a**, **b** Jessie M. Harris; **c** Dan Tenaglia, http:// missouriplants.com; **d** Charles Schurch Lewallen

340 Top: a Richard Old, http:// www.xidservices.com; **b**, **c** Jessie M. Harris; **d** Dan Tenaglia, http://missouriplants.com **Bottom: a**, **b** Michael Charters, http://calflora.net; **c** Lewis E. Epple*

341 Top: a James M. André; **b***(ins)* Keir Morse; **c** Christopher L. Christie **Bottom: a** Ben Legler; **b** Teresa Prendusi, U.S. Forest Service; **c** William R. Gray, cyberflora@xmission.com

342 Top: a Mark S. Brunell, University of the Pacific;

b Ben Legler; **c** Mark S. Brunell, University of the Pacific **Bottom: a**, **b** Al Schneider, http:// swcoloradowildflowers.com; **c** Mary Ellen Harte; **d** Misa Milliron; **e** Dr. Dean Taylor, Jepson Herbarium

343 Top: a Spectrum Photofile; **b** Tom Barnes, University of Kentucky; **c** Jessie M. Harris; **d** John Hilty; **e** Spectrum Photofile **Bottom: a** Michael Charters, http://calflora.net; **b** Spectrum Photofile; **c** Lee Dittmann

344 Top: a Roger L. Hammer; **b** Leroy Simon, Pink Guppy; **c** Gil Nelson, http://www. gilnelson.com/stockimages **Bottom: a** Bob Harms; **b** Hazel L. Topoleski; **c** http:// fireflyforest.com

345 Top: a Charles Schurch Lewallen; **b**, **c** Kurt Schaefer **Bottom: a** Richard Old, http:// www.xidservices.com; **b** R. Spellenberg; **c***(ins)* Lewis E. Epple*

346 Top: a Linda Lee, University of South Carolina Herbarium; **b***(ins)* Jessie M. Harris **Bottom: a** David Liebman, Pink Guppy; **b**, **c** Charles Schurch Lewallen; **d***(ins)* Gerald D. Carr

347 Top: a Fred Nation **Bottom: a** Dan Tenaglia, http://missouriplants.com; **b**, **c** Jessie M. Harris

348 Top: a, **b** Gil Nelson, http://www.gilnelson. com/stockimages; **c** Jessie M. Harris **Bottom: a** Bud Kovalchik Photography; **b** Matt Goff, http://www. sitkanature.org; **c** Derrick Ditchburn; **d** Steve Matson

349 Top: a Jessie M. Harris; **b** Shirley Denton **Bottom: a** Christopher L. Christie

350 Top: a Gerald D. Carr; **b** Jessie M. Harris; **c** Karen A. Burgess **Bottom: a** Adolf Ceska; **b** Ben Legler; **c** Dan Tenaglia, http://missouriplants.com

351 Top: a Ray Collett **Bottom: a** Ben Legler; **b***(ins)* Gerald D. Carr

352 Top: a Charles R. Hutchins; **b** David Liebman, Pink Guppy; **c** Wilbur H. Duncan **Bottom: a** Al Schneider, http:// swcoloradowildflowers.com;

b Christopher L. Christie
53 Top: a Adolf Ceska; **b** Jessie M. Harris; **c** Christopher L. Christie **Bottom: a** Melissa A. Carr; **b** Roger L. Hammer
54 Top: a, b Dan Tenaglia, http://missouriplants.com; **c** James M. André; **d** http://fireflyforest.com **Bottom: a** Robert Sivinski; **b(ins)** Michael Charters, http://calflora.net; **c** Ronald J. Taylor
55 Top: a, b Charles R. Hutchins; **c, d** R. Spellenberg **Bottom: a** Ronald J. Taylor; **b** Charles R. Hutchins; **c** R. Spellenberg; **d(ins)** Noble Proctor, Photo Researchers, Inc.
56 Top: a Forest & Kim Starr; **b** R. Spellenberg; **c** Haskel Bazell **Bottom: a** University of Florida: Center for Aquatic and Invasive Plants; **b** R. J. Bielesch
57 Top: a Linda Lee, University of South Carolina Herbarium; **b, c(ins)** Charles Schurch Lewallen; **d, e(ins)** University of Florida: Center for Aquatic and Invasive Plants **Bottom: a** Shirley Denton
58 Top: a Ronald J. Taylor; **b** Campbell and Lynn Loughmiller, Lady Bird Johnson Wildflower Center
59 Top: a Ben Legler; **b** Norden Cheatham, Photo Researchers, Inc.; **c** Bill Bouton **Bottom: a** Matt Below; **b** Christopher L. Christie; **c** Neal Kramer; **d** Keir Morse
60 Top: a Dr. Dean Taylor, Jepson Herbarium; **b** Michael Charters, http://calflora.net; **c** Keir Morse; **d** Michael Charters, http://calflora.net **Bottom: a** Keir Morse; **b** Jorg Fleige, http://westernwildflowers.com; **c** Michael Charters, http://calflora.net; **d** Gary A. Monroe @ National Plants Database
61 Top: a John C. Dittes; **b** Jessie M. Harris; **c** Gerald D. Carr; **d** Richard Old, http://www.xidservices.com **Bottom: a** John J. Kehoe; **b** Michael Charters, http://calflora.net; **c** Ben Legler
62 Top: a Gary A. Monroe @ National Plants Database; **b** Adolf Ceska; **c** Janet Novak **Bottom: a** Kenneth M. Highfill, Photo Researchers, Inc.; **b**

Charles Schurch Lewallen; **c** Roger L. Hammer; **d** Gil Nelson, http://www.gilnelson.com/stockimages
363 Top: a Charles R. Hutchins; **b** Lewis E. Epple*; **c** Van Vives; **d** Hartmut Wisch, Eaton Canyon Nature Center **Bottom: a** Jessie M. Harris; **b(ins)** Mike Haddock
364 Top: a Dan Tenaglia, http://missouriplants.com; **b** Charles Schurch Lewallen; **c** Dan Tenaglia, http://missouriplants.com **Bottom: a, b(ins), c** Charles Schurch Lewallen; **d** Robert Sivinski; **e** Al Schneider, http://swcoloradowildflowers.com
365 Top: a Dan Tenaglia, http://missouriplants.com; **b** Jessie M. Harris; **c(ins)** Charles Schurch Lewallen **Bottom: a(ins)** Saint Mary's College of California; **b** Gerald D. Carr; **c** Lewis E. Epple*
366 Top: a, b(ins) Trent M. Draper **Bottom: a, b(ins)** Christopher L. Christie
367 Top: a William R. Gray, cyberflora@xmission.com; **b(ins)** Steve Matson; **c** Christopher L. Christie **Bottom: a** John C. Dittes; **b** Steve Matson; **c** Christopher L. Christie; **d, e** Keir Morse
368 Top: a, b Christopher L. Christie; **c** Lewis E. Epple* **Bottom: a** Charles E. Jones; **b** William R. Gray, cyberflora@xmission.com; **c** Christopher L. Christie
369 Top: a, b(ins) Michelle Cloud-Hughes **Bottom: a** University of Florida: Center for Aquatic and Invasive Plants; **b** Dan Tenaglia, http://missouriplants.com; **c** Linda Lee, University of South Carolina Herbarium
370 Top: a Kenneth Highfill, Photo Researchers, Inc.; **b** Bob Bierman, Atlas of Florida Vascular Plants, http://florida.plantatlas.usf.edu **Bottom: a** Keir Morse; **b** Michael R. Clapp, http://nwnature.net; **c** Walter Muma
371 Bottom: a Penn Martin, Shasta Wildflowers Project; **b** Richy J. Harrod
372 Top: a Ronald A. Coleman; **b** Jessie M. Harris **Bottom: a, b** Jessie M. Harris; **c** Charles

Schurch Lewallen; **d** William R. Gray, cyberflora@xmission.com
373 Top: a Steve Matson; **b** Ben Legler; **c(ins)** Steve Matson; **d** Ronald A. Coleman; **e** Steve Matson **Bottom: a** Charles Schurch Lewallen; **b** Richard Worthington; **c** Ronald A. Coleman; **d(ins)** Charles Schurch Lewallen
374 Top: a David G. Smith, http://delawarewildflowers.org; **b** Dan Tenaglia, http://missouriplants.com; **c** David G. Smith, http://delawarewildflowers.org **Bottom: a** Charles Schurch Lewallen; **b** Alan Cressler; **c** Linda Lee, University of South Carolina Herbarium
375 Top: a Al Schneider, http://swcoloradowildflowers.com; **b** Ron Wolf; **c** Ronald A. Coleman **Bottom: a, b(ins)** Jessie M. Harris
376 Top: a Ronald A. Coleman; **b** Jessie M. Harris; **c** Ronald A. Coleman **Bottom: a** Jessie M. Harris; **b(ins)** Alfred Schotz
377 Top: a Philip Kauth; **b** Roger L. Hammer; **c** Dan Tenaglia, http://missouriplants.com **Bottom: a** Dan Tenaglia, http://missouriplants.com; **b** http://southeasternflora.com; **c** Betty Wargo, Atlas of Florida Vascular Plants, http://florida.plantatlas.usf.edu
378 Top: a Alfred Schotz; **b(ins)**, **c, d** Jessie M. Harris **Bottom: a** Ronald A. Coleman; **b, c** Charles Schurch Lewallen; **d(ins)** Ronald A. Coleman
379 Top: a Jessie M. Harris; **b** Vernon H. Oswald; **c** Ronald A. Coleman **Bottom: a** Don and Priscilla Eastman; **b(ins)** John Game; **c** Jessie M. Harris
380 Top: a(ins) David G. Smith, http://delawarewildflowers.org; **b** William R. Gray, cyberflora@xmission.com **Bottom: a** Gil Nelson, http://www.gilnelson.com/stockimages; **b** Jessie M. Harris; **c** Ronald A. Coleman
381 Top: a Alfred Schotz; **b** Jessie M. Harris; **c** Eleanor Saulys **Bottom: a** Gil Nelson, http://www.gilnelson.com/stockimages; **b** Dale A. Zimmerman Herbarium, Western New Mexico University; **c** William F. Jennings; **d(ins)** Dan Tenaglia,

Bottom: a Jessie M. Harris; **b** Lynn Watson; **c** Ben Legler
442 Top: a Dan Tenaglia, http://missouriplants.com; **b** Mike Haddock; **c** Dan Tenaglia, http://missouriplants.com **Bottom: a, b** Al Schneider, http://swcoloradowildflowers.com
443 Top: a, b(ins) Charles R. Hutchins **Bottom: a** Arizona Game and Fish Department; **b** Charles R. Hutchins; **c** Linda Lee, University of South Carolina Herbarium; **d** Ken Brate, Photo Researchers, Inc.
444 Top: a Michael Charters, http://calflora.net; **b, c(ins)** http://fireflyforest.com **Bottom: a** David Hosking, Photo Researchers, Inc.; **b** Adolf Ceska; **c** Al Schneider, http://swcoloradowildflowers.com
445 Top: a Jessie M. Harris; **b** Ben Legler; **c** Lewis E. Epple* **Bottom: a** Neal Kramer; **b(ins)** Ben Legler
446 Top: a Doug Waylett ; **b** Robert Potts, California Academy of Science **Bottom: a** Dennis Flaherty, Photo Researchers, Inc.; **b** Jessie M. Harris; **c** Steve Matson; **d** William R. Gray, cyberflora@xmission.com
447 Top: a Daniel Mathews; **b** Al Schneider, http://swcoloradowildflowers.com **Bottom: a(ins)** Gail Jankus, Photo Researchers, Inc.; **b** Jessie M. Harris; **c** William R. Gray, cyberflora@xmission.com
448 Top: a Alfred Schotz; **b** Steve Matson; **c** Ben Legler **Bottom: a** Charles Schurch Lewallen; **b, c** Shirley Denton; **d(ins)** Linda Lee, University of South Carolina Herbarium
449 Top: a, b Don and Priscilla Eastman **Bottom: a** David G. Smith, http://delawarewildflowers.org
450 Top: a Dan Tenaglia, http://missouriplants.com; **b** Jessie M. Harris; **c** David Liebman, Pink Guppy; **d** Gerald D. Carr **Bottom: a, b** Jessie M. Harris; **c** Kenneth J. Sytsma
451 Top: a Ben Legler **Bottom: a** Daniel Mathews; **b** Wilbur H. Duncan; **c** Gerald D. Carr
452 Top: a Jessie M. Harris; **b** Adolf Ceska; **c** Dave Powell, USDA Forest Service, Bugwood.org **Bottom: a** William R. Gray, cyberflora@xmission.com; **b** Ben Legler
453 Top: a Don and Priscilla Eastman; **b(ins)** Adolf Ceska; **c** George W. Hartwell **Bottom: a** Charles Schurch Lewallen; **b(ins)** Jessie M. Harris
454 Top: a Gerald D. Carr; **b(ins)** Dan Tenaglia, http://missouriplants.com **Bottom: a** Jessie M. Harris; **b** William R. Gray, cyberflora@xmission.com; **c** Jessie M. Harris; **d** Gregory K. Scott, Photo Researchers, Inc.
455 Top: a BONAP; **b** Dan Tenaglia, http://missouriplants.com; **c** Jessie M. Harris **Bottom: a** Jessie M. Harris; **b** Larry West, Photo Researchers, Inc.; **c, d** Gerald D. Carr
456 Top: a Jessie M. Harris; **b, c** Don and Priscilla Eastman **Bottom: a** Dan Tenaglia, http://missouriplants.com; **b(ins)** Bill Johnson
457 Top: a Jessie M. Harris **Bottom: a, b, c** http://southeasternflora.com
458 Top: a Rod Planck, Photo Researchers, Inc.; **b, c** Jessie M. Harris **Bottom: a** Dan Tenaglia, http://missouriplants.com; **b** Ben Legler
459 Top: a Jessic M. Harris; **b** Matt Below **Bottom: a** Dan Tenaglia, http://missouriplants.com; **b** Jessie M. Harris; **c** Al Schneider, http://swcoloradowildflowers.com; **d, e** Dan Tenaglia, http://missouriplants.com
460 Top: a James M. André; **b** http://southeasternflora.com; **c** Mike Haddock **Bottom: a** Benjamin Fleming; **b(ins)** Al Schneider, http://swcoloradowildflowers.com; **c** Gregory G. Dimijian, M.D., Photo Researchers, Inc.; **d** Ben Legler
461 Top: a Andy Fyon, http://www.ontariowildflower.com; **b** Keir Morse; **c** William R. Gray, cyberflora@xmission.com **Bottom: a** Dan Tenaglia, http://missouriplants.com; **b(ins)** Stephen Parker, Photo Researchers, Inc.; **c, d(ins)** Michael Charters, http://calflora.net; **e** Jessie M. Harris
462 Top: a Tom Barnes, University of Kentucky; **b** Mrs. W. D. Bransford, Lady Bird Johnson Wildflower Center; **c** Gil Nelson, http://www.gilnelson.com/stockimages; **d** Melody Lytle, Lady Bird Johnson Wildflower Center **Bottom: a** Carol J. Lim; **b** Keith A. Bradley; **c** Jon Mark Stewart; **d** William R. Gray, cyberflora@xmission.com
463 Top: a Scott Camazine, Photo Researchers, Inc.; **b(ins)** Eleanor Saulys; **c** Steve Matson **Bottom: a** John Brew; **b, c** Eleanor Saulys
464 Top: a Eleanor Saulys; **b** Keir Morse; **c** Gerald D. Carr **Bottom: a** Neil Gilham; **b(ins)** Paula J. Brooks; **c** Yvona Momatiuk, Photo Researchers, Inc.; **d** Jessie M. Harris
465 Top: a Jessie M. Harris; **b** William R. Gray, cyberflora@xmission.com; **c** Jessie M. Harris **Bottom: a** Jessie M. Harris; **b** Steve Matson; **c** William R. Gray, cyberflora@xmission.com
466 Top: a Jessie M. Harris; **b** Richard Old, http://www.xidservices.com; **c** William R. Gray, cyberflora@xmission.com; **d** Doug Waylett; **e** Robert W. Freckmann **Bottom: a** Christopher L. Christie; **b(ins)** Ben Legler; **c** Christopher L. Christie; **d** Steve Matson
467 Top: a Ben Legler; **b** Jessie M. Harris; **c** Robert Sivinski **Bottom: a** Ben Legler; **b** Vernon H. Oswald; **c** Keir Morse; **d, e** Ben Legler
468 Top: a Charles Schurch Lewallen; **b** Aaron Schusteff; **c** Jessie M. Harris; **d** Mary Ellen Harte **Bottom: a** Jessie M. Harris; **b** Christopher L. Christie
469 Top: a Richy J. Harrod; **b** Wynn Anderson, Chihuahuan Desert Gardens at University of Texas at El Paso; **c** S. J. Krasemann, Photo Researchers Inc. **Bottom: a** Jim Steinberg, Photo Researchers, Inc.; **b** Doug Waylett ; **c** Kenneth W. Fink, Photo Researchers, Inc.
470 Top: a Jessie M. Harris; **b** R. Spellenberg; **c** William F. Jennings **Bottom: a** Dan Tenaglia, http://missouriplants.com; **b** Steve Matson; **c** Keir Morse; **d** Jessie M. Harris

471 Top: a Vernon H. Oswald; **b** Christopher L. Christie **Bottom: a** Linda Lee, University of South Carolina Herbarium; **b** Dan Tenaglia, http://missouriplants.com; **c** Jessie M. Harris

472 Top: a Jessie M. Harris; **b**, **c** Ben Legler; **d** Ron Lance **Bottom: a** Jessie M. Harris; **b(ins)** John Hilty

473 Top: a, **b**, **c** Ben Legler **Bottom: a** Adolf Ceska; **b** Ben Legler; **c** Keir Morse

474 Top: a Al Schneider, http://swcoloradowildflowers.com; **b(ins)** James M. André **Bottom: a**, **b**, **c** Ben Legler

475 Top: a, **b(ins)** H. Wayne Phillips **Bottom: a** Barry Breckling; **b** Christopher L. Christie; **c**, **d** Steve Matson

476 Top: a Ben Legler; **b** Michael Charters, http://calflora.net; **c** Jessie M. Harris; **d** Ben Legler **Bottom: a** Michael Charters, http://calflora.net; **b**, **c**, **d** Steve Matson

477 Top: a Jessie M. Harris; **b** Doreen Smith, Marin CNPS; **c** Gerald & Buff Corsi, Focus on Nature, Inc. **Bottom: a** Jeffrey S. Pippen, http://www.duke.edu/~jspippen/nature.htm; **b** Jessie M. Harris; **c** Daniel W. Reed, http://2bnthewild.com

478 Top: a Dan Tenaglia, http://missouriplants.com; **b** Ben Legler **Bottom: a** William R. Gray, cyberflora@xmission.com; **b(ins)** Jessie M. Harris

479 Top: a Al Schneider, http://swcoloradowildflowers.com; **b** Mary Ellen Harte; **c** William R. Gray, cyberflora@xmission.com; **d** Paul B. Slichter **Bottom: a**, **b(ins)** Ben Legler; **c(ins)** Jessie M. Harris

480 Top: a Lewis E. Epple*; **b** Jessie M. Harris; **c** Louis-M. Landry; **d** J. S. Peterson, http://plants.usda.gov **Bottom: a** Jessie M. Harris

481 Top: a Will Chatfield-Taylor; **b** Merel R. Black, http://wisplants.uwsp.edu; **c** William R. Gray, cyberflora@xmission.com **Bottom: a** Lewis E. Epple*; **b** Ben Legler; **c** Jessie M. Harris

482 Top: a Jessie M. Harris; **b(ins)** Steve Matson **Bottom: a**, **b(ins)** Louis-M. Landry; **c** James Henderson, Gulf

South Research Corporation, Bugwood.org

483 Top: a Paul S. Drobot, Plant Stock Photos, http://www.plantstockphotos.com; **b** Katy Chayka; **c** Paul S. Drobot, Plant Stock Photos, http://www.plantstockphotos.com **Bottom: a** Valerie Giles, Photo Researchers, Inc.; **b**, **c**, **d** Dan Tenaglia, http://missouriplants.com; **e** Charles Schurch Lewallen

484 Top: a, **b**, **c** Dan Tenaglia, http://missouriplants.com **Bottom: a** Janet Novak; **b** Louis-M. Landry; **c** Janet Novak; **d** Al Schneider, http://swcoloradowildflowers.com

485 Top: a R. Spellenberg; **b(ins)** Michael Giannechini, Photo Researchers, Inc. **Bottom: a** Ben Legler; **b** Steve Matson; **c** Gail Jankus, Photo Researchers, Inc.; **d** Jessie M. Harris

486 Top: a Carly Gibson; **b** Jessie M. Harris; **c** Daniel Mathews **Bottom: a** Shirley Denton; **b** Gil Nelson, http://www.gilnelson.com/stockimages; **c** Gary Fewless, Cofrin Center for Biodiversity, University of Wisconsin-Green Bay

487 Top: a Chris Evans, River to River CWMA, Bugwood.org; **b** Jessie M. Harris; **c** Will Cook, http://carolinanature.com; **d** Gary Fewless, Cofrin Center for Biodiversity, University of Wisconsin-Green Bay; **e** Gil Nelson, http://www.gilnelson.com/stockimages **Bottom: a** Ben Legler; **b** Jessie M. Harris

488 Top: a John Game; **b** Ben Legler; **c** Jessie M. Harris; **d** Louis-M. Landry **Bottom: a**, **b(ins)** Jessie M. Harris

489 Top: a Ronald J. Taylor; **b(ins)** Charles R. Hutchins **Bottom: a** Linda Lee, University of South Carolina Herbarium; **b** Lewis E. Epple*; **c** BONAP

490 Top: a Linda Lee, University of South Carolina Herbarium; **b** Alan Cressler; **c** Robert Sivinski; **d** Richard Old, http://www.xidservices.com **Bottom: a** Dan Tenaglia, http://missouriplants.com; **b** Jessie M. Harris; **c** Bill Carr, The Nature Conservancy of Texas

491 Top: a, **b** Jessie M. Harris; **c**, **d** Steve Matson **Bottom:**

a Richard Old, http://www.xidservices.com; **b(ins)** Steve Matson; **c** Jessie M. Harris; **d** Robert B. Coxe

492 Top: a Ben Legler; **b** Ken Bowles, http://www.kenbowles.net; **c** Lynn Watson; **d** Ben Legler **Bottom: a**, **b(ins)** Linda Lee, University of South Carolina Herbarium

493 Top: a Charles Schurch Lewallen; **b** Gil Nelson, http://www.gilnelson.com/stockimages; **c** Wilbur H. Duncan; **d** Linda Lee, University of South Carolina Herbarium **Bottom: a** Daniel Mathews; **b** Adolf Ceska; **c(ins)** Merel R. Black, http://wisplants.uwsp.edu

494 Top: a Melissa A. Carr; **b** Steven Thorsted; **c** George W. Hartwell **Bottom: a** Samuel R. Maglione, Photo Researchers, Inc.; **b** Jeffrey Lepore, Photo Researchers, Inc.; **c** Jessie M. Harris; **d(ins)** Gil Nelson, http://www.gilnelson.com/stockimages

495 Top: a Jessie M. Harris; **b**, **c** Jeffrey Lepore, Photo Researchers, Inc.; **d** Gregory K. Scott, Photo Researchers, Inc. **Bottom: a** Michael Charters, http://calflora.net

496 Top: a Linda Lee, University of South Carolina Herbarium; **b(ins)** Jessie M. Harris **Bottom: a** Don and Priscilla Eastman; **b** Gerald D. Carr

497 Top: a Gerald D. Carr; **b**, **c(ins)** Ben Legler; **d** Jessie M. Harris **Bottom: a(ins)** Jeffrey Lepore, Photo Researchers, Inc.; **b** James Steinberg, Photo Researchers, Inc.; **c** Al Schneider, http://swcoloradowildflowers.com; **d** Jessie M. Harris

498 Top: a Ben Legler; **b** Gerald D. Carr; **c** Ben Legler **Bottom: a** Ben Legler; **b**, **c**, **d** Keir Morse

499 Top: a Ronald J. Taylor; **b** Robert Sivinski; **c(ins)** Keir Morse **Bottom: a**, **b** Jessie M. Harris; **c(ins)** Charles Schurch Lewallen

500 Top: a Gerald D. Carr; **b** Ben Legler; **c** Gerald D. Carr; **d** Jessie M. Harris; **e** Steven J. Baskauf, http://bioimages.vanderbilt.edu **Bottom: a** Jessie M. Harris; **b(ins)** Gail Jankus, Photo Researchers, Inc.

557 Top: a Jessie M. Harris;
b Linda Lee, University
of South Carolina
Herbarium Bottom: a Dan
Tenaglia, http://missouriplants.
com; b Ben Legler
558 Top: a William R. Gray,
cyberflora@xmission.com;
b, c Jessie M. Harris Bottom:
a Dennis D. Horn, Tennessee
Native Plant Society; b George
W. Hartwell; c Vernon H.
Oswald; d Jessie M. Harris
559 Top: a Jessie M. Harris; b
Wilbur H. Duncan; c Gary
W. Sherwin, President, http://
americanvioletsociety.org
Bottom: a Dan Tenaglia, http://
missouriplants.com; b Tom
Barnes, University of Kentucky
560 Top: a Merel R. Black, http://
wisplants.uwsp.edu; b Jessie M.
Harris; c Dan Tenaglia, http://
missouriplants.com; d Charles
Schurch Lewallen Bottom:
a Dan Tenaglia, http://
missouriplants.com; b(ins) c
Charles Schurch Lewallen; d
Steve Matson; d Thayne Tuason
561 Top: a Linda Lee, University
of South Carolina Herbarium;
b Mike Haddock; c Jessie M.
Harris Bottom: a G. Yatskievych,
Missouri Botanical Garden
562 Top: a R. Spellenberg
Bottom: a Lewis E. Epple*;
b James M. André
563 Top: a Dan Tenaglia, http://
missouriplants.com
564 Row 1: a Vernon H. Oswald;
b Michael Charters, http://
calflora.net Row 2: a Derral R.
Herbst; b Michael Charters,
http://calflora.net Row 3: a Jessie
M. Harris; b Dan Tenaglia,
http://missouriplants.com
Row 4: a Steven J. Baskauf,
http://bioimages.vanderbilt.edu;
b Jessie M. Harris
565 Row 1: a Jessie M. Harris;
b Charles R. Hutchins;
c Louis-M. Landry; d Dan
Tenaglia, http://missouriplants.
com Row 2: a, b Ben Legler;
c Michael Charters, http://
calflora.net Row 3: a Virginia
Tech Weed ID Guide; b Ben
Legler; c Dan Tenaglia, http://
missouriplants.com Row 4: a
Ben Legler; b Dan Tenaglia,
http://missouriplants.com; c
Charles Schurch Lewallen
566 Row 1: a, b Richard Old,

http://www.xidservices.com;
c David L. Marrison, Assistant
Professor, The Ohio State
University Row 2: a Ben
Legler; b Richard Old, http://
www.xidservices.com
Row 3: a, b Richard Old, http://
www.xidservices.com
Row 4: a Jessie M. Harris;
b Richard Old, http://
www.xidservices.com
567 Row 1: a Christopher L.
Christie; b Dan Tenaglia,
http://missouriplants.com
Row 2: a CDFA; b BonTerra
Consulting Row 3: a Charles
Schurch Lewallen; b Richard
Old, http://www.xidservices.com;
c George W. Hartwell Row 4: a
Don and Priscilla Eastman; b
Eric Wrubel; c Ana Cojocariu
568 Row 1: a Perennou
Nuridsany, Photo Researchers,
Inc.; b Charles Schurch Lewallen;
c Perennou Nuridsany, Photo
Researchers, Inc. Row 2:
a Dan Tenaglia, http://
missouriplants.com; b Richard
Old, http://www.xidservices.com
Row 3: a John C. Dittes; b
William R. Gray, cyberflora@
xmission.com Row 4: a, b
Forest & Kim Starr; c Frank
Soltes, Atlas of Florida
Vascular Plants, http://florida.
plantatlas.usf.edu
569 Row 1: a Ben Legler; b Jessie
M. Harris Row 2: a, b Ben
Legler; c Gerald D. Carr Row 3:
a, b Bob Harms; c Ben Legler;
d Steve Matson Row 4: a Don
and Priscilla Eastman; b Louis-
M. Landry; c William R. Gray,
cyberflora@xmission.com
570 Row 1: a, b Dan Tenaglia,
http://missouriplants.com;
c Charles Schurch Lewallen
Row 2: a Ben Legler; b Richard
Old, http://www.xidservices.
com; c Vernon H. Oswald Row
3: a Ben Legler; b Richard Old,
http://www.xidservices.com; c
Ben Legler Row 4: a, b Richard
Old, http://www.xidservices.com
571 Row 1: a Richard Old, http://
www.xidservices.com; b Jessie
M. Harris; c Richard Old, http://
www.xidservices.com Row
2: a Ben Legler; b Jessie M.
Harris Row 3: a Ben Legler;
b Richard Old, http://www.
xidservices.com Row 4: a Bob
Gibbons, Photo Researchers,

Inc.; b Jessie M. Harris
572 Row 1: a, b Eleanor Saulys
Row 2: a Nigel Cattlin, Photo
Researchers, Inc.; b Jessie M.
Harris; c Richard Old, http://
www.xidservices.com
Row 3: a, b William R. Gray,
cyberflora@xmission.com
Row 4: a Derek S. Anderson,
Freckmann Herbarium,
University of Wisconsin-
Stevens Point; b Amadej
Trnkoczy; c Gerald D. Carr
573 Row 1: a, b Ben Legler
Row 2: a, b Richard Old,
http://www.xidservices.com
Row 3: a Dan Tenaglia, http://
missouriplants.com; b William
R. Gray, cyberflora@xmission.
com; c Dan Tenaglia, http://
missouriplants.com
Row 4: a, b Dan Tenaglia,
http://missouriplants.com
574 Row 1: a Dan Tenaglia,
http://missouriplants.com;
b Charles Schurch Lewallen;
c Jessie M. Harris; d Ben Legler;
e Jessie M. Harris Row 2: a
Jessie M. Harris; b Donald
M. Zouras II; c John W. Bova,
Photo Researchers, Inc. Row 3:
a Merel R. Black, http://wisplants
uwsp.edu; b Ken Bowles,
http://www.kenbowles.net;
c Ben Legler Row 4: a Jessie M.
Harris; b Gerald D. Carr
575 Row 1: a Richard Old, http://
www.xidservices.com; b
Joseph M. DiTomaso; c Ben
Legler Row 2: a Michael
Charters, http://calflora.net;
b Jessie M. Harris; c Richard
Old, http://www.xidservices.
com Row 3: a Shirley Denton;
b Don and Priscilla Eastman;
c Richard Old, http://www.
xidservices.com Row 4: a
William R. Gray, cyberflora@
xmission.com; b Michael
Charters, http://calflora.net;
c Carol W. Witham
576 Row 1: a William R. Gray,
cyberflora@xmission.com;
b, c Richard Old, http://www.
xidservices.com Row 2: a Don
and Priscilla Eastman; b Richard
Old, http://www.xidservices.
com Row 3: a, b Dan Tenaglia,
http://missouriplants.com Row
4: a Richard Old, http://www.
xidservices.com; b Jessie M.
Harris
577 Row 1: a Charles Schurch

Lewallen; **b** Gerald D. Carr
Row 2: a, b Ben Legler
Row 3: a Don and Priscilla Eastman; **b** Richard Old, http://www.xidservices.com
Row 4: a, b Jessie M. Harris
578 Row 1: a Dan Tenaglia, http://missouriplants.com; **b** Ben Legler **Row 2: a** Dan Tenaglia, http://missouriplants.com; **b** BONAP **Row 3: a, b, c** Ben Legler **Row 4: a** Dan Tenaglia, http://missouriplants.com; **b** Richard Old, http://www.xidservices.com; **c** Ann Pickford, Photo Researchers, Inc.
579 Row 1: a Ben Legler; **b** Dan Tenaglia, http://missouriplants.com; **c** Steve Matson **Row 2: a** Richard Old, http://www.xidservices.com; **b** Charles R. Hutchins **Row 3: a** Charles Schurch Lewallen; **b** Gilbert S. Grant, Photo Researchers, Inc. **Row 4: a, b** Linda Lee, University of South Carolina Herbarium; **c** Charles Schurch Lewallen
580 Row 1: a, b Jessie M. Harris **Row 2: a, b** Richard Old, http://www.xidservices.com **Row 3: a** Gerald D. Carr; **b, c** Forest & Kim Starr **Row 4: a** George W. Hartwell; **b** Dan Tenaglia, http://missouriplants.com
581 Row 1: a Richard Old, http://www.xidservices.com; **b** Jessie M. Harris; **c** Amadej Trnkoczy **Row 2: a** University of Florida: Center for Aquatic and Invasive Plants; **b** Forest & Kim Starr; **c** Harold St. John **Row 3: a** Richard Old, http://www.xidservices.com; **b** Ben Legler; **c** Dan Tenaglia, http://missouriplants.com **Row 4: a, b, c** Ben Legler
582 Row 1: a, b Dan Tenaglia, http://missouriplants.com; **c** Ben Legler **Row 2: a** Gilbert S. Grant, Photo Researchers, Inc.; **b** Ron Lance; **c** Dan Tenaglia, http://missouriplants.com **Row 3: a** Jessie M. Harris; **b, c** Dan Tenaglia, http://missouriplants.com **Row 4: a, b** Ben Legler; **c** Al Schneider, http://swcoloradowildflowers.com
583 Row 1: a, b, c Ben Legler **Row 2: a** BONAP; **b** Ben Legler **Row 3: a** Charles Schurch Lewallen; **b** Dan Tenaglia, http://missouriplants.com; **c** Ben Legler **Row 4: a**

William R. Gray, cyberflora@xmission.com; **b** Charles Schurch Lewallen
584 Row 1: a Dan Tenaglia, http://missouriplants.com; **b, c, d** Ben Legler **Row 2: a, b** Linda Lee, University of South Carolina Herbarium **Row 3: a, b** Dan Tenaglia, http://missouriplants.com; **c** Shirley Denton **Row 4: a** Jessie M. Harris; **b** William R. Gray, cyberflora@xmission.com
585 Row 1: a Ben Legler; **b** Steve Matson; **c** Charles Schurch Lewallen **Row 2: a, b, c** Jessie M. Harris **Row 3: a** Gail Jankus, Photo Researchers, Inc.; **b** Michael Charters, http://calflora.net **Row 4: a, b** Ben Legler
586 Row 1: a Robert B. Coxe; **b** Linda Lee, University of South Carolina Herbarium **Row 2: a, b** Richard Old, http://www.xidservices.com **Row 3: a** Ben Legler; **b** Linda Lee, University of South Carolina Herbarium **Row 4: a** Chris Evans, River to River CWMA, Bugwood.org; **b** Linda Lee, University of South Carolina Herbarium; **c** John Hilty
587 Row 1: a Ben Legler; **b** Michael Charters, http://calflora.net **Row 2: a** Gerald D. Carr; **b** Charles R. Hutchins **Row 3: a** Dan Tenaglia, http://missouriplants.com; **b** Charles Schurch Lewallen **Row 4: a** Ohio State Weed Lab Archive, The Ohio State University; **b, c** Dan Tenaglia, http://missouriplants.com
588 Row 1: a Jessie M. Harris; **b** Dan Tenaglia, http://missouriplants.com **Row 2: a** Charles Schurch Lewallen; **b** William R. Gray, cyberflora@xmission.com; **c** Richard Old, http://www.xidservices.com **Row 3: a, b** Dan Tenaglia, http://missouriplants.com; **c** Richard Old, http://www.xidservices.com **Row 4: a** Nigel Cattlin, Photo Researchers, Inc.; **b** Vernon H. Oswald
589 Row 1: a Jessie M. Harris; **b, c** Dan Tenaglia, http://missouriplants.com **Row 2: a** John Hilty; **b, c** Dan Tenaglia, http://missouriplants.com **Row 3: a** Bildagentur-online, TH Foto-Werbung, Photo

Researchers, Inc.; **b** Luigi Rignanese **Row 4: a** Gerald D. Carr; **b, c** Ben Legler
590 Row 1: a, b University of Florida: Center for Aquatic and Invasive Plants **Row 2: a** William R. Gray, cyberflora@xmission.com; **b** University of Florida: Center for Aquatic and Invasive Plants; **c** Ann Pickford, Photo Researchers, Inc. **Row 3: a** Janet Novak; **b** Jessie M. Harris; **c** Ronald A. Coleman **Row 4: a** Jessie M. Harris; **b** Richard Old, http://www.xidservices.com
591 Row 1: a Jessie M. Harris; **b** Vernon H. Oswald **Row 2: a** Jessie M. Harris; **b** BONAP; **c** Amadej Trnkoczy **Row 3: a, b** Dan Tenaglia, http://missouriplants.com **Row 4: a** Dan Tenaglia, http://missouriplants.com; **b, c** Ben Legler
592 Row 1: a T. Ann Williams, Atlas of Florida Vascular Plants, http://florida.plantatlas.usf.edu; **b, c** Matt Merritt **Row 2: a** Dan Tenaglia, http://missouriplants.com; **b** Ben Legler; **c** Louis-M. Landry **Row 3: a** Dan Tenaglia, http://missouriplants.com; **b** Richard Old, http://www.xidservices.com; **c** Steven J. Baskauf, http://bioimages.vanderbilt.edu **Row 4: a** University of Florida: Center for Aquatic and Invasive Plants; **b** Roger L. Hammer
593 Row 1: a Dan Tenaglia, http://missouriplants.com **Row 2: a** Linda Lee, University of South Carolina Herbarium; **b** Gerald D. Carr; **c** William R. Gray, cyberflora@xmission.com **Row 3: a** Janet Novak; **b** Eleanor Saulys **Row 4: a** Richard Old, http://www.xidservices.com; **b** Jessie M. Harris
594 Row 1: a Dan Tenaglia, http://missouriplants.com; **b** Jessie M. Harris **Row 2: a** Janet Novak; **b** Louis-M. Landry; **c** Ben Legler **Row 3: a** Gail Jankus, Photo Researchers, Inc.; **b** Richard Old, http://www.xidservices.com **Row 4: a** William R. Gray, cyberflora@xmission.com; **b** Jessie M. Harris; **c** David Fenwick, http://davefenwick.com
595 Row 1: a John Hilty; **b** Emmet Judziewicz, University of Wisconsin-Stevens Point;

Species Index

Boldface type indicates a main species entry.